Virginia Cooperative Extension Master Gardener Handbook

VIRGINIA
COOPERATIVE EXTENSION
GARDENER HANDBOOK

VIRGINIA COOPERATIVE EXTENSION

PDF and EPUB free online at: https://doi.org/10.21061/vcegardener

© Virginia Polytechnic Institute and State University, 2023. The original edition of the Virginia Master Gardener Handbook was printed January 1985. The handbook was revised in January 1986, January 1987, July 1990, November 1994, December 1999, July 2009, December 2015, and February 2018.

Virginia Cooperative Extension Gardener Handbook by Virginia Cooperative Extension is licensed under a Creative Commons Attribution-NonCommercial-ShareAlike 4.0 International License, except where otherwise noted.

You are free to copy, share, adapt, remix, transform, and build on the material for any primarily noncommercial purpose as long as you follow the terms of the license: https://creativecommons.org/licenses/by-nc-sa/4.0.

  You must:
  - Attribute—You must give appropriate credit, provide a link to the license, and indicate if changes were made. You may do so in any reasonable manner, but not in any way that suggests the licensor endorses you or your use.
  - ShareAlike—If you remix, transform, or build on the material, you must distribute your contributions under the same license as the original.

  You may not:
  - NonCommercial—You may not use the work for primarily commercial use.
  - Additional restrictions—You may not add any legal terms or technological measures that legally restrict others from doing anything the license permits.

Suggested citation: Virginia Cooperative Extension (2023). Virginia Cooperative Extension Gardener Handbook. Blacksburg: Virginia Cooperative Extension. https://doi.org/10.21061/vcegardener. Licensed with CC BY-NC-SA 4.0. https://creativecommons.org/licenses/by-nc-sa/4.0.

Publisher: This work is published by the Virginia Cooperative Extension
State Administrative Office, 101 Hutcheson Hall (0402)
250 Drillfield Drive, Blacksburg, VA 24061 USA
https://ext.vt.edu

Accessibility statement: Virginia Tech is committed to making its publications accessible in accordance with the Americans with Disabilities Act of 1990. The Pressbooks (HTML) and ePub versions of this text are tagged structurally and include alternative text, which allows for machine readability.

Publication cataloging information:
Virginia Cooperative Extension, author
Virginia Cooperative Extension Gardener Handbook / Virginia Cooperative Extension
Pages cm
ISBN 978-1-957213-48-4 (PDF)
ISBN 978-1-957213-49-1 (ePub)
ISBN 978-1-957213-47-7 (Pressbooks) https://pressbooks.lib.vt.edu/emgtraining
ISBN 978-1-957213-42-2 (Print)
URI (Universal Resource Identifier): http://hdl.handle.net/10919/112743
DOI: https://doi.org/10.21061/vcegardener
  1. Gardening--Virginia--Handbooks, manuals, etc.
     Title: Virginia Cooperative Extension Gardener Handbook
     SB453.2.V8 2023
     635.09755

Disclaimer: The figures in this book have varying licenses. Please check the figure references at the end of each chapter before redistributing.

Educators, please let us know you are using the book: https://bit.ly/interest-vcegardener
Report an error: https://bit.ly/report-error-vcegardener
Errata: https://bit.ly/errata-vcegardener

Cover images: Kathleen Wellington (CC BY-NC-SA 4.0); U.S. Department of Agriculture (public domain) via Flickr (https://flic.kr/p/2a7hMVD, https://flic.kr/p/WKHf26, https://flic.kr/p/dPjWUD)
Cover design: Kindred Grey

CONTENTS

Introduction	xiv
Acknowledgments	xv
About This Resource	xvii
Chapter 1: Botany	1
Plant Cell Structure and Function	1
Anatomy: Plant Parts and Functions	2
Physiology: Plant Growth and Development	20
Environmental Factors Affecting Plant Growth	23
Taxonomy: Biological Classification	26
Additional Resources	35
References	35
Attributions	35
Image Attributions	35
Chapter 2: Soils and Nutrient Management	38
Components of Soil	38
Soil Horizons	41
Physical Properties of Soils	42
Soil Testing	49
Soil pH	50
Building Healthy Soil	53
Understanding Fertilizers	56
Applying Fertilizer	60
Soil and Nutrient Problems	62
Additional Resources	65
References	65
Attributions	66
Image Attributions	66

Chapter 3: Entomology 67
    Benefits and Value of Insects 67
    Insect Form and Structure—Morphology 68
    Insect Development—Metamorphosis 71
    Identifying Insects 73
    Types of Insect Injury 74
    Insects of Importance to the Gardener 76
    Commonly Encountered Non-Insect Arthropods 85
    Taxonomy 89
    Additional Resources 92
    Attributions 92
    Image Attributions 92
Chapter 4: Plant Pathology 95
    Plant Diseases in History 95
    Diseases Defined: Cause of Disease 96
    Steps to Disease Diagnosis 97
    Symptoms (Change in Plant Appearance) of Plant Disease 98
    Signs (Visible Structures Produced by Pathogens) of Plant Disease 101
    Disease Development 102
    Methods and Tools to Control Diseases 103
    Summary 107
    Additional Resources 107
    Attributions 107
    Image Attributions 108

Chapter 5: Abiotic Stress Effects on Plant Growth and Development — 109
- Definition of Plant Stress — 109
- Abiotic Stress — 109
- Chemical Stress — 111
- Plant Nutrient Stress — 113
- Salinity Stress — 118
- Herbicide Injury — 119
- Physical Stress — 121
- Chilling and Freezing Stress — 123
- Light Stress — 124
- Mechanical Stress — 124
- Summary of Physical Stresses — 125
- Additional Resources — 126
- References — 126
- Attributions — 126
- Image Attributions — 126

Chapter 6: Diagnosing Plant Damage — 128
- A Systematic Approach to Diagnosing Plant Damage — 128
- Define the Problem — 130
- Look for Patterns — 131
- Determine Causes — 134
- Diagnostic Keys — 148
- Additional Resources — 189
- Attributions — 189
- Image Attributions — 189

Chapter 7: Integrated Pest Management and Pesticide Safety — 191
- What Is a Pest? — 191
- Integrated Pest Management — 191
- Pesticide Safety — 196
- Additional Resources — 208
- Attributions — 208
- Image Attributions — 209

Chapter 8: Plant Propagation — 210
- Sexual Propagation — 210
- Asexual Propagation — 217
- Additional Resources — 228
- Attributions — 228
- Image Attributions — 228

Chapter 9: The Vegetable Garden — 230
- Planning the Vegetable Garden — 230
- Soil Preparation — 232
- Selecting Gardening Equipment — 236
- Seed for the Garden — 239
- Transplants for the Garden — 245
- Irrigating the Home Garden — 246
- Fertilizing the Garden — 248
- Weed Control in the Garden — 248
- Vegetable Planting Guide — 250
- Intensive Gardening Methods — 251
- Container Gardening — 255
- Vegetable Gardening in the Fall — 258
- Season Extenders — 263
- Culinary Herbs — 265
- Organic Vegetable Gardening — 269
- Additional Resources — 273
- References — 273
- Attributions — 273
- Image Attributions — 273

Chapter 10: Fruits in the Home Garden — 275
    Planning a Tree Fruit Planting — 275
    Buying Trees — 278
    Planting Fruit Trees — 279
    Fruit Tree Management — 280
    Pest Management for Fruit Trees — 282
    Planning the Small Fruit Garden — 285
    Blueberries — 287
    Caneberries — 290
    Grapes — 293
    Strawberries — 297
    Additional Resources — 301
    Attributions — 302
    Image Attributions — 302

Chapter 11: Lawns — 303
    Establishing a Lawn — 303
    Renovating an Old Lawn — 306
    Recommended Turfgrass Varieties for Virginia — 308
    Purchasing Quality Seed — 312
    Purchasing Quality Sod — 314
    Annual Lawn Maintenance — 314
    Additional Resources — 325
    Attributions — 325
    Image Attributions — 325

Chapter 12: Indoor Plants — 326
- Purchasing an Indoor Plant — 326
- Factors Affecting Plant Growth Indoors — 327
- Growing Media — 330
- Containers — 331
- Repotting — 332
- Training and Grooming — 333
- Common Indoor Plant Pests — 333
- Care of Specific Plants — 335
- Terrariums and Dish Gardens — 337
- Plant Lists — 339
- Additional Resources — 343
- Attributions — 343
- Image Attributions — 343

Chapter 13: Woody Landscape Plants — 344
- What is a Woody Plant? — 345
- Species Diversity and Monoculture — 348
- Hardiness — 348
- Growth Rate — 351
- Functions of Woody Plants — 352
- Choice of Nursery Stock — 354
- Right Plant for the Right Place and Right Function — 355
- Invasive Plants — 357
- Challenge — 357
- Additional Resources — 357
- References — 357
- Attributions — 358
- Image Attributions — 358

Chapter 14: Pruning … 359
- Reasons for Pruning … 359
- Pruning Tools … 360
- Pruning Techniques … 361
- Controlling Size … 363
- Maintaining or Improving Plant Health … 363
- Reducing the Risk of Personal Injury or Property Damage … 370
- Training the Plant … 370
- Improving the Quality of Plants, Flowers, and Ornamental Features … 371
- Pruning for Fruit … 374
- Training and Pruning Small Fruit … 381
- Additional Resources … 385
- Attributions … 385
- Image Attributions … 385

Chapter 15: Herbaceous Landscape Plants … 387
- Annuals … 388
- Perennials … 388
- Biennials … 389
- Tropicals … 389
- Geophytes … 390
- Pond and Bog Plants … 390
- Ornamental Grasses … 391
- Ferns (Pterophytes) … 392
- Succulents … 393
- Planning the Herbaceous Border … 394
- Containers and Hanging Baskets … 397
- Additional Resources … 398
- Attributions … 398
- Image Attributions … 398

Chapter 16: Landscape Design — 400
- Plans and Maps — 400
- Site Analysis — 401
- User Analysis — 405
- Elements and Principles of Design — 406
- Sustainability — 409
- Planting Design (Plan) — 410
- Energy Conservation through Landscaping — 411
- Maintenance — 412
- Themes — 413
- Additional Resources — 413
- Attributions — 414
- Image Attributions — 414

Chapter 17: Water Quality and Conservation — 416
- Watersheds — 416
- Surface, Ground, and Storm Waters — 417
- Water Pollution — 418
- Water Quality Standards — 420
- State Regulatory Information — 422
- Water-Wise Landscaping — 423
- Stormwater Best Management Practices (BMPs) — 425
- Additional Resources — 432
- Attributions — 433
- Image Attributions — 433

Chapter 18: Habitat Gardening for Wildlife — 434
- Habitat Loss and Declining Wildlife Populations — 434
- Habitat Principles — 435
- Conservation Landscaping and Habitat Gardening — 441
- Selected Habitat Gardens that Sustain Wildlife Diversity — 448
- Troubleshooting Wildlife Conflicts — 456
- Additional Resources — 465
- References — 467
- Attributions — 468
- Image Attributions — 468

Chapter 19: Virginia Native Plants 469
    8 Reasons to Plant Native Plants 470
    Virginia's History of Native Plants 471
    What is a Native Plant? 472
    Native Plants Outside of Academia 475
    Natives: Why Now? 475
    The Flora of Virginia 475
    Choosing Native Plants to Match Your Site 477
    Going Native, but to What Degree? 484
    Why Are Native Plants Important? 485
    Virginia Invasives: 8 More Reasons to Plant Native Plants 488
    Additional Resources 489
    References 490
    Attributions 492
    Image Attributions 493

Glossary 495
Version Notes 517
    Overall or Major Changes 517
    Chapter Numbering 517
    New Chapter Order 517
    "Call out Box" Topics and Authors: 518
    Specific Chapter-Level Changes 518

INTRODUCTION

The Virginia Extension Gardener Handbook is the training manual for Extension Master Gardener volunteers (EMG) in Virginia. This manual will provide the basics of horticulture and gardening in Virginia and help to build a strong foundation of gardening knowledge. We encourage readers to take a deeper dive into the topics that interest them and continue their gardening and learning journey. Resources for additional reading can be found at the end of each chapter.

Virginia Cooperative Extension (VCE) is the outreach and engagement branch of Virginia Tech and Virginia State University, the land grant universities in Virginia. Extension Agents, specialists, and volunteers work to bring scientific knowledge to the citizens of Virginia in order to help improve quality of life. VCE has more than 100 local offices across the commonwealth, many of which have volunteer programs. There are Extension Master Gardeners, Virginia Master Naturalists, Master Food Volunteers, Master Financial Education Volunteers, 4-H volunteers, and more! Extension offices also offer a number of learning opportunities throughout the year. You can learn more about VCE at ext.vt.edu.

Extension Master Gardener volunteers in Virginia are an essential part of the fabric of Virginia Cooperative Extension in the Commonwealth. These volunteers are community educators who embody the EMG Program mission of "Sharing Knowledge. Empowering Communities." Our volunteers receive at least 50 hours of training through their local Extension office and volunteer on projects specific and relevant to their local community. Anyone can become an Extension Master Gardener volunteer. All that is needed is an interest in gardening and a desire to give back to your community.

EMGs take part in a wide array of volunteer projects in their communities. Projects are tailored to their local area and will often change in scope from year to year based on what the community needs. Types of projects commonly undertaken by EMGs include:

Youth: Extension Master Gardener volunteers throughout the state engage with youth of all ages through garden education projects that help kids learn and get excited about the natural world. Volunteers can work in school, after school, or with after school organizations to provide education and resources to the youth of their communities. School garden projects offer important opportunities for kids to experience the joy of growing plants and learn where their food comes from.

Food Security: Volunteers with Extension help to meet the needs of their community, including engaging with issues of food security. Food security projects include providing vegetable and fruit gardening classes and demonstrations for all scales of gardens, partnering with food pantries and other local food organizations, supporting the work of (or creating) community gardens, setting up educational booths at farmers markets, assisting with "share the spare" or "plant a row" programs, and more.

Environmental Care: Extension Master Gardener volunteers have a passion for the outdoors and the natural world. Many units throughout the commonwealth work to educate and demonstrate sustainable gardening practices. They work to minimize their impact on the Earth and build sustainable systems. Projects can include water quality and conservation initiatives (such as rain barrel education or shoreline evaluation), working one-on-one with homeowners to share conservation landscaping practices, invasive species monitoring and education, and education about gardening in a changing climate.

Virginia Cooperative Extension is a partnership of Virginia Tech, Virginia State University, the U.S. Department of Agriculture, and local governments. Its programs and employment are open to all, regardless of age, color, disability, gender, gender identity, gender expression, national origin, political affiliation, race, religion, sexual orientation, genetic information, military status, or any other basis protected by law.

ACKNOWLEDGMENTS

Thank you to contributors and editors of this handbook including:

- Kathleen Reed (2022 project advisor, editor, and contributor)
- Devon Johnson (2022 project manager and image author)
- Kindred Grey (2022 image author and Pressbooks formatting)
- Stacey Morgan Smith (2022 handbook editor)
- Emma Freeborn (2022 alt text and editorial assistance)
- Anita Walz and the Virginia Tech Publishing team (2022)
- The 2021/22 Handbook Review Team: Barb Wilson, Beth Kirby, Carol King, Courtney Soria, Doug Levin, Elaine Mills, Elizabeth Brown, Fern Campbell, JC Gardner , Jim Revell, Khosro Aminpour, Maraea Harris, Margaret Brown, Meagan Shelley, Melanie Thompson, Michael Cole, Mimi Rosenthal, Nancy Brooks, Nancy Butler, Patricia Lust, Ralph Morini, Sabrina Morelli, Shawn Jadrnicek, Sherry Kern, Stacey Morgan Smith, Susan Dudley, Susan Perry, Wendy Silverman and all other volunteers who contributed

Previous versions:

- Dave Close, State Coordinator, VCE Master Gardener Program & Consumer Horticulture Specialist (2015 project advisor)
- John Freeborn, Assistant State Coordinator, VCE-MG Program (2015 editor)
- Sue Edwards (2015 editorial assistant)
- Diane Relf, Retired Extension Specialist, Environmental Horticulture (original compilation, revision, and editing)
- Judith Schwab (original compilation, revision, and editing)
- Elissa Steeves (original compilation, revision, and editing)
- R. Peter Madsen (original compilation, revision, and editing)
- Virginia Nathan (original compilation, revision, and editing)

Thank you to the many Extension Master Gardener volunteers and agents who contributed feedback or made suggestions for this handbook over the years.

> This version of the Extension Gardener Handbook was made possible in part by financial and technical support from the Open Education Initiative at the University Libraries https://guides.lib.vt.edu/oer. Additional financial support was provided by the Virginia Tech School of Plant and Environmental Sciences.

Thank you to the following Virginia Tech, Virginia State University faculty and Extension agents:

Susan Day, Associate Professor, Department of Horticulture; Laurie J. Fox, Horticulture Associate, Hampton Roads AREC; J. Roger Harris, Retired Professor, Department of Horticulture; Stephanie Huckestein, Education & Outreach Coordinator, Hahn Horticulture Garden; Alex X. Niemiera, Professor, School of Plant and Environmental Sciences; Jim Owen, Assistant Professor, Hampton Roads AREC; Jayesh B. Samtani, Extension Specialist, Small Fruit Production, Hampton Roads AREC; Holly Scoggins, Former Associate Professor, School of Plant and Environmental Sciences; Tony K. Wolf, Professor, Viticulture, Alson H. Smith Jr. AREC; Mike Goatley, Jr., Extension Specialist, Turfgrass, Department of Crop and Soil Environmental Sciences; Michael Weaver, Professor & Program Director, Virginia Tech Pesticide Programs; Stephanie Blevins, Consumer Education Project Coordinator, Virginia Tech Pesticide Programs; Eric Day, Insect Identification Lab Manager, Department of Entomology; Theresa Dellinger, Collections Manager, Department of Entomology; Thomas P. Kuhar, Professor, Department of Entomology; Mary Ann Hansen, Plant Diagnostician & Instructor, Department of Plant Pathology, Physiology, and Weed Science; David M. Orcutt, Professor Emeritus, Department of Plant Pathology, Physiology, and Weed Science; Eric Beers, School of Plant and Environmental Sciences; Keith S. Yoder, Extension Specialist, Tree Fruit

Pathology, Alson H. Smith Jr. AREC, School of Plant and Environmental Sciences; Pattie Bland, Urban Conservationist, Hanover-Caroline Soil & Water Conservation District; Thomas Bolles, Environmental Educator, VCE-Prince William; Adria Bordas, Extension Agent, VCE-Fairfax; Leonard Githinji, Assistant Professor, Virginia State University & Extension Specialist Sustainable and Urban Agriculture; Carol A. Heiser, Education Section Manager & Habitat Education Coordinator, VA Department of Wildlife Resources; Cathryn Kloetzli, Extension Agent, VCE-Albemarle; J. Christopher Ludwig, Chief Biologist, Virginia Department of Conservation & Recreation; Dan Nortman, Extension Agent, VCE-York/Poquoson; Tim Ohlwiler, Extension Agent, VCE-Fauquier; Reza Rafie, Extension; Specialist, Horticulture, Virginia State Cooperative Extension; Lisa Sanderson, Former Extension Agent, VCE-Henrico; Pamela H. Smith, EMG; Coordinator, VCE-Fairfax; Stuart Sutphin, Extension Agent, VCE-Danville City; Paige Thacker, Extension Agent, VCE-Prince William; Megan Tierney, Extension Agent, VCE-York/Poquoson; Meredith Hoggatt, Extension Agent, Montgomery.

Thank you to original contributors to past versions of the handbook, including the Northern Virginia Master Gardeners, the Utah Cooperative Extension Service, and the Georgia Cooperative Service for use of their handbook material and the Texas Agricultural Extension Service and N.C. State for the use of their revised and expanded versions of this handbook (circa 2009). According to the 2009 version of this handbook, "material was taken from many Extension publications written in Virginia and other states." We have worked to identify, rewrite, and attribute this content.

The original edition of the Virginia Master Gardener Handbook was printed January 1985. The handbook was revised January 1986, January 1987, July 1990, November 1994, December 1999, July 2009, and December 2015.

Original content of this handbook was compiled from many sources. We have made every effort to identify and attribute original sources of material.

Virginia Cooperative Extension Gardener Handbook by Virginia Cooperative Extension Master Gardener Program is licensed under a Creative Commons Attribution-NonCommercial-ShareAlike 4.0 International License, except where otherwise noted. Please see the image attributions at the end of each chapter for copyright information for specific images.

ABOUT THIS RESOURCE

What is an Open Textbook?

This is an open textbook with a Creative Commons NonCommercial ShareAlike 4.0 (CC BY-NC-SA 4.0) license (https://creativecommons.org/licenses/by-nc-sa/4.0). That means that this book is freely available and you are welcome to use and share this book with attribution. The CC BY-NC-SA 4.0 license on this book allows customization and redistribution which is noncommercial, that is, "not primarily intended for or directed towards commercial advantage or monetary compensation."

Many, but not all images, illustrations, etc., in this book are licensed under Creative Commons licenses.

Best practices for attribution are provided at https://wiki.creativecommons.org/wiki/ Best_practices_for_attribution.

How to Access This Book

The main landing page for the book is https://doi.org/10.21061/vcegardener.

This page includes:

- Links to multiple electronic versions of the textbook
    - PDF (http://hdl.handle.net/10919/112743)
    - ePub (http://hdl.handle.net/10919/112743)
    - HTML/Pressbooks (https://pressbooks.lib.vt.edu/emgtraining – note that the Pressbooks platform offers customization/remixing)
- Link to errata document (https://bit.ly/errata-vcegardener)
- Link to report errors (https://bit.ly/report-error-vcegardener)

Sharing Resources You've Created

Have you created any supplementary materials for use with this book such as presentation slides, activities, test items, or a question bank? If so, please consider sharing your materials related to this open textbook by using this form: https://bit.ly/interest-vcegardener.

Educators reviewing, adopting, or adapting this textbook are encouraged to register at https://bit.ly/interest-vcegardener. This assists the Open Education Initiative at Virginia Tech in assessing the impact of the book and allows us to more easily alert instructors using this book of additional resources, features, and opportunities.

CHAPTER 1: BOTANY

Chapter Contents:

- Plant Cell Structure and Function
- Anatomy: Plant Parts and Functions
- Physiology: Plant Growth and Development
- Environmental Factors Affecting Plant Growth
- Taxonomy: Biological Classification
- Additional Resources

Horticulturists work with a wide array of plants, both as garden friend or foe. This range of different plants brings an enjoyable diversity to the garden and landscape, yet on close observation many similarities become evident. These similarities in basic plant structures and functions, along with the environmental factors that affect plant growth, are the basis of this chapter. The information provided in this chapter will primarily focus on the higher flowering plants because they are most significant in the garden and landscape. This chapter will cover terminology to help enhance your understanding of botanical references in the future and to gain a perspective on the practices discussed in later chapters.

Hundreds of millions of years of evolution have produced an amazingly diverse and complex array of plants. Land plants are primarily divided into two groups: **gymnosperms** and **angiosperms**. Angiosperms are flowering plants that produce seeds enclosed in a fruit. There are over 300,000 species of angiosperms distributed all over the world. The gymnosperms, numbering around 700 species, are primarily the evergreen species of the temperate zones. They produce naked seeds, which are usually borne in cones. Gymnosperms generally also have narrow or needle-like leaves, while angiosperms usually have broad leaves.

Angiosperms are first subdivided into two major subclasses based on their vascular (or vein) arrangement. The **dicots** include most of the broadleaf herbs, shrubs, and trees. **Monocots** include such orders as lilies, palms, and grasses.

Plant Cell Structure and Function

Cells are the structural and functional units of life. Large organisms are made up of trillions of cells, while small organisms may be composed of only a single cell. Both plants and animals are made of cells, though plant and animal cells are somewhat different.

Plant cells consist of a **cell wall** containing cellulose, a chemical compound. Inside the cell wall, a plant cell has some of the same features as animal cells: a **cell membrane**, **mitochondria** (which are responsible for respiration, or energy production), a **nucleus** (which contains the genetic information for the organism and controls the activities of the cell), and numerous other organelles necessary to carry out the mechanisms of life. Plant cells also develop one (or more) large liquid-filled cavity called a **vacuole**.

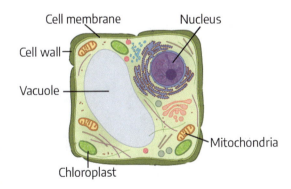

Figure 1-1: Plant cell diagram: This plant cell is surrounded by a rigid cell wall and then a cell membrane. It contains important organelles including the vacuole (storage cavity), chloroplast (responsible for photosynthesis), mitochondria (responsible for respiration), and nucleus (contains genetic material).

Plant cells have special structures called **chloroplasts**. Chloroplasts are the sites of photosynthesis and contain chlorophylls and carotenoid pigments. Chlorophyll is responsible for the green color of plants. Carotenoids are yellow and orange pigments that are masked by the more numerous chlorophyll pigments in green leaves. Chloroplasts are found only in plants and green algae (Evert and Eichhorn, 2012).

Plant cells grow and divide in different directions, creating all the structures of the plant like roots, stems, leaves, and more.

Anatomy: Plant Parts and Functions

Stem Anatomy

Stems are structures that support buds and leaves and serve as conduits for water, minerals, and sugars. The three major internal parts of a stem are the xylem, phloem, and cambium. The xylem and phloem are the major components of a plant's vascular system. The vascular system transports food, water, and minerals and offers support for the plant. **Xylem** tubes conduct water and minerals to the leaves, while **phloem** tubes conduct sugars and other metabolic products away from the leaves.

The xylem and phloem make up the vascular system of the stem and are arranged in distinct strands called **vascular bundles** that run the length of the stem. When viewed in cross section, the vascular bundles of dicot stems are arranged in a ring. In plants with stems that live for more than one year, these individual bundles grow together (producing growth rings). In monocot stems, the vascular bundles are randomly scattered throughout the stem.

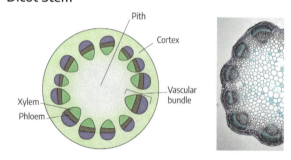

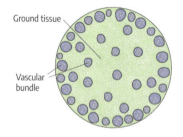

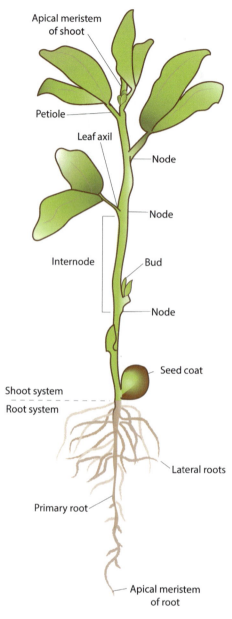

Figure 1-2: A few principal parts of a vascular plant include the stem, buds, leaves, and root system. The apical meristem of the root/shoot is the site of cell division that makes the plant elongate.

Figure 1-3: Stem drawing: Illustrates the difference between a typical dicot and monocot stem. In the dicot stem, xylem and phloem are arranged into vascular bundles which are arranged circularly around the perimeter of the stem. Vascular bundles in the monocot stem are arranged randomly.

The difference in the vascular system of the two groups is of practical interest to the horticulturist because certain herbicides are specific to either monocots or dicots. An example is 2,4-D, an herbicide that only kills dicots. In contrast, dicots may be more readily grafted as it is easier to align the vascular rings of the two stem pieces compared to the scattered bundles in monocots.

A part of the stem where a bud is located is called a **node**. This is where leaves are attached to the stem, and buds are located in these leaf axils (angle between stem and bud/leaf).

The stem section between nodes is called the **internode**. The length of an internode may depend on many factors. Internode length varies with the season. Growth produced early in the season has the greatest internode length; length decreases as the growing season nears its end. Decreasing fertility will decrease internode length. Too little light will result in a long internode, causing a spindly stem. This situation is known as stretch or etiolation. Vigorously growing plants tend to have greater internode lengths than less vigorous plants. Internode length will also vary with competition from surrounding stems or developing fruit. If the energy for a stem has to be divided among three or four stems, or if the energy is diverted into fruit growth, internode length will be shortened.

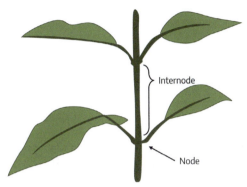

Figure 1-4: Stem nodes are where leaves or buds grow from. The space between nodes is called the internode.

A **bud** is a small package of partially preformed tissue which becomes leaves/stems or flowers. In some cases, buds contain partially preformed flower tissue (**flower bud**), and usually have a different appearance from a **vegetative bud**, a bud that contains partially preformed leaf and stem tissue. Some buds contain both floral and vegetative tissues.

Modified stems

The presence of leaves (regular or modified) or buds distinguishes a stem. Although typical stems are above-ground trunks and branches with great distances between leaves and buds, there are modified stems that can be found above ground and below ground. The above-ground modified stems are crowns, stolons, and spurs; and the below-ground stems are bulbs, corms, rhizomes, and tubers.

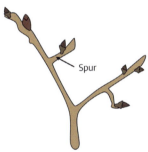

Above-ground stems

Spurs are short, stubby, side stems that arise from the main stem. They are common on such fruit trees as pears, apples, and cherries, and are capable of bearing fruit. If severe pruning is done close to fruit-bearing spurs, the spurs can revert to a long, nonfruiting stem.

Figure 1-5: Spurs are short side stems.

Crowns (seen in strawberries, dandelions, and African violets) are another type of compressed stem having leaves and flowers on short internodes. A **crown** is a region of compressed stem tissue from which new shoots are produced, generally found near the surface of the soil. Crowns are located at soil level so that roots support them upright and the central growing point is never covered with soil. Many herbaceous perennials, such as Shasta daisy, also develop crowns that enlarge with branching over successive years. These crowns persist over winter with buds that develop into elongated aerial stems during the growing season. A **stolon** is a horizontal stem that is fleshy or semi-woody and lies along the top of the ground. The spider plant has stolons. A **runner** is a type of stolon. It is a specialized stem that grows on the soil surface and forms a new plant at one or more of its nodes.

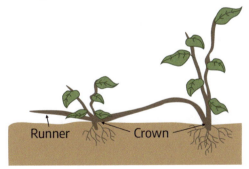

Figure 1-6: Diagram of a crown (region of compressed stem tissue from which new shoots are produced) and runner (type of stolon that grows on soil surface).

Strawberry runners are examples of stolons. Remember, all stems have nodes and buds or leaves. The leaves on strawberry runners are small, but are located at the nodes, which are easy to see. The nodes on the runner are the points where roots begin to form.

Below-ground stems, such as the potato tuber, the tulip bulb, gladiolus corm, and the iris rhizome, store food for the plant.

Figure 1-7: Stolon (horizontal stem that lies along the top of the ground).

Below-ground stems

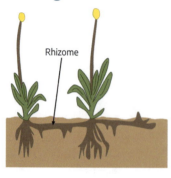

Figure 1-8: Rhizome (horizontal stem that grows underground).

Rhizomes are similar to stolons but grow underground. Some rhizomes are compressed and fleshy, such as those of iris; they can also be slender with elongated internodes, such as bentgrass. Bermudagrass is both an effective lawn grass and a hated weed principally because of the spreading capability of its rhizomes.

Tulips, lilies, daffodils, and onions are plants that produce **bulbs** — shortened, compressed, underground stems surrounded by fleshy scales (leaves) that envelop a central bud located at the tip of the stem. If you cut through the center of a tulip or daffodil bulb, you can see major plant parts within the bulb. Many bulbs require a period of low-temperature exposure before they begin to send up the new shoot. Both the temperature and length of this treatment are of critical importance to commercial growers who force bulbs for holidays.

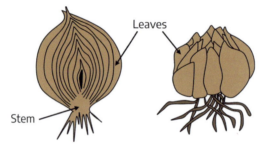

Figure 1-9: Bulb (shortened, compressed underground stems surrounded by fleshy scales).

Corms are not the same as bulbs. They have shapes similar to bulbs, but do not contain fleshy scales. A corm is a solid, swollen stem whose scales have been reduced to a dry, leaf-like covering. Examples of corms include gladiolus and crocus.

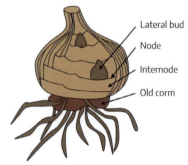

Figure 1-10: Corm (solid, swollen stem with dry leaf-like scales).

Figure: 1-11: Tuberous begonia stem with leaves growing from the crown.

A **tuber** is an enlarged portion of an underground stem. The tuber, like any other stem, has nodes that produce buds. The eyes of a potato are actually the nodes on the stem. Each eye contains a cluster of buds.

Some plants produce a modified stem referred to as a **tuberous stem**. Examples are tuberous begonia and cyclamen. The stem is shortened, flattened, enlarged, and underground. Buds and shoots arise from the crown, and fibrous roots are found on the bottom of the tuberous stem.

In addition, some plants, such as dahlia and sweet potato, produce an underground storage organ called a **tuberous root**, which is often confused with a bulb or tuber. However, these are roots, not stems, and have neither nodes nor internodes.

It may sometimes be difficult to distinguish between roots and stems, but one sure way is to look for the presence of nodes with their leaves and buds. Stems have nodes; roots do not.

Types of stems

A **shoot** is a young stem with leaves present. A **twig** is a stem that is less than one year old and has no leaves since it is still in the winter-dormant stage. A **branch** is a stem that is more than one year old and typically has lateral stems. A **trunk** is a main stem of a woody plant. Most trees have a single trunk.

Trees are perennial woody plants, usually with one main trunk and usually more than 12 feet tall at maturity.

Figure 1-12: Tuberous dahlia root.

Shrubs are perennial woody plants that have one or several main stems, and usually are less than 12 feet tall at maturity. The distinction between a small tree and large shrub is blurry, and often botanists will describe these plants as small trees or large shrubs.

A **vine** is a plant that develops long, trailing stems that grow along the ground unless they are supported by another plant or structure. Some twining vines circle their support clockwise (hops or honeysuckle), while others circle counter-clockwise (e.g., pole beans or Dutchman's pipe vine). Clinging vines are supported by aerial roots (e.g.,English ivy or poison ivy). A tendril is a modified plant part (leaf, stem, or flower, depending on the plant) that encircles the supporting object (e.g., cucumber, gourds, grapes, and passionflowers). Some tendrils have adhesive tips (e.g., Virginia creeper and Japanese creeper).

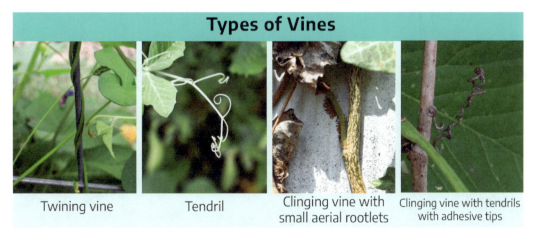

Figure 1-13: Types of vines include twining vines, tendrils, clinging vines with aerial rootlets, and clinging vines with tendrils that have adhesive tips.

Texture and growth of stems

Woody stems contain relatively large amounts of hardened xylem tissue in the central core and are typical of most fruit trees, ornamental trees, and shrubs.

A **cane** is a stem that has a relatively large pith (the central, strength-giving tissue of stem) and usually lives only one or two years. Examples of plants with canes include rose, grape, blackberry, and raspberry.

Herbaceous or succulent stems contain only small amounts of xylem tissue and usually live for only one growing season. If the plant is perennial, it will develop new shoots from a crown or underground part. An example of a plant with herbaceous stems is mayapple (*Podophyllum peltatum*), a native perennial that grows back each year from underground roots.

The edible portion of cultivated plants such as asparagus and kohlrabi is an enlarged succulent stem. The edible parts of broccoli are composed of stem tissue, flower buds, and a few small leaves. The edible part of potato is a fleshy, underground tuber. Although the name suggests otherwise, the edible part of the cauliflower is immature inflorescence (flowers) and flower stalk.

Plant life cycles

Plants are classified by the number of growing seasons required to complete a life cycle.

- **Annuals** pass through their entire life cycle from seed germination to seed production in one growing season, then die.
- **Biennials** are plants that start from seeds and produce vegetative structures and food storage organs the first season. In most biennials, during the first winter a hardy evergreen rosette of basal leaves persists. During the second season, flowers, fruit, and seeds develop to complete the life cycle. The plant then dies. Carrot, beet, cabbage, and celery are biennial plants. Hollyhock, Canterbury Bells, and Sweet William are biennials commonly grown for their attractive flowers.
    - Plants that typically develop as biennials may, in some cases, complete the cycle of growth from seed germination to seed production in only one growing season. This situation occurs when drought, variations in temperature, or other climatic conditions cause the plant to physiologically pass through the equivalent of two growing seasons in a single season.
- **Perennial** plants live for many years, and after reaching maturity, may produce flowers and seeds each year, though many only flower every few years. Perennials are classified as herbaceous if the top dies back to the ground each winter and new stems grow from the roots each spring. If significant xylem develops in the stem and the top persists, as in shrubs or trees, then they are classified as woody plants.

Leaf Anatomy

Parts of a leaf

Leaves are the principal site of photosynthesis (food manufacturing) in plants. This process requires light and water from the plant's vascular system, and carbon dioxide from the air. The petiole and leaf blade provide good exposure to sunlight and air. Other structures in the leaf are involved in accomplishing photosynthesis and protecting the soft leaf tissues from desiccation (drying out).

The **blade** of a leaf is the expanded, thin structure on either side of the midrib. The blade is usually the largest and most conspicuous part of a leaf. Conifers (gymnosperm class) have a different structure in that the leaf blade is a narrow angle needle. These needles occur singly or in clusters of two or more with their bases enclosed in a sheath. The **petiole** is the stalk that supports the leaf blade; it varies in length and may be lacking entirely in some cases where the leaf blade is described as sessile (attached directly by its base), as in conifers, grass, or zinnias.

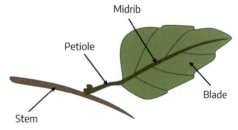

Figure 1-14: Broadleaf diagram showing stem, petiole (which attaches leaf to stem), midrib (primary vein in the center of the leaf), and leaf blade.

Sheath   Needle

Figure 1-15: Conifer leaf diagram.

The leaf blade is composed of several layers. On both the top and bottom is a layer of thickened, tough cells called the epidermis. The primary function of the epidermis is protection of leaf tissue. The way the cells in the epidermis are arranged determines the texture of the leaf surface. Some leaves have hairs that are an extension of certain cells of the epidermis. The African violet has so many hairs that the leaf feels like velvet.

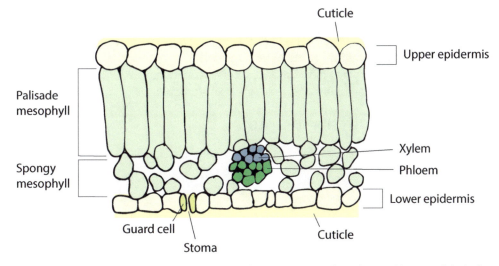

Figure 1-16: Cross section of a leaf showing the cuticle as the outer surface of top and bottom of the leaf (protecting it from dehydration), the epidermis, palisade and spongy mesophyll, and the vascular bundle containing the xylem and phloem. The lower epidermis contains stomata (plural of stoma) surrounded by guard cells.

Part of the epidermis is the **cuticle**, which is composed of a waxy substance called cutin that protects the leaf from dehydration and prevents penetration of some diseases. The amount of cutin is a direct response to sunlight, increasing with increasing light intensity. For this reason, plants grown in the shade should be moved into full sunlight gradually over a period of a few weeks to allow the cutin layer to build and to protect the leaves from the shock of rapid water loss or sunscald. The waxy cutin also repels water and can shed pesticides if spreader-sticker agents or soaps are not used. This is the reason many pesticide manufacturers include some sort of spray additive to adhere to or penetrate the cutin layer.

Stomata (singular: stoma) are openings in leaves that allow passage of water and gasses into and out of the leaf. **Guard cells** are epidermal cells located around a stoma. They help regulate gas exchange by opening and closing in response to weather conditions.

The middle layer of the leaf is the mesophyll and is located between the upper and lower epidermis. This is the layer where photosynthesis occurs. The mesophyll is divided into a dense upper layer called the palisade, and a spongy lower layer that contains a great deal of air space, called the parenchyma layer. The cells in these two layers contain chloroplasts which are the actual site of the photosynthetic process.

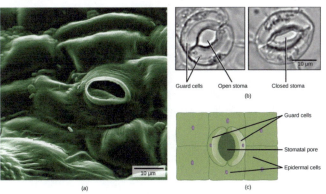

Figure 1-17: Images of stoma: (a) electron micrograph shows closed stoma on a dicot; (b) shows stoma opening and closing; (c) diagram of stomal pore with guar cells on either side, entirely surrounded by epidermal cells that make up the leaf surface.

Types of leaves

A number of rather distinct types of leaves occur on plants. Leaves commonly referred to as foliage are the most common and conspicuous and, as previously stated, serve as the manufacturing centers where the photosynthetic activity of the plant occurs. **Scale leaves, or cataphylls**, are found on rhizomes and are the small, leathery, protective leaves that enclose and protect buds. **Seed leaves, or cotyledons**, are modified leaves that are found on the embryonic plant and commonly serve as storage organs. **Spines** as found on barberry and cactus, are specialized modified leaves that protect the plant. **Storage leaves**, as found on bulbous plants and succulents, serve as food storage organs. Other specialized leaves include **bracts**, which are often brightly colored. The showy structures on dogwoods and poinsettias are bracts, not petals.

The leaf blade is the principal edible part of several horticultural crops, including chive, collard, dandelion, endive, kale, leaf lettuce, mustard, parsley, spinach, and Swiss chard. The edible part of leek, onion, and Florence fennel is a cluster of fleshy leaf bases. The petiole of the leaf is the edible product in celery and rhubarb. In Brussels sprout, cabbage, and head lettuce, the leaves — in the form of a large, naked bud — are the edible product.

Leaves as a means of identifying plants

Leaves are useful in identifying species and varieties of horticultural plants. Characteristics of leaf composition, arrangement, and venation pattern can be readily recognized.

Composition:

Simple leaves are those with a leaf blade that is a single continuous unit.

A compound leaf is composed of several separate leaflets arising from the same petiole. Some leaves may be doubly compound, having divisions of the leaflets. Compound leaves are further described by the **palmate** (as in palm of the hand) or **pinnate** (like a feather) arrangement of the leaflets.

Figure 1-18: Simple leaf.

Palmate compound Pinnate compound Double pinnate compound

Figure 1-19: Three examples of compound leaves: palmate, pinnate, and double pinnate compound.

Deciding if a specimen is a compound leaf or a branch with several simple leaves can be difficult because petioles and young stems appear similar. However, remember that leaves attach to stems at a node, and there is a bud only at the node. **The presence of a bud identifies where the leaf begins.**

Leaf arrangement along a stem: In a **rosulate** leaf arrangement, the basal leaves form a rosette around the stem with extremely short nodes. **Opposite** leaves are positioned across the stem from each other, two leaves at each node. **Alternate** leaves are arranged in alternate steps along the stem with only one leaf at each node. **Whorled** leaves are arranged in circles along the stem.

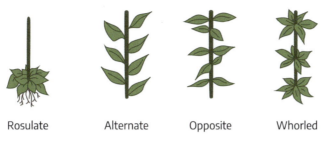

Figure 1-20: Types of leaf arrangements.

Venation of leaves

The vascular tissues from the stem extend as bundles through the petiole and spread out into the blade. The term venation refers to the pattern of vein distribution in the blade. Two principal types of venation are parallel-veined and net-veined.

Parallel-veined leaves are those with numerous veins that run essentially parallel to each other and are connected laterally by minute, straight veinlets. Possibly the most common type of parallel veining is that found in plants of the grass family, where the veins run from the base to the apex of the leaf. Another type of parallel venation is found in plants such as banana, calla, and pickerel-weed, where the parallel veins run laterally from the midrib. Parallel-veined leaves mainly occur on monocot plants.

Figure 1-21: Three examples of venation in leaves: parallel, pinnate, and palmate.

Net-veined leaves, also called reticulate-veined, have veins that branch from the main rib(s), then subdivide into finer veinlets which then unite in a complicated network. This system of enmeshed veins gives the leaf more resistance to tearing than most parallel-veined leaves. Net venation may be either pinnate or palmate. In pinnate venation, the veins extend laterally at an angle from the midrib to the edge, as in apple, cherry, and peach.

Palmate venation occurs in grape and maple leaves where the principal veins extend outward, like the ribs of a fan, from the petiole near the base of the leaf blade. Net-veined leaves occur on dicot plants..

Leaf shape

Common leaf blade shapes (found in leaves and leaflets):

- Acicular: Needle-like
- Subulate: Awl-shaped with tapering point
- Linear: Narrow, several times longer than wide; approximately the same width throughout
- Oblong: Leaf is 2-3x as long as it is wide and has parallel sides
- Elliptical: Two or three times longer than wide; tapering to an acute or rounded apex and base
- Ovate: Egg-shaped, basal portion wide; tapering toward the apex
- Obovate: Leaf is broadest above the middle and about 2x as long as wide
- Lanceolate: Longer than wide; tapering toward the apex and base
- Oblanceolate: Leaf is 3x longer than wide and broadest above the middle
- Spatulate: Generally narrow leaves widening to a round shape at the tip
- Reniform: Leaves wider than they are high
- Hastate: Arrowhead shaped leaves
- Deltoid: Triangular
- Cordate: Heart-shaped, broadly ovate; tapering to an acute apex, with the base turning in and forming a notch where the petiole is attached

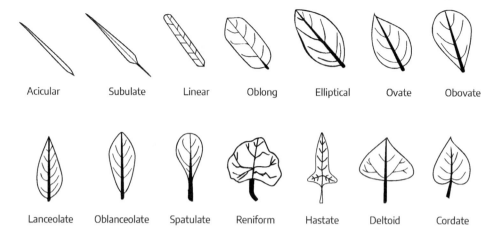

Figure 1-22: Leaf blade shapes.

Leaf apex shapes:

- Acute: Ending in an acute angle with a sharp, but not acuminate, point
- Acuminate: Tapering to a long, narrow point
- Aristate: Has a bristle at the tip
- Cuspidate: Tip is sharp with two curves meeting at tip
- Mucronate: Tip ends in a small sharp point projecting from the midrib
- Obtuse: Tapering to a rounded edge
- Retuse: Rounded with a very shallow notch at apex
- Emarginate: Shallowly notched at the apex

Figure 1-23: Leaf apex shapes.

Leaf base shapes:

- Cuneate: Wedge-shaped, gradually narrowed towards base
- Attenuate: Tapering with concave margins
- Obtuse: Blunt, forming a wide angle at the base
- Cordate: Rounded double lobes
- Auriculate: Ear-like appendages at the base
- Sagittate: Arrowhead-shaped, with two pointed lower lobes
- Truncate: Relatively square end

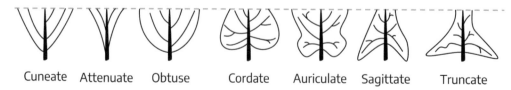

Figure 1-24: Leaf base shapes.

Leaf margins (studying leaf margins is especially useful in the identification of certain varieties of fruit plants):

- Entire: A smooth edge with no teeth or notches
- Sinuate: Having a pronounced sinuous or wavy margin
- Crenate: Having rounded teeth
- Dentate: Having teeth ending in an acute angle, pointing outward
- Serrate: Having small, sharp teeth pointing toward the apex
- Serrulate: Edges with smaller, more evenly-spaced serrations than a serrated leaf
- Double serrate: Small serrations on larger serrations
- Incised: Margin cut into sharp, deep, irregular teeth or incisions
- Lacerate: Irregular, appearing torn
- Pectinate: Prominent serrated teeth
- Ciliate: Fringed or fuzzy hairs along the margin
- Lobed: Incisions extend less than halfway to the midrib
- Cleft: Incisions extend more than halfway to the midrib
- Parted: Cut or dissected almost to the midrib

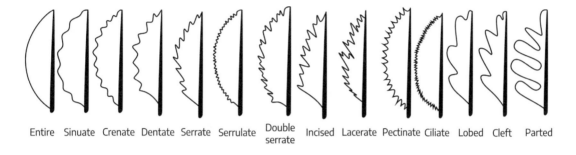

Figure 1-25: Leaf margin shapes.

Bud Anatomy

A bud is an undeveloped shoot from which embryonic leaves or flower parts arise. The buds of trees and shrubs of the temperate zone typically develop a protective outer layer of small, leathery bud scales. Annual plants and herbaceous perennials have naked buds with outer leaves that are green and somewhat succulent.

Buds of many plants require exposure to a certain number of days below a critical temperature (a period of rest) before they will resume growth in the spring. This time period varies for different plants. The flower buds of forsythia require a relatively short rest period and will grow at the first sign of warm weather. Many peach varieties require from 700 to 1000 hours of temperatures below 45°F (7°C) before they will resume growth. During rest, dormant buds can withstand very low temperatures, but after the rest period is satisfied, buds become more susceptible to weather conditions and can be damaged easily by cold temperatures or frost.

A **leaf bud** is composed of a short stem with embryonic leaves, with bud primordia (early bud embryo) in the axils and at the apex. Such buds develop into leafy shoots. Leaf buds are often less plump and more pointed than flower buds.

A **flower bud** is composed of a short stem with embryonic flower parts. In some cases, the flower buds of plants that produce fruit crops of economic importance are called fruit buds. This terminology is objectionable because, although flowers have the potential for developing into fruit, this development may never occur because of adverse weather conditions, lack of pollination, or other unfavorable circumstances. The structure is a flower bud and should be so designated since it may never set fruit.

Types of buds

Buds are named for their location on the stem. **Terminal buds** are located at the apex of a stem. **Lateral buds** are borne on the sides of the stem. Most lateral buds arise in the leaf axils and are called **axillary buds**. In some instances, more than one bud is formed. **Adventitious buds** are those arising at sites other than in the terminal or axillary position. They may develop from the internode of the stem, at the edge of a leaf blade, from callus tissue at the cut end of a stem or root, or laterally from the roots of a plant.

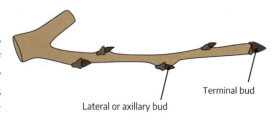

Figure 1-26: Twig diagram.

Enlarged buds or parts of buds form the edible portion of some horticultural crops. Cabbage and head lettuce are examples of unusually large terminal buds. Succulent axillary buds of Brussels sprouts become the edible part of this plant. In the case of globe artichoke, the fleshy basal portion of the bracts of the flower bud are eaten along with the solid stem portion of the bud. Broccoli is the most important horticultural plant having edible flower buds that are consumed. In this case, portions of the stem as well as small leaves associated with the flower buds are eaten.

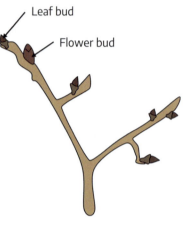

Figure 1-27: Leaf and buds of Elm.

Root Anatomy

A thorough knowledge of the root system of plants is essential for understanding their growth, flowering, and fruiting responses. The structure and growth habits of roots have a pronounced effect on the size and vigor of the plant, method of propagation, adaptation to certain soil types, and response to cultural practices and irrigation. The roots of certain vegetable crops are important as food.

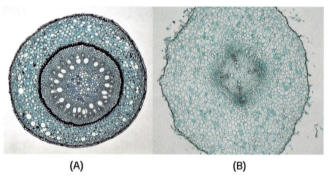

Roots typically originate from the lower portion of a plant or cutting. They possess a root cap, have no nodes, and never bear leaves or flowers directly. The principal functions of roots are to absorb nutrients and moisture, to anchor the plant in the soil, to furnish physical support for the stem, and to serve as food storage organs. In some plants, they may be used as a means of propagation.

Figure 1-28: (A) Cross section of monocot *Smilax* spp. root showing vascular cylinder with xylem arranged in circular pattern around outside of the cylinder; (B) Cross section of immature dicot *Ranunculus* spp. root with vascular cylinder in center and xylem arranged in x pattern inside the cylinder.

Types of roots

A **primary (radicle) root** originates at the lower end of the embryo of a seedling plant. A **taproot** is formed when the primary root continues to elongate downward into the soil and becomes the central and most important feature of the root system, with a somewhat limited amount of secondary branching. Some trees, especially nut trees like pecan, have a long taproot with very few lateral or fibrous roots. This makes them difficult to transplant and necessitates planting only in deep, well-drained soil.

A **lateral**, or secondary, root is a side or branch root that arises from another root.

A **fibrous** root system is one where the primary root ceases to elongate, leading to the development of numerous lateral roots which branch repeatedly and form the feeding root system of the plant. One factor that causes shrubs and dwarf trees to remain smaller than standard trees is the inactivity of the cambium tissue in the roots.

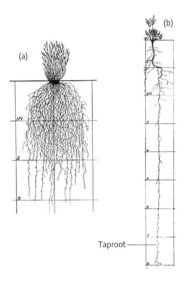

Figure 1-29: (a) Fibrous root system of *Aristida purpurea*, a grass native to the western two-thirds of the U.S.; (b) Taproot of loco weed (*Aragallus lambertii*), a legume native to the central U.S. In this figure, each line represents one foot of depth.

If plants that normally develop a taproot are undercut so that the taproot is severed early in the plant's life, the root will lose its taproot characteristic and develop a fibrous root system. This is done commercially in nurseries so trees, which naturally have tap roots, will develop a compact, fibrous root system. This allows a higher rate of transplanting success.

The quantity and distribution of plant roots are very important because these two factors have a major influence on the absorption of moisture and nutrients. The depth and spread of the roots are dependent on the inherent growth characteristics of the plant and the texture and structure of the soil. Roots will penetrate much deeper in a loose, well-drained soil than in a heavy, poorly drained soil. A dense, compacted layer in the soil will restrict or stop root growth.

During early development, a seedling plant absorbs nutrients and moisture from the few inches of soil surrounding it. Therefore, the early growth of most horticultural crops that are seeded in rows benefits from band applications of fertilizer, placed several inches to each side and slightly below the seeds.

As plants become well established, the root system develops laterally and usually extends far beyond the spread of the branches. The greatest concentration of fibrous roots occurs in the top foot of soil, but significant numbers of laterals may grow downward from these roots to provide an effective absorption system several feet deep. **Tuberous roots** are modified lateral roots that are enlarged to function as a storage organ.

The enlarged root is the edible portion of several vegetable crops. The sweet potato is a tuberous root. Carrot, parsnip, salsify, and radish are elongated taproots.

Parts of a root

Internally, there are three major parts of a root. The **meristem** is at the tip and manufactures new cells; it is an area of cell division and growth. Behind it is the zone of elongation, where cells increase in size through food and water absorption. These cells, by increasing in size, push the root tip through the soil. The third major root part is the maturation zone, where cells undergo changes to become specific tissues, such as epidermis, cortex, or vascular tissue. The epidermis is the outermost layer of cells surrounding the root. These cells are responsible for the absorption of water and minerals dissolved in water. Cortex cells are involved in the movement of water from the epidermis and in food storage. Vascular tissue is located in the center of the root and transports food and water.

Externally, there are two areas of importance. **Root hairs** are found along the main root and perform much of the actual work of water/nutrient absorption. The **root cap** is the outermost tip of the root and consists of cells that are sloughed off as the root grows through the soil. The root cap covers and protects the meristem.

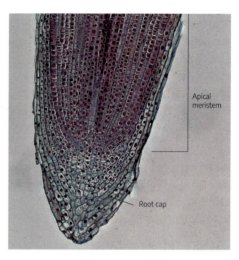

Figure 1-30: Apical meristem of *Allium* spp. root tip. Cells composing the root cap are shaded blue with the cells composing the apical meristem in purple.

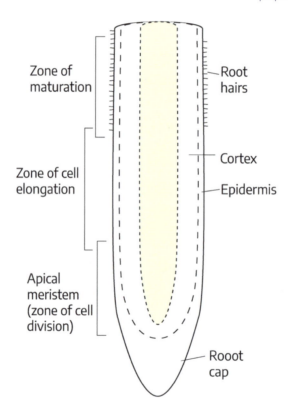

Figure 1-31: Zones of elongation. In early stages of primary development of the root tip, the apical meristem (zone of cell division) contains cells engaged in division. These cell divisions overlap with the zone of cell elongation, where cells grow and get longer, and with the zone of maturation, where different root tissues (like the vascular system) mature at different rates and root hairs develop.

Flower Anatomy

The sole function of the flower, which is generally the showiest part of the plant, is sexual reproduction. Its attractiveness and fragrance have not evolved to please humans but to ensure the continuance of the plant species. Fragrance and color are devices to attract pollinators — insects that play an important role in the reproductive process.

Parts of a flower

As the reproductive part of the plant, the flower contains the male pollen and/or the female ovule plus accessory parts such as petals, sepals, and nectar glands.

Sepals are small, green, leaf-like structures on the base of the flower that protect the flower bud. The sepals collectively are called the **calyx**.

Petals are highly colored portions of the flower. They may contain perfume as well as nectar glands. The number of petals on a flower is often used in the identification of plant families and genera. The petals collectively are called the **corolla**. Flowers of dicots typically have sepals and/or petals in multiples of four or five. Monocots typically have these floral parts in multiples of three.

The **pistil** is the female part of the plant. It is generally shaped like a bowling pin and located in the center of the flower. It consists of the stigma, style, and ovary. The stigma is located at the top and is connected to the ovary by the style. The ovary contains the eggs, which reside in the ovules. After the egg is fertilized, the ovule develops into a seed.

The **stamen** is the male reproductive organ. It consists of a pollen sac (anther) and a long, supporting filament. This filament holds the anther in position so the pollen it contains may be dispersed by wind or carried to the stigma by insects or birds.

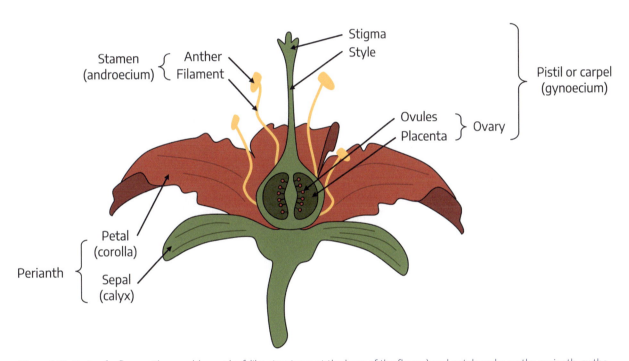

Figure 1-32: Parts of a flower. The sepal (green leaf-like structures at the base of the flower) and petals make up the perianth, or the outer part of the flower. The pistil contains the sigma, style, and ovary and is the female part of the plant. The stamen contains the anther and filament and is the male part of the plant.

Types of flowers

If a flower has a stamen, pistils, petals, and sepals, it is called a **complete** flower. If one of these parts is missing, the flower is designated incomplete.

If a flower contains functional stamens and pistils, it is called a **perfect** flower. (Stamens and pistils are considered the essential parts of a flower.) If either of the essential parts is lacking, the flower is imperfect.

Pistillate (female) flowers are those that possess a functional pistil(s), but lack stamens. **Staminate** (male) flowers contain stamens, but no pistils.

Because cross fertilization combines different genetic material and produces stronger seed, cross-pollinated plants are usually more successful than self-pollinated plants. Consequently, more plants reproduce by cross pollination than by self pollination.

As previously mentioned, there are plants that bear only male flowers (staminate plants) or only female flowers (pistillate plants). Species in which the sexes are separated into staminate and pistillate plants are called **dioecious**. Most hollies are dioecious, which means a male and a female plant are necessary to obtain berries. **Monoecious** plants are those with male and female flower parts on the same plant. Corn plants and pecan trees are examples. Some plants bear only male flowers at the beginning of the growing season, but later develop flowers of both sexes; examples are cucumbers and squash.

How seeds form

Pollination is the transfer of pollen from an anther to a stigma. This may occur by wind or by pollinators. Wind-pollinated flowers lack showy floral parts and nectar since they don't need to attract a pollinator. Flowers are brightly colored or patterned and contain a fragrance or nectar when they must attract insects, animals, or birds. In the process of searching for nectar, these pollinators will transfer pollen from flower to flower.

The stigma contains a chemical that stimulates activity of pollen from the same type of plant, causing it to grow a long pollen tube down the inside of the style to the ovules inside the ovary. The sperm from the pollen grain moves down the tube, and fertilization typically occurs. Fertilization is the union of the male sperm nucleus (from the pollen grain) and the female egg (in the ovule). If fertilization is successful, the ovule will develop into a seed.

Types of inflorescences

Some plants bear only one flower per stem and are called solitary flowers. Other plants produce an inflorescence, a term that refers to a cluster of flowers and how they are arranged on a floral stem. Most inflorescences may be classified into two groups — racemes and cymes.

In the racemose group, the florets, which are individual flowers in an inflorescence, bloom from the bottom of the stem and progress toward the top. Some examples of racemose inflorescence include spike, raceme, corymb, umbel, and head. A spike is an inflorescence where many stemless florets are attached to an elongated flower stem, or peduncle. A raceme is similar to a spike, except the florets are borne on small stems attached to the peduncle. A corymb is made up of florets with stalks, or pedicels, that are arranged at random along the peduncle in such a way that the florets create a flat, round top. An umbel is similar, except that the pedicels all arise from one point on the peduncle. A head, or composite, inflorescence is made up of numerous stemless florets and is characteristic of daisy inflorescence.

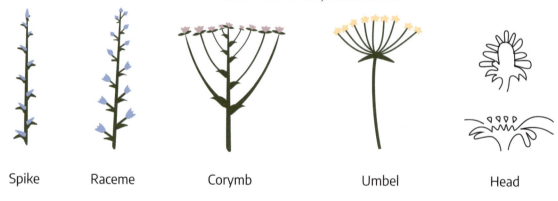

Figure 1-33: Racemose.

In the cyme group, the top floret opens first and blooms downward along the peduncle. A dichasium cyme has florets opposite each other along the peduncle. A **helicoid** cyme is one where the lower florets are all on the same side of the peduncle. A scorpioid cyme is one where the florets are alternate to each other along the peduncle.

Figure 1-34: Cyme.

Fruit Anatomy

Parts of fruit

A fruit is a ripened ovary. Fruit consists of the fertilized and mature ovules (called seeds) and the ovary wall, which may be fleshy (as in melons), or dry and hard (as in a pecan nut). The only parts of the fruit that are genetically representative of both the male and female flowers are the seeds (mature ovules). The rest of the fruit arises from the maternal plant, and is therefore genetically identical to that parent. Many fruits have additional maternal tissues develop along with the ovary; for example, the core of an apple is the ovary containing the seeds, while the part consumed develops from the receptacle that supported the ovary in the flower.

Types of fruit

Fruits can be classified as simple fruits, aggregate fruits, or multiple fruits. **Simple fruits** develop from a single ovary. There are several types oof simple fruits:

- Berry: Fleshy pericarp (ovary) surrounding the seeds (e.g., tomatoes, grapes, eggplant, blueberries)
- Drupe: Hard, stony endocarp (where seed is located) surrounded by fleshy mesocarp (middle section of ovary) like a peach
- Pepo: A modified berry with a hard rind (e.g., cucumbers, pumpkin, watermelon)
- Legume: A simple fruit that splits along 2 seams (e.g., bean, peanut)
- Achene: Small, thin-walled (papery seed) dry fruit that does not spit open at maturity (e.g., dandelion, strawberry seeds)
- Pome: A type of accessory fruit where the edible part is a swollen receptacle and the center consists of fused carpels
- Samsara: A winged achene
- Nut: A seed surrounded by a thick, hard ovary wall (pericarp) (e.g. acorns and chestnuts are true nuts)

Aggregate fruits, such as raspberries, come from a single flower with many ovaries. The flower appears as a simple flower with one corolla, one calyx, and one stem, but with many pistils or ovaries. The ovaries are fertilized separately and independently. If ovules are not pollinated successfully, the fruit will be misshapen and imperfect. Strawberry and blackberry are also aggregate fruits with the addition of an edible, enlarged receptacle. For this reason, they are sometimes termed aggregate-accessory fruits.

Multiple fruits are derived from a tight cluster of separate, independent flowers borne on a single structure. Each flower has its own calyx and corolla. Examples of multiple fruits are pineapple, fig, and the beet seed. Multiple fruits are not common in Virginia.

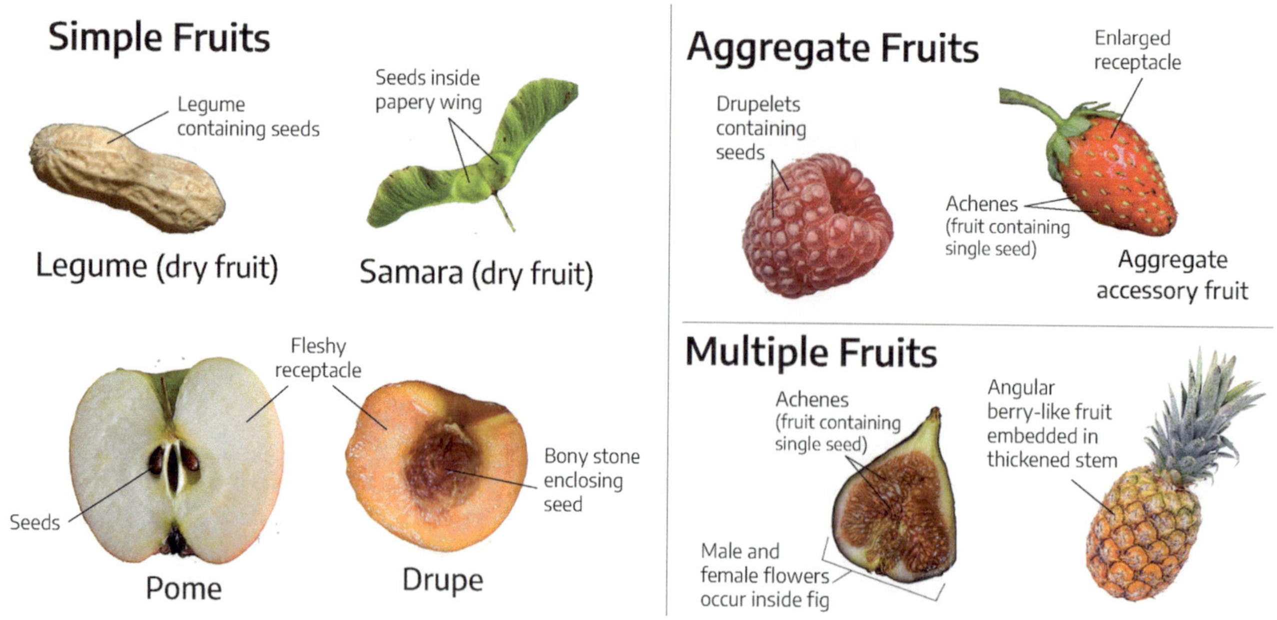

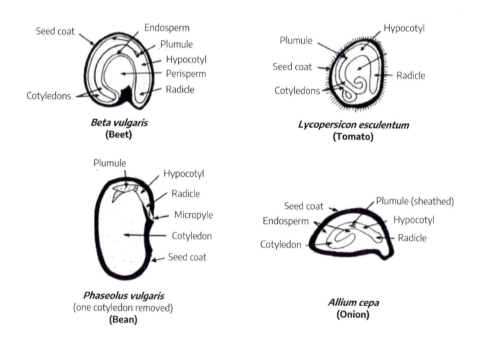

Figure 1-35: Types of fruit.

Seed Anatomy

The seed, or matured ovule, is made up of three parts. The embryo is a miniature plant in an arrested state of development. Most seeds contain a built-in food supply called the **endosperm** which can be made up of proteins, carbohydrates, or fats. (Orchid is an exception in producing no endosperm, while in some other mature seeds, the endosperm has been absorbed and stored within the embryo.) The third part is the hard outer covering, called a seed coat, which protects the seed from disease and insects and prevents water from entering the seed (this would initiate the germination process before the proper time).

Figure 1-36: Parts of a seed.

Seedlings

Germination is the resumption of active embryo growth. Prior to any visual signs of growth, the seed must absorb water through the seed coat. In addition, the seed must be in the proper environmental conditions; that is, exposed to oxygen, favorable temperatures, and for some, correct light. The **radicle** is the first part of the seedling to emerge from the seed. It will develop into the primary root from which root hairs and lateral roots develop. The portion of the seedling between the radicle and the first leaf-like structure is called the **hypocotyl**. Above the hypocotyl is the **plumule**, which is the embryonic shoot. The seed leaves, or **cotyledons**, encase the embryo and are usually different in shape from the leaves that the mature plant will produce. Plants producing one cotyledon fall into the group of monocotyledons or **monocots**. Plants producing two seed leaves are called dicotyledons or **dicots**. A **micropyle** a small pore located in the seedcoat that allows water absorption and gas exchange.

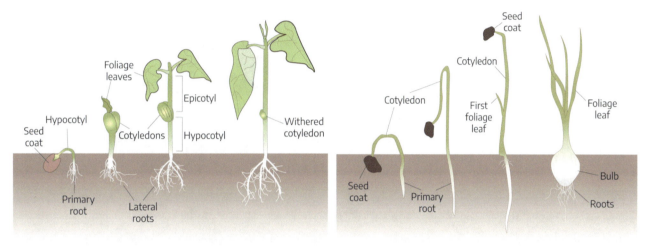

Figure 1-37: Germination of a dicot bean seed and monocot onion seed.

Green Spring Gardens "Planting Seeds of Hope" A Master Gardener approach to Therapeutic Gardening

By Kathleen Wellington, Extension Master Gardener, Green Spring Gardens

Since 2016, Green Spring Extension Master Gardeners in Fairfax County have implemented and sustained on-going therapeutic gardening projects. Green Spring Extension Master Gardeners (GSEMG's) provide education and therapeutic focused hands-on gardening experiences for individuals with mental health and substance abuse challenges at the Fairfax County Wellness Circle Crisis Stabilization Program and at the USO Resiliency Garden at Fort Belvoir.

During the initial phases of implementing these projects, the GSEMG's met with unanticipated challenges that jeopardized the success of the projects. Staff uninterested in gardening, lack of management support, along with a lack of understanding of the benefits of gardening for individuals with special needs were just some of the challenges encountered.

Out of these challenges originated Green Spring's "Planting Seeds of Hope" initiative: a replicable framework to implement successful gardening for individuals with special needs.

Here are some examples of things that have made our horticulture therapy projects successful:

1. Master Gardener and program staff training – including modules pertaining to definition and theoretical information about horticulture therapy, benefits of gardening, and practical applications to special populations for GSEMG's. Program staff training includes an understanding of the mission of the Master Gardener program and education on therapeutic gardening and its relevance to the program objectives.
2. Development of project goals – developed with program staff consistent with the needs of the clients, along with a plan to implement and measure progress.
3. Therapeutic focused education and hands-on gardening that is not "show or tell" but "do with" education adapted to the comprehension level of clients.
4. Development of self-sustaining gardening manuals for the program, including "how to" garden education that connects the task with the therapeutic/wellness benefits.
5. Coordination with staff recognizing that staff are experts on their clients but GSEMG's can help staff work more successfully with clients through therapeutic gardening techniques (sensory stimulation, development of skill sets, metaphors, etc.).

Sustainable funding/community partnerships including awareness of the difference in fundraising guidelines between nonprofits and government entities. Collaboration with program management to understand the best opportunities for funding such as inclusion in program budget, fund raising, partnerships with community organizations and the value of media recognition.

Figure 1-38: The bounty from the Resiliency Garden at Fort Belvoir.

Physiology: Plant Growth and Development

The five major plant functions that are the basics for plant growth and development are photosynthesis, respiration, transpiration, absorption, and translocation.

Photosynthesis

One of the major differences between plants and animals is the ability of plants to internally manufacture their own food (called **autotrophy**). To produce food for itself, a plant requires energy from sunlight, carbon dioxide from the air, and water from the soil. If any of these ingredients is lacking, **photosynthesis**, or food production, will stop. If any factor is removed for a long period of time, the plant will die. Photosynthesis literally means "to put together with light."

$$6\ CO_2 + 6\ H_2O + \text{sunlight} \longrightarrow C_6H_{12}O_6$$

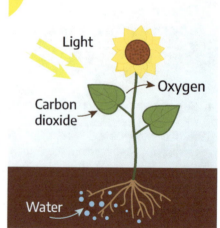

Figure 1-39: Photosynthesis: Plants use light from the sun to make energy, a process which involves turning carbon dioxide into oxygen.

Plants first store the energy from light in simple sugars, such as glucose ($C_6H_{12}O_6$). Some of these sugars are converted back to water and carbon dioxide, releasing the stored energy through the process called respiration. This energy released from respiration is required for all living processes and growth. Simple sugars are also converted to other sugars and starches (carbohydrates) which may be transported to the stems and roots for use or storage, or may be used as building blocks for more complex structures (e.g., oils, pigments, proteins, cell walls).

Any green plant tissue is capable of photosynthesis. **Chloroplasts** in these cells contain the green pigment chlorophyll which traps the light energy. However, leaves are generally the site of most food production due to their special structure. The internal tissue (mesophyll) contains cells with abundant chloroplasts in an arrangement that allows easy movement of water and air. The protective upper and lower epidermis (skin) layers of the leaf include many stomata that regulate movement of the gases involved in photosynthesis into and out of the leaf.

Photosynthesis is dependent on the availability of **light**. Generally speaking, as sunlight increases in intensity, photosynthesis increases. This results in greater food production. Many garden crops, such as tomatoes, respond best to maximum sunlight. Tomato production is cut drastically as light intensities drop. Only two or three varieties of "greenhouse" tomatoes will produce any fruit when sunlight is minimal in late fall and early spring.

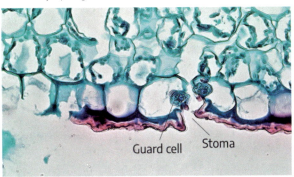

Figure 1-40: Guard cells surrounding open stoma in epidermis of succulent xerophyte leaf.

Water (H_2O) plays an important role in photosynthesis in several ways. First, it maintains a plant's **turgor**, the firmness or fullness of plant tissue. Turgor pressure in a cell can be compared to air in an inflated balloon. Water pressure or turgor is needed in plant cells to maintain shape and ensure cell growth. Second, water is split into hydrogen and oxygen by the energy of the sun that has been absorbed by the chlorophyll in the plant leaves. The oxygen (O_2) is released into the atmosphere, and the hydrogen is used in manufacturing carbohydrates. Third, water dissolves minerals from the soil and transports them up from the roots and throughout the plant where they serve as raw materials in the growth of new plant tissues. The soil surrounding a plant should be moist, not too wet or too dry. Water is pulled through the plant by evaporation of water through the leaves (**transpiration**).

Photosynthesis also requires carbon dioxide (CO_2) which enters the plant through the stomata. Carbon and oxygen are used in the manufacturing of carbohydrates. Carbon dioxide in the air is plentiful enough so that it is not a limiting factor in plant growth. However, since carbon dioxide is consumed in making sugars and is not released by plants at an equal rate, a tightly closed greenhouse in midwinter may not let in enough outside air to maintain an adequate carbon dioxide level. Under these conditions, improved crops of roses, carnations, tomatoes, and certain other crops can be produced if the carbon dioxide level is raised with CO_2 generators or, in small greenhouses, with dry ice.

Although not a direct component in photosynthesis, temperature is an important factor. Photosynthesis occurs at its highest rate in the temperature range 65 to 85°F (18 to 27°C) and decreases when temperatures are above or below this range.

Respiration

Carbohydrates made during photosynthesis are of value to the plant when they are converted into energy. This energy is used in the process of building new tissues (plant growth). The chemical process by which sugars and starches produced by photosynthesis are converted into energy is called **respiration**. It is similar to the burning of wood or coal to produce heat (energy). This process in cells is shown most simply as:

$$C_6H_{12}O_6 + 6\,O_2 \longrightarrow 6\,CO_2 + 6\,H_2O + \text{Energy released}$$

This equation is precisely the opposite of that used to illustrate photosynthesis, although more is involved than just reversing the reaction. However, it is appropriate to relate photosynthesis to a building process, while respiration is a breaking-down process.

Table 1-1: Photosynthesis vs respiration

Photosynthesis	Respiration
Produces food	Uses food for plant energy
Stores energy	Releases energy
Occurs in cells containing chloroplasts	Occurs in all cells
Releases oxygen	Uses oxygen
Uses water	Produces water
Uses carbon dioxide	Produces carbon dioxide
Occurs in sunlight	Occurs in darkness and light

By now, it should be clear that respiration is the reverse of photosynthesis. Unlike photosynthesis, respiration occurs at night as well as during the day. Respiration occurs in all life forms and in all cells. The release of accumulated carbon dioxide and the uptake of oxygen occurs at the cell level. In animals, blood carries both carbon dioxide and oxygen to and from the atmosphere by means of the lungs or gills. In plants, there is simple diffusion into the open spaces around the cells, and exchange occurs through the stomata on leaves and stems, or through root hairs.

Transpiration

Transpiration is the process by which a plant loses water, primarily from leaf stomata. Transpiration is a necessary process that involves the use of about 90% of the water that enters the plant through the roots. The other 10% of the water is used in chemical reactions and in plant tissues. Transpiration is involved in the movement of water, minerals, and at times, stored sugars from the roots to other parts of the plant. This occurs in the xylem.

Transpiration and turgor pressure: The amount of water lost from the plant depends on several environmental factors such as temperature, humidity, and wind or air movement. An increase in temperature or air movement decreases humidity outside the leaf and increases the rate of transpiration. This presents a continuing danger to plants as the rate of water loss may not be matched by the rate of water absorption from dry soil into the roots. A water deficit in the plant may only lead to temporary wilting (loss of turgor pressure) from which the plant may rapidly recover when the transpiration rate decreases later in the day or stops overnight. The guard cells respond to the loss of turgor by shrinking and closing the stomata. While this significantly reduces further damaging water loss, it also impedes carbon dioxide entry for photosynthesis. Repeated temporary wilting can lead to stunted plants due to reduction of the food supply and other metabolic changes, especially in cell division and enlargement. A plant maintains adequate turgor pressure when the amount of water loss due to transpiration is equal to the amount of water absorbed into the plant.

Absorption

Absorption is the process by which substances, particularly water and minerals, are moved into the plant. This occurs mainly through the roots in the tip region where root hairs are present, but it may also occur through leaf surfaces. Water absorption into roots may be a passive process due to a "pulling" action, drawing water through the xylem tubes to replace water lost from the leaves through transpiration. Other water absorption is an active process linked to active absorption of mineral nutrients. This is discussed later in the section on plant nutrition.

Translocation

Translocation is the movement of sugars, amino acids, and other plant chemicals from the leaves to other parts of the plant through the **phloem**. This translocation is often an active process requiring respiration energy as the substances are moved upward and downward in the plants to growing areas or storage.

Environmental Factors Affecting Plant Growth

Plant growth and distribution are limited by the environment. If any one environmental factor is less than ideal, it will become a limiting factor in plant growth. Limiting factors are also responsible for the geography of plant distribution. For example, only plants adapted to limited amounts of water can live in deserts. Most plant problems are caused by environmental stress, either directly or indirectly. Therefore, it is important to understand the environmental aspects that affect plant growth. These factors are light, temperature, water, humidity, and nutrition. For more about how these factors impact plants, see Chapter 5: "Abiotic Stress."

Light

Light has three principal characteristics that affect plant growth: quantity, quality, and duration.

Light **quantity** refers to the intensity or concentration of sunlight and varies with the season of the year. The maximum is present in the summer and the minimum in winter. The more sunlight a plant receives (up to a point), the better capacity it has to produce plant food through photosynthesis. As the sunlight quantity decreases, the photosynthetic process decreases. Light quantity can be decreased in a garden or greenhouse by using cheesecloth shading above the plants. It can be increased by surrounding plants with white or reflective material, or supplemental lights.

Light **quality** refers to the color or wavelength reaching the plant surface. Sunlight can be broken up by a prism into respective colors of red, orange, yellow, green, blue, indigo, and violet. On a rainy day, raindrops act as tiny prisms and break the sunlight into these colors, producing a rainbow. Red and blue light have the greatest effect on plant growth. Green light is least effective to plants as they reflect green light and absorb none. It is this reflected light that makes them appear green to us. Blue light is primarily responsible for vegetative growth or leaf growth. Red light, when combined with blue light, encourages flowering in plants. Fluorescent, or cool-white, light is high in the blue range of light quality and is used to encourage leafy growth. Such light would be excellent for starting seedlings. Incandescent light is high in the red or orange range, but generally produces too much heat to be a valuable light source. Fluorescent "grow" lights have a mixture of red and blue colors that attempts to imitate sunlight as closely as possible, but they are costly and generally not of any greater value than regular fluorescent lights.

Light **duration**, or photoperiod, refers to the amount of time that a plant is exposed to sunlight. When the concept of photoperiod was first recognized, it was thought that the length of periods of light triggered flowering. The various categories of response were named according to the light length (i.e., short-day and long-day). It was then discovered that it is not the length of the light period, but the length of uninterrupted dark periods that is critical to floral development. The ability of many plants to flower is controlled by photoperiod. Plants can be classified into three categories depending upon their flowering response to the duration of darkness. These are short-day, long-day, or day-neutral plants.

Short-day plants form their flowers only when the day length is less than about 12 hours in duration. Short-day plants include many spring- and fall-flowering plants, such as chrysanthemum and poinsettia. **Long-day** plants form flowers only when day lengths exceed 12 hours (short nights). They include almost all of the summer-flowering plants, such as rudbeckia and California poppy, as well as many vegetables, including beet, radish, lettuce, spinach, and potato. **Day-neutral** plants form flowers regardless of day length. Some plants do not really fit into any category, but may be responsive to combinations of day lengths. The petunia will flower regardless of day length, but flowers earlier and more profusely under long daylight. Since chrysanthemums flower under the short-day conditions of spring or fall, the method for manipulating the plant into experiencing short days is very simple. If long days are predominant, a shade cloth is drawn over the chrysanthemum for 12 hours daily to block out light until flower buds are initiated. To bring a long-day plant into flower when sunlight is not present longer than 12 hours, artificial light is added until flower buds are initiated.

Temperature

Temperature affects the productivity and growth of a plant, depending on whether the plant variety is a warm- or cool-season crop. If temperatures are high and day length is long, a cool-season crop such as spinach will **bolt** (flower prematurely) rather than produce the desired flower. Temperatures that are too low for a warm-season crop such as tomato will prevent fruit set. Adverse temperatures also cause stunted growth and poor quality. For example, the bitterness in lettuce is caused by high temperatures.

> The USDA classifies geographic areas into a series of "plant hardiness zones" based on the average annual minimum winter temperature, divided into 10-degree F zones. The most recent (2012) version is based on weather data from 1976–2005. To check your USDA hardiness zone, go to: https://planthardiness.ars.usda.gov.

Sometimes temperatures are used in connection with day length to manipulate the flowering of plants. Chrysanthemums will flower for a longer period of time if daytime temperatures are around 59°F (15°C). The Christmas cactus forms flowers as a result of short days and low temperatures. Daffodils are forced to flower by putting the bulbs in cold storage in October at 35 to 40°F (2 to 4°C). The cold temperatures allow the bulb to break dormancy. The bulbs are transferred to the greenhouse in midwinter where growth begins. The flowers are then ready for cutting in three to four weeks.

Thermoperiod refers to the daily range of temperatures a plant is exposed to. Plants produce maximum growth when exposed to a day temperature that is about 10 to 15° higher than the night temperature. This allows the plant to photosynthesize (build up) and respire (break down) during an optimum daytime temperature and to curtail the rate of respiration during a cooler night. High temperatures cause increased respiration, sometimes above the rate of photosynthesis. This means that the products of photosynthesis are being used more rapidly than they are being produced. This causes plant growth to slow down or even stop. For growth to occur, photosynthesis must be greater than respiration.

Low temperatures can result in poor growth. Photosynthesis is slowed down at low temperatures. Since photosynthesis is slowed, growth is slowed, and this results in lower yields. Not all plants grow best in the same temperature range. For example, snapdragons grow best when night temperatures are 55°F (12°C); the poinsettia prefers 62°F (17°C). Florist cyclamen does well under very cool conditions, while many bedding plants prefer a higher temperature. Recently, it has been found that roses can tolerate much lower night temperatures than previously believed. This has meant a conservation in energy for greenhouse growers.

However, in some cases, a certain number of days of low temperatures are needed by plants to grow properly. This is true of crops growing in cold regions of the country. Peaches are a prime example; most varieties require 700 to 1000 hours between 45°F (7°C) and 32°F (0°C) before they break their rest period and begin growth. Lilies need 6 weeks at 33°F (1°C) before blooming.

Plants can be classified as either hardy or nonhardy (tender), depending on their ability to withstand cold temperatures. Winter injury can occur to nonhardy plants if temperatures are too low or if unseasonably low temperatures occur early in the fall or late in the spring. Winter injury may also occur because of desiccation (drying out) — plants need water during the winter. When the soil is frozen, the movement of water into the plant is severely restricted. On a windy winter day, broadleaved evergreens can become water-deficient in a few minutes; the leaves or needles then turn brown. Wide variations in winter temperatures can cause premature bud break in some plants and consequent bud-freezing damage. Late spring frosts can ruin entire peach crops. If temperatures drop too low during the winter, entire trees of some species are killed by the freezing and splitting of plant cells and tissue.

Water

As mentioned earlier, water is a primary component of photosynthesis. It maintains the turgor pressure or firmness of tissue and transports nutrients throughout the plant. In maintaining turgor pressure, water is the major constituent of the protoplasm (living material) of a cell. By means of turgor pressure and other changes in the cell, water regulates the opening and closing of the stoma, thus regulating transpiration. Water also provides the pressure to move a root through the soil. Among water's most critical roles is that of the solvent for minerals moving into the plant and for carbohydrates moving to their site of use or storage.

Relative humidity is the ratio of water vapor in the air to the amount of water the air could hold at a given temperature and pressure, expressed as a percent.

$$\mathrm{RH} = \frac{\text{Water in the air}}{\text{Water the air could hold (at constant temperature and pressure)}}$$

For example, if a kilogram of air at 75°F could hold 4 grams of water vapor and there are only 3 grams of water in the air, then the relative humidity (RH) is:

$$\mathrm{RH} = \tfrac{3}{4} = 0.75$$

Expressed as a percent = 75%

Warm air can hold more water vapor than cold air; therefore, if the amount of water in the air stays the same and the temperature increases, the relative humidity decreases.

Water vapor will move from an area of high RH to one of low RH. The greater the difference in humidity, the faster water will move.

The relative humidity in the air space between the cells within the leaf approaches 100%; therefore, when the stomate is open, water vapor rushes out. As the vapor moves out, a cloud of high humidity is formed around the stomate. This cloud of humidity helps slow down transpiration and cool the leaf. If air movement blows the humid cloud away, transpiration will increase.

Nutrition

Many people confuse plant nutrition with plant fertilization. **Plant nutrition** refers to the needs and uses of the basic chemical elements in the plant. **Fertilization** is the term used when these materials are supplied to the environment around the plant. A lot must happen before a chemical element supplied in a fertilizer can be taken up and used by the plant.

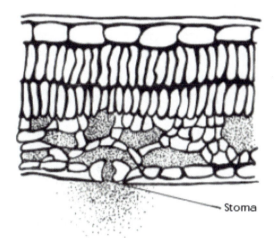

Figure 1-41: Cross section of a leaf (dots represent relative humidity): In this example, an area of lower humidity exists outside the leaf and the stoma is open, allowing the higher relative humidity inside the leave to escape.

Plants need 16 elements for normal growth. Carbon, hydrogen, and oxygen are found in air and water. Nitrogen, potassium, magnesium, calcium, phosphorous, and sulfur are found in the soil. These six elements are used in relatively large amounts by the plant and are called **macronutrients** (nitrogen, potassium, and phosphorous are the primary macronutrients and magnesium, sulfur and calcium are the secondary macronutrients). There are seven other elements called **micronutrients** (or trace elements) and are used in much smaller amounts. Micronutrients are found in the soil: iron, zinc, molybdenum, manganese, boron, copper, and chlorine. All 16 elements, both macronutrients and micronutrients, are essential for plant growth.

Most of the nutrients that a plant needs are dissolved in water and then absorbed by the roots. Many nutrient combinations in fertilizers dissolve easily, and those nutrients can be readily absorbed. Sometimes two dissolved nutrients will combine into a product that has very low solubility. Availability of both nutrients to the plant is then severely reduced. This can occur with calcium and phosphorus and the micronutrients. Nutrient solubility is also affected by soil pH. High (alkaline) pH levels drastically reduce the solubility and availability of micronutrients (a factor in iron deficiency in azaleas), while low (very acidic) pH levels make some micronutrients (and non-nutrient minerals such as aluminum) so highly available as to injure the plant. Another consideration is the nutrient balance in the soil. For example, calcium and magnesium are absorbed similarly, but magnesium is absorbed more readily. The root does not select the nutrient to be absorbed; if both are present at the absorption site, the magnesium will be absorbed. This is why a soil test may indicate that, while there is sufficient calcium in the soil, a plant can suffer calcium deficiency because of an excess of magnesium competing for absorption.

The process whereby nutrients are absorbed varies. Water and nutrients can move between the outer cells of the root, but eventually they must cross a membrane to enter a cell. Water and some nutrients can do this easily (a passive process) while other nutrients are too large for the 'holes' in the membrane, and energy is needed to move these nutrients into the cell (an active process). Absorption is generally a combination of these processes: certain nutrients are actively absorbed, others enter passively to maintain a chemical balance.

Anything that lowers or prevents the production of sugars in the leaves can lower nutrient absorption. If the plant is under stress due to low light or extremes in temperature, nutrient deficiency problems may develop. The stage of growth or rate of growth may also affect the amount of nutrients absorbed. Many plants go into a rest period, or dormancy, during part of the year. During this dormancy, few nutrients are absorbed. Plants may also absorb different nutrients just as flower buds begin to develop.

Foliar absorption: A special case

Under normal growing conditions, plants absorb most nutrients except carbon, hydrogen, and oxygen from the soil. However, some nutrients can also be absorbed by the leaves if they are sprayed with a dilute solution. The factors that affect absorption by the cell are still important because the nutrient must enter the cell to be used by the plant. Care must be taken that the concentration of the nutrient is not too high or the leaf will be injured. The nutrient must get around or through the waxy leaf cuticle before it can enter the cell.

Taxonomy: Biological Classification

Taxonomy is the science of biological classification of plants and animals. The purpose of taxonomy is to develop a convenient and precise method of classifying human knowledge. This method thus preserves knowledge and makes it accessible. In this chapter, we will learn how plants are classified, then learn how to go about identifying a plant by the use of a leaf key.

Classification of Landscape Plants

There are many ways to classify or categorize the thousands of plants used in the landscape. The validity of any system depends on consistency, clarity, and utility. For example, the classification of plants based on use, such as ornamentals in contrast to edibles, seems logical until you consider some species which are both ornamental and edible. Other ways of classifying plants, such as through the relationships of their growth habits, are also descriptive though frequently not a basis for easy differentiation. For example, differences between some trees and shrubs or between evergreen, semi-evergreen, and deciduous trees and shrubs may depend on geographical location. Other divisions include length of life (annual, biennial, or perennial) and type of stem tissue (woody or herbaceous).

Among woody plants, a major distinction is made between those that lose their leaves during part of the year (deciduous) and those with leaves that persist during the entire year (evergreen). There are also those that hold their leaves late into the winter when others are leafless, but eventually lose their leaves or turn brown (semi-evergreen). In fact, even evergreen plants ultimately lose their leaves, though it is usually after new leaves have been formed. Some evergreens hold their leaves only one year, but most hold them two or more years.

In addition to the very general horticultural classifications outlined previously, plants are further differentiated for landscape purposes by size, growth habit, usage, and adaptability to specific environmental conditions. See Chapter 16: "Landscape Design" for more information.

Finally, landscape plants are classified according to tolerance of various environmental conditions or on the basis of their requirement of certain conditions. This is particularly true of plants with growth that is unique to a specific habitat, such as bog plants and indoor or outdoor plants. Major categories related to environment are tropical, subtropical, and temperate. Within each of these categories and locations, plants are classified either as hardy or tender, depending on whether or not the plant will survive the winter of a particular region. These, along with the scientific classification, ought to provide you with sufficient background to build upon as you become increasingly experienced.

Scientific Classification

Various methods of classifying plants have been used throughout history, including some of the approaches already mentioned; however, it was the effort of Carolus Linnaeus (1707-1778) that revolutionized plant classification and gave form to the present scientific system. This system uses structural (morphological) similarities and differences, particularly in the reproductive organs, as a basis for classification. These plant parts are the least likely to be influenced by environmental conditions and, therefore, provide stable distinguishing features.

Plant classification begins by dividing the plant kingdom into major divisions, separated on an evolutionary basis. The division that will be of importance to you is the most advanced division containing the so-called higher plants. This division, known as Tracheophyta, are plants with roots, stems, leaves, and vascular systems. Further divisions can be illustrated by using as an example a cultivar of beautyberry called 'Early Amethyst': *Callicarpa dichotoma* 'Early Amethyst.'

Callicarpa dichotoma 'Early Amethyst' is described by each of the following categories. The precision of the description increases as the list descends.

Kingdom: Plant
   Division: Tracheophyta
     Class: Magnoliopsida
       Order: Lamiales
         Family: Lamiaceae
           Genus: *Callicarpa*
             Species: *C. dichotoma*
               Cultivar: 'Early Amethyst'

The family has very specific distinguishing characteristics that can be used for identification purposes. This is particularly true of reproductive (flower) parts, but frequently holds true for non-reproductive structural features such as leaf and bud arrangements. Family names end in aceae. For example, apples, cherries, and peaches are in the Rosaceae family (rose family). Historically, plants have been grouped into families based on flower and fruit characteristics; currently, DNA sequencing is being used to clarify the true identity of plants and their relationships to other species/genera. While the family concept is not generally used in the nursery and landscape industries, knowledge of the family can prove to be helpful. For example, species in the Rosacea family may be prone to pest problems, and species in the Ericaceae (heath) family (e.g., azaleas and blueberries) generally require well drained acid soils.

Below family, plants are grouped in a particular **genus** and these plants are very similar morphologically. Sometimes members of the same genus but different species usually can cross pollinate among themselves, but usually not with members of other genera (plural of genus).

Below genus the basic unit of this taxonomy system is the **species**. Distinct and repeated variation within a species is often observed. This results in the naming of a subspecies or variety or **cultivar** (cultivated variety). A **hybrid** is a genetic cross of two different plants, usually from two different varieties of the same species. The following discussion will help you understand the **binomial system of nomenclature**. Note that the species and variety names always include the genus name.

Common Plant Names

All plants bear at least one common name, a vernacular name that is commonly attached to a plant. Examples of common names are red maple, American beech, white pine, and redbud. The issues of using these familiar names are that 1) a plant often has more than one common name, 2) names can vary from region to region, and 3) names vary from one language to another. Furthermore, two completely unrelated tree species can share the same or similar common name. For example, the common name of a conifer commonly seen throughout Virginia is eastern red cedar (*Juniperus virginiana*). Eastern red cedar is a juniper and not a type of cedar; it is not even in the same plant family as a true cedar (genus = *Cedrus*). Thus, referring to common names in horticultural plant commerce is a very unreliable way to describe a plant.

Plants also have a scientific name which is essential to correctly identify, propagate, sell, purchase, use, assess, and diagnose plants in many horticultural applications. Most wholesale plant catalogs list plants by scientific name, and anyone in the horticultural realm needs to know plants by their scientific name. Scientific names are "relatively" stable; botanists occasionally reclassify plants resulting in family and species names being changed. In general, common names are written in lower case with the exception of proper names (e.g., American beech).

Many garden centers and virtually all wholesale plant vendors list their plants by the scientific name, so knowing both names is important. Knowing plant names also helps you understand the relationships (plant growth relative to light, water, soil, and climate aspects) between plants when observing plants in natural or man-made landscapes. The use of a plant's scientific name is the best and most reliable way to describe a plant.

Scientific Names

Genus and Specific Epithet = Species

All known living things are given a two-word Latin scientific name, a generic name followed by a specific name. Latin was chosen because it is a dead language (not commonly spoken and no longer evolving). This two-word name (binomial) is descriptive of only one plant (i.e., species) and is composed of a **genus** and a **specific epithet** (species). For example, humans are *Homo sapiens*; *Homo* is the genus (a generic name) and *sapiens* is the specific epithet (a specific name). Collectively, the genus followed by the specific epithet is a species.

The scientific name is very important to know in most situations since there is no ambiguity on the interpretation of the name. For example, the common name of *Acer rubrum* is red maple. However, red maple is also called scarlet maple and swamp maple. Adding to the confusion is that there are a few maples that can have red foliage. However, if the *Acer rubrum* name is used, then one knows exactly which species is being referred to.

A **genus** is a group of somewhat closely related individuals (a group name) comprising one or more species. For example, the genus name for all maples is *Acer*, and the genus name for all oaks is *Quercus*. A genus name is always a noun and a single species name is either an adjective or another supporting noun. The specific epithet relates to such things as plant attributes, the place it was originally found, or the discoverer. The specific epithet is the second word of the Latin binomial that usually functions as an adjective (or sometimes named after an individual) and indicates or describes the member of the genus. For example, the species name for sugar maple is *Acer saccharum* and the species name for white oak is *Quercus alba*. Again, the genus followed by the specific epithet comprises a species. A **species** is a group of individuals that can be characterized by a set of identifiable characteristics that distinguishes them from other types; thus, all sugar maples (*Acer saccharum*) look more or less alike and can be differentiated from other maple species.

There are rules for writing a species name. The genus name is capitalized and either italicized or underlined. For example, the genus for maples is written as *Acer* (or Acer). The plural of genus is genera. The specific epithet is written in lower case and is italicized or underlined. For example, the Japanese maple is *Acer palmatum* (or Acer palmatum). Italics or underline designates the names are in a foreign language. The plural of species is species; the abbreviation for a species (singular) is sp. and the abbreviation for more than one species is spp. (plural). For example, one maple species is *Acer* sp. and more than one species is *Acer* spp. In paragraph style, after the first mention of a species, e.g., *Acer palmatum*, the following references to that species use a first letter abbreviation of the genus term, e.g., *A. palmatum*. Here is review example for the proper designation of a scientific plant name, *Acer palmatum*:

Species: *Acer palmatum*
Genus: *Acer*
Specific epithet: *palmatum*
Common name: red maple

Knowing the Latin meaning of the binomial can often help one remember the species name. For example, in the species *Cornus florida*, flowering dogwood, the genus *Cornus* means horn, referring to the very hard wood of this species. The specific epithet, *florida*, means flowering referring to the very showy flowers. Not all binomial names have meanings that are linked with tangible nouns or adjectives. For example, the genus *Pinus* (pine) refers to the name historically given to pine trees.

A scientific name and a common name may be learned with equal ease. We just need to make the association with the plant. Most people never really take a close look at the scientific name because it appears so foreign, hard to remember, impossible to pronounce, and of no help at all in remembering the plant. In fact, the Latin genus and species may be quite familiar to us and help more than we may think in making the plant-to-name association. Pronunciation does not need to be an undue burden either.

Pronouncing Latin names

Latin pronunciations of plant names have evolved from the classical form of the language to a more comfortable, modernized form. The following guide may help in understanding and using the pronunciations.

Table 1-2: Consonants

Letter	Sound	Example
C-	soft (as in city) when followed by E, I, Y, AE, or OE hard (as in call) when followed by A, O, U, AU, OI, or a consonant	Cycas = SIGH-kus Coccinea - kok-SIN-ee-uh
G-	soft (as in gem) when followed by E, I, Y, AE, or OE hard (as in go) when followed by A, O, U, AU, or OI	Ginkgo = JINK-go
CH-	always as K (as in chemist) unless part of a proper name	Chamaedorea = kam-ee-DOR-ee-uh Pachysandra = pak-ih-SAN-druh Veitchia = VEETCH-ee-uh (for English Nursery)

Table 1-3: Vowels

Letter	Sound
A-	long as in fate (sometimes fat), short as in idea
E-	long as in be; short as in bell
I-	long as in pine (sometimes machine); short as in pin. Species names ending in -ii have the first pronounced as machine and the second as in side (-ii = ee-eye)
O-	long as in note; short as in not
U-	long as in rule; short as in up
Y-	long as in type; short as in symbol

Table 1-4: Dipthongs

Dipthong	Sound	Example
ae-	as in Caeser	*dracaena* = dra-SEE-nuh
oe-	as in oenology	*amoena* - a-MEE-nuh
au-	as in author	*centaurea* = cen-TAU-ree-uh
eu-	as in neuter	*leucothoe* = loo-KOTH-oh-ee
oi-	as in coin	*deltoides* = del-TOY-deez

Accents: Final syllables are never accented. When the name has three or more syllables, the next to last is generally accented. If that syllable is very short (especially if a single vowel), the accent is commonly placed on the preceding syllable. Note: Common usage sometimes interferes with these rules, and some plant dictionaries may even disagree.

> *Gypsophila* = jip-so-PHIL-uh rather than jip-SOPH-il-uh
> *Pittosporum* = pit-oh-SPOR-um rather than pit-TOSS-pore-um
> *Araucaria* = ar-au-CARE-ee-uh rather than ar-au-care-EE-uh

Examples:

> *Cordyline terminalis:* kor-dih-LYE-nee ter-mih-NAY-lis
> *Kalachoe blossfeldiana:* kal-an-KOH-ee bloss-fel-dee-AYN-uh
> *Sedum acre:* SEE-dum AY-kree

Many Latin genus names have been adopted into our common name vocabularies, such as Aucuba, Begonia, Dieffenbachia, Draceana, Forsythia, Gladiolus, Petunia, and Philodendron. (They are not italicized or underlined when used as English common names, but still must be when including the Latin species.) Other times, the common name is a direct English version of the Latin genus, as in juniper from *Juniperus*, lily from *Lilium*, pine from *Pinus*, rose from *Rosa*, and spirea from *Spiraea*. For other genera, the name derivation is not as direct, but with repetition, it is equally easy to relate *Acer* as maples, *Dianthus* as pinks, *Ilex* as hollies, *Ligustrum* as privets, or *Taxus* as yews.

Looking at these Latin words may offer instant recognition or be challenging. Further help could really benefit our learning effort. One good reference is *Botanical Latin* (W.T. Stearn, 2004, Hafner Publishing Co., New York) is more for the taxonomist than the gardener. Another is *A Dictionary of Botanical Terms* (F.A. Swink, 1990, American Nurseryman Publishing Co.). A favorite is the soft-bound, pocket-size *New Pronouncing Dictionary of Plant Names* (rev. 2006). As the title says, both pronunciations and translations are provided for a wide array of genus and species names. It also may be obtained from American Nurseryman Publishing.

Plant Classifications Subordinate to a Species (Subspecies, Variety, Cultivar, Hybrid)

Plants of a particular species are not identical. They may have a different form, leaf size, flower color, growth rate. To appreciate this phenomenon, consider the wide variety of **phenotypic** (visual appearance as a result of DNA expression) traits that makes each one of us who we are: hair, eye, and skin color, height, hand size, and body type are a few traits that make each one of us unique. The same phenotypic variation occurs in plant populations. So, in a population of 1,000 seed-grown redbud trees (*Cercis candensis*), most plants will have the typical leaf size, flower color, and tree height. A small proportion will, however, have large leaves or small leaves, some have light pink flowers and some will have dark pink/purplish or even white flowers, some will have a showy yellow fall foliage color and others not, and so on. This variation is termed **intra-specific (within a species) variation**. The reason for this variation is sex. All offspring derived from seeds are the result of the mixing of male and female genetic material from each parent. In the case of plants, pollen grains (male) unite with an "egg" (female) to form a seed.

There are a few important nomenclature categories that are subordinate to a species. They are subspecies, variety, and cultivar.

Subspecies

A **subspecies** is a grouping within a species used to describe geographically isolated variants. It is a category above variety and is indicated by the abbreviation "subsp." Not all species have subspecies.

An example of subsp. use is *Hydrangea anomala* subsp. *petiolaris* (climbing hydrangea). There is usually a wide range of intra-specific variation for numerous traits in a population of a seed-propagated species. In addition to obvious traits such as leaf and flower sizes and colors, vigor, plant form, and dwarfism, there may also be differences in less obvious traits, such as tolerances to external influences such as pests, low and high temperatures, and soil moisture aspects. You should have an appreciation for **intraspecific (within a species) variation.** Why? First, this wide degree of variation is necessary for plants to adapt to the dynamic nature of the environment. For example, the genetic capacity to produce small leaves may be advantageous in climates/environments where rainfall is relatively low since small leaves lose less water via transpiration (water vapor that exits leaf pores) than large leaves. Conversely, the genetic capacity to produce large leaves may be advantageous in climates/environments with ample rainfall to have a larger leaf surface to capture more sunlight and produce more sugars via photosynthesis. Secondly, having a keen eye for this variation may make you rich. You may discover an individual plant that has a particularly unique, attractive, and marketable trait. You can introduce, trademark, and perhaps patent this clone. New-to-the-trade plants are very popular and generate a lot of plant sales and profit.

Variety

A **variety** is a subpopulation of a species that has a distinctive trait that distinguishes it from the rest of the species and occurs in nature. Many species variety traits are inheritable, and succeeding seedling generations will express that trait; hence varieties are "true to seed." True to seed refers to the phenomenon where a distinctive trait is usually inherited and expressed when propagated via seeds (sexual propagation). For example, most redbuds (*Cercis canadensis*) produce pinkish flowers in the spring, whereas the variety alba of redbud (*Cercis canadensis* var. *alba*) produces white flowers. Thus, seed from *Cercis canadensis* var. *alba* will result in most, but probably not all, of those seedlings ultimately producing white flowers. Another example, the common honeylocust, *Gleditsia triacanthos*, has very large thorns. The thornless subpopulation of this species is the variety inermis (meaning thornless; *Gleditsia triacanthos* var. *inermis*). As in the redbud example, most plants produced from seeds from *Gleditsia triacanthos* var. *inermis* will be thornless.

A variety is part of the scientific name and the word variety is abbreviated, var., and placed after the specific epithet and the italicized variety term follows var. Thus, the scientific name for redbud (usually pink-flowered) with white flowers is *Cercis canadensis* var. *alba*. Note that the var. term is lower case and not italicized. Here is an example for the proper designation of a plant variety name, *Cercis canadensis* var. *alba*

> ***Cercis canadensis* var. *alba***
> Genus: Cercis
> Specific epithet: *canandensis*
> Variety abbreviation: var.
> Variety term: *alba*

Cultivar

Another species subclassification is a **cultivar**. The word cultivar is the shortened version of a **culti**vated **var**iety, which is a variety that was developed or selected by humans. A cultivar is an assemblage of plants that has been selected for a particular attribute or combination of attributes and that is clearly distinct, uniform, and stable in these characteristics and that retains those characteristics when propagated. Most cultivars must be propagated asexually. The cultivar name is not in Latin. The first letter of each word (if more than one word) is upper case, and put in single quotes. For example, the purple-leaved cultivar of redbud is *Cercis canadensis* 'Forest Pansy.'

Cercis canadensis 'Forest Pansy'
Genus: Cercis
Specific epithet: *canadensis*
Cultivar: 'Forest Pansy'

In some cases there are cultivars of a variety such as the thornless common honeylocust cultivar ('Sunburst') that has chartreuse new foliage. The name for this plant is *Gleditsia triacanthos* var. *inermis* 'Sunburst'. There are three main distinctions between a cultivar and a variety.

1) Whereas a variety has a natural connotation, a cultivar has a commercial connotation (used in horticultural commerce).

2) Most woody plant cultivars are not discovered as a subpopulation, but are the result of a bud sport (bud mutation), a seedling plant with a distinctive trait, a witches' broom (plant tissue that usually arises from a microorganism invading plant tissue and causing dwarfism), or human-mediated mutagenic alterations. In the case of a bud sport, when a bud (small package of embryonic tissue which becomes a leaf, stem, or flower) is forming, a mutation occurs that can give rise to a distinctive trait.

3) To introduce the third distinction, you should know that grasses and some annuals (non-woody plants) are generally "true-to-seed." This means that the offspring of true-to-seed species will exhibit the characteristics of the parents (due to "well behaved" gene mixing during reproduction). This is why we can plant seed of corn, turfgrass species, and marigolds, for example, and get plants that will exhibit the cultivar characteristics of those mother plants. In contrast, most woody plant cultivars are **not** true-to-seed (due to a more random mixing of genes during reproduction). Hence, woody plants must be asexually propagated (e.g., cuttings, grafting, layering, and micro-propagation) to maintain their cultivar characteristic. For example, if you plant a seed from a 'Delicious' apple, you will not get an apple tree that produces fruit with the characteristic shape and sweet taste traits of a 'Delicious' apple; you will get an apple that may be round and bitter since the genetic makeup of a 'Delicious' apple was not preserved during seed formation. Accordingly, seedlings from a 'Sunburst' honeylocust (*Gleditsia triacanthos* var. *inermis* 'Sunburst') will not have the chartreuse new foliage characteristic, but most of them will be thornless. This is because the cultivar characteristic is usually not true-to-seed for woody plants, whereas the variety characteristic (thornlessness) is usually true-to-seed. Thus, to propagate a woody plant cultivar with a distinctive trait, one must clone the plant by an asexual propagation technique (e.g., cuttings or grafting). The distinction between variety and cultivar gets fuzzy because woody plant varieties are commonly sold in the horticultural trade (sometimes as cultivars), and there are a very few woody plant cultivars that are true-to-seed.

Cultivar traits and trait stability

There are numerous cultivar traits such as variegated (colors other than the species' characteristic green) leaves, plant size/form, flower color/size/petal number/fragrance, fruit size/color, disease resistance, and growth rate. For example, *Acer platanoides* 'Drummondii' (Drummondii Norway maple) has variegated foliage, leaves with broad white edges. If a cultivar partly or totally ceases to express its cultivar characteristic trait and produces an appearance that is the same as the species, then that cultivar has reverted (reversion) to the species characteristics. Portions of an *Acer platanoides* 'Drummondii' tree characteristically revert to the all green leaves. Thus when reversion occurs, the "genetic switch" to control the expression of the cultivar trait (leaf variegation in this case) is turned off, and the "genetic switch" controlling the expression of the normal species leaf color is turned on. Some cultivar traits are very stable and rarely revert to the species form, some cultivars revert occasionally, and some cultivars revert commonly. Commonly, and in some cases occasionally, reverting cultivars make poor landscape plants since they do not retain their unique cultivar trait and plants have to be pruned to remove the reversions. Of course, if a reversion occurs in the upper portion of a tree, then the reverted branch would be difficult to remove.

The popular dwarf Alberta spruce (*Picea abies* 'Conica'), a dwarf, slow-growing, compact, cone-shaped form of white spruce, will occasionally revert to the species characteristics (medium tree with a faster growth rate, much larger needles and wide-spaced branches). In this case the branch sport (reversion) exhibiting the species characteristics will ultimately outgrow the plant and the result will be a very awkward looking specimen. To avoid this, the reversion should be cut out as soon as possible to maintain the character of the cultivar.

Taxon

A **taxon**, an abbreviation of "taxonomic group" or "taxonomic unit," is any taxonomic group/category; the plural is taxa. For example, a genus is a taxon, a cultivar is a taxon, and a genus, species, and cultivars are three taxa.

Trademark

The primary role of a trademark is to indicate the source of goods and is not intended to label an individual product or cultivar. For example, the very popular Wave™ petunia series includes Wave™ Blue, Wave™ Misty Lilac, and Wave™ Purple. Cultivar names are the domain of the public, and therefore cannot be trademarked. There are two types of trademarks. The common use trademark is designated with the superscript TM, such as in the previously mentioned Wave™ petunia series. Common business use of trademark name grants a business the rights to that name. The second trademark type is a registered trademark in which the trademark is registered by the United States Patent and Trademark Office. A registered trademark is designated by a superscript ®, is valid for 10 years, and is renewable. By ascribing a trademark name (either type) to a plant, a company has the sole right to selling a plant by that trademark name. However, another company can sell that plant by its cultivar name.

Unfortunately, some plant catalogs and text books incorrectly put trademark names in single quotes (cultivar designation). Such errors result in considerable confusion between cultivar and trademark names. Due to the proliferation of new plant introductions, many of which have been trademarked, many plants are known by their trademark name, and some of these trademark names are erroneously put in single quotes.

Plant patent

A **plant patent** gives the patent owner the sole right to reproduce, sell, or use an asexually propagated plant. A patent grant lasts for 20 years from the date of filing the patent application, and is not renewable. Patented plants are generally trademarked. Patented plants have the letters PP (plant patent) next to their name. Plants in the process of being patented have the acronym PPAF (plant patent applied for) which carries no legal validity.

Hybrids

A **hybrid** is the result of a sexual cross, transfer of pollen (sperm) of one plant to the pistil (contains ovary/egg) of another plant, between two or more plants that are somewhat related. Most of the time, a hybrid is a cross between two different varieties of the same species. Occasionally two different species of the same genus are crossed. The resulting plant is called an **interspecific (between species) hybrid.** For example, two *Abelia* species, *A. chinensis* and *A. uniflora* were crossed, and the relatively common landscape shrub *A.* ×*grandiflora* (glossy abelia) was produced.

> ***Abelia* ×*grandiflora***
> Genus: *Abelia*
> Multiplication symbol: × (represents a genetic cross)
> Specific epithet (no space between × and specific epithet): *grandiflora*

As seen in this example, an interspecific hybrid is designated by placing a multiplication symbol (or lowercase x) immediately (no space) before the specific epithet. An **intergeneric (between genera) hybrid** is a cross between two genera and is a very rare occurrence. An intergeneric hybrid is designated by placing the × symbol immediately in front of the genus, for example, ×*Sycoparrotia semideciuda* which is a hybrid between *Parrotia persica* and *Sycopsis sinensis*.

What Do Those Words Mean?

This short list of Latin words used in plant names offers a glimpse of the information they provide. Adjectives here are presented in the masculine form to go with a masculine noun (genus). The endings would differ for a feminine or neuter genus, but the root portion would stay the same.

Designating Plant Habitat

aquaticus = in water
arvensis = in fields
maritimus = by the sea
palustris = in swamps
pratensis = in meadows
sativus = cultivated
sylvestris, sylvaticus = in woods

Designating Plant Geography

americanus = Americas

australis = southern
borealis = northern
canadensis = Canada (N. US)
carolinianus = Carolinas
chinensis, sinensis = China
occidentalis = western (New World)
virginianus = Virginias
orientalis = eastern (Old World)

Designating Plant Attributes

annus = annual
officianales = medicinal
communis, vulgaris = common
parennes = perennial
pulchellus = beautiful
rugosus = wrinkled
setaceus = bristle-like
spectabilis = handsome, showy
vernus = spring flowering

Designating Plant Appearance

gracilis = graceful, slender
humilus = low
procumbens = trailing
pubescens = downy hair surface
pumilus, nanus = dwarf
repans, reptans = creeping
scandens = climbing
tuberosus = forming tubers

Designating Plant Parts

carpus = fruit
caulis = stem
florus, anthos = flower
folium, phyllon = leaf

Designating Color

albus = white
atropurpureus = dark purple
aureus = golden
bicolor = of two colors
coccineus = scarlet
concolor = same color both sides
discolor = different color each side
flavus, luteus = yellow
glaucus = whitish with a bloom
niger = black
ruber = red
sanguineus = blood-red
variegatus = variegated
viridis = green

Designating the Collector

(*occasionally capitalized*)
fortunei = from Fortune
halliana = from Hall
sargentii = from Sargent
thunbergii = from Thunberg

Numerical Prefixes

uni-, mono- = one
bi-, di- = two
tri- = three
quadri-, tetra- = four
quinque-, penta- = five
multi- = many
a- = without, lacking

Descriptive Prefixes

albi-, leuco- = white
alterni- = alternate
angusti- = narrow
brevi- = short
grandi- = large
hetero- = differing
lati- = broad
longi- = long
micro- = small
macro- = large, long
rotundi- = round
semper- = always

Identification With an Analytical Key

The ability to identify plants is something like learning people's names. When you are introduced to someone by name, you may concentrate on associating the name with particular features of that person, whether they are facial or other physical features. If you meet a person only once, you will probably soon forget who the person is. However, after you have been associated with a person for a long time and have called him or her by name a number of times, you will then be able to identify that person when you see him/her anywhere. If you do not see him/her for a few years, you may find that you have forgotten the name, but it will only take a short reminder to re-familiarize yourself with that person. The same process is involved in identifying plants. The significant difference between identifying plants and identifying people is that plants can't tell you who they are. Consequently, various guides have been prepared to assist in determining the identity of various plants. The bibliography at the end of this section lists several of these manuals.

The identification of an unknown plant usually requires an analytical key, or identification tool, which is a part of most identification manuals. These keys list plant features, such as leaf arrangement, leaf shape, leaf color and hairiness, various twig features, and many other identifying characteristics that are evident at various times of the year. Usually the keys are based on vegetative features, even though the first separation of plants by species was based on differences in sexual structures. Unfortunately, the flowering stages do not last long enough to use this as a general means of identifying plants.

The use of a key is a step-by-step process of elimination, beginning with the most general characteristics (for example, evergreen vs. deciduous) and progressing to the most specific characteristics. Most manuals will begin with instructions for their use, as well as definitions of the various characteristics. The terms used in the definitions can differ slightly between manuals, so review of this section is important.

Additional Resources

- "Name that Plant – The Misuse of Trademarks in Horticulture (https://www.plantdelights.com/blogs/articles/name-that-plant)
- Evert, Ray F. and Eichhorn, Susan E. *Raven Biology of Plants*. 2012. W. H. Freeman.
- For more on absorption: "How Vegetable Plant Roots Absorb Nutrients" by Mosaic Crop Nutrition (https://www.cropnutrition.com/resource-library/how-vegetable-plant-roots-absorb-nutrients)

References

"Plant Cell Structure and Function" section adapted from Evert, Ray F. and Eichhorn, Susan E. *Raven Biology of Plants*. 2012. W. H. Freeman.

Leaf blade shapes adapted from Colorado State University Extension Master Gardener Training, "CMG GardenNotes #134: Plant Structures: Leaves." 2017. https://cmg.extension.colostate.edu/Gardennotes/134.pdf

Attributions

- Susan Dudley, Norfolk Extension Master Gardener (2021 reviser)
- Wendy Silverman, New River Valley Extension Master Gardener Coordinator (2021 reviser)
- Lisa Sanderson, Extension Agent, Agriculture and Natural Resources (2015 reviser)
- Stuart Sutphin, Extension Agent, Agriculture and Natural Resources (2015 reviser)
- J. Christopher Ludwig, Chief Biologist, Virginia Department of Conservation and Recreation (2015 reviewer)
- Alan McDaniel, Extension Specialist, Horticulture (2009 reviser)
- Thank you to Dr. Eric Beers, School of Plant and Environmental Sciences, Virginia Tech

Image Attributions

- Figure 1-1: Plant cell diagram. Johnson, Devon. 2022. CC BY-NC-SA 4.0. Includes CNX OpenStax. 2016. Figure 04 03 01b.png CC BY-NC-SA 4.0. From WikimediaCommons
- Figure 1-2: Principal parts of a vascular plant. Johnson, Devon. 2022. CC BY-NC-SA 4.0. Adapted from "1–9 A modern vascular plant" in *Raven Biology of Plants*. 2012. by Eichhorn, Susan E., and Evert, Ray F. Originally from W. Troll. 1937.

Vergleichende Morphologie der Hoheren Pflanzen, vol. 1, pt. 1, Verlage von Gebru ̈ der Borntraeger, Berlin.
- Figure 1-3: Three examples of organization of vascular system in stem, shown in cross-section. Johnson, Devon. 2022. CC BY-NC-SA 4.0. Adapted from "25–8 Three basic types of organization in the primary structure of stems, as seen in transverse section" in *Raven Biology of Plants*. 2012. by Eichhorn, Susan E., and Evert, Ray F.
- Figure 1-4: Stem nodes. Grey, Kindred. 2022. CC BY-NC-SA 4.0.
- Figure 1-5: Spur. Grey, Kindred. 2022. CC BY-NC-SA 4.0.
- Figure 1-6: Diagram of a crown and runner. Grey, Kindred. 2022. CC BY-NC-SA 4.0.
- Figure 1-7: Image of a stolon. Grey, Kindred. 2022. CC BY-NC-SA 4.0.
- Figure 1-8: Image of a rhizome. Grey, Kindred. 2022. CC BY-NC-SA 4.0.
- Figure 1-9: Image of a bulb. Grey, Kindred. 2022. CC BY-NC-SA 4.0.
- Figure 1-10: Image of a corm. Grey, Kindred. 2022. CC BY-NC-SA 4.0.
- Figure 1-11: Image of a tuberous stem. Johnson, Devon. 2022. CC BY-NC-SA 4.0.
- Figure 1-12: Tuberous root of dahlia. Johnson, Devon. 2022. CC BY-NC-SA 4.0.
- Figure 1-13: Types of vines. Johnson, Devon. 2022. CC BY-NC-SA 4.0.
- Figure 1-14: Broadleaf diagram. Grey, Kindred. 2022. CC BY-NC-SA 4.0.
- Figure 1-15: Conifer leaf diagram. Grey, Kindred. 2022. CC BY-NC-SA 4.0.
- Figure 1-16: Cross section of a leaf. Johnson, Devon. 2022. CC BY-NC-SA 4.0.
- Figure 1-17: Images of stoma. CNX OpenStax. 2016. Figure_30_02_05abc.jpg. CC BY-NC-SA 4.0. From WikimediaCommons
- Figure 1-18: Simple leaf. Grey, Kindred. 2022. CC BY-NC-SA 4.0.
- Figure 1-19: Three examples of compound leaves; palmate, pinnate, and double pinnate compound. Grey, Kindred. 2022. CC BY-NC-SA 4.0.
- Figure 1-20: Types of leaf arrangements. Grey, Kindred. 2022. CC BY-NC-SA 4.0.
- Figure 1-21: Three examples of venation in leaves; parallel, pinnate, and palmate. Johnson, Devon. 2022. CC BY-NC-SA 4.0.
- Figure 1-22: Leaf blade shapes. Grey, Kindred. 2022. CC BY-NC-SA 4.0.
- Figure 1-23: Leaf apex shapes. Grey, Kindred. 2022. CC BY-NC-SA 4.0.
- Figure 1-24: Leaf base shapes. Grey, Kindred. 2022. CC BY-NC-SA 4.0.
- Figure 1-25: Leaf margin shapes. Grey, Kindred. 2022. CC BY-NC-SA 4.0.
- Figure 1-26: Twig diagram. Grey, Kindred. 2022. CC BY-NC-SA 4.0.
- Figure 1-27: Leaf and buds of Elm. Grey, Kindred. 2022. CC BY-NC-SA 4.0.
- Figure 1-28: (A) Cross section of monocot *Smilax* spp. root... Berkshire Community College Bioscience Image Library. Flickr. 2014. Public Domain. and "Young Herbaceous Dicot Root: Ranunculus." Berkshire Community College Bioscience Image Library. Flickr. 2014 Public Domain.
- Figure 1-29: Fibrous root system of *Aristida purpurea*. Includes "Fig. 43 — Wire grass (*Aristida purpurea*)" and " Fig. 46.— A loco weed (*Aragallus lambertii*)" by Weaver, John E. 1926. *Root Development of Field Crops*. McGraw-Hill, New York. Public Domain. Accessible here.
- Figure 1-30: Apical meristem of *Allium* spp. Berkshire Community College Bioscience Image Library. Flickr. Public Domain.
- Figure 1-31: Zones of elongation. Johnson, Devon. 2022. CC BY-NC-SA 4.0.
- Figure 1-32: Parts of a flower. Grey, Kindred. 2022. CC BY-NC-SA 4.0.
- Figure 1-33: Racemose. Grey, Kindred. 2022. CC BY-NC-SA 4.0.
- Figure 1-34 Cyme. Grey, Kindred. 2022. CC BY-NC-SA 4.0.
- Figure 1-35: Types of fruit. Johnson, Devon. 2022. CC BY-NC-SA 4.0. Includes Isolated Pineapple by Schwarzenarzisse on Pixabay and Raspberry Fruit by L_cwojdzinski on Pixabay and Blue Jay Eating Peanut by edbo23 on Pixabay.
- Figure 1-36: Parts of a seed. Grey, Kindred. 2022. CC BY-NC-SA 4.0. Adapted from *Master Gardener Training Handbook*, Virginia Cooperative Extension, 2018.
- Figure 1-37: Germination of a dicot bean seed and monocot onion seed. Johnson, Devon. 2022. CC BY-NC-SA 4.0. Adapted from *Master Gardener Training Handbook*, Virginia Cooperative Extension, 2018.
- Figure 1-38: The bounty from the Resiliency Garden at Fort Belvoir. Wellington, Kathleen. GSEMG: Wellness Circle and USO Resiliency Gardens. CC BY-NC-SA 4.0.
- Figure 1-39: Photosynthesis. Johnson, Devon. 2022. Adapted from Photosynthesis_en.svg by At09kg, Wattcle, and Nefronus. 2016. WikimediaCommons. CC BY-NC-SA 4.0.

- Figure 1-40: Guard cells surrounding open stoma in epidermis of succulent xerophyte leaf. Berkshire Community College Bioscience Image Library form Flickr. 2014. Public Domain.
- Figure 1-41: Cross section of a leaf (dots represent relative humidity). CC BY-NC-SA 4.0. from *Master Gardener Training Handbook*, Virginia Cooperative Extension, 2018.

CHAPTER 2: SOILS AND NUTRIENT MANAGEMENT

Chapter Contents:

- Components of Soil
- Soil Horizons
- Physical Properties of Soils
- Soil Testing
- Soil pH
- Building Healthy Soil
- Understanding Fertilizers
- Applying Fertilizer
- Soil and Nutrient Problems
- Additional Resources

Soil is formed when rock (parent material) is broken down by climate and vegetation over a period of time. Soil is weathered rock fragments and decaying remains of plants and animals (organic matter). It also contains varying amounts of air, water, and microorganisms. It furnishes mechanical support and nutrients for growing plants.

Components of Soil

A desirable surface soil in good condition for plant growth contains approximately 50% solid material and 50% open pore space. Most of the soil solids are a mineral component, which is usually made up of many different kinds and sizes of particles, ranging from those visible to the unaided eye to particles so small that they can only be seen with the aid of a very powerful (electron) microscope. This mineral material comprises about 45% to 48% of the total volume. **Organic matter** makes up about 2% to 5% of the volume and may contain both plant and animal material in varying stages of decomposition. Under ideal or near-ideal moisture conditions for growing plants, soil pore spaces contain about 25% air and 25% water based on the total volume of soil.

The percentage of mineral matter and organic matter in a cubic foot of surface soil varies from one soil to another and within the same soil, depending on the kinds of crops grown, frequency of tillage, and wetness or drainage of the soil. Content of organic matter will usually be high in soils that have not been cultivated over long periods of time. Soils that are tilled frequently and have relatively small amounts of plant residues worked into the soil are usually low in organic matter. Plowing and tilling the soil increases the amount of air in the soil, which increases the rate of organic matter decomposition. Soils with poor drainage or high water tables usually have a higher organic matter content than those that are well drained, because water excludes air from the soil mass.

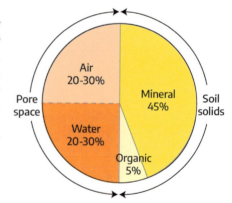

Figure 2-1: Soil composition: Air and water occupy pore space while mineral and organic components compose soil solids.

Since either air or water fills pore spaces, the amount of air in a soil at a particular time depends on the amount of water present in the pore spaces. Immediately after a rain, there is more water and less air in the pore spaces. Conversely, in dry periods, a soil contains more air and less water. Increasing organic matter content usually increases water-holding capacity, but adding large amounts of undecomposed organic material reduces water-holding capacity until the material has partially decomposed.

Organic Matter

Organic matter in soil consists of the remains of plants and animals. When temperature and moisture conditions are favorable in the soil, earthworms, insects, bacteria, fungi, and other types of plants and animals use the organic matter as food, breaking it down into **humus** (the portion of organic matter that remains after most decomposition has taken place) and soil nutrients. Through this process, materials are made available for use by growing plants.

The digested and decomposing organic material also helps develop good air-water relationships. In very sandy soil, organic material occupies some of the space between the sand grains, binding them together, and increasing water-holding capacity. In a finely textured soil (e.g., loam, clay loam), organic material creates aggregates of the fine soil particles, allowing water to move more rapidly around these larger particles. This grouping of the soil particles into aggregates, or **peds,** makes it easier to work.

Organic matter content depends primarily on the kinds of plants that have been growing in a soil, the long-term management practices, temperature, and drainage. Soils that have native grass cover for long periods usually have a relatively high organic matter content in the surface area. Those that have native forest cover usually have relatively low organic matter content. In either case, if the plants are grown on a soil that is poorly drained, the organic matter content is usually higher than where the same plants are grown on a well-drained soil. This is due to differences in available oxygen and other substances needed by the organisms that attack and decompose the organic material. Soils in a cool climate often have more organic matter than those in a warm climate.

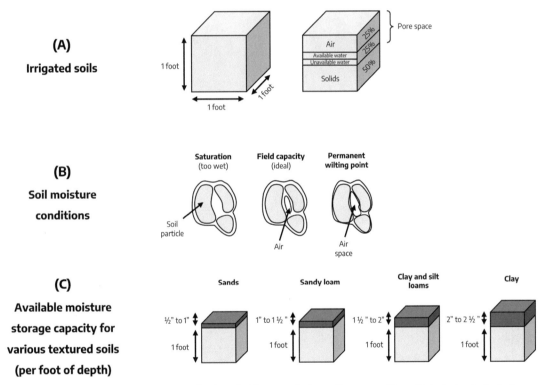

Figure 2-2: Effects of texture on capacity of soils to hold water. A) shows the composition of irrigated soils, including pore space (25% air, 25% water) and soil solids (50%). B) shows the amount of air space in a saturated soil particle (no air space), a soil particle at field capacity (small space of air), and permanent wilting point (large air space). C) shows available moisture storage capacity for various textured soils for each foot of depth. Sandy soil has the least moisture storage capacity, while clay has the most moisture storage capacity.

Water and Air

All water in the soil ultimately comes from precipitation (rain, snow, hail, or sleet), entering the soil through cracks, holes, and openings between the soil particles. As the water enters, it pushes the air out. Oxygen is taken up by plant roots for respiration. If air is unavailable for too long, the roots will die.

Some water is used by plants, some is lost by evaporation, and some moves so deep into the soil that plant roots cannot reach it. If it rains very hard or for a long time, some of the water is lost through run-off.

When organic matter decomposes in the soil, it gives off carbon dioxide. This carbon dioxide replaces some of the oxygen in the soil pores. As a result, soil air contains less oxygen and more carbon dioxide than the air above the soil surface.

Carbon dioxide is dissolved by water in the soil to form a weak acid. This solution reacts with the minerals in the soil to form compounds that can be taken up and used as nutrients by the plants.

Table 2-1: A Guide for Estimating Moisture Content of Soil

Adapted from: Craig, C.L. 1976. "Strawberry Culture in Eastern Canada." Agric. Canada Publication 1585:19. Observations based on soil sample from 4 to 6 inch depth. For an explanation of sand, silt, loam, and clay, see "Texture" under "Physical Properties of Soil" below.

% of Field Capacity	Adequacy of Soil Moisture for Plant Growth	Response to Physical Manipulation: Loamy sand, sandy loam	Response to Physical Manipulation: Silt loam, loam	Response to Physical Manipulation: Silty clay loam
100 plus	Saturated soil - too much moisture and too little air in the soil; can damage plants if this condition persists	Free water appears on soil when squeezed	Same as sandy loam	Same as sandy loam
100	Excess moisture has drained into subsoil after rainfall or irrigation and optimum amounts are available in the root zone for plant growth	When squeezed, no free water appears on the surface, but it leaves a wet outline on your hand. Forms weak ball; usually breaks when bounced in hand, will not stick	Same as sandy loam. Forms a very pliable ball; sticks readily	Same as sandy loam. Ribbons out (can be formed into a thin strand when rolled between thumb and forefinger), has a slick feeling.
75	Adequate moisture for plant growth. (As field capacity drops below 75%, it reaches marginal moisture for plant growth.)	Tends to ball under pressure, but breaks easily when bounced in hand	Forms a ball, somewhat plastic, sticks slightly with pressure	Forms a ball, ribbons out between thumb and forefinger, has slick feeling.
50	Inadequate moisture for plant growth	Appears too dry; will not form a ball with pressure	Somewhat crumbly, but holds together with pressure	Somewhat pliable, balls under pressure
25	Moisture in soil unavailable for plant growth	Dry, loose, falls through fingers	Powdery, sometimes crusty, but easily broken down into a powdery condition	Hard, cracked, difficult to break down to powdery condition

Plant Nutrients

Plants need 16 elements for normal growth. Carbon, hydrogen, and oxygen (which come from air and water) and nitrogen (which is in the soil) make up 95% of plant solids. Although the atmosphere is 78% nitrogen, it is unavailable for plant use. However, certain bacteria that live in nodules on the roots of legumes are able to fix (convert) nitrogen from the air into a form available to plants.

The other 12 essential elements are phosphorus, potassium, calcium, magnesium, sulphur, iron, copper, manganese, zinc, boron, chlorine, and molybdenum. These elements come from the soil. With the exception of phosphorus, potassium, calcium, and magnesium, there is usually a large enough quantity of each of these elements in the soil for cultivation of crops.

Table 2-2: Macronutrient Elements

Element	Symbol	Chemical form most frequently absorbed
Carbon	C	
Hydrogen	H	
Oxygen	O	O_2
Nitrogen	N	NO_3^- NH_4^+
Potassium	K	K^+
Calcium	Ca	Ca^{++}
Phosphorus	P	$H_2PO_4^-$ HPO_4^+
Magnesium	Mg	Mg^{++}
Sulfur	S	SO_4^+

Table 2-3: Micronutrient Elements

Element	Symbol	Chemical form most frequently absorbed
Molybdenum	Mo	MoO_4^{2-}
Copper	Cu	Cu^+ Cu^{++}
Zinc	Zn	Zn^{++}
Manganese	Mn	Mn^{++}
Iron	Fe	Fe^{++} Fe^{+++}
Boron	B	BO_3^- $B_4O_7^-$
Chlorine	Cl	Cl^-

Soil Horizons

Most soils have four distinct principal layers or horizons. Each layer can have two or more sub-horizons. The principal horizons (collectively called the soil profile) are: O – leaf litter, A – surface soil or topsoil, E – the subsurface, and B – the subsoil. Beneath the soil profile lies: C – the parent material, and R -rock, similar to that from which the soil developed. Horizons usually differ in color, texture, consistency, and structure. In addition, there are usually considerable differences in chemical characteristics or composition.

The **surface horizon** and **subsurface** are usually the coarsest layers. The surface soil contains more organic matter than the other soil layers. Organic matter gives a gray, dark-brown, or black color to the surface horizon, the color imparted depending largely upon the amount of organic matter present. Soils that are highest in organic matter usually have the darkest surface colors. The surface layer is usually most fertile and has the greatest concentration of plant roots; plants obtain much of their nutrients and water from the surface soil.

The **subsoil** layer is usually finer and firmer than the surface soil. Organic matter content of the subsoil is usually much lower than that of the surface layer. Subsoil colors are strong and bright; shades of red, brown, and yellow are frequently observed. The subsoil supports the surface soil and may be considered the soil reservoir, providing storage space for water and nutrients for plants, aiding in temperature regulation of the soil, and supplying air for the roots of plants.

The bottom horizon, or **parent material,** is decomposed rock that has acquired some characteristics of the subsoil and retained some characteristics of the rock from which it weathered. It is not hard, like rock, but may show the form or structure of the original rocks or layering if it is in a water-laid deposit. The parent material influences soil texture, natural fertility, rate of decomposition (and thus rate of soil formation), acidity, depth, and in some cases, topography (or lay of the land) on which the soil is formed.

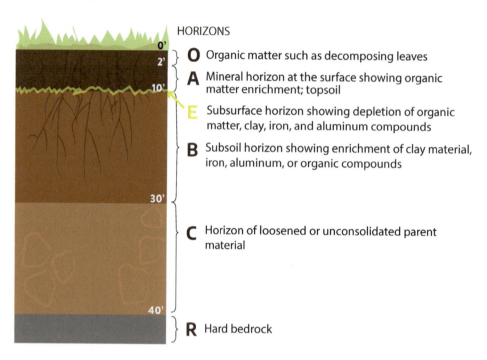

Figure 2-3: Soil horizon diagram. Horizons include: O horizon (organic matter such as decomposing leaves), A horizon (topsoil horizon, at or near the surface), E horizon (mineral horizon underlain by B horizon), B horizon (subsoil horizon), C horizon (made up of rock, parent material, and only a little organic matter) R horizon (bedrock).

Physical Properties of Soils

There are physical, chemical, and biological aspects of soil. The physical properties of soil are those characteristics which can be seen with the eye or felt between the thumb and fingers. They are the result of soil parent materials being acted upon by climatic factors (such as rainfall and temperature), and affected by topography (slope and direction, or aspect) and vegetation (kind and amount, such as forest or grass) over a period of time. A change in any one of these influences usually results in a difference in the type of soil formed. Important physical properties of a soil are color, texture, structure, drainage, depth, and surface features (stoniness, slope, and erosion).

Both the physical properties and chemical composition largely determine the suitability of a soil for its planned use and the management requirements to keep it most productive. Soil physical properties usually control the suitability of soil as growth medium; chemical composition is also important in determining **fertility** (the ability of soil to sustain plant growth).

Color

When soil is examined, color is one of the first things noticed. It indicates extremely important soil conditions. It can indicate if soil is dry or saturated or if there are excess minerals; for example, clay soils contain an excess of iron oxide that gives them a red color. In general, soil color is determined by: (1) organic matter content, (2) drainage conditions, and (3) degree of oxidation (extent of weathering).

Surface soil colors vary from almost white, through shades of brown and gray, to black. Light colors indicate a low organic matter content and dark colors can indicate a high content. Light or pale colors in the surface soil are frequently associated with relatively coarse texture, highly leached conditions, and high annual temperatures. Dark colors may result from high water table conditions (poor drainage), low annual temperatures, or other influences that induce high organic matter content and, at the same time, slow the oxidation of organic materials. However, soil coloration may be due to the colors imparted by the parent material. Shades of red or yellow, particularly where associated with relatively fine textures, usually indicate that subsoil material has been incorporated in the surface layer.

Subsoil colors, in general, are indications of air, water, and soil relationships and the degree of oxidation of certain minerals in the soil. Red and brown subsoil colors indicate relatively free movement of air and water allowed by the soil. If these or other bright colors persist throughout the subsoil, aeration is favorable. Some well-aerated subsoils will appear mottled (have mixed colors), in shades of red and brown.

Yellow-colored subsoils usually indicate some drainage impediment. Most mottled subsoils, especially those where gray predominates, have too much water and too little air (oxygen) much of the time. The red-to-brown color of subsoils comes from iron coatings under well-aerated conditions. In wet soils with low oxygen levels, the iron coatings are chemically and biologically removed, and the gray color of background soil minerals shows.

Drainage

Soil drainage is defined as the rate and extent of water movement in the soil, including movement across the surface as well as downward through the soil. Slope is a very important factor in soil drainage. Other factors include texture, structure, and physical condition of surface and subsoil layers. Soil drainage is indicated by soil color.

Clear, bright subsoil colors indicate well-drained soils. Mixed, drab, and dominantly gray colors indicate imperfection in drainage. Low-lying areas within the landscape receive run-off water. Frequently, the water from these areas must escape by lateral movement through the soil or by evaporation from the surface, as poor structure and other physical influences do not allow drainage.

Too much or too little water in the soil is equally undesirable. With too much water, most plants will suffocate. Where there is too little water, plants will wilt and eventually die. The most desirable soil moisture situation is one in which approximately 1/2 of the pore space of the surface soil is occupied by water.

Texture

Texture refers to the relative amounts of differently sized soil particles (i.e., percent sand, silt, and clay), or the fineness/coarseness of the mineral particles in the soil. In each texture class, there is a range in the amount of sand, silt, and clay that class contains.

Sand is the coarser mineral particles of the soil. These particles vary in size. Most sand particles can be seen without a magnifying glass. All feel rough when rubbed between the thumb and fingers.

Silt are relatively fine soil particles that feel smooth and floury. When wet, silt feels smooth but is not slick or sticky. When dry, it is smooth, and if pressed between the thumb and finger, will retain the imprint. Silt particles are so fine that they cannot usually be seen by the unaided eye and are best seen with a microscope.

Clays are the finest soil particles. Clay particles can be seen only with the aid of a very powerful (electron) microscope. They feel extremely smooth when dry, and become slick and sticky when wet. Clay will hold the form into which it is molded.

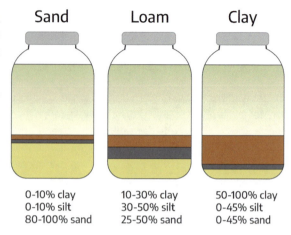

Figure 2-4: Soil composition can be determined by placing a sample in water and allowing components to settle. For many gardeners, this is a far more reliable way of determining soil composition than soil feel.

Loam is a textural class of soil that has moderate amounts of sand, silt, and clay. Loam contains approximately 7% to 27% clay, 28% to 50% silt, and 23% to 50% sand. Loams are desirable for plant growth.

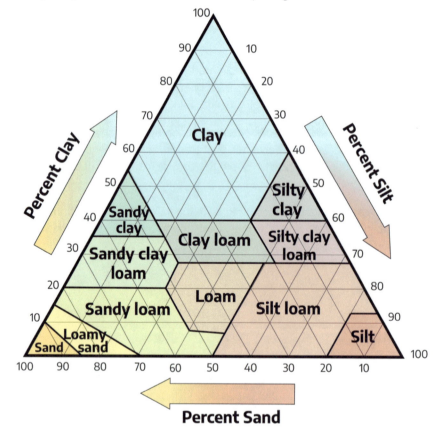

Figure 2-5: Soil texture triangle. Used to classify the texture of soil. The sides of the triangle are scaled according to percent content of silt, sand, and clay.

Determining soil texture

Soil texture (the proportions of sand, silt, and clay particles) can be accurately determined by a lab. A fairly good estimate can be made at home, however, using the texture-by-feel method. The first part of this test determines the amount of clay in your soil. Take a small amount of soil from your representative sample, moisten it, and knead it into a smooth, walnut-sized ball in your hand. If it is impossible to form a ball, it is a sand soil. Using your thumb, gently push a ribbon of soil of even thickness out between your thumb and crooked forefinger. A loamy sand soil will form no ribbon at all. A ribbon less than 1 inch indicates a loam, 1 to 2 inches, a clay loam, and more than 2 inches, a clay soil.

The second part of the test will further qualify the soil texture as sandy or silty, if necessary. Take a pinch of soil, place it in your palm, and thoroughly wet it. Rub your finger in the soil and note if it feels very smooth and floury (silty), very gritty (sandy), or equally smooth and gritty (no further qualification of the texture you determined in the first part of the test is needed). For example, if your soil forms a 1.5 inch ribbon (a clay loam), and feels very smooth and floury in the second part of the test (silty), then your soil texture is a silty clay loam.

Although there are approximately 20 classes of soil texture, most surface soils in Virginia fall into five general textural classes. Each class name indicates the size of the mineral particles that are dominant in the soil. Texture is determined in the field by rubbing moist-to-wet soil between the thumb and fingers. These observations can be checked in the laboratory by mechanical analysis or by separation into clay, silt, and various sized sand groups. Regardless of textural class, all soils in Virginia contain sand, silt, and clay, although the amount of a particular particle class may be small.

Principal soil classes found in Virginia:

- Loam – When rubbed between the thumb and fingers, approximately equal influence of sand, silt, and clay is felt.
- Sandy loam – Varies from very fine loam to very coarse. Feels quite sandy or rough, but contains some silt and a small amount of clay. The amount of silt and clay is sufficient to hold the soil together when moist.
- Silt loam – Silt is the dominant particle in silt loam, which feels quite smooth or floury when rubbed between the thumb and fingers.
- Silty clay loam – Noticeable amounts of both silt and clay are present in silty clay loam, but silt is a dominant part of the soil. It is smooth to the touch when dry, but when moist, it becomes somewhat slick/sticky.
- Clay loam – Clay dominates a clay loam, which is smooth when dry and slick/sticky when wet. Silt and sand are usually present in noticeable amounts in this texture of soil, but are overshadowed by clay.

Other textural designations of surface soils are sands, loamy sands, sandy clay loams, and clays. In each textural class there is a range in the amount of sand, silt, or clay that class may contain. The composition of each textural class does not allow for overlap from one class to another.

Texture of soil influences many different characteristics. A brief comparison between sandy and clay soils will highlight these points. Coarse-textured or sandy soils allow water to enter at a faster rate and to move more freely than in a clay. In addition, the relatively low water-holding capacity and the large amount of air present in sandy soils allows them to warm up faster than fine-textured soils. Sandy soils are also more easily tilled. They are well-suited for the production of special crops such as vegetables, flue-cured tobacco, peanuts, and certain fruits.

Soil orders found in Virginia

Soil orders are based on two or more physical or chemical characteristics that differentiate them from one another. Soil surveys of the state's naturally occurring soils indicate 7 of the 12 USDA, NRCS soil orders are prevalent throughout the state. These are in the order of occurrence in Virginia by percentage:

- **Ultisols** (last formed) are highly weathered and strongly leached, infertile mineral soils with significant subsoil clay accumulation that formed under deciduous, coniferous, or mixed forest and woodland vegetation. Farming, silvopasture, and silviculture requires inputs of lime and fertilizer.
- **Alfisols** are moderately leached soils with significant subsoil clay accumulation and relatively high natural fertility. These soils have mainly formed under forest and have a subsurface horizon in which clays have accumulated. The higher mineral content results in a more productive soil and permits a greater variety of crops than Ultisols.
- **Inceptisols** (beginning) are mineral soils relatively new in origin and are characterized by having subsoil horizons just beginning to exhibit a moderate degree of soil development. Inceptisols lack significant clay accumulation in the subsoil and may be naturally fertile or infertile.
- **Entisols** (newly formed) exhibit little soil development other than the presence of an identifiable topsoil horizon. These soils occur in unstable environments of recently deposited sediments such as active flood plains, dunes, and landslide areas. They may be naturally fertile or infertile.
- **Mollisols** (soft, deep, fertile) are the soils forming in alluvium eroded from limestone and dolomite bedrock. They are characterized by a thick, dark surface horizon which results from the long-term addition of organic matter. Mollisols are extensively used for forests in Virginia but are among the most productive and fertile soils of the world. They occur in flood plains draining limestone and dolomite such as those around the the Shenandoah, Roanoke, and James Rivers.
- **Spodosols** (sandy, acidic) have a strongly leached surface layer and a subsoil in which an amorphous mixture of organic matter and aluminum, with or without iron, accumulates in a subsoil horizon. Most Spodosols have little silicate clay and have the appearance of white sugar sand. These are soils formed under coniferous forests such as the longleaf pine growing near Zuni.
- **Histosols** (organic, wet) are deep, poorly drained organic soils consisting of muck, peat, or mucky peat. They are usually highly deficient in plant nutrients and often highly acidic. Most of these soils are saturated year-round and occur in marshes and low-energy swamps along some estuaries.

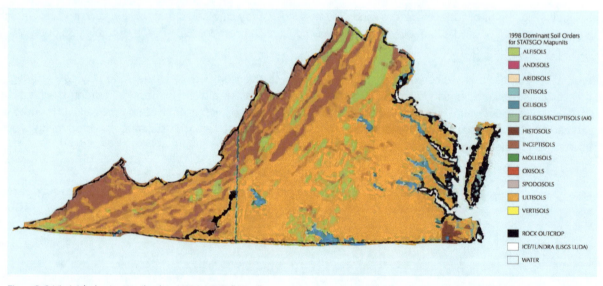

Figure 2-6: Virginia's dominant soil orders, USDA-NRCS (https://www.nrcs.usda.gov/Internet/FSE_MEDIA/stelprdb1237749.pdf). Utisols (represented by orange) cover the largest area of the commonwealth.

Structure

Soil particles are grouped together to form structural pieces called **peds** or aggregates. In surface soil, the structure will usually be granular unless it is disrupted. The soil aggregates will be rounded and vary in size from that of a very small shot pellet to that of a large pea. If organic matter content is low and the soil has been under continuous cultivation, the soil structure may be quite indistinct. If the soil is fine-textured, it may have a blocky subsoil structure.

Air and water movement within the soil is closely related to its structure. Good structure allows rapid movement of air and water, while poor structure slows down this movement. Water can enter a surface soil that has granular structure more rapidly than one that has little structure. Since plant roots move through the same channels in the soil as air and water, good structure allows extensive root development while poor structure discourages it. Water, air, and plant roots move more freely through subsoils that have blocky structure than those with a platy horizontal structure. Good structure of the surface soil is promoted by an adequate supply of organic matter, and by working the soil only when moisture conditions are correct.

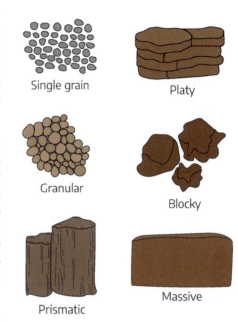

Figure 2-7: Soil structure including single grain, platy, granular, blocky, prismatic, and massive.

Plant root growth also changes the soil structure, sending roots into the soil for mechanical support and to gather water and nutrients. As they grow, the roots of plants tend to enlarge the openings in the soil. When they die and decay, they leave channels for movement of air and water. In addition to the plants that we see, there are bacteria, molds, fungi, and other very small plants growing in the soil which can be seen only with the aid of a microscope. These organisms also enrich the soil as they die.

Table 2-4: Examples of soil structure

Name	Description	Where commonly found in soils
Single Grain	Usually individual sand grains not held together	Sandy or loamy textures
Granular	Porous granules held together by organic matter and some clay	"A" horizons with some organic matter
Platy	Aggregates that have a thin vertical dimension with respect to lateral dimensions	Compacted layers and sometimes "E" horizons
Blocky	Roughly equidimensional peds usually higher in clay than other structural aggregates	"B" horizons with clay
Prismatic	Structural aggregates that have a much greater vertical than lateral dimension	In some "B" horizons
Massive	No definite structure or shape; usually hard	"C" horizons or compact transported material

Depth

The effective depth of a soil for plant growth is the vertical distance into the soil from the surface to a layer that essentially stops the downward growth of plant roots. The barrier layer may be rock, sand, gravel, heavy clay, or a partially cemented layer.

- **Very shallow**: Soil surface is less than 10 inches from a layer that retards root development
- **Shallow**: Soil surface is 10 to 20 inches from a layer that retards root development
- **Moderately deep**: Soil surface is 20 to 36 inches from a layer that retards root development
- **Deep**: Soil surface is 36 to 60 inches from a layer that retards root development
- **Very deep**: Soil surface is more than 60 inches from a layer that retards root development

Soils that are deep, well drained, and have desirable texture and structure are suitable for the production of most crops. Deep soils can hold more plant nutrients and water than can shallow soils with similar textures. The depth of a soil and its capacity for nutrients and water frequently determine the yield from a crop, particularly annual crops grown through the summer months. Gardeners with very shallow soil often benefit from establishing raised beds.

Plants growing on shallow soils also have less mechanical support than those growing in deep soils. Trees growing in shallow soils are more frequently blown over by wind than are those growing in deep soils.

Northern Neck Shoreline Evaluation Program

By Ian Cheyne, Extension Master Gardener, Northern Neck

In the early 2000s, Northern Neck Master Gardeners (NNMG) began to engage in living shoreline installations. They recognized that, in the right situations, this was a way for homeowners to protect their property and also contribute to the restoration of the Chesapeake Bay. Where homeowners and plants are involved, Extension Master Gardeners (EMGs) should be too.

In 2004, the opportunity arose to participate in a project to install a demonstration living shoreline in Reedville in Northumberland County. The project involved Bethany United Methodist Church's waterfront property adjacent to the Reedville Fishermen's Museum. The eroding shoreline and stormwater runoff from the church and its parking lot were contaminating the adjacent creek. To address these issues, a living shoreline was proposed. The implementation was a collaboration among between the church, the Fishermen's Museum, the Virginia Institute of Marine Science (VIMS), NNMG, and several other local non-profits. The project was successfully completed in 2005 and has been maintained by NNMG volunteers since then. The installation demonstrates the benefits and beauty of a living shoreline.

Figure 2-8: Reedville Demonstration Living Shoreline.

Enthused by their initial involvement, the EMGs wondered how they could do more. Then opportunity struck. In 2009, the Great Recession resulted in state budget cuts and one victim was the VIMS homeowner shoreline advisory service. Seeing an opportunity and already having a relationship with VIMS, the EMGs proposed to offer a similar service on the

Northern Neck. VIMS welcomed the idea and agreed to provide training and consulting support. Thus, the Shoreline Evaluation Program (SEP) was conceived.

Before the program launched in 2012, the SEP team received training from VIMS and also qualified as EMG Water Stewards, an advanced training available to current Extension Master Gardeners. They documented necessary procedures, performed practice evaluations around the Northern Neck, and developed a strategic plan.

The SEP mission is to encourage homeowners to adopt shoreline protection methods that also protect habitats and their adjacent waters. To that end, SEP offers shoreline management advice through individual on-site evaluations and educational outreach to the public.

The educational outreach includes an annual shoreline management seminar, presentations to individual community groups, and a presence at farmers markets and other local events. To date, SEP has conducted over 300 individual shoreline evaluations and interacts directly with approximately 600 people each year through its evaluations, seminars, and outreach. The program is also continually adapting to changing legislation and the growing effects of climate change.

Figure 2-9: EMGs conduct a shoreline management class.

Collaboration has been a key ingredient to the program's success. The living shoreline project was a collaboration. The relationship with VIMS continues as a collaboration. Recently, the James City County Williamsburg Master Gardeners in partnership with the Colonial Soil and Water Conservation District decided to launch SEP in their district. NNMG has played a role in training and transferring know-how to the new program, and the groups will maintain a collaborative relationship.

It has been a tremendously rewarding experience to see attitudes towards waterfront property management gradually change as homeowners realize they can protect their property in ways that can also contribute to the restoration of the Chesapeake Bay.

Soil Testing

The purpose of a soil test is to supply the homeowner with enough information to make wise decisions about the purchase and application of lime and fertilizer. A soil test from Virginia Tech will provide information on the soil pH and the plant available levels of phosphorus, potassium and seven other essential elements or nutrients. A Virginia Tech Soil Test report will also provide an estimated Cation Exchange Capacity (CEC), which gives an indication of a soil's ability to retain nutrients (Ca^{++}, Mg^{++} & K^+) against leaching. Soil tests should be performed if such tests have never before been conducted or if past soil test results are unavailable. A soil test is unnecessary more often than every 3-4 years.

The accuracy of the soil test is a reflection of the sample taken. Be sure the sample is representative of the area to be treated; sampling should be specific and occur for one landscape type or use (e.g. vegetable garden, turf, landscape bed). Sample the soil from 10 or more random areas of the garden to a depth of 6 inches. Avoid sampling unusual areas such as those near gravel roads, manure or compost spots, brush piles, or under eaves. Place the samples in a clean plastic pail or container, and mix the soil thoroughly. Contact your local Extension office for soil sampling boxes and proper sampling procedures. For more information, visit the Soil Testing Lab website (http://www.soiltest.vt.edu/).

A soil test is the only way to determine if nutrients must be added or if a pH adjustment is needed. The soil test results suggest how much of each nutrient to add. Without a soil test, any application of fertilizer could be detrimental to the landscape and surrounding environment or ecosystem. Over-application or application of unneeded materials could result in salt injury to plants, cause nutrient imbalances unsuitable for plant growth, and has the potential to become an environmental pollutant.

Most nutrients move very slowly through the soil profile, so to be most effective, they should be incorporated into the top 4-6 inches. However, these elements can be surface applied, but the nutrients will be less readily available to the plants.

Magnesium may be deficient, especially in low pH soils. If magnesium levels and soil pH are low, dolomitic limestone can be used to raise the pH and supply the needed magnesium. To add magnesium without affecting the pH, Epsom salts ($MgSO_4$) can be applied, either by incorporating into soil or as a soil drench (dissolved in water and applied near roots). Potassium can be surface applied, if needed. It is possible to over-apply potassium which can lead to deficiencies of other nutrients, particularly magnesium, so follow soil test recommendations closely.

Nitrogen is the nutrient that most frequently limits plant growth, and is often the only nutritional element that accelerates the growth of ornamental plants.

Unfortunately, nitrogen is also the most challenging nutrient to manage. Unlike other nutrients, it is not possible to accurately determine from a soil test how much nitrogen will be available during a plant's growth. Nitrogen readily moves or leaches in the soil. The challenge is to provide adequate nitrogen levels when needed to meet the plant growth requirements. A soil test will recommend the amount and time to apply nitrogen based upon established annual requirements for the specified plant to be grown.

Nitrogen can be supplied with two different approaches and both work very well. Nitrogen can be applied as (1) a water soluble form which includes liquid feed and granular fertilizers or (2) slow release forms. See chapters on specific plant groups (i.e., lawns, woody ornamentals, etc.) and the chapter on water quality for more information on fertilizer application.

Cation Exchange Capacity (CEC)

The **cation exchange capacity** (CEC) is a measure of the net negative charge per unit of clay. Nutrient cations (such as CA^{++}, Mg^{++}, K^+), which have a positive charge, are readily attracted to clay particles which have a net negative charge. A water molecule's positive polar ends are also attracted to clay. Humus also has a high CEC and may also be adsorbed to clay. If the CEC is too low, cations and water are not adsorbed strongly and are easily drained or leached away. Soils with little clay, such as sand textures, and highly weathered clays and oxides have very low CEC. The CEC determines a soil's ability to adsorb nutrients, and is related to potential fertility. Although many factors affect cation exchange between the clays or humus and the plants, we are most interested when nutrient cations and anions (which have a negative charge) are exchanged across root cell walls and taken into the root. The plant root releases hydrogen ions (H^+), which then replaces the cations in the soil for uptake into the plant. Uptake of phosphate anions requires some energy expenditure by the plant.

Soil pH

A pH is a reading taken from a scale that measures the hydrogen (acid-forming) ion activity of soil or growth media. The reading expresses the degree of acidity or alkalinity in terms of pH values. The scale of measuring acidity or alkalinity contains 14 divisions known as pH units. It is centered around pH 7 which is neutral. Values below 7 constitute the acid range of the scale and values above 7 make up the alkaline range.

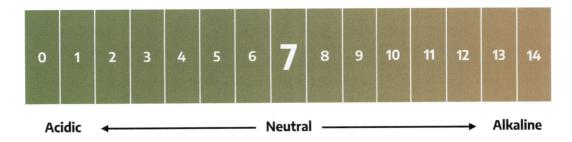

Figure 2-10: pH range scale.

The measurement scale is not a linear scale but a logarithmic scale. That is, a soil with a pH of 8.5 is ten times more alkaline than a soil with a pH of 7.5, and a soil with a pH of 4.5 is ten times more acid than a soil with a pH of 5.5.

The pH condition of soil is one of a number of environmental conditions that affects the quality of plant growth. A near-neutral or slightly acidic soil is generally considered ideal for most plants. Some types of plant growth can occur anywhere in a 3.5 to 10.0 range. With some notable exceptions, a soil pH of 6.0 to 7.0 requires no modification of soil pH to improve plant growth.

The major impact that pH extremes have on plant growth is the availability of plant nutrients and concentration of the plant-toxic minerals. In highly acidic soils, calcium, phosphorous, and magnesium become tied up and unavailable, and manganese can be available in toxic levels. At pH values of 7 and above, phosphorus, iron, copper, zinc, boron, and manganese become less available.

How soil pH affects availability of plant nutrients

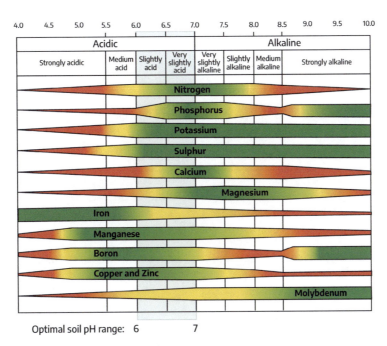

Figure 2-11: Nutrient availability by pH.

Ground limestone and rarely sulfur are used to adjust pH that is not in the ideal range for plant growth. Limestone raises pH and sulfur lowers it. To avoid under or over applying these materials, applications should be based on a soil test. Preferably, any applied lime should be thoroughly tilled into the soil prior to planting.

Table 2-5 presents some approximate amounts of ground limestone needed to increase the pH of five soil types. Table 2-6 presents some approximate amounts of ground sulfur needed too decrease the pH of two soil types. These values are only representative and should not be taken as recommendations. To avoid under or over applying liming material, applications should be based on a soil test. In order to ascertain a more precise lime requirement recommendation, the Virginia Tech Soil Testing Laboratory not only performs a soil pH using distilled water, but it also determines a pH using a buffered solution to measure the total (active plus reserve) acidity and buffering capacity for a particular soil sample. Preferably, any applied lime should be thoroughly tilled into the soil prior to planting. As with soil testing for fertilizer needs, amendments to improve aeration and/or drainage should be applied prior to testing soil pH.

Table 2-5: Approximate amount of limestone needed to increase the pH of the upper 7 inches of soil to 6.5

Table shows the amount of lime to apply in lbs./1000 square feet. Lime recommendations are based on using a ground limestone with a neutralizing value of 90%

Soil texture (Upper 7 inches)	pH range 4.5 to 4.9	pH range 5.0 to 5.4	pH range 5.5 to 5.9	pH range 6.0 to 6.4
Sand	115	92	69	23
Loamy sand	138	115	92	46
Sandy loam	184	138	115	69
Clay and silty clay	270	230	184	92
Clay loam and loam	230	184	138	92

Table 2-6: Approximate amount of ground sulfur needed to decrease the pH of the soil to 6.5

Sulfur recommendations are based on using a ground sulfur material containing 95% S. This information was provided by D.A. Bailey, Department of Horticulture Science, NCSU

Soil Texture	pH range 7.0 to 7.5	pH range 7.6 to 8.0	pH range 8.1 to 8.5	pH range 8.6 to 9.0
Sandy soils	9-13	22-34	34-45	45-68
Clay soils	18-22	34-45	34-45	----

If the soil pH is too high and must be lowered, elemental sulfur or aluminum sulfate can be incorporated into the soil to reduce alkalinity. If only a small decrease in pH is required, acid-forming fertilizer such as ammonium nitrate can be used as a nitrogen source.

Most ornamental plants require slightly to strongly acidic soil. When grown in soils in the alkaline range, these species may develop trace metal deficiencies (such as iron or manganese, trace metal deficiency symptoms will first appear on new leaves).

While there is likely plenty of iron in the soil, when the pH is not in a favorable range for the plant being grown, the iron is unavailable to the plant. This problem can be corrected by applying chelated iron. The term chelate comes from the Greek word for claw. **Chelates** are chemical claws that help hold metal ions, such as iron, in solution, so that the plant can absorb them. Different chemicals can act as chelates, from relatively simple natural chelates like citrate to more complex, manufactured chemicals. When a chelated metal is added to the soil, the nutrient held by the chelate will remain available to the plant for a longer period of time than if added as a salt form such as iron sulfate.

Most nutrients do not require the addition of a chelate to help absorption. Only a few of the metals, such as iron, benefit from the addition of chelates.

Building Healthy Soil

Well-formed soil structure can have a positive impact on nutrient retention. Organic matter is a great soil improver for both clay and sandy soils. Good sources of organic matter include manures, leaf mold, sawdust, and straw. These materials are decomposed by soil organisms. Various factors such as moisture, temperature, and nitrogen availability determine the rate of decomposition through their effects on these organisms. Adequate water must be present, and warm temperatures will increase the rate at which the microbes work. The proper balance of carbon and nitrogen is needed for rapid decomposition. Fresh green wastes, such as grass clippings, are higher in nitrogen than dry material. The addition of nitrogen may be necessary if large amounts of undecomposed high-carbon substances such as dried leaves, straw, or sawdust are used. In the process of breaking down the organic matter. Nitrogen is used by the microbes and, therefore, may become deficient in the plants.

Tilling

Tilling is a good way to loosen soil and break up soil clods in new beds as well as in the yearly preparation of annual flower and vegetable gardens. It is also a good opportunity to incorporate organic matter and nutrients into the soil, though excessive tillage can be detrimental to soil organisms and soil structure. The best time to till is when soil is very slightly moist. Tilling in the fall for spring planting helps kill insects and weeds and allows winter freezing and thawing to help build soil structure.

However, tillage of the soil, especially deep tilling practices, can negatively affect the physical and biological properties of the soil. For more about alternatives to tilling, see "No-till or low-till methods" in Chapter 9 "The Vegetable Garden."

Compost

Organic matter should make up 5% or more (by weight) of a healthy soil. Many Virginia soils, especially urban soils, are low in organic matter. The regular application of compost to lawns and landscape beds will add organic matter and improve the overall health of the soil.

The carbon in compost feeds a variety of beneficial bacteria, fungi and other organisms. As these organisms feed they convert nutrients into plant available forms. For example, nitrogen in ammonium (NH_4^+) and ammonia (NH_3^-) is converted to the more plant available form of nitrate (NO_3^-).

Some specialized fungi form symbiotic relationships with plants that provide plants with nutrients and water, essentially acting as an extension of the root system.

As compost-fed soil organisms thrive they break up compacted soil and exude natural glues that allow soil particles to form aggregates. These aggregates help preserve pore space that allows for the passage of water, gasses and roots.

The organic matter in compost can also act as a reserve for food and water. This is especially important in sandy soils where high infiltration rates and low cation exchange capacities would otherwise require frequent applications of water and fertilizer.

The quality of compost is not uniform. Both home-made and commercial compost can vary in chemistry from batch to batch. While there is an effort to standardize commercial compost, it is not mandatory and does not cover home-made compost.

Compost should be dark, brown, fluffy, and crumbly with an earthy odor when ready to use. It should not be moldy, have a rotten smell, or be decomposed to a point of being powdery. Except for some woody pieces, the source materials that went into the compost should not be recognizable and finished compost should have a stable pH near neutral and be low in soluble salts.

Cover Crops

Another source of inexpensive soil improvement that should not be underestimated is the cover crop. Cover crops, sometimes called green manures, can be used to increase organic matter, break up hard soils, suppress weeds, prevent erosion, and hold and increase soil nutrients. Most cover crops have multiple uses. Cereal rye, for example, can absorb soil nutrients and hold them over the winter while also suppressing weeds.

The best time to seed a cover crop depends on the species being planted and when the previous crop is harvested. Often, cover crops are planted in the garden in the fall for incorporation in the spring. In a fall garden, plant cover crops between the rows and in any cleared areas. Cover crops can also be used in late spring and summer to suppress weeds or provide a nitrogen boost before the next crop is planted.

Table 2-7: Table of common cover crops

Type	Legume (L)/Non-Legume (N)	Amount to Sow/100 ft2 (Oz.)	When to Sow	When to Turn Under	Effects	Notes
Alfalfa (spring sow)	L	0.5	Spring Late Summer	Fall Spring	Fixes 150-250 lbs. N/ac./yr; deep roots break up hard soil, trace elements to surface.	Loam, fairly fertile soil; needs warm temps. for germination. Lime if pH is low. Hardy. In mountains sow by Aug 10. Drought tolerant. Inoculate.
Barley	N	4	Fall Spring	Spring Fall	Adds organic matter; improves soil aggregation.	Prefers medium-rich, loam soil. Lime if pH is low. Not as hardy as rye. Tolerates drought.
Buckwheat	N	2.5	Spring Summer	Summer Fall	Mellows soil; rich in potassium	Must leave part of garden in cover crop during season. Grows quickly. Not hardy.
Crimson Clover	L	0.33	Spring Fall	Fall Spring	Fixes 100-150 lbs. N/ac./yr.	Not reliably hardy. Sow before mid-Sept. in Piedmont and mountains. Not drought tolerant. Lime if pH is low. White clover is a bit hardier.
Fava Beans	L	Plant 8" apart	Early Spring Late Summer	Early Summer Fall	Some types fix 70-100 lbs. N/ac./yr in as little as 6 weeks. Use small seeded rather than large seeded table types.	Will grow on many soil types. Medium drought tolerance. Likes cool growing weather. Good for mountain areas. If planted in early spring can grow late vegetables. Inoculate with same bacteria as hairy vetch.
Forage Radish	N	Plant 4" apart with 15" row spacing,	Fall, 4-10 weeks before expected killing frost	Spring	Reduces soil compaction, suppresses weeds, increase soil infiltration, captures and holds up to 170 lb N/ac/yr	Will die off once the temperature reaches 25°F but roots will slowly decompose leaving open channels that will help infiltration
Oats	N	4	Spring Fall	Summer Spring	Adds organic matter; improves soil aggregation.	Needs adequate manganese. Not hardy; tolerates low pH
Rye, winter	N	3.5	Fall	Spring	Adds organic matter; improves soil aggregation.	Very hardy. Can plant until late October.
Vetch, hairy	L	2.5	Early Fall	Spring	Fixes 80-100 lbs. N/ac./yr.	Inoculate; slow to establish. Fairly hardy. Till under before it seeds; can become a weed.
Wheat, winter	N	4	Fall	Spring	Adds organic matter; improves soil aggregation.	Prefers medium-rich, loam soil. Lime if pH is low. Not as hardy as rye. Tolerates drought.

Cover cropping provides additional organic matter, holds nutrients that might have been lost over the winter, and helps reduce erosion and loss of topsoil. Legume cover crops can increase the amount of nitrogen in the soil and reduce fertilizer needs over time. A deep-rooted cover crop allowed to grow for a season in problem soil can help break up a hardpan and greatly improve soil tilth. Planting multiple species of cover crops together has shown to increase the diversity of soil organism communities.

Incorporate green manures at least 2 weeks before planting vegetables. In most cases, cover crops should not be allowed to go to seed.

The regular addition of manures, compost, cover crops, and other organic materials can raise the soil nutrient level to a point where the need for synthetic fertilizers is greatly reduced. This highly desirable soil quality does not come about after a single or even several additions of organic material and requires a serious soil-building program. For more information, see Chapter 9: "The Vegetable Garden."

Soil Food Web

The soil food web is built of a wide range of organisms. This complex system includes organisms such as bacteria, algae, fungi, protozoa, nematodes and micro-arthropods, as well as earthworms, insects, small vertebrates, and plants. From the microscopic to the visible, each organism plays an important role in this ecosystem. Decomposition of organic matter, sequestration of nitrogen, fixing of nitrogen from the atmosphere to make it available for plants, and aerating the soil are just a few of the specific tasks these organisms can play in the soil food web.

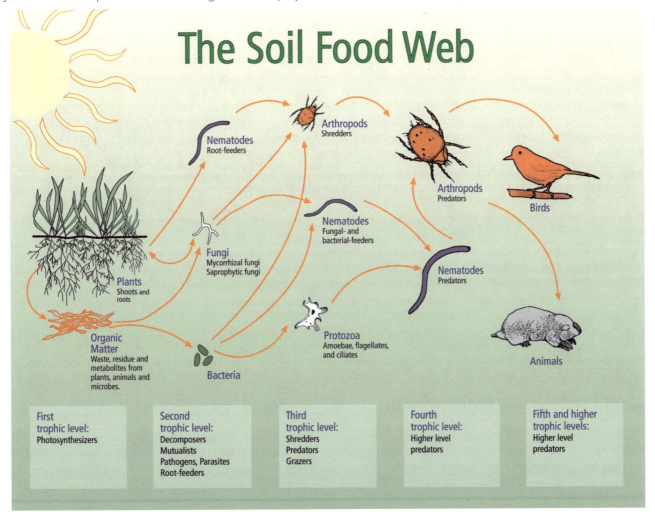

Figure 2-12: The soil food web: Organization of organisms into trophic levels; photosynthesis first; second decomposers, mutualists, pathogens, parasites, and root-feeders; third shredders, predators, and grazers; fourth higher level predators; fifth higher level predators.

Understanding Fertilizers

There are 16 elements essential to plant growth, as described in Table 2-2 and 2-3. Carbon, hydrogen, and oxygen come from air and/or water. Nitrogen, phosphorous and potassium are considered fertilizer macronutrients because plants require them in a relatively large quantity for maximum growth. Calcium, magnesium, and sulfur are secondary macronutrients but usually are either present in sufficient quantities or are added coincidentally with other materials (e.g., lime). The other seven nutrients, called micronutrients, are just as important but are required in smaller amounts. To review the roles of the elements in plant growth, please see the section, "Physiological and Biochemical Functions of Essential Elements in Plants" in Chapter 5 "Abiotic Stress."

If plants are low in any of these elements, they exhibit signs of nutrient deficiency. High levels may contribute to nutrient toxicity. Some of these symptoms are given in the discussion of nutrients in Chapter 5 "Abiotic Stress."

Fertilizer Analysis

Some fertilizer packaging includes an analysis of nutrient content, represented by three numbers which refer to the percentage by weight of nitrogen (N), phosphate (P_2O_5), and potash (K_2O) respectively.

Often, to simplify matters, these numbers are said to represent nitrogen, phosphorus, and potassium, or N-P-K. We should remember that it is not N-P-K, but N-P_2O_5-K_2O. For example, a bag of 10-10-10 fertilizer contains 10% N, 10% P_2O_5, and 10% K_2O by weight. For example, if we have a 100-pound bag of this fertilizer labeled 10-10-10, there are 10 pounds of N, 10 pounds of P_2O_5, and 10 pounds of K_2O in that bag.

In some fertilizers, a filler is sometimes added to bulk up the fertilizer. This is done to lower the analysis, or dilute the concentration, allowing a more even spreading pattern as compared to trying to spread a small amount of a high analysis fertilizer over an area. A filler is generally an inert material such as sand or ground corn cobs. Some fillers are used to enhance the fertilizer's handling qualities.

The information contained on fertilizer labels has been well standardized, and the consumer is protected by state laws requiring manufacturers to guarantee the claimed nutrients. In some cases, a fertilizer will contain secondary nutrients or micronutrients not listed on the label because the manufacturer does not want to guarantee their exact amounts.

Figure 2-13: Fertilizer will be labeled with three numbers giving percentage by weight of nitrogen, phosphate, and potash.

On fertilizer labels, the initials WIN and WSN stand for Water Insoluble Nitrogen and Water Soluble Nitrogen. Water soluble nitrogen (WSN) dissolves readily and is usually in a simple form, such as ammoniacal nitrogen (ammonium, NH_4^+) or nitrate (NO_3^-) nitrogen. Nitrogen, which will not dissolve readily, may exist in other forms in the fertilizer. Water insoluble nitrogen (WIN) is referred to as a slow-release nitrogen (SRN) source and delivers nitrogen at different rates according to the amount and kind of material in its composition. WIN is also sometimes referred to as slowly-available nitrogen (SAN).

The best fertilizer to use depends on many factors, such as the nutrients needed, soil structure, soil chemistry, and method of applying the fertilizer.

Complete versus Incomplete

A complete fertilizer contains nitrogen, phosphorus, and potassium. Common examples of complete fertilizers are 10-10-10 and 20-10-5. An incomplete fertilizer is missing one or two of the major components. Examples of incomplete fertilizers are indicated on the following chart.

Manufacturers can blend different incomplete fertilizers to create many different fertilizer ratios found on store shelves.

The fertilizer ratio indicates the proportion of nitrogen, phosphate, and potash contained in the fertilizer. The specific fertilizer ratio you will need depends on the soil nutrient level, and the plants being grown.

Table 2-8: Common incomplete (agricultural) fertilizers

Type of fertilizer	% Nitrogen	% Phosphate (P2O5)	% Potash (K$_2$O)
Ammonium nitrate	34	0	0
Ammonium sulfate	21	0	0
Monoammomium phosphate	11	48	0
Muriate of potash (Potassium chloride)	0	0	60
Potassium sulfate	0	0	52
Superphosphate	0	20	0
Triple superphosphate	0	46	0
Urea	46	0	0
Ureaformaldehyde (Urea form)	38	0	0

Fertilizer Formulation

Fertilizer formulation determines how quickly nutrients will be available to plants. Some of the formulations available to the homeowner are: water-soluble powders, slow-release pellets, slow-release collars or spikes, liquids, tablets, and granular solids.

Liquid fertilizers come in a variety of different formulations, including complete formulas, special incomplete formulations, and types that offer just one or two micronutrients. All liquid fertilizers are made to be diluted with water, some are concentrated liquids, and others are powder or pellets. Growers of container plants often use liquid fertilizers (which typically contain more WSN) at half concentration twice as frequently, so that the plants receive a more continuous supply of nutrients.

Special-Purpose Fertilizers

When shopping for fertilizer, you will find fertilizers packaged for certain uses or types of plants such as Camellia Food, Rhododendron and Azalea Food, or Rose Food. Some of the compounds used in these fertilizers are chosen because they have an acid reaction, or provide the plant with its preferred nutrient source, such as ammoniacal N, so they are especially beneficial to acid-loving plants where soil is naturally neutral or alkaline.

A soil test should be performed before the purchase of any expensive, special-purpose fertilizers. It is not possible to make a blanket statement that one fertilizer is best for every area. It is true that different plants use different nutrients at different rates. What is unknown is the reserve of nutrients already in the soil. This will change with soil type and location.

Slow-release fertilizers

Plants can absorb nutrients continuously, so it is beneficial to provide them with a balance of nutrients throughout their growth. Perhaps the most efficient way to achieve this is to apply a slow-release fertilizer, which releases nutrients at a rate that makes them available to the plants over a long period. Slow-release fertilizers contain one or more essential elements and can be categorized according to their release mechanism. The three major types of nutrient release mechanisms are: (1) materials that dissolve slowly, (2) materials requiring microorganisms to release nitrogen, and (3) granular materials with membranes made of resin or sulfur to control the rate of nutrient release into the soil.

Sulfur-coated urea is a slow-release fertilizer with a covering of sulfur around each urea particle. The rate of nitrogen release is determined by the thickness of the coating. Sulfur-coated urea applied to the soil's surface releases nitrogen more slowly than if incorporated into the soil. This material generally costs less than other slow-release fertilizers, and it supplies the essential element sulfur.

When fertilizer products coated with multiple layers of resin come into contact with water, the layers swell and increase the pore size in the resin so that the dissolved fertilizer can move into the soil. Release rate depends on the coating thickness, temperature, and water content of the soil. There is often a large release of fertilizer during the first 2 or 3 days after application. Release timing can be from 0 to 6 months, depending on the coating.

Slow-release fertilizers need not be applied as frequently as other fertilizers, and higher amounts can be applied without danger of burning. Plants may use the nitrogen in slow-release fertilizers more efficiently than nitrogen in other forms, since it is released over a longer period of time and in smaller quantity. Slow-release fertilizers are generally more expensive than other types, but they require much less frequent application than conventional fertilizers.

Urea formaldehyde and sulfur-coated urea have been used as turf fertilizer, while resin-coated fertilizers are predominantly used in container growing.

Caution should be used when applying slow-release fertilizers around trees or shrubs as this can encourage late summer growth that may not harden off completely, exposing the plant to winter damage.

Table 2-9: Comparison of slow-release fertilizers, conventional fertilizers, and manure or sludge

Type of Fertilizer	Advantages	Disadvantages
Slow-Release Fertilizers	- Fewer applications - Low burn potential - Release rate varies depending on fertilizer characteristics - Comparatively slow release rate	- Unit cost is high - Availability is limited
Conventional Fertilizers	- Fast-acting - Some are acid-forming - Lower cost	- Greater burn potential - Solidifies in the bag when wet - Nitrogen leaches readily
Manure or Sewage Sludge	- Low burn potential - Relatively slow release - Contains micronutrients - Conditions the soil	- Salt could be a problem (except for fresh chicken manure) - Bulky, hard to handle - Odor - Expensive per pound of actual nutrient - Weed seeds are a problem - Cannot select a needed formulation; usually low in N, high in P, and sometimes high in K. Best applied based on P needs (add additional conventional fertilizer for any remaining N needs) - Heavy metals may be present in sewage sludge from large cities or industrial areas

Organic fertilizers

Although compost is fertilizer, home gardeners might seek additional sources of organic fertilizer. The nutrients in organic fertilizers are derived solely from the remains or by-products of a once-living organism (and not necessarily "organic" in the sense of the term used in organic gardening). Cottonseed meal, blood meal, bone meal, hoof and horn meal, and all manures are examples of organic fertilizers. When packaged as fertilizers, these products will have the fertilizer ratios included on the label. Some organic materials, particularly composted manures and sludge, are sold as soil conditioners and do not have a nutrient guarantee, although small amounts of nutrients are present. Some are fortified with nitrogen, phosphorus, or potash for a higher analysis. In general, organic fertilizers release nutrients over a fairly long period, first releasing quickly available nutrients and then additional mineral nutrients become available later via decomposition. The potential drawback is that they may not release enough of their principal nutrient at a time to give the plant what it needs for best growth. Organic fertilizers depend on soil organisms to break them down to release nutrients, so most are only effective when soil is moist and warm enough for the soil organisms to be active.

Cottonseed meal is a by-product of cotton manufacturing and is frequently used for fertilizing acid-loving plants such as azaleas, camellias, and rhododendrons. Formulas vary slightly, but generally contain 6% nitrogen, 3% phosphate, and 2%

potash. Cottonseed meal is readily available to plants in warm soils, and there is little danger of burn. For general garden use, apply 2 to 5 pounds per 1000 square feet.

Blood meal is dried, powdered blood collected from beef processors. It is a rich source of nitrogen — so rich, in fact, that it may do harm if used in excess. The gardener must be careful not to use more than the amount recommended on the label. In addition to supplying nitrogen, blood meal supplies many of the essential trace elements, including iron.

Urea is a synthetic organic fertilizer, an organic substance manufactured from inorganic materials.

Fish emulsion, a complete fertilizer, is a partially decomposed blend of finely pulverized fish. No matter how little is used, the odor is intense — but it dissipates within a day or two. Fish emulsion is high in nitrogen and is a source of several trace elements. In the late spring, when garden plants have sprouted, an application of fish emulsion followed by a deep watering will boost the plant's early growth spurt. Contrary to popular belief, too strong a solution of fish emulsion can burn plants, particularly those in containers.

Manure is also a complete fertilizer and varies in nutrient content depending on the animal and its diet, but a fertilizer ratio of 1-1-1 is typical. Manures are best used as soil conditioners instead of nutrient sources. Commonly available manures include horse, cow, pig, chicken, and sheep. The actual nutrient content varies widely, but is highest when manures are fresh. Fresh manure should not be used where it will contact tender plant roots. As it is aged, leached, or composted, nutrient content is reduced. However, the subsequent reduction in salts will reduce the chances of burning plants. Typical rates of manure applications vary from a moderate 70 pounds per 1,000 square feet to as much as half a ton per 1,000 square feet.

Compared to synthetic fertilizer formulations, organic fertilizers contain relatively low concentrations of actual nutrients, but they perform other important functions which the synthetic formulations do not. Some of these functions are: increasing organic content of the soil, improving physical structure of the soil, adding micronutrients, and increasing bacterial and fungal activity.

Fertilizer application rate examples

Example 1

Determine the amount of ammonium sulfate needed by a 5000 square-foot lawn if 1 pound of nitrogen per 1000 square feet is recommended.

- Lawn: 5000 square feet
- Fertilizer: ammonium sulfate (21-0-0)
- Rate: 1 pound of nitrogen per 1000 square feet

Since we need 1 pound of nitrogen for every 1000 square feet and we have 5000 square feet, we need 5 pounds of nitrogen.

Ammonium sulfate is 21% nitrogen (round to 20%).

20% is the same as 0.20 or 1/5 . This means that we need 5 pounds of fertilizer to get 1 pound of nitrogen.

Since we need 5 pounds of nitrogen, 5 x 5 = 25 pounds of fertilizer.

Total fertilizer needed =

$$\frac{\text{N application rate (lbs. per 100 sq. ft.)}}{\text{N content of fertilizer}} \times \frac{\text{Lawn size (sq. ft.)}}{1000} = \frac{1}{0.20} \times \frac{5000}{1000} = 25 \text{ lb. fertilizer}$$

Example 2

Determine how much 10-10-10 needs to be applied to ensure 2 pounds of nitrogen per thousand square feet in a garden that measures 20 x 10 feet.

Garden: 20 x 10 = 200 square feet

Fertilizer: 10-10-10 = 10 percent nitrogen

Rate: 2 pounds of nitrogen per 1000 square feet

Total fertilizer needed =

$$\frac{2}{0.10} \times \frac{200}{1000} = 4 \text{ lb. fertilizer}$$

Fertilizers Combined With Pesticides

Fertilizers can be combined with pesticides by the manufacturer or the applicator but must be applied at the appropriate time and rate. Always read the label carefully.

Applying Fertilizer

Fertilizer Application Rate

The amount of fertilizer applied is determined by the amount of nitrogen because it is the nutrient most easily lost from the soil. In the following chart, you can see how the amount to be applied decreases as the percentage of nitrogen increases.

Nitrogen fertilizers do not burn or damage plants if they are applied correctly. Fertilizers are salts, much like our familiar table salt, except that they contain various plant nutrients. Salts in the fertilizer begin to diffuse or move away from the place where they had been applied. This dilutes the fertilizer and distributes it through a much larger area. If tender plant roots are close to the area where the fertilizer is placed, water will be drawn from these roots and from the surrounding soil. The more salt or fertilizer applied, the more water will be drawn from nearby roots. As water is drawn from the roots, plant cells begin to dehydrate and collapse, and the plant roots burn or dehydrate to a point from which they cannot recover. If soil moisture is limited, most of the water drawn towards the salt will come from plant roots and the damage will be more severe.

Two rules should be kept in mind when applying a fertilizer during hot weather when soil moisture is limited: 1) do not over-apply nitrogen fertilizers, and 2) make sure adequate moisture is present after applying fertilizers high in salts.

Soluble salts accumulate when fertilizer is applied repeatedly without sufficient water to leach or wash the old fertilizer's salts through the soil. It also occurs when water evaporates from the soil and leaves previously dissolved salts behind. Soluble salts will accumulate on top of the soil in a container and form a yellow-to-white crust. A ring of salt deposits may form around the pot at the soil line or around the drainage hole. Salts may also build up on the outside of clay pots.

As the salts in the soil become more concentrated, plants find it harder to take up water. If salts build up to an extremely high level, water can be taken out of the root tips, causing them to die.

Table 2-10: Fertilizer application rates as determined by goal N content

Formula	Lbs. Fertilizer applied per 1000 square feet
5-10-10	3.5
6-18-6	2.9
8-12-4	2.2
10-10-10	1.8
12-6-6	1.5
16-16-16	1.1

Timing and Method of Application

Soil type dictates the frequency of fertilizer application. Sandy soils require more frequent applications of nitrogen and other nutrients than do clay-type soils. Factors affecting the type and rate of fertilizer application include: the type of crop, the level of crop productivity required, frequency and amount of water applied, and the type of fertilizer applied and its release rate.

Timing

The type of crop influences timing and frequency of application since some crops are heavier feeders of particular nutrients than others. Root crops (such as carrots) require less nitrogen fertilization than do leafy crops (such as greens). Corn is a heavy feeder of nitrogen, while most trees and shrubs are generally light nitrogen-feeders. A general rule of thumb is that nitrogen is for leafy top growth, phosphorus is for root and fruit production, and potassium is for cold hardiness, disease resistance, and general durability.

Proper use of nutrients can control plant growth rate and character. Nitrogen is the most critical nutrient in this regard. If tomatoes are fertilized too heavily with a nitrogen fertilizer or side-dressed before fruit set, the plants may be all vegetative (shoot, stem, leaf) and no fruit. This is also the case with potatoes, which will show excess vining and poor tuber formation. If slow-release fertilizers or heavy amounts of manure are used on crops that form fruit or vegetables, vegetative growth will continue into late summer, and fruit and vegetable development will occur very late in the season. Late nitrogen fertilization can also prevent perennial plants from becoming cold-hardy, inducing cold weather injury.

Remember that a nitrogen application will have its greatest effect for 3-4 weeks after application. If tomatoes are fertilized heavily on June 1, there may be no flower production until July 1, which will, in turn, delay fruit ripening until late August. For this reason, it is important to plant crops with similar fertilizer needs close together to avoid improper rates of application.

Late fertilization (after July 1) of trees and shrubs can cause new flushes of growth to occur on woody plants that are normally adjusting themselves for the coming winter. This may delay dormancy of woody plants and cause severe winter dieback in new growth. Gardeners should be aware that individual species within these groups vary considerably. Refer to Chapter 17: "Water Quality and Conservation," for information on fertilizer use and water quality.

Application methods

There are different methods of applying fertilizer depending on its formulation and the crop needs.

Broadcasting

A recommended rate of fertilizer is spread over the entire growing area and left to filter into the soil or incorporated into the soil with a roto tiller or spade. Broadcasting is used over large garden areas or when time or labor is limited.

Banding

Narrow bands of fertilizer are applied in furrows 2 to 3 inches from the garden seeds and 1 to 2 inches deeper than the seeds or plants. Careless placement of the fertilizer band too close to the seeds will burn the roots of the seedlings. The best technique is to stretch a string where the seed row is to be planted. With a corner of a hoe, dig a furrow 3 inches deep, 3 inches to one side, and parallel with the string. Spread half the suggested rate of the fertilizer in the furrow and cover it with soil. Repeat the banding operation on the other side of the string, then sow seeds underneath the string.

For widely spaced plants, such as tomatoes, fertilizers can be placed in bands 6 inches long for each plant or in a circle around the plant. Place the bands 4 inches from the plant base. If used in the planting hole, place the fertilizer at the bottom of the hole, work it into the soil, and add a layer of soil about 2 inches deep over the fertilized soil before putting the plant in the hole.

Banding is one way to satisfy the needs of many plants (especially tomatoes) for phosphorus as the first roots develop. When fertilizers are broadcast and worked into soil, much of the phosphorus is locked up by the soil and is not immediately available to the plant. By concentrating the phosphorus in the band, the plant is given what it needs even though much of the phosphorus stays locked up.

Starter solutions

Another way to satisfy the need for phosphorus when setting out transplants of vegetables and flowers is through the use of a liquid fertilizer high in phosphorus as a starter solution. Follow directions on the label.

Side-dressing

Dry fertilizer is applied as a side dressing after annuals are up and growing. Scatter fertilizer on both sides of the row 6 to 8 inches from the plants. Rake it into the soil and water thoroughly.

Foliar feeding

Foliar feeding (spray of fertilizer applied to foliage) is used when insufficient fertilizer was used before planting, when a quick growth response is wanted, when micronutrients (such as iron or zinc) are locked into the soil, or when the soil is too cold for the plants to use the fertilizer applied to the soil. Foliar-applied nutrients are absorbed and used by the plant quite rapidly. Absorption begins within minutes after application and, with most nutrients, it is completed within 1 to 2 days.

Foliar nutrition can be a supplement to soil nutrition at a critical time for the plant, but not a substitute. At transplanting time, an application of phosphorus spray will help in the establishment of the young plant in cold soils. For perennial plants, early spring growth is usually limited by cold soil, even when the air is warm. Under such conditions, soil microorganisms are not active enough to convert nutrients into forms available for roots to absorb; yet, if the nutrients were available, the plants could grow. A nutrient spray to the foliage will provide the needed nutrients immediately, allowing the plants to begin growth.

Soil and Nutrient Problems

Erosion

Soils that have lost part or all of their surface are usually harder to till and have lower productivity than those that have desirable thickness of surface soil. To compensate for surface soil loss, better fertilization, liming, and other management practices should be used. Increasing the organic matter content of an eroded soil often improves its tillage characteristics, as well as its water and nutrient holding capacity.

The principal reasons for soil erosion in Virginia are:

- Insufficient vegetative cover
- Overexposure through the use of cultivated crops on soils not suited to cultivation
- Improper equipment and methods used in preparation and tillage of the soil

Soil erosion can be held to a minimum by:

- Producing crops to which the soil is suited
- Mulching
- Thorough soil preparation
- Proper tillage methods
- Adequate fertilization and liming to promote vigorous growth of plants

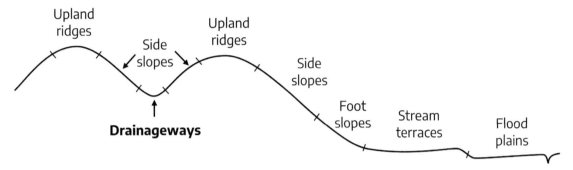

Figure 2-14: Drainage slope: This diagram shows the sections of a drainage slope, including upland ridges with drainageways in between side slopes and downward-draining side slopes that lead to foot slopes, stream terraces, and flood plains.

Nutrients as Pollutants

Nitrogen and phosphorus are currently major sources of pollution in our waterways. Excess nutrients come from sewage treatment plants, automobile exhaust, animal wastes, excess nutrients applied to agricultural fields, excess nutrients applied to home lawns and gardens or failing septic fields. These pollutants can come from organic or synthetic sources. Once these nutrients are in the water, they become available for algae growth. A large, quick growth of algae is referred to as an algae bloom. Once the algae has used up the available flush of nitrogen and phosphorus, it quickly dies and bacteria begins to break it down. This bacteria uses oxygen to help break down the algae, causing oxygen levels in the water to crash. Water low in dissolved oxygen causes fish and other aquatic animals to perish.

Nitrogen is mobile in the soil. It can easily leach out of the soil or run off the soil surface with the movement of water and easily end up in waterways where it contributes to algae blooms. Phosphorus on the other hand is not usually mobile in the soil. Phosphorus binds with clay particles and organic matter in the soil. Plants are then able to use the phosphorus associated with organic material and soil particles. Phosphorus usually becomes a pollutant in our waterways when it is washed into streams, and creeks while attached to a soil particle. Thus it is important to limit the amount of soil erosion. Another factor that makes phosphorus toxic to our waterways is the fact that algae are much more responsive to phosphorus than to nitrogen. Thus, a small amount of phosphorus can trigger the same algae bloom as a much larger amount of nitrogen.

Since nitrogen and phosphorus have been identified as pollutants, one might expect Virginia Cooperative Extension to recommend not using fertilizers on lawns and gardens in the future. The answer is much more nuanced than this. When plants have the nutrients they need available to them, they are healthier, grow thicker and denser, and their roots are stronger. They hold soil better and limit erosion. Thus, these plants help to limit the amount of nitrogen and phosphorus that end up in our waterways. Conversely, if plants don't have enough nutrients to thrive and stay healthy, they are often spindly and small, and they may not be able to hold soils in place as well as we would like and may contribute to soil erosion. Thus, the results of a soil test are invaluable to help determine the need for nutrient amendments, as well as the form and amount needed. Nutrients applied correctly are beneficial. When misapplied, they can become pollutants.

Our communities are making concerted efforts to help limit the excess nutrients that end up in our waterways. Virginia law prohibits the sale of synthetic fertilizers with phosphorus for maintenance purposes. Phosphorus fertilizers are, however, allowed to be used for establishing new plantings or for use on sites that are low in phosphorus according to a soil test.

Areas inappropriate for fertilizer application

Some locations are inappropriate for fertilizer application. They create a high potential for runoff and/or leaching, in which case the fertilizer then becomes an environmental pollutant. Detailed information on each of these types of locations is given below.

- **Impervious surfaces:** Driveways, sidewalks and other paved areas should not have fertilizers applied to them. During lawn fertilization some fertilizer may spread to these areas and this fertilizer should be swept or blown back into the planting areas. Fertilizers should not be used as deicers in the winter.
- **Soils with high water table:** Fertilizer is more likely to move into water where there are soils that do not drain well or there is a high water table. Individuals should be cautious about applying fertilizers in these areas.
- **Stream and pond banks:** In places where a lawn goes directly to the edge of a stream or pond, a buffer should be left in place. An area of turf grass that is 20 feet from the water should not be fertilized and ideally there is an area of vegetation that is thicker and taller than a lawn that is typically mowed weekly during the growing season.
- **Well heads and rock outcroppings:** Both of these sites have the potential to take surface water directly into local ground water. And as such a buffer or no fertilization zone should be left around these sites.
- **Karst bedrock**: Many areas of Virginia have limestone based bedrock. This limestone dissolves over time and often there are channels or sinkholes that provide immediate movement of surface water into ground water. Use fertilizers in these areas cautiously.
- **Steep slopes:** Steep slopes have a high potential to have fertilizers wash away. Slow release fertilizers work best in these situations.

Figure 2-15: Areas inappropriate for fertilizer application include impervious surfaces (sweep any fertilizer back into planting area), stream banks, and steep slopes.

Keeping soils covered with healthy plants is the best way to limit the amount of nutrients that end up in local waterways. But where plants are absent it is helpful to have the soil covered. Hardwood or pine bark mulch and other plant based mulches can be helpful to limit erosion and nutrients reaching water.

Compaction

Compaction is the process in which a stress applied to a soil causes loss of pore space, such as equipment traffic on wet soils. The measure of soil bulk density, which is the ratio of dry weight of a soil sample divided by its volume, determines the bulk density or compaction. As the dry weight increases relative to the volume, porosity in the soil decreases and compaction increases. This situation restricts root, air and water movement and leads to plant stress. Urban soils tend to be moderately to heavily compacted because of the amount of traffic they receive during construction or landscaping.

Urban Soils

Soils in urban environments provide unique challenges. One primary challenge is to provide the functions of the natural environment in a built environment. While some plants are adaptable to a fairly wide range of environmental conditions, others have a narrow range in which they will grow well. For example, urban soils will often have a higher pH than surrounding rural areas due to limestone-containing materials in the urban environment (Bassuk, Curtis, Marranca, and Neal). For plants that require a specific pH range in order to thrive, the higher pH of urban soils can cause stress to the plant. Other challenges of urban soil are compaction and the removal of topsoil during construction. For more about urban soils, see the VCE Master Gardener Tree Steward Manual (https://pressbooks.lib.vt.edu/treesteward/chapter/6).

Salinity

Soil salinity falls into two categories:

Primary salinity is the result of natural processes such as erosion. It can also be seen in land near the ocean, where salts are accumulated through salt spray brought by wind and deposited in the soil by rain. Primary salinity can occur over very long periods of time.

Secondary salinity results from human activity and occurs more quickly than primary salinity. Continuous irrigation and fertilization of agricultural areas results in a buildup of salts in the top layers of the soil. Removal of natural vegetation to make space for annual agricultural crops destroys perennials that have adapted to their environment. Removing perennials and planting annuals often requires irrigation that can expose plants to higher salinities. For more information about salinity and the problems it can cause plants, see Chapter 5 "Abiotic Stress Effects on Plant Growth and Development."

Additional Resources

- Virginia Tech Soil Testing Lab (http://www.soiltest.vt.edu/)
- "Making Compost from Yard Waste" 426-703
- "Compost – What Is It and What Is It to You" 452-231
- Shrivastava, P., & Kumar, R. (2015). Soil salinity: A serious environmental issue and plant growth promoting bacteria as one of the tools for its alleviation. *Saudi journal of biological sciences*, 22(2), 123–131. https://doi.org/10.1016/j.sjbs.2014.12.001
- USDA NRCS Soil Health information (https://www.nrcs.usda.gov/wps/portal/nrcs/main/soils/health/)
- USDA NRCS Soil Classification educational website (https://www.nrcs.usda.gov/wps/portal/nrcs/main/soils/survey/class/)

References

"Soil Food Web" section adapted from "Soil Food Web" By Elaine R. Ingham, USDA Natural Resources Conservation Service. https://www.nrcs.usda.gov/wps/portal/nrcs/detailfull/soils/health/biology/?cid=nrcs142p2_053868

"Urban Soils" section adapted from VCE Master Gardener *Tree Steward Manual* Chapter 6: Soil Properties and Management by Gwen Harris and Cherilyn Kern. https://pressbooks.lib.vt.edu/treesteward/chapter/6/#chapter-246-section-4

"Salinity" section adapted from Chapter 5: Abiotic Stress by David Orcutt

"Soil orders found in Virginia" section from VCE Master Gardener *Tree Steward Manual* Chapter 6: Soil Properties and Management by Gwen Harris and Cherilyn Kern. https://pressbooks.lib.vt.edu/treesteward/chapter/6/#chapter-246-section-4

Citations

- Bassuk, N., Curtis, D., Marranca, B.Z., Neal, B. (n.d.) *Recommended Urban Trees: Site Assessment and Tree Selection for Stress Tolerance*. Urban Horticulture Institute, Department of Horticulture, Cornell University. http://www.hort.cornell.edu

Attributions

Adapted from the Soils and Nutrient Management chapters in the 2015 Extension Master Gardener Handbook.

- Mimi Rosenthal, Norfolk Extension Master Gardener (2021 reviser and contributor)
- Ralph Morini, Albemarle/Charlottesville Extension Master Gardener (2021 reviser)
- Doug Levin, Washington County Extension Master Gardener (2021 reviser)
- Paige Thacker, Extension Agent, Agriculture and Natural Resources (Prepared 2015 Nutrient Management chapter)
- Thomas Bolles, Environmental Educator (Prepared 2015 Nutrient Management chapter)
- Tim Ohlwiler, Extension Agent, Agriculture and Natural Resources (Prepared 2015 Nutrient Management chapter)
- Jim Owen, Assistant Professor of Agriculture (2015 Nutrient Management chapter reviewer)
- Dan Nortman, Extension Agent, Agriculture and Natural Resources (2015 Soils chapter reviser)
- Pattie Bland, Urban Conservationist, Hanover-Caroline Soil and Water Conservation District (2015 Soils chapter reviewer)
- Stephen J. Donahue, Extension Specialist, Soil Testing and Plant Analysis (2009 Soils chapter reviser)
- Steve Heckendorn, Laboratory Manager, Virginia Tech Department of Crop and Soil Environmental Science (2009 Soils chapter reviser)
- Louis Judson, VCE Master Gardener (2009 Soils chapter reviser)

Image Attributions

- Figure 2-1: Soil composition. Johnson, Devon. 2022. CC BY-NC-SA 4.0.
- Figure 2-2: Effects of texture on capacity of soils to hold water. Grey, Kindred. 2022. CC BY-NC-SA 4.0.
- Figure 2-3: Soil horizon diagram. Johnson, Devon. 2022. CC BY-NC-SA 4.0.
- Figure 2-4: Soil composition diagram. Johnson, Devon. 2022. CC BY-NC-SA 4.0.
- Figure 2-5: Soil texture triangle. Johnson, Devon. 2022. CC BY-NC-SA 4.0.
- Figure 2-6: Virginia's dominant soil orders. USDA-NRCS. Public Domain.
- Figure 2-7: Soil structure. Johnson, Devon. 2022. CC BY-NC-SA 4.0.
- Figure 2-8: Reedville Demonstration Living Shoreline. Cheyne, Ian. 2021. CC BY-NC-SA 4.0.
- Figure 2-9: EMGs conduct a shoreline management class. Duhring, Karen. 2021. CC BY-NC-SA 4.0.
- Figure 2-10: pH range. Grey, Kindred. 2022. CC BY-NC-SA 4.0.
- Figure 2-11: Nutrient availability by pH. Johnson, Devon. 2022. CC BY-NC-SA 4.0.
- Figure 2-12: Soil food web. USDA-NRCS. Public Domain.
- Figure 2-13: Fertilizer will be labeled with three numbers giving percentage by weight of nitrogen, phosphate, and potash. Johnson, Devon. 2022. CC BY-NC-SA 4.0.
- Figure 2-14: Drainage slopes. Grey, Kindred. 2022. CC BY-NC-SA 4.0.
- Figure 2-15: Areas inappropriate for fertilizer application include impervious surfaces (sweep any fertilizer back into planting area), stream banks, and steep slopes. Johnson, Devon. 2022. CC BY-NC-SA 4.0.

CHAPTER 3: ENTOMOLOGY

Chapter Contents:

- Benefits and Value of Insects
- Insect Form & Structure – Morphology
- Insect Development – Metamorphosis
- Identifying Insects
- Types of Insect Injury
- Insects of Importance to the Gardener
- Commonly Encountered Non-Insect Arthropods
- Taxonomy
- Additional Resources

Insects are among the oldest, most numerous, and most successful creatures on earth. Insect fossils date back to over 350 million years. Estimates of insect diversity range from 5–80 million different species, with only about one million formally described so far. Insects can be found in nearly every ecosystem and habitat except the open ocean. In the typical backyard, there may be hundreds of different species of insects present at any given time.

The vast majority of insect species are beneficial or harmless to humans. Insects pollinate fruits and vegetables. They provide food for birds, fish, and other animals, including humans in some cultures. They have been a source of inspiration for the arts and sciences. They produce useful products such as honey, wax, shellac, and silk, as well as help degrade plant debris, dung, and animal carcasses. In addition, some insects feed on other insects that are considered pests by humans. Insects are an integral part of our ecosystems, and through the study of entomology, gardeners can better understand and appreciate the unique role they play in our natural world.

Benefits and Value of Insects

Not all insects are harmful or destructive. People have often gone to great trouble or expense to destroy insects only to learn that the insects were an important part of their garden, were not causing that much damage, or were actually helpful by eating other insects. A good rule of thumb is that pest insects will usually be abundant and associated with plant damage. Beneficial insects, or those that are harmless, are generally less abundant and not associated with plant damage. If all else fails, make note of the insects you see in your yard. If you are unsure if they are pests or not, monitor and revisit areas where you saw them. Take action against them only if you find plant damage.

Insects are beneficial to the gardener in many ways. Insects aid in the production of fruit, seeds, vegetables, and flowers by pollinating the blooms. Many of our common fruits and vegetables are pollinated by insects. Squash, tomatoes, beans, okra, peppers, apples, peaches, citrus, berries, and grapes all require insect activity to set fruit. Insects also pollinate many ornamental plants. The lack of insect activity in greenhouses can be a problem if the plant requires an insect pollinator to produce fruits or seeds. Insects can attack undesirable weeds in the same way they injure crop plants. Insects improve the physical condition of the soil and promote soil fertility by burrowing through the surface layers. Their droppings and dead bodies fertilize the soil. Insects scavenge and consume dead plants, dead animals, and dung.

Insects offer many services to our environment – from feeding fish, birds, and other animals to pollinating flowers. One service offered by insects is the control of plant-feeding insects by insect predators and parasitoids. Predators are insects (or other animals) that catch and eat other animals (their prey), usually in a single meal. Prey animals are usually small and weaker than the predator. Ladybugs, lacewings, assassin bugs, and dragonflies are good examples of predators. In contrast, parasitoids are insects that live on or in the bodies of another living animal (the host), from which they get their food for at least one stage of their development. The hosts of parasites are usually larger and stronger than the parasitoid, but parasitoids eventually kill their host. Most parasitoids are found in the orders Hymenoptera and Diptera. These are important natural enemies of many plant-feeding pests.

Insect Form and Structure–Morphology

All adult members of class Insecta are identifiable by having three body regions, three pairs of legs, and one pair of antennae. Most adult insects have two pairs of wings, although some have only one pair and some are wingless. The legs, antennae, wings, mouthparts, and other appendages are often greatly modified to suit the habitat where the insect lives and what it eats. These appendages can be very useful in determining the order to which an insect belongs.

The three regions of the adult insect body are the head, thorax, and abdomen. Sometimes the division between two regions is not always obvious. It is helpful to remember that the eyes, mouthparts, and antennae are found on the head and the legs and wings are found on the thorax. The abdomen is primarily important for digestion and reproduction.

Insects do not have an internal bony skeleton. The insect body is supported by an exoskeleton, a tough outer body wall. The outer layer of the exoskeleton, the **cuticle**, is made of **chitin**, a strong and flexible material. However, chitin is not very hard so the body wall also includes **sclerites**, hardened plates that offer stronger protection. Together, this combination of sclerites connected by thin, flexible cuticle is a structural feature that has helped arthropods colonize nearly every habitat on Earth. In addition, the cuticle has an outer layer of wax that limits water loss and prevents desiccation, a very important survival feature for insects. The cuticle of an immature insect is often softer than that of the adult.

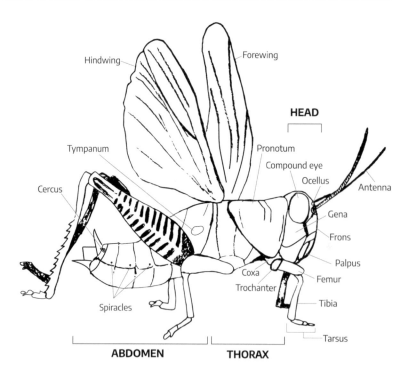

Figure 3-1: Insect body parts: The three main parts of an insect are the head, thorax, and abdomen.

Head

The insect head is primarily involved with eating and sensory perception. The main features of the insect head are the eyes, antennae, and mouthparts. These organs may be highly specialized among orders and families.

Antennae

The antennae are a prominent and distinctive feature of many insects. Adult insects have one pair of antennae located usually between or in front of the compound eyes. Antennae are segmented and vary greatly in form and complexity. The antennae are primarily organs of smell, but may serve as organs for taste, touch, and/or hearing.

Mouthparts

Insect mouthparts are complicated structural features, and they vary greatly in form and function. Most types of insect mouthparts can be divided into two broad categories: those adapted for chewing and those adapted for sucking. There are also intermediate types of mouthparts: rasping-sucking, as found in thrips, and chewing-lapping, as found in honey bees, wasps, and bumble bees. Piercing-sucking mouthparts are typical of the Hemiptera (bugs, aphids, scales, and mealybugs), blood-sucking lice, fleas, mosquitoes, and the biting flies. Butterflies and moths have siphoning mouthparts for feeding on nectar. House flies and many other flies have sponging mouthparts.

The mouthparts of immature insects may differ from the adults. Larvae generally have chewing mouthparts regardless of the kind possessed by the adults. Nymphs have mouthparts similar to those of the adults. In some adult insects, the mouthparts are vestigial (rendered functionless) because the adults do not feed.

Some types of insect mouthparts are diagrammed in figure 3-2: a) chewing-lapping (honey bee), b) sponging (house fly), c) piercing-sucking (mosquito), d) siphoning, coiled (butterfly), e) chewing (grasshopper).

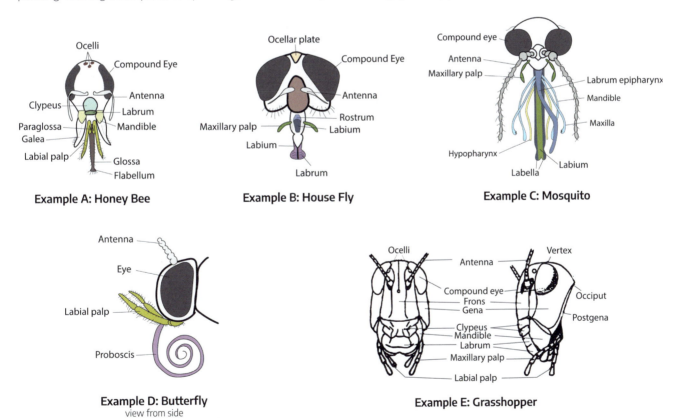

Figure 3-2: Diagram of mouthparts demonstrating different adaptations: a) chewing-lapping (honey bee), b) sponging (house fly), c) piercing-sucking (mosquito), d) siphoning, coiled (butterfly), and e) chewing (grasshopper).

Thorax

The thorax is made up of three segments, each bearing a pair of legs. Most adult insects possess two pairs of wings that are attached to the second and third segments of the thorax.

Legs

The most important characteristic for identifying something as an insect is the presence of three pairs of jointed legs. These are almost always present on adult insects and are generally present in the other stages as well. In addition to walking and jumping, insects often use their legs for digging, grasping, feeling, swimming, carrying loads, building nests, and cleaning parts of the body. The legs of insects vary greatly in size and form and are frequently used in insect classification.

Leg adaptations of some insects are diagrammed below, (left to right): swimming (diving beetle), grasping (praying mantis), jumping (grasshopper), running (beetle), digging (mole cricket).

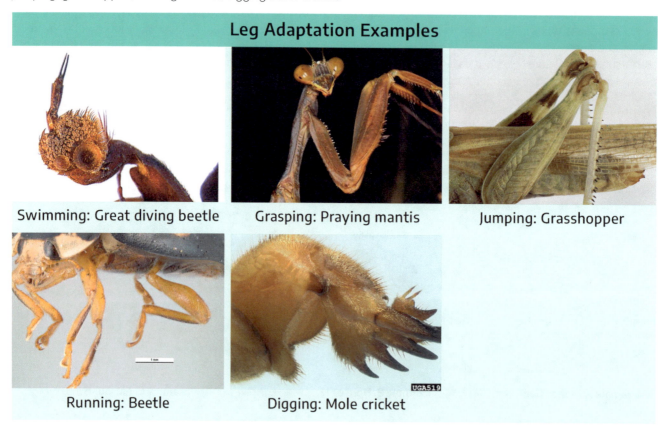

Figure 3-3: Leg adaptations. Swimming: Great diving beetle (*Dytiscus marginalis*), Grasping: praying mantis (*Sphodromantis viridis*), Jumping: southwestern dusky grasshopper (*Encoptolophus subgracilis*), Running: multicolored Asian lady beetle (*Harmonia axyridis*), and Digging: northern mole cricket (*Neocurtilla hexadactyla*).

Wings

Wings are also important features of insects and the variations of wing forms can help identify insect families, genera, and even different species. Wing venation (the arrangement of veins in wings) also serves as a means of identifying insects to family or sometimes species. Wing surfaces may be covered with fine hairs or scales or they may be bare or membranous; these characteristics can be used for identification as well. Note that the names of most insect orders end in "-ptera," which comes from the Greek word meaning "with wings." Many order names describe some feature of the wings. Hemiptera means "half-winged" and refers to the appearance of the wings of true bugs, while Diptera means "two-winged" and refers to the fact that flies have only one pair of wings.

Only adult insects possess wings, although wing pads (areas where the wings are developing) are sometimes noticeable on older nymphs.

Figure 3-4: Types of wings. Diptera: common hoverfly fly (*Simosyrphus grandicornis*), Lepidoptera: painted lady butterfly (*Vanessa cardui*), Ephemeroptera: mayfly (*Callibaetis* sp.), Neuroptera: goldeneyed lacewing (*Chrysopa oculata*), and Hymenoptera: carpenter bee (*Xylocopavirginica*).

Abdomen

The insect abdomen may have 11–12 segments, but in most cases they are difficult to see clearly because the segments are short or they are covered by wings. Some insects have appendages called **cerci** at the tip of the abdomen. Cerci can be short, as seen in grasshoppers, termites, and cockroaches; extremely long, as in mayflies; or curved, as in earwigs.

Insect Development–Metamorphosis

As immature insects feed and grow, eventually their exoskeleton gets too tight and the insect must shed the outer skeleton in a process called "molting." At various stages of growth, the immature insect will split open the exoskeleton and pull itself out of it wearing a soft, new exoskeleton it formed under the old one. The new exoskeleton will harden to protect the insect while giving it sufficient room to grow once it hardens. The stage of life between each molt is called an instar. The number of instars, or the frequency of molts, varies with each species and to some extent with food supply, temperature, and moisture.

In addition to molting, insects also undergo a distinctive phenomenon called metamorphosis at certain stages of their development. The term is a combination of two Greek words: "meta," meaning change, and "morphe," meaning form. Metamorphosis is a biological process in which an insect undergoes an abrupt change in its form from one stage of development to the next. A familiar example of metamorphosis is the change a caterpillar undergoes when it becomes a pupa, or when the adult butterfly emerges from the pupa.

Types of Metamorphosis

Without metamorphosis (ametabolous): Insects increase in size throughout their life cycle but do not change basic body structure and arrangement. The adult is wingless and looks very similar to the immature form. This is considered the most evolutionarily 'primitive' form of metamorphosis. Silverfish are a good example of an insect with ametabolous metamorphosis. Example orders: Protura, Diplura, Thysanura, Collembola.

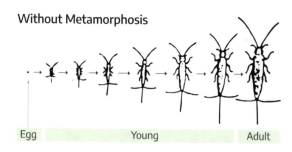

Figure 3-5: Without metamorphosis: The insect increases in size throughout its life cycle but does not change basic body structure.

Gradual metamorphosis: Insects increase in size while maintaining the same basic characteristics throughout the life of the insect. This is the most common type of metamorphosis seen in insects. There are three stages of development in hemimetabolous insects: egg, immature, and adult.

Hemimetabolous insects are usually terrestrial. The immatures, called nymphs, share similar food sources with the adult insects. Some hemimetabolous insects are aquatic, such as the dragonflies. Immature aquatic insects are called naiads and they have a different food source than the terrestrial adults. In both terrestrial and aquatic hemimetabolous insects, fully functioning wings are found only in the adult stage. These wings will appear as developing wing buds in the immature stage. Example orders that undergo gradual metamorphosis: Orthoptera, Hemiptera. Orders that undergo incomplete metamorphosis: Ephemeroptera, Odonata, Plecoptera.

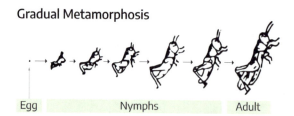

Figure 3-6: Gradual metamorphosis in terrestrial hemimetabolous insects: The insect increases in size but maintains the same basic characteristics.

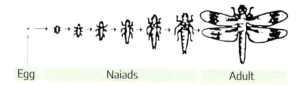

Figure 3-7: Incomplete metamorphosis in aquatic hemimetabolous insects: The insect increases in size but maintains the same basic characteristics.

Complete metamorphosis (holometabolous): Insects go through four distinct stages: egg, larva, pupa, and adult. The immature larvae differ greatly in appearance from their adult form. The profound change from larvae to adult takes place during the pupal stage. Many tissues and structures, such as the prolegs of caterpillars, are completely broken down, and true legs, antennae, wings, and other structures of the adult are formed. The larvae of holometabolous insects often use different food sources from the adults. These are considered to be the most evolutionarily advanced and biodiverse insect orders. Example orders: Coleoptera, Lepidoptera, Diptera.

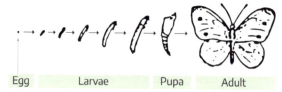

Figure 3-8: Complete metamorphosis: Insects undergo four distinct stages: egg, larva, pupa, and adult.

Regardless of the type of metamorphosis, the adult stage of an insect focuses on reproduction rather than feeding and growth. Some adults are very short-lived and they may not feed at all.

Identifying Insects

Some home gardeners recognize insects by the common name of their order, such as beetle, wasp, ant, or butterfly. Common names are sometimes regional and occasionally inaccurate. For example, a June bug in one area may be called a May beetle in another location. However, these common names can be helpful when conversing with clients who are not familiar with insects or their scientific names.

While there are many apps and online tools available to help ID insects, becoming familiar with insect orders and basic entomology can help gardeners assess the accuracy of ID recommendations from apps (which are not always correct) and provide a starting point for online searches.

The ability to classify an insect to its correct order gives a gardener access to valuable information about that insect. This information includes the type of mouthparts the insect has, which provides clues to the type of plant damage caused by members in that order and which methods may be effective in controlling those insects. Familiarity with the life cycle of an insect can help the planning for the proper use and timing of best management practices to avoid pest problems.

Because of the sheer number of insects, their overall diversity, and their relatively small size, identification can be difficult for the beginner. Outside of having a local expert identify them, the best way for gardeners to learn insect classification is to practice using a dichotomous key. Dichotomous keys are based on an organized series of choices between mutually exclusive characteristics, arranged hierarchically from the more general to the more specific. By working through the organized set of couplets and carefully selecting answers, you can arrive at the correct identification of an organism. These keys require knowledge of insect characteristics and time spent becoming familiar with how to use the keys, but this effort will allow the gardener to quickly classify insects to the order level or even higher levels. The goal of order level keys is to familiarize the user with the basic characteristics so that eventually the keys will become no longer necessary except as a reminder when memory fails.

While the identification of adult insects can be learned with some practice, immature insects often present a greater challenge. With the exception of colorful caterpillars and some odd-looking species, many immature insects are difficult to differentiate from each other and their adult counterparts. Sometimes the immature stages look nothing like the adult stage. There are some rules of thumb to describe immature insects in relation to their adult counterparts. The following table illustrates some of the main differences.

Table 3-1: Features of immature and mature insects

Immature Insects	Adult Insects
Sometimes worm-like or grubs	Three body regions
Number of legs can vary	Three pairs of legs
Body generally soft and/or fleshy	Usually with tough body wall
Lack wings	May have wings
Most move slowly	Most can move quickly

In some cases we are more dependent upon host and habitat information to help us identify insects in question. Knowing the host plant can go a long way to figuring out the insect (for example, tomato hornworms aren't usually found on oak trees). Some key questions can offer important clues to the identification of the immature insect. Where were the insects found? What are the insects eating? What kind of mouthparts do they have? Do they have legs? If so, how many legs? What color are the insects?

For your reference, the insect orders have been divided into three sections: those containing insects important to the gardener, those containing insects of lesser importance to the gardener, and common "noninsect" pests in Virginia. The orders containing insects of importance to home gardeners will be considered in detail.

Resources for Identifying Insects

There are many insect identification keys available in textbooks, field guides, scientific papers, and on the Internet. Start with keys that are simple, such as those for the order level, and do not rely on scientific terminology. A good key for beginners are the following books: *A Field Guide to Insects North of Mexico*, by Donald J. Borrer and Richard E. White; *Garden Insects of North America: The Ultimate Guide*, by Whitney Cranshaw; and *Bugs Rule!, An Introduction to the World of Insects* by Whitney Cranshaw. In addition the website bugguide.net is a fabulous resource for images of insects and other arthropods. Experts on this website may be able to assist with the identification of an arthropod if a high-quality image can be uploaded to the site. Most of the characteristics used to identify an insect to order can be seen with a 10X magnifier, although it is easier with a dissecting microscope and a good light source. Once an insect has been identified to order it can be more easily cross-referenced with other resources that narrow down possible suspects by habitat or food source.

Insect ID Lab

Insects can be submitted to Virginia Tech's Insect ID Lab for identification. Important information that must be included is: host plant or location found, date, description of damage, when it was first found, and if control information is required. Since an Extension office is an excellent resource on local pests, identifications can often be obtained at that office without sending a sample to state identifier.

Types of Insect Injury

Sometimes it is useful to classify insects in groups according to how they feed or damage plants. Members of these groups, also called guilds, all share a common manner of injuring plants even though they may belong to different insect orders.

Injury by Chewing Insects

Insects take their food in a variety of ways. Many insects feed by chewing off the external parts of a plant, so they are called "chewing insects." Examples of this type of plant injury are easy to find. Perhaps the best way to appreciate the prevalence of this type of damage is to look for leaves of plants in late summer that have no sign of leaf chewing. Cabbage worms, armyworms, grasshoppers, Colorado potato beetle, and fall webworm are common examples of chewing insects. Often chewing insects merely browse the leaves and do not cause a significant amount of plant damage beyond aesthetics. Significant plant damage occurs when large numbers of insects defoliate a significant portion of the leaf and impair its ability to make food for the plant. Plant species differ in their responses to insect damage, and this should be a consideration in pest management.

Chewing Damage

Cabbage white/imported cabbage worm

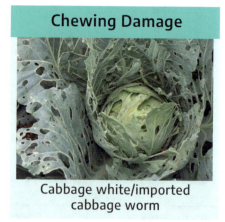

Figure 3-9: Chewing damage.

Injury by Piercing-Sucking Insects

Other insects feed by piercing plant tissue and sucking sap from the plant's cells. Only internal liquids from the plant are ingested, not portions of the tissue. Insects that feed this way have slender, sharp mouthparts that are inserted into the plant and used like a straw. The injury to the plant is physically small and very difficult to see with the naked eye, but the withdrawal of sap can result in: minute, spotty discolorations on leaves, fruit, and stems; curling or puckering of leaves; deformed fruit and seeds; **witch's broom** growths; or a general wilting and dying of the entire plant. Aphids, squash bugs, scale insects, leafhoppers, and other members of the order Hemiptera are all piercing-sucking insects. Many of these pests also carry plant diseases and transmit them when they feed.

Piercing-Sucking Damage

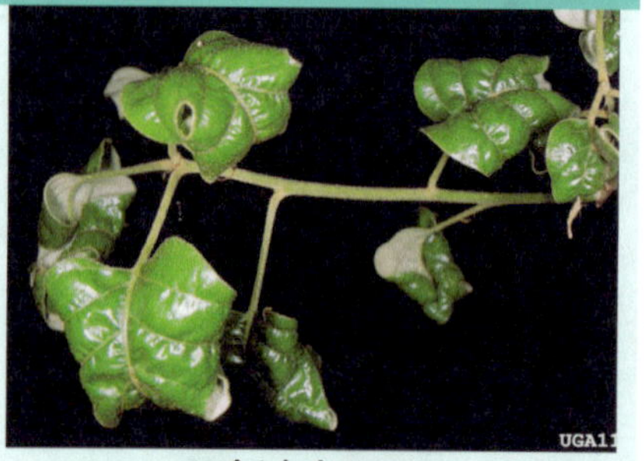

Aphid damage

Figure 3-10: Piercing-sucking damage.

Injury by Internal Feeders

Some insects feed within plant tissues for all or part of their development. They gain entrance to plants either when an adult female inserts her eggs into part of a plant, or by eating their way into the plant after hatching from eggs deposited on the plant. In either case, the entrance hole is small and hard to see. Large holes in fruit, seeds, stems, or trunks usually indicate where an insect has left the plant, not where it entered.

The chief guilds of internal plant feeders share a common name for their group. Borers feed in wood or pith; worms or weevils are found in fruits, nuts, or seeds; leaf miners live within the thin layers of leaf tissue; and gall insects form characteristic homes from leaves, stems, twigs, and roots. These guilds are some of the most important insect pests. Nearly all internal feeding insects live inside the plant only during part of their lives and usually emerge as adults. Control measures are most effective when aimed at emerging adults or the immature stages before they enter the plant, where they are hidden from sight and well protected.

Figure 3-11: Internal feeder damage.

Injury by Subterranean Insects

Insects that attack plants below the surface of the soil are also hidden from sight. These subterranean insects include chewing and sucking insects, root borers, and gall insects. Some subterranean insects spend their entire life cycle below ground. For example, the woolly apple aphid sucks sap from the roots of apple trees as both nymph and adult, causing the development of tumors and subsequent decay of the tree roots. Other subterranean insects have at least one life stage found above ground. Examples include wireworms, root maggots, strawberry root weevil, and corn rootworm. These larvae are root feeders while the adults live above ground.

Injury by Egg Laying

Probably 95% of the plant injury caused by insects is due to their feeding in the various ways just described. Some insects also cause damage by laying eggs in critical plant tissues. The periodical cicada deposits eggs in 1-year-old-growth of deciduous trees, splitting the wood so much that the twig may break and die. When they hatch, the nymphs drop to the ground and feed on roots in the soil but cause no further damage to the canopy.

Figure 3-12: Subterranean damage.

Female gall insects lay eggs in plant tissues. The plant responds by forming a gall where the female laid her eggs, which houses and feeds the developing immature insects. Galls are abnormal growths of deformed stem, leaf, root, or bud tissue. They can be distinctive enough that the attacking insect can be identified to species based solely on the size and shape of the gall. Gall formation is likely initiated by chemicals produced by the female laying her eggs, but continued development of the gall relies on the mechanical damage by larval feeding and secretions from the developing grubs.

Figure 3-13: Egg laying damage.

Use of Plants for Nest Materials

Insects sometimes remove parts of plants for the construction of nests or to provision nests. Leaf-cutter bees neatly cut circular pieces of foliage from roses and other plants to line the brood cells of their young.

Insects as Vectors for Plant Diseases

There are over 200 plant diseases spread by insects. Viruses produce the majority of plant diseases vectored by insects, followed by fungi, bacteria, and some protozoa. One example is fire blight of apples and related fruit trees, which is caused by bacteria and spread by honey bees and other pollinators.

Insects can spread plant disease in the following ways:

- By creating wounds when feeding, laying eggs, or boring into plants. These are entrance points for a disease that is not actually carried by the insect.
- By carrying and disseminating the causative agent of a disease in or on their bodies from one plant to the next. This is a passive transfer of pathogens.
- By carrying pathogens in or on their bodies and actively transferring the pathogen into the host as they feed.
- By serving as an essential host for some part of the pathogen's life cycle. The pathogen could not survive without the insect host.

Examples of diseases where the insect is the vector:

- The fungus responsible for Dutch elm disease and the elm bark beetle.
- The virus responsible for tomato curly top and the beet leafhopper.
- The virus responsible for tomato spotted wilt and thrips.
- The bacteria responsible for Stewart's disease in corn and corn rootworm and flea beetles.
- The virus responsible for rose rosette disease and eriophyid mites.

Insects of Importance to the Gardener

Orthoptera: Grasshoppers, Crickets, Katydids

- Adults can be moderate to large insects, often with hard bodies.
- Hind legs are modified for jumping. Antennae can be very long.
- They undergo gradual metamorphosis. Nymphs resemble adults but lack wings.
- Adults have two pairs of wings. The forewings are elongated, narrow, and hardened. Hindwings are membranous with extensive folded areas. Some species have reduced wings or may be wingless.
- Many orthopterans "sing" or chirp by rubbing one part of their body against another.

Figure 3-14: Orthoptera includes grasshoppers (pictured: differential grasshopper *Melanoplus differentialis*), crickets (pictured: field cricket *Gryllus pennsylvanicus*), and katydids (pictured: walkingstick *Diapheromera femorata*).

Blattodea: Cockroaches and Termites

- Both cockroaches and termites have chewing mouthparts.
- Both cockroaches and termites undergo gradual metamorphosis. Nymphs generally resemble the adults but without wings.
- Cockroaches have oval, flattened bodies and are usually dark brown to reddish in color. They can be small to large insects. Adults may have wings, or they may be reduced in size or absent. Cockroaches are known for being fast runners.
- Termites somewhat resemble ants in shape and size, but they lack the "waist" seen in ants. They are soft-bodied and live in colonies with a complex social system. Termites feed on cellulose and are very destructive to wood. Reproductive termites have two pairs of wings, but they may shed them quickly.

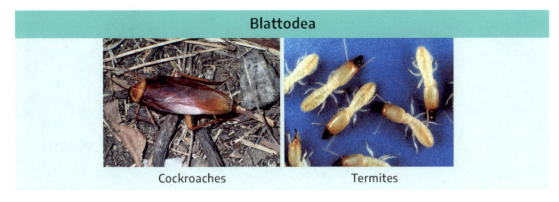

Figure 3-15: Blattodea includes cockroaches (pictured: American cockroach *Periplaneta americana*) and termites (pictured: eastern subterranean termite *Reticulitermes flavipes*).

Mantodea: Praying Mantises, Mantids

- Adults can be moderate to large insects.
- They have elongated bodies, large eyes, and front legs modified for catching their prey.
- Adults have two pairs of wings. The forewings are elongated, narrow, and hardened. Hindwings are membranous with extensive folded areas.
- They undergo gradual metamorphosis. Nymphs resemble adults but lack wings.
- Both nymphs and adults have chewing mouthparts and eat other arthropods.

Phasmida: Walkingsticks

- Largely resemble brown or green twigs with long legs and antennae.
- They undergo gradual metamorphosis. Nymphs resemble small adults.
- Both nymphs and adults have chewing mouthparts and feed on foliage of trees.
- Typically very slow moving and may hold themselves to look like twigs.

Figure 3-16: Mantodea includes mantids, pictured Chinese mantis *(Tenodera sinensis sinensis)*.

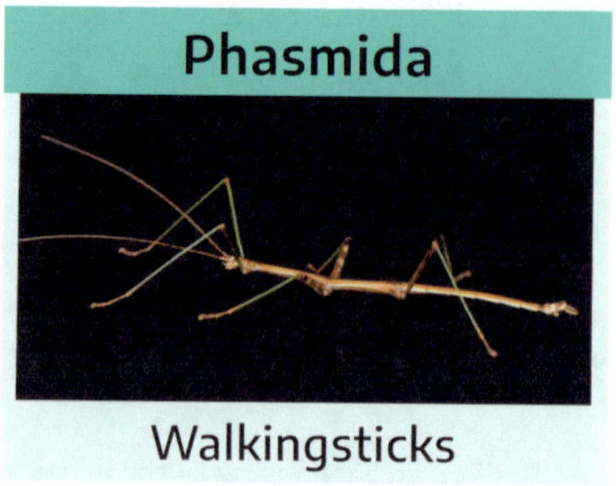

Figure 3-17: Phasmida includes walkingsticks, pictured walkingstick *(Diapheromera femorata)*.

Dermaptera: Earwigs

- Adults are moderate-sized insects.
- They undergo gradual metamorphosis with both the nymphs and adults being similar in appearance.
- They are elongated and flattened, with strong, moveable forceps at the tip of the abdomen. Some species can pinch with their forceps. The forceps in the immature are somewhat weaker.
- Adults have short, hardened outer wings that cover the folded, membranous inner wings. Some adults are wingless.
- Both adult and immature earwigs possess chewing mouthparts.

Figure 3-18: Dermaptera includes earwigs, pictured European earwig *(Forficula auricularia)*.

Hemiptera: True Bugs, Cicadas, Hoppers, Aphids, Scales, and Allies

- This is a very large and diverse group of insects with considerable differences in appearances and life histories.
- Range from being generally small, soft-bodied insects to the large, hard-bodied cicadas.
- They undergo gradual metamorphosis, but some (like the aphids) have complex life cycles involving alternate plant hosts.
- Nymphs of true bugs (such as squash bug and stink bugs) generally resemble the adults.
- Adult true bugs usually have two pairs of wings. The first pair are "half-wings" with a thickened part close to the body and a membranous bottom half. The second pair of wings is fully membranous.
- Other adult hemipteran species may have both winged and wingless forms.
- Nymphs of scales, mealy bugs, and whiteflies can look very different from the adults.
- All homopterans (suborder of Hemiptera) have piercing-sucking mouthparts. Most are plant feeders, but some feed on blood.
- Many plant feeders transmit plant pathogens; some blood feeders carry human and animal diseases.

Figure 3-19: Hemiptera includes aphids, cicada (*Tibicen davisi*), euonymus scale (*Unaspis euonymi*), wax scales (*Ceroplastes* sp.), mealybug (*Ferrisia dasylirii*) whitefly (*Bemisia afer*), brown marmorated stink bug (*Halyomorpha halys*), wheel bug (*Arilus cristatus*), and large milkweed bug (*Oncopeltus fasciatus*).

Thysanoptera: Thrips

- Called thrips whether there is one thrips or several.
- Small, soft-bodied insects.
- Metamorphosis includes a mix of gradual and complete stages.
- Mouthparts are rasping-sucking.
- Can be found on flowers or foliage of plants and may transmit plant diseases.
- Adults have two pairs of slender wings with a fringe of hairs resembling feathers.

Figure 3-20: Thysanoptera includes thrips, pictured tobacco thrips *(Frankliniella fusca)*.

Coleoptera: Beetles, Weevils, Borers, White Grubs

- Adults often have a hardened exoskeleton, but some species have soft bodies as adults.
- Adults usually have two pairs of wings; the outer pair (the elytra) is hard and protects the membranous inner pair. The elytra usually cover the abdomen but some species have very short elytra that do not completely cover the abdomen.
- Both adult and immature beetles possess chewing mouthparts.
- Adults usually have noticeable antennae, sometimes in very distinctive forms that can be useful in identifying them to the family level.
- Adult beetles range in size from the very tiny, approximately 1 mm long, to an inch or more in the larger species.
- They undergo complete metamorphosis. The larvae are often called grubs.
- Larvae have a head capsule, three pairs of legs on the thorax, and no legs on the abdomen. Weevil larvae, however, do not have any legs.

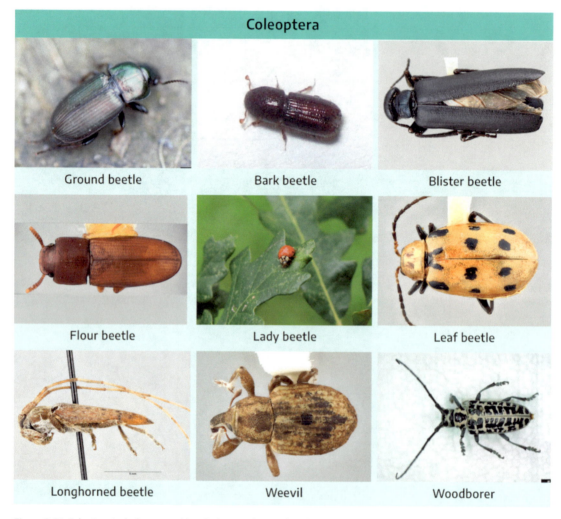

Figure 3-21: Coloptera includes ground beetle (pictured *Harpalus distinguendus*), bark beetles (pictured subfamily Scolytinae), blister beetle (pictured *Linsleya californica*), flour beetle (pictured small-eyed flour beetle *Palorus ratzeburgi*), leaf beetle (*Isotes mexicana*), longhorned beetles (pictured flat-faced longhorned beetle *Neohebestola humeralis*), weevils (pictured marsh weevil *Onychylis meridionalis*), and woodboring beetles (pictured cottonwood borer *Plectrodera scalator*).

Diptera: Flies, Mosquitoes, Gnats, Midges

- Adult flies have one pair of wings, are usually soft-bodied, and often covered with hairs or bristles.
- Flies undergo complete metamorphosis.
- Most larvae are legless with chewing mouthparts or mouth "hooks."
- Adults have sponging mouthparts, or in blood-feeders like mosquitoes, piercing mouthparts.
- Larvae of advanced flies (such as house flies) lack a head capsule, possess mouth hooks, and are called maggots.
- Larvae of lower forms (such as mosquitoes and fungus gnats) possess a head capsule.
- Blood-feeding flies (such as mosquitoes, horse flies, biting midges, and black flies) are a nuisance and can transmit diseases.

Figure 3-22: Diptera includes crane flies (pictured *Tipula* sp.), flower fly (pictured *Helophilus* sp.), midges (pictured aphid predatory midge *Aphidoletes aphidimyza*), syrphid flies (pictured *Syrphus* sp.), tachina flies (pictured spiny tachina fly *Paradejeania rutilioides*), and vinegar fly (pictured *Scaptomyza* sp.).

Hymenoptera: Bees, Ants, Wasps, Sawflies, Horntails

- Adults usually have two pairs of membranous wings. (Female velvet ants do not have wings.)
- Larvae have no legs except for the sawflies, with three pairs of legs on the thorax and at least six pairs of legs on the abdomen.
- Adults have chewing mouthparts and soft or slightly hard bodies.
- They undergo complete metamorphosis.

Figure 3-23: Hymenoptera includes bees (pictured honey bee *Apis mellifera*), Braconid wasp (*Wroughtonia occidentalis*), Chalcid wasp (*Torymus druparum*), Ichneumonid parasitoid wasps (*Enicospilus* sp.), horntail wasps (pictured blue horntail woodwasp *Sirex cyaneus*), sawflies (pictured redheaded pine sawfly *Neodiprion lecontei*), mud daubers (pictured black and yellow mud dauber *Sceliphron caementarium*), and ants (pictured *Formica* sp.).

Asian giant hornet look-alikes in Virginia

Vespa mandarinia, or the Asian giant hornet, has not been found in Virginia (in the U.S., it has only been confirmed in the Pacific Northwest). A few look-alike species are found in Virginia and these are often mistaken for the Asian giant hornet. For example, the European hornet, Asian hornet/yellow-legged hornet, and the cicada killer are large insects that can be mistaken for the Asian giant hornet. For more information, see Virginia Tech's Asian giant hornet fact sheet here.

Lepidoptera: Butterflies, Moths, Caterpillars, Cutworms

- Adults are soft-bodied with two pairs of well-developed wings covered with scales.
- They undergo complete metamorphosis.
- Larvae have chewing mouthparts while adults have a coiled, sucking tube adapted for feeding on nectar and other liquids.
- Larvae are called caterpillars; they are worm-like, voracious feeders on plants.
- Caterpillars have three pairs of legs on the thorax as well as multiple pairs of legs on the abdomen.

3-24: Lepidoptera adults includes: cabbage white or imported cabbage worm (*Pieris rapae*), Nickerl's fritillary (*Melitaea aurelia*), imperial moth (*Eacles imperialis*), luna moth (*Actias luna*), polyphemus moth (*Antheraea polyphemus*), and codling moth (*Cydia pomonella*).

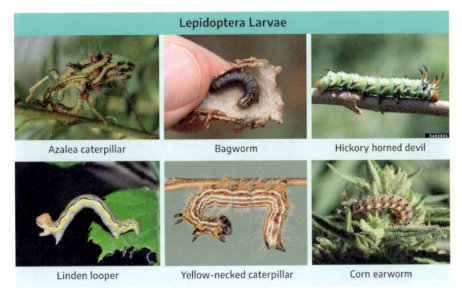

Figure 3-25: Lepidoptera larvae includes: azalea caterpillar (*Datana major*), evergreen bagworm (*Thyridopteryx ephemeraeformis*), hickory horned devil (*Citheronia regalis*), linden looper (*Erannis tiliaria*), yellownecked caterpillar (*Datana ministra*), and corn earworm or tomato fruitworm (*Helicoverpa zea*).

Neuroptera: Lacewings, Antlions, Snakeflies, Dobsonflies

- Many neuropterans are predators of other insects.
- Some are aquatic.
- Adults have two pairs of membranous wings held "roof-like" over the abdomen.
- Adults have chewing mouthparts and long antennae.
- They undergo complete metamorphosis.

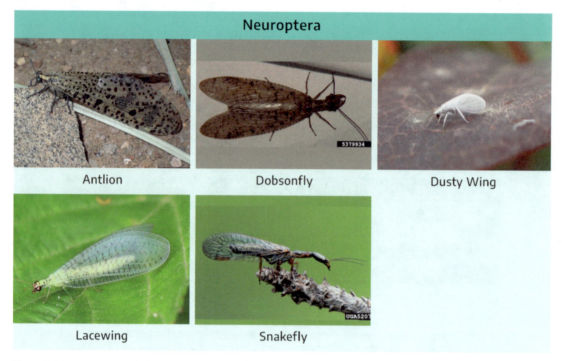

Figure 3-26: Neuroptera includes giant antlion (*Palpares* sp.), dobsonfly (*Corydalus cornutus*), dusty-wings, lacewings (family *Chrysopidae*), and snakeflies (order Raphidioptera).

Table 3-2: Insect orders of lesser importance

(Examples, not a comprehensive list)

Order	Example Insects
Ephemeroptera	Mayflies
Embiidina	Webspinners
Mecoptera	Scorpionflies
Odonata	Dragonflies, damselflies
Plecoptera	Stoneflies
Psocoptera	Booklice, barklice, parasitic lice
Siphonaptera	Fleas
Strepsiptera	Twisted-wing insects
Trichoptera	Caddisflies
Zoraptera	Angel insects
Zygentoma	Silverfish

Commonly Encountered Non-Insect Arthropods

There are a variety of other arthropods seen in the average backyard. The following are some of the more common ones found in Virginia.

Arachnida: Spiders, Mites, Ticks, Daddy-Longlegs

Spiders are soft-bodied arthropods with two distinct body regions. Spiders have four pairs of legs, although some of their specialized mouthparts may be mistaken for legs. Spiders are important predators of insects and other arthropods. Many spiders spin webs to catch their prey but others ambush or actively hunt for food. Only a few species of spiders in Virginia have venom considered potentially harmful to humans. For more information, see the VCE publication "Spiders of Medical Concern" ENTO-346NP.

Mites superficially resemble very tiny spiders. They have two body regions that appear undivided and lack antennae. Most adult mites have four pairs of legs while some of the immature stages have only three pairs of legs. Many mites are plant feeders, but some are predators of other mites while others feed on animals. Spider mites that attack plants often produce noticeable sheets of webbing when their populations are large.

Ticks look much like large mites. Adults have four pairs of legs while the youngest immature stage has only three pairs of legs. They are exclusively parasitic, feeding on the blood of animals. Some species are important vectors of diseases. For more information, see the VCE publication "Common Ticks of Virginia" ENTO-487NP.

Daddy-longlegs are also known as harvestmen. These familiar arachnids have small bodies and long legs that are often several times longer than the length of the body. They are harmless and do not possess venom.

Figure 3-27: Arachnida includes: black widow spider (*Latrodectus mactans*), wolf spiders (family *Lycosidae*), mites (pictured twospotted spider mite *Tetranychus urticae*), American dog tick (*Dermacentor variabilis*), lone star tick (*Amblyomma americanum*), and daddy longlegs or harvestmen (*Leiobunum* sp.).

Tick populations densest in suburban forests

By David Gaines, State Public Health Entomologist Virginia Dept. of Health, Office of Epidemiology

Suburban forests are the most important tick prone environments for people, and persons whose homes are adjacent to suburban forests are at higher risk of exposure to ticks and the diseases that they carry than people who do not live next to such forests.

Deer hunting is generally prohibited in suburban forests due to the dangers posed to people and homes by firearms and flying projectiles. Therefore, deer population densities often become much higher in suburban forests than in rural forests. Because populations of the two most important human-biting, disease-vector tick species in Virginia (blacklegged ticks and lone star ticks) mainly use deer as their mating ground and as a source of blood used by mated female ticks to nourish the thousands of eggs she will lay, tick population densities will generally be greatest where deer population density is highest.

Blacklegged tick adults mostly meet and mate on deer during the fall and early winter season, and lone star tick males and females mostly meet and mate on deer during the late winter and early spring season. The male ticks often encounter and mate with the female ticks on a deer as the females are engorging on deer blood, and each mated female tick that has filled up with deer blood can nourish up to 3000 to 4000 eggs to lay. The fully engorged female ticks often drop off the deer and lay their eggs in these same suburban forests.

Immature lone star ticks often pick up the *ehrlichia* disease agents that they transmit to people by feeding on an infected deer, and immature blacklegged tick larvae that have recently hatched out of eggs often become infected with Lyme disease, or other associated disease agents, by feeding on white-footed mice (which are primarily a rodent species associated with suburban forests or forest environments that have been altered or fragmented by human activity). Additionally, suburban forest environments often offer mouse nesting habitats such as firewood piles, scrap lumber piles, leaf piles, sheds, or junk piles for the mice to nest under.

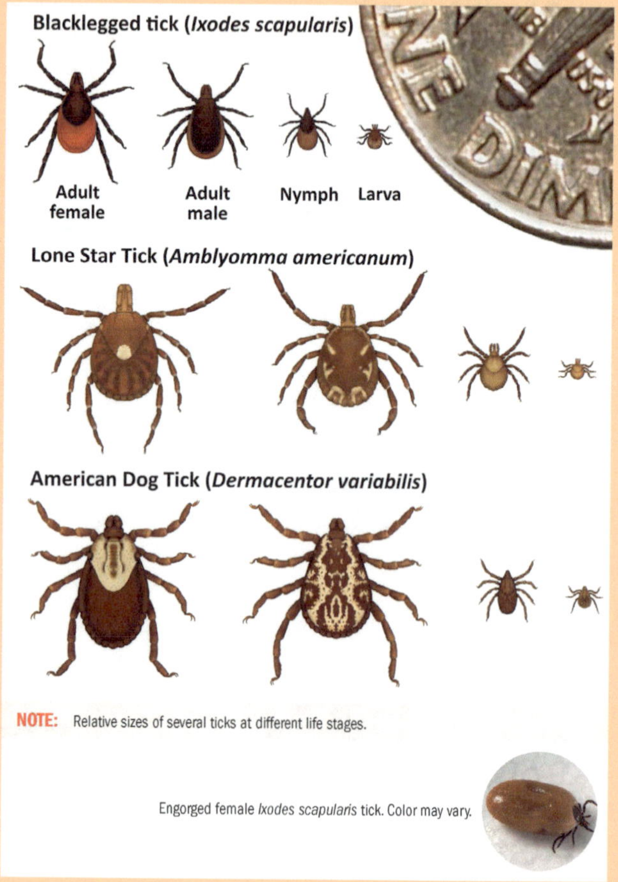

Reduce your risk:

Virginia has three tick species that can bite people and transmit diseases (lone star tick *Amblyomma americanum*, American dog tick *Dermacentor variabilis*, and blacklegged tick *Ixodes scapularis*), and at least 12 different disease agents and/or health conditions that can be caused by tick bites to people, including ehrlichiosis, Lyme disease, and alpha-gal syndrome (also called acquired red meat allergy).

Probably the best means of reducing the risk of blacklegged or lone star tick bites is to wear permethrin-treated shoes, socks and pants, and to always tuck the treated pants legs into the treated socks. That is because the ticks, which are

Figure 3-28: Ticks that commonly bite humans.

primarily found in shaded areas on the ground, on leaf litter, or on very low vegetation on the forest floor, generally climb onto a person's shoes first, and then crawl upwards until they can find some skin to attach to and feed from. Therefore, if one's shoes, socks, and pants are treated with permethrin, and are tucked, by the time a blacklegged nymph has been forced to crawl across the treated shoes and socks, it will also be forced to climb up the treated pants legs, and will become too intoxicated from the permethrin to go much further.

Lone star nymphs move much faster than blacklegged nymphs, so they may climb up a person's treated shoes, socks and pants, to reach the shirt level, and then may go between the buttons looking for skin to attach to. However, because that tick has crossed a large amount of permethrin-treated clothing, it typically dies inside one's shirt without ever biting. On the other hand, if one is wearing shorts or will have a lot of hand contact with the forest floor, it is best to wear treated shoes, socks, shorts and shirt, and apply a band of deet around the ankles and wrists to serve as a deterrent/barrier to the ticks climbing any higher. Clothing that has been treated with permethrin stays effective even after a few wash cycles, and may remain effective for a full season.

For more information about ticks, see the Virginia Department of Health website (https://www.vdh.virginia.gov/environmental-epidemiology/bugs-human-health/?tab=3) and their publication "Ticks and Tick-Borne Disease of Virginia." (https://www.vdh.virginia.gov/content/uploads/sites/12/2019/08/Tick-borne-Disease-in-Virginia-Flyer-8.5-x-11-format-for-website-.pdf)

Diplopoda: Millipedes

Millipedes are long arthropods whose bodies are rounded in cross section and made up of many segments. All but the first four or five body segments behind the head have two pairs of legs. Millipedes move slowly and are found in leaf litter or on the soil. They prefer humid habitats. Most are detritivores, feeding on decaying organic matter. Sometimes they can be pests to tender young plants or in greenhouses.

Chilopoda: Centipedes

Centipedes are also long arthropods made up of many segments. They tend to be flatter than millipedes, with longer antennae and only one pair of legs per body segment. The last pair of legs is held extended behind the body. Centipedes are fast-moving predators of other arthropods, with a pair of legs modified into "poison claws" that they use to inject venom into their prey. Despite their fearsome appearance, most centipedes are too small to be of medical concern to humans.

Isopoda: Sowbugs, Roly Poly, Pill Bugs, Woodlice

These are small, oval arthropods with highly segmented, hard bodies and seven pairs of legs. They require high humidity for survival. Only some isopods can roll themselves into a ball. Isopods feed on decaying plant matter and are generally harmless, but sometimes they attack young, tender plants.

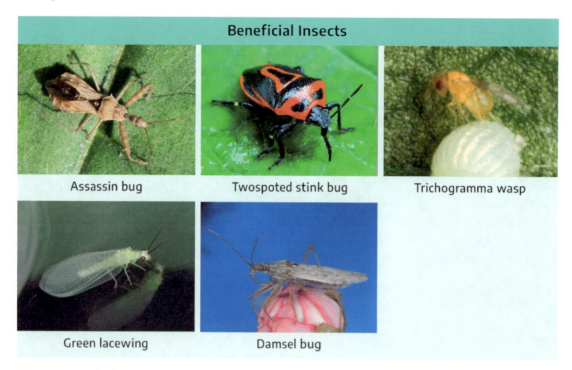

Figure 3-29: Beneficial insects: Assassin bug (pictured spined assassin bug *Sinea diadema*), Predaceous stink bugs (pictured twospotted stink bug, *Perillus bioculatus* (F.), Trichogramma wasps (pictured *Trichogramma ostriniae*), Green lacewing (pictured *Chrysoperla rufilabris*), and Damsel bug (pictured common damsel bug *Nabis americoferus*).

Table 3-3: Commonly seen classes of phylum arthropoda

Class	Examples	Body Regions	Pairs of Legs	Importance
Arachnida	Spiders, mites, ticks, harvestmen, scorpions, chiggers, etc.	1-2	4 (immature ticks have 3 pairs)	Spiders prey on insects; some mites are major plant pests while others are beneficial predators; ticks, some mites and spiders, and scorpions are of medical importance
Chilopoda	Centipedes	15+	15+, 1 pair per segment	Predators of insects, spiders, and other small animals; some are household pests
Collembola	Springtails	3	3	Feed on decaying organic matter can be pests of houseplants
Diplopoda	Millipedes	2 (body can have many segments)	Generally 2 pairs per segment	Feed on decaying organic matter
Diplura	Two-pronged bristletails	3		Feed on decaying organic matter
Insecta	Beetles, true bugs, flies, butterflies, wasps, fleas, etc.	3	3	Mostly beneficial with some pest species
Malacostraca	Crabs, lobsters, shrimp, sowbugs	2	5	Many aquatic orders; some considered delicacies; predators and scavengers
Protura	Coneheads	3	3	Feed on decaying organic matter
Symphyla	Symphylans, garden centipedes	2 (body can have many segments)	10-12	Feed on decaying organic matter; can be pests in agriculture

Taxonomy

Taxonomy is the science of classifying life into a hierarchical scheme with categories of varying ranks. Identification of the hundreds of thousands of species of insects would be impossible if they were not organized around a standard classification system that groups organisms according to their shared characteristics. All life on Earth is divided into six kingdoms, the highest level of the classification system: Eubacteria, Archaeabacteria, Protista, Fungi, Animalia, and Plantae. Each kingdom is further divided into smaller phyla. For example, several of the phyla that contain agricultural and horticultural pests in the animal kingdom are:

- Arthropoda (insects, spiders, mites, crayfish, millipedes)
- Nematoda (roundworms, trichina)
- Platyhelminthes (flatworms, flukes, tapeworms)
- Mollusca (snails, slugs, clams)

Classification Mnemonic:

Kingdom = Keep

Phylum = Putting

Class = Coffee

Order = On

Family = For

Genus = Good

Species = Students

Phyla are subdivided into classes, which are composed of orders. Orders are composed of families, which contain genera, in which the species are ultimately placed. High school biology students may remember the phrase "Keep Putting Coffee On For Good Students," or a similar mnemonic device to help remember the whole classification arrangement of kingdom through species.

Phylum Arthropoda and its Classes

Insects belong to the phylum Arthropoda. Arthropods are a very important group of animals, representing more than 80% of all described living animal species. Familiar arthropods include spiders, ticks, crabs, scorpions, shrimp, barnacles, and insects. All arthropods share some common characteristics, such as segmented bodies, paired segmented appendages, bilateral symmetry, and an exoskeleton (an outer "skin" or "shell" that serves as an external skeleton) that is periodically shed as the arthropod grows. Insects belong to the class Insecta.

Orders of the class Insecta

Classes are further divided into orders. Orders in the class Insecta are based on the type of metamorphosis, mouthparts, and wings an insect may have. Insect orders are further broken down into smaller groupings called the family. Each family is a more select group of very closely related insects. Family names end with "-idae." Aphidae (aphids), Muscidae (house flies), and Acrididae (grasshoppers) are examples of families of insects.

Families are divided into genera, which are finally divided into species. These are the most finite levels of our classification system. The house fly, *Musca domestica*, serves here as an example of specific classification:

- Phylum: Arthropoda
- Class: Insecta
- Order: Diptera
- Family: Muscidae
- Genus: Musca
- Species: domestica
- Common name: house fly

Musca domestica is the scientific name for the house fly. The scientific name of an organism includes both its genus and species names. The scientific name is always italicized and only the genus name is capitalized. Many insects, but not all, have common names; sometimes a single species will have several common names. For example, *Heliothis zea* is called the corn earworm when found on corn, but it is a tomato fruitworm when found on tomatoes. Using scientific names eliminates the confusion that can occur when an insect has several common names, or if one common name is used for more than one species. Common names can also refer to large groups of insects, such as families or orders. The entire order Coleoptera is known as the beetles. The term moth refers to thousands of species in the order Lepidoptera.

Note: Invertebrate taxonomy often changes to reflect ongoing research into the relationships among organisms. Species are moved from genus to genus, whole families can be combined with another family, and changes sometimes occur even at the level of orders. One resource that stays up-to-date on the current state of insect taxonomy is the website bugguide.net. This website has a wealth of material on insects, spiders, and related arthropods, including a fantastic gallery of photos.

Table 3-4: Commonly seen orders of the class Insecta

Order	Common Name	Habitat	Metamorphosis	Mouthparts	Wings
Zygentoma	Silverfish	Leaf litter and soil; indoors	Gradual	Chewing	None
Ephemeroptera	Mayflies	Aquatic or near water	Gradual	Vestigial	2 pairs
Odonata	Dragonflies, damselflies	Aquatic or near water	Gradual	Chewing	2 pairs
Dermaptera	Earwigs	On vegetation; leaf litter	Gradual	Chewing	2 pairs, sometimes reduced in size or absent
Plecoptera	Stoneflies	Aquatic or near water	Gradual	Chewing	2 pairs, sometimes reduced in size or absent
Orthoptera	Grasshoppers, crickets, katydids	On vegetation; leaf litter	Gradual	Chewing	2 pairs, sometimes reduced in size or absent
Phasmida	Walkingsticks	On vegetation	Gradual	Chewing	In the U.S., none or 2 pairs very reduced in size

Table 3-4: Commonly seen orders of the class Insecta (continued)

Order	Common Name	Habitat	Metamorphosis	Mouthparts	Wings
Mantodea	Mantids	On vegetation	Gradual	Chewing	2 pairs
Blattodea	Cockroaches, termites	Leaf litter and woody plant debris; in buildings; subterranean	Gradual	Chewing	2 pairs on reproductive termites; 2 pairs, sometimes reduced in size, on cockroaches
Thysanoptera	Thrips	On vegetation	Intermediate between simple and complex	Rasping-sucking	2 pairs
Hemiptera	True bugs, cicadas, aphids, leafhoppers, scales, and allies	On vegetation; aquatic; in leaf litter	Gradual	Piercing-sucking	2 pairs, sometimes reduced or absent
Psocodea	Booklice, barklice, and parasitic lice	Booklice are found in buildings; barklice on trees; parasitic lice on birds and mammals	Gradual	Chewing; piercing-sucking	2 pairs, sometimes reduced or absent in booklice and barklice; none in parasitic lice
Neuroptera	Dobsonflies, antlions, lacewings, and allies	Aquatic or near water; on vegetation; in soil and leaf litter	Complete	Chewing	2 pairs
Coleoptera	Beetles	Everywhere	Complete	Chewing	2 pairs, sometimes reduced in size or absent
Hymenoptera	Ants, bees, wasps, sawflies	Everywhere	Complete	Chewing-lapping	2 pairs, sometimes reduced in size or absent
Lepidoptera	Butterflies, moths	On vegetation or plant materials	Complete	Chewing siphoning	2 pairs, sometimes absent
Siphonaptera	Fleas	In association with birds and mammal hosts	Complete	Piercing-sucking	None
Diptera	Flies	Everywhere	Complete	Piercing-sucking, sponging	1 pair

Summary

The class Insecta is larger than all of the other classes in the Animal kingdom combined. Insect species vary greatly in size, color, shape, life history, and favored habitat. Most insects are harmless or even beneficial, but the few that cause damage have tremendous impact on the world. Insects can usually be recognized with practice and some knowledge of their host, habitat, and life cycle. Feeding damage by pest insects varies according to the type of mouthparts possessed by the insect.

Additional Resources

- Resources for Entomology section on the VCE publications website (https://www.pubs.ext.vt.edu/tags.resource.html/pubs_ext_vt_edu:department/entomology)
- *A Field Guide to Insects North of Mexico*, by Donald J. Borrer and Richard E. White
- *Garden insects of North America: The Ultimate Guide*, by Whitney Cranshaw
- *Bugs Rule!, An Introduction to the World of Insects* by Whitney Cranshaw
- Bugguide.net

Attributions

- Elizabeth Brown, Bedford Extension Master Gardener (2021 reviser)
- Jim Revell, Bedford Extension Master Gardener (2021 reviser)
- Theresa Dellinger, Collections Manager, Virginia Tech Insect Collection, Department of Entomology (2021 image advice and revisions)
- Theresa Dellinger, Collections Manager, Virginia Tech Insect Collection, Department of Entomology (2015 reviser)
- Eric Day, Manager, Insect Identification Lab, Department of Entomology (2015 reviser)
- Additional Contributions by Dan Nortman, Extension Agent, Agriculture and Natural Resources (2015), Peter Warren, Extension Agent, Agriculture and Natural Resources (2009)

Image Attributions

- Figure 3-1: Insect body parts. Johnson, Devon. 2022. CC BY-NC-SA 4.0. Adapted from *Master Gardener Training Handbook*, Virginia Cooperative Extension, 2018.
- Figure 3-2: Mouthparts. Johnson, Devon. 2022. CC BY-NC-SA 4.0. Adapted from *Master Gardener Training Handbook*, Virginia Cooperative Extension, 2018.
- Figure 3-3: Leg adaptations. Johnson, Devon. 2022. CC BY-NC-SA 4.0. Includes image "Male front leg from underside" by Siga from Wikipedia, public domain, image 5190034 by Natasha Wright, Braman Termite & Pest Elimination, Bugwood.org (CC BY-NC 3.0 US), image 5524210 by Keren Levy, Bugwood.org (CC BY-NC 3.0 US), image 5552100 by Seastone, L. and B. Parks, Museum Collections: Orthoptera, USDA APHIS PPQ, Bugwood.org (CC BY-NC 3.0 US), and image 5465396 by Pest and Diseases Image Library, Bugwood.org (CC BY-NC 3.0 US).
- Figure 3-4: Types of wings. Johnson, Devon. 2022. CC BY-NC-SA 4.0. Includes image 5296002 by Forest and Kim Starr, Starr Environmental, Bugwood.org (CC BY-NC 3.0 US), image 5582501 by Steven Katovich, Bugwood.org (CC BY-NC 3.0 US), image 5376044 by David Cappaert, Bugwood.org (CC BY-NC 3.0 US), image 1236053 by Clemson University – USDA Cooperative Extension Slide Series , Bugwood.org (CC BY-NC 3.0 US), and image 5530014 by David Stephens, Bugwood.org (CC BY-NC 3.0 US).
- Figure 3-5: Without metamorphosis. Johnson, Devon. 2022. CC BY-NC-SA 4.0. Adapted from *Master Gardener Training Handbook*, Virginia Cooperative Extension, 2018.
- Figure 3-6: Gradual metamorphosis. Johnson, Devon. 2022. CC BY-NC-SA 4.0. Adapted from *Master Gardener Training Handbook*, Virginia Cooperative Extension, 2018.
- Figure 3-7: Incomplete metamorphosis. Johnson, Devon. 2022. CC BY-NC-SA 4.0. Adapted from *Master Gardener Training Handbook*, Virginia Cooperative Extension, 2018.
- Figure 3-8: Complete metamorphosis. Johnson, Devon. 2022. CC BY-NC-SA 4.0. Adapted from *Master Gardener Training Handbook*, Virginia Cooperative Extension, 2018.
- Figure 3-9: Chewing damage. Johnson, Devon. 2022. CC BY-NC-SA 4.0. Includes image 5443232 by Whitney

Cranshaw from Bugwood.org (CC BY 3.0 US).
- Figure 3-10: Piercing-sucking damage. Johnson, Devon. 2022. CC BY-NC-SA 4.0. Includes image 1150004 by Andrew J. Boone from Bugwood.org (CC BY-NC 3.0 US).
- Figure 3-11: Internal feeder damage. Johnson, Devon. 2022. CC BY-NC-SA 4.0. Includes image 5378685 by Milan Zubrik from Bugwood.org (CC BY-NC 3.0 US), image 1263040 by National Plant Protection Organization, the Netherlands from Bugwood.org (CC BY-NC 3.0 US), and image 5443216 by Whitney Cranshaw from Bugwood.org (CC BY 3.0 US).
- Figure 3-12: Subterranean damage. Johnson, Devon. 2022. CC BY-NC-SA 4.0. Includes image 0284074 by James Solomon from Bugwood.org (CC BY 3.0 US).
- Figure 3-13: Egg laying damage. Johnson, Devon. 2022. CC BY-NC-SA 4.0. Includes image 1669003 by Bruce W. Kauffman from Bugwood.org (CC BY-NC 3.0 US) and image 1398081 by Steven Katovich from Bugwood.orgCC BY 3.0 US).
- Figure 3-14: Orthoptera includes grasshoppers, crickets, and katydids. Johnson, Devon. 2022. CC BY-NC-SA 4.0. Includes image 5602869 by Gerald Holmes from Bugwood.org (CC BY-NC 3.0 US), image 5573940 by Joseph Berger from Bugwood.org (CC BY 3.0 US), and image 2158015 by David Cappaert from Bugwood.org (CC BY-NC 3.0 US).
- Figure 3-15: Blattodea includes cockroaches and termites. Johnson, Devon. 2022. CC BY-NC-SA 4.0. Includes image 5581708 by Whitney Cranshaw from Bugwood.org (CC BY 3.0 US) and image 1324033 by USDA ARS Photo Unit from Bugwood.org (CC BY 3.0 US).
- Figure 3-16: Mantodea includes mantids, pictured Chinese mantis *(Tenodera sinensis sinensis)*. Johnson, Devon. 2022. CC BY-NC-SA 4.0. Includes image 5604040 by Gerald Holmes from Bugwood.org (CC BY-NC 3.0 US).
- Figure 3-17: Phasmida includes walkingsticks, pictured walkingstick *(Diapheromera femorata)*. Johnson, Devon. 2022. CC BY-NC-SA 4.0. Includes image 5490116 by David Cappaert from Bugwood.org (CC BY-NC 3.0 US).
- Figure 3-18: Dermaptera includes earwigs, pictured European earwig *(Forficula auricularia)*. Johnson, Devon. 2022. CC BY-NC-SA 4.0. Includes image 5443277 by Whitney Cranshaw from Bugwood.org (CC BY 3.0 US).
- Figure 3-19: Hemiptera includes aphids, cicada, euonymus scale, wax scale, mealybug, whitefly, stink bug, wheel bug, milkweed bug. Johnson, Devon. 2022. CC BY-NC-SA 4.0. Includes image 5445767 by Dani Barchana from Bugwood.org (CC BY-NC 3.0 US), image 5565787 by Paul Langlois from Bugwood.org (CC BY-NC 3.0 US), image 5560871 by Chris Evans from Bugwood.org (CC BY-NC 3.0 US), image 1626029 by John A. Weidhass from Bugwood.org (CC BY 3.0 US), image 5599978 by Matthew Borden from Bugwood.org (CC BY 3.0 US), image 5581522 by Henry Juarez from Bugwood.org (CC BY-NC 3.0 US), image 5612242 by Rebekah D. Wallace from Bugwood.org (CC BY-NC 3.0 US), image 9009079 by Herbert A. 'Joe' Pase III from Bugwood.org (CC BY-NC 3.0 US), and image 5347031 by William M. Ciesla from Bugwood.org (CC BY-NC 3.0 US).
- Figure 3-20: Thysanoptera includes thrips, pictured tobacco thrips *(Frankliniella fusca)*. Johnson, Devon. 2022. CC BY-NC-SA 4.0. Includes image 1389005 by David Jones from Bugwood.org (CC BY 3.0 US).
- Figure 3-21: Coloptera includes ground beetle (pictured *Harpalus distinguendus*), bark beetles (pictured subfamily Scolytinae), blister beetle (pictured *Linsleya californica*), flour beetle (pictured small-eyed flour beetle *Palorus ratzeburgi*), leaf beetle (*Isotes mexicana*), longhorned beetles (pictured flat-faced longhorned beetle *Neohebestola humeralis*), weevils (pictured marsh weevil *Onychylis meridionalis*), and woodboring beetles (pictured cottonwood borer *Plectrodera scalator*). Johnson, Devon. 2022. CC BY-NC-SA 4.0. Includes image 5581934 by Mary C Legg from Bugwood.org (CC BY-NC 3.0 US), image 5598826 by Mohammed El Damir from Bugwood.org (CC BY 3.0 US), image 5594932 by Hanna Royals from Bugwood.org (CC BY-NC 3.0 US), image 5550056 by Hanna Royals from Bugwood.org (CC BY-NC 3.0 US), image 5598022 by Ryan Armbrust from Bugwood.org (CC BY-NC 3.0 US), image 5607975 by Paul Langlois from Bugwood.org (CC BY-NC 3.0 US), image 5599996 by Paul Langlois from Bugwood.org (CC BY-NC 3.0 US), image 5607890 by Paul Langlois from Bugwood.org (CC BY-NC 3.0 US), and image 5511473 by Robert J. Bauernfeind from Bugwood.org (CC BY-NC 3.0 US).
- Figure 3-22: Diptera includes crane flies (pictured *Tipula* sp.), flower fly (pictured *Helophilus* sp.), midges (pictured aphid predatory midge *Aphidoletes aphidimyza*), syrphid flies (pictured *Syrphus* sp.), tachina flies (pictured spiny tachina fly *Paradejeania rutilioides*), vinegar fly (pictured *Scaptomyza* sp.). Johnson, Devon. 2022. CC BY-NC-SA 4.0. Includes image 5424150 by David Cappaert from Bugwood.org (CC BY-NC 3.0 US), image 5443509 by Jon Yuschock from Bugwood.org (CC BY-NC 3.0 US), image 5598726 by Ward Strong from Bugwood.org (CC BY-NC 3.0 US), image 5595559 by Ansel Oommen from Bugwood.org (CC BY-NC 3.0 US), image 5382157 by Whitney Cranshaw from Bugwood.org (CC BY 3.0 US), and image 5402545 by Joseph Berger from Bugwood.org (CC BY 3.0 US).
- Figure 3-23: Hymenoptera includes bees (pictured honey bee *Apis mellifera*), Braconid wasp

94 | CHAPTER 3: ENTOMOLOGY

(*Wroughtonia occidentalis*), Chalcid wasp (*Torymus druparum*), Ichneumonid parasitoid wasps (*Enicospilus* sp.), horntail wasps (pictured blue horntail woodwasp *Sirex cyaneus*), sawflies (pictured redheaded pine sawfly *Neodiprion lecontei*) , mud daubers (pictured black and yellow mud dauber *Sceliphron caementarium*), and ants (pictured *Formica* sp.). Johnson, Devon. 2022. CC BY-NC-SA 4.0. Includes image 5598195 by Hanna Royals from Bugwood.org (CC BY-NC 3.0 US), image 5583935 by Paul Langlois from Bugwood.org (CC BY-NC 3.0 US), image 5583921 by Paul Langlois from Bugwood.org (CC BY-NC 3.0 US), image 5611811 by Rebekah D. Wallace from Bugwood.org (CC BY-NC 3.0 US), image 5458756 by Pest and Diseases Image Library from Bugwood.org (CC BY-NC 3.0 US), image 9009072 by Herbert A. 'Joe' Pase III from Bugwood.org (CC BY-NC 3.0 US), image 5482934 by USDA Forest Service – Southern Research Station from Bugwood.org (CC BY-NC 3.0 US), and image 5598442 by Ward Strong from Bugwood.org (CC BY-NC 3.0 US).

- Figure 3-24: Lepidoptera adults includes: cabbage white or imported cabbage worm (*Pieris rapae*), Nickerl's fritillary (*Melitaea aurelia*), imperial moth (*Eacles imperialis*), luna moth (*Actias luna*), polyphemus moth (*Antheraea polyphemus*), and codling moth (*Cydia pomonella*). Johnson, Devon. 2022. CC BY-NC-SA 4.0. Includes image 5559869 by Hanna Royals from Bugwood.org (CC BY-NC 3.0 US), image 5582245 by Mary C Legg from Bugwood.org (CC BY-NC 3.0 US), image 2089014 by Lacy L. Hyche from Bugwood.org (CC BY 3.0 US), image 5424219 by David Cappaert from Bugwood.org (CC BY-NC 3.0 US), image 5585710 by Sturgis McKeever from Bugwood.org (CC BY 3.0 US), and image 5578713 by Mourad Louadfel from Bugwood.org (CC BY-NC 3.0 US).
- Figure 3-25: Lepidoptera larvae includes: azalea caterpillar (*Datana major*), evergreen bagworm (*Thyridopteryx ephemeraeformis*), hickory horned devil (*Citheronia regalis*), linden looper (*Erannis tiliaria*), yellownecked caterpillar (*Datana ministra*), and corn earworm or tomato fruitworm (*Helicoverpa zea*). Johnson, Devon. 2022. CC BY-NC-SA 4.0. Includes image 2118035 by Chris Evans from Bugwood.org (CC BY-NC 3.0 US), image 5603961 by Gerald Holmes from Bugwood.org (CC BY-NC 3.0 US), image 5482801 by Johnny N. Dell from Bugwood.org (CC BY-NC 3.0 US), image 5493120 by William M. Ciesla from Bugwood.org (CC BY-NC 3.0 US), image 0014042 by Gerald J. Lenhard from Bugwood.org (CC BY 3.0 US), and image 5596837 by Whitney Cranshaw from Bugwood.org (CC BY 3.0 US).
- Figure 3-26: Neuroptera includes giant antlion (*Palpares* sp.), dobsonfly (*Corydalus cornutus*), dusty-wings, lacewings (family *Chrysopidae*), and snakeflies. Johnson, Devon. 2022. CC BY-NC-SA 4.0. Includes image 5577750 by Whitney Cranshaw from Bugwood.org (CC BY 3.0 US), image 5379934 by Jessica Louque from Bugwood.org (CC BY 3.0 US), image 5596739 by Whitney Cranshaw from Bugwood.org (CC BY 3.0 US), image 5564611 by Johnny N. Dell from Bugwood.org (CC BY-NC 3.0 US), and image 5207007 by David Leatherman from Bugwood.org (CC BY-NC 3.0 US).
- Figure 3-27: Arachnida includes: black widow spider (*Latrodectus mactans*), wolf spiders (family *Lycosidae*), mites (pictured twospotted spider mite *Tetranychus urticae*), American dog tick (*Dermacentor variabilis*), lone star tick (*Amblyomma americanum*) and daddy longlegs or harvestmen (*Leiobunum* sp.). Johnson, Devon. 2022. CC BY-NC-SA 4.0. Includes image 5361242 by Frank Peairs from Bugwood.org (CC BY 3.0 US), image 1528004 by Sturgis McKeever from Bugwood.org (CC BY-NC 3.0 US), image 5387671 by Joseph Berger from Bugwood.org (CC BY 3.0 US), image 5532835 by Mohammed El Damir from Bugwood.org (CC BY 3.0 US), image 0001049 by Centers for Disease Control and Prevention from Bugwood.org (CC BY 3.0 US), and image 1225122 by Edward L. Manigault from Bugwood.org (CC BY 3.0 US).
- Figure 3-28: Ticks that commonly bite humans. Centers for Disease Control and Prevention. (retrieved 2022). Public Domain.
- Figure 3-29: Beneficial insects: Assassin bug (pictured spined assassin bug *Sinea diadema*), Predaceous stink bugs (pictured twospotted stink bug, *Perillus bioculatus* (F.), Trichogramma wasps (pictured *Trichogramma ostriniae*); Green lacewing (pictured *Chrysoperla rufilabris*), Damsel bug (pictured common damsel bug *Nabis americoferus*). Johnson, Devon. 2022. CC BY-NC-SA 4.0. Includes image 5367980 by Russ Ottens from Bugwood.org (CC BY 3.0 US), image 5175038 by Kevin D. Arvin from Bugwood.org (CC BY 3.0 US), image 5526014 by Peggy Greb from Bugwood.org (CC BY-NC 3.0 US), image 1386016 by Joseph Berger from Bugwood.org (CC BY 3.0 US), and image 5435576 by Joseph Berger from Bugwood.org (CC BY 3.0 US).

CHAPTER 4: PLANT PATHOLOGY

Chapter Contents

- Plant Diseases in History
- Diseases Defined: Cause of Disease
- Steps to Disease Diagnosis
- Symptoms (change in plant appearance) of plant disease
- Signs (visible structures produced by pathogens) of plant disease
- Disease Development
- Methods & Tools to Control Diseases
- Summary
- Additional Resources

Organisms that cause plant disease can damage plants from the time the seed is put into the ground until the time the crop is harvested and in storage. Some diseases are capable of totally destroying a crop, while others may cause only cosmetic damage. However, cosmetic damage may be equivalent to total destruction in the case of ornamental plants. While many biological entities can cause plant diseases, the vast majority of plant pathogens are fungi.

Plant Diseases in History

Certain diseases have had tremendous impacts on our society. Perhaps one of the most widely known among these is *Phytophthora* late blight, which caused the potato famine in Ireland (1845). As a result of this epidemic, approximately two million people either starved to death or emigrated, many to the United States.

Grape downy mildew ruined the French wine industry until Bordeaux mixture (a combination of copper sulfate, lime, and water) was accidentally found to control the fungus.

Two forest tree diseases that caused great economic and aesthetic losses in the U.S. are Dutch elm disease and chestnut blight. Both were introduced accidentally to the U.S. Chestnut blight destroyed the most valuable trees in the Appalachians, while Dutch elm disease continues its destruction today. More recently, dogwood anthracnose (which appeared in the 1980s in our area) has caused the long-term prospects of natural dogwood populations in cool, moist locations to become questionable.

These examples are prominent because they caused extensive damage. However, plant diseases cause variable amounts of damage from year to year, depending weather patterns.

Table 4-1: Infectious agents

Disease Cause	Description	Common Symptoms
Fungi	Usually filamentous (threadlike) organisms without chlorophyll. They are the most common causes of plant disease. The fungal filaments usually grow and ramify inside the plant tissue, but may also develop on the surface. Fungi typically reproduce, spread, and persist by minuscule spores. Fungus structures may be visible with the unaided eye (for example, mold, mildew, mushrooms, and conks), or may be microscopically small (for example, many fungi that cause leaf spots). There are thousands of different fungal plant pathogens.	Leaf spots and blights Fruit, stem, root, wood, and seedling rots Cankers Vascular wilts Galls Mildew Rust
Bacteria	Minute, one-celled organisms, much smaller and simpler than fungi. Sometimes, large masses of bacterial cells can be visible as bacterial slime or ooze, but more commonly nothing is visible without a microscope. There are several hundred different bacterial plant pathogens. Mycoplasmas or phytoplasmas are specialized bacteria that look like bacteria in the lab, but "behave" more like viruses in the field (for example, they are usually spread by insects and cause symptoms more similar to viruses).	Leaf spots and blights Stem and fruit rot Cankers Galls Vascular wilts
Viruses	Infectious molecules (or "clumps" of molecules) that take over plant metabolism and use the plant cell to produce more virus. Several hundred different viruses attack plants. Viroids are similar but even smaller.	Poor growth Mottling and mosaic Ring spots and wavy line patterns Leaf crinkling Distortion
Nematodes	A group of nonsegmented roundworms. The fact that these animals are usually covered in plant pathology texts or chapters, while insects and mites are treated separately, is purely an accident of history. Plant-parasitic nematodes are always small (less than 2 millimeters long, usually very thin and thus not easily visible without magnification), and many live in the soil, feeding on roots. A few kinds may live inside leaves or shoots.	Poor root development (and thus poor plant growth and wilt or yellowing) Root galls Swollen root tips Abnormal root branching

Diseases Defined: Cause of Disease

A plant disease may be defined as any disturbance that prevents the normal development of a plant and reduces its economic or aesthetic value. Plant disease is the rule rather than the exception. Every plant has disease problems of one sort or another. Fortunately, plants either tolerate these maladies, or the maladies are not very serious in most years. According to this broad definition, plant disease is caused by a large array of **biotic** (living) agents such as fungi, nematodes, bacteria, and viruses; by a large array of **abiotic** (nonliving) factors such as nutrient deficiencies and water or temperature stress; or sometimes by a combination or complex of these factors (Figure 4-1). Terms such as "disorder" and "damage" are often used to refer to abiotic problems, whereas the term "disease" is used to refer to biotic problems, but the boundaries are indistinct.

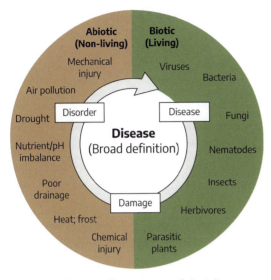

Figure 4-1: Abiotic and biotic causes of plant diseases.

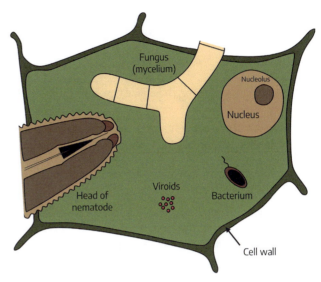

Figure 4-2: Schematic diagram of the shapes and sizes of certain plant pathogens in relation to a plant cell. Viruses are the smallest, while bacteria are larger, but not as large as funguses or nematodes.

Steps to Disease Diagnosis

See Chapter 6 "Diagnosing Plant Damage" for more details.

- Study the symptoms and signs; together, they form the disease syndrome. **Symptoms** are physical expressions of disease in the host tissue, e.g., changes in color, appearance, integrity, etc. Primary symptoms are symptoms at the point where the pathogen is active. Secondary symptoms are the result of pathogen activity somewhere else in the plant. For example, if a fungus invaded the roots of a plant, the resulting root rot is the primary symptom; the above-ground symptoms of poor growth, leaf yellowing, wilting, etc., are secondary symptoms. For correct diagnosis it is very important to find the primary symptoms, because it's only there that the pathogen can be found. A **lesion** is a well-defined area of diseased or injured tissue, often dead spots or areas. Lesions are often a primary symptom. **Signs** are structures or products of the pathogen itself on a host plant. Examples of signs are mold, fungal fruiting bodies, and bacterial slime/ooze. Examination with a hand lens may sometimes reveal structures that can aid in diagnosis. Placing the plant sample in a moist chamber (closed container or plastic bag) for a day or two may stimulate production of such structures. The presence of tiny, pimple-like, dark fruiting bodies in the spot indicate the presence of a fungus and may provide sufficient information for diagnosing the disease.
- Collect background information on the history of and patterns in the problem's development. For instance, the cause of sudden death of shoot tips is more easily diagnosed once one realizes that a night frost has occurred a few days earlier. If identical symptoms develop on several different species of plants, it is highly likely that the cause is abiotic (for instance, herbicide damage). The diagnostic form used by Virginia Cooperative Extension requires much information that may be helpful in diagnosis, but one should always be on the lookout for additional clues.
- Consult reference books and the internet to compare syndromes with descriptions and pictures. Keep in mind that not all possible problems may be described or pictured in books, especially non plant-specific abiotic problems, which may be omitted. Be aware that not all web sites have been carefully reviewed by professional plant pathologists.
- Narrow down the possibilities by searching online for research-based information. Try adding "site:edu" to the end of your search query to see results from universities, or go to the Extension search page (https://extension.org/search/). Refer to a lab for further testing if the diagnosis in unclear.

The Plant Disease Clinic (https://spes.vt.edu/affiliated/plant-disease-clinic.html) at Virginia Tech is a wonderful resource for assistance with diagnostic problems and staying informed about diseases in Virginia.

Symptoms (Change in Plant Appearance) of Plant Disease

Chlorosis

Chlorosis is the yellowing of normally green tissue. Pattern of the discoloration may be helpful in diagnosis

- **General Chlorosis:** Yellowing of entire leaf or plant. Causes: Nutrient deficiencies, root problems, nematodes
- **Interveinal Chlorosis**: Yelllowing of the leaf tissue between veins while the veins themselves remain green. Causes: Poor root functioning, root rot, nematodes, nutrient deficiencies, improper pH, chemical injury
- **Chlorosis along the Veins:** Chlorotic areas along the veins. Causes: Viruses, some herbicides
- **Marginal Chlorosis**: Yellowing of leaf edges. Causes: Chemical injury, nutrient toxicity
- **Mosaic, mottle:** Irregular light and dark green areas on the leaves, with distinct (mosaic) or less distinct (mottle) margins. Chlorotic areas may be on or between veins, pattern is more random on or between veins, pattern is more random than for interveinal chlorosis. Causes: Commonly virus, sometimes genetic abnormality, some nutrient deficiencies (esp. mottle)
- **Ringspot:** A circular area of chlorosis or necrosis with a green center. Causes: Viruses, cold weather (African violet)
- **Line Patterns:** Irregular patterns or wavy lines; on some plants lines may form a more regular pattern in the outline of an oak leaf. Causes: Viruses, chemical injury

Other Color Changes

- **Color Breaking**: Abnormal streaks of different color in colored plant organs (usually flowers). Causes: Virus, genetic (streaks usually more regular if genetic than with virus)
- **Purpling, Reddening:** Development of abnormal purple or red colors in normally green tissue. Causes: Phosphorus or boron deficiency, some herbicides, cold temperatures
- **Bronzing:** Foliage takes on gold or copper metallic appearance. Causes: Insects, mites, cold injury
- **Browning:** Plant tissue turns brown and may also become dry and brittle. Usually associated with tissue death. Browning is sometimes diagnostic, as with vascular browning in vascular plants. Causes: Many
- **Russeting:** Superficial roughening of plant epidermis (surface tissue) (e.g., apple) due to cork formation. Causes: Some fungal diseases (e.g., powdery mildew), frost injury, some chemicals, nematodes (e.g., root knot on potato tubers)

Figure 4-3: Marginal necrosis and chlorosis on cantaloupe; Sweet Potato Feathery Mottle Virus (*Potyvirus SPFMV*) on sweet potato; and Ringspot caused by *Mycosphaerella brassicicola*.

Necrosis (Tissue Death)

- **Spot:** Distinct necrotic areas on leaves and superficial lesions on fruits and herbaceous stems. May be round, angular, or irregular; they may have concentric rings or be surrounded by purple rims or chlorotic haloes. Commonly caused by fungi, but can also be caused by bacteria and abiotic factors (e.g., paraquat drift), uncommonly caused by viruses or nematodes.
- **Blight:** A general killing of plant parts (twigs, limbs, leaves, flowers, or shoots). Sometimes called Blast. May be primary or secondary symptom, for example, due to root disease or a canker girdling a stem or trunk. Causes: Many
- **Blotch:** Large, superficially discolored areas of irregular shape on leaves, shoots, fruits, and stems. Causes: Fungi, bacteria, chemical injury, sun scald
- **Scorch, Marginal Necrosis:** "Burning" of leaf margins. Causes: Drought, excess salt or fertilizer, root problems, cankers, vascular fungi, bacteria
- **Rot:** Affected tissues discolored, disintegrated (decayed), and often softened. Examples: wood rot (fungal), root rot (usually fungal), and soft rot (bacterial). Causes: Fungi, bacteria
- **Canker:** Necrotic areas in the bark of woody or herbaceous stems or twigs. Surfaces may be smooth or rough, sunken with raised margins, or swollen and cracked. Raised margins may sometimes have concentric rings = target shape. Causes: Usually fungi, bacteria
- **Damping-Off:** Seed, seedling rot, or canker-like lesions girdling seedlings and young herbaceous plants at the ground-line that cause the seedling to fall over and rot. Seedling death before emerging above ground is pre-emergence damping off. Seedling death after emergence is called post-emergence damping off. Causes: Usually fungi, sometimes insects, or soil conditions
- **Shot-Hole:** Dead areas of leaf spots fall away leaving holes in the leaves. Leaves may have tattered appearance if holes are numerous. Holes may be irregular in shape. Causes: Fungi, bacteria, insect-feeding
- **Dieback:** Twigs, limbs, or shoots die from the tip back. Similar to, if not the same as, blight. Causes: See blight
- **Anthracnose:** Disease caused by a certain group of fungi that produce acervuli (a type of fruiting body — a small blister on the lesion surface which in moist area may become pink from spore masses). Symptoms may vary from leaf spots to fruit or twig lesions. Causes: Fungi (per definition)
- **Water-Soaked Appearance:** Translucent appearance of tissue due to the intercellular spaces being filled with water. Often the first visible symptom of cell death. Causes: Bacteria, fungi, frost injury

Figure 4-4: Impatiens necrotic spot virus (INSV) (Tospovirus *INSV*) on touch-me-not (*Impatiens* spp. L.); Diplodia tip blights (*Diplodia* spp. Fr.); early blight (*Alternaria solani*) on potato; Seiridium cankers (*Seiridium* sp.); damping off (general) on cotton; and anthracnose (*Colletotrichum orbiculare*) on pumpkin surface.

Miscellaneous Symptoms

- **Dwarfing, Stunting:** Failure of a plant part or whole plant to attain normal size. Causes: Many
- **Gall, Tumor, Knot:** Localized enlargement of plant parts. Examples: root gall, crown gall, leaf gall. Causes: Some fungi, some bacteria, some viruses, some nematodes (roots), MANY insects and mites
- **Witches' Broom:** A dense, broom-like clustering of branches resulting from development of numerous adventitious buds at one region. Causes: Fungi, phytoplasmas, some mites
- **Leaf Curl:** Leaf curl is due to irregular growth; parts grow excessively or growth of parts is retarded compared to the rest of the leaf blade. Causes: Viruses, some fungi, herbicides, ethylene, aphids
- **Wilt:** Plant parts limp from lack of water. Causes: Drought, root rot, root damage from nematodes, other root problems, vascular pathogens (fungi, bacteria), walnut toxicity
- **Leaf drop, Abscission:** Falling off of leaves, flowers, fruit, or other tissues. Causes: Leaf spot pathogens, root pathogens, growth regulators, various abiotic conditions
- **Epinasty:** Downward curvature of leaves due to abnormal growth in part of the petiole. Causes: Vascular wilt pathogens, ethylene injury, some herbicides
- **Gummosis:** Production and exudation of a thick gummy liquid in response to injury or disease. Causes: Insects, fungal or bacterial infection, normal plant response to injury (e.g., in *Prunus* species)

Figure 4-5: Dwarfing caused by potato yellow dwarf virus on potato; oak leaf gall (*Polystepha pilulae*); witches' brooming caused by rose rosette disease (RRD) (*Emaravirus* RRD) on rose; leaf curl caused by tomato yellow leaf curl virus (TYLCV) (Begomovirus TYLCV) on tomato; aphid induced leaf curl on southern red oak (*Quercus falcata* Michx.); and melon plants showing Fusarium wilt infection caused by *Fusarium oxysporum*.

Signs (Visible Structures Produced by Pathogens) of Plant Disease

- **Mildew:** Grayish or whitish growth of fungus, of two groups: downy mildew, (grayish, often on lower leaf surface) and powdery mildew (whitish, on both upper and lower leaf surfaces – the most common). The names reflect the appearance; the two groups are quite different in their biology.
- **Mold:** Fungus mycelium and/or fruiting structures, similar to mildew but of different groups of fungi. Molds may be many colors, commonly gray, white, black, blue, or green.
- **Sooty Mold:** Black fungal growth on plant surface which can be scraped off. Caused by dark-colored fungi that grow on sticky secretions of sucking insects, such as aphids, whiteflies, and scale insects. Sooty mold fungi do not infect the plant itself.
- **Rust:** Spore pustules of a certain group of fungi called the rust fungi (sometimes also orange leaf spots and galls or cankers). Color of pustules may be yellow, orange, red, brown, or black.
- **Smut:** Spore masses of a certain group of fungi called the smut fungi, usually brown or black and powdery. May occur in inflorescences (for example wheat loose smut, corn smut), leaves (stripe smut of grasses), sometimes on stems (corn smut galls).
- **Mushroom:** Large fruiting body of certain fungi, few are plant pathogens, most are secondary decay organisms.
- **Conk:** Large, woody, shelf-like fruiting body of many of the wood decay fungi
- **Bacterial Slime:** Drops of sap containing bacteria. Found on the surface of plants infected by bacteria, or Slime especially under humid conditions.

Figure 4-6: Cucumber foliage showing symptoms of cucurbit downy mildew (*Pseudoperonospora cubensis*); pumpkin foliage showing symptoms of cucurbit downy mildew (*Pseudoperonospora cubensis*); basil downy mildew (*Peronospora belbahrii*) on underside of basil leaf; powdery mildew (*Podosphaera fuliginea*) on watermelon leaf; powdery mildew (*Erysiphe polygoni*) infection of bean plants; sooty mold on California laurel; cedar apple rust disease (*Gymnosporangium juniperi-virginianae*) on apple tree; corn smut (*Mycosarcoma maydis*) on corn cob; and young birch conk (*Piptoporus betulinus*).

Disease Development

Development and severity of disease is determined by three conditions. First, it is necessary to have a susceptible **host** plant. Each species of plant is capable of being infected by only certain pathogens. The plant must be in a stage of development susceptible to infection by the disease agent. The second requirement is the presence of an active pathogen in a stage of development conducive to infecting the host plant. If there is no or little inoculum of the pathogen present, there can be no or only a little disease. The third condition is an environment suitable for the pathogen to infect the plant. Temperature and moisture are important factors.

Disease Cycle

The chain of events involved in disease development is the disease cycle, which summarizes answers to questions such as:

- *What are sources and forms of inoculum?* (**Inoculum** is part of a pathogen that can cause infection). Possibilities include: other infected plants, plant materials (for example, seed, tubers, cuttings, and transplants), plant debris (dead leaves, stems, and roots) from infected plants, or infested soil.
- *When or under what conditions does the pathogen infect?* (**Infection** means to become established on/in the plant and initiate disease development). For example, most fungi and bacteria that cause leaf spots and blights can infect only when leaves are wet. Some of these pathogens may infect only young, developing leaves, while others infect only old, senescent leaves.
- *How long does it take for the pathogen to colonize the plant and for symptoms to develop?* This may range from a few days to a few weeks or sometimes months. During this stage, although symptoms do not yet show, it is often already too late to prevent a problem.
- *After how long and under what conditions does the pathogen reproduce?* Fungi and bacteria often need high humidity to produce more inoculum.
- *How and under what conditions does the pathogen spread?* Means of dispersal include: wind, water drip and splash, soil, anything that moves soil (e.g. shoes), running water (run-off, irrigation water), vectors (for example, aphids for many virus diseases, beetles for Dutch elm disease), equipment, tools, and moving plants from one location to another.
- *How and where does the pathogen survive adverse conditions (for example, winter, dry spell, period of absence of host)?* See above under sources of inoculum. Some pathogens produce specialized structures that are highly resistant to extremes in temperature or moisture (e.g. sclerotia of the fungus that causes southern blight).

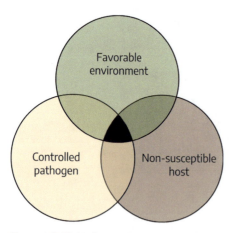

Figure 4-7: Slight disease: A non-susceptible plant in a favorable environment with a controlled pathogen will only experience slight disease.

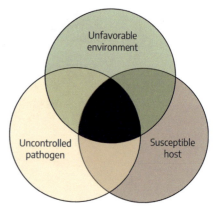

Figure 4-8: Severe disease: A susceptible plant in an unfavorable environment with an uncontrolled pathogen will experience severe disease.

Methods and Tools to Control Diseases

Cultural Practices to Control Diseases

Plant only certified-as-disease-free seed or planting stock

- Certified seed is only free of those diseases for which it has been tested ! Quality depends on the program.
- General nursery inspection program — tries to make sure that only materials free of (important) diseases and pests are sold.

Sanitation

- Removal of diseased plants or plant parts (pruning, roguing).
- Removal and/or destruction of plant debris and leaf litter that may contain inoculum.
- Removal of other hosts (including weeds) of the pathogen.
- Prevention of introduction and spread of pathogens: clean tools, equipment, clothes, etc.

Importance of disinfecting tools to prevent spread of plant disease

By Mary Ann Hansen, Extension Plant Pathologist, Virginia Tech

One way to help prevent the spread of some plant diseases is to sanitize garden tools before using them on healthy plants. This is especially important for preventing diseases that can be transmitted from diseased plant tissue to healthy plant tissue.

A good example of a disease for which sanitizing tools is especially important is boxwood blight. If infested plant debris remains on pruning shears after being used on a diseased plant, the disease could be transmitted to the next stem that is pruned with the shears. To sanitize tools effectively, it is important first to wash any visible plant debris from the surface of the tool before treating it with the sanitizer.

Figure 4-9: Pruning tools soaking in a 1:14 household bleach solution.

The tool should either be sprayed with the sanitizer and allowed to air dry or dipped in the sanitizer for the recommended length of time. Wiping tools with sanitizing wipes is NOT an effective way to sanitize a tool! Some readily available sanitizers include ethanol (70% or greater), sodium hypochlorite (a 1:14 solution of 8.25% household bleach), and Lysol Brand Concentrate Disinfectant. (Bleach can be corrosive to tools, so remember to rinse tools well after sanitizing them with bleach.)

There are also commercial sanitizer products labeled for use by professional applicators. Since sanitizing tools can be time-consuming in the home garden, try, at a minimum, to sanitize tools before moving to a new plant and/or location. More detail on appropriate use of sanitizers for preventing spread of boxwood blight can be found on the Virginia Boxwood Blight Task Force website (https://ext.vt.edu/agriculture/commercial-horticulture/boxwood-blight.html).

Tillage and cultivation

- Buries plant debris with inoculum, leads to faster degradation.
- May also bring inoculum to the surface where it is exposed to sun and drying cycles.

Crop rotation

- Rotation with a species of plant that is not a host for a particular pathogen prevents buildup of that pathogen over the years, and allows inoculum to decline due to natural causes.

Temperature management (make it optimum for crop, but unfavorable for pathogen)

- Direct: greenhouse, storage facilities.
- Indirect: shading, mulching to affect soil temperature, timing of planting (planting warm-season crops into cold soils may predispose them to damping-off diseases), solarization.

Moisture management (make conditions less favorable for pathogen)

- **Irrigation**: Furrow and flood irrigation may spread pathogens and may saturate soil, which promotes some root diseases. Sprinkler irrigation may lead to splash dispersal of pathogens, and makes the leaves wet, creating conditions favorable for infection by many leaf pathogens. Timing may be important (late afternoon may be bad – leads to long periods of leaf wetness). To prevent pathogen dispersal and leaf wetness, it is usually best to water at the base of the plant, if possible. Drip irrigation reduces chances of spreading pathogens and creating conditions favorable for disease.
- **Drainage**: Avoid planting in poorly drained areas or choose plants that are adapted to wet sites. Install drainage tile before planting in poorly drained soil. Plant on raised beds to allow water to drain away from the roots.
- **Relative humidity**: Direct management: greenhouse, storage facilities. Indirect management: pruning and thinning for better canopy ventilation; foliar diseases tend to be more severe in shaded areas because the leaves stay wet longer.
- **Management of fertilization and soil pH**: Some diseases are worse when fertilization is excessive; others are worse when fertility is poor. Some diseases are favored by acid soil, others by alkaline soil.
- **Soil amendments and mulches:** Organic matter may stimulate soil microbial activity that may inhibit growth of pathogens. Adding organic matter can also help to improve drainage.
- **Repel or control vectors:** For example, by insecticides or by placing reflective aluminum foil around young plants to repel aphids.
- **Plant at proper planting depth:** Roots may not get enough oxygen or the crown may rot when plants are too deep.
- **Avoid injury, which can invite decay organisms.**

A program approach to control diseases

Plant disease control has never placed sole reliance on **chemicals**. Other major pillars are **cultural practices** and **resistant cultivars**. The use of several simultaneous control practices is usually required for effective disease management. A combination of methods is always required to manage the numerous diseases (Integrated Disease Management) and other pests (Integrated Pest Management) that threaten a specific garden or landscape.

A complete program for an annual plant might include the following steps (with modifications for establishment of perennial plants):

- Assess inoculum based on experience from past years. Identify possible sources.
- Use cultural practices or treatments that reduce inoculum. For example:

    - Rotate out of susceptible crop
    - Eradicate reservoir hosts (weeds, etc.)
    - Remove or bury infested or diseased plant debris
    - Steam or bleach (e.g., pots, flats, soil, tools)

- Select top-quality seed or planting stock that is:

    - Adapted to the area and site
    - Disease-free (from a reputable source)
    - Disease-resistant (Note that few plants are resistant to all diseases; choose plants that are resistant to the diseases that have been previously diagnosed in that plant)

- Purchase treated seed (fungicide/insecticide) if experience shows it is needed.
  Plant at optimum time, row spacing, and seeding rate; apply fertilizer and pesticide treatments as needed.
- Monitor plants for early detection of disease problems:

    - Get an accurate diagnosis of the problem. County Extension personnel can provide advice or forward sample to a lab for diagnosis.
    - Apply chemicals as needed. Most sprays are PREVENTATIVE.
    - Cultural practices — e.g., canopy management

- Harvest at proper time; handle and store produce properly.
- Remove and destroy plant debris to reduce survival of pathogens. Do not compost weeds or diseased plant material – place in trash.
- Plan for next year. Take steps to prevent future problems (rotations, etc.). Keep accurate records and maps that show pest and disease problems.

Plant Resistance to Control Diseases

- Genetically resistant cultivars may be partially resistant (some disease develops; nevertheless, these plants can be very useful) or completely resistant to a particular disease (but not necessarily to other diseases).
- Genetic resistance may be defeated when a pathogen develops new strains that can attack the resistant cultivars. Resistance may also sometimes "break down" when plant is under excessive stress, or when several pathogens attack at the same time.
- "Physiological" resistance refers to reducing the susceptibility of the plant by management of water, nutrients, light, and other cultural practices.

Chemical Controls

Both organic and synthetic chemicals are available for controlling plant diseases. **Organic** methods involve growing and maintaining healthy plants without using synthetic (man-made) fertilizers, pesticides, hormones, and other materials (as defined in the National List of Allowed and Prohibited Substances (https://www.ams.usda.gov/rules-regulations/organic/national-list)). In organic disease control, natural materials (things found in nature or that exist in the environment) can be used to inhibit or prevent the activity of plant pathogens. The most common organic controls used against diseases are mineral fungicides, such as copper and sulfur. A few biological fungicides, such as *Bacillus subtilis* (bacterium), have also been developed in recent years. Sprays of copper and sulfur are effective in preventing disease, but they are not effective in clearing up a disease once it becomes established. Note that just because a product is organic, it does not mean you should not take precautions. Read the pesticide label, which gives you information about the product and its toxicity. Some organic products do have their consequences too; you must weigh the options in every control method. For example, copper materials sprayed on an area year after year can accumulate in the soil and cause harm to beneficial microbial populations. Planting disease-resistant varieties, practicing crop rotation, maintaining balanced soil fertility, and using a trickle irrigation system rather than overhead irrigation should allow one to avoid disease while minimizing the use of chemical sprays.

Regulatory Practices to Control Diseases

- Quarantine laws and inspections at the borders to keep foreign pathogens out.
- Certification of seed and planting stock to minimize initial inoculum.

Control of Diseases: Avoiding Attack

Keep host and pathogen out of striking distance from each other by:

- Exclusion – keep pathogen away from the crop.

    - Keep pathogen out of the country, state. Quarantine regulations ban importation of certain types of plant material; other kinds of plant material must be inspected before being admitted.
    - Keep pathogen out of the garden. Avoid spread of contaminated soil, equipment, boots, irrigation water, etc. Use pathogen-free planting material.

- Avoidance or evasion – keep plants away from the pathogen.

    - Do not plant in already infested sites or in areas where the pathogen is a major problem.
    - Grow plants in areas, during times, and under conditions that are not favorable for pathogen development. Reduce or eradicate inoculum. Complete eradication of a pathogen from an area or a country is rare.

- Reduction of inoculum by sanitation, deep plowing, crop rotation, etc., is common and often effective.
- Protect plants by reducing or eliminating chances for infection (using both cultural and chemical protection).
- Plant resistant plants (another way to protect the plant).

Physical Methods to Control Diseases

- Soil treatment with steam to eliminate pathogens, weed seeds, and insects. This is done mostly in greenhouses and seedbeds; it is not very practical for homeowners.
- Soil "solarization" in warm climates during the hot season by covering soil for several weeks with clear plastic. High temperatures eliminate many pathogens and weeds. This is most effective in tropical or subtropical areas where there is a long period of continuous sunlight and high temperatures.
- Hot-water treatment of seed and planting stock (not very practical for homeowners).

Biological Control

- Apply organisms that inhibit, eat, or parasitize plant pathogens. Currently, there are *only a few* commercially available examples of this available for home use.
- Stimulate naturally occurring beneficial organisms by organic soil amendments, water management, etc.

Summary

Plant diseases are to be expected. Fortunately, in most years there are few truly devastating diseases.

For disease to occur, there must be a susceptible host, a suitable environment, and a living pathogen. When all three conditions are met, disease occurs. Severity of the disease depends on the degree to which the conditions are met.

Diagnosis depends on a careful evaluation of symptoms, but also on evaluation of the history and patterns of disease development.

Disease control involves more than the use of chemicals. Planting resistant cultivars, destruction of inoculum sources, and a variety of cultural practices should be considered first. A combination of control methods, based on understanding of the biology of the pathogen, will give best results.

Additional Resources

- Virginia Tech Plant Disease Clinic (https://spes.vt.edu/affiliated/plant-disease-clinic.html)
- VCE Master Gardener Common Plant Diseases video playlist (https://www.youtube.com/playlist?list=PLnWrSBjZVh9ftUgg09O2jq17VaVAIGQBr)

Attributions

- Sherry Kern, Virginia Beach Extension Master Gardener (2021 reviser)
- Adria C. Bordas, Extension Agent, Agriculture and Natural Resources (2015 reviser)
- Mary Ann Hansen, Department of Plant Pathology, Physiology, and Weed Science (2015 reviewer)
- Anton Baudoin, Department of Plant Pathology, Physiology, and Weed Science (2009 reviser)
- Mary Ann Hansen, Department of Plant Pathology, Physiology, and Weed Science (2009 reviser)

Image Attributions

- Figure 4-1: Abiotic and biotic causes of plant diseases. Grey, Kindred. 2022. CC BY-NC-SA 4.0.
- Figure 4-2: Schematic diagram of the shapes and sizes of certain plant pathogens in relation to a plant cell. Grey, Kindred. 2022. CC BY-NC-SA 4.0.
- Figure 4-3: Marginal necrosis and chlorosis on cantaloupe, Sweet Potato Feathery Mottle Virus (*Potyvirus SPFMV*) on sweet potato, Ringspot caused by *Mycosphaerella brassicicola*. Johnson, Devon. 2022. CC BY-NC-SA 4.0. Includes image 5605913 by Gerald Holmes from Bugwood.org (CC BY-NC 3.0 US), image 1576917 by Gerald Holmes from Bugwood.org (CC BY-NC 3.0 US), and image 5549138 by Penn State Department of Plant Pathology & Environmental Microbiology Archives from Bugwood.org (CC BY-NC 3.0 US).
- Figure 4-4: Impatiens necrotic spot virus (INSV) (*Tospovirus INSV*) on touch-me-not (*Impatiens spp.* L.), Diplodia tip blights (*Diplodia spp.* Fr.), early blight (*Alternaria solani*) on potato, Seiridium cankers (*Seiridium sp.*), damping off (general) on cotton, anthracnose (*Colletotrichum orbiculare*) on pumpkin surface. Johnson, Devon. 2022. CC BY-NC-SA 4.0. Includes image 5549122 by Penn State Department of Plant Pathology & Environmental Microbiology Archives from Bugwood.org (CC BY-NC 3.0 US), image 0590020 by Robert L. Anderson from Bugwood.org CC BY 3.0 US), image 5606707 by Gerald Holmes from Bugwood.org (CC BY-NC 3.0 US), image 5435276 by Jennifer Olson from Bugwood.org (CC BY-NC 3.0 US), image 1572331 by Gerald Holmes from Bugwood.org (CC BY-NC 3.0 US), and image 1576761 by Gerald Holmes from Bugwood.org (CC BY-NC 3.0 US).
- Figure 4-5: Dwarfing caused by potato yellow dwarf virus on potato, oak leaf gall (*Polystepha pilulae*), witches' brooming caused by rose rosette disease (RRD) (*Emaravirus RRD*) on rose, leaf curl caused by tomato yellow leaf curl virus (TYLCV) (*Begomovirus TYLCV*) on tomato, aphid induced leaf curl on southern red oak (*Quercus falcata* Michx.), melon plants showing Fusarium wilt infection caused by *Fusarium oxysporum*. Johnson, Devon. 2022. CC BY-NC-SA 4.0. Includes image 0162085 by American Phytopathological Society from Bugwood.org (CC BY-NC 3.0 US), image 5507614 by Bruce Watt from Bugwood.org (CC BY-NC 3.0 US), image 5485808 by Mary Ann Hansen from Bugwood.org (CC BY 3.0 US), image 5411469 by Don Ferrin from Bugwood.org (CC BY 3.0 US), image 1150004 by Andrew J. Boone from Bugwood.org (CC BY-NC 3.0 US), and image 5365875 by Howard F. Schwartz from Bugwood.org (CC BY 3.0 US).
- Figure 4-6: Cucumber foliage showing symptoms of cucurbit downy mildew (*Pseudoperonospora cubensis*), pumpkin foliage showing symptoms of cucurbit downy mildew (*Pseudoperonospora cubensis*), basil downy mildew (*Peronospora belbahrii*) on underside of basil leaf, powdery mildew (*Podosphaera fuliginea*) on watermelon leaf, powdery mildew (*Erysiphe polygoni*) infection of bean plants, sooty mold on California laurel, cedar apple rust disease (*Gymnosporangium juniperi-virginianae*) on apple tree, corn smut (*Mycosarcoma maydis*) on corn cob, young birch conk (*Piptoporus betulinus*). Johnson, Devon. 2022. CC BY-NC-SA 4.0. Includes image 5602753 by Gerald Holmes from Bugwood.org (CC BY-NC 3.0 US), image 5602737 by Gerald Holmes from Bugwood.org (CC BY-NC 3.0 US), image 5551704 by Rebecca A. Melanson from Bugwood.org (CC BY-NC 3.0 US), image 5077043 by David B. Langston from Bugwood.org (CC BY 3.0 US), image 5358902 by Howard F. Schwartz from Bugwood.org (CC BY 3.0 US), image 1427010 by Joseph OBrien from Bugwood.org (CC BY 3.0 US), image 5486242 by James Chatfield from Bugwood.org (CC BY-NC 3.0 US), image 5604984 by Daren Mueller from Bugwood.org (CC BY-NC 3.0 US), and image 2187099 by Joseph LaForest from Bugwood.org (CC BY-NC 3.0 US).
- Figure 4-7: Slight disease. Grey, Kindred. 2022. CC BY-NC-SA 4.0.
- Figure 4-8: Severe disease. Grey, Kindred. 2022. CC BY-NC-SA 4.0.
- Figure 4-9: Pruning tools soaking in a 1:14 household bleach solution. Johnson, Devon. 2022. CC BY-NC-SA 4.0.

CHAPTER 5: ABIOTIC STRESS EFFECTS ON PLANT GROWTH AND DEVELOPMENT

Chapter Contents

- Definition of Plant Stress
- Abiotic Stress
- Chemical Stress
- Plant Nutrient Stress
- Salinity Stress
- Herbicide Injury
- Physical Stress
- Chilling and Freezing Stress
- Light Stress
- Mechanical Stress
- Summary of Physical Stresses
- Additional resources

This chapter is devoted to understanding the effects of abiotic stresses (chemical and physical) on the growth and development of plants. Crop losses due to abiotic stress is considered to be the principal cause of crop yield loss worldwide. Economic losses are in the billions of dollars and with increased global temperatures, extreme weather events, and climate change, it is increasingly important to have an understanding of how abiotic stress affects plant growth and distribution. Not only are commercial crops impacted by abiotic stresses but landscapes, home gardens and natural ecosystems are also affected. The goal of this chapter is to provide a framework for understanding how plants respond to abiotic stress. This chapter covers the basics of this topic. There are a number of other resources and research out there on this topic for those interested in taking a deeper dive.

Definition of Plant Stress

One way of defining **stress** is any change in environmental conditions that adversely affects survival, growth, development and yield in plants. Stress can be divided into two different types, biotic and abiotic. Biotic stresses are caused by another living organism, whereas, abiotic stresses are caused by the physical/chemical environment. In this chapter we are going to be concerned with the abiotic stresses and their impact on plant growth and development.

Abiotic Stress

Abiotic stress can divide into physical and chemical stresses. Physical stresses include: water (drought/flooding), temperature (high/low), light (quantity/quality), and mechanical (ice/snow/wind). Chemical stresses include nutrient (high/low), salinity, soil characteristics (pH/soil composition), air pollution (CO_2/O_2/NO_2/SO_2) and pesticides (herbicides/insecticides/fungicides). Each of these types of stress will be discussed in this chapter.

Plant Responses to Abiotic Stress

Plant responses to stress depend on the severity, duration, number of exposures and if a single stress or multiple stresses are involved. Rarely are plants in nature exposed to a single stress. For example, if a plant is exposed to freezing temperatures, the duration and frequency of exposure may be critical. If the temperature is low enough to freeze the soil in which the plant is growing, the plant may suffer from water deficit as well as nutrient deficiency.

Plant part, stage of development and genetics are all plant characteristics that can determine susceptibility to stress. Using freezing temperatures as an example, young actively growing tissues are more susceptible to freezing than old, slower growing tissues. Flowering in fruit trees may be reduced during freezing temperatures resulting in failure of fruits to develop. Some plants such as spinach and peas are genetically more resistant to cold than are tomato plants.

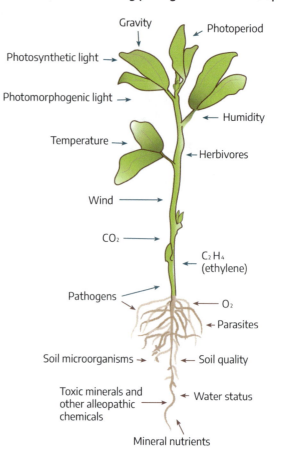

Figure 5-1: Factors affecting plant growth and development: Factors act on the stem (gravity, wind, herbivores) and on the roots (soil microorganisms, water status, soil quality). Pathogens can affect both root and stem.

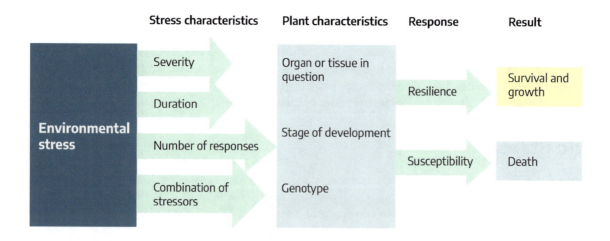

Figure 5-2: Environmental stressors effects' on plants, response, and result.

Chemical Stress

Air Pollution Stress

There are many chemicals that comprise what is referred to as air pollution. Such chemicals include: carbon dioxide, ozone, sulphur dioxide, hydrogen fluoride, oxides of nitrogen, olefins such as ethylene (a natural plant hormone), ammonia, chlorine, hydrogen chloride and metals. The burning of fossil fuels, natural processes, industrial activities, and atmospheric photochemical activity can produce air pollution. In this section only carbon dioxide, ozone, nitrous oxide, sulphur dioxide and ozone will be discussed. These are produced directly or indirectly from the combustion of fossil fuels.

Carbon dioxide pollution

Burning of fossil fuels, or any carbon-containing substance, produces carbon dioxide (CO_2) as a result of combining carbon with atmospheric O_2 under high temperature.

Increasing CO_2 concentrations can influence plant growth directly through its effects on photosynthesis. As a greenhouse gas, it also affects plant growth by impacting atmospheric CO_2 levels, which could be a contributor to global warming and global climate change. Atmospheric CO_2 levels have increased from about 315 ppm in the mid 1950s to 412.5 ppm in 2020. Plants use CO_2, sunlight and water in photosynthesis to produce sugars that are used as an energy source to make other constituents necessary for plant growth and development.

Figure 5-3 illustrates how CO_2 levels have changed over the past 800,000 years compared to today's levels and Figure 5-4 shows how CO_2 levels have changed since 1961.

Effects of increased CO_2 levels on plant growth, development, and distribution

All plants are not the same with respect to how they will respond to rising CO_2 levels. These differences have to do with how a plant captures (fixes) CO_2 from the air and processes it into sugar.

Plants can be divided into 3 groups based on how they remove CO_2 from the atmosphere. These are referred to as C_3, C_4, and CAM plants. Each plant type has adapted to a different environmental niche and has a different way to fix CO_2 from the atmosphere.

Most **C_3 plants** are found in temperate to cold climates with high moisture environments and represent the majority of plant species. They typically are slower-growing plants than C_4 plants and use CO_2 less efficiently as a result of an energy-wasting process called photorespiration. There are 250,000 known C_3 species (1854 weed species). Examples of C_3 plants include: forest trees, woody shrubs, cool season grasses, soybean, wheat and most vegetable crops.

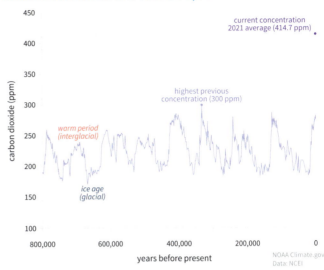

Figure 5-3: Carbon dioxide over 800,000 years.

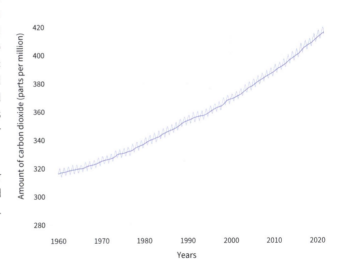

Figure 5-4: Atmospheric carbon dioxide (1960-2021).

C₄ plants are found in hot, dry, subtropical to tropical environments. They are fast growers and have higher rates of photosynthesis than C₃ plants. Because C₄ plants do not photorespire, they are more efficient in fixing CO_2 than C₃ plants, and thus when growing under high light and limited water conditions, C₄ plants can outperform C₃ plants. There are 7500 known C₄ species (146 weed species). Corn, crab grass, millet, sorghum, sedge, nut grass and sugar cane are considered C₄ plants. Interestingly, although C₄ plants comprise only about 5% of the world's biomass, they fix roughly 30% of the terrestrial CO_2.

CAM plants are found in very hot dry desert areas. Like C₄ plants, CAM plants are not susceptible to photorespiration because, unlike C₃ and C₄ plants, they open their stomata at night, thus conserving water and fixing CO_2 and storing it for use during the day to make sugar. There are 16,000 known CAM species. Pineapple, yucca, cactus, orchids, and jade plants are CAM plants.

The types of environments occupied by C₃, C₄ and CAM plants can be observed in the United States as one travels from the east coast to the west. The eastern deciduous forests (mostly C₃ plants) start in the east and end near the border of Oklahoma, followed by the grasslands (mostly C₄ plants) of the prairie states and into the deserts (CAM plants) of the far west.

Possible responses of C₃, C₄, and CAM plants to increasing temperature and elevated CO_2

Experiments have shown that C₃ and C₄ plants grown at elevated CO_2 levels grow faster. However, the growth response is usually greater in C₃ plants because they are considered to be CO_2-limited compared to C₄ plants. In some cases, increased growth in C₃ plants has been shown to be temporary, and some C₄ plants do not respond to elevated CO_2 levels at all. A recent long term 15-year field experiment using C₃ and C₄ grasses demonstrated that elevated CO_2 levels may not affect C₃ and C₄ plants as previously predicted using short-term studies. The authors found elevated CO_2 caused a slight increase in biomass of C₃ plants over time, but the total yield declined for both elevated CO_2 plants and controls (ambient CO_2) until about year 10, when no further decline occurred and yield was about the same. In C₄ grasses, little difference in yield occurred between elevated CO_2 plants and ambient plants, but after 10 years, ambient CO_2 plants had increased yields and elevated CO_2-treated plants had greater yield than controls (Reich 2018). But photosynthesis also depends on temperature and the amount of light and water available. Since C₄ plants have greater water use efficiency and are more heat tolerant than C₃ plants, it is possible that as temperature increases and water availability declines, C₄ plants may have an advantage over C₃ plants. In other words there may be a cross-over point where higher temperature and lower water availability favor C₄ plants over C₃ plants even though C₃ plants may benefit more from elevated CO_2 levels.

Although not as much has been done with CAM plants relative to how climate change will affect these plants, it appears that CAM plants will benefit from elevated CO_2 levels as well. On average, when CO_2 levels are doubled, the biomass of CAM plants has been observed to increase as much as 35%. This suggests that this group of plants may do well as temperature and CO_2 levels increase and occupy an expanded environmental niche in which C₃ and C₄ plants cannot exist.

All of this has ramifications for plant competition in natural ecosystems as well as in agro-ecosystems. As global warming increases, natural plant communities are shifting toward northern latitudes or alpine environments. Agricultural production areas and types of plants that grow in specific regions may have to be adjusted to accommodate climate change, with the possibility that entire regions once productive agriculturally may cease to be productive, and competition from weeds may produce new challenges with respect to control. Recently, USDA issued new growth zone designations for the United States in which climate zones have been pushed toward northern latitudes.

Nitrogen oxides, sulphur dioxide, and ozone pollution

Oxides of carbon (CO_2 and CO), sulfur (SO_2) and nitrogen (NO and NO_2) are considered to be primary air pollutants because they come directly from a source such as automobile exhausts, burning of coal, refuse, or natural sources such as vegetation fires and volcanic activity. In the air, some of these pollutants (SO_2 & NO_2) combine with water to form acids and can fall as acid precipitation, or nitrogen oxides can undergo photochemical reactions to produce ozone (O_3). These are considered to be secondary pollutants formed from the primary pollutants.

Effects of acid rain from nitrogen oxides and sulfur oxides on plant growth

Figure 5-5: Sulfur dioxide injury on sumac.

Considerable research has been conducted on acid rain effects on forest trees. Results suggest that acid rain can impact forest ecosystems by leaching nutrients from leaves and/or affecting soil pH by making it more acidic. This in turn affects nutrient availability either directly or through leaching of nutrients out of the soil. Also, at these lower soil pH levels, aluminum in soils is more readily available to plants and may be at toxic levels affecting tree growth. As a result, this weakens trees and makes them more susceptible to disease, insects, cold, drought and other air pollutants such as O_3 (ozone). There may be a more direct effect on trees that grow in elevated areas where they may be exposed to acid fog/clouds, resulting in longer exposure of leaves to acid conditions.

Agricultural crops are not as drastically affected by acid rain as are plants in natural ecosystems. One reason for this is that a grower can control soil pH and nutrient levels as needed.

The good news about atmospheric levels of nitrogen oxides and sulfur oxides is they have declined since 1980. EPA estimates indicate that emissions in 1980 of nitrogen oxides and sulfur oxides were 26 and 27 million tons, respectively, while in 2013 they were 5 and 13 million tons, respectively.

O_3 effects on plant growth

Ozone is a strong oxidizing agent. It enters the plant through stomata during the day. It impacts plants by oxidizing and degrading membrane lipids and proteins that control permeability and biochemical reactions. Photosynthesis is very susceptible to O_3 and is part of the reason reductions in growth and yield have been observed in crop plants. Dicots appear to be more susceptible to O_3 than monocots. This may be because many monocots are C_4 plants and more efficient than C_3 plants at fixing CO_2 and conserving water under high temperature dry conditions. USDA has determined that soybean yields can be reduced by 10% at O_3 levels of 50 ppb, amounting to $1 billion in losses per year just from that single crop. Peanuts and cotton show reductions of 11% and 8%, respectively, at 50 ppb O_3. Sorghum and field corn, both C_4 plants, show little to no reductions in yield at that concentration. From 1980 to 2013, O_3 levels have dropped by 33% but are still high enough to cause significant damage to natural and agricultural vegetation.

The following links are good references for more information on O_3 and its effects on crop plants: "Ozone Research and Vegetative Impacts" by Ray Knighton, USDA CSREES, 2006, (https://www.nrcs.usda.gov/Internet/FSE_DOCUMENTS/nrcs143_008861.pdf) and "National Air Quality: Status and Trends of Key Air Pollutants," US EPA website. (https://www.epa.gov/air-trends#airquality)

Plant Nutrient Stress

Nutritional stress in plants can be caused by either high or low concentrations of essential elements in the soil. It is important to have the soil analyzed for the concentrations of essential elements and also to determine the pH of the soil before planting (see Chapter 2 "Soils" for more information on soil testing). This will prevent addition of too much or too little fertilizer if the soil needs amending. Determining pH is important because soils may have plenty of nutrients that are simply are not available because extremes in pH can influence their availability to plants.

Essential Elements Needed for Plant Growth

Plants generally require thirteen elements, which they absorb as inorganic ions. This is in addition to carbon, hydrogen and oxygen, which they obtain from carbon dioxide, water and molecular oxygen. Six of these elements are required in greater amounts than the others and are called "macro-nutrients" or "major" elements. They are nitrogen, phosphorus, potassium, sulfur, calcium, and magnesium. The seven "micro-nutrients," "minor," or "trace" elements are iron, manganese, boron, copper, zinc, chlorine, and molybdenum. Several elements are required by some species but not by others. For example, sodium is required for certain blue-green algae and the halophyte *Atriplex vescicaria*. Cobalt is a micro-nutrient for some microorganisms and symbionts, although it has not been demonstrated to be essential for green plants. Silicon is indispensable for diatoms, and vanadium is reported to be essential for the green alga *Scenedesmus obliquus*. Twelve of the thirteen elements in Table 5-2 are derived from parent rock and are, therefore, "mineral elements." The ultimate source of nitrogen is molecular nitrogen (N_2) of the earth's atmosphere. However, aside from those plants that fix atmospheric nitrogen (blue-green algae/bacteria either alone or symbiotically (nitrogen fixing bacteria on legume roots), nitrogen is absorbed as an inorganic ion (nitrate or ammonium). If any one of these elements is missing, plants will not grow and reproduce. For more detailed information about the role of essential elements in plants, see Chapter 1 "Botany."

Table 5-1: Essential micronutrient elements and form absorbed by most plants

Element	Symbol	Chemical form most frequently absorbed	Conc. in Dry Tissue (ppm)
Molybdenum	Mo	MoO_4	0.1
Copper	Cu	Cu^+ Cu^{++}	6
Zinc	Zn	Zn^{++}	20
Manganese	Mn	Mn^{++}	50
Iron	Fe	Fe^{++} Fe^{+++}	100
Boron	B	BO_3^- $B_4O_7^-$	20
Chlorine	Cl	Cl	100

Table 5-2: Essential macronutrient elements and form absorbed by most plants

Element	Symbol	Ions Most Frequently Absorbed	Conc. in Dry Tissue (ppm)
Nitrogen	N	NO_3^- NH_4^+	15000
Potassium	K	K^+	10000
Calcium	Ca	Ca^{++}	5000
Phosphorus	P	$H_2PO_4^-$ HPO_4^+	2000
Magnesium	Mg	Mg^{++}	2000
Sulfur	S	SO_4^+	1000

Functions of Nutrients and Diagnosing Deficiencies

Diagnosing nutrient deficiencies is not an easy task. Familiarity with a particular plant species helps since nutrient deficiencies are not always expressed the same in all plants. In addition, other environmental factors have to be considered because plants may express symptoms similar to nutrient deficiency when exposed to pathogens, insects, air pollutants, pesticides and abiotic stresses.

Chapter 6 "Diagnosing Plant Damage" outlines under "Key to Symptoms of Chemical Disorders," the general descriptions of symptoms associated with nutrient deficiencies in plants.

Nutrient deficiencies are typically initiated in old leaves, new leaves or terminal buds. If terminal buds are dying or dead, and the leaves appear leathery, then the plant is likely deficient in either boron or calcium. If symptoms develop in both old and young leaves, then the element lacking is likely Zn. If symptoms show in the old leaves you can narrow the elements down to N, P, K, Mg or Mo. These elements are mobile in plant tissues. This means as the older leaves die, because of a lack of one of these elements, those elements that are remaining are moved out of those leaves to sustain the actively growing terminal meristems.

If symptoms develop in young terminal leaves then the deficiency is likely due to a lack of S, Fe, Mn, or Cu. These elements are considered to be immobile in plants since they are tightly bound to organic molecules in the healthy plant tissues and cannot be moved to the new leaves to support growth.

These groups of elements are further subdivided based on whether the leaves have dead spots and green or yellow veins.

Effects of pH on nutrient deficiencies and toxicities

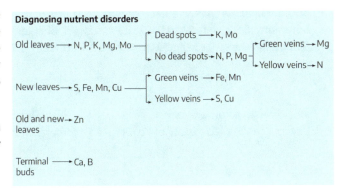

Figure 5-6: Diagnosing nutrient disorders.

pH is a measure of the hydrogen ion concentration in the soil (see the Soils Chapter for more details). The higher the hydrogen ion concentration the more acid is the soil. pH ranges from 0-14, with zero being the most acidic and 14 the most alkaline or basic. A pH of 7 is neutral and most plants grow best around 6.5 to 7. Some plants, like azaleas and rhododendrons, prefer a more acid pH and desert plants prefer a more alkaline pH.

Nutrient uptake by plants is affected by pH. Generally, an acid soil tends to make micronutrients more readily available to plants, and at extremes can result in toxic levels. The element Mo is the exception and its availability decreases. Macronutrients on the other hand are more available in slightly acid to slightly alkaline soils. "Figure 2-8: Nutrient availability by pH" in Chapter 2 demonstrates how pH affects nutrient availability. This chart does not represent all soil types since the chemistry, structure and composition of soils varies. Aberrations in uptake of some elements, such as B and P, is a result of the nature of the soil and complex chemical reactions that occur between soil particles and the element at different pH.

Physiological and biochemical functions of essential elements in plants

The list below reviews some of the functions elements have in plants. Limiting any single element would significantly limit plant growth and development. C, H, and O (not listed) make up the greatest percentage of elements in plants and represent the basic building blocks of plant tissues. Some elements are listed as beneficial since they have not been shown to be essential for growth in all plants. For example some plants may substitute Na for K to control osmotic relations in tissues. Others such as diatoms (a unicellular alga) have an absolute requirement for Si in the cell wall. Heavy metals are frequently toxic to plants, particularly under extremely acidic conditions.

Essential Elements

- **Nitrogen (N):** Constituent of many compounds, amino acids, nucleic acids, chlorophyll
- **Phosphorus (P):** Constituent of nucleic acids, phospholipids, ATP, NAD, NADP
- **Potassium (K):** Cofactor for enzyme reactions; osmotic balance particularly stomata
- **Sulfur (S):** Constituent of proteins; coenzyme A
- **Calcium (Ca):** Calcium pectate of middle lamella; important in membrane selectivity
- **Magnesium (Mg):** Constituent of chlorophyll, important in nucleic acid structure, coenzyme
- **Iron (Fe):** Constituent of cytochromes, ferredoxin; needed for chlorophyll synthesis
- **Manganese (Mn):** Coenzyme for numerous reactions; Krebs cycle, nitrate reductase
- **Copper (Cu):** Coenzyme – oxidases in plastocyanin a carrier in photosynthetic phosphorylation
- **Zinc (Zn):** Needed for IAA synthesis and protein synthesis; cofactor numerous dehydrogenases
- **Molybdenum (Mo):** Important in nitrate reduction and nitrogen fixation; probably also a cofactor
- **Boron (B):** Uncertain. Possibly involved in sugar translocation cross cell membranes, may alter hormone balance in plants
- **Chlorine (Cl):** Photosynthesis (deficiency never seen in nature)

Beneficial Elements

- **Cobalt (Co)** Nitrogen fixation

- **Sodium (Na)** Can partly replace K
- **Selenium (Se)** Can reverse P toxicity in susceptible plants
- **Silicon (Si)** Can improve growth in cereals. Reduces Fe, Mn toxicity by precipitation

Toxicity

- Most heavy metals are toxic.
- Low pH can lead to toxicity of Fe, Mn, Al particularly, in tropical soils.

Macronutrient deficiency outline

Nitrogen (N)
Leaches from soil
Mobile in plant
Nitrogen excess:
Succulent growth, dark green color, weak spindly growth, few fruits, may cause brittle growth especially under high temperatures
Nitrogen deficiency:
Reduced growth, yellowing (chlorosis), reds and purples may intensify with some plants, reduced lateral branching; symptoms appear first on older growth
Action notes:
Uptake of N is inhibited by high P levels. Indoors, the best N/K ration is 1/1 unless light is extremely high. In soils with a high C:N ratio, more N should be supplied

Phosphorus (P)
Does not leach from soil readily
Mobile in plant
Phosphorus excess:
Shows up as micronutrient deficiency of Zn, Fe, or Co
Phosphorus deficiency:
Reduced growth, color may intensify, browning or purpling in foliage of some plants, thin stems, reduced lateral breaks, loss of lower leaves, reduced flowering
Action notes:
Rapidly "fixed" on soil particles when applied. Under acid conditions fixed with Fe, Mg, and Al. Under alkaline conditions fixed with Ca. Important for young plants and seedling growth. High P interferes with micronutrient absorption and N absorption. Used in relatively small amounts when compared to N and K. May leach from soil high in bark or peat

Potassium (K)
Leaches from soil
Mobile in plant
Potassium excess:
Causes N deficiency in plants and may affect the uptake of other positive ions
Potassium deficiency:
Reduced growth, shortened internodes, marginal burn or scorch (brown leaf edges), necrotic (dead) spots in the leaf, reduction of lateral branching and tendency to wilt readily
Action notes:
N/K balance is important; high N/low K favors vegetative growth; low N/high K promotes reproductive growth (flower, fruit)

Magnesium (Mg)
Leaches in soil
Mobile in plant
Magnesium excess:
Interferes with Ca uptake
Magnesium deficiency:
Symptoms are reduction in growth, marginal chlorosis or interveinal chlorosis (yellow between the veins) of the older leaves in some species, reduction in seed production, and cupped leaves
Action notes:
Mg is commonly deficient in foliage plants because it is leached and not replaced. Epsom salts at a low rate of 1 teaspoon per gallon may be used two times a year. Mg can also be absorbed by leaves if sprayed with a weak solution. Dolomitic limestone can be applied in outdoor situations to rectify a deficiency

Calcium (Ca)
Moderately leachable from soil
Not mobile in plant
Calcium excess:
Interferes with Mg absorption. High Ca usually causes high pH which then precipitates many of the micronutrients so that they become unavailable to the plant
Calcium deficiency:
Inhibition of bud growth, death of root tips, cupping of mature leaves, weak growth, blossom end rot of many fruits, pits on root vegetables
Action notes:
Ca is important to pH control and is rarely deficient if the correct pH is maintained. Water stress (too much or too little) can affect Ca relationships within the plant causing deficiency in the location where Ca was needed at the time of stress

Sulphur (S)
Leaches from soil
Not mobile in plant
Sulfur excess:
Sulfur excess is usually in the form of air pollution
Sulfur deficiency:
Sulfur is often a carrier or impurity in fertilizers and is rarely deficient. It may also be absorbed from the air and is a by-product of combustion. Symptoms are a general yellowing of affected leaves or entire plant
Action notes:
Sulfur excess is difficult to control

Micronutrient deficiency outline

The majority of the micronutrients are not mobile; thus, deficiency symptoms are usually found on new growth. Their availability in the soil is highly dependent upon the pH and the presence of other ions. The proper balance between the ions present is important, as many micronutrients are antagonistic to each other. This is especially true of the heavy metals where an excess of one element may show up as a deficiency of another. If the pH is maintained at the proper level and a fertilizer which contains micronutrients is used once a year, deficiency symptoms (with the exception of iron deficiency symptoms) are rarely found on indoor plants. Many of the micronutrients are enzyme activators.

Iron (Fe)
Iron excess:
Rare except on flooded soils
Iron deficiency:
Interveinal chlorosis primarily on young tissue, which may become white. Fe deficiency may be found under the following conditions even if Fe is in the soil: soil high in Ca, poorly drained soil, soil high in Mn, high pH, high P, soil high in heavy metals (Cu, Zn), oxygen deficient soils or when nematodes attack the roots. Fe should be added in the chelate form; the type of chelate needed depends upon the soil pH.

Boron (B)
Boron excess:
Blackening or death of tissue between veins
Boron deficiency:
Failure to set seed, internal breakdown, death of apical buds

Zinc (Zn)
Zinc excess:
Appears as Fe deficiency. Interferes with MG
Zinc deficiency:
"Little leaf," reduction in leaf size, short internodes, distorted or puckered leaf margins, interveinal chlorosis

Copper (Cu)
Copper excess:
Can occur at low pH; shows up as Fe deficiency
Copper deficiency:
New growth small, misshapen, wilted; may be found in soil peat soils

Manganese (Mn)
Manganese excess:
Reduction in growth, brown spotting on leaves; shows up as Fe deficiency found under acid conditions
Manganese deficiency:
Interveinal chlorosis of leaves followed by brown spots producing a checkered red effect

Molybdenum (Mn)
Molybdenum deficiency:
Interveinal chlorosis on older or midstem leaves, twisted leaves (whiptail)

Chlorine (Cl)
Chlorine excess:
Salt injury, leaf burn, may increase succulence
Chlorine deficiency:
Wilted leaves which become bronze then chlorotic and may die; club roots

Cobalt (Co)
Necessary to recently established plants
Essential for nitrogen fixation
Little is known about its deficiency or excess (toxicity) symptoms

Salinity Stress

The Origin of High Saline Soils

There are two types of salinity relative to how such soils are formed.

Primary salinity results from natural causes such as weathering and erosion or from land near the ocean that accumulates salt as a result of salt spray carried inland by wind and deposited in the soil by rain. Primary salinity can occur over very long periods of time depending on location and weather conditions.

Figure 5-7: Pecan death caused by soil salinization.

Secondary salinity results from human activity such as irrigation and removal of natural vegetation and can occur much more quickly than primary salinity. Continuous irrigation and fertilization of agricultural areas results in a build up of salts in the top layers of the soil unless salts are leached out by rainfall or carefully controlled irrigation practices. The source of irrigation water may also have high levels of salts in the water that contribute to salt accumulation. Removal of natural vegetation often destroys deep-rooted perennials that have adapted to environments where water would be unavailable to shallow-rooted annual crop plants. Removing perennials and replacing them with annual crops often requires irrigation that ultimately raises the water table in the soil profile and exposes plants to higher salinities. Evaporation of high salinity irrigation water also contributes to increased soil salinity in the upper soil profile.

Differences Between Saline and Sodic Soils

Soils with high salt concentrations are further divided into saline and sodic soils. Saline soils have a high concentration of soluble salts, particularly sodium salts, whereas sodic soils have low concentrations of soluble salts. In sodic soils, monovalent cations such as sodium, displace divalent cations that hold clay particles together. This causes clay particles to dissociate and disperse. Over time dispersed particles are leached deeper into the soil profile-blocking pores in the soil leading to water logging and poor drainage. Alkaline soils are a type of sodic soil with a high pH and are typical of semi-arid to arid regions. Salts typical of saline soils include: $NaCl$, Na_2SO_4, while salts typical of sodic/alkaline soils are: Na_2CO_3, $NaHCO_3$. Salts of the cations Na^+, Ca^{2+}, Mg^{2+}, and K^+, and the anions Cl^-, SO_4^{2-}, HCO_3^-, CO_3^{2-}, and NO_3^- can also form in soils.

About 6.5% of the world's soils are considered to be sodic or saline. Approximately 20% of all irrigated land is either sodic or saline.

Plant Responses to High Salinity Environments

Plants can be classified relative to salinity tolerance as glycophytes, halophytes, obligate halophytes, and facultative halophytes. Glycophtes cannot tolerate salinity levels in excess of 10mM (millimolar), halophytes can tolerate a concentration up to 50mM, obligate halophytes do not grow well below 10mM but grow well between 10-50mM, and facultative halophytes only become halophytic after being exposed to moderate soil salinity.

Two problems develop in plants as a result of high saline conditions. One is an osmotic problem due to high salt concentrations in the soil. This results in drought stress for the plant since water moves out of the plant into the soil. The other problem is one of toxic ion accumulation in the tissues of the plant.

The osmotic problem is countered in some plants by producing organic solutes in the cytoplasm that retain the water in the plant instead of allowing water to move into the soil. This requires metabolic expenditure of energy and thus slows the growth of the plant. Another adjustment the plant may make is the uptake of potassium ions or other low toxicity ions to counter the soil salt concentrations. Controlling ionic balance in the plant is critical in maintaining pH conducive to enzyme function and metabolism.

Toxic ion accumulation is prevented in some plants by exclusion by the roots, or prevention of transport in the shoots, to growing meristems of the plant. If salts reach the shoots and leaves, they can be compartmentalized in vacuoles or extruded by way of salt glands in some plants. If salts are not excluded or compartmentalized they can have deleterious effects on proteins and cell membranes and ultimately decrease growth and result in death. The following list summarizes some of the physiological effects of salinity stress on plants:

Salinity Stress Effects on Plants

- High Na^+ transport to shoot
- Low K^+ uptake
- High Cl^- uptake
- Low P and Zn uptake
- Preferential accumulation of Na^+ in old leaves
- Increase in non-toxic organic solutes
- Increase in free radical oxygen species
- Lower fresh and dry weight of shoots and roots
- Low germination of seeds
- Partial closure of stomata in response to water deficit

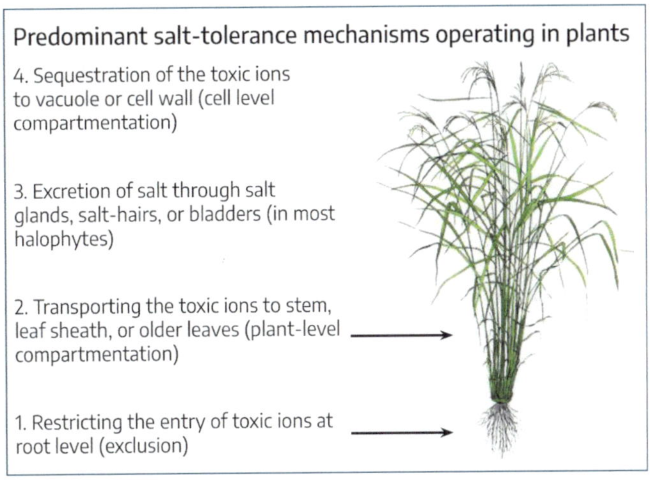

The tolerance of a plant depends on its ability to exclude, compartmentalize, or remove salt from tissues. In addition, adjusting the ion balance in the plant and the production of organic chemicals that help to retain water in the plant are fundamental to tolerance.

Figure 5-8: Predominant salt-tolerance mechanisms operating in plants.

Symptoms of Salinity Stress in Plants

In the home landscape, like many other stresses, it is difficult to determine if the stress is caused by high salinity or some other stress presenting similar symptoms. One must carefully examine the environment in which the plant is growing to determine the surroundings of the plant in order to eliminate other possibilities.

Some of the symptoms of salinity stress in plants include: reduced shoot growth, marginal necrosis of leaves, delay in bud break and flowering, premature defoliation, early leaf color formation, crown thinning, and twig death.

Salt injury to plants along roadways is common as a result of using salts to melt snow and ice. Sources of salt damage can include salt spray from passing vehicles or salt that has seeped into the soil around plant roots. Symptoms usually start to show in the early to late spring, depending on the amount of salt to which the plant is exposed, soil types and weather conditions. Symptoms may not develop for quite some time if soils are affected. Homeowners using salt on driveways and sidewalks may also experience salt damage to their plants. Watering plants with softened water may also contribute to salt injury in sensitive plants.

Herbicide Injury

Figure 5-9: Atrazine drift damage on potato.

Herbicide injury to landscape plants is most likely a result of using herbicides on lawns unless you live near an agricultural production area.

There are several ways non-target plants can be exposed to herbicides and include:

- **Drift and volatilization**: Herbicides should never be applied on windy days because they can drift to non-target plants and cause injury. Some pesticides are volatile and can vaporize in the hot sun. The vapors are then carried by wind to other plants. When applying herbicides, spray particle size is also important. The smaller the particle size of the spray, the more likely it can be carried by the wind or be vaporized.

- **Leaching and run-off from the soil**: Some herbicides are applied to soils and are referred to as pre-emergence herbicides. These form a thin layer of chemical on the soil and when newly germinating seedlings attempt to break through the soil, they are killed by the herbicide. Some of these chemicals can run off in rain water and affect other plants or potentially leach down through the soil and possibly be taken up by deep-rooted plants such as trees.
- **Misapplication**: Bottom line, read the label on the product you are using. Only use the herbicide on plants listed on the label and follow the recommended rates.
- **Soil or soil amendment application**: Make sure you know the history and source of any top soils or soil amendments you may use around plants. Be particularly aware of agricultural fertilizers and compost that may have originated from previous treatment of hay fields with weed control herbicides. These can be carried over in livestock manure and compost.

Herbicide Application and Effects on Plants

Herbicides are either applied to soils (pre-emergence) to control newly germinating seedlings or directly to shoots and foliage (post-emergence) to control already established growing plants. Herbicides can further be divided based on whether the chemical affects the plant at the site of application (contact) or whether it moves around in the vascular system of the plant (systemic). Herbicides can be selective, that is some will kill only broadleaf plants or only grasses, or they can be non-selective and kill both. Factors such as how the herbicide is used (pre/post-emergence), and whether it is a contact or systemic herbicide, or whether it is selective or non-selective has to do with the herbicide's mode of action. The mode of action refers to how a chemical affects the physiology, biochemistry, and development of the plant.

Differentiating herbicide damage in plants from other environmental stresses is sometimes difficult. Nutrient, air pollution, salinity, pathogens, insects and other environmental stress can sometimes mimic herbicide damage symptoms. However, if one can eliminate these other potential stress factors, knowledge of herbicide modes of action can be helpful in determining if a specific herbicide may have caused the damage.

Herbicide Modes of Action

The following outlines the different categories of herbicides relative to their mode of action and how they affect plant metabolism.

- Amino acid synthesis inhibitors prevent the synthesis of aromatic and branched chain amino acids required for the synthesis of enzymes and membrane proteins.
- Plant growth regulator herbicides mimic or disrupt auxin (indole acetic acid) functions in plants. Auxin controls many aspects of plant development including: cell division, sex, tropisms, and polarity.
- Pigment inhibitors prevent the formation of carotenoids in plants that are crucial for protection of chlorophyll from photodecomposition. These are also called bleaching herbicides because the leaves of treated plants are white.
- Photosynthesis inhibitors prevent the light reactions of photosynthesis from functioning. Photosynthesis is divided into two phases: the light reactions, which captures the energy of light (photons) and stores it as stable chemical energy, and the dark reactions, which uses the energy produced in the light reactions to make sugar.
- Cell membrane disruption herbicides oxidize membranes directly and cause membranes to break down and decompose. Contact herbicides are examples.
- Seedling growth inhibitors affect apical cell division of roots and shoots.
- Lipid synthesis inhibitors affect plant cell membranes and membranes surrounding chloroplasts, mitochondria, vacuoles and other organelles in the cell. This disrupts the ability of each to perform a specific function.
- Nitrogen metabolism inhibitors affect the metabolism of ammonium into amino acids, which can accumulate to toxic levels in the plant.

The VCE "Pest Management Guide: Home Grounds and Animals" 456-018 lists a variety of herbicides that are approved for use on Virginia lawns. Most of these are used to control broadleaf weeds, nuisance grasses, and sedges. Although there is a possibility that any of these could be used in lawns, it is most probable that the plant growth regulator (PGR) type herbicides are going to be the most prominent since they are found most frequently in weed and feed fertilizers. So where weed and feed fertilizers are used in lawn care and non-target plants show injury symptoms, the most likely suspect would be the PGR group of herbicides.

Physical Stress

The Importance of Water to Plants

Water is important to plants for maintaining tissue turgidity. That means there needs to be an internal water content that allows cells and tissues to maintain maximum cell volume and thus tissue surface area. A tissue that is not turgid is said to be flaccid and often is accompanied by wilting. Wilting is a defensive mechanism to reduce water loss from the plant, but it also reduces leaf surface area to sunlight and thus reduces photosynthesis and growth (for more information on this topic, see the Chapter 1 "Botany").

Water is also important for transporting nutrients from the soil to the tissues of the plant. The xylem is the main water and nutrient transport system, extending from the roots through the stems and into the veins of the leaf. In the leaf, water is lost through the stomata when they are open during the day, thus providing another important function for water and that is cooling the leaf surface through the process referred to as **evapo-transpiration**. Water is also required for photosynthesis.

Drought Stress

Causes of drought stress in plants

High temperature, low soil moisture, low humidity, wind, frozen soil, high salt concentrations and low genetic tolerance to moisture stress all contribute to water deficit stress in plants. Many of these stresses can act at the same time and frequently do. Each deprives the plant of moisture through the lack of availability as in low soil moisture and frozen soils, or through moisture removal from the plant as a result of high salt concentrations, high wind, and low humidity.

Plant control of water loss: Physiological/developmental responses

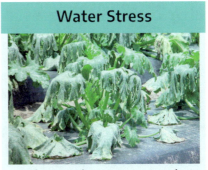

Figure 5-10: Flagging leaves on squash plants indicate water stress.

One of the primary ways plants control water loss is through opening and closing stomata on the surface of leaves. Stomata in most plants are open during the day and close at night. The exception being: plants growing in hot dry climates such as CAM plants that open stomata at night to conserve precious water during the day. However, most plants under water deficit stress can partially or totally close stomata during the day to conserve water. Other responses plants have include leaf drop, flower drop, and fruit drop, early flowering, die back in trees, increased root growth, wilting/leaf rolling and internal production of molecules in cells that help retain water. All of these reflect survival strategies at the expense of growth.

Plant control of water loss: Genetic adaptations for conserving water

Plant adaptations to low moisture environments include: More stomata on under surface of leaves than on the top, sunken stomata, thick leaf cuticle and high wax production, modified leaves (no leaves to narrow pointed leaves), hairy and light-colored leaf surfaces, low plant profile, different strategies for opening and closing stomata, and leaf movements to avoid direct sun exposure.

Water use in plants

Plants are part of the hydrologic cycle and are important in recycling of water from the soil to the air. Some plants are more efficient at water usage than others. It has been estimated that about 1/3 of the rainfall that falls on a forested ecosystem is transpired through evapotranspiration back to the atmosphere. Generally, C_4 plants are more efficient than C_3 plants in water use. However, even a C_4 plant, such as corn, uses considerable amounts of water to grow. It has been estimated that it takes about 16.6 gallons of water to produce an ear of corn, and at a planting rate of about 30,000 plants per acre, that translates to 500,000 gallons per acre not including the water needed for the vegetative growth of the corn stalk.

Trees also transpire large amounts of water during the summer. For example, a 46' silver maple tree can transpire as much as 60 gallons per hour.

Flooding Stress

Effects of flooding on soils

When a soil is saturated with water after a heavy rain or during a flood, it can impact plant growth severely. Short periods of flooding can have significant impacts on crops and plants in general. Flooding deprives plants of O_2 (anaerobic conditions) in the root system and prevents CO_2, due to respiration, from escaping from the soil into the air. This creates an O_2 deficit in the soil and inhibits root growth. As CO_2 builds up, carbonic acid is formed from the reaction of CO_2 with water making the soil more acidic. In so doing, it makes some elements in the soil more readily available sometimes in toxic amounts. Other essential elements such as nitrogen can be leached from the soil or made less available because of acidic conditions. In addition, anaerobic bacteria become more active, producing toxic metabolites such as methane, ethylene, and hydrogen sulfide. These conditions weaken the plant root system, making it more susceptible to root pathogens. This scenario can also be applied to overwatering of potted plants in the home or nursery.

Physiological changes in flooded plants

Flooding puts plants into a survival mode rather than a growth mode. Plants respond by growing adventitious roots on the stem near the water line thus being closer to available atmospheric O_2. Ethylene production increases, which is a natural plant hormone that inhibits growth rate and induces a condition called epinasty in the leaves. Plants showing epinasty appear wilted. This is not wilting as a result of lack of available water but rather a loss of turgidity of petiole basal cells in response to ethylene. In woody plants, flooding causes an increased production of openings in the bark called lenticels, which facilitate gaseous exchange. Also, plants that are flooded for extended periods produce a type of tissue in the roots called aerenchyma, which is a degradation of root cellular structure in order to facilitate movement of O_2 among plant tissues and removal of CO_2. Interestingly, plants that normally live in aquatic environments, such as cattails, normally have this type of tissue in root systems and stems. Finally, some plants that normally live in aquatic environments such as mangroves, produce structures called pneumatophores, which have been shown to be involved with O_2 transfer to the roots of these plants. Analogous structures in cypress do not appear to have that function.

Heat Stress

Water deficit stress is most frequently linked to high temperature or heat stress. All plants have an optimum temperature for good growth. Exceeding that temperature can have profound effects on the physiology and biochemistry of the plant. When temperature exceeds the optimum for a given plant, a number of things start to happen. Stomata start to close or shut down completely to limit water loss. However, this limits CO_2 uptake, causing a reduction in photosynthesis. Also, O_2 cannot get out of the leaves and builds up in the leaf tissues and can result in the formation of free radical O_2, which oxidizes cell membrane lipids, making them leaky and non-functional. Respiration increases in the cells, causing an increased use of stored energy in the plant thus resulting in reduced growth and possibly death of the plant depending on the severity and length of exposure.

Plants tolerant to heat stress are capable of altering their membranes to protect from oxidation. They also produce molecules (heat shock proteins) that can be incorporated into plant membranes or used to help conserve cellular water and make them less susceptible to heat stress.

Chilling and Freezing Stress

The Difference Between Chilling and Freezing Stress

Chilling stress occurs in plants sensitive to temperatures in the range of 68-32° F. These include plants that are tropical to subtropical in origin, such as many indoor species, beans, corn, rice, tomatoes, squash and bananas.

Freezing stress occurs in plants sensitive to temperatures below the freezing point of water or 32°F. Some plants are frost hardy and can acclimate to temperatures just below freezing and can recover if the temperature is not too prolonged. Peas, spinach, lettuce are examples of such plants.

Other plants are cold hardy and include temperate trees and woody shrubs, some of which can with withstand temperatures of -70°F and lower.

Physiological and Biochemical Differences Between Cold Sensitive and Tolerant Plants

Several things are involved biochemically and physiologically that separate plants that are sensitive from those that are tolerant to cold temperatures. Plants that are freezing tolerant can prevent ice from forming inside the cell. If this occurs in plants, it is lethal. Plants that are susceptible to freezing temperatures cannot do this. Cold tolerance is accomplished through changes in membrane composition and the production of substances inside the cell that lower the freezing point.

Structurally the plant cell is comprised of an outer cell wall comprised of cellulose, and immediately inside the cell wall is the cytoplasmic membrane. The membrane controls the movement of water and dissolved substances in and out of the cell. Membranes also surround important organelles inside the cell, including chloroplasts, mitochondria, vacuoles as well as many other structures. Plant membrane composition changes with temperature. Membranes are comprised primarily of lipid (with some protein and carbohydrate), and lipids can change viscosity with changing temperature. That is, they become more fluid-like with elevated temperature and more solid-like at lower temperatures. The challenge for the plant is to control how fluid or how solid the membrane becomes, because this affects the ability of the membrane to transport water and dissolved substances across it. Plants can control this fluid/solid nature by interjecting unsaturated or saturated fats into the membrane structure. If you have ever baked pastries you have experienced saturated and unsaturated fats. An example of an unsaturated fat is vegetable oil, which is liquid at room temperature. On the other hand, lard is a saturated fat and is solid at room temperature. So this is basically what you find in plant membranes: combinations of saturated and unsaturated fats that change with temperature to affect membrane permeability and function when it gets too hot or too cold. So when plants experience increasing cold temperatures, they interject unsaturated fatty acids so as to maintain a more fluid membrane, which is functional at lower temperatures. Conversely, when it gets hot, membranes can become more permeable and the plant injects more saturated fats into the membrane to make it less fluid. This is basically what happens when you harden off your tomato plants in early spring. The ability to make such changes in membrane structure is genetically determined and is part of the basis for differences in temperature sensitivity in plants.

Along with membrane changes, plant cells also produce substances called sugar alcohols that lower the freezing point of the cytoplasm so it does not form ice crystals. Some plants have the ability to move water out of the cell into the area of the cell wall where freezing is less likely to damage the cell. When ice starts to form, however, water diffuses out of the cell to form more ice. This may be both beneficial or harmful depending on how much water is removed. Some plants, mostly trees, undergo a process called supercooling where water can stay liquid down to a temperature of -70°F.

The Symptoms, Cellular, and Physiological Effects of Chilling and Freezing

Symptoms: reduced growth, leaf necrosis or damage, water soaking and a flaccid appearance of plant tissues.

Cellular effects: loss of membrane function, dehydration, salt injury, membrane rupture as a result of ice formation, air bubbles(embolisms) in the xylem.

Physiological effects: decreased photosynthesis, protein degradation, reduced transport in vascular tissues, increased respiration.

Light Stress

Light is important in promoting photosynthesis, affecting plant orientation, promoting/inhibiting flowering, germination and dormancy, stomatal opening and closing and developmental processes (photomorphogenesis).

Plants can either be exposed to too much light, too little light (quantity), or the wrong kind of light (quality). Some plants are considered to be sun plants in that they grow well in full sunlight while others prefer shade or partial sun. Characteristics of sun plants include: reduced leaf area, thick leaves and cuticle, and abundant stomata. Shade plants have the opposite characteristics.

The quality of light is important as well in that red and blue wavelengths of light are needed for photosynthesis, phototropism (growth of plants toward light), stomatal opening, and solar tracking (plants adjusting leaves during the day to follow the sun). Red light and far-red light are important in flowering, seed germination and dormancy. UVB light can damage plants and inhibit growth. This is particularly true at higher elevations.

Plants growing in the under-story of a forest have the ability to capture what little light that may penetrate the canopy in a very efficient way. When walking through the forest on a sunny, slightly windy day, you may have noticed the flickers of light that come and go with the tree canopy movements. These flickers of light are referred to as sun flecks and are important in the growth of under-story plants.

Mechanical Stress

Mechanical stress includes wind, rain, hail, snow, ice and animal movement. Plants can sense touch or movement that may be caused by any of the above mechanical stimuli. In some cases the response is not obvious, but in others such as the Venus fly trap (*Dionaea muscipula*) or the sensitive plant (*Mimosa pudica*), perception of touch can be very rapid and obvious.

Effects of Mechanical Stress on Plants

Wind is probably one of the most prevalent mechanical stresses and causes plants to respond in several ways. Wind can be beneficial as well as harmful to plants. When wind is strong it can cause physical damage to the plant but subtle and less obvious effects are changes in photosynthesis. On a calm clear warm day, plants have their stomata open and O_2 from photosynthesis diffuses out and CO_2 goes in. However, on calm days a layer of high humidity produced from evaporative transpiration forms near the surface of leaves called a boundary layer. This layer creates a resistance to the exchange of gases between the atmosphere and the leaf, slows down photosynthesis, and retains O_2, which slows growth. Consequently a slight breeze can be beneficial to plants in that the boundary layer is removed and allows gas exchange more efficiently.

However, if the wind is rapid it could create a water deficit stress for the plant. The stomata close and again photosynthesis is reduced and growth is slowed.

There is still another effect that is a result of constant flexing and movement of plant leaves and branches as a result of wind or other mechanical stimuli. This results in chemical signals that are transmitted in the tissues of the plant causing changes in growth patterns, usually reducing the height of plants and increasing the diameter of shoots or branches. If you have ever observed trees growing on mountaintops, you have observed the effects of wind on growth. Such plants are usually small and misshapen, reflecting the wind direction.

Practical applications of this knowledge have been used in fruit and nursery production. For example, attaching weights to fruit tree branches or bending branches down and tying them to the ground causes the branches to increase in diameter and shortens elongation growth, thus providing a stronger branch that is capable of supporting a larger, heavier fruit load without causing damage to the tree. Researchers have also shown that by using mechanical devices, which gently pass across the tops of greenhouse-grown plants, they can cause decreases in height growth and increased stem diameter. This is beneficial to growers in that it prevents plants from becoming leggy and better able to support inflorescences. It also avoids the use of plant growth regulator chemicals often used for this purpose.

Rain, hail, snow and ice can cause observable mechanical damage to plants, such as leaf tearing/removal and limb damage but can also induce similar responses as wind, causing changes in growth distribution in tissues. However, these conditions are usually short term as opposed to almost daily plant encounters with wind.

Effects of Soil Compaction on Root and Seedling Growth

Soil compaction also impacts differential growth in plant tissues, particularly the roots and germinating seeds. Persistent pedestrian traffic, animal grazing, construction machinery and the nature of the soil can cause soil compaction. Compaction can affect many things that influence plant growth including gas exchange in the soil and water and nutrient movement. However, soil compaction also imparts a physical resistance to the growth of plant roots and the growth and penetration of germinating seedlings. This resistance causes roots and shoots to increase in diameter in a similar fashion to wind stress. This is thought to give the root or young shoot a greater mechanical advantage to penetrate and grow through a compacted soil. Certainly soil compaction will affect growth and survival of plants depending on plant species.

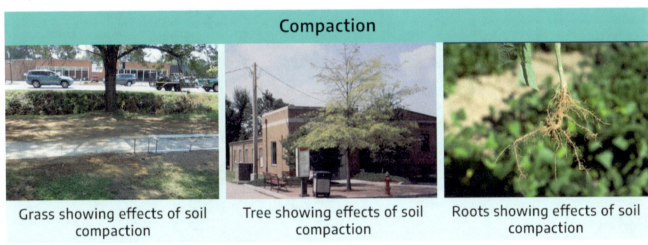

Figure 5-11: Soil compaction and root damage, tree showing signs of abiotic stress from soil compaction in urban area, dry bean roots showing the effects of soil compaction.

Summary of Physical Stresses

We now know that creating and defining microclimates in crops (wind breaks/terraces) and in urban landscapes (plantings around buildings etc.) can influence the physiology of plants in favorable and unfavorable ways. So when considering all of the physical and chemical stresses plants must endure to grow well, it is important that we know as much about how these stresses impact plants as we can, so we can make the best decisions for optimum plant growth.

Additional Resources

Acid Rain:

- Effects of Acid Rain, U.S. EPA (https://www.epa.gov/acidrain/effects-acid-rain)
- National Air Quality: Status and Trends of Key Air Pollutants, U.S. EPA (http://www.epa.gov/airtrends/aqtrends.html#airquality)

Nutrient deficiency:

- Boron Deficiency, Haifa Knowledge Group (https://www.haifa-group.com/online-expert/deficiency-pro/b-boron)
- Visual Guide to Nutrient Deficiencies, Grow Abundant (https://growabundant.com/nutrient-deficiencies/)

Salinity:

- Salt Damage in Landscape Plants, Purdue (https://www.extension.purdue.edu/extmedia/id/id-412-w.pdf)

Herbicide damage:

- Herbicides: How they Work and Damage They Cause, Texas Agricultural Extension (http://twig.tamu.edu/B6081.pdf)

Physical stress:

- Plant Responses to Wind, Agriculture, Ecosystems, and the Environment (journal) (https://www.sciencedirect.com/science/article/pii/0167880988900084)
- Effects of Mechanical Stress on Cotton Growth and Development, PLOS One (journal) (https://journals.plos.org/plosone/article?id=10.1371/journal.pone.0082256)
- *Arabidopsis thaliana* Responses to Mechanical Stimulation Do Not Require ETR1 or EIN2, Plant Physiology (journal) (https://academic.oup.com/plphys/article/116/2/643/6085816)

References

Reich, P.B. et al. (2018). Unexpected reversal of C_3 versus C_4 grass response to elevated CO_2 during a 20-year field experiment. *Science* 360(6386), 317-320.

Attributions

Written by David M. Orcutt, Professor Emeritus, Plant Physiology (2015)

- Reviewed by Daivid M. Orcutt, Professor Emeritus, Plant Physiology (2021)

Image Attributions

- Figure 5-1: Factors affecting plant growth and development. Johnson, Devon. 2022. CC BY-NC-SA 4.0 Adapted from "Figure 18.1" in "Signal Perception and Transduction" by A. Trewavas. *Biology*. 2002.
- Figure 5-2: Environmental stressors effects' on plants, response, and result. Johnson, Devon. 2022. CC BY-NC-SA 4.0. Adapted from "Risposta delle colture in serra agli stress ambientali" by Anonymous, 2018.
- Figure 5-3: Carbon dioxide over 800,000 years. NOAA Climate.gov image from "Climate Change: Atmospheric Carbon

Dioxide" 2022. Public domain.
- Figure 5-4: Atmospheric carbon dioxide (1960-2021). NOAA Climate.gov image from "Climate Change: Atmospheric Carbon Dioxide" 2022. Public domain.
- Figure 5-5: Sulfur dioxide injury on sumac. Johnson, Devon. 2022. CC BY-NC-SA 4.0 Includes image 1634216 by Penn State Department of Plant Pathology & Environmental Microbiology Archives from Bugwood.org CC BY-NC 3.0 US.
- Figure 5-6: Diagnosing nutrient disorders. Johnson, Devon. 2022. CC BY-NC-SA 4.0. Adapted from *Master Gardener Training Handbook*, Virginia Cooperative Extension, 2018.
- Figure 5-7: Pecan death caused by soil salinization. Johnson, Devon. 2022. CC BY-NC-SA 4.0 Includes image 5545229 by Jonas Janner Hamann from Bugwood.org CC BY 3.0 US.
- Figure 5-8: Predominant salt-tolerance mechanisms operating in plants. Johnson, Devon. 2022. CC BY-NC-SA 4.0. Adapted from "Predominant salt tolerance mechanisms operating in plants," Knowledge Bank.
- Figure 5-9: Atrazine drift damage on potato. Johnson, Devon. 2022. CC BY-NC-SA 4.0. Includes image 5553953 by Jed Colquhoun from Bugwood.org CC BY-NC 3.0 US.
- Figure 5-10: Flagging leaves on squash plants indicate water stress. Johnson, Devon. 2022. CC BY-NC-SA 4.0 Includes image 5602899 by Gerald Holmes from Bugwood.org CC BY-NC 3.0 US.
- Figure 5-11: Soil compaction and root damage, tree showing signs of abiotic stress from soil compaction in urban area, dry bean roots showing the effects of soil compaction. Johnson, Devon. 2022. CC BY-NC-SA 4.0. Includes image 5334099 by Mary Ann Hansen from Bugwood.org CC BY 3.0 US, image 5454888 by Jason Sharman from Bugwood.org CC BY-NC 3.0 US, and image 5358725 by J.G. Davis from Bugwood.org CC BY 3.0 US.

CHAPTER 6: DIAGNOSING PLANT DAMAGE

Chapter Contents

- A Systematic Approach to Diagnosing Plant Damage
- Define the Problem
- Look for Patterns
- Determine Causes
- Diagnostic Keys
- Additional Resources

Diagnosis of plant problems is often a very difficult task since there can be many different causes for a given symptom, not all of which are pathogenic organisms. Soil nutrition and texture, weather conditions, lighting, and many other environmental and cultural conditions influence the overall health of a plant. Insect damage can sometimes be confused with plant disease caused by microorganisms or abiotic factors. Knowing a complete history of the plant is essential to making an accurate diagnosis. Also, a plant specimen should be in the early stages of deterioration when it is examined in order for an accurate diagnosis to be made. Once it has decayed, secondary organisms invade the tissue and evidence of the primary pathogen is often obscured.

For these reasons, it is difficult to construct a foolproof key for the diagnosis of plant problems. Even with the necessary laboratory equipment at one's disposal, it is often difficult to determine the exact cause of a plant's problem.

The following pages provide an aid to diagnosing some of the common problems of urban plants. This chapter was constructed to help solve consumer's plant problems — it is not meant for diagnosis of commercial problems or use by laboratory diagnosticians. The information provided is by no means comprehensive, and other resources will be needed for many of your diagnoses.

A Systematic Approach to Diagnosing Plant Damage

Determining what factors caused damage to a plant requires an inquisitive, investigative approach combined with careful observation and the ability to put all the pieces together to reconstruct the event(s) that produced the plant damage. Accurate diagnosis must be made before corrective action can be taken. Even if no corrective measures are available, there is satisfaction in simply knowing what the problem is and what its future development might be.

Living (biotic) factors: Living organisms such as pathogens (fungi, bacteria, viruses, nematodes), and pests (insects, mites, mollusks, rodents, etc.). With living factors, "Something is missing, and something is gained."

Nonliving (abiotic) factors: Mechanical factors (breakage, abrasions, etc.), physical/environmental factors (extremes of temperature, light, moisture, oxygen, lightning), and chemical factors (chemical phytotoxicities, nutritional disorders, etc.).

If we suspect that it is a living damaging factor, we will look for signs and symptoms to distinguish between pathogens and pests. If the accumulated evidence suggests that it is a pathogen, we will seek evidence to distinguish among fungal, bacterial, viral pathogens, and nematodes. If the evidence indicates the damaging factor is an insect or other animal, we will seek further evidence to distinguish between sucking and chewing types.

The probability of a correct diagnosis based on only one or two clues or symptoms is low. Similarities of symptoms produced on the same plant by completely different factors frequently make the use of symptoms alone inadequate.

In diagnosing plant damage, a series of deductive steps can be followed to gather information and clues from the big, general situation down to the specific, individual plant or plant part. Through this systematic, diagnostic process of deduction and elimination, the most probable cause of the plant damage can be determined. Steps to follow in gathering diagnostic information are presented below. Each step will then be expanded and guidelines presented as we proceed through the diagnostic process. We will first identify the problem, then attempt to distinguish between living and nonliving damaging factors based on the observed damage patterns, development of the patterns with time, and other diagnostic signs.

Factors causing plant damage can be grouped into two major categories: If evidence indicates that the damage is being caused by a nonliving factor, we will seek further evidence as to whether the initial damage is occurring in the root or aerial environment. We will then attempt to determine if the damage results from mechanical factors, from extremes in physical factors (such as extremes of temperature, light, moisture, or oxygen), or from chemical factors (phytotoxic chemicals or nutritional disorders). Once we have identified the plant and limited the range of probable causes of the damage, we can obtain further information to confirm our diagnosis from reference books, specialists such as plant pathologists, entomologists, horticulturists, and/or laboratory analyses.

Model for Diagnosing Plant Damage

I. Define the Problem: Determine that a "real" problem exists.

1. Identify plants and know characteristics. Establish what the "normal" plant would look like at this time of year. Describe the "abnormality": Symptoms & Signs.
2. Examine the entire plant and its community. Determine the primary problem and part of the plant where initial damage occurred.

II. Look for Patterns: On more than one plant? On more than one plant species?

1. Understand nonuniform damage pattern (scattered damage on one or only a few plant species) is indicative of living factors (pathogens, insects, etc.).
2. Understand uniform damage pattern over a large area (i.e., damage pattern on several plant species) and uniform pattern on the individual plant and plant parts indicates nonliving factors (mechanical, physical, or chemical factors).
3. Compare patterns of living and nonliving factors on plant community, plant, plant part.

III. Delineate Time-Development of Damage Pattern

1. Progressive spread of the damage on a plant onto other plants or over an area with time indicates damage caused by living organisms.
2. Damage occurs, does not spread to other plants or parts of the affected plant. There is a clear line of demarcation between damaged and undamaged tissues. These clues indicate nonliving damaging factors.

IV. Determine Causes of the Plant Damage: Ask questions and gather information.

1. Distinguish among living factors:
    - Symptoms and signs of pathogens
    - Symptoms and signs of insects, mites, and other animals
2. Distinguish among nonliving factors:
    1. Mechanical factors
    2. Physical factors (temperature extremes, light extremes, oxygen and moisture extremes)
    3. Chemical factors (damage patterns in fields and other plantings, injury patterns on individual plants, pesticide-pollutant

phytotoxicities/damage patterns, nutritional disorders)

3. References (check reports of damaging factors on identified plant); may need laboratory analysis to narrow range of probable causes.

V. Synthesis of Information to Determine Probable Causes

Define the Problem

Identify Plant and Know Characteristics

Is the growth and appearance of the identified plant normal? Is it abnormal?

Determine that a real problem exists. It is essential that the plant be identified (genus, species, and cultivar or variety) so that the normal appearance of that plant can be established either by personal knowledge or by utilizing plant reference books. Many horticultural plants or structures on those plants such as fruits, seeds, lenticels, etc. may appear to be abnormal to the person who is not familiar with the specific plant. For example, the 'Sunburst' honey locust might appear to be suffering from a nutrient deficiency because of its chlorotic yellow-green leaf color, but it was selected because of this genetic characteristic. It is not abnormal for this plant; therefore, it is not a problem.

Always compare the typical diseased plant with a healthy or normal plant, since normal plant parts or seasonal changes are sometimes mistakenly assumed to be evidence of disease. Examples are the brown, spore-producing bodies on the lower surface of leaves of ferns.

These are the normal propagative organs of ferns. Also in this category are the small, brown, club-like tips that develop on arborvitae foliage in early spring. These are the male flowers, not deformed shoots. Small galls on the roots of legumes, such as beans and peas, are most likely nitrogen-fixing nodules essential to normal development and are not symptoms of root-knot nematode infection. The leaves of some plants, such as some rhododendron cultivars, are covered by conspicuous fuzz-like epidermal hairs. This is sometimes thought to be evidence of disease, but it is a normal part of the leaf. Varieties of some plants have variegated foliage that may resemble certain virus diseases. These examples illustrate the importance of knowing what the normal plant looks like before attributing some characteristic to disease.

In describing the plant "abnormality," distinguish between symptoms and signs. Symptoms are changes in the growth or appearance of the plant in response to living or nonliving damaging factors. Many damaging factors can produce the same symptoms; symptoms are not definitive. Signs are evidence of the damaging factor (pest or pathogen life stages, secretions, mechanical damage, chemical residues, records of weather extremes or chemical applications, damage patterns). Patterns of damage are excellent signs and are definitive diagnostic clues.

Examine the Entire Plant and Its Community

In defining a plant problem, it is essential to determine the real primary problem. There are foliage symptoms that may occur due to root damage. The primary problem would be root damage, not **chlorosis** of the foliage — examine the roots. In general, if the entire top of the plant or entire branches are exhibiting abnormal characteristics, examine the plant downward to determine the location of the primary damage. Look for the factor causing the damage at the periphery of the plant damage.

Some pathogens and insects as well as nonliving factors are only damaging if the plant has been predisposed by other primary factors. For example, borers generally only attack trees that are already predisposed by moisture or other physical stress. Premature dropping of leaves by foliage plants (like *Ficus benjamina*) and of needles by conifers frequently causes alarm. Evergreen plants normally retain their leaves for 3-6 years and lose the oldest gradually during each growing season.

This normal leaf drop is not noticed. However, prolonged drought or other stress factors may cause the tree as a whole to take on a yellow color for a short period and may accelerate leaf loss. If the factors involved are not understood, this often causes alarm. The leaves that drop or turn yellow are actually the oldest leaves on the tree, and their dropping is a protective mechanism which results in reduced water loss from the plant as a whole.

Normal versus abnormal needle drop or leaf drop from evergreens

Non-deciduous plants normally retain their leaves for several years but eventually they fall. This drop is usually gradual, and production of new leaves obscures the loss of older leaves.

Normal: If drop is confined to older leaves, alarm is unnecessary because it is a normal response to a condition of stress (e.g., drought). Unfavorable growing conditions such as drought may accelerate leaf fall so that it becomes apparent and of concern.

Abnormal: If newly produced leaves are lost, it is a problem. The drop of current year's leaves may result from a pathogen or insect attack or from chemical deficiencies or toxicities.

Figure 6-1: Normal leaf drop among older leaves nearer to trunk (top) versus abnormal leaf drop from newer leaves towards tip of branch (bottom).

Look for Patterns

Here is where we start making the distinction between living and nonliving factors that cause plant damage.

Understand Nonuniform Damage Pattern

Living factors

There is usually no discernible, widespread pattern of damage on a planting. Damage produced by living organisms, such as pathogens or pests, generally results from their using the plant as a food source. Living organisms are generally rather specific in their feeding habits and do not initially produce a wide-spread, discernible damage pattern. Plants become abnormal. Tissues are destroyed or removed, become deformed, or proliferate into galls.

Living organisms are specific (damage may be greatest on or limited to one species of plant).

Living organisms multiply and grow with time; therefore, they rarely afflict 100% of the host plants at one time. The damage is progressive over time. Likewise, the damage generally is initially limited to only one part of the plant and spreads from that initial point of attack with time.

Living organisms usually leave "signs" like excrement, cast skins, mycelium, eggs, etc.

Understand Uniform Damage Pattern

Nonliving factors

Damage patterns produced by nonliving factors such as frost or applications of toxic chemicals are generally recognizable and widespread. Damage will appear on all leaves of a certain age (for example, on all the leaves forming the plant canopy at the time a toxic spray was applied) or exposure (all leaves not shaded by overlapping leaves on the southwest side of a plant may be damaged by high temperatures resulting from intense sunlight). Damage will likely appear on more than one type or species of plant (look for similar damage patterns on weeds, neighboring plants, etc.) and over a relatively large area.

Compare Patterns

The following figures provide a comparison of patterns of living and nonliving factors on plant community, plant, and plant part and discuss these factors.

A. Entire or major portion of top dying: If all or a major portion of a tree or shrub dies, suspect a problem with the roots. Look for damaging factors at junction of normal and abnormal plant tissue.

Gradual decline of entire plant or a major portion of it is caused by living factors such as Armillaria root rot, Verticillium wilt, and root weevil.

Sudden decline is generally caused by a nonliving factor such as a toxic chemical in the soil or drastic climatic changes such as freezing or drought.

B. Single branch dying: If scattered damage occurs in the plant canopy, suspect that the primary problem is related to the foliage or aerial environment, not the roots.

Gradual death of a branch: If scattered branches start to decline and eventually die, suspect a living organism such as a canker pathogen, a shoot blight, or borers.

Sudden death of a branch: If a branch dies suddenly, and especially if affected branches are concentrated on one side of the plant, suspect a nonliving factor such as weather (wind, snow, etc.), animal damage, or chemical drift.

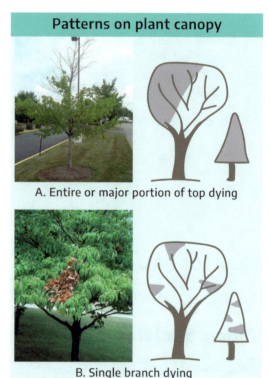

Figure 6-2: Patterns of dieback on plant canopy. A. Shows canopy death due to urban tree decline B. shows branch death due to dogwood twig borer (*Oberea tripunctata*).

A. Shoot dieback caused by nonliving factors: Sudden dying back of a shoot usually indicates a nonliving cause such as climatic or chemical damage, not a living factor. Damage caused by nonliving factors usually results in a sharp line between affected and healthy bark.

If dieback is more gradual and there is also cracking of the bark and wood, suspect winter injury.

B. Shoot dieback (blight) caused by living factors: Gradual decline of shoots and retention of dead leaves may indicate a living factor.

The margin between affected and healthy tissue is often irregular and sunken.

There may be small, pin-like projections or bumps over the surface of dead bark. These are spore-producing structures of pathogenic fungi.

However, small, woody bumps radiating from all sides of twigs of dwarf Alberta spruce are **pulvinus**, woody projections where needles were attached. This is a taxonomic identifying characteristic of spruce.

Figure 6-3: A. Dieback on branch due to cold injury B. Dieback on branch due to Phomopsis blight (Phomopsis juniperivora).

Death of the tips of conifer needles producing a uniform pattern usually indicates a nonliving factor such as a toxic chemical or unfavorable climatic condition. Air pollutants frequently cause tip burn on conifers as do certain soil-applied herbicides or excess fertilizer.

Drought and freezing may have a similar effect. In these cases all needles of a specific growth period are usually affected, and usually the same length on each needle is affected.

The margin between the affected tissue (usually reddish brown) and healthy tissue is sharp and distinct.

Damage by living organisms, such as fungi and insects, to needles usually occurs in a random, scattered pattern and rarely kills all needles of a particular growth period. Needles are usually affected over varying lengths and often appear straw yellow or light tan in color. Black fruiting bodies of causal fungus may be present on diseased needles.

Figure 6-4: Needle damage.

Delineate Development

As already mentioned, another clue for distinguishing between living and nonliving factors causing plant damage is to observe the development of the pattern.

Living organisms generally multiply with time and produce an increasing spread of the damage over a plant or planting with time, and therefore are progressive.

Spots are usually uniformly and evenly distributed over the leaf surface, and generally will be of uniform size. Color is usually uniform across the spot.

Injury from chemicals taken up by plants from soil through roots or from air through leaves usually results in scorching (necrosis) of leaf margins and interveinal areas. If severe, necrotic tissue may drop out giving a ragged appearance. Similar patterns are produced by moisture stress. If uptake of toxic chemical is to a fully expanded leaf, toxicity is marginal and interveinal. If uptake is to an unexpanded leaf, toxicity occurs in veins.

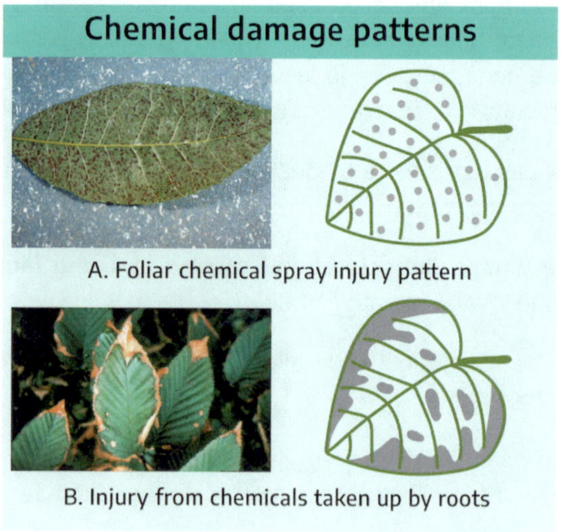

Nonliving factors generally damage the plant at a given point in time; for example, death of leaf tissue caused by a phytotoxic chemical is immediate and does not spread with time. There are exceptions. If a nonliving damaging factor is maintained over time, the damage will also continue to intensify with time. For example, if a toxic soil or air chemical is not removed, damage to plants within the contaminated area will continue to develop, but damage will not spread to plants in uncontaminated areas. Nonliving factors are not progressive. This again reemphasizes the necessity of piecing together multiple clues to identify the most probable factor causing plant damage.

Figure 6-5: Chemical damage from: A. Sulfur dioxide in a consistent pattern across pecan leaf; B. Flouride injury on birch which is concentrated around leaf margins.

Determine Causes

Patterns of damage distribution and time patterns in development of damage have been valuable in making the gross distinction between damage caused by living factors and damage caused by nonliving factors. Additional clues must be obtained to distinguish among factors within the living and nonliving categories.

Distinguish Among Living Factors

To further identify which subcategory of living factor caused the damage, a close examination of the symptoms and signs is required.

Symptoms are the modified appearance of the affected plant, for example necrotic tissues, chlorosis, cankers, galls, leaf distortion.

Signs are the presence of the actual organism or evidence directly related to it: visual observation of the insect on the leaf, presence of fungal mycelium, spores, insect egg masses, insect frass, mite webbing, etc. Signs can be used as clues in identifying the specific living organism that produced the plant damage.

A combination of clues from both symptoms and signs are required for preliminary distinction between pathogen and insect-mite damage.

Symptoms and Signs of Pathogens: Differentiating between bacterial and fungal pathogens is not always clear cut.

Table 6-1: Symptoms and signs of fungal and bacterial leaf spots

Abnormality	Fungal	Bacterial
Water-Soaking	Uncommon	Common
Texture	Dryish-papery	Slimy-sticky
Odor	Usually none	Fishy, rotten
Pattern	Circular with concentric rings	Irregular-angular; initially does not cross veins
Disintegration	Uncommon	Common
Color Changes	Common: red, yellow, purple halos	Uncommon
Pathogen Structures	Common -mycelia, spores, etc.	Uncommon

Fungal diseases

Fungal leaf spots and stem rots are characterized by various symptoms: dry texture, concentric rings, discoloration, and fruiting structures. Fungal leaf spots and stem rots are usually dry or papery. This is especially true in dry climates. The most distinguishing clue of a fungal disease is the presence of signs: mycelium and fruiting bodies of the fungus itself. The fruiting bodies range in size from microscopic to those easily detected with the naked eye. They are found within the leaf spot or stem rot area. Each type of fungus has its own characteristic structures which enable plant pathologists to identify them.

Zones of different color or texture may develop, giving the spot a bull's eye effect. The dead tissue (tan) is in the center of the spot where the fungal spore germinated. Then as the fungal mycelium front moves outward from the point of dead tissue to healthy, not yet infected tissue on the perimeter, the foliage color changes from dead tan in the center to healthy green on the perimeter.

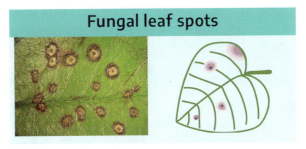

Figure 6-6: Example of fungal leaf spots. Photo shows entomosporium leaf spot. Spots usually vary in size, are generally round, and occasionally elongate on stems. (*Diplocarpon mespili*) on chokeberry leaf.

Spots are not limited by leaf veins since mycelium grows on leaf surface.

Foliar pathogens: The leaf spots caused by fungi generally have distinct margins. Many times they are circular with concentric rings resulting from growth of the mycelium from the center point of initial infection outward (much like crocheting a doily). The condition of the leaf tissue and associated color ranges from dead (necrotic tan) in the center, to recently dead (darker brown ring), to dying (darker ring with possible light yellow, chlorotic edge indicating the advancing edge of the fungal infection). The margins of fungal leaf spots (Figure 6-6) and stem rots can be brightly discolored, such as purple (Fusarium stem rot) or yellow (Helminthosporium leaf spot), making these symptoms quite striking.

Root and stem Pathogens: Root rot and vascular wilt result from fungal infection and destruction of root and stem tissues. The most common visual symptom is gradual wilting of the above-ground shoots.

Bacterial diseases

Bacteria do not actively penetrate healthy plant tissue like fungi. They enter through wounds or natural openings such as leaf stomata or twig lenticels. Once bacteria enter the plant, they reproduce rapidly, killing the plant cells.

Bacterial leaf spots are often angular because they are initially limited by the leaf veins.

Color of the bacterial spots is usually uniform. Bacteria are one-celled organisms that kill as they go. Tissue may first appear oily or water-soaked when fresh, but upon drying becomes translucent and papery tan.

Bacterial galls: In some cases, toxic materials are produced that cause plant tissues of roots, stems, or leaves to grow abnormally as in crown gall.

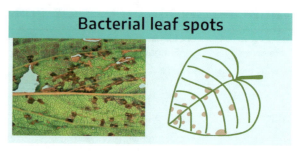

Figure 6-7: Example of bacterial leaf spots on leaf, photo shows bacterial spot of stone fruits (*Xanthomonas arboricola* pv. *pruni*) on plum leaf.

Bacterial leaf spot disease: The bacteria usually enter through leaf stomata. Symptoms include water-soaking, slimy texture, fishy or rotten-odor, confined initially between leaf veins resulting in discrete spots that have straight sides and appear angular. Many bacterial leaf spots, such as Xanthomonas leaf spot on Philodendron (also called red edge disease), expand until they reach a large leaf vein. This vein frequently acts as a barrier and inhibits the bacteria from spreading further. A chlorotic halo frequently surrounds a lesion. Lesions may enlarge through coalescence to develop blight lesions. Some lesions exude fluid containing bacteria. Water-soaking frequently occurs in bacterial leaf spot diseases such as Erwinia blight of Dieffenbachia. Holding the leaf to light usually reveals the water-soaking. The ability of bacteria (usually *Erwinia* species) to dissolve the material holding plant cells together results in a complete destruction of leaf or stem integrity. Some fungi also produce this symptom but not usually as extensively as *Erwinia*. In general, bacterial infections show this characteristic more than fungal infections. In final stages, cracks form in the tissue and disintegration follows.

Vascular wilt: In some cases the bacteria poison or plug the water conducting tissue and cause yellowing, wilting, browning, and dieback of leaves, stems, and roots.

Viral diseases

Viruses are "submicroscopic" entities that infect individual host plant cells. Once inside a plant cell they are able to infect other cells. Viruses are obligate parasites. They can only replicate themselves within a host's cell. Because the virus commandeers the host cell to manufacture viruses identical to itself, the plant cell is unable to function and grow normally. In the virus infected plant, production of chlorophyll may cease (chlorosis, necrosis); cells may either grow and divide rapidly or may grow very slowly and be unable to divide (distortion, stunting).

Figure 6-8: Vein clearing, photo shows Tobacco etch virus (Potyvirus TEV) on tobacco leaf.

Vein clearing (chlorosis) with interveinal tissue remaining green usually indicates a virus disease or uptake and xylem translocation of a herbicide such as diuron. This is in contrast to the leaf veins remaining green with surrounding chlorotic tissue associated with nutrient deficiencies such as iron deficiency.

Mosaic is a patchwork of green and yellow areas over the surface of a leaf. The leaf may also be puckered and distorted. These symptoms usually indicate a virus disease, especially if yellow areas blend gradually into green areas. If margins are distinct, mottling may indicate a nutritional problem or genetic variegation.

The symptoms of most virus diseases can be put into four categories:

1. Lack of chlorophyll formation in normally green organs:

Foliage may be mottled green and yellow, mosaic, or ringed (yellow or other pigmented ring patterns), or be a rather uniform yellow (virus yellows).

Veins: Vein clearing is a common first symptom of some viral diseases. The veins have a somewhat translucent or transparent appearance. In vein banding there is a darker green, lighter green or yellow band of tissue along the veins.

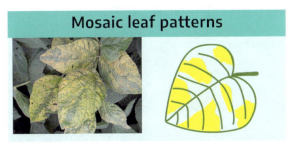

Figure 6-9: Mosaic leaf pattern, photo shows alfalfa mosaic (Alfamovirus Alfalfa mosaic virus) on soybean leaf.

2. Stunting or other growth inhibition: The reduction in photosynthesis due to less chlorophyll leads to shorter internodes, smaller leaves and blossoms, and reduced yield.

3. Distortions of leaves and flowers: Witches' brooms or rosettes result from non-uniform growth within a tissue or uncontrolled growth.

4. Necrotic areas or lesions: Being obligate parasites, viruses require the survival of their host plant for their own procreation. Hence, viruses rarely cause death. Necrosis that does occur is usually confined to discrete areas of the plant; necrosis rarely occurs to such an extent that the entire plant is killed.

Viruses typically discolor, deform, or stunt plants rather than induce necrosis or cause death. Expressed symptoms (chlorosis, stunting, distortions) can be valuable clues for virus identification, but can be easily confused with symptoms induced by other problems such as nutritional disorders, spray injuries, or certain feeding damage induced by mites or insects. In addition, because of their extremely small size, the virus or signs of the virus are not visible to the unaided eye. The virus particles are detectable within the plant cell through the electron microscope.

Viruses are transmitted from plant to plant by insects, mites, fungi and nematodes, rubbing, abrasion, or other mechanical means (including grafting or other forms of vegetative propagation). Viruses are occasionally transmitted in seed. Because of the nature of virus transmission, virus symptoms generally spread with time from one infected plant tissue to other plant tissues or from one infected plant to other plants in the community.

Nematodes

Plant nematodes are microscopic roundworms that damage plant tissues as they feed on them. Many feed on or in root tissues. A few feed on foliage or other above-ground organs.

Shoot nematodes: (*Aphelenchoides* spp.)**:** Foliar nematodes feed inside leaves between major veins causing chlorosis and necrosis. Injury is most often seen at the base of older foliage. When plants with a net-like pattern of veins become infested with foliar nematodes, the tissues collapse in wedge-shaped areas and then change color.

Root nematodes: The most common above-ground symptoms caused by root-infesting nematodes result from damaged root systems. Moisture and nutrient stress symptoms and general stunting are common. The root lesion nematodes (*Pratylenchus* spp.) and burrowing nematodes (*Radopholus similis*) destroy the root cortex tissues as they feed. The root-knot nematodes (*Meloidogyne* spp.) inject growth-regulating substances into root tissues as they feed, stimulating growth of large tender cells to provide themselves a permanent feeding site, and causing overgrowth of root tissues around them to form visible, swollen galls or knots. Other root nematodes stunt growth, apparently by killing root meristems.

Symptoms and Signs of Insects, Mites, and Other Animals

Insects

The location of the feeding damage on the plant caused by the insect's feeding, and the type of damage (damage from chewing or from sucking mouth parts) are the most important clues in determining that the plant damage is insect-caused and in identifying the responsible insect.

An insect's life cycle (complete or incomplete) is important when attempting to detect the insect or design a control program.

Feeding habits

Chewing damage or rasping damage

- **Entire leaf blade consumed:** Entire leaf blade may be consumed by various caterpillars, canker worms, and webworms. Only tougher midvein remains.
- **Distinct portions of leaf missing:** Distinct notches cut from leaf margin (black vine weevil adult), circular holes cut from margin of leaf (leaf cutter bees), small randomly scattered holes in leaf (beetles, chafers, weevils, grasshoppers).
- **Leaf surfaces damaged:** "Skeletonization" of leaf surface. Slugs, beetle larvae, pear slug (pear sawfly larvae), elm leaf beetle, and thrips.
- **Leaves "rolled":** Leaves that are tied together with silken threads or rolled into a tube often harbor leafrollers or leaftiers (e.g., omnivorous leaftier, *Cnephasia longana*).
- **Leaf miner damage:** Leaf miners feed between the upper and lower leaf surfaces. If the leaf is held up to the light, one can see either the insect or frass in the damaged area (discolored or swollen leaf tissue area). Examples: boxwood, holly, birch, elm leaf miners.
- **Petiole and leaf stalk borer damage:** Petiole and leaf stalk borers burrow into the petiole near the blade or near the base of the leaf. Tissues are weakened and leaf falls in early summer. Sectioning petiole reveals insect-larva of small moth or sawfly larva. Examples: maple petiole borer.
- **Damage from twig girdlers and pruners:** Twig girdlers (like the twig girdling beetle) may chew all the way around (or girdle) branches of the host plant. Pruners like the vine weevil may eat irregular holes in plants.
- **Borer damage:** Borers feed under the bark in the cambium tissue or in the solid wood or xylem tissue. Examples: Mountain pine beetle and smaller European elm bark beetle galleries. Damage is often recognized by a general decline of the plant or a specific branch. Close examination will often reveal the presence of holes in the bark, accumulation of frass or sawdust-like material or pitch. Examples: raspberry crown borer, Sequoia pitch moth.
- **Root feeder damage:** Larval stages of weevils, beetles, and moths cause general decline of plant, chewed areas of roots. Examples: sod webworm, Japanese beetle, root weevil.

Sucking damage

In addition to direct mechanical damage from feeding, some phloem-feeding insects cause damage by injecting toxic substances when feeding. This can cause symptoms which range from simple stippling of the leaves to extensive disruption of the entire plant. Insect species which secrete phytotoxic substances are called toxicogenic (toxin-producing) insects. The resulting plant damage is called "phytotoxemia" or "toxemia."

Figure 6-10: The highly invasive spotted lanternfly is a phloem-feeding insect.

- **Spotting or stippling:** Results from little diffusion of the toxin and localized destruction of the chlorophyll by the injected enzymes at the feeding site. Aphids, leafhoppers, and lygus bugs are commonly associated with this type of injury.
- **Leaf curling or puckering:** More severe toxemias such as tissue malformations develop when toxic saliva causes the leaf to curl and pucker around the insect. Severe aphid infestations may cause this type of damage.

- **Systemic Toxemia:** In some cases the toxic effects from toxicogenic insect feeding spread throughout the plant, resulting in reduced growth and chlorosis. Psyllid yellows of potatoes and tomatoes and scale and mealy bug infestations may cause systemic toxemia.
- **General (uniform) "stipple," flecking, or chlorotic pattern on leaf:** Examples: adelgid damage on spruce needles and bronzing by lace bugs.
- **Random stipple pattern on leaf:** Examples: leafhoppers, mites.
- **Leaf and stem "distortion":** Associated with off-color foliage = aphids (distortion often confused with growth regulator injury). Examples: rose aphid, black cherry aphid, leaf curl plum aphid.
- **Galls, swellings:** May occur on leaf and stem tissue and may be caused by an assortment of insects. Examples: aphids, wasps, midge, mossyrose gall wasp, poplar petiole gall midge, azalea leaf gall.
- **Damaged twigs are split:** Damage resembling split by some sharp instrument is due to egg laying (oviposition) by sucking insects such as tree hoppers and cicadas. Splitting of the branch is often enough to kill the end of the branch. Examples: cicada.
- **Root, stem, branch feeders:** General decline of entire plant or section of a plant as indicated by poor color, reduced growth, dieback. Examples: Scales, mealybugs, pine needle scale.

Insect life cycles

Knowledge of life cycles assists in identifying the damaging insect.

Incomplete life cycle: Insects resemble the adult upon hatching, except they are smaller and without wings. As the insect grows, it sheds its skin or molts, leaving cast skins as a diagnostic sign. The adult stage is most damaging. Lygus bugs, leafhoppers, and grasshoppers are examples of insects with incomplete life cycles.

Complete life cycle: Eggs, larva (wormlike or grub-like creature that may feed on various plant parts), pupa (relatively inactive, often enclosed in some form of cocoon), and adult insect are completely different in appearance. The larval stage with chewing and rasping feeding is most damaging. Examples of insects with complete life cycles are butterflies, moths, weevils, beetles, and flies.

Other animal damage

Arachnids have sucking mouth parts and 8 legs instead of 6 like the insects. Spider mites have an incomplete life cycle (mite resembles adult throughout life cycle). Damage is often a characteristic stipple pattern on leaf which then becomes pale color on underside (severe infestation causes leaf bronzing and death). Presence of "dirty" foliage indicates small fine webbing on the underside of the foliage mixed with eggs and frass. *Eriophyid mites* cause distorted new growth, leaf margins roll, leaf veins swell, and distort the leaf (symptoms often confused with growth regulator damage).

Crustacea: Sow bugs and pill bugs feed on decaying vegetation. Not considered to be damaging to live plants.

Mollusca: Slugs and snails. Feeding injury to low-growing foliage resembles skeletonizing or actual destruction of soft tissue. Signs: Presence of 'silvering' and slime trails on foliage.

Miscellaneous animals: Millipedes and centipedes (arthropods) feed on decaying plant vegetation (many small legs, brownish or white in color, vary in size from 1/2 – 2"). Not considered to be injurious to live plants.

Small mammals: Chewing of bark and cambium tissue on small trees and shrubs is most frequently by rodents (mice, rabbits, squirrels, and possibly beavers). Signs: Note teeth marks.

Large mammals: Branches torn or clean cut by cattle, goats, deer, and horses.

Birds: Yellow-bellied sap-sucker (even rows of holes in the tree trunk). Missing flower petals, puncture splitting of bark.

Distinguishing Among Nonliving Factors

If patterns of damage in the field planting and on the individual plant are uniform and repeated, this indicates that a nonliving factor is the probable cause of the damage. We will now examine additional information and clues to determine whether the nonliving damaging factor was a mechanical, physical, or chemical factor.

Look for changes in the three categories of nonliving factors of the affected plant's environment:

- Mechanical Factors – (damage/breakage) – plant damage caused by site changes – "construction damage," transplanting damage, "lawn mower blight," abrasion, bruising.
- Physical Factors – environment or weather changes causing extremes of temperature, light, moisture, aeration.
- Chemical Factors – chemical pesticide applications, aerial and soil pollutants, nutritional disorders.

Mechanical factors

Close visual examination and questioning will often determine if the stems or roots have been broken or girdled or if the leaves have been bruised, punctured, or broken. For example, if a large *Ficus elastica* is dropped while being transplanted and the stem is broken, rapid wilting of the portion of the plant above the break will occur. Examine the plant site for signs of recent excavation, construction, paving, etc.

Physical factors (environmental factors)

Primary sources of diagnostic information are damage patterns and weather records to pinpoint time and location of weather extremes. Records are "signs" of the factor that caused the plant damage.

Temperature extremes

Heat: The highest leaf temperatures will occur in the early afternoon when the sun is located in the southwest quadrant of the sky. Therefore, lethal leaf temperatures produced by solar radiation absorption will occur primarily on unshaded leaves on the outer surface of the plant canopy on the southwest side. Portions of leaves shaded by other leaves or leaves on the shaded northeast side may be undamaged. Most severe damage occurs on the leaves most exposed and furthest from the vascular (roots, stem, leaf vein) source of water, on leaves on the outer perimeter of the plant, leaf tips, and interveinal areas. A recognizable pattern related to leaf tissue that would have the highest potential temperature and be most readily desiccated will occur uniformly over all plants in the area.

Cold: Damage will occur on the least hardy plants and will be most severe on the least hardy tissues of those specific plants. In fall acclimation, cold hardiness is first achieved by the terminal buds, and then with time the lower regions achieve hardiness; the branch crotches are often the last tissues to achieve cold hardiness. Generally the root systems will not survive as low a temperature as will the tops – root systems are damaged at higher temperatures than are the tops. On the other hand, after hardiness has been achieved, if warm temperatures induce deacclimation (for example, in the early spring), the terminals (buds) are first to become less cold hardy.

The portion of plant damaged will indicate if low temperature damage occurred before the plant achieved cold hardiness in the fall, or if it occurred after cold hardiness was lost in the spring. Reverse patterns are produced.

Figure 6-11: Examples of cold injury, includes damage on Scots pine (*Pinus sylvestris* L.) and freeze damage on sugar beet (*Beta vulgaris* ssp.).

On a given structure (like a leaf or bud), the damage will be death of exposed, nonhardy tissues in a recognizable (repeated) pattern. **Frost damage to foliage** (e.g., conifer needles) in the spring will uniformly kill all needles of a given age from the tip of the needle back toward the stem a given distance on each needle. Frost cracks are longitudinal separations of the bark and wood generally on the southwest sides of the trunk -most likely to occur because of daily, wide temperature fluctuations. **Freezing death** of dividing cells on outer portions of leaf folds inside the bud will cause distorted or lace-like leaf blade because of non-uniform cell division and growth during leaf expansion. Cold damage to the root system is primarily a concern with container-grown plants where the root temperature fluctuates more and can be expected to reach lower temperatures than would occur with the same plant if field-grown. **Cold damage to the root system** can be detected by examining the roots. Damage generally occurs from the periphery of the root ball (near the container edge) and evidence includes blackened or spongy roots with lack of new growth or new root hairs. Above ground symptoms generally will not be evident until new shoot growth in the spring; at that time leaf expansion may be incomplete (small leaf size) because of the restricted uptake of water and nutrients by the damaged root system. With increased air temperatures, the water loss from the shoots and leaves may exceed the root uptake capacity, and the plants may defoliate due to this water deficiency.

Plants Vary in their Cold Tolerance: The cold tolerance (hardiness) of various plants in the landscape has been rated by the USDA. The most recent (2012) version is based on weather data from 1976–2005. To check your USDA hardiness zone, check the USDA Plant Hardiness Zone Map (https://planthardiness.ars.usda.gov/)

Light extremes

Plants can acclimate to various conditions, but the primary requirement for acclimation is time. Plants respond adversely to rapid changes in the environment. Rapid change from low to high light intensity will result in destruction of the chlorophyll pigments in the leaf (yellowing and necrosis = sunburn). Rapid change from high to low light intensity will result in reduced growth and leaf drop; new leaves will be larger. "Sun leaves" are smaller, thicker and lighter green in color than are "shade leaves." Flowering will be reduced, delayed, or absent under low light.

Oxygen and moisture extremes

Here we are primarily considering the root environment where oxygen and moisture are inversely related. Water logging (moisture saturation) of the root environment results in oxygen deficiency. Without oxygen, root metabolism and growth come to a standstill. Consequently, uptake of water and nutrients is restricted with subsequent wilting and nutritional deficiency symptoms occurring on the above-ground portions of the plant. Drought and water logging produce many of the same symptoms on the above-ground portion of the plant. The first symptoms will be chlorosis and abscission of older leaves. Under severe, continuing moisture stress, wilting and necrosis will occur on tips and interveinal regions of recently expanded leaves and new growth.

Chemical factors

Chemical injury patterns on an individual plant

A general uniform pattern of damage occurring over several plant species and over a relatively large area indicates a nonliving factor such as a chemical phytotoxicity. Questions-answers, records, the plant symptoms, and knowledge about the mobility within the plant of the common chemicals (nutrients and pesticides) should help determine which chemical caused the damage.

Patterns of injury symptoms on an individual plant that develop because of deficiency, excess, or toxicity of a chemical differ, depending primarily upon whether the chemical causes damage directly on contact or is absorbed and distributed within the plant through phloem-translocation or through xylem-translocation.

Symptoms from direct contact of chemicals with the plant

Shoot foliage contact: Symptoms from shoot contact chemicals occur over the general plant canopy. If the toxic chemical is applied directly to the above-ground parts of the plant (shoot-foliage contact chemical), the physical pattern of application may be detected (e.g., spray droplet size, etc.). If the toxic chemical is spray-applied, the pattern of spray droplets or areas where spray accumulated to runoff along the leaf edges will show the most severe damage. If it is a toxic gas (a volatile chemical acting as an aerial pollutant), the areas between the leaf veins and along the leaf margins where the concentration of water within the leaf is lower will be the first to show damage. Injury from foliar applications of insecticides, fungicides, and fertilizers is primarily of the direct-contact type and is typified by chlorotic-necrotic spotting, especially interveinally and along leaf edges and other areas where chemical concentrates and is least diluted by inter-cellular moisture. Examples of shoot-foliage contact chemicals are foliar-applied fertilizer salts and the herbicides paraquat, acifluorfen, dinoseb, and herbicidal oils.

Root contact: Toxic contact chemicals in the root zone, including excess fertilizer, result in poor root development. Symptoms from root-contact chemicals are localized where the chemical contacts the root, but produce general symptoms in the shoot. The shoots may show water and nutrient stress symptoms (e.g., reduced growth, wilting, nutrient deficiency symptoms). The injury symptoms on the shoot and foliage from root damage by direct contact with toxic chemicals or excessive salts resembles a drying injury; the roots are unable to obtain water. Roots are injured and root tips may be killed. This will result in a general stunting of the plant. In severe cases, wilting can occur even though the soil is wet. Lower leaves generally wilt first and this is followed by a marginal drying of the leaves. Many factors injuring or inhibiting root growth may produce similar shoot symptoms. Nematodes, soil compaction, cold weather, salinity, nutritional disorders, and certain herbicides (dinitroanilines, DCPA, and diphenamid) cause root inhibition.

Symptoms of deficient or toxic translocated chemicals

The effects of mobile chemicals absorbed by the plant are dependent upon whether the chemical is transported in the **phloem** or in the **xylem**. If transported solely in the xylem system, the chemical will move upward in the plant in the xylem-transpiration stream. Toxic symptoms from xylem-translocated chemicals occur primarily in the older foliage. Deficiency symptoms of xylem-transported (phloem-immobile) nutrient ions will occur first in the new growth.

If the chemical is translocated in the phloem, it may move multidirectional from the point of absorption (i.e., it may move from the shoot to the root or the reverse). Toxic symptoms from phloem-translocated chemicals occur primarily in the new growth and meristematic regions of the plant. Deficiency symptoms of phloem-retranslocated nutrient ions occur first in the older foliage.

Xylem translocated chemicals move primarily upward in the plant to the foliage. A chemical is translocated upward in the xylem (apoplastic movement) of the plant from the point of absorption. Symptoms occur in tissues formed after the toxicity or deficiency occurs.

Toxic chemicals, xylem translocated: When toxic chemicals are translocated to fully expanded, older leaves, the toxicity symptoms generally appear on the leaf margins and interveinal areas. When toxic chemicals are translocated to immature, young leaves, the toxicity symptoms generally appear associated with the veins, especially the midrib.

- Photosynthetic-inhibiting chemicals: Injury from translocated toxic chemicals is primarily to the foliage. Plant injury generally progresses from the lower, older foliage to the top. Individual leaves show greatest injury (chlorosis) along their tips and margins or along the veins. Examples of xylem-translocated herbicides include the photosynthetic inhibitors such as the triazine, urea, and uracil herbicides.
- Shoot-inhibiting chemicals: Examples of toxic chemicals absorbed by the roots and translocated in the xylem to the shoots are the "shoot inhibiting herbicides." The shoot inhibitors cause malformed and twisted tops with major injury at the tips and edges of the leaves; looping of the leaves may occur since the base of the leaf may continue to grow while the leaf tips remain twisted together. Thiocarbamate herbicides cause these symptoms on both grasses and broadleaves. Alachlor and metolachlor herbicides cause similar injury symptoms on grasses.

Deficient nutrient ions, xylem-translocated (phloem immobile): Several nutrient ions are immobile after upward translocation in the xylem and incorporation in plant tissue. They cannot be withdrawn when deficiencies develop in the root zone and retranslocated in the phloem to the new growth. Deficiency symptoms of phloem-immobile nutrient ions develop on the new growth. Boron and calcium are quite phloem-immobile, which means that if the external supply becomes deficient, the symptoms of boron and calcium deficiency will appear first on the new growth. And, with severe deficiencies, the terminal bud dies. Iron, manganese, zinc, copper, and molybdenum are also relatively phloem-immobile and are not readily withdrawn from the older leaves for translocation through the phloem to younger leaves and organs. Deficiency symptoms are most pronounced on the new growth. Phloem-translocated chemicals move multidirectionally from point of application or source of the chemical to the meristematic regions.

Toxic chemicals, phloem translocated: Injury from phloem-translocated toxic chemicals is primarily to new leaves and roots because of translocation of chemical to the meristems. Whether taken up by the roots or shoots, these compounds are moved through the living plant cells and phloem (symplastic movement) to both the root and shoot tips. The young tissue (shoots or roots) will be discolored or deformed and injury may persist for several sets of new leaves. Examples of phloem-translocated toxic chemicals, whether absorbed by the roots or shoots, include the herbicides 2,4-D, dicamba, picloram, glyphosate, amitrole, dalapon, sethoxydim, and fluazifopbutyl. These compounds move to the meristems and typically injure the youngest tissues of the plant.

Deficient nutrient ions, phloem mobile: If phloem mobile nutrient ions become deficient in the root zone, these ions may be withdrawn from the older plant tissue and retranslocated in the phloem to the new growth. In such situations, deficiency symptoms will first occur on the older leaves. Elements that may be withdrawn from older leaves and retranslocated in the phloem to younger leaves and storage organs include nitrogen, phosphorus, potassium, magnesium, chlorine, and in some plant species, sulfur. In plant species where sulfur can be withdrawn from the older leaves and translocated to the newer growth, deficiency symptoms may initially occur on the older leaves or over the plant in general. In plants where sulfur is not readily retranslocated, the older leaves may remain green and the sulfur deficiency symptoms occur only on the new growth.

Key to symptoms of chemical disorders

I. Symptoms appearing first or most severely on new growth (root and shoot tips, new leaves, flowers, fruits, buds).

A. Terminal bud usually dies. Symptoms on new growth:

1. **Boron deficiency:** Basal part of young leaves and internal tissues of organs may become necrotic. One of the earliest symptoms is failure of the root tips to elongate normally. Terminal shoot meristems also die giving rise to a witch's broom. Young leaves become very thick, leathery, and chlorotic; in some species young leaves may be crinkled because of necrotic spots on leaf edge during development. Young leaves of terminal buds become light green then necrotic and stem finally dies back at terminal bud. Rust colored cracks and corking occur on young stems, petioles, and flower stalks. "Heart rot" of beets, "stem crack" of celery.

2. **Calcium deficiency:** Necrosis occurs at tip and margin of leaves, causing a definite hook at leaf tip. Calcium is essential for the growth of shoot and root tips (meristems). The growing point dies. Margins of young leaves are scalloped and abnormally green and, due to inhibition of cell wall formation, the leaf tips may be "gelatinous" and stuck together, inhibiting leaf unfolding. Stem structure is weak and peduncle collapse or shoot topple may occur. Roots are stunted. Premature shedding of fruit and buds is common. Downward curl of leaf tips (hooking) occurs near terminal bud. Ammonium or magnesium excess may induce a calcium deficiency in plants.

    ◦ Differentiating between calcium and boron deficiency symptoms: when calcium is deficient, there is a characteristic hooking of the youngest leaf tips. However, when boron is deficient, the breakdown occurs at the bases of the youngest leaves. Death of the terminal growing points is the final result in both cases.

3. **Ammonium excess**: Tissue breakdown – necrosis and firing of the tip and margins of the leaf. The ammonium cation in itself may become phytotoxic and result in breakdown of the plant tissue (proteolysis breakdown of plant proteins) initially producing a wet, dark-green, "steamed" appearance at the leaf tips and margins. This destroyed tissue eventually desiccates and becomes a light tan color. Excess ammonium may also induce calcium deficiency (abnormally dark green foliage, scalloped leaf margins, weak stem structure, death of terminal bud or growing point of the plant, premature shedding of the blossoms and buds).

B. Terminal bud remaining alive. Symptoms on new growth.

Interveinal chlorosis on young leaves:

1. **Iron deficiency**: Interveinal chlorosis on young leaves with larger veins only remaining green. Necrotic spots usually absent; however, with extreme deficiencies, young leaves are almost white and may have necrotic margins and tips; necrotic spots may extend inward. Potassium, zinc or copper excess can inhibit uptake of iron. High pH may also induce iron deficiency.

   - Iron deficiency symptoms are similar to those of magnesium deficiency but iron deficiencies occur in young leaves first. Iron accumulated in older leaves is relatively immobile in the phloem.

2. **Manganese deficiency:** Interveinal chlorosis with smallest veins remaining green producing a checkered or finely netted effect. Grey or tan necrotic spots usually develop in chlorotic areas; the dead spots of tissue may drop out of the leaf, giving a ragged appearance. Poor bloom–both size and color. Potassium excess can inhibit uptake of manganese.

3. **Zinc deficiency:** Stunted new growth with interveinal chlorosis: young leaves are very small ("little leaf"), sometimes missing leaf blades altogether, and internodes are short, giving a rosette appearance.

Interveinal chlorosis is not the main symptom on new growth:

1. **Copper deficiency:** Wilting and loss of turgor of young, terminal leaves and stem tips is common. Symptoms are highly dependent upon plant species. In some species younger leaves may show interveinal chlorosis while tips and lobes of older leaves remain green followed by veinal chlorosis and rapid, extensive necrosis of leaf blade.

   - There are no known reports of H_2PO_4 toxicity; however, plants may take up the phosphate anion in luxury amounts.
   - **Phosphorus excess:** Phosphorus excess is associated with impeded uptake and possible deficiency of copper and sometimes of zinc.

2. **Sulfur deficiency:** Leaves light green, veins lighter in color than adjoining interveinal areas. Leaves over entire plant may become yellowish-green, roots and stems are small in diameter and are hard and woody. Young leaves may appear to be uniformly yellow. Some necrotic spots.

3. **Xylem- translocated "shoot-inhibiting chemicals":** Shoot inhibition causing malformed and twisted tops with major injury at the tips and edges of the leaves.

   - Examples of toxic xylem-translocated chemicals include the thiocarbamate herbicides (symptoms on grasses and broadleaves) and alachlor and metolachlor (symptoms on grasses).

4. **Xylem- translocated chemicals:** Young tissues discolored or deformed and injury may persist for several sets of new leaves.

   - Examples of toxic phloem-translocated chemicals include the herbicides 2, 4-d, dicamba, picloram, glyphosate, amitrole, dalapon, sethoxydim, and fluazifopbutyl.

II. Symptoms do not appear first or most severely on youngest leaves: effect general on whole plant or localized on older, lower leaves.

A. Chlorosis general, no interveinal chlorosis. Effects usually general on whole plant.

1. **Nitrogen deficiency:** Visible symptoms include yellowing and dying of older leaves. Foliage light green, growth stunted, stems slender, yellow.

    ◦ Plants receiving enough nitrogen to attain limited growth exhibit deficiency symptoms consisting of a general chlorosis, especially in older leaves. In severe cases, these leaves become completely yellow and then light tan as they die. They frequently fall off the plant in the yellow or tan stage.

2. **Zinc excess:** Older leaves wilt. Entire leaf is affected by chlorosis, but edges and leaf tissues near main veins often retain more color (chlorophyll).

B. Vein-clearing, chlorosis-necrosis at leaf tips and margins on older-younger foliage.

1. **Xylem- transported photosynthetic- inhibitors**: When toxic chemicals are xylem-translocated to older, fully-expanded leaves, the toxicity symptoms generally occur on the margins and interveinal areas of the leaf. When translocated to young, expanding leaves, toxicity symptoms are generally associated with the veins, especially the midrib. Examples of xylem-translocated, photosynthetic inhibitors include the triazine, urea, and uracil herbicides.

C. Interveinal chlorosis. Interveinal chlorosis first appears on oldest leaves.

1. **Magnesium deficiency:** Older leaves chlorotic, usually necrotic in late stages. Chlorosis along leaf margins extending between veins produces a "Christmas tree" pattern. Veins normal green. Leaf margins may curl downward or upward with puckering effect. Necrosis may suddenly occur between veins. Potassium or calcium excess can inhibit uptake of magnesium.

    ◦ When the external magnesium supply is deficient, interveinal chlorosis of the older leaves is the first symptom because as the magnesium of the chlorophyll is remobilized, the mesophyll cells next to the vascular bundles retain chlorophyll for longer periods than do the parenchyma cells between them. Leaves lose green color at tips and between veins followed by chlorosis or development of brilliant colors, starting with lower leaves and proceeding upwards. The chlorosis/brilliant colors (unmasking of other leaf pigments due to the lack of chlorophyll) may start at the leaf margins or tips and progress inward interveinally producing a "Christmas tree" pattern. Leaves are abnormally thin, plants are brittle, and branches have a tendency to curve upward. Twigs are weak, subject to fungus infection, usually leaves drop prematurely; plant may die the following spring.

2. **Manganese excess:** Smaller veins in older leaves may turn brown. Small necrotic spots in older leaves spread margins inwards, and finally desiccate the entire leaf blade. At severe, advanced stages, young leaves also display this spotting.

3. **Molybdenum deficiency:** Chlorotic areas (pale yellow) on whole plant; leaf edges curl upwards. General symptoms are similar to those of nitrogen deficiency. Interveinal chlorosis occurring first on the older or midstem leaves, then progressing to the youngest. Sometimes, as in the "whiptail" disease, plants grown on ammonium nitrogen may not become chlorotic, but develop severely twisted young leaves which eventually die. Other characteristic molybdenum deficiency symptoms include marginal scorching and rolling or cupping of leaves. With molybdenum deficiency, nitrogen deficiency symptoms may develop in the presence of adequate levels of nitrate nitrogen in the root environment and high levels of nitrate nitrogen in the plant. Nitrate nitrogen must be reduced in the plant before it can be utilized. Molybdenum is required for this reduction, and if it is deficient, nitrate may accumulate to a high level in the plant, yet at the same time the plant may exhibit nitrogen deficiency symptoms. Molybdenum differs from other trace nutrients in that many plants can develop in its absence, provided that ammonium nitrogen is present. Molybdenum appears to be essential for the nitrate-reducing enzyme to function.

4. **Fluoride, Fluorine excess:** Foliar marginal necrosis is the most common symptom of fluoride toxicity along with chlorosis. Chlorosis along and between the veins occurs in fluorine-sensitive plants. With many plants, the marginal necrosis is preceded by the appearance of gray or light-green, water-soaked lesions which later turn tan or reddish-brown. Injury generally occurs at the tips of the leaves first, then moves inward and downward until a large part of the leaf is affected.

D. Leaf chlorosis is not the dominant symptom. Symptoms appear on older leaves at the base of the plant.

Plant dark green:

1. **Phosphorus deficiency:** At first, all leaves are dark green and growth is stunted. Purple pigment often develops in older leaves, particularly on the underside of the leaf along the veins. Leaves drop early. Phosphorus deficiency is not readily identified by visual symptoms alone. Visual symptoms of phosphorus deficiency are not always definite, but many phosphorus deficient plants exhibit off-color green foliage with purple venation, especially on the underside of leaves, and plants are stunted and remain stunted even when fertilizers supplying potassium and nitrogen are applied. Older leaves assume a purple-bronze color. Small growth, especially root development; spindly growth with tips of older leaves often dead. Phosphorus is retranslocated by the phloem from older leaves to new growth.
2. **Aluminum excess:** Aluminum appears to affect root growth in particular: root tips blacken, no longer lengthen, but become thickened. Excess aluminum accumulation in roots reduces their capacity for translocating phosphorus. Amelioration involves suppression of aluminum activity, for example by liming to bring the medium's pH above 5.5, and not by addition of phosphorus. The toxic amount of aluminum in a soil will depend upon other soil properties such as pH and phosphorus content and upon the plant grown. Media amendments such as perlite may release toxic quantities of aluminum if the media pH is extremely acid.

Leaves are thick, brittle, and deep green: (In acute toxicity, older leaves wilt and scorch from the margins inward)

1. **Nitrate excess**

Necrotic spots develop on older leaves:

1. **Potassium deficiency:** Margins of older leaves become chlorotic and then burn, or small, chlorotic spots progressing to necrosis appear scattered on old leaf blades. Calcium excess impedes uptake of potassium cations.

    - Potassium deficiency symptoms first appear on the recently matured leaves of the plant (not on the young, immature leaves at the growing point). In some plants, the first sign of potassium deficiency is a white specking or freckling of the leaf blades. With time, the symptoms become more pronounced on the older leaves, and they become mottled or yellowish between the veins and scorched at the margins. These progress inward until the entire leaf blade is scorched. If sodium cations are present and taken up in place of K+, leaf flecking (necrotic spots scattered on leaf surface) and reduced growth occur. Seed or fruit is shriveled. Potassium is retranslocated by the phloem from old leaves to new growth.

2. **Boron excess:** Tips and edges of leaves exhibit necrotic spots coalescing into a marginal scorch. Symptom from the plant's base upwards with older leaves being affected first. In advanced, severe toxicity, necrotic spots with a pale brown center also appear in the inner parts of the leaf blade.
3. **Direct-contact of toxic chemical with shoot and foliage:** Mottling and necrotic spots primarily on margin and interveinally may be due to excessive amounts of fertilizers or pesticides applied as foliar sprays. Examples of shoot direct-contact toxic chemicals include the shoot-foliage applied herbicides paraquat, acifluofen, dinoseb, and the herbicidal oils which produce this type of symptom.
4. **Direct-contact injury by toxic chemicals** (or other factors in the root zone, e.g., low temperatures, nematodes, root weevils)**:** Reduced growth and wilting of older leaves with development of chlorotic and necrotic spots. Roots become stunted in length and thickened, or club-shaped, near the tips: the shoots remain normal but may show nutrient and moisture stress. Under severe conditions, root tips may be killed, causing general stunting of the plant and wilting followed by marginal drying of the lower leaves first. Examples of root direct-contact toxic chemicals include excess salts or presence of toxic chemical such as the herbicides dcpa, dinitroanilines, diphenamid.
5. **Chloride deficiency:** Leaves often eventually become bronze colored.
6. **Excess salt or sodium excess:** Marginal scorching that may progress to general leaf scorching. Generally no spotting.

7. **Molybdenum excess:** Intense yellow or purple color in leaves. Molybdenum excess or toxicity in field grown plants is rarely observed. Plants appear to tolerate relatively high tissue concentrations of molybdenum. Isolated reports of symptoms from excess molybdenum include development of intense yellow color in tomato leaves and intense purple color in cauliflower leaves.

Summary: Systematic approach to diagnosing plant damage

I. Define the problem (determine a "real" problem exists).

1. Identify plant and know characteristics. Establish what the "normal" plant would look like at this time of year. Describe the "abnormality": symptoms and signs.
2. Examine the entire plant and its community. Determine the primary problem and part of the plant where initial damage occurred.

II. Look for patterns: On more than one plant? On more than one plant species?

1. Understand nonuniform damage pattern (scattered damage on one or only a few plant species) is indicative of living factors (pathogens, insects, etc.).
2. Understand uniform damage pattern over a large area (i.e., damage pattern on several plant species) and uniform pattern on the individual plant and plant parts indicates nonliving factors (mechanical, physical, or chemical factors).
3. Compare patterns of living and nonliving factors on plant community, plant, plant part.

III. Delineate time-development of damage pattern.

1. Progressive spread of the damage on a plant onto other plants or over an area with time indicates damage caused by living organisms.
2. Damage occurs, does not spread to other plants or parts of the affected plant. Clear line of demarcation between damaged and undamaged tissues. These clues indicate nonliving damaging factors.

IV. Determine causes of the plant damage. Ask questions and gather information.

1. Distinguish among living factors.
    1. Symptoms and signs of pathogens.
    2. Symptoms and signs of insects, mites, and other animals.
2. Distinguish among nonliving factors.
    1. Mechanical factors.
    2. Physical factors.
        1. Temperature extremes.
        2. Light extremes.
        3. Oxygen and moisture extremes.
    3. Chemical factors.
        1. Analyze damage patterns in fields and other plantings.
        2. Injury patterns on individual plants.

3. Pesticide-pollutant phytotoxicities – damage, patterns.
4. Nutritional disorders-key to nutritional disorders.

3. References (check reports of damaging factors on identified plant); may need laboratory analyses to narrow range of probable causes.

V. Synthesis of information to determine probable causes.

Diagnostic Keys

These are useful keys to keep at help desks. Use them to match common problems with their causes and control methods. For specific control recommendations, always refer to the "Pest Management Guide: Home Grounds and Animals" 456-018.

Vegetable Diagnostic Key

Tree Fruit & Nuts Diagnostic Key

Small Fruits Diagnostic Key

Ornamental Shrubs and Trees Diagnostic Key

Annual and Perennial Flowers Diagnostic Key

To access the fully accessible tables, visit https://pressbooks.lib.vt.edu/emgtraining/chapter/6/#:~:text=determine%20probable%20causes.-,Diagnostic%20Keys,-These%20are%20useful.

Table 6-2: Vegetable Diagnostic Key

	Symptoms	Possible Causes	Controls & Comments
All Vegetables			
All vegetables	Poor fruit yield; fruit may be small and have poor taste	Uneven moisture	Supply water during dry periods
		Poor soil fertility or improper soil pH	Soil test
	Plants grow slowly; leaves light green	Insufficient light	Thin plants; do not plant in shade
		Cool weather	
		Poor soil fertility or improper soil pH	Soil test
		Excess water	Do not overwater; improve drainage
		Seed corn maggots	Replant with insecticidal seed treatment
		Insufficient water	Supply water
	Seedlings don't emerge	Dry soil	Supply water
		Seeds washed away	
		Damping-off (fungal or oomycete disease)	Do not overwater; treat seed with registered fungicide
		Incorrect planting depth	
		Slow germination due to cool weather	Plant when ground is warm
		Root maggots	Use registered soil insecticide
	Wilted seedlings; seedlings fall over	Dry soil	Supply water
		Damping-off (fungal or oomycete disease)	Do not overwater; treat seed with registered fungicide
		Cutworms	Use registered soil insecticide; use plant collars
		Root maggots	Use registered soil insecticide
	Chewed seedlings	Rodents, rabbits, or birds	Fence or netting
		Slugs	Use slug bait (beer or commercial slug bait)
		Various insects	Submit insect for identification; use registered insecticide for specific insect (see PMG)
	Wilted plants; bottom leaves may turn yellow	Dry soil	Supply water
		Root rot (fungal or oomycete disease)	Do not overwater; remove old plant debris; rotate
		Vascular wilt (fungal or bacterial disease: mainly affecting tomato, potato, eggplant, pepper)	Submit sample for laboratory diagnosis; refer to controls for specific disease in PMG; use resistant varieties; rotate
		Root knot (nematode problem)	Check roots for galls; rotate; grow cover crops antagonistic to nematodes before replanting crop; incorporate organic matter into soil to stimulate microbial activity antagonistic to nematodes; plant French

All Vegetables			marigolds to infested area for one year and incorporate into soil to reduce nematode populations; use resistant varieties if available
		Various root-feeding nematodes	Submit soil sample for nematode analysis; rotate; grow cover crops antagonistic to nematodes before replanting crop; incorporate organic matter into soil to stimulate microbial activity antagonistic to nematodes; plant French marigolds to infested area for one year and incorporate into soil to reduce nematode populations; use resistant varieties if available
		Walnut wilt (mainly affecting tomato)	Rule out vascular wilt disease with laboratory diagnosis; do not plant tomatoes near walnut or butternut trees; sever roots bordering garden and place barrier between tree and garden
		Waterlogged soil	Improve drainage
		Insects with sucking mouthparts, such as aphids and true bugs	Submit insect for identification; use registered insecticide for specific insect (see PMG)
	General leaf yellowing; no wilting	Nutrient or mineral deficiency; improper soil pH	Soil test
		Insufficient light	Thin plants
	Leaves stippled with tiny white spots	Spider mites	Treat with registered miticide
		Air pollution (ozone)	
		Leafhoppers, thrips, or aphids	Submit insect for identification; use registered insecticide for specific insect (see PMG)
	Leaf margins turn brown and shrivel	Dry soil	Supply water
		Salt damage	Do not place garden where de-icing salt may have been applied on nearby concrete
		Fertilizer burn	Soil test for soluble salts level; do not over-apply fertilizer; flush soil with water
		Potassium deficiency	Soil test
		Cold injury	
		Thrips	Treat with registered insecticide
		Mites	Treat with registered miticide
	Discrete brown spots on leaves; some spots may coalesce	Fungal or bacterial leaf spot disease	Submit sample for laboratory diagnosis; refer to controls for specific disease in PMG
		Chemical injury from contact burn-type chemical	Do not apply chemicals that are not registered for use on the plant; apply chemicals at registered rates; some chemical injury occurs from drift
		Four-lined plant bugs	Use registered insecticide

All Vegetables	White powdery growth on upper and lower leaf surfaces	Powdery mildew (fungal disease)	Use registered fungicide; use resistant varieties
	Leaves shredded or stripped from plant	Hail damage	
		Rodents	Place fence around garden
		Slugs	Use slug bait
		Dead tissue dropping out, following fungal or bacterial infection	Submit sample for laboratory diagnosis; refer to controls for specific disease in PMG
		Various insects	Submit insect for identification; use registered insecticide for specific insect (see PMG)
	Leaves with yellow and green mosaic or mottled pattern; leaves may be puckered and plant stunted	Viral disease	Use resistant varieties if available; weed control; remove affected plants; remove old plant debris; insect control
	Leaves curled, puckered, or distorted	Herbicide injury from growth regulator-type herbicide (common on tomato, cucumber, bean)	If lawn herbicides are used, apply after wind has died down and do not apply in heat of day; avoid using mulch from herbicide-treated fields, manure from animals fed on herbicide-treated fields or grass clippings from herbicide-treated lawns
		Viral disease	Use resistant varieties if available; weed control; remove affected plants; remove old plant debris; insect control
		Aphids, leafhoppers, or thrips (insects)	Use registered insecticide; keep plants well watered; use reflective mulch
Asparagus			
Asparagus	Tops turn yellow, brown, and die back; reddish-brown, orange or black pustules appear on stems and leaves	Rust (fungal disease)	Cut tops close to ground in fall and destroy cuttings; use registered fungicide; use resistant varieties
	Shoots wilt, turn yellow, then brown; roots are reddish color	Fusarium wilt (fungal disease)	Destroy infected plants; rotate for 2-4 years; use resistant varieties
		Root rot (fungal or oomycete disease)	Rotate; remove old plant debris; plant in well-drained area
	Small spears	Immature plants	Asparagus produces small spears for the first 2-3 years after planting
		Overharvested plants	Do not harvest late into the season; plants cannot store enough carbohydrates for following season
		Poor fertility or improper soil pH	Soil test
		Poor drainage	Do not overwater; plant in well-drained area
	Spears crooked or bent at tip	Mechanical injury from windblown sand or mishandling	
		Insect injury	Control asparagus beetles with registered insecticide

		Cold injury	
Asparagus	Spears turn brown and soft	Frost injury	Protect spears with mulch on nights when cold temperatures are expected
		Root rot (fungal or oomycete disease)	Remove old plant debris; rotate; plant in well-drained area
	Leaves chewed; slime may be present on leaves; no evidence of insects	Slugs (emerge at night and hide during the day)	Use slug bait
	Spears and leaves chewed or scarred	Asparagus beetles	Use registered insecticide

Basil

Basil	Leaves with irregular browning or yellowing as if declining early; fuzzy, gray growth (looks like soil) may be present on lower leaf surface	Downy mildew (oomycete disease)	Use resistant varieties
	Wilt; leaf chlorosis; black streaking on stems	Fusarium wilt (fungal disease)	Remove affected plants; rotate with plants not in the mint family for at least 3 years; avoid high-ammonium fertilizers; varieties with resistance to Fusarium wilt are available, but they are not resistant to downy mildew

Bean

Bean	Plants wilted or are stunted; leaves may turn yellow	Dry soil	Supply water
		Root rot (fungal or oomycete disease)	Remove old plant debris; rotate; plant in well-drained area
		Root knot (nematode problem)	Check roots for galls; rotate; grow cover crops antagonistic to nematodes before replanting crop; incorporate organic matter into soil to stimulate microbial activity antagonistic to nematodes; plant French marigolds to infested area for one year and incorporate into soil to reduce nematode populations; use resistant varieties if available
		Poor fertility or improper pH	Soil test
		Root maggots	Use registered insecticide
	Failure to set pods	High temperatures, causing blossoms to drop	
		Dry soil	Supply water
		Wet soil, causing lack of oxygen to roots	Do not overwater; plant in well-drained soil
		Mature pods left on vines, causing seed production rather than pod set	Pick pods regularly
	Rust-colored, powdery spots surrounded by yellow haloes form on leaves, stems, and pods	Rust (fungal disease)	Use resistant varieties; use registered fungicide; remove old plant debris
	Soft, watery spots on leaves, stems, and pods; white moldy growth on affected plant parts; plants wilt and die	White mold (fungal disease)	Use registered fungicide; rotate; remove old plant debris

	Symptom	Cause	Control
Bean	Thin, white powdery growth on leaves and pods	Powdery mildew (fungal disease)	Use resistant varieties; use registered fungicide; rotate; remove old plant debris
	Small, brown spots surrounded by yellow haloes on leaves; leaves wither	Bacterial blight	Avoid overhead watering, which spreads the disease; use fixed copper bactericide if available; rotate
	Brown spots without yellow haloes appear on leaves, pods and seeds; leaves wither	Fungal disease (any of several)	Submit sample for laboratory diagnosis; refer to controls for specific disease in PMG
		Stink bugs	Use registered insecticide
	Leaves skeletonized; copper colored beetles with black spots or yellow grubs present	Mexican bean beetle	Hand pick beetles and grubs or use registered insecticide
	Leaves with white flecks	Spider mites	Use registered miticide
		Thrips	Use registered insecticide; keep plants well watered; use reflective mulch
	Young leaves curled, distorted, and yellow; clusters of tiny insects on leaves and stems	Aphids	Use registered insecticide
Beets			
Beets	Small, circular spots with light centers and dark borders on leaves	Cercospora leaf spot (fungal disease)	Pick off and destroy affected leaves, fungicides are not warranted
	Roots cracked; black areas on surface and inside root; plants stunted	Boron deficiency	Soil test; maintain pH between 6 and 7; apply solution of household borax if necessary (1 T household borax per 12 gal water per 100 ft row)
	Leaf margins rolled upward; leaves brittle and puckered along veins; plants stunted	Viral disease	Control leafhoppers, which spread the disease; weed control
	Misshapen roots	Overcrowding	Thin beets early
		Lumpy soil	
	Leaves riddled with tiny holes	Flea beetles	Treat early with registered insecticide
	Irregular, tan blotches on leaves	Leafminers	Use registered insecticide; root is still edible
	Root scarred or tunneled	Carrot weevil, carrot rustfly, or wireworms	Destroy infested plants; next year work in a soil insecticide at planting
Carrots			
Carrots	Brown spots on leaves; spots may appear on carrots also	Fungal or bacterial disease (any of several)	Submit sample for laboratory diagnosis; refer to controls for specific disease in PMG
	Inner leaves yellowed, outer leaves reddish purple; roots stunted and bitter	Aster yellows (phytoplasma disease)	Remove affects plants; weed control; leafhopper control with registered insecticide
	Root tops green	Root tops exposed to sunlight	Cover exposed roots with soil or mulch
	Roots misshapen	Overcrowding	Thin carrots early
		Lumpy soil	
		Root knot (nematode problem)	Check roots for galls; rotate; grow cover crops antagonistic to nematodes before replanting crop; incorporate organic matter into soil to stimulate microbial activity antagonistic to nematodes; plant French

			marigolds to infested area for one year and incorporate into soil to reduce nematode populations; use resistant varieties if available
	Plants stunted and yellowed; roots misshapen; small knots on fibrous roots	Root knot (nematode problem)	Check roots for galls; rotate; grow cover crops antagonistic to nematodes before replanting crop; incorporate organic matter into soil to stimulate microbial activity antagonistic to nematodes; plant French marigolds to infested area for one year and incorporate into soil to reduce nematode populations; use resistant varieties if available
	Tiny holes on leaves	Flea beetles	Use registered insecticide
	Light brown blotches or tunnels in leaves	Leafminers	Use registered insecticide
Celery			
Celery	Stalks tough and bitter	High temperatures	
		Dry soil	Celery requires high moisture
		Poor fertility	Soil test
		Overmaturity	Harvest when tender
	Plants stunted and yellowed; stalks twisted and brittle	Aster yellows (phytoplasma disease)	Remove affects plants; weed control; leafhopper control with registered insecticide
	Leaves curled and petioles twisted; small, sunken, light brown, elliptical lesions on stalks; pale green leaves and stalks; slimy, dark rot of celery hearts may be present	Anthracnose (fungal disease)	Avoid overhead irrigation; avoid planting celery near garlic or strawberries; rotate; plant less susceptible varieties, e.g. Meringo, Hadrian, Geronimo, Balada
	Plants wilted; soft, watery rot on leaves and stalks; heart of plant may be black	Fungal or bacterial crown rot	No adequate controls; rotate and remove old plant debris
		Black heart (due to calcium deficiency)	Calcium deficiency results from uneven water supply or improper pH; water during dry periods; soil test; maintain soil pH between 6.5 and 8
	Brown or gray spots on leaves and stalks	Fungal or bacterial disease (any of several)	Submit sample for laboratory diagnosis; refer to controls for specific disease in PMG
Cole Crops (Broccoli, Brussels Sprouts, Cabbage, Cauliflower, Kale, Turnip)			
Cole	Cracking of cabbage heads	Excess water taken up by the plant causes head to burst	Harvest heads as soon as mature
	Poor heading	Overcrowding	Thin plants early
		Dry soil	Supply water
		High temperatures	
		Poor fertility or improper soil pH	Soil test
		Root knot (nematode problem)	Check roots for galls; rotate; grow cover crops antagonistic to nematodes before replanting crop; incorporate organic matter into soil to stimulate microbial activity

Cole			antagonistic to nematodes; plant French marigolds to infested area for one year and incorporate into soil to reduce nematode populations; use resistant varieties if available
		Clubroot (fungal disease)	Check roots for large, spindle-shaped swellings (larger than root knot galls); rotate cole crops out of affected area for 7 years
		Root rot (fungal or oomycete disease)	Rotate; remove old plant debris; plant in well-drained soil
	Discolored cauliflower heads	Exposure to sun	Tie leaves over head when heads form
	Brown spots on leaves	Fungal, bacterial or oomycete disease (any of several)	Submit sample for laboratory diagnosis; refer to controls for specific disease in PMG
	Plants wilt and turn yellow; roots have large, spindle-shaped swellings (not to be confused with smaller root knots)	Clubroot (fungal disease)	7-year rotation
	Plants wilt and turn yellow; roots are discolored and poorly developed; roots may be hard and brittle	Blackleg (fungal disease)	Use western-grown, hot-water-treated seed; rotate; remove old plant debris
		Cabbage maggots	Work in a registered soil insecticide at planting time
	Plants stunted and yellowed (esp. cabbage), roots not discolored	Dry soil	Supply water
		Poor fertility or improper soil pH	Soil test
		Fusarium yellows (fungal disease)	Use resistant varieties; rotate
		Cabbage maggots	Work in a registered soil insecticide at planting time
	Heads soft and rotted	Soft rot of broccoli (bacterial disease)	Grow broccoli varieties that shed water (conical head)
		Bottom rot of cabbage (fungal disease)	Rotate; plant in well-drained soil
	Rough, brown, raised areas on undersurface of leaves	Oedema, physiological problem due to uneven water supply	Water during dry periods
	Leaves riddled with tiny holes	Flea beetles	Use registered insecticide
	Leaves chewed	Imported cabbage worm, cabbage looper, diamondback moth, cross-striped cabbage worm, or flea beetle	Submit insect for identification; use registered insecticide for specific insect (see PMG)
	Some leaves curled and yellowed; clusters of small gray or green insects on affected plant parts	Aphids	Use registered insecticide
Corn			
Corn	Ears not completely filled with kernels	Poor pollination	Plant in blocks of at least 3-4 short rows instead of 1 long row; hand pollinate
		Birds	Put paper bag over ear after pollination
		Western corn rootworm	Rotate

	Symptom	Cause	Control
	White smooth or black, oily galls on stalk, leaves, ears, or tassels	Smut (fungal disease)	Cut off galls before they turn black; remove old plant debris; use tolerant varieties
Corn	Brown lesions on stalks near joints; stalks rotted inside; kernels pink or brown and moldy	Fungal stalk and ear rot (any of several)	No adequate controls; remove old plant debris
	Plants wilted and stunted; long, irregular brown streaks on leaves; brown cavities in stalks near soil line	Bacterial wilt	Control flea beetles and cucumber beetles; remove affected plants; use tolerant varieties
	Yellowish or tan elliptical spots, initially on lower leaves	Fungal leaf spot (any of several)	Submit sample for laboratory diagnosis; refer to controls for specific disease in PMG
	Plants stunted with yellow and green stripe or mosaic pattern, older leaves pale yellow	Maize dwarf mosaic (viral disease)	Weed control, esp. Johnsongrass; aphid control; destroy affected plants; do not handle healthy plants after handling affected ones
	Small pustules containing rust-colored, powdery substance on leaves	Rust (fungal disease)	Use resistant varieties; remove old plant debris
	Plants fall down after rain	Western corn rootworm	Rotate
	Numerous tiny brown spots on leaves	Fungal leaf spot (any of several)	Submit sample for laboratory diagnosis; refer to controls for specific disease in PMG
	Leaves reddish on margins	Phosphorus deficiency	Soil test
		Viral disease	Weed control before corn emerges; aphid control; remove affected plants
	Distorted leaf or stalk: leaves may fail to unfurl or stalk may be bent	Herbicide injury (growth regulator-type herbicide)	Follow label rates and precautions when applying herbicides
	Feeding on the tip of the ear	Corn earworm	Apply registered insecticide during silking to prevent infestation
	Young plants chewed off at ground level	Cutworms	Use registered insecticide

Cucurbits (Cantaloupe, Cucumber, Pumpkin, Squash, Watermelon)

	Symptom	Cause	Control
Cucurbits	No fruit produced	Poor pollination	Be patient; male and female flowers are not produced at the same time at first; bee activity may be low due to cool weather or use of insecticides; spray insecticides in late afternoon when pollinators are not active
	Misshapen or bitter fruit	Poor pollination	See above for no fruit produced
		Dry soil	Supply water
		Poor soil fertility or improper soil pH	Soil test
	Watersoaked, sunken, brown or black spot at blossom end of fruit only	Calcium deficiency, usually caused by uneven soil moisture and poor supply of calcium to fruit during early development	Water during dry periods; apply calcium foliar spray
	Watersoaked, sunken, brown or black spots on fruit not restricted to blossom end	Fungal, bacterial or oomycete fruit rot (any of several)	Submit sample for laboratory diagnosis; refer to controls for specific disease in PMG
	Wilted plants	Dry soil	Supply water
		Bacterial wilt	Control cucumber beetles
		Root rot (fungal or oomycete disease)	Improve drainage; rotate; remove old plant debris

Cucurbits		Fusarium wilt (fungal disease)	Use tolerant varieties if available; rotate
		Root knot (nematode problem)	Check roots for galls; rotate; grow cover crops antagonistic to nematodes before replanting crop; incorporate organic matter into soil to stimulate microbial activity antagonistic to nematodes; plant French marigolds to infested area for one year and incorporate into soil to reduce nematode populations; use resistant varieties if available
		Squash vine borer	Destroy affected vine; use registered insecticide
	Wilted plants; if a cut stem piece is propped up in a glass of water so that the cut end remains suspended in the water (not touching bottom), a white, milky substance streams out within 15 minutes (make sure what you see is not debris or soil)	Bacterial wilt	Control cucumber beetles; remove affected plants
	Circular or irregular brown spots on leaves and/or fruit	Fungal, bacterial or oomycete disease (any of several)	Submit sample for laboratory diagnosis; refer to controls for specific disease in PMG
	White, powdery growth on leaves; may be on both leaf surfaces	Powdery mildew (fungal disease)	Use resistant varieties; use registered fungicide; remove old plant debris
	Yellow or brown, angular spots on upper leaf surfaces; grayish fuzzy growth on underside of spots (visible with hand lens)	Downy mildew (oomycete disease)	Use resistant varieties; use registered fungicide; remove old plant debris
	Yellow and green mottled pattern on leaves; leaves have strapped appearance i.e. abnormally narrow with leaf veins extending beyond leaf margins so that leaves appear feathery	Viral disease	Weed control before plants emerge; aphid control; remove affected plants
		Herbicide injury (growth regulator-type herbicide)	If lawn herbicides are used, apply after wind has died down and do not apply in heat of day; avoid using mulch from herbicide-treated fields, manure from animals fed on herbicide-treated fields or grass clippings from herbicide-treated lawns
	Holes chewed in leaves and stems; yellow-green beetles with black stripes or spots	Cucumber beetles	Use registered insecticide
	Squash and pumpkin leaves wilt, eventually become black and crisp; dark gray bugs 1/2 inch long present	Squash bug	Use registered insecticide
Garlic			
Garlic	Leaves turn yellow, wilt and die back; tiny, black, spherical structures the size of a pin head appear on surface of bulb	White rot (fungal disease)	Avoid moving infested soil to other areas on shoes, tools, etc., as sclerotia (the tiny black structures) overwinter and are long-lived in soil; carefully remove affected plants and the soil around them and discard; rotate with non-allium crops; use only healthy garlic for planting
Eggplant			
Eggplant	Blossoms drop; no fruit develops	Poor pollination due to unfavorable temperatures	Be patient, fruit will set when temperatures become more favorable

	Symptom	Probable Cause	Control
Eggplant	Plants wilt; bottom leaves may turn yellow	Dry soil	Supply water
		Verticillium wilt or Fusarium wilt (fungal diseases) or bacterial wilt	Submit sample for laboratory diagnosis; rotate; remove old plant debris; do not plant tomatoes, strawberries, potatoes, or brambles in the same area; use resistant varieties for specific disease
		Waterlogged soil	Improve drainage
		Root knot (nematode problem)	Check roots for galls; rotate; grow cover crops antagonistic to nematodes before replanting crop; incorporate organic matter into soil to stimulate microbial activity antagonistic to nematodes; plant French marigolds to infested area for one year and incorporate into soil to reduce nematode populations; use resistant varieties if available
	Plants wilt; bottom leaves may turn yellow, brown discoloration inside stem	Verticillium wilt or Fusarium wilt (fungal diseases) or bacterial wilt	Submit sample for laboratory diagnosis; rotate; remove old plant debris; do not plant tomatoes, strawberries, potatoes, or brambles in the same area; use resistant varieties for specific disease
		Waterlogged soil	Improve drainage
		Walnut wilt	Rule out vascular wilt disease with laboratory diagnosis; do not plant garden near walnut or butternut trees; sever roots between garden and tree and put in barrier
	Circular or irregular brown spots on leaves and/or fruit	Fungal or bacterial disease (any of several)	Submit sample for laboratory diagnosis; refer to controls for specific disease in PMG
	Leaves riddled with tiny holes	Flea beetles	Use registered insecticide
Lettuce			
Lettuce	Bolting; may taste bitter	Weather too hot	Lettuce is a cool season crop; plant early or late
	Sunken, water-soaked spots appear on lower leaves, which turn brown and slimy; heads turn brown	Rhizoctonia bottom rot (fungal disease)	Rotate; remove old plant debris; plant in well-drained area
		Sclerotinia drop (fungal disease)	Rotate; remove old plant debris; plant in well-drained area
	Sunken, water-soaked spots appear on lower leaves, which turn brown and slimy; head turns brown and slimy; hard, black, pea-sized pellets found in mold between dead leaves	Sclerotinia drop (fungal disease)	Rotate; remove old plant debris; plant in well-drained area
	Stem and lower leaves rotted; dense, fuzzy gray mold on affected areas	Botrytis gray mold (fungal disease)	Rotate; remove old plant debris; plant in well-drained area
	Yellow or brown, angular blotches on upper leaf surfaces; white, fuzzy mold on underside of blotches (visible with hand lens)	Downy mildew (oomycete disease)	Rotate; use registered fungicide; use resistant varieties
	Plants stunted; yellowed; youngest leaves curled; head soft	Aster yellows (phytoplasma disease)	Remove affected plants; weed control; insect control

Lettuce		Virus	Remove affected plants; weed control; insect control
		Nutrient deficiency or improper soil pH	Soil test
	Leaf veins and area adjacent to veins turns light yellow causing a "big vein" effect	Big vein (viroid disease)	Plant in well-drained soil: viroid (virus-like particle) is spread by a soil fungus; remove affected plants; rotate out of area for 10 years

Onion

Onion	Watersoaked spots appear on the leaves and rapidly turn brown; spots become purplish with a dark margin and surrounded with a yellow halo; spots become covered with brown, dusty mold in moist weather	Purple blotch (fungal disease)	Use registered fungicide
	Numerous small white flecks on leaves; leaves die from tips back and turn brown	Botrytis blast (fungal disease)	Use registered fungicide
		Downy mildew (oomycete disease)	Use registered fungicide
		Onion thrips (insect)	Use registered insecticide; keep plants well watered; use reflective mulch
	White flecks form on leaves and expand into elongated leaf lesions; white to purplish mold (visible with hand lens), develops on spots during moist weather; leaves drop and dry up	Downy mildew (oomycete disease)	Rotate; Use registered fungicide
	Leaves yellow and die back from tips; bulbs are soft and rotted	Fungal or bacterial bulb rot (any of several)	Rotate; remove old plant debris; plant in well-drained soil
	Dark green or black smudge up to 1 inch in diameter on bulb or neck; dark smudge is covered with stiff bristles (visible with hand lens)	Smudge (fungal disease)	Rotate; remove old plant debris; plant in well-drained soil
	Plants grow slowly, wilt, and die; white maggots inside bulb	Onion maggots	Work registered insecticide into soil; destroy infested onions
	White streaks or blotches on leaves	Onion thrips	Use registered insecticide; keep plants well watered; use reflective mulch

Peas

Peas	Plants stop producing pods; leaves turn yellow, then brown and die	Hot weather	Peas are cool-season vegetables; plant early in spring; plant heat-tolerant varieties
		Root rot (any of several fungi or oomycetes)	Rotate; plant in well-drained soil; remove old plant debris
		Fusarium wilt (fungal disease)	Use resistant varieties; rotate; remove old plant debris
	Plants stunted; lower leaves yellowed; internal stem tissue discolored brown	Fusarium wilt (fungal disease)	Use resistant varieties; rotate; remove old plant debris
		Waterlogged soil	Improve drainage
	White, powdery mold develops on upper and then lower surfaces of leaves; leaves and pods may be distorted	Powdery mildew (fungal disease)	Rotate; remove old plant debris

	Symptoms	Cause	Management
Peas	Brown or white spots on leaves, pods, and/or stems	Fungal or bacterial disease (any of several)	Submit sample for laboratory diagnosis; refer to controls for specific disease in PMG
		Thrips, aphids, or leafhoppers	Submit insect for identification; use registered insecticide for specific insect (see PMG)
	Yellowish areas on leaves; blister-like ridges on undersides of leaves and on pods; pod distortion	Pea enation mosaic virus	Use resistant varieties; weed control; insect control; remove affected plants
	Light-colored leaf veins; rosetting of shoot tips; plants stunted with poor pod set	Pea stunt virus	Weed control; insect control; remove affected plants
	Yellow and green mottle or mosaic pattern on leaves; plants stunted	Viral disease (any of several)	Use resistant varieties if available; weed control; insect control
Peppers			
Peppers	Large, sunken, tan, watersoaked spot develops on blossom end of fruit; spot turns black and mold may grow on surface	Blossom end rot, caused by calcium deficiency to developing fruits	Calcium deficiency is a problem when developing fruits receive uneven moisture; supply water during dry periods; mulch plants
	Thin, wrinkled tan areas develop on fruit and become white and papery	Sunscald	Control leaf diseases with registered pesticides to prevent leaf drop, which exposes fruit to sun
	Brown frass-filled tunnels in fruit	European corn borer	Use registered insecticide
	Dark brown, sunken spots develop on fruit (not restricted to blossom end) and leaves	Fungal or bacterial disease (any of several)	Submit sample for laboratory diagnosis; refer to controls for specific disease in PMG
	Small tan to dark brown, watersoaked spots develop on leaves; small brown, dry raised spots appear on fruit	Bacterial spot	Use fixed copper bactericide (e.g. Kocide) if available; use bleach-treated or western grown, hot-water-treated seed; avoid overhead watering
	Tiny, brown specks with pale white haloes develop on fruit; fruit may be distorted around specks	Stink bug injury	Use registered insecticide
	Brown spots on leaves	Fungal or bacterial disease (any of several)	Submit sample for laboratory diagnosis; refer to controls for specific disease in PMG
	Plants stunted; leaves with yellow and green mottle; leaves curled; fruit misshapen with brown streaks, rings or yellow, green, and red mottle	Viral disease (any of several)	Use resistant varieties if available; weed control; insect control; remove old plant debris
	Plants wilted; dark brown canker at base of stem	Fungal or bacterial disease (any of several)	Submit sample for laboratory diagnosis; refer to controls for specific disease in PMG
	Plants wilted; dark brown canker at base of stem; small, hard, brown pellets form on soil and rotted plant tissue	Southern blight (fungal disease)	Rotate; remove old plant debris
	Plants wilt; lower leaves may turn yellow	Fungal or bacterial vascular wilt disease	Submit sample for laboratory diagnosis; refer to controls for specific disease in PMG
		Dry soil	Supply water
		Waterlogged soil	Improve drainage
		Root rot (fungal or oomycete disease)	Rotate; remove old plant debris; plant in well-drained soil

Potato			
Potato	Potato tuber is green	Exposure to sun	Mound soil up around plants; do not eat green parts of potatoes
	Tubers with tunneling white worms present	Potato tuberworm	Provide adequate soil coverage when hilling potatoes; harvest as soon as crop is mature; destroy any culled potatoes as soon as possible; store tubers below 52F; screen storage area to prevent entry of moths
	Brown spots on leaves and/or stems	Various fungal diseases	Submit sample for laboratory diagnosis; refer to controls for specific disease in PMG
	Plants wilt; bottom leaves may turn yellow	Dry soil	Supply water
		Vascular wilt (fungal or bacterial disease)	Rotate; remove old plant debris
		Root rot (fungal or oomycete disease)	Rotate; remove old plant debris; plant in well-drained soil
		Root knot (nematode problem)	Check roots for galls; rotate; grow cover crops antagonistic to nematodes before replanting crop; incorporate organic matter into soil to stimulate microbial activity antagonistic to nematodes; plant French marigolds to infested area for one year and incorporate into soil to reduce nematode populations; use resistant varieties if available
		Waterlogged soil	Improve drainage
	Plants wilt; dark brown or black canker at base of stem	Fungal or bacterial disease (any of several)	Submit sample for laboratory diagnosis; refer to controls for specific disease in PMG
	Brown, corky scabs or pits on tubers; plants do not wilt	Scab (bacterial disease)	Soil test; acidify soil with aluminum sulfate if necessary to maintain pH of 5.0-5.5; rotate out of area for 3-4 years; use tolerant varieties; use certified seed pieces
	Plants stunted; leaves turn bronze to yellow color; plants wilt; tubers have raised, knotty areas	Root knot (nematode problem)	Check roots for galls; rotate; grow cover crops antagonistic to nematodes before replanting crop; incorporate organic matter into soil to stimulate microbial activity antagonistic to nematodes; plant French marigolds to infested area for one year and incorporate into soil to reduce nematode populations; use resistant varieties if available
	Tubers show irregular white or brown cavities when cut open	Hollow heart, caused by plants growing too rapidly	Do not over-fertilize or plant too far apart
	Shoot tips stunted, forming rosette; leaves turn yellow, then brown between veins; leaf margins curl upward; individual shoots may wilt; tubers show dark brown discolored ring internally when cut open	Ring rot (bacterial disease)	Submit sample for laboratory diagnosis; ring rot and brown rot are difficult to distinguish; discard infected tubers; plant certified seed pieces
		Brown rot (bacterial disease)	Submit sample for laboratory diagnosis; ring rot and brown rot are difficult to distinguish; discard infected tubers; plant certified seed pieces

Potato	Irregular brown discoloration in tubers	Early frost	
		Drought	Supply water
		Viral disease (any of several)	Use resistant varieties if available; weed control; insect control
	Leaves stippled with dark specks; have bronzed appearance and die starting with lowest leaves	Ozone injury	
	Deformed tubers, e.g. dumbbell or other shapes	"Second growth" due to extremes in moisture and/or temperature	Maintain uniform moisture by watering and mulching
	Tubers have slimy, smelly rot	Soft rot (bacterial disease)	Plant in well-drained soil; hill plants to encourage water runoff; wait until vines turn yellow and die to dig; store properly
	Leaves roll upward, turn light green to yellow and leathery; plants stunted	Leaf roll (viral disease)	Plant certified seed pieces; insect control; weed control
	Leaves roll upward, turn purple or yellow; plants stunted; aerial tubers form	Aster yellows (phytoplasma disease)	Leafhopper control; weed control
	Tunnels in tubers	Wireworms	Use a registered soil insecticide at planting time
	Leaves chewed; fat, red, humpbacked grubs or orange beetles with black stripes present	Colorado potato beetles	Hand pick beetles or use registered insecticide

Radish

Radish	Yellow spots develop on upper leaf surfaces and later turn brown with bluish-black lace-like markings; white mold develops on undersurface of spots (visible with hand lens); inner root tissue may be discolored	Downy mildew (oomycete disease)	Remove old plant debris; rotate
	Purple to black spots develop on root surface; black discoloration extends inward in radial streaks; roots remain firm	Black root (fungal disease)	Plant in well-drained soil; rotate; remove old plant debris
	Leaves riddled with tiny holes	Flea beetles	Use registered insecticide

Spinach

Spinach	Bolting	Hot weather and long days	Spinach is a cool-season crop; plant in early spring
	Pale yellow spots appear on upper leaf surfaces; grayish purple mold develops on underside of spots (visible with hand lens); whole leaves may wither	Downy mildew (oomycete disease)	Fungicides are registered but usually not practical; remove affected leaves and old plant debris
	White, blister-like spots with a yellow halo appear on undersides of leaves; upper surfaces are pale green to yellow	White rust (oomycete disease)	Fungicides are registered but usually not practical; remove old plant debris; 3-year rotation
	Irregular tan blotches or tunnels appear on leaves; tunnels are translucent when held up to light	Leafminers	Use registered insecticide before leafminer eggs are laid

Sweet Potato			
	Large cracks in potato skin	Growth cracks, caused by moisture extremes	Supply water during dry periods
	Brown or black spots on potato skin; discoloration extends beneath skin	Various fungal diseases	Submit sample for laboratory diagnosis; refer to controls for specific disease in PMG
	Brown, irregular blotches on potato skin; discoloration does not extend beneath skin	Scurf (fungal disease)	3-4 year rotation; use disease-free slips; eat infected potatoes soon since they will dry out rapidly
Tomato			
	Uniformly small (1/8") chocolate brown spots or dark spots with tan centers develop on leaves from bottom of plant to top; spots sometimes form on stems but never on fruits; leaves shrivel	Septoria leaf spot (fungal disease)	Use registered fungicide; remove old plant debris
		Bacterial spot	Not as common as Septoria leaf spot; use bleach-treated seed and fixed copper (e.g. Kocide) spray if available.
	Dark brown irregular spots with target rings and yellow haloes develop on leaves, stems, and fruit; spots on fruit are often at stem end and are sunken	Early blight (fungal disease)	Use resistant varieties; use registered fungicide; remove old plant debris
		Phoma rot (fungal disease)	Phoma rot is not as common as early blight; use registered fungicide; remove old plant debris
	Light tan spots on upper leaf surfaces; dense, olive green moldy growth on undersurface of spot	Gray leaf mold (fungal disease)	Mainly a greenhouse problem: provide adequate ventilation to avoid high humidity; fungicides used to control other diseases will control this disease in the garden
	Small (1/8") chocolate brown spots on leaves and fruit; spots on fruit are raised and scabby	Bacterial spot	Use bleach-treated seed; avoid overhead watering; used fixed copper bactericide (e.g. Kocide) if available; remove old plant debris; rotate
	Very tiny, raised specks on fruit; no white haloes around spots	Bacterial speck	Same controls as for bacterial spot
	Very tiny raised specks surrounded by white haloes on fruit; plants wilt; center of stem appears discolored brown when cut longitudinally; marginal leaf scorch with a band of chlorosis inside the brown scorched edge	Bacterial canker	Difficult to diagnose without fruit spots; same controls as for bacterial spot and speck
	Brown spots on leaves that do not fit above descriptions	Various fungal leaf spots	Submit sample for laboratory diagnosis; refer to controls for specific disease in PMG
	Dark brown, leathery spot on blossom end of fruit only; mold may grow on spot	Blossom end rot, caused by calcium deficiency to developing fruits during dry periods; moldy growth is secondary on dead tissue	Calcium deficiency is a problem when fruits receive uneven moisture during early development; supply water; apply calcium foliar spray; mulch
	Dark brown, sunken spots on fruits	Various fungal fruit rots	Submit sample for laboratory diagnosis; refer to controls for specific disease in PMG
	General browning of tomato skin; brown speckling of walls between seed cavities apparent when fruit is cut open	Internal browning (viral disease)	Use resistant varieties (resistant to Tobacco Mosaic Virus); weed control; do not handle healthy plants after diseased ones; remove affected plants

Tomato	Extreme malformation and scarring of fruit during fruit formation	Catfacing, caused by cool weather or herbicide injury from growth regulator-type herbicide	If lawn herbicides are used, apply after wind has died down and do not apply in heat of day; avoid using mulch from herbicide-treated fields, manure from animals fed on herbicide-treated fields or grass clippings from herbicide-treated lawns
	Yellow-orange blotches that do not ripen at stem end of fruit or white, papery spot on side of fruit facing sun	Sunscald	Prevent foliar diseases that cause leaf drop and expose fruits to sun
	Leaves distorted with strapped or feathery look (leaves narrower than normal, tips stretched out into thin projection, veins very close together)	Herbicide injury (growth regulator-type herbicide)	If lawn herbicides are used, apply after wind has died down and do not apply in heat of day; avoid using mulch from herbicide-treated fields, manure from animals fed on herbicide-treated fields or grass clippings from herbicide-treated lawns
		Cucumber mosaic (viral disease)	It is impossible to distinguish Cucumber Mosaic Virus from herbicide injury based on symptoms alone; however, if samples comes during spring when lawn herbicides are being sprayed, strongly suspect herbicide injury; virus is controlled by removing affected plants, weed control and aphid control
	Leaves roll upward, feel leathery, but remain green; plants are not stunted	Excess water	Common physiological disorder after wet periods; varieties Big Boy, Floramerica, and Beefsteak are especially susceptible
	Plants wilted; bottom leaves may turn yellow; brown discoloration inside stem (in vascular ring)	Fungal or bacterial vascular wilt disease	Submit sample for laboratory analysis; resistant varieties are available for some vascular wilt diseases
		Walnut wilt, caused by toxin from walnut tree	Rule out vascular wilt disease with laboratory diagnosis; do not plant tomatoes near walnut or butternut trees; sever roots bordering garden and place barrier between tree and garden
	Plants stunted, wilted, and yellowed; nodules on roots	Root knot (nematode problem)	Check roots for galls; rotate; grow cover crops antagonistic to nematodes before replanting crop; incorporate organic matter into soil to stimulate microbial activity antagonistic to nematodes; plant French marigolds to infested area for one year and incorporate into soil to reduce nematode populations; use resistant varieties if available
	Young plants cut off at ground level	Cutworms	Use cutworm collars or registered insecticide
	Young plants with many tiny holes in leaves	Flea beetles	Tomatoes will tolerate a lot of flea beetle damage if they are healthy; when necessary, use a registered insecticide
	Tiny, white-winged insects on undersides of leaves	Whiteflies	Yellow sticky boards (smeared with grease) will attract and trap adults or use registered insecticide

Table 6-3: Tree Fruit & Nuts Diagnostic Key

	Symptoms	Possible Causes	Controls & Comments
Problems Common to Many Trees Bearing Fruits and Nuts			
Many	Premature fruit drop	Natural thinning	Many trees produce more fruit than they need and thin themselves naturally
		Spring frost	Frost often kills developing fruits or buds
		Poor pollination	Tree may require an appropriate pollinator tree nearby to pollinate it; be careful not to kill bees with insecticides
		Environmental stress	Drought, cold, or hear can cause fruit to drop
		Disease stress	See controls under specific diseases
		Use of Sevin insecticide	Sevin causes some fruit thinning; do not misuse
		Various insects	Submit insect for laboratory identification
	Poor fruit development (small number of fruit on tree)	Poor pollination	Tree may require an appropriate pollinator tree nearby to pollinate it; be careful not to kill bees with insecticides
		Biennial bearing	Some apples and pears may produce a heavy crop one year and few fruits the following year
		Improper pruning	Do not prune off fruit-bearing wood during the dormant season; consult pruning chapter for proper pruning timings
		Frost injury	
	Fruits too small	Failure to prune or thin fruit	Peaches, nectarines, plums, and apples tend to produce many small fruits if not pruned; consult pruning chapter for proper instructions
		Poor soil fertility	Soil test
	Fruit misshapen; "cat faces"	Tarnished plant bug	Follow spray schedule
	Many small twigs broken off	Squirrel damage	Squirrels prune twigs for nest-building and often prune more than they need
		Wind damage	
	Oozing sap on branches or trunk	Natural gummosis	Cherries, plums, apricots, and peaches naturally ooze sap
		Environmental stress	Drought or waterlogging can cause fruit trees to ooze sap excessively
		Mechanical injury	
		Disease or insect damage	See section on specific diseases and insects
		Shothole borer	Promote vigorous growth

Many	Large areas of split bark; no decay evident	Frost cracks	Frost can split tree trunks if sap in trunk expands; use tree-wrap to protect bark from sun to prevent extremes in temperature
		Sunscald	Thin-barked trees, e.g. young ones, split when exposed to intense sunlight; use tree wrap or block sun with board on bright days
		Mechanical injury, e.g. lawn mower	Dig up grass around trunk and replace with mulch to avoid mowing too closely to base of tree
		Lightning injury	
	Large areas of split bark; decay evident in wood	Secondary decay of any of the wounds described above	No adequate controls; remove loose bark; water and fertilize tree when necessary
		Fungal or bacterial (any of several)	Same as for secondary decay canker
	Gray or white powdery growth on leaves or flowers; leaves and fruit may be distorted	Powdery mildew (fungal disease)	Use registered fungicide
	Black, sooty growth on leaves, stems, and/or fruit	Sooty mold (fungus that grows on honeydew substance secreted by aphids and other insects)	Identify insect then control as warranted
	Brown dead areas on leaf margins	Leaf scorch, caused by insufficient transport of water to leaves	Water tree deeply during dry periods; scorch is usually caused by hot, dry weather, but root rot or other root problems can cause leaf scorch, as well.
		Cold injury	This would appear suddenly. Check weather history.
	Trees wilted/may have poor color	Dry soil	Water deeply during drought
		Root rot (fungal disease)	Improve drainage
		Root knot or root feeding nematodes	Submit soil sample for nematode assay
		Various fungal, bacterial, or viral diseases	Submit for laboratory analysis
		Waterlogged soil	Improve drainage
	Interveinal yellowing of leaves; no wilting	Nutrient or mineral deficiency; incorrect soil pH	Soil test
		Waterlogged soil, resulting in poor transport of nutrients to leaves	Improve drainage
	Large, corky galls at base of tree and on roots	Crown gall (bacterial disease)	Some galls can be pruned out, but it is best to consult with a certified arborist; trees may live for many years in spite of galls; avoid wounding trees and choose rootstock that is resistant to crown gall
	Young leaves curled and distorted; clusters of insects on undersides of leaves	Aphids	Use registered insecticide; thoroughly cover undersides of leaves
	Silk tents in branch crotches in spring	Eastern tent caterpillar	Physically remove tents or use registered insecticide when caterpillars are small
	Silk tents on ends of branches in mid or late summer	Fall webworm	Same as for Eastern tent caterpillar

Many	Crescent-shaped scars on fruit; whitish legless grubs with brown heads present	Plum curculio	Use registered insecticide on a regular schedule
	Leaves with tiny white spots, often dirty with webbing	Spider mites	Use registered miticide
	Bark encrusted with tiny, slightly raised bumps; apples may have red spots with white centers	San Jose scale	Use a dormant oil spray or treat with registered insecticide when eggs are hatching; consult PMG for timing

Apple and Pear

Apple and Pear	Leaf spots with brown to yellowish-brown centers with dark brown border; spots on fruit are initially small and brown; progression of rot is slow and decayed tissue is firm; the fungus can also cause cankers on twigs and limbs	Frogeye leaf spot, also called black rot (fungal disease)	Follow apple/pear fungicide spray schedule; remove mummied fruit and prune out cankered wood back to healthy tissue; infection of the fruit can occur at any time and also post-harvest; fire blight infected limbs and freeze damaged limbs may develop large black rot fungal cankers
	Initial leaf spots small, circular brown to blackish, later becoming irregularly shaped with a dark border (frogeye); when leaf petioles are infected leaves yellow and defoliation occurs; no branch/twig symptoms; no fruit infection on majority of cultivars	Alternaria blotch (fungal disease)	Follow apple/pear spray schedule; prune out diseased shoots and remove fallen leaves
	Olive-brown velvety spots on leaves and young fruit; fruit spots develop into brown corky lesions and mature fruit is distorted	Scab (fungal disease)	Plant scab resistant cultivars; follow apple/pear spray schedule for susceptible cultivars
	Bright yellow spots with orange or black centers on upper surface of leaves; cuplike pustules on lower leaf surface; greenish/yellowish spots on fruit; leaf infection results in defoliation	Cedar Apple Rust (fungal disease)	Plant cedar apple rust resistant cultivars; follow apple/pear spray schedule for susceptible cultivars; do not plant Eastern red cedar (*Juniperus virginiana*) trees, which are the alternate hosts of the fungus
	Brown, roughly circular leaf spots not fitting above descriptions	Fungal leaf spot (any of several)	Submit sample for laboratory analysis
		Chemical injury	Some fungicides can cause spotting on certain varieties of fruit trees
	Sunken, light brown circular spots that grow rapidly and develop concentric rings of salmon colored specks (spore masses) on fruit; fruit mummies form and hang on tree; apple tastes bitter; cankered branches	Bitter rot (fungal disease)	Use apple/pear fungicide spray schedule; remove fruit mummies from tree and ground; prune out cankered branches back to healthy wood
	Circular clusters of tiny black specks and small sooty smudges on fruit	Fly speck and sooty blotch (two fungal diseases that commonly occur together)	fruit is still edible; specks can be rubbed off; since this is a cosmetic problem fungicide sprays are not needed for the home garden; the apple/pear spray schedule can be used if the appearance of the fruit is critical
	Unlike cedar apple rust this rust does not affect foliage; typically near the calyx end of fruit sunken, deformed lesions develop that are dark green to brown; lesions extend deep into fruit leading to fruit loss	Cedar-quince rust (fungal disease)	Use apple/pear spray schedule; do not plant Eastern red cedar (*Juniperus virginiana*) trees, which are the alternate hosts of the fungus
	Small, necrotic, dry, brown lesions on fruit skin and/or flesh; taste of lesion is bitter; usually appears in storage	Bitter pit (physiological problem)	Often associated with certain cultivars and/or environmental and cultural conditions; very susceptible cultivars

Apple and Pear			include Cortland, Honeycrisp, Cox's Orange Pippin; since various causal factors background info may help pinpoint the cause(s)
	Spots on fruit that do not fit above descriptions	Fungal disease	Submit sample for laboratory analysis
		Various insects	Use apple/pear insecticide program
	Bark on young branches is rough and pimply; tissue beneath bark has brown spots	Measles, believed to be a nutrient imbalance	Soil test
	In springtime, leaves wilt, curl, and cling to twigs; shoot tip may be curved into "shepherd's crook"; sunken, black or wine-colored cankers on young twigs, larger branches, or trunk.	Fire blight (bacterial disease)	Plant trees and rootstock resistant to fire blight; prune out affected branches on which bacteria overwinter; in late summer remove young suckers as they appear since they are very susceptible to fire blight; do not plant apples near pears which are highly susceptible
	Tree breaks off at graft union during strong winds	Poorly constructed graft	Purchase young transplants from reliable dealer
		Virus infection at graft union	Submit soil sample for nematode analysis; some of these viruses are transmitted by nematodes in the soil
	Pink-white worms bore into blossom end of apple; clusters of round, brown frass pellets inside fruit	Codling moth	Use registered insecticide on a regular schedule
	Apples dimpled with faint brown areas in flesh	Apple maggot ("railroad streaks in the flesh worm")	Use registered insecticide on a regular spray schedule
Stone fruits (Apricot, cherry, peach, plum, and nectarine)			
Stone	Initial symptoms are small, angular, gray leaf spots that later turn purple, then necrotic; shothole may also occur; leaves with multiple spots may drop and susceptible cultivars may defoliate; the bacterium also causes twig cankers/dieback and spots on fruit that are first visible several weeks after petal fall and can progress to cracking, gum exudation and fruit loss	Bacterial spot (bacterial disease) Nitrogen deficiency OR a captan + oil spray can cause similar symptoms on leaves and defoliation, so accurate diagnosis is important	Plant cultivars of stone fruit that are resistant to bacterial spot. Once symptoms are observed it is too late to control the bacterium. Prune out diseased twigs back to healthy wood, since the bacterium overwinters in twig cankers. Ensuring adequate fertility is also important in avoiding this disease, since weakened trees are more susceptible. Appropriately labeled copper fungicides can be used for suppression, but phytotoxicity is a risk if applied during the growing season. Apply at leaf fall in the autumn and/or before bud break.
	Small, circular, olive-green spots on young fruit; spots eventually turn brown and velvety; similar spots on leaves	Scab (fungal disease)	Use spray schedule for stone fruits; prune properly so that sprays penetrate the canopy
	Purple spots appear on upper surfaces of cherry leaves; leaf spots drop out leaving holes, and turn yellow; fruit may also be spotted	Cherry leaf spot (fungal disease)	Plant resistant cherry cultivars; use fungicidal spray program recommended for stone fruits
	Peach or nectarine leaves puckered, thickened, and curled from the time they first appear in the spring; leaves red or orange at first but turn yellow; shoots swollen and stunted	Peach leaf curl (fungal disease on peaches and nectarines)	Follow stone fruit spray schedule for peach and nectarine

Stone	Blossoms and young twigs wilt and decay during bloom; sunken cankers with gummy ooze develop on twigs; circular brown spots which develop tufts of gray spores during moist weather form on fruit; rot may cover large portion of fruit	Brown rot (fungal disease common to all stone fruit)	Follow stone fruit fungicidal spray schedule; remove all diseased fruit from tree and on ground: decayed fruit turns into a "mummy" on which the fungus overwinters
	Sunken cankers on twigs, larger branches and/or trunk; leaves above canker wilt	Fungal or bacterial disease (any of several)	Submit branch samples that include the junction of healthy and dead tissue for laboratory analysis. Prune out dead wood on branches back to healthy tissue. There are no management recommendations for cankers on the trunk.
	Swellings that split the bark appear on plum or cherry branches and later turn coal-black; leaves may wilt above swellings	Black knot (fungal disease of plum and cherry only)	Follow spray schedule. Prune out affected twigs at least 4" below knots; if practical remove wild plum and wild cherry trees in the area, since they provide inoculum for initial infections. There are plum cultivars with resistance to this disease and these are recommended for new plantings.
	Shoot tips stunted; leaves yellow and curled upward; severe defoliation; trees tend to break off near ground in strong winds; base of trunk may be swelled	Stem pitting (viral disease; primarily of peach)	Submit soil sample for nematode analysis; nematodes can transmit the virus or it can come in on the transplants; remove and destroy the affected trees
		Nutrient deficiency	Tissue analysis to check for nitrogen deficiency (private laboratory), soil test and analyze fertilization regime.
		Various other viral diseases	Purchase certified virus-free plants; remove any virus-infected plants; manage weeds. There are no control options for viruses other than avoidance and removal of diseased plants. Since different viruses are spread by different mechanisms, identifying the specific virus can help determine appropriate control tactics. Testing for specific viruses is limited, so it is advisable to start with submission of a digital sample.
	New growth at tip of twig wilts and dies; resin at tip of twig; maturing fruit may contain 1/2 long pinkish worms	Oriental fruit moth	Use registered insecticide to prevent damage; peach will tolerate a lot of natural pruning by this insect, so insecticides may not be necessary
	Gum oozes from holes at base of trunk or lower branch crotches; sawdust may be evident	Peach tree borers	Use registered insecticide on bark only
	Many small round holes in twigs and branches	Shothole borer	Remove and destroy all dead or dying wood; use registered insecticide to protect healthy trees
	Tiny white, flat insects encrusting bark	White peach scale	Use a dormant oil or treat with registered insecticide; refer to PMG for application timings
Pecan			
Pecan	Small, olive-colored spots on twigs and undersides of leaves; tiny black dots on shucks enlarge to form black lesions; nuts drop prematurely	Scab (fungal disease)	Plant scab-resistant cultivars of pecan. Raking and removing fallen leaves and nuts will reduce fungal inoculum for next season infection period.

Pecan	Leaf spots; no spots on nuts	Fungal disease (any of several)	Rake and remove fallen leaves to reduce inoculum available for future infections. Submit sample for laboratory analysis. There are limited fungicide controls for pecans in the home garden.
	Poor nut fill and/or premature nut drop	"Pops" – often a result of poor pollination	Poor pollination can result from stressful environmental conditions, such as drought, during nut development. Plant at least two different cultivars, spaced approximately 60 to 80 feet apart, to increase chances of good pollination. Another abiotic problem that can cause poor nut fill in pecans is called "water stage fruit split". Cultivars vary in susceptibility to this problem. Maintaining good soil moisture during the last two weeks prior to nuts reaching full size can help to prevent the problem. Other causes of premature nut drop include nutrient deficiency, which may be due to a soil problem, inadequate fertilization, inadequate water, crowded trees, etc. Also, bearing pecan trees require fertilizer. Soil samples can be submitted to check for soil nutrient deficiencies. In general, Virginia does not provide an optimum climate for pecan production.
	Nutmeats (kernels) have brown or black blotches and may be distorted	Feeding punctures (several species of plant bugs and stink bugs)	Remove any nearby weeds; treat with insecticide if insects found
	Small, cream-colored worms in immature nuts or in the green shucks after shells have hardened	Hickory shuckworm	Clean up and destroy fallen nuts to eliminate overwintering larvae

Walnut

See section on general problems. Most walnut diseases are difficult to diagnose without consulting a diagnostic laboratory.

Table 6-4: Small Fruits Diagnostic Key

	Symptoms	Possible Causes	Controls & Comments
Problems common to many small fruits			
Many	Grayish or white moldy growth on leaves	Powdery mildew (fungal disease)	Follow appropriate pesticide spray schedule.
Many	Galls at base of plant, on roots, or on canes; plants stunted	Crown gall (bacterial disease)	Avoid wounding plants, which predispose plants to infection by this bacterium. Purchase disease-free plant material. Prune out galled tissue back to healthy tissue, if possible; there are no chemical controls for home growers.
Many	Plants wilt; leaves may turn yellow	Dry soil	Supply water
Many		Waterlogged soil	Plant in well-drained area
Many		Wilting can be caused by various abiotic and biotic (disease) problems.	Submit a plant and soil sample for diagnosis.
Many	Green and yellow mosaic or mottle pattern on leaves; plants may be stunted	Viral disease (any of several)	Purchase certified virus-free plants; remove any virus-infected plants to avoid spread; manage weeds, which may harbor virus inoculum. There are no control options for viruses other than avoidance and removal of diseased plants. Since viruses are spread by different mechanisms, both abiotic and biotic, identifying the specific virus can be helpful. However, testing for specific viruses is limited, so it is advisable to start with submission of a digital sample.
Many	Leaves rolled or tied together; small caterpillars feeding inside	Leafrollers	Follow spray schedule
Blueberry			
Blueberry	Plants stunted and foliage off-color	Improper soil pH	Blueberries require acidic soil conditions; submit a soil sample for analysis
Blueberry		Nutrient deficiency	Submit a soil sample for analysis
Blueberry		Viral disease (any of several)	Purchase certified virus-free plants; remove any virus-infected plants to avoid spread; manage weeds, which may harbor virus inoculum. There are no control options for viruses other than avoidance and removal of diseased plants. Since viruses are spread by different mechanisms, both abiotic and biotic, identifying the specific virus can be helpful. However, testing for specific viruses is limited, so it is advisable to start with submission of a digital sample.
Blueberry	This fungus can infect shoots soon after bud break and also berries; white or pale-colored blueberries among normal berries are symptomatic of this disease; infected berries appear normal when green, then as they near maturity, turn cream and eventually tan or white; such berries become shriveled and hard and drop	Mummy berry (fungal disease)	Burying dropped diseased berries two inches in the soil or covering with 2" of fresh mulch will reduce inoculum for future infections.

Symptom	Cause	Management
The most common symptom of this disease is flagging and death the upper two to six inches of shoots during summer with leaves turning reddish and remaining attached to the twig; however, whole canes can also be affected	Phomopsis canker and twig dieback (fungal disease)	Prune out affected twigs or branches back to healthy tissue. Avoid planting in sites that are prone to spring frost, which can predispose plants to disease. Manage plants to discourage late season growth by irrigation and fertilizing according to recommendations. Refer to blueberry spray schedule for pesticide recommendation.
Branches die back; cankers may be evident	Fungal canker (any of several)	Submit sample for laboratory analysis
	Winter injury	Damage is commonly observed in spring or early in the growing season
Ripening berries soft and mushy	Blueberry maggot	Use registered insecticide on a regular schedule

Brambles

Symptom	Cause	Management
Shoots are stunted and leaves turn yellow at bottom of plant, wilt and drop; overall plant wilts and dies back; stem may show dark blue color (not on red raspberry) at base; internal stem tissue may be discolored	Verticillium wilt (fungal disease)	Laboratory diagnosis needed; use certified disease-free plants; use resistant varieties, 3-4-year rotation
Plants wilt, but yellowing and wilting does not begin at the bottom of the cane; stunting and foliar yellowing or marginal scorch; progressing to dieback	Dry soil	Supply water
	Waterlogged soil	Improve drainage and/or modify irrigation
	Phytophthora rot (oomycete disease)	Laboratory diagnosis needed; correct soil drainage; use a registered fungicide on adjacent non-symptomatic plants and replacement plants; remove affected plants
	Root knot (nematode problem)	Check roots for knots; rotate
	Planted too deeply (brambles do not tolerate deep planting)	Plant at proper depth
Ripening berries covered with tufts of gray, green, white, or black moldy growth	Fungal fruit rot (any of several)	Harvest berries before they are over-ripe; cool immediately
Small light grayish spots on canes that grow and develop dark border around a gray center; spots may be sunken; canes may crack; dieback; small spots on leaves are gray with purple margins; defoliation not typical	Anthracnose (fungal disease)	Submit sample for laboratory analysis; plant disease-free brambles; thin, prune and remove dead canes annually; prune out diseased canes; remove wild brambles in the vicinity; follow fungicide spray schedule
Wilting; dieback; discoloration on canes; canes may be pimply, cracked or brittle	Fungal cane canker (any of several)	Submit sample for laboratory analysis; thin, prune and remove dead canes annually; prune out cankered canes
Leaves curl downward; leaves smaller than usual; internodes shorter than normal	Leaf curl (viral disease)	Plant certified virus-free stock; remove affected canes; if more than 20% of canes are affected, remove entire planting; control aphids with registered insecticide; remove nearby wild brambles
	Aphids or blackberry psyllid	Look for clusters of small gray insects on undersides of leaves; control with registered insecticide
	Herbicide injury	Obtain background information on herbicides used in the vicinity

Symptoms	Cause	Management
Only on red or purple raspberry: yellow spore masses on fall fruit; powdery, yellow spore masses on undersides of leaves; leaves may drop	Late leaf rust (fungal disease)	Plant disease-free plants; plant resistant red and purple raspberry; promote foliar drying by cleaning out dead canes and manage weeds; remove infected canes post-season
On black raspberry, blackberry and purple raspberry: In spring leaves on new shoots are stunted, deformed and off-color and shoots are spindly and many; blisters form on lower leaf surfaces and develop bright orange, powdery spores	Orange rust (fungal disease)	Plant disease-free plants and resistant cultivars; remove infected plants as soon as symptoms are observed; thin planting annually and manage weeds; remove nearby wild brambles
Tip dies; rows of punctures around twig	Raspberry cane borer	Prune and destroy dead tips
On blackberry: Leaf spots with a brown whitish center and a brown or purplish margin	Septoria leaf spot (fungal disease)	Space plants to allow proper air circulation and thin and remove dead canes annually; manage weeds; follow fungicide spray schedule for anthranose

Currant

Symptoms	Cause	Management
Orange-brown blisters containing yellow spores appear on undersides of leaves; leaves turn yellow	White pine blister rust (fungal disease which has white pine as alternate host)	Use resistant varieties (Viking and Red Dutch); plant certified disease-free stock
Stems die back; cankers with tiny black pimple-like structures appear on stems	Fungal dieback (any of several)	Prune out affected stems
Brown leaf spots with tiny black pimply structures	Septoria leaf spot (fungal disease)	Use registered fungicide
Brown leaf spots without tiny black pimply structures	Fungal leaf spot (any of several)	Submit sample for laboratory analysis

Grape

Symptoms	Cause	Management
Brown spots with dark borders on leaves; grapes turn black, shrivel up like raisins; and remain attached to stem	Black rot (fungal disease)	Use grape fungicide spray schedule; remove mummified berries since fungus overwinters on them
Brown leaf spots	Fungal leaf spot (any of several)	Submit sample for laboratory analysis
Small yellow spots appear on upper leaf surfaces; white cottony growth forms on undersides of spots (do not confuse white leaf hairs of some varieties with fungus)	Downy mildew (fungal disease)	Use grape fungicide spray schedule; Concord grape is resistant
Fruit rot not resembling black rot	Fungal fruit rot (any of several)	Submit sample for laboratory analysis
Canes die back; dark lesions on canes; tiny black lesions on leaves	Fungal dieback (most common one is Phomopsis dieback)	Prune well below cankers; use grape fungicide spray schedule
Leaf resembles a fan: main veins are drawn together and teeth along margins are elongated; plants stunted	Fan leaf (viral disease)	Purchase certified virus-free stock; submit soil sample for nematode analysis; remove affected plants
	Herbicide injury	Fan leaf and herbicide injury symptoms are identical: if symptoms occur in spring when lawn herbicides are being applied, herbicide injury is a good bet; do not apply lawn herbicides during hot or windy conditions
Small, green, seedless grapes are intermingled with ripe grapes in the cluster	Shot berry (physiological)	May be related to genetic, nutritional and environmental factors; no control

Grapes and/or leaves webbed together; some grapes collapsed	Grape berry moth	Use registered insecticide on regular schedule
Green or red irregular swellings on leaves, canes, or tendrils	Grape tomato gall (insect problem)	Prune out and destroy heavily infested leaves and canes before the insects inside have matured
Small, rough galls the size of a small pea on the undersides of leaves; swellings on roots	Grape phylloxera (insect)	Use resistant varieties; no chemical controls

Strawberry

Small spots with white or tan centers and reddish-brown borders on leaves	Mycosphaerella leaf spot (fungal disease)	Use resistant varieties; use strawberry fungicide spray program
Purplish or brown spots on leaves not fitting above description	Fungal or bacterial leaf spot (any of several)	Submit sample for laboratory analysis
White or gray crusty material covering leaves, stems, and/or fruits	Slime mold (fungus)	Slime molds grow on plant surfaces during wet weather and disappear again in dry weather; no need for control
Gray, fuzzy mold on fruit, especially during wet periods and after frost	Gray mold (fungal disease)	Do not crowd plants; do not apply fertilizer in spring since dense foliage delays drying of berries after rains; follow strawberry spray schedule
Plants wilt; leaves may turn brown at margins; roots and/or crown appear discolored when cut open	Root and/or crown rot (fungal or oomycete disease)	Submit sample for laboratory diagnosis. If many plants show symptoms, replant in another area; plant in well-drained area; purchase disease-free transplants
	Nematode injury	Submit soil sample for nematode analysis; soil fumigation
Fruit is hard and leathery with brown spots	Leather rot (oomycete disease)	Mulch with straw or bark to avoid fruit and soil contact; plant in well-drained location; rotate if high incidence.
	Environmental stress	Poor growing conditions can cause berries to become dry and hard
Fruit is soft with brown spots	Fungal fruit rot (any of several)	Laboratory diagnosis is needed. Mulch; Follow strawberry fungicide spray schedule if fungal disease is diagnosed
Malformed berries: look like several berries have grown together	Fasciation; a response to environmental conditions	Common in certain varieties in fall and spring
Berries seedy at tips	Insect injury	Use strawberry insecticide spray program
	Mites	Use registered miticide
	Frost injury	Protect plants from frost by mulching
	Nutrient deficiency	Soil test
Flower buds droop, turn brown and may drop to ground	Strawberry bud weevil	Use registered insecticide during the bud stage
Small holes in leaves; poor growth	Strawberry rootworm	Rotate to new area

Table 6-5: Ornamental Shrubs and Trees Diagnostic Key

	Symptoms	Possible Causes	Controls & Comments
Problems common to many ornamental trees and shrubs			
Many	Many small twigs broken off	Squirrel damage	Squirrels prune twigs for nest-building and often prune more than they need
		Wind breakage	
		Twig pruner, twig girdler (insects)	Rake up and destroy fallen twigs
	Vertical splitting of bark along the trunk; sudden appearance; no decay evident	Frost cracks or southwest injury	Frost can split thin bark, particularly on young trees on the southwest side of the main stem/trunk; use tree-wrap to protect bark from temperature fluctuations
		Sunscald	Thin-barked trees, e.g., young ones, split when exposed to intense sunlight; use tree-wrap or block sun with board on bright days; avoid heavy fertilization in late summer and in fall
		Lightning injury	Use lightning rod
	Other trunk damage, not vertical splitting of bark	Mechanical injury, e.g. lawn mower, weed whacker, etc.	Avoid injury to trunk. Mulch in donut shape around the tree, so that mulch does not contact the trunk. Mulch should be in a shallow layer, approximately 2" or less.
	Large areas of split bark; decay evident in wood	Secondary decay of any of the mechanical damage described above	No chemical controls; if practical provide deep irrigation to trees during drought and fertilize, if recommended by a soil test
		Fungal or bacterial canker (any of several)	Wood decay is often difficult for a remote laboratory to diagnosis; it is advisable to begin with a digital sample; if decay is in the trunk there are no controls
	Gray or white powdery growth on leaves; leaves may be distorted	Powdery mildew (fungal disease)	Use registered fungicide
	Black, sooty growth on leaves and/or stems	Sooty mold (fungus that grows on honeydew substance secreted by aphids and other insects)	Sooty molds are not pathogenic to plants, but unsightly and can block sunlight; control insect problem to avoid honeydew
	Brown dead areas on leaf margins	Leaf scorch	Anything that interferes with adequate water uptake can cause leaf scorch and an abiotic or biotic factor could be the cause. Try to determine/rule out possible abiotic factors, such as establishment stress, lack of adequate water, etc. Submit a sample for a diagnosis.
		Cold injury	Cold damage would be distinguished by a sudden appearance. Look at weather history.
	Tree or shrub wilted and may have poor color	Wilted and off-color foliage may result from various abiotic (e.g. poor planting, establishment stress, lack of	Collect background history of plant to determine if the problem may be abiotic. If no abiotic cause (e.g. overly wet soil

		irrigation, etc.) or biotic cause (e.g. root rot, decay in the main stem, girdling roots, vascular disease).	conditions, drought, establishment stress, etc.) is identified, then submit a sample for diagnosis.
	Interveinal yellowing of leaves; no wilting	Nutrient deficiency	Soil test
	Large, corky galls at base of shrub or on roots	Crown gall (bacterial disease)	Avoid wounding shrubs since that provides an entry point for the crown gall bacterium. Some galls can be pruned out if not on main stem; shrubs may live for many years in spite of a gall.
	Few or no flowers	Cold injury	
		Improper pruning	Some plants flower only on old wood
		Overfertilization with nitrogen	This stimulates leaf production and reduces flower production
		Shade	Grow plants in proper amount of light for the species
		Incorrect fertility	Soil test
	Galls on upper branches	Fungal disease (any of several)	Submit sample for laboratory analysis; prune out galled branches
		Various insects	Most are harmless; prune out galled branches
	Proliferation of branches at specific points on the plant, forming a "witches' broom" disease effect	Insect injury	For all of these, the only control is to prune out affected branches
		Fungal, viral, or mycoplasma	
		Mistletoe	
Many	Pustules containing yellow, orange, or black powdery substance on leaves; may be on both leaf surfaces	Rust (fungal disease)	Fungicides may be useful for management, if warranted, but must be timed appropriately and that depends on the particular rust. Submit sample for diagnosis.
	Brown, gray, green, or yellow crusty, leaflike growths on trunk and branches	Lichens	Lichens are a combination of algae and fungi; they grow on bark and do not harm the plant
	Early leaf drop	Can be a result of various environmental stress factors or foliar disease or arthropod problem	Collect background information and try to determine if an abiotic factor is involved. If none is found, then submit for laboratory diagnosis.
	Browning of tips of conifer needles; faint yellow bands about 1/8" wide at the same location across groups of needles	Ozone injury	No controls; white pine is especially sensitive but individual trees vary in sensitivity
	General browning of conifer needles	Could be a result of abiotic e.g. (salt injury, gas leak, waterlogged soil, transplant shock, stem girdling roots, soil compaction) or a biotic problem.	Collect background information to try to determine if an abiotic factor could be involved. If an abiotic factor is not identified then any biotic-associated problem would likely be in the main trunk/stems or roots. Pinewood nematode is also a possibility on pines not native to north America. Submit a sample for laboratory diagnosis.
		Fungal canker	Check trunk and branches for cankers; prune out affected branches
		Mites	Use miticide

Many	Sour-smelling sap oozes from cracks in the trunk	Slime flux (bacterial disease)	Avoid wounding the tree, protect tree from other stresses such as soil compaction, and promote tree vigor.
	Yellow and green mottle or mosaic pattern on leaves; leaves may be distorted	Viral disease	No controls; removal of plant may be necessary if virus is easily spread
	Sunken cankers on trunk or branches; plant may wilt or have poor growth	Fungal or bacterial canker	Submit sample for laboratory analysis; prune out affected branches well below canker. There are no remedies for cankers on the trunk.
	Oozing sap on trunk	Normal	Some trees naturally ooze sap
		Environmental stress	Drought or waterlogging can cause trees to ooze excessively
		Mechanical injury	Prevent lawn mower injury, other wounds
		Disease or insect damage	See section on specific diseases
	Brown leaf spots	Fungal or bacterial disease (any of several)	See section on specific diseases or submit sample for laboratory analysis
		Chemical injury	
	Leaves chewed or completely eaten	Various caterpillars, sawflies, leaf beetles, etc.	Use registered insecticide while insects are small and before damage is extensive; consult PMG
	Fish scale-like structures tightly attached to leaves, twigs, or branches	Various scale insects	Submit sample for laboratory analysis; use dormant oil
	Young leaves puckered, curled, or distorted; clear, sticky substance on leaves; clusters of small insects on undersides of leaves	Aphids	Use registered insecticide
	Leaves off-color with tiny white or yellow spots; may appear dirty due to fine webbing and dust that leaves collect	Spider mites	Use registered miticide
	Galls (abnormal growths on leaves, stems, or other tissues)	Various insects or mites	There are no chemical controls for gall insects, but the plants will not be seriously harmed

Birch

Birch	Leaves sparse, especially at top of tree; swollen ridges in bark	Bronze birch borer	Use registered insecticide on bark in mid-May, early, mid, and late June

Boxwood

Boxwood	Large portions of shrub turn yellow, bronze or brown; on some leaves, the browning may only occur at leaf margins.	Winter injury	Often the damage is most severe or limited to the top of the boxwood. The symptoms typically appear in the spring. Prune out dead branches but wait until June to be sure branches are dead.
		Volutella blight (fungal disease)	Prune out affected branches
	Sectional dieback with leaves turning straw-colored. Blackened woody tissue on lower affected stems just beneath the bark.	Colletotrichum dieback	Submit for laboratory diagnosis. Currently there are no effective disease management tactics for this disease, so removal of diseased boxwood is recommended.

	Symptoms	Cause	Recommendation
	Large portions of shrub turn yellow or brown; roots rotted; brown discoloration may be evident in wood when base of trunk is cut open	Phytophthora root rot (fungal disease)	Submit sample for laboratory analysis. Improve soil drainage. Fungicides will not benefit boxwood already showing symptoms, but can protect adjacent boxwood. Use registered fungicide.
		English boxwood decline (fungal disease)	Submit sample for laboratory analysis; only a problem on English boxwood; replace shrub with boxwood other than English
		Root feeding nematodes	Submit soil sample for nematode analysis.
	Leaf spots leading to severe defoliation; green stems have longitudinal black cankers	Boxwood blight	Submit sample for confirmatory laboratory diagnosis since removal of affected susceptible boxwood (English) is recommended. Plant boxwood blight resistant boxwood to avoid the disease and purchase boxwood from nurseries that participate in the Boxwood Blight Cleanliness Program.
	Leaves are brown and have tiny black specks on them	Macrophoma leaf spot (fungal disease) (see photo 1K)	Secondary problem; prune out branches damaged by winter injury or disease
	Leaves blistered; small yellowish maggots inside	Boxwood leafminer	Use registered insecticide in early June
	Leaves at stem tips cupped	Boxwood psyllid	Use registered insecticide just as new growth starts appearing
	Tiny white or yellow flecks on leaves	Boxwood mite	Use registered miticide as soon as damage is noticed
Cotoneaster			
Cotoneaster	Individual twigs die back, turn black, and have curved tips; sunken cankers may be evident on wood	Fire blight (bacterial disease) (see photo 1L)	Prune out affected branches or remove plant if you do not observe the blackening or curved tips; problem could be drought or root rot; blackening that can be rubbed off is sooty mold
Dogwood			
Dogwood	Late season brown leaf spots	Septoria Leaf Spot (fungal disease) (see photos 1M & 1N)	Septoria leaf spot is a late season disease that is not a threat to the health of the tree.
	Tiny purplish spots with tan centers or that appear on leaves and flowers in the spring; leaves may be distorted	Spot anthracnose	This is a springtime disease and can be severe in wet springs, but the problem will dissipate with summer. No controls are needed.
	Brown leaf and bract spots with purple margins; spots vary widely in size and may blight entire leaves; lower branches die back and whole tree may eventually die; leaves cling to tree in winter	Discula anthracnose (fungal disease) (see photos 1O & 1P)	Use registered fungicide
	Subtle symptoms of off-color leaves or reddish-purplish to brown areas on leaves. Leaves may become scorched, cupped and drop early.	Powdery mildew (fungal disease)	Often laboratory confirmation is needed since symptoms are subtle. Plant dogwood resistant to powdery mildew. Use registered fungicide
	Leaves wilt and leaf margins turn brown	Scorch, due to hot, dry weather	Dogwood should be planted in reduced sunlight; it is very susceptible to scorch; irrigate regularly and deeply during establish

Dogwood		Fungal canker	No controls; water and fertilize
		Dogwood borer, dogwood twig borer	Use registered insecticide to protect trees; prune out dead and dying branches
		Lawn mower injury	
Elm			
Elm	Leaves wilt, curl, turn yellow, and drop off; branches die back	Dutch elm disease (fungal disease transmitted by beetles)	Submit sample of many medium-sized affected twigs for laboratory analysis
		Various other fungal wilt disease	Submit sample for laboratory analysis
		Phloem necrosis (mycoplasma disease)	Submit sample for laboratory analysis
	Leaves eaten between veins and appear lacy; may turn brown and drop off	Elm leaf beetle	Use registered insecticide
Hemlock			
Hemlock	Resinous bleeding near base of trunk on young (3-7 year old) trees; browning under bark	Bleeding canker	No controls known; cause has not been determined
	Needles with brown specks, especially near base; fine webbing between needles; foliage gray and dirty	Spruce mite	Use registered insecticide
Holly			
Holly	Dieback of part or all of foliage; blackened roots	Black root rot (fungal disease)	Common problem on Japanese hollies and inkberry holly. Plant hollies that are not susceptible to black root rot. A registered fungicide can be used preventatively, but will not benefit plants already showing symptoms.
	Tan winding trails or blotches on leaves; tiny brown dots on undersides of leaves	Leafminers	Use registered insecticide in early June
	Leaves with tiny yellow spots; leaves small and off-color	Southern red mite	Use registered miticide
Juniper			
Juniper	Tips of branches turn brown; black pimple-like structures can be seen on brown needles or stems	Various fungal tip blights (see photos 2D & 2E)	Submit sample for laboratory analysis; fungicides are registered for some of these tip blights
	Browning of parts or all of plant	Root rot (fungal or oomycete disease)	Submit sample for laboratory analysis; fungicides are registered for Phytophthora root rot
		Winter injury	Prune out dead branches
		Drought	Water deeply during dry periods
		Vole damage	Check for vole tunnels in the soil around plants and signs of vole chewing.
	Brick-red or brown galls form on branches; in spring, orange jelly-like horns form on the galls; galls turn brown with age	Cedar-apple rust (fungal disease)	Controls are not recommended for juniper. Spores from the galls spread to infect apple trees.

	Needles gray, dirty-looking, and covered with tiny yellow specks	Spruce mite	Use registered miticide

Lilac

	Description	Cause	Treatment
Lilac	Brown spots appear on leaves in early spring; leaves are distorted, turn black and die; flowers die	Bacterial blight	Prune out affected branches
		Frost injury	Prune out affected branches
	Stems swollen and cracked near ground; sawdust may be present	Lilac borer	Use registered insecticide on bark in early May and mid-June
	Bark chewed off	European hornet	Carefully destroy the hornet's nest

Magnolia

	Description	Cause	Treatment
Magnolia	Twigs with powdery white or tan bumps the size of half a bean	Magnolia scale	Use registered insecticide in early September or dormant oil
	Marginal browning of older leaves or sometimes all leaves	Winter injury	Water deeply in fall before ground freezes; apply anti-desiccant before winter

Maple

	Description	Cause	Treatment
Maple	Large, irregular grayish blotches on leaves; concentric ring pattern in spots are evident when leaves are held up to light	Zonate leaf spot (fungal disease)	No fungicides registered; rake up and burn or bury fallen leaves; this is a late season disease; fungicides are not warranted
	Irregular, shiny black, tar-like spots, about 1/2" in diameter on upper leaf surfaces	Tar spot (fungal disease)	Use registered fungicide; rake up and destroy fallen leaves
	Irregular, brown spots on leaves; on Norway maple, brown areas follow leaf veins; tree otherwise healthy	Anthracnose (fungal disease)	Use registered fungicide; rake up and destroy fallen leaves
		Scorch, caused by hot, dry weather	Water tree deeply; Anthracnose can be confused with scorch if the leaf spots have enlarged and coalesced; in early stages, it should be possible to distinguish between the two; scorch is mainly at the leaf margins
	Brown, dry areas on margins of leaves only	Scorch, caused by hot, dry weather and/or lack of adequate water	Water tree deeply during drought and during establishment
	Leaves on tree suddenly wilt and may turn yellow and drop off; wilt may occur on one side of tree only; tree may die suddenly or decline over a period of years; no external trunk or branch damage evident; some branches may have brown streaks in wood	Verticillium wilt (fungal disease) (see photos 2F & 2G)	Fertilizing heavily with nitrogen sometimes helps the tree to recover: distribute nitrogen in holes rather than on soil surface or grass may die; if tree dies, do not replant in the spot or replant with a species immune to Verticillium wilt; water tree deeply
		Drought	Water tree deeply
	Tree shows "stagheading", i.e., top branches die back; leaves discolored and small	Poor site	Maple is a shallow-rooted tree and cannot withstand stresses such as soil compaction, being planted near roads and sidewalks, etc.
		Maple decline, a disease thought to be associated with several pathogens and environmental stresses	Watering and fertilizing may help
		Fungal or bacterial canker	Prune out cankered branches; water fertilize

Maple	Cottony egg sacs on twigs and leaves	Cottony maple scale, cottony maple leaf scale	Use registered insecticide when egg sacs first appear
	Small red, green, or black globular growths on upper leaf surfaces	Gall mites	No control, but the tree will not be harmed
Oak			
Oak	General yellowing of tree or yellowing sections of tree; no wilting	Iron chlorosis, esp. on pin and willow oak	Soil test; iron deficiency can usually be corrected by adjusting soil pH to 6.0; in severe cases, injections of iron can be made
	Puckered, circular areas 1/2" in diameter on leaves; blisters are yellowing at first, then turn brown; leaves may drop	Oak leaf blister (fungal disease)	Rake up and destroy affected leaves
	Brown, dead areas on leaves, extending out to leaf margins; no trunk damage evident	Anthracnose (fungal disease)	Use registered fungicide; rake up and destroy fallen leaves
		Various other fungal leaf spots (anthracnose is probably the most common)	Submit sample for laboratory analysis; rake up and destroy fallen leaves
	Brown leaf spots that may progress to general leaf browning and defoliation	Tubakia leaf spot	This is typically a late season disease that can be severe in wet seasons and cause premature defoliation but is not a serious threat to the health of the tree. Rake and remove fallen leaves.
	Marginal leaf scorch; eventually branch dieback, progression of dieback varies	Bacterial scorch (bacterial disease)	Often there is a yellow line between brown tissue and green tissue with this disease, but it is not always present. Submit sample for laboratory analysis. No control; progression of the disease varies.
		Scorch, caused by hot, dry weather or inadequate water	Anthracnose can be confused with scorch if leaf lesions have enlarged and coalesced; if browning is mainly at leaf margins, it is probably scorch or the disease bacterial scorch
	Leaves wilt, turn bronze color, and drop off; no trunk damage evident	Dry soil	Water tree deeply
		Oak wilt (fungal disease)	To date we have not diagnosed oak wilt in Virginia and old reports of the disease have not been confirmed.
		Soil compaction	Correct compaction; consult certified arborist
	Galls on leaves or branches	Gall wasps	Oaks are subject to attack by dozens of species of gall wasps. The tree is not harmed even by heavy infestations
Photinia			
Photinia	Circular, gray leaf spots with purplish borders; tiny black specks in centers of spots; defoliation	Entomosporium leaf spot (fungal disease) (see photo 2H)	Use registered fungicide on a regular basis throughout the season; avoid pruning and fertilizing plants in summer
Pine			
Pine	Cream-colored pustules containing bright orange or yellow spores form on needles;	Needle rust (fungal disease)	Fungicides usually not necessary; remove goldenrods and asters around pines: these are alternate hosts of the fungus

	Symptom	Cause	Recommendation
Pine	sides of pustules are papery in appearance; needles may drop		
	Rough, elongated, swollen areas with yellowish orange color develop on trunk and branches; sap may flow from these cankers; needles turn brown	White pine blister rust (fungal disease)	Submit sample for laboratory analysis; remove all currant and gooseberry bushes in a 1000-foot radius of tree (alternate hosts); prune out cankers
		Various other fungal cankers	Submit sample for laboratory analysis
	Black, sooty substance covers needles and stems	Sooty mold, fungus very common on pine, grows on honeydew excreted by aphids and other insects	Not a disease; control aphids with registered insecticide to avoid honeydew on which sooty molds grow
	Small, circular spots or bands on needles; some needles may be brown from a spot all the way out to the tip	Brown spot or other needle cast	Submit sample for laboratory analysis; time of fungicide application depends on which disease it is
	Needles turn reddish brown and remain attached to tree	Pine wood nematode, esp. on Japanese black pine and some other pines not native to North America	Submit sample of lower branches for nematode analysis; remove and destroy affected trees; control longhorn beetles with registered insecticide
		Dry soil	Water tree deeply
		Other environmental stress; e.g. soil compaction, gas leak	
		Fungal canker	Prune out cankers on branches; there are no controls for cankers that form on the trunk
		Fungal tip blight (any of several)	Submit sample for laboratory analysis
		Mites	Use registered miticide
	Needles turn brown from tips of branches back	Fungal tip blight (any of several)	Submit sample for laboratory analysis
		Dry soil	Water tree deeply
	Tips of needles turn brown; two yellow bands about 1/8-1/4" wide appear across groups of needles; tree is otherwise healthy	Ozone injury, esp. on white pine	Tree will recover if damage is not severe
	Clusters of caterpillar-like insects feeding on needles in groups	Sawflies	Use registered insecticide
	Leader wilts, droops, and dies	White pine weevil	Prune out infested terminals; spray leader with registered insecticide in early April

Rhododendron and Azalea

	Symptom	Cause	Recommendation
Rhododendron and Azalea	Fleshy, thick, white galls form on leaves and/or flowers	Azalea leaf and petal gal (fungal disease) (see photo 21)	Pick off and destroy galls
	General leaf yellowing on all or part of plant	Improper soil pH	Soil test; rhododendron and azalea require acid soil
		Nutrient deficiency	Soil test
	Small, pale, circular spots appear on undersides of flower petals; spots enlarge and appear white on colored flowers and brown on white flowers; flowers become limp and covered with white, fuzzy spore mass	Ovulinia petal blight (fungal disease), mainly on azalea	Use registered fungicide

Rhododendron and Azalea	Marginal leaf browning; leaves curl downward on rhododendron	Winter injury	Very common on rhododendron; always suspect this on samples submitted in early spring
		Scorch, caused by hot, dry weather	Supply water
		Salt injury	Do not overapply de-icing salt on sidewalks or drives near shrubs or trees
		Phytophthora root rot (oomycete disease) (see photos 2J & 2K)	Submit sample (include roots) for laboratory analysis
		Phytophthora dieback (oomycete disease that attacks stem tips)	Submit sample for laboratory analysis
		Botryosphaeria dieback (fungal disease)	Very common problem. Submit sample for laboratory analysis; prune out dead branches; consult pruning manual for proper technique when doing routine pruning; the fungus often invades pruning wounds or stressed tissue; protect plants from winter injury
	Brown spots on leaves	Various fungal leaf spots	Submit sample for laboratory analysis
		Physiological leaf spot, cause unknown	Easily confused with fungal leaf spot
	Leaves with yellow specks on upper surface; black, shiny spots on undersurface	Lace bugs	Use registered insecticide
Rose			
Rose	Black, circular lea spots with feathery edges surrounded by yellow halo; leaves drop	Black spot (fungal disease) (see photo 2L)	Use registered fungicide; plant resistant cultivars
	Spots of various colors on leaves that do not fit black leaf spot description	Various fungal leaf spots	Submit sample for laboratory analysis
	Various patterns of yellow and green on leaves, including streaks, rings, vein clearing (yellow veins), or blotches	Viral disease	Common on roses; these viruses mainly enter through grafts and are not transmitted from plant to plant; purchase healthy stock; maintain shrub vigor by watering and fertilizing; not necessary to remove shrub
	General or interveinal chlorosis	Nutrient deficiency	Soil test
		Waterlogged soil	Improve drainage
	Branches die back; sunken or swollen discolored areas which may be covered with tiny black specks appear on branches	Various fungal cankers	Very common problem on rose; prune out cankers; no fungicides are registered; prevents stress from other diseases and environmental problems; prune near side shoot or bud; do not leave long pruning stubs
	Plants wilt; lower leaves may turn yellow	Dry soil	Supply water
		Verticillium wilt (fungal disease)	Use resistant varieties; do not replant in same area
		Root knot (nematode problem)	Check roots for knots; plant in another area
		Waterlogged soil	Improve drainage
		Transplant shock	Water regularly after transplanting

	Symptoms	Possible Causes	Controls & Comments
Rose	Flowers wilt, develop spots, or fail to open and become covered with fuzzy, grayish mold	Botrytis blight (fungal disease)	Remove and destroy affected flowers; fungicides for black spot should control this disease
Rose	Shoots and foliage have an abnormal red color; stems appear thick and succulent; rapidly elongating shoots; shoots with shortened internodes; stems with an overabundance of pliable thorns; new growth may have many branches that create a witch's broom (similar to glyphosate injury); distorted or dwarfed leaves (similar to 2,4-D injury); deformed buds and flowers; abnormal flower color; lack of winter hardiness	Rose rosette virus (viral disease)	Virus is spread by eriophyid mites; choose healthy nursery stock without any of the symptoms mentioned here; remove any wild multiflora roses within 100 yards of the landscape; space plants well to allow for mature growth to slow potential of mites from spreading from plant to plant; remove any roses diagnosed with this virus, including the roots to avoid spread. Can be mistaken for glyphosate injury, so laboratory diagnosis is recommended.
Rose	Flower buds fail to open; blooms are deformed with brown streaks or spots on petals	Thrips	Use registered insecticide
Spruce			
Spruce	Needles on branches near ground turn brown; branches die back; needles may drop or remain attached; dried, white pitch may ooze from bark	Cytospora canker (fungal disease) especially on Colorado and Norway spruce	Prune dead branches back to trunk
Spruce	Older, inner needles of branches appear speckled with dull yellowish blotches; later these needles turn brown or purple from tips back and drop; tiny black specks in rows on needles can be seen with a hand lens	Rhizosphaera needle blight (fungal disease)	Use registered fungicide
Spruce		Stigmina needle cast (fungal disease)	Laboratory diagnosis is needed to distinguish these two fungi, but the control recommendation is the same for both.
Willow			
Willow is very susceptible to a number of different fungal cankers. See general section for description of canker symptoms. Prune out and destroy cankered branches. There are no remedies for cankers on the trunk.			

Table 6-6: Annual and Perennial Flowers Diagnostic Key

	Symptoms	Possible Causes	Controls & Comments
Problems common to many annuals and perennials			
Many	Plants wilt; flowers may drop and leaves may turn yellow	Dry soil	Supply water
Many		Waterlogged soil	Improve drainage
Many		Transplant shock	Do not transplant in heat of day; water regularly after transplanting
Many		Verticillium wilt (fungal disease)	Submit sample for laboratory diagnosis; replant new plants in another area
Many		Root and stem or corm rot (fungal, bacterial or oomycete disease)	Plant in well-drained soil; destroy affected plants

	Seedlings wilt, stems turn brown and soft and may be constricted at the soil line	Damping-off (fungal or oomycete disease)	Plant in well-drained soil; avoid planting too early in the growing season; destroy affected plants
	Plants fail to produce flowers	Wrong season	Plants have specific day length requirements for flowering
		Cool weather	
		Insufficient light	Do not plant sun-loving plants in shade
		Too much nitrogen	Do not over-fertilize; nitrogen stimulates foliage, not flowers
		Immature plants	Biennials and perennials often do not flower in the first year
		Undersized bulbs	
	Plants produce too many small flowers	Plants not disbudded	Some flowers; e.g. chrysanthemum, need to have some buds removed to produce large flowers
	Tall, "leggy" plant; stem and foliage pale or yellow	Insufficient light	Plant in location where species will receive adequate light
	General yellowing of leaves; yellowing may be interveinal; plants may be stunted; no wilting	Nutrient deficiency or improper soil pH	Soil test
Many	Grayish white powdery growth on leaves	Powdery mildew (fungal disease)	Use registered fungicide
	Pustules containing orange, yellow, or brown powdery substance	Rust (fungal disease)	Use resistant varieties if available; use registered fungicide
	Brown, dead spots on leaves	Fungal, bacterial, or foliar nematode disease (any of several)	Submit sample for laboratory diagnosis; refer to controls for specific disease in PMG
	Brown, dead areas on margins of leaves	Scorch, due to hot, dry weather	Supply water
		Salt injury	Do not plant near walkways or driveways that were treated with deicing salt in winter
	Flowers wilt or fail to open; grayish mold appears on flowers in moist weather	Gray mold (fungal disease)	Pick off and destroy affected flowers; use registered fungicide
	Yellow and green mottle or mosaic pattern on leaves	Viral disease (any of several)	Remove affected plants; do not touch healthy plants after diseased ones; control insects
	Tiny, white flecks on leaves	Ozone injury	
		Spider mites	Use registered miticide
		Thrips	Use registered insecticide
	Clusters of insects on stems or undersides of leaves; leaves may be curled or distorted	Aphids	Use registered insecticide
	Leaves chewed or completely eaten	Various insects	Submit insect for laboratory identification; refer to controls for specific insect in PMG
		Slugs	Use slug bait
	Light-colored tunnels or blotches in leaves	Leafminers	Use registered insecticide

Many	Tiny, white-winged insects on undersides of leaves	Whiteflies	Use yellow sticky boards (smeared with grease) to trap insects or use registered insecticide
	White, cottony masses on leaves or stem	Mealybugs	Use registered insecticide

Chrysanthemum

Chrysanthemum	Flowers distorted and abnormally colored; rosetting of florets may occur; yellow and green mosaic, mottle or ring pattern may appear on leaves	Viral disease (any of several)	Remove affected plants; control insects
	Green-colored flowers instead of normal color; upper branches of flowering stem are yellowish and upright	Aster yellows (phytoplasma disease)	Remove affected plants; weed control; insect control
	Brown, dead flowers	Thrips	Prune out affected flowers; use registered insecticide
		Gray mold (fungal disease)	Pick off and destroy affected flowers; use registered fungicide

Daylily

Daylily	Irregular brown streaks on leaves; yellow streak along midvein of leaf, starting at leaf tip; general leaf yellowing	Daylily leaf streak (fungal disease)	Avoid overhead irrigation; cut back and remove old leaves in fall; keep notes on which varieties are most affected and plant those that consistently look better; use a registered fungicide
	Yellow leaf spots and streaks; powdery, orange pustules associated with spots on lower leaf surface	Daylily rust (fungal disease)	Use resistant varieties; remove old plant debris at the end of the season; use a registered fungicide

Geranium

Geranium	Corky, raised spots on lower leaf surfaces	Oedema, a physiological problem associated with overwatering	Do not overwater; ivy geraniums are especially prone to oedema
	Plants wilt; brown or black rotted area evident at base of stem; brown spots may be present on leaves	Fungal or bacterial root and stem rot (any of several)	Plant in well-drained soil; remove dead plants
	Pie-shaped brown areas or small brown spots with yellow haloes on leaves; rot may be present on lower stems	Bacterial stem rot and leaf spot	Plant in well-drained soil; avoid overhead watering; remove and destroy affected plants and plant debris

Gladiolus

Gladiolus	White streaked flowers	Viral disease	Destroy affected plants; control insects; do not plant near vegetable garden since two major gladiolus viruses also infect plants in bean and cucumber family
	Plants are thin with weak leaves that turn yellowish green; flower spikes are twisted and distorted and may be green	Aster yellows (phytoplasma disease)	Destroy affected plants; weed control; insect control
		Poor growing conditions	Aster yellows could be confused with poor growing conditions, but twisted flowers are an indication of disease
	Plants stunted; flowers small and faded; leaves yellow from tips back; corm may be rotted; corm discolored internally	Fusarium yellows (fungal disease)	Destroy affected plants; practice 4-year rotation; soak corms in registered fungicide before planting

Gladiolus		Various fungal corm rots	Same as above
		Waterlogged soil	Improve drainage
	Plants stunted and yellowed; corm rotted with blue-green, powdery mold on surface	Penicillium corm rot (fungal disease)	Destroy all affected corms; store corms in cool, dry place before planting; dip corms in registered fungicide before planting; rotate
	Sunken, black lesions covered with shiny, varnish-like substance surrounded by raised, brittle rims on corms; after planting, tiny, raised reddish-brown specks appear on leaf bases; leaf specks become soft	Scab (bacterial disease)	Destroy affected corms; rotate
	Whitish streaks on leaves; flowers deformed and discolored	Gladiolus thrips	Keep plants well-watered; use registered insecticide

Hollyhock

Hollyhock	Yellow to orange spots on upper leaf surfaces; small, brown pustules on corresponding lower leaf surfaces	Rust (fungal disease)	Pick off and destroy affected leaves; use registered fungicide; note that symptoms of rust on hollyhock are slightly different from those caused by rust on other plants (described in the general section). This rust does not have an alternate host. Destroy all aboveground diseased plant tissue in the fall.

Iris

Iris	Leaves turn yellow and wilt; if pulled gently, leaves detach from plant; soft, slimy, smelly rot at base of plant; rhizomes may have holes	Bacterial soft rot, spread by iris borer	Dispose of infested plants in fall; use registered insecticide to control iris borer when plants are 5-6" tall
	Oval, watersoaked leaf spots that later turn tan and blight the entire leaf	Cladosporium leaf spot (fungal disease, formerly "Heterosporium leaf spot")	Remove all old leaf debris in the fall: use a registered fungicide when leaves are 4-6" tall

Marigold

Marigold	Plants wilt; leaves wither; lower stem discolored inside and out	Fungal stem rot	Destroy affected plants; rotate; plant in well-drained soil
		Fusarium wilt (fungal disease)	Same as for stem rot
	Round, corky galls on lower stem	Crown gall (bacterial disease)	Destroy affected plants; rotate
		Herbicide injury (growth regulator-type herbicide)	If lawn herbicides are used, apply after wind has died down and do not apply in heat of day; avoid using mulch from herbicide-treated fields, manure from animals fed on herbicide-treated fields or grass clippings from herbicide-treated lawns
	Numerous small brown spots on leaves, stems, and flowers	Alternaria blight (fungal disease)	Use registered fungicide

Peony

	New shoots wilt and turn black; flowers, buds, leaves, and stems turn brown and	Gray mold (fungal disease)	Prune out affected plant parts; use registered fungicide

	leathery; gray fuzzy mold may appear in wet weather	Phytophthora blight (oomycete disease)	Same as for gray mold
		Cold injury	

Petunia			
	Wilt; leaves light green or yellowed; stems may have soft rot at base; roots rotted	Root and stem rot (oomycete disease)	Plant in well-drained soil; remove affected plants

Snapdragon			
Snapdragon	Pale, yellow spots appear on upper leaf surfaces; reddish pustules of spores appear on upper leaf surfaces in concentric rings	Rust (fungal disease)	Use registered fungicide; note that symptoms of rust on snapdragon are slightly different from those of rust on other plants (described in the general section); pustules form concentric rings on snapdragon

Tulip			
Tulip	Stems are very short and flowers bloom at ground level	Warm spring and/or inadequate winter cooling	Place tulip bulbs in paper bags in fall and chill in refrigerator before replanting
	Light or dark-colored spots on leaves and flowers; spots enlarge to form large, gray blotches; fuzzy brown or gray growth appears on spots during wet weather; leaves and stems are distorted	Botrytis blight (fungal disease)	Destroy affected plants; rotate; do not plant spotted bulbs; use registered fungicide
	Flowers streaked, spotted, or mottled in an irregular pattern; leaves may also be streaked or mottled	Viral disease (any of several)	Destroy affected plants; insect control; do not plant variety Rembrandt near other tulips: its showy streak patterns are caused by a virus that may infect other plants; Parrot tulips also streak but this is genetic and not caused by a virus

Zinnia			
Zinnia	Small, dark brown, angular spots on leaves and flowers; flowers may be completely blighted	Bacterial spot	Submit sample for laboratory diagnosis; use bleach-treated seed
		Various fungal diseases	Submit sample for laboratory diagnosis; refer to controls for specific disease in PMG
	Reddish-brown, circular spots with grayish white centers; flowers may also have spots	Alternaria blight (fungal disease)	Use registered fungicide

Additional Resources

- *The Ortho Problem Solver* by Michael D. Smith

Attributions

Prepared by James L. Green, Extension Horticulture Specialist, Oregon State University; adapted for Virginia (2009)

- Sabrina Morelli, Arlington Extension Master Gardener (2021 reviser)
- Elizabeth Brown, Bedford Extension Master Gardener (2021 reviser)
- Adria C. Bordas, Extension Agent, Agriculture and Natural Resources (2015 reviser)
- Diagnostic Key revised by Mary Ann Hansen, Plant Disease Diagnostician (2009, 2022) and Eric Day, Insect Identification Lab Manager, Virginia Tech (2009)

Image Attributions

- Figure 6-1: Normal leaf drop among older leaves nearer to trunk versus abnormal leaf drop from newer leaves towards tip of branch. Johnson, Devon. 2022. CC BY-NC-SA 4.0.
- Figure 6-2: Patterns of dieback on plant canopy. A. Shows canopy death due to urban tree decline B. shows branch death due to dogwood twig borer (*Oberea tripunctata*). Johnson, Devon. 2022. CC BY-NC-SA 4.0. Includes image 5454691 by Jason Sharman from Bugwood.org CC BY-NC 3.0 US and image 3056077 by James Solomon from Bugwood.org CC BY 3.0 US.
- Figure 6-3: A. Dieback on branch due to cold injury B. Dieback on branch due to Phomopsis blight (*Phomopsis juniperivora*). Johnson, Devon. 2022. CC BY-NC-SA 4.0. Includes image 5049098 by Joseph OBrien from Bugwood.org CC BY 3.0 US and image 0485003 by David J. Moorhead from Bugwood.org CC BY-NC 3.0 US.
- Figure 6-4: Needle damage. Johnson, Devon. 2022. CC BY-NC-SA 4.0. Includes image 1241649 by Susan K. Hagle from Bugwood.org CC BY-NC 3.0 US and image 1241572 by USDA Forest Service from Bugwood.org CC BY-NC 3.0 US.
- Figure 6-5: Chemical damage from: A. Sulfur dioxide in a consistent pattern across pecan leaf; B. Flouride injury on birch which is concentrated around leaf margins. Johnson, Devon. 2022. CC BY-NC-SA 4.0. Includes image 1505014 by USDA Forest Service – Region 8 – Southern from Bugwood.org CC BY 3.0 US and image 1494137 by University of Georgia Plant Pathology from Bugwood.org CC BY 3.0 US.
- Figure 6-6: Example of fungal leaf sports, photo shows entomosporium leaf spot. Spots usually vary in size, are generally round, and occasionally elongate on stems. (*Diplocarpon mespili*) on chokeberry leaf. Johnson, Devon. 2022. CC BY-NC-SA 4.0. Includes image 5368844 by Paul Bachi from Bugwood.org CC BY-NC 3.0 US.
- Figure 6-7: Example of bacterial leaf spots on leaf, photo shows bacterial spot of stone fruits (*Xanthomonas arboricola pv. pruni*) on plum leaf. Johnson, Devon. 2022. CC BY-NC-SA 4.0. Includes image 0162018 by U. Mazzucchi from Bugwood.org CC BY-NC 3.0 US.
- Figure 6-8: Vein clearing, photo shows Tobacco etch virus (Potyvirus TEV) on tobacco leaf. Johnson, Devon. 2022. CC BY-NC-SA 4.0. Includes image 1440033 by R.J. Reynolds Tobacco Company from Bugwood.org CC BY 3.0 US
- Figure 6-9: Mosaic leaf pattern, photo shows alfalfa mosaic (Alfamovirus Alfalfa mosaic virus) on soybean leaf. Johnson, Devon. 2022. CC BY-NC-SA 4.0. Includes image 5605168 by Craig Grau from Bugwood.org CC BY-NC 3.0 US.
- Figure 6-10: The highly invasive spotted lanternfly is a phloem-feeding insect. Image 5524251 from Joseph OBrien, USDA Forest Service, Bugwood.org, CC BY 3.0 US

190 | CHAPTER 6: DIAGNOSING PLANT DAMAGE

- Figure 6-11: Examples of cold damage. Johnson, Devon 2022. CC BY-NC-SA 4.0. Includes image 5049093 by Joseph OBrien, USDA Forest Service, Bugwood.org CC BY 3.0 US and image 5363644 by Howard F. Schwartz, Colorado State University, Bugwood.org, CC BY 3.0 US

CHAPTER 7: INTEGRATED PEST MANAGEMENT AND PESTICIDE SAFETY

Chapter Contents:

- What Is a Pest?
- Integrated Pest Management
- Pesticide Safety
- Additional Resources

What Is a Pest?

Most organisms are not considered pests. However, certain situations may occur that prompt an organism to be labeled a pest. Organisms are considered pests when they

- Damage food, fiber, structures, or other materials that humans need or value.
- Cause or spread disease.
- Live or grow where they are not wanted.
- Cause general annoyance or anxiety.

A pest can be an invertebrate (e.g., insect, mite, tick, slug), pathogen (e.g., bacteria, fungi, virus), plant (weed), vertebrate (e.g., deer, rodent), or other unwanted organism. It is important to correctly define an organism as a pest, and verify the identity of a pest, before making any pest management decisions.

Integrated Pest Management

Integrated pest management (IPM) is an ecosystem-based strategy that focuses on long-term prevention of pests or their damage through a combination of appropriate control tactics. These tactics can be preventative, curative, or both and are often combined to provide the best possible results. An IPM program proactively seeks to determine and correct the cause of a pest problem while also minimizing risks to human health and the environment. In short, IPM can be thought of as best practices for managing pests. IPM plans can be developed for virtually any setting where pests occur such as gardens, farms, natural areas, homes, or schools.

Figure 7-1: Integrated pest management offers many tools gardeners can use to control pests.

When dealing with any pest issue, there are important questions to ask and decisions to make. Start by identifying or describing the problem. Ask yourself these questions:

- Is the problem actually caused by a pest?
- If so, what kind of pest?
- Is the problem severe enough to require action?
- Can the pest be controlled at this stage of its life or growth cycle?
- What control options are available? Which control options are compatible?
- If pesticides are needed, are there effective, legal, and manageable chemical control options for this site and

situation?

The process of answering these questions will help you begin implementing an integrated pest management plan.

Understanding IPM

The purpose of IPM is to provide practical, cost-effective solutions for managing pests while protecting people, animals, and the environment. A major goal of IPM is to reduce reliance on pesticides by using a variety of control methods. Integrating multiple control methods has the added benefit of helping to avoid or delay development of resistance to any one pest control technique or tactic. However, before focusing on the methods for managing pests, it is important to first think about your pest control goals.

The objective of IPM in most outdoor situations is not to eliminate the pest population, but to suppress pest numbers or damage to a tolerable level. In many cases, a certain level of pest presence can be tolerated because the complete eradication of a pest species may be prohibitively expensive or technically impossible. In indoor areas, eradication of a pest population is often more feasible because the environment is smaller, less complex, and more easily controlled than outdoor areas. In either case, determining what a tolerable level is for your situation is essential during the goal setting process. When establishing tolerance levels, a number of factors can be considered such as the potential damage (economic, aesthetics, health, etc.) from the pest's activities and the cost and/or time involved to control the pest.

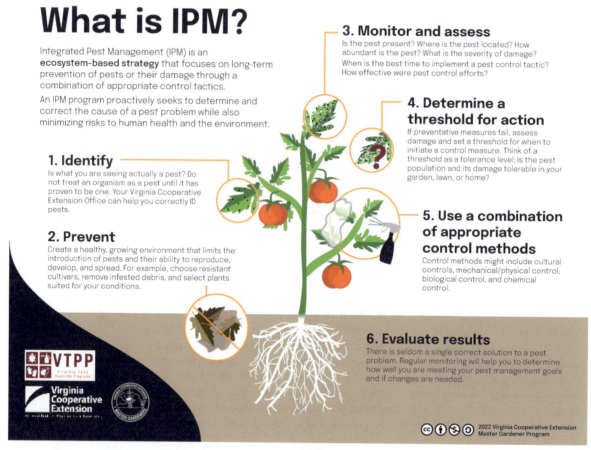

Figure 7-2: What is IPM infographic: IPM is an ecosystem-based strategy that focuses on long-term prevention of pests or their damage through a combination of appropriate control tactics including: 1. Identify the problem, for example flea beetles illustrated on the tomato plant here, 2. Prevent the problem by limiting pests' ability to reproduce, for example by removing debris each year, 3. Monitor and assess, 4. Determine a threshold for action, 5. Use a combination of appropriate control methods, in this case physical controls such as agricultural fabric to exclude the flea beetles or pesticides, and 6. Evaluate results.

Once pest control goals have been established, you can begin developing your IPM plan. Although IPM plans can vary with each situation, they all follow a similar process:

- Identify the pest(s) to be managed.
- Use prevention strategies to deter the pest(s).
- Monitor pest populations and assess their damage.
- Determine a guideline (threshold) for when control action(s) is needed.
- Use a combination of appropriate control actions to reduce pest populations.
- Evaluate the results of control efforts.

Together, these actions enable informed and intelligent decision-making regarding pest control.

Prevention Strategies

Prevention strategies can help limit the factors that contribute to pest issues in our gardens, homes, lawns, and other areas. Preventative measures taken before a pest appears can result in fewer rescue treatments, and should be used first if practical and available. It may be easier and more effective to remove the reason why the pest is present in the first place, as opposed to controlling the pest after the fact. Prevention strategies are used to create a healthy, growing environment that limits the introduction of pests and their ability to reproduce, develop, and/or spread. Preventative tactics can include:

- Selecting plants that are best suited to the existing site conditions (e.g., hardiness zone, sun exposure, soil type, drainage).
- Choosing disease or pest resistant plant cultivars/varieties.
- Using pest-free seeds or transplants.
- Cleaning and disinfecting tools, equipment, and potting materials.
- Ensuring that appropriate growing practices are implemented (e.g., providing adequate moisture and fertilization, proper maintenance).

Pest Identification

Correct identification of the pest or problem is the foundation of any IPM plan and can be considered the most important step. It starts with asking yourself if what you are seeing is actually a pest. **Do not treat an organism as a pest until it has proven to be one**. Make sure the damage observed is due to the pest and not another cause.

Proper identification will provide you with important information about the pest. This can include its preferred habitat, life cycle, and the factors that influence its spread and development. The more information that can be gathered about a pest, the greater the opportunity for cost-effective and successful pest control. Although identifying a pest can sometimes be difficult, there are several Virginia Cooperative Extension resources that can help.

- Virginia Tech Diagnostic Labs:
    - Insect ID Lab (http://www.ento.vt.edu/idlab.html)
    - Weed ID Clinic (https://agweedsci.spes.vt.edu/extension/weedid.html)
    - Plant Disease Clinic (https://spes.vt.edu/affiliated/plant-disease-clinic.html)
- Virginia Cooperative Extension Publications:
    - General Information (http://www.pubs.ext.vt.edu/)
    - "Pest Management Guide: Home Grounds and Animals" 456-018 (https://www.pubs.ext.vt.edu/456/456-018/456-018.html)
- Your Local Extension Agent (https://ext.vt.edu/offices.html)
- Your Local Extension Master Gardeners (https://ext.vt.edu/lawn-garden/master-gardener.html)

Monitoring and Assessment

Another key component to a successful IPM plan is regular monitoring of pest populations or their damage. Monitoring can answer several important questions:

- Is the pest present?
- Where is the pest located?
- How abundant is the pest?
- What is the severity of damage?
- When is the best time to implement a pest control tactic?
- How effective were pest control efforts?

To aid monitoring efforts, it is important to learn about the preferences and common problems relevant to the system being managed. For example, in a vegetable garden it is important to know what healthy plants look like, so you can quickly notice if something is abnormal or does not quite look right. Pest management guides can be used to familiarize yourself with some of the common pests and problems in the systems being managed.

Regular monitoring of a garden, lawn, home, or other site will allow for early detection of pests, which can help prevent or minimize a pest outbreak. Specifics on how often monitoring should be conducted depends on the system being managed and the pest. Regardless, it is often easier to control a pest problem in the early stages before populations have increased in size and spread.

Pest populations can vary from one location to another and from year to year. For this reason, it is important to consider keeping records of your monitoring activities. Records can help you manage pests during the current growing season, evaluate current control methods, and predict problems in the future.

Determining Thresholds

If preventative measures fail to control a pest population, you will need to assess their damage and set a threshold for when to initiate a control measure or rescue treatment. A threshold can be thought of as a tolerance level. In other words, is the pest population and its damage tolerable in your garden, lawn, or home? Or is it causing economic, aesthetic, or other losses? Remember, finding a single pest or low levels of a pest may not indicate you should take action for its control. Only when the pest and/or its harm surpass a set level of tolerable damage should controls be implemented. Determining a threshold for each pest you are assessing will help you move forward with implementing control tactics only when necessary.

For some pests and commodities, thresholds have been developed based on economic or other considerations and are often based on monitoring data. For example, in tree fruit, if captures of codling moth in pheromone baited traps exceeds five moths per trap per week, control is necessary to prevent economic losses from this pest. For other pests, thresholds may involve some other assessment such as percent defoliation, leaf wetness duration, or population numbers per unit area.

In some situations, thresholds cannot be developed or have limited value. This is particularly true for many plant diseases, disease vectors (e.g., mosquitoes, ticks, fleas), or newly invasive species, which essentially have a threshold of zero. Controls for these pests are often initiated preventively or immediately upon detection.

Control Methods

When pest populations and/or their damage exceed established thresholds, it is time to initiate a control measure or rescue treatment. In an IPM program there are nonchemical and chemical control methods available. Nonchemical control methods should be used first if available and feasible. The techniques or tactics you choose will depend on the target pest and the kind and amount of control needed. IPM promotes the use of four basic pest control methods, as explained below.

Cultural Control: Controlling a pest with cultural methods involves modifying or disrupting the pest environment to make it less habitable. Many cultural control tactics can be thought of as preventative because they keep pest populations from developing or delay their impact. Examples of cultural control tactics include:

- Sanitation practices (e.g., removing plant residues or other food sources from the site).
- Eliminating alternative hosts or habitats (e.g., removing nearby weedy species that serve as a reservoir for pests and diseases).
- Crop rotations.
- Varying the time of planting.
- Intercropping.

Mechanical/Physical Control: This method involves the use of hands-on techniques or simple equipment/devices to reduce or prevent the spread of pest populations. This is often achieved through activities that directly remove or exclude the pest from the system. Examples of removal include the use of traps to remove rodents from a structure, or hand removal of weeds from a garden bed. Techniques that focus on removal can be particularly effective if pest populations have not already reached high levels. Exclusionary tactics limit pest access into the system. Examples of exclusion include the use of row covers or fencing to prevent pests from feeding on plants in a garden, or the use of tight-fitting screens on windows and doors to prevent pest entry into a home.

Biological Control: This method involves the use of living organisms (i.e., natural enemies) to reduce pest populations (typically insects and weeds). Introducing or encouraging natural enemies can reduce the severity of potential pest outbreaks. Natural enemies can typically be grouped as predators, parasitoids, or pathogens. Predators feed on multiple prey throughout their life (e.g., insects, spiders, birds, fish). Parasitoids feed and develop on or within another invertebrate host, eventually killing it (e.g., parasitic wasps and flies). Pathogens are microorganisms that cause disease in their host (e.g., bacteria, fungi, nematodes, viruses).

Conservation of natural enemies (i.e., protecting and maintaining existing populations) is a readily available form of biological control for gardeners. Common conservation practices include limiting the use of broad-spectrum pesticides that kill a wide range of organisms, and providing habitat that promotes the establishment and survival of natural enemies.

Chemical Control: This method involves the use of pesticides to reduce pest populations. A **pesticide** is any substance that is used to prevent, destroy, repel, or mitigate any pest. Pesticides can be synthetic (man-made), or natural products derived from plants, microorganisms, or inorganic elements. Although a major goal of IPM is to reduce reliance on pesticides, they are sometimes necessary to control pests and their damage. When selecting a pesticide, it is important to choose a product that is compatible with any nonchemical control methods that may already be in place. Safe use and other considerations regarding pesticides will be discussed in further detail later in this chapter.

Cultural

  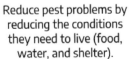

Reduce pest problems by reducing the conditions they need to live (food, water, and shelter).

Mechanical/physical

Reduce pest problems by physically preventing access to the area or removing them if they are already there.

Biological

Reduce pest problems by introducing predators, parasitoids, or pathogens to control the population.

Chemical

Reduce pest problems by using pesticides to control the pest population.

Figure 7-3: Control methods: Control can be undertaken by means other than chemical application (reducing pest problems by using pesticides to control the pest population). Options include: cultural control (reduce pest problems by reducing the conditions they need to live: food, water and shelter), mechanical/physical control (reduce pest problems by physically preventing access to the area or removing them if they are already there), biological control (reduce pest problems by introducing predators, parasitoids, or pathogens to control the population), and chemical control (reduce pest problems by using pesticides to control the pest population).

Evaluating Results

An important, but often overlooked, step is to evaluate the results of your control efforts. Because of the variability present in any biological system, the effectiveness of an IPM plan may change over time or between sites. Understand that IPM plans are not static, but constantly evolve as more information is collected and new control tactics are developed. There is seldom a single correct solution to a pest problem. Regular monitoring will help you to determine how well you are meeting your pest management goals and if changes are needed. Be aware that some control tactics may be slow to show noticeable results. It is also important to evaluate any potential negative impacts your control efforts may have on the target treated, natural enemies present, and the environment before deciding to continue using them in the future.

Pesticide Safety

If you decide to include chemical control in your pest management plan, do so safely. Proper selection and proper use of pesticides is key for not only controlling the pest, but protecting yourself, others, and the environment. Following safety precautions and using common sense can prevent pesticides from causing unintended and unnecessary harm. Always read the pesticide product label before purchasing, using, storing, or disposing of a pesticide product or its container.

When selecting a pesticide, choose a product that is labeled for the site you need to treat and effective against the pest you need to control. Consider only those products you have the equipment and expertise to handle. If there is a choice of several products, select the least hazardous product with the lowest toxicity. For pest management recommendations, contact your local Extension office or consult the Virginia Cooperative Extension "Pest Management Guide: Home Grounds and Animals" 456-018

Some pesticides are specifically intended for home use. These products are packaged in small quantities (i.e., pints, quarts, and ounces) and are often ready-to-use. Their label directions are less technical than those intended for occupational users. Most pesticide products intended for home use are low in toxicity but can still be dangerous if used improperly. It is important to read and follow all label directions to help prevent pesticide related accidents.

Some pesticide products available for purchase are intended for agricultural and professional/commercial use. These products will have statements on the front of the label that indicate the intended user. You should not purchase these products. Often, these products are higher in toxicity because they are highly concentrated or contain higher amounts of active ingredients. They may require special protective clothing and application equipment. They are also sold in larger containers, which means the homeowner will have more material than can be used in a reasonable amount of time. Additionally, application rates are often given on a per-acre basis, making them difficult to mix.

Reading the label before purchasing a pesticide is the only way to be sure you can use the product as directed. Be sure you have the proper handling and measuring devices, application equipment, and protective clothing. Read the mixing instructions and application directions. Note any special handling instructions, specific warnings, and precautions.

Pesticides and the Law

The U.S. Environmental Protection Agency (EPA) and the Virginia Department of Agriculture and Consumer Services, Office of Pesticide Services (VDACS-OPS) are the regulatory agencies charged with enforcing pesticide laws and regulations. Under the Federal Insecticide, Fungicide, and Rodenticide Act, it is illegal to use a pesticide on a site unless that site (plant, animal, place) is listed on the label. You may not exceed the application rate or other special use restrictions as directed by the label.

You are liable for misuse of pesticides on your property, which includes applications you may make or the applications of any commercial applicators you hire. Serious misuse may result in drift on to other people's property, leaching of a pesticide into water supplies, or other problems related to application of a pesticide contrary to label directions.

Some pesticide products are extremely hazardous to humans and/or the environment. The EPA classifies these products as restricted use pesticides (RUPs). A certificate issued by VDACS-OPS is required to purchase and use RUP products. If a person intends to use RUPs to produce agricultural commodities on their farm or land they lease, they are required to have private pesticide applicator certification. Anyone who uses RUPs as a part of their job duties, must obtain a commercial pesticide applicator or registered technician certification. The process of certification and use of RUP products is NOT intended for the home gardener.

Pesticide Terminology

The words "insecticides" and "pesticides" are often used interchangeably. However, these two words have different meanings. As you can see in Table 7-1, an insecticide is just one type of pesticide.

Table 7-1: Types of Pesticides and Functions

Type of Pesticide	Function
Acaricide	Controls mites, ticks, and spiders.
Attractant	Lures pest (to trap or bait).
Disinfectant/Antimicrobial	Controls microorganisms.
Fungicide	Controls fungal plant pathogens.
Herbicide	Controls plants.
Insecticide	Controls insects.
Miticide	Controls mites.
Nematicide	Controls nematodes.
Plant Growth Regulator	Stops, speeds up, or otherwise changes normal plant development processes.
Repellent	Keeps pests away.
Rodenticide	Controls rodents.

Pesticides work in different ways. They can be grouped in any of several ways on the basis of their chemistry, how/when they work, or their site of action (see Table 7-2 for examples).

Table 7-2: Pesticide Activity - How Pesticides Work

Pesticide Activity	Explanation of Effect
Selective	Affects only certain kinds of plants or animals. For example, the herbicide 2,4-D is used to control weeds in lawns because it kills many broadleaf plants but does not harm grasses.
Nonselective	Kills a wide variety of pests.
Contact	Kills the pest simply by touching it.
Systemic	Are absorbed or ingested and circulate throughout the sap of a plant or blood of an animal.
Translocated	Are absorbed and move from the point of initial application to circulate throughout the plant.
Stomach Poison	Kills pests when swallowed, or when treated materials are eaten.
Protectant	Prevents certain diseases. Protectants must be applied before the disease has a chance to invade.
Curative/Eradicant	Cures fungal diseases.

The Pesticide Label

In order for a pesticide to be sold, purchased, or used in the United States, the pesticide must be registered by the EPA. Registration decisions are based on the agency's examination of the

- Ingredients of the pesticide.
- Intended application site.
- Amount, frequency, and timing of use.
- Storage and disposal practices.

The EPA assesses both risks and benefits of a product. They only register pesticide products that the agency has determined will not pose unreasonable adverse effects to humans, the environment, and nontarget species when used according to label directions. A product cannot be legally sold, purchased, or used as a pesticide until it is registered with the EPA's Office of Pesticide Programs.

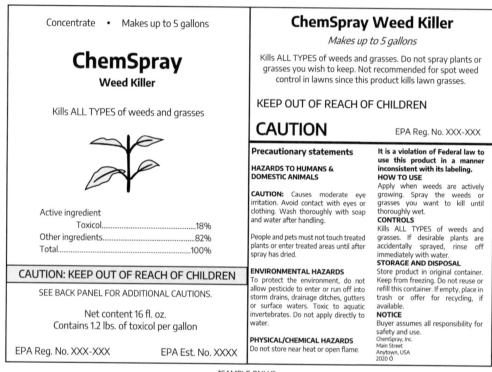

Figure 7-4: Pesticide label sample: This sample label shows the kinds of information found on pesticide labels, including the brand name, ingredients, EPA registration and establishment numbers (bottom left side), signal word (in this case, "Caution"), and more.

Another category of available products is Section 25(b), minimum-risk pesticides. Minimum-risk pesticides are exempt from federal registration by the EPA because they have been determined to pose little to no risk to human health or the environment. Minimum-risk pesticides are often derived from plant and food compounds and therefore are considered relatively benign. Although EPA does not require federal registration of Section 25(b), minimum-risk pesticides, many states require them to be registered with their state pesticide regulatory agency. In Virginia, these products must be registered with the VDACS-OPS if they are to be manufactured, distributed, sold, or used within the state. Be aware that because minimum-risk pesticides are exempt from the federal registration process, their labels may offer limited information on safety and efficacy. Exercise caution and follow all label directions if using minimum-risk pesticides no matter how natural the ingredients appear.

Federal law defines pesticide labeling as all of the print information and graphics (label, booklet) attached to or sold with the product. The pesticide label is a binding legal agreement among three parties: the product registrant (manufacturer), the EPA, and the end user.

The pesticide label must provide the user with all the necessary information on safe and effective use, proper storage, and proper disposal of the pesticide and its container. Pesticide users are required to follow all label directions. Using a pesticide in any manner that is inconsistent with the labeling is against the law.

Specific parts of the label identify the product, its hazards and precautions for handlers, and directions for proper use, storage, and disposal. The following section lists the information commonly found in specific parts of the pesticide label.

Brand Name: Each company uses brand names to identify their products. The brand name is displayed prominently on the front panel of the label.

Ingredients Statement: The ingredients statement lists the active ingredients (the chemicals that affect or control the target pest). It must list the chemical name and amount of each active ingredient (as a percentage by weight of the total product). The label must also show what percent of the total contents are other (inert) ingredients.

> Pesticides have complex chemical names describing their chemical composition. Many chemical names are shortened into common names to make them easier to identify. A product label may use the chemical name, common name, or both to identify the active ingredient(s).

EPA Registration Number: A registration number must be on every pesticide label. This number shows that the product has been registered with the EPA for the uses listed on the label. EPA registration numbers are unique to each individual pesticide product.

EPA Establishment Number: The establishment number identifies the facility where the pesticide was produced.

Name and Address of Manufacturer: The law requires the manufacturer or distributor of a pesticide product to print the name and address of their company on the label.

Net Contents: The front panel of a pesticide states how much product is in the container. This can be listed as pints, pounds, quarts, gallons, or other units of measure.

Type of Pesticide: The front panel usually indicates in general terms what the pesticide will control. This statement might also indicate how the product may be used.

Type of Formulation: A pesticide formulation is the mixture of chemical ingredients (active and inert) that allows the product to be used effectively for the purpose claimed. Pesticide formulations can be sold as ready-to-use (meaning no further mixing is required) or as concentrated formulations, which require mixing and/or application equipment. Sometimes the formulation of a specific product is written on the label or is part of the product name (e.g., bait, dust, granule).

"Restricted Use" Designation: When a pesticide is classified as restricted use, the label will state "Restricted Use Pesticide" in a box at the top of the front panel. There may also be a statement describing the reason for the restricted use classification. Restricted use pesticides are not for home and garden use and should only be used by a certified pesticide applicator.

Precautionary Statements: Precautionary statements identify hazards associated with the use of the product, how to avoid them, and first aid for various exposure situations. The product's toxicity is described by the signal word. All pesticide products carry the child hazard warning statement "Keep Out of Reach of Children." The precautionary statements section of a label may also include personal protective equipment (PPE) requirements, user safety requirements and recommendations, environmental hazards, and physical or chemical hazards.

Signal Words and Symbols: You can tell how acutely toxic a pesticide product is by the signal word on the label.

Table 7-3: Signal Words and Meaning

Signal Word	Toxicity Level	Lethal Oral Dosage	Skin, Eye, or Respiratory Injury
DANGER/POISON or DANGER	High	A drop to a teaspoonful.	Corrosive; permanent or severe damage.
WARNING	Moderate	A teaspoonful to a tablespoonful.	Moderate damage.
CAUTION	Low (or relatively nontoxic)	More than an ounce.	Mild damage or irritation.

Pesticides with the signal word DANGER are typically not sold in the lawn and garden trade.

First Aid (Statement of Practical Treatment): The label provides emergency first aid instructions and describes the types of exposure requiring medical attention. Four routes of exposure can be harmful: ingestion (swallowing), inhalation (inhaling vapors), ocular (eyes) exposure, and dermal (skin) exposure.

Personal Protective Equipment (PPE): The label lists all protective clothing and equipment you must use when handling the product. At minimum, you should always wear long pants, a long-sleeved shirt, socks, and closed-toed shoes.

Hazards to Humans and Domestic Animals: This section must be included if a product is hazardous to humans or domestic animals. It will tell you if and how a product may harm people and animals. It will also describe any special steps necessary to avoid exposures.

Environmental Hazards: The label tells you how to avoid harm to the environment — including water, soil, air, and beneficial insects, plants, and/or wildlife. Some examples of hazard statements are:

- "This product is highly toxic to bees. Do not apply this product to blooming crops or weeds when bees are actively visiting the treatment area."
- "This product is highly toxic to fish. Do not apply directly to water."

Physical and Chemical Hazards: This section lists any specific fire, explosive, or chemical hazards the product may have.

Directions for Use: This section describes where, when, and how to apply the product, how much to use, and how to handle the product from start to finish. These instructions will:

- Identify the sites (whether it is crops, animals, or other locations) that can be treated legally and safely with the product.
- Describe anything you must do — or not do — to prevent contamination or exposure to sensitive areas and nontarget species.
- List the pests the product will control.
- Explain how the product should be applied (application equipment or methods to use).
- Tell you when to apply this product (season; pest or host growth stage; restrictions based on temperature, weather, or time of day, if any).
- List the restricted entry interval and pre-harvest interval* (if applicable).
- Tell you how much to use (how much to mix).
- Give you instructions regarding storage and disposal.

> All pesticide labels have a restricted entry interval (REI). The REI indicates how long to stay out of treated areas. Some products instruct you to keep people or pets out of the treated area for a short period of time, or until certain conditions are met. For example, the label may state, "Do not allow people or pets to enter the treated area until sprays have dried."
>
> *Pesticides labeled for use on food crops have a pre-harvest interval (PHI). The PHI is a period between the time of application and the time it is safe to pick and use the crop. A pre-harvest interval is usually written as "days to harvest."

Misuse Statement: This section will remind you that it is a violation of federal law to use a product in a manner that is inconsistent with its labeling.

In summary, pesticide product labels provide instructions for all steps of pesticide use. Applicators must read, understand, and follow label directions carefully. Remember:

- Pesticides may not be applied to any plant, animal, or site not listed on the product label.
- Pesticides may not be applied at higher rates or more frequently than the label directs.
- Pesticide applicators are required to follow label directions for transport, mixing, loading, application, storage, and disposal of pesticide products and their containers.

Pesticide label directions are NOT advice; they are legal requirements. Read the label before you purchase a pesticide product and before, during, and after each use. **THE LABEL IS THE LAW!**

Pesticide Formulations

The pesticide formulation describes the physical state of a pesticide. Pesticides are usually formulated as a mixture of active and other (inert) ingredients. The active ingredient is the chemical that affects or controls the target pest. The inert ingredients dilute the pesticide and make it easier or safer to handle.

Pesticide active ingredients are often formulated as liquid or dry materials. In some cases, abbreviations on the pesticide label are used to describe the formulation. The same pesticide active ingredient may be available in more than one formulation. You should choose a formulation that is right for the job. Common pesticide formulations are listed below.

- **Aerosols (A)**: These are low-concentrate solutions that are applied as a fine spray or mist. Ready-to-use aerosols are generally sold in pressurized cans that release pesticide when the nozzle valve is triggered. Use caution with these products as they pose a risk of inhalation exposure. Examples of aerosols include wasp or hornet control products.
- **Baits (B)**: These are made by adding the active ingredient to an edible or attractive substance. They are ready-to-use but require careful placement to avoid contact with nontarget wildlife, children, and pets. Examples of baits include ant and cockroach control products.
- **Dusts (D)**: These are made by adding the active ingredient to a fine, inert powder or talc. Most dusts are ready-to-use and do not require further dilution or mixing. They must be used with caution as they have the potential to drift offsite and can cause inhalation exposure.
- **Emulsifiable Concentrates (EC or E):** These contain an oil-soluble liquid active ingredient, one or more petroleum-based solvents, and an emulsifier (mixing agent). The emulsifier allows the product to mix with water to form an emulsion. Emulsifiable concentrates are a popular formulation for agricultural pest control.
- **Granules (G)**: These are similar to dust formulations, except the carrier particles are larger and heavier. Granular pesticides are ready-to-use but do require application equipment to broadcast the coarse particles. Examples of granules include "weed and feed" type products for lawns, which contain both herbicides (for weed control) and fertilizer.
- **Pellets (P)**: These are similar to granules but are more uniform in their shape and size. Pellets are ready-to-use and

are often used as spot treatments.
- **Solution (S):** These are often diluted with water to form a true solution that will not settle out or separate. Solutions are a popular formulation in household pest control products. They can be sold as ready-to-use products or as **concentrates (C)** which require mixing before use.
- **Ready-to-Use (RTU):** As the name implies, these formulations are ready for use. No further dilution or mixing is required. Ready-to-use products are packaged in their application equipment. RTU liquid formulations may come in a spray bottle or aerosol can. RTU dry formulations like dusts are packaged in application canisters. Many pesticide products are sold ready-to-use to make applications safer and easier for consumers.
- **Wettable Powders (WP):** These are made by combining the active ingredient with a fine powder. A wettable powder may look like a dust, but it is made to be mixed with water and applied as a spray with its particles suspended in water. Wettable powders need continuous agitation to keep the particles in suspension, which can make them difficult for home gardeners to use. In contrast, **soluble powders (SP)** dissolve readily in water to form a true solution and are much easier to mix and apply.

Adjuvants

Adjuvants are added to a pesticide mix to improve the action of the pesticide or to modify the properties of the formulation or mix for better application. There are many types of adjuvants. They include wetting agents, spreaders, stickers, emulsifiers, plant penetrants, drift control additives, buffers or pH modifiers, and antifoaming agents. If an adjuvant is not already present in the formulation, recommendations for adding adjuvants will appear on the label as necessary. Adjuvants are sold separately from pesticides unless they are already included in a formulation. Make sure to follow all label directions and recommendations concerning adjuvants exactly.

Personal Safety

In general, two factors determine your risk when using a pesticide: your exposure to the product and its toxicity. The best way to manage risk is by reducing exposure through use of personal protective equipment. PPE provides an additional line of defense to prevent accidental exposure. Select ready-to-use products that are sold in an application device whenever possible. This will help minimize or eliminate the need to handle pesticides during mixing, measuring, or loading. In addition, careful product selection, such as choosing the least toxic chemical (based on the label's signal word), can further help to minimize risk. Always read and follow the product label before you purchase or apply any pesticide.

Never eat, drink, or smoke while handling pesticides. Before applying a pesticide, clear all people, pets, and livestock from the area. If possible, to reduce your own exposure while spraying, aim the spray so you will not walk through just-treated areas. After using any pesticide, wash your hands and arms thoroughly with soap and water. If you have been doing a lot of spraying or dusting, take a shower as soon as possible.

Personal Protective Equipment

The product label lists the minimum personal protective equipment required for handling the pesticide. Requirements and recommendations for PPE vary and depend on the toxicity and the formulation of the product. Any time you handle pesticides, wear at a minimum a long-sleeved shirt, long pants, socks, and close-toed shoes. Additional activities such as mixing and loading may require further PPE like unlined chemical-resistant gloves, an apron, and/or goggles. Consider wearing additional PPE for:

- Mixing concentrates and loading an application device.
- Making a broadcast spray application with hand-held equipment.
- Walking into a recently treated area.
- Treating an enclosed space.
- Using an aerosol or powder duster (especially indoors).
- Making an overhead application (like spraying fruit trees).

Protective clothing and equipment should be laundered separately from the family wash. After laundering, run an empty load (hot water and detergent) through your washing machine to rinse out any leftover pesticide residues. Line dry items on a sunny day to help break down remaining pesticide residues. Do not dry your protective clothing in a dryer.

If you spill pesticide on yourself or your clothing, shower immediately. Follow the first aid procedures on the pesticide label. Any clothing that was fully saturated should be discarded.

Safety Precautions

Pesticides can cause severe illness or even death if misused. It is important to follow all label directions for use (PPE, application instructions, storage, disposal) to help prevent accidents. Applicators can become ill from mishandling or accidental spills. Always use safety precautions and treat all pesticides with respect. Keep all pesticides in their original containers and out of the reach of children and pets.

Figure 7-5: Personal protective equipment: Any time you handle pesticides wear at a minimum a long-sleeved shirt, long pants, socks, and close-toed shoes.

Symptoms of Pesticide Poisoning

Awareness of the early symptoms and signs of a pesticide poisoning is important. Unfortunately, all pesticide poisoning symptoms are not the same and can resemble other illnesses like the flu or heat stress. It is important to monitor yourself after working with pesticides. If symptoms develop, they will come in stages, usually in this order:

- **Mild Poisoning or Early Symptoms of Acute Poisoning:** Fatigue, headache, dizziness, blurred vision, excessive sweating and salivation, nausea and vomiting, stomach cramps, or diarrhea.
- **Moderate Poisoning or Intermediate Symptoms of Acute Poisoning:** Symptoms described above become more severe. In addition, new symptoms may include the inability to walk, weakness, chest discomfort, muscle twitches, or constriction of the pupil of the eyes.
- **Severe Poisoning or Advanced Symptoms of Acute Poisoning:** Unconsciousness, severe constriction of the pupil of the eyes, muscle twitches, convulsions, secretions from the mouth and nose, and difficulty breathing. Death may occur without medical treatment.

In cases of acute poisoning, ill effects will appear soon after exposure — usually within 24 hours. Acute effects are usually obvious and often reversible if the person receives proper medical treatment. Talk with your physician if you begin feeling ill after working with pesticides.

Emergency Procedures

Read the first aid section on the label before using a product. The directions can save lives. In pesticide emergencies, the best first aid is to stop the exposure as soon as possible. The pesticide label directions describe how to handle each type of exposure (i.e., dermal, ocular, inhalation, and ingestion).

In case of acute poisoning, seek medical attention immediately. If you call a physician, give the victim's name, age, and sex. Identify yourself and your relationship to the victim. As with any poisoning incident, have the pesticide packaging on hand. Tell the physician what chemical was involved (and how much) and how the victim was exposed. Describe the incident to the best of your ability. If you take a victim to a hospital, take the pesticide container or the labeling with you. Transport the pesticide product safely. Never carry a pesticide container in the passenger space of a car or truck.

In the case of a poisoning emergency, assistance is available from Virginia's Poison Control Centers. The telephone number of the nearest Poison Control Center, along with other emergency information, is listed in the introductory sections of the Virginia Cooperative Extension Pest Management Guides. To purchase one of these guides or to ask about emergency information in advance, contact your local Extension agent.

Protecting the Environment

Pollinator Protection: Gardeners should give special consideration to protecting pollinators and other beneficial insects from pesticide poisoning. There is detailed information about pollinator protection in the Virginia Cooperative Extension, "Pest Management Guide: Home Grounds and Animals." Often, pesticide labels recommend restricted application times to protect pollinators. In general, bees are less active in the late evening and early morning. Do not apply insecticides to plants in bloom. If possible, choose an active ingredient that is relatively nontoxic to bees. Also, if possible, use products formulated as granules, liquid concentrates, or ready-to-use spray solutions rather than dusts, or sprays made from dry formulated materials.

Pesticide Movement: Pesticides cause problems when they move off target. This may mean drifting in the form of airborne dust or fine mist, moving with soil particles through erosion, leaching through the soil, being carried as residues on crops or livestock, or evaporating into vapors and moving with air currents.

Pesticides should be directed to the target. To minimize drift, do not apply them on windy days. Applications can be managed in a light, steady breeze. However, if strong or gusty winds begin while you are working, stop immediately. Generally, the safest time of day to spray to reduce the hazard of drift is early morning or late in the evening.

Vaporization (or volatilization) is the evaporation of a pesticide during or after application. Pesticide vapors can cause injury to highly sensitive plants like grapevines and tomatoes. High temperatures increase vaporization. Some pesticide products and formulations are very volatile and can move for miles under favorable conditions. Choose pesticide formulations that do not volatilize easily, if possible. Check the pesticide label for temperature restrictions relating to application.

Do not mix or load where a spill will contaminate water. Do not apply pesticides close to a well, creek, pond, or other water supply.

Pesticide Application Equipment

Using the same spray equipment for weed and insect control is neither safe nor desirable. No matter how well a tank is rinsed after using some herbicides, a residue may be left in the tank, gaskets, hoses, and other parts. If the same equipment is then used to spray a plant with insecticide or fungicide, the herbicide residue may kill or injure the plant. The wisest policy is to maintain two sprayers: one for herbicides and another for insecticides and fungicides. Have them clearly labeled according to use pattern.

Sprayers should be rinsed after each use. Do not forget to flush the hoses and nozzles. Proper rinsing will keep sprayers clean and in good working order. Also, replace nozzles when they begin to show signs of wear and tear.

Pesticide application equipment comes in all shapes, sizes, types, and prices. Select equipment that best suits your application needs.

Backpack Sprayer and Compressed-Air Sprayer: These sprayers have a small tank, generally one to four gallons, where the pesticide is mixed with a diluting agent such as water. A hand-operated pump supplies pressure for the application, and a single nozzle releases the spray at the end of a hand-held wand. Backpack sprayers are carried over the shoulders like a knapsack. Compressed-air sprayers have a small tank carried by a handle. These types of sprayers typically do not have in-tank agitation. As a result, some formulations, like wettable powders, would be difficult to apply because the product in the spray mix will settle out due to lack of agitation.

Hand Duster: The duster may consist of a squeeze tube or shaker, a plunger that slides through a tube, or a fan powered by a hand crank. Uniform coverage of target surfaces is often difficult to achieve with many dusters. Dusts are more subject to drift than liquid formulations due to their light weight and poor sticking qualities. Many dust formulations are sold in dispenser canisters.

Figure 7-6: Pesticide application equipment including a compressed air sprayer, hand duster, hose-end sprayer, and a backpack sprayer.

Hose-End Sprayer: These hand-held sprayers attach to a garden hose to deliver the spray mix from a quart-sized tank. Some hose-end sprayers are set to apply the spray mix at a fixed rate, while others may have a dial that allows for an adjustable rate. Fixed rate versions typically come ready-to-use, while adjustable rate versions require product to be added to the tank.

Spreaders: (not pictured) These are designed to apply granule or pellet formulations to lawns or crop fields. The two main types of spreaders are drop spreaders and rotary (or broadcast) spreaders. As the name implies, drop spreaders let pesticide drop from the opening under the spreader onto the ground directly below. Rotary spreaders release pesticide onto a turning disk that broadcasts it out in a circular pattern around the spreader.

Equipment Calibration and Care

Calibration is the process of measuring and adjusting the amount of pesticide that a piece of application equipment distributes over a target area. There are different processes for calibrating different types of equipment (e.g., backpack sprayer versus rotary spreader). For assistance with equipment calibration, contact your local Extension agent.

When and how you calibrate will depend on the pesticide label. All pesticide labels have mixing and application instructions. Some pesticides give application rates in teaspoons, tablespoons, or ounces per gallon. For example, an herbicide label may direct the user to make a 1% solution by mixing three tablespoons per gallon of water and then spray the target plants until their foliage is wet. In this instance, there is no need to calibrate the application equipment. However, the spray must be directed to the target, and coverage instructions must be followed.

Other labels give rates of application in volume per unit area; for example, teaspoons per 100 square feet or ounces per 1,000 square feet. This is often true for lawn herbicides and insecticides. Pesticides with rates given in volume per unit area must always be delivered with properly calibrated equipment.

Regular equipment maintenance is critical to accurate pesticide application. Always check spray equipment for leaking hoses or connections and plugged, worn, or dripping nozzles before adding pesticide. This will help prevent accidental spillage of chemicals. Check openings/gates of granular application devices (rotary or drop spreaders) to be sure they are clean and free of debris.

Storage and Disposal

Storage: Always read the pesticide label for specific storage requirements. The chemical and container in which it is purchased must be maintained in good condition. This is necessary to ensure the material remains useful and to avoid environmental or human health hazards.

Design or designate a pesticide storage area that has the following characteristics:

- Secure.
- Well-ventilated and dry.
- Protected from temperature extremes.
- Constructed in such a manner that leaks and/or spills may be contained.

A good storage area is safe from unwanted visitors — especially children and animals. Proper ventilation is important to protect the health of anyone using the storage area. It is essential to store pesticides where their fumes cannot invade areas used by people or pets. Dampness is a serious problem, as it reduces the shelf life of many chemicals and causes metal and paper containers to decompose. It is imperative that storage areas be designed so that there is no danger of chemicals being washed into storm drains or other water sources by flooding or accidental spills. Freezing and high heat are dangerous because temperature extremes may cause containers to rupture. Extreme heat and cold can also cause physical or chemical changes in some pesticide formulations. This can make the product less effective over time. Pesticide product labels often list temperature storage requirements. Finally, the storage area should be set up so that leaks and spills can be contained. Contained spills can be cleaned up without compromising the soil and water quality in the vicinity.

Keep cleanup materials (absorbent [e.g., kitty litter], broom, dustpan, water) separate but in close proximity to your storage area. Keep pesticides in their original containers. Do not store pesticides with or near food, medicine, cleaning supplies, seed, or animal feed. Do not store flammable materials with pesticides. Routinely inspect your storage area, and check containers for damage or leaks.

Disposal: Waste minimization and careful planning can reduce or eliminate disposal problems. Buy only the amount of pesticide you need for a job or the growing season. Consider small volume containers, even if you pay more for the active ingredient. Look for pesticides packaged in ways that reduce or eliminate container waste. Choose product formulations that simplify measuring and mixing. Often, ready-to-use products are the best choice for small pest-management jobs.

Never pour pesticides down the sink, into the toilet, or down any sewer or street drains. Never dump, bury, or burn excess pesticides. The best way to dispose of unmixed pesticide product is through proper use. Other methods for disposal include:

- Following label disposal directions.
- Participating in a local household hazardous waste collection program.
- Participating in a state pesticide collection program (check the VDACS Pesticide Collection Program website for more information: https://www.vdacs.virginia.gov/pesticide-collection.shtml).

Careful planning should prevent the problem of dealing with excess mixed pesticides. Once a pesticide has been mixed for an application, it should NOT be stored. The best disposal option for excess pesticide mix is to apply it to a legal site according to label directions. This means that the site (plant, place) must be listed on the product label, and the amount applied does not exceed the application rate allowed on the pesticide label. The best way to deal with leftover pesticide mixes is to avoid having any.

Be sure that rinse water does not become a pollutant. Water collected from cleaning pesticide-contaminated equipment can be applied to a properly labeled site.

Empty, properly rinsed, and drained pesticide containers should be disposed of according to label directions. In many cases, these can be placed in household trash or offered for recycling if available in your locality. Empty pesticide containers should be punctured to prevent re-use before discarding. However, you should never puncture (or burn) a pressurized container such as an aerosol can because it can explode. Always refer to the pesticide label for directions on container disposal.

If you have questions about proper pesticide disposal, contact your local solid waste authority; the VDACS-OPS (https://www.vdacs.virginia.gov/pesticides.shtml); or your local Extension office (https://ext.vt.edu/offices.html).

Spill Management: The best defense against pesticide spills is to work carefully. Keep PPE and spill cleanup materials handy — close to the place where you are mixing and loading application equipment. In case of an accident, refer to the product label for directions for spill management. If there are no specific directions regarding spill remediation, remember the three C's: control, contain, and clean up.

Control the spill by first taking steps to protect yourself and others. Put on PPE if you need to handle a leaking container or may be exposed when controlling a spill. Then, stop the source of the spill. This may be as simple as placing a leaking container into a larger, chemical-resistant one or setting a fallen container upright. Do not leave a spill unattended until it is cleaned up.

Contain a liquid spill by confining it with soil, kitty litter, newspaper, vermiculite, sand, or absorbent pads. You can contain dry pesticides such as dusts, granules, or powders by covering them up with a sheet of plastic. Do not apply water — that will just spread the material over a wider area and make clean up more difficult.

Clean up a liquid spill by using a broom and dustpan to sweep up any absorbent materials you used to contain the spill, and place it into a heavy-duty plastic bag or bucket. Clean up a dry spill by sweeping up the pesticide with a broom and dustpan. If the pesticide was not contaminated, you may use it for a later application. If too much debris is mixed with the spilled pesticide, place the pesticide into a heavy-duty plastic bag or bucket. Decontaminate the spill site by washing the area with water and heavy-duty detergent (only use enough water to clean the area). Cover the area again with absorbent material, sweep up the contents, and add them to your heavy-duty bag or plastic bucket. These materials will need to be properly disposed of according to label directions. Clean all PPE and equipment used during the spill cleanup. Then be sure to wash yourself thoroughly with soap and water.

Things to keep on hand in case you need to handle a small spill include:

- Chemical-resistant gloves and absorbent materials for containing/absorbing liquid spills.
- A broom, dustpan, and heavy-duty detergent.
- A heavy-duty plastic bag or bucket.
- Any other spill cleanup materials specified on the labels of the products you use.
- Emergency contact information.

Choosing the Right Pesticide

Avoid problems by taking the time to study your pesticide needs carefully. Your local Extension agent or certified nursery employee can help with pesticide recommendations and suggest ways you can tailor the pesticide application to the intended site. Personal and environmental safety are prime concerns when selecting pesticides.

Consider the Site: Read the label of each product under consideration to ensure it can be used in the place and manner you intend. For example, if the label indicates the pesticide is toxic to fish, do not use the product on plants that border a pond. If the label requires that you wait two weeks from the time you spray until the time you harvest, do not use the product on vegetables or fruits that are almost ripe. If the product label lists only ornamental uses, do not apply it to fruits or vegetables. If a specific product gives application instructions for some types of vegetables but not others, use it ONLY on the crops listed in the "Directions for Use" section of the label. Consider all uses of the site to which the pesticide will be applied. Protect children, pets, and wildlife by careful pesticide selection and use.

Application Equipment and PPE: Do you have the right equipment and PPE? If not, are you willing to purchase, use, and maintain it? Do you want a pesticide that must be mixed and loaded into a sprayer? If you do not have the right PPE and equipment, you might consider other pesticide options that will suit your needs. A ready-to-use product may get the job done while saving you time and money.

Minimize Waste: Purchase only the amount of pesticide you anticipate using in one season. Most pesticides have a limited shelf life. If pesticides are stored, they must be protected from temperature extremes and moisture, and they must be kept in a secure location. Read the storage section of the product label prior to purchase, and do not buy a product that you cannot store as directed. Remember, pesticides must be kept in their original containers with the label intact.

Choose the Least Toxic Product: Compare pesticides based on how hazardous they are. The signal word on the label indicates a product's acute toxicity. For example, products marked CAUTION are less toxic than products marked WARNING, and should be considered first.

Environmental Hazards: Be especially cautious with pesticides that contain warnings regarding impacts on water, fish, birds, and pollinator health.

Disposal Directions: Be sure you can properly dispose of any unused or unwanted pesticide product and its container according to the label recommendations.

Pesticides can be valuable gardening tools and an important part of a well-planned IPM program, but they must be selected with personal and environmental safety in mind. As with other tools, it is important to use the right pesticide for the job. Care and planning before pesticides are purchased can ensure safe and proper use.

Additional Resources

- Virginia Tech Pesticide Programs (https://vtpp.ento.vt.edu/)
- Virginia Department of Agriculture Office of Pesticide Services (https://www.vdacs.virginia.gov/pesticides.shtml)
- "An Introduction to IPM " ENTO-365NP (https://www.pubs.ext.vt.edu/ENTO/ENTO-365/ENTO-365.html)
- "Reading Pesticide Product Labels" ENTO-390NP (https://www.pubs.ext.vt.edu/content/pubs_ext_vt_edu/en/ENTO/ENTO-390/ENTO-390.html)
- "Myth-busting Integrated Pest Management for Extension Master Gardeners" ENTO-388NP (https://www.pubs.ext.vt.edu/ENTO/ENTO-388/ENTO-388.html)

Attributions

Written by Stephanie Blevins Wycoff, Extension Associate, Virginia Tech Pesticide Programs; and Daniel Frank, Director, Virginia Tech Pesticide Programs (2022)

Edited by Dana Beegle, Publications Manager, Virginia Tech Pesticide Programs (2022)

Reviewed by Elizabeth Brown, Bedford Extension Master Gardener (2022)

Image Attributions

- Figure 7-1: IPM Toolbox. Grey, Kindred. 2022. CC BY-NC-SA 4.0.
- Figure 7-2: What is IPM Infographic. Johnson, Devon. 2022. CC BY-NC-SA 4.0.
- Figure 7-3: Control Methods. Grey, Kindred. 2022. CC BY-NC-SA 4.0.
- Figure 7-4: Pesticide label. Grey, Kindred. 2022. CC BY-NC-SA 4.0.
- Figure 7-5: Personal protective equipment. Grey, Kindred. 2022. CC BY-NC-SA 4.0.
- Figure 7-6: Application methods. Grey, Kindred. 2022. CC BY-NC-SA 4.0.

CHAPTER 8: PLANT PROPAGATION

Chapter Contents:

- Sexual Propagation
- Asexual Propagation
- Additional Resources

Plant propagation is the process of multiplying the numbers of or perpetuating a species or a specific individual plant. There are two types of propagation: sexual and asexual. Sexual reproduction requires the union of the sperm and egg and results in a plant with a new combination of genes. It involves the floral parts of a plant. Asexual propagation involves taking a part of one plant and causing it to regenerate itself into a new plant. Genetically it is identical to its "parent." Asexual propagation involves the vegetative parts of a plant: stems, roots, or leaves.

There can be advantages to sexual propagation. Sexual propagation may be quicker than other methods for some species, may be the only way to obtain new varieties and strong hybrids, may be the only viable method for propagation in some species, and can help avoid transmission of certain diseases. Asexual propagation has advantages as well. It may be easier and faster in some species, may be the only way to perpetuate some cultivars, and it bypasses the juvenile characteristics of certain species.

Sexual Propagation

Sexual propagation involves the union of the sperm (male) with the egg (female) to produce a seed. The seed is made up of three major parts: the outer seed coat, which protects the seed, the food reserve (usually the endosperm), and the embryo, which is the young plant itself (refer to Chapter 1: "Botany"). When a seed is mature, not in dormancy, and placed in a favorable environment, it will germinate, or begin active growth. In the following section, seed germination and transplanting of seeds will be discussed.

Seed

To obtain quality plants, start with good quality seed from a reliable supplier. Select varieties to provide the size, color, and habit of growth desired. Choose varieties adapted to your area which will reach maturity before an early frost. Many new vegetable and flower varieties are **hybrids** (a hybrid is the result of a sexual cross between two or more plants that are somewhat related), which cost a little more than **open pollinated** types (open pollinated seed is self or cross-pollinated by wind or insects and is produced by isolating plants from other plants of different varieties to produce seed that is "true to type"). However, hybrid plants usually have more vigor, more uniformity, and better production than non-hybrids and sometimes have specific disease resistance or other unique cultural characteristics.

Although some seeds will keep for several years if stored properly, it is advisable to purchase only enough seed for the current year's use. Good seed will not contain seed of any other crop, weeds, or other debris. The seed packet usually indicates essential information about the variety, the year for which the seeds were packaged, germination percentage you may typically expect, and notes of any chemical seed treatment. If seeds are obtained well in advance of the actual sowing date or are stored surplus seeds, keep them in a cool, dry place. Laminated foil packets help ensure dry storage. Paper packets are best kept in tightly closed containers and maintained around 40°F in a low humidity environment.

Some gardeners save seed from their own gardens; however, if such seed are the result of random pollination by insects or other natural agents, they may not produce plants typical of the parents. This is especially true of the many hybrid varieties. (See Chapter 9: "The Vegetable Garden" for information on saving vegetable seed.) Most seed companies take great care in handling seeds properly. Generally, do not expect more than 65% to 80% of the seeds to germinate, with lower rates as time passes. From those germinating, expect about 60% to 75% to produce satisfactory, vigorous, sturdy seedlings.

Germination

There are four environmental factors which affect germination: water, oxygen, light, and heat.

Water for germination

The first step in the germination process is the imbibition or absorption of water. Even though seeds have great absorbing power due to the nature of the seed coat, the amount of available water in the germination medium affects the uptake of water. An adequate, continuous supply of water is important to ensure germination. Once the germination process has begun, a dry period will cause the death of the embryo.

Light for germination

Light is known to stimulate or to inhibit germination of some seed. The light reaction involved here is a complex process. Some crops which have a requirement for light to assist seed germination are ageratum, begonia, browallia, impatiens, lettuce, and petunia. Conversely, calendula, centaurea, annual phlox, verbena, and vinca will germinate best in the dark. Other plants are not specific at all. Seed catalogs and seed packets often list germination or cultural tips for individual varieties. When sowing light-requiring seed, do as nature does and leave them on the soil surface. If they are covered at all, cover them lightly with fine peat moss or fine vermiculite. These two materials, if not applied too heavily, will permit some light to reach the seed without limiting germination and will help keep soil uniformly moist. When starting seed in the home, supplemental light can be provided by fluorescent or LED fixtures suspended 6 to 12 inches above the seeds for 16 hours a day.

Oxygen for germination

Respiration takes place in all viable seed. The respiration in dormant seed is low, but some oxygen is required. The respiration rate increases during germination, therefore, the medium in which the seeds are placed should be loose and well-aerated while still holding adequate water. If the oxygen supply during germination is limited or reduced, germination can be severely retarded or inhibited.

Heat for germination

A favorable temperature is another important requirement of germination. It not only affects the germination percentage but also the rate of germination. Some seeds will germinate over a wide range of temperatures, whereas others require a narrow range. Many seeds have minimum, maximum, and optimum temperatures at which they germinate. For example, tomato seed has a minimum germination temperature of 50°F and a maximum temperature of 95°F, but an optimum germination temperature of about 80°F. Where germination temperatures are listed, they are usually the optimum temperatures unless otherwise specified. Generally, 65 to 75°F is best for most plants. This often means the germination flats may have to be placed in special chambers or on radiators, heating cables, or heating mats to maintain optimum temperature. The importance of maintaining proper medium temperature to achieve maximum germination percentages cannot be overemphasized.

Germination will begin when certain internal requirements have been met. A seed must not be in a dormant state, have a mature embryo, contain a large enough endosperm to sustain the embryo during germination, and contain sufficient hormones or auxins to initiate the process.

Methods of breaking dormancy

One of the functions of dormancy is to prevent a seed from germinating before it is surrounded by a favorable environment. In some trees and shrubs, seed dormancy is difficult to break, even when the environment is ideal. Various treatments are performed on the seed to break dormancy and begin germination. Most vegetable and flowering annuals do not have significant dormancy.

Seed scarification

Seed **scarification** involves breaking, scratching, or softening the seed coat so that water can enter and begin the germination process. There are several methods of scarifying seeds. In mechanical scarification, seeds are filed with a metal file, rubbed with sandpaper, or cracked with a hammer to weaken the seed coat. Hot water scarification involves putting the seed into hot water (170 to 212°F). The seeds are allowed to soak in the water, as it cools, for 12 to 24 hours before being planted. A fourth method is one of warm, moist scarification. In this case, seeds are stored in non-sterile, warm, damp containers where the seed coat will be broken down by decay over several months. Acid scarification involves dissolving the seed coat with acid.

Seed stratification

Seeds of some fall-ripening trees, shrubs, some perennials and other plants of the temperate zone will not germinate unless chilled underground as they overwinter. Gardeners can replicate this with **cold stratification,** or exposing seeds to a period of cold temperatures to break their dormancy cycle.

The following procedure is usually successful. Put sand or vermiculite in a clay pot to about 1 inch from the top.

Place the seeds on top of the medium and cover with 1/2 inch of sand or vermiculite. Wet the medium thoroughly and allow excess water to drain through the hole in the pot. Place the pot containing the moist medium and seeds in a plastic bag and seal. Place the bag in a refrigerator. Periodically check to see that the medium is moist, but not wet. Additional water will probably not be necessary. After 10 to 12 weeks, remove the bag from the refrigerator. Take the pot out and set it in a warm place in the house. Water often enough to keep the medium moist. Soon the seedlings should emerge. When the young plants are about 3 inches tall, transplant them into pots to grow until they are ready to be set outside.

Another procedure that is usually successful uses sphagnum moss or peat moss. Wet the moss thoroughly, then squeeze out the excess water with your hands. Mix seed with the sphagnum or peat and place in a plastic bag. Seal the bag and put it in a refrigerator. Check periodically. If there is condensation on the inside of the bag, the process will probably be successful. After 10 to 12 weeks remove the bag from the refrigerator. Plant the seeds in pots to germinate and grow. Handle seeds carefully. Often the small roots and shoots are emerging at the end of the stratification period. Care must be taken not to break these off. Temperatures in the range of 35 to 45°F (2 to 7°C) are effective. Most refrigerators operate in this range. Seeds of most fruit and nut trees can be successfully germinated by these procedures. Seeds of peaches should be removed from the hard pit. Care must be taken when cracking the pits. Any injury to the seed itself can be an entry path for disease organisms.

Starting Seed Indoors

Media

A wide range of materials can be used to start seeds, from plain vermiculite or mixtures of soilless media to the various amended soil mixes. With experience, you will learn to determine what works best under your conditions. However, keep in mind what the good qualities of a germinating medium are. It should be rather fine and uniform (to promote good seed to soil contact), yet well-aerated and loose. It should be free of insects, disease organisms, and weed seeds. It should also be of low fertility or total soluble salts and capable of holding and moving moisture by capillary action. Traditionally, one mixture which has been used to supply these factors is a combination of 1/3 sterilized soil, 1/3 sand or vermiculite or perlite, and 1/3 peat moss. Ideally seedlings are started in a mixture compound of sphagnum peat moss and vermiculite. **Do not use garden soil by itself to start seedlings; it is not sterile, is too heavy, and will not drain well.**

The importance of using a sterile medium and container cannot be overemphasized. The home gardener can treat a small quantity of soil mixture in an oven. Place the slightly moist soil in a heat-resistant container in an oven set at about 250°F. Use a candy or meat thermometer to ensure that the mix reaches a temperature of 180°F for at least 1/2 hour. Avoid overheating as this can be extremely damaging to the soil. Be aware that the heat will release very unpleasant odors in the process of sterilization. This treatment should prevent damping-off and other plant diseases, as well as eliminate potential plant pests. Growing containers and implements should be washed to remove any debris, then rinsed in a dilution of 9 parts water to 1 part 5.25% sodium hypochlorite (bleach) or 14 parts water to 1 part 8.25% sodium hypochlorite.

An artificial, soilless mix also provides the desired qualities of a good germination medium. The basic ingredients of such a mix are sphagnum peat moss and vermiculite, both of which are generally free of diseases, weed seeds, and insects. Sphagnum peat moss also contains anti-fungal properties which can be beneficial for seedlings. The ingredients are also readily available, easy to handle, lightweight, and produce uniform plant growth. "Peat-lite" mixes or similar products are commercially available or can be made at home using this recipe: 4 quarts of shredded sphagnum peat moss or coconut coir, 4 quarts of fine vermiculite, 1 tablespoon of superphosphate, and 2 tablespoons of ground limestone. Mix thoroughly. These mixes have little fertility, so seedlings must be watered with a diluted fertilizer solution soon after they emerge.

Containers

Flats and trays can be purchased or you can make your own containers for starting seeds by recycling such things as cottage cheese containers, styrofoam cups, the bottoms of milk cartons or bleach containers, recycled newspaper pots, and pie pans, as long as good drainage is provided. You can also purchase tools to make your own compressed soil blocks for starting seed.

Clay or plastic pots can be used, and numerous types of pots and strips made of compressed peat are also on the market. Plant bands and plastic cell packs are also available. Each cell or minipot holds a single plant which reduces the risk of root injury when transplanting. Peat pellets, peat or fiber-based blocks, and expanded foam cubes can also be used for seeding.

Seeding

The proper time for sowing seeds for transplants depends upon when plants may safely be moved outdoors in your area. This period may range from 4 to 12 weeks prior to transplanting, depending upon the speed of germination, the rate of growth, and the cultural conditions provided. A common mistake is to sow the seeds too early and then attempt to hold the seedlings back under poor light or improper temperature ranges. This usually results in tall, weak, spindly plants which do not perform well in the garden.

After selecting a container, fill it to within 3/4-inch of the top with moistened growing medium. For very small seeds, at least the top 1/4-inch should be a fine, screened mix or a layer of vermiculite. Firm the medium at the corners and edges with your fingers or a block of wood to provide a uniform, flat surface.

For medium and large seeds, make furrows 1 to 2 inches apart and 1/8 to 1/4-inch deep across the surface of the container using a narrow board or pot label. By sowing in rows, good light and air movement results, and if damping-off fungus does appear, there is less chance of it spreading. Seedlings in rows are easier to label and handle at transplanting time than those which have been sown in a broadcast manner. Sow the seeds thinly and uniformly in the rows by gently tapping the packet of seed as it is moved along the row. Lightly cover the seed with dry vermiculite or sifted medium if they require darkness for germination. A suitable planting depth is usually about twice the diameter of the seed.

Do not plant seeds too deeply. Extremely fine seed such as petunia, begonia, and snapdragon are not covered, but lightly pressed into the medium or watered in with a fine mist. If these seeds are broadcast, strive for a uniform stand by sowing half the seeds in one direction, then sowing the other way with the remaining seed in a crossing pattern.

Large seeds are frequently sown directly into some sort of a small container or cell pack which eliminates the need for early transplanting. Usually 2 or 3 seeds are sown per unit and later thinned to allow the strongest seedling to grow.

Pregermination

Another method of starting seeds is **pregermination**. This method involves sprouting the seeds before they are planted in pots (or in the garden). This reduces the time to germination, as the temperature and moisture are easy to control. A high percentage of germination is achieved since environmental factors are optimum. Lay seeds between the folds of a cotton cloth, paper towel, or on a layer of vermiculite in a shallow pan. Keep moist, in a warm place. When roots begin to show, place the seeds in containers or plant them directly in the garden. While transplanting seedlings, be careful not to break off tender roots. Continued attention to watering is critical.

Watering

After the seed has been sown, moisten the planting mix thoroughly. Use a fine mist or place the containers in a pan or tray which contains about 1 inch of warm water. Avoid splashing or excessive flooding which might displace small seeds. When the planting mix is saturated, set the container aside to drain. The soil should be moist but not wet.

Ideally, seed flats should remain sufficiently moist during the germination period without having to add water. One way to maintain moisture is to slip the whole flat or pot into a clear plastic bag after the initial watering. The plastic should be at least 1 inch from the soil. Many home gardeners cover their flats with panes of glass instead of using a plastic sleeve. Keep the container out of direct sunlight, otherwise the temperature may rise to the point where the seeds will be harmed. Be sure to remove the plastic bag or glass cover as soon as the first seedlings appear. Surface watering can then be practiced if care and good judgement are used.

Temperature and light after germination

Several factors for good germination have already been mentioned. The last item, and by no means the least important, is temperature. Since most seeds will germinate best at an optimum temperature that is usually higher than most home night temperatures, often special warm areas must be provided. Seed starting mats are an excellent method of providing constant heat.

After germination and seedling establishment, move the flats to a light, airy, cooler location, at a 55 to 60°F night temperature and a 65 to 70°F day reading. This will prevent soft, leggy growth and minimize disease troubles.

Some crops, of course, may germinate or grow best at a different constant temperature and must be handled separately from the bulk of the plants. Check the packet for proper germination temperature.

Seedlings grown indoors must receive bright light after germination, and natural daylight (even that from a south-facing window) is most often not adequate enough to produce viable seedlings indoors. Instead, place the seedlings under a fluorescent or LED light. Position the plants 6 inches from the tubes and keep the lights on about 16 hours each day. As the seedlings grow, the lights should be raised. When seedlings have formed 1 to 2 sets of true leaves, they are ready to be transplanted. For more information on planting seeds outdoors, see Chapter 9: "The Vegetable Garden."

Table 8-1: Seed germination requirements

Plant	Approximate time to seed before last spring frost	Approximate germination time (days)	Germination Temperature (°F)	Germinate in light (L) or dark (D) conditions
Begonia	12 weeks or more	10-15	70	L
Browallia	12 weeks or more	15-20	70	L
Geranium	12 weeks or more	10-20	70	L
Larkspur	12 weeks or more	5-10	55	D

Table 8-1: Seed germination requirements (continued)

Plant	Approximate time to seed before last spring frost	Approximate germination time (days)	Germination Temperature (°F)	Germinate in light (L) or dark (D) conditions
Pansy (Viola)	12 weeks or more	5-10	65	D
Vinca	12 weeks or more	10-15	70	D
Dianthus	10 weeks	5-10	70	-
Impatiens	10 weeks	15-20	70	L
Petunia	10 weeks	5-10	70	L
Portulaca	10 weeks	5-10	70	D
Snapdragon	10 weeks	5-10	65	L
Stock	10 weeks	10-15	70	-
Verbena	10 weeks	15-20	65	D
Ageratum	8 weeks	5-10	70	L
Alyssum	8 weeks	5-10	70	-
Broccoli	8 weeks	5-10	70	-
Cabbage	8 weeks	5-10	70	-
Cauliflower	8 weeks	5-10	70	-
Celosia	8 weeks	5-10	70	-
Coleus	8 weeks	5-10	65	L
Dahlia	8 weeks	5-10	70	-
Eggplant	8 weeks	5-10	70	-
Head lettuce	8 weeks	5-10	70	L
Nicotiana	8 weeks	10-15	70	L
Pepper	8 weeks	5-10	80	-
Phlox	8 weeks	5-10	65	-
Aster	6 weeks	5-10	70	D
Balsam	6 weeks	5-10	70	-
Centaurea	6 weeks	5-10	65	-
Marigold	6 weeks	5-10	70	D
Tomato	6 weeks	5-10	80	-
Zinnia	6 weeks	5-10	70	-
Cucumber	4 weeks or less	5-10	85	-
Cosmos	4 weeks or less	5-10	70	-
Muskmelon	4 weeks or less	5-10	85	-
Squash	4 weeks or less	5-10	85	-
Watermelon	4 weeks or less	5-10	85	-

Transplanting and Handling

If the plants have not been seeded in individual containers, they must be transplanted to give them proper growing space. One of the most common mistakes made is leaving the seedlings in the seed flat too long. The ideal time to transplant young seedlings is when they are small and there is little danger from setback. This is usually when the first set of true leaves appear above or between the cotyledon leaves (the cotyledons or seed leaves are the first leaves the seedling produces). Don't let plants get hard and stunted or tall and leggy.

Seedling growing mixes and containers can be purchased or prepared similar to those mentioned for germinating seed. The medium should contain more plant nutrients than a germination mix, however. Some commercial soilless mixes have fertilizer already added.

Containers for transplanting

There is a wide variety of containers from which to choose for transplanting seedlings. These containers should be economical, durable, and make good use of space. The type selected will depend on the type of plant to be transplanted and individual growing conditions. Standard pots are not recommended for the transplant from germination flats as they waste a great deal of space and may not dry out rapidly enough for the seedling to have sufficient oxygen for proper development.

There are many types of containers available commercially. Those made out of pressed peat can be purchased in varying sizes. Individual pots or strips of connected pots fit closely together, are inexpensive, and can be planted directly in the garden. When setting out plants grown in peat pots, be sure to cover the pot completely. If the top edge of the peat pot extends above the soil level, it will act as a wick, and draw water away from the soil in the pot. To avoid this, tear off the top lip of the pot and then plant flush with the soil level. Compressed peat pellets, when soaked in water, expand to form compact, individual pots. They waste no space, don't fall apart as badly as peat pots, and can be set directly out in the garden. If you wish to avoid transplanting seedlings altogether, compressed peat pellets are excellent for direct sowing.

Community packs are containers in which there is room to plant several plants. These are generally inexpensive. The main disadvantage of a community pack is that the roots of the individual plants must be broken or cut apart when separating them to put out in the garden. Cell packs, which are strips of connected individual pots, are also available in plastic and are frequently used by commercial bedding plant growers, as they withstand frequent handling. In addition, many homeowners find a variety of materials from around the house useful for containers. These homemade containers should be deep enough to provide adequate soil and have plenty of drainage holes in the bottom. For example, styrofoam egg cartons make good cell packs.

Transplanting

Carefully dig up the small plants with a knife or plant label. Avoid tearing roots in the process. Let the group of seedlings fall apart and pick out individual plants. Gently ease them apart in small groups which will make it easier to separate individual plants. Handle small seedlings by their leaves, not their delicate stems. Punch a hole in the medium into which the seedling will be planted. Make it deep enough so the seedling can be put at the same depth it was growing in the seed flat. After planting, firm the soil and water gently. Keep newly transplanted seedlings in the shade for a few days, or place them under fluorescent lights. Keep them away from direct heat sources. Begin a fertilization program. When fertilizing, use a soluble house plant fertilizer, at the dilution recommended by the manufacturer, about every 2 weeks after the seedlings are established. Remember that young seedlings are easily damaged by too much fertilizer, especially if they are under any moisture stress.

Hardening plants

Hardening is the process of altering the quality of plant growth to withstand the change in environmental conditions which occurs when plants are transferred from a greenhouse or home to the garden. A severe check in growth may occur if plants produced in the home are planted outdoors without a transition period. Hardening is most critical with early crops, when adverse climatic conditions can be expected. To avoid sun scorch, cold shock, and/or wind damage, plants must be hardened off.

Hardening can be accomplished by gradually lowering temperatures and relative humidity and reducing water. This procedure results in an accumulation of carbohydrates and a thickening of cell walls. A change from a soft, succulent type of growth to a firmer, harder type is desired.

This process should be started at least 2 weeks before planting in the garden. If possible, plants should be moved to a 45 to 50°F temperature indoors or outdoors in a shady location. A coldframe is excellent for this purpose. When put outdoors, plants should be shaded, then gradually moved into sunlight. Each day, gradually increase the length of exposure. Don't put tender seedlings outdoors on windy days or when temperatures are below 45°F. Reduce the frequency of watering to slow growth, but don't allow plants to wilt. Even cold-hardy plants will be hurt if exposed to freezing temperatures before they are hardened. After proper hardening, however, they can be planted outdoors and light frosts will not damage them.

The hardening process is intended to slow plant growth. If done too quickly, growth will stop and significant damage can be done to certain crops. For example, cauliflower will make thumb size heads and fail to develop further if hardened too severely.

Propagation by Spores

Though ferns are more easily propagated by other methods, some gardeners like the challenge of raising ferns from spores. One tested method for small quantities follows:

Put a solid, sterilized masonry brick (bake at 250°F for 30 minutes) in a pan and add water to cover the brick. When the brick is wet throughout, squeeze a thin layer of moist soil and peat (1:1) into the top of the brick. Pack a second layer (about an inch) on top of that. Sprinkle spores on top. Cover with plastic (not touching the spores) or put in a plastic shoe box and put in a warm place in indirect light. It may take a month or more for the spores to germinate. Keep moist at all times. A prothallus (one generation of the fern) will develop first from each spore, forming a light green mat. Mist lightly once a week to maintain high surface moisture; the sperm must be able to swim to the archegonia (female parts). After about three weeks, fertilization should have occurred. Pull the mat apart with tweezers in 1/4-inch squares and space them 1/2-inch apart in a flat containing a 2-inch layer of sand, 1/4-inch of charcoal, and about 2 inches of soil/peat mix. Cover with plastic and keep moist. When fern fronds appear and become crowded, transplant to small pots. Gradually reduce the humidity until they can survive in the open. Light exposure may be increased at this time.

Asexual Propagation

Asexual propagation is the best way to maintain some species, particularly an individual that best represents that species.

The major methods of asexual propagation are cuttings, layering, division, and budding/grafting. Cuttings involve rooting a severed piece of the parent plant. Layering involves rooting a part of the parent and then severing it. Budding and grafting are joining two plant parts from different varieties. **Clones** are groups of plants that are identical to their one parent and that can only be propagated asexually. The Bartlett pear (1770) and the Delicious apple (1870) are two examples of clones that have been asexually propagated for many years.

Rooting Media

Rooting media for asexual propagation should be clean and sterile. Cuttings are not susceptible to damping-off, but are attacked by other fungi and bacteria which may come along in the medium. Most commercially prepared media are purchased clean.

This media needs a combination of good aeration and water-holding capacity. In order for a plant to form a new root system, it must have a ready moisture supply at the cut surface. Oxygen, of course, is required for all living cells. The coarse-textured media choices often meet these requirements.

The media should be low in fertilizer, as discussed for sexual propagation. Excessive fertility will damage or inhibit new roots.

100% coarse perlite can be used to start some cuttings. This doesn't hold much water for long, but it is fine for rooting cuttings of cactus-type plants which would ordinarily rot in higher moisture media. 100% coarse vermiculite has excellent water holding capacity and aeration, but may dry out rapidly via evaporation if not covered in some way. 50% peat moss and 50% perlite is a good mix that favors aeration. An equal mix of peat moss, vermiculite, and perlite is also a good mix which favors moisture retention.

Plain water can be used to propagate some cuttings. This is possible and actually works quite well for some species which root easily. It certainly provides the needed moisture, but if the water is not changed on a weekly basis it will become stagnant, oxygen deficient, and inhibitory to rooting. Furthermore, roots produced in 100% water are different than those produced in solid media; they may undergo greater transplant shock with a greater incidence of death. So it is not the most desirable, but certainly feasible.

Rooting Enhancement Conditions

Once you've selected the right medium, your first priority is to get roots produced as quickly as possible. The consequences of slow rooting invariably mean death because the cutting must rely on its limited water reserves. Water is required for major chemical reactions in plants which will be shut down in its absence. Even though the exposed cells on the cut surface of the cutting ordinarily transport water throughout the plant, they are not equipped to absorb it from the medium. This can only be done in most plants by roots, and particularly root hairs. Root hairs are tiny, single-cell projections from the larger roots.

Make sure the medium is moist prior to inserting cuttings. If incompletely moist, then the cut surface may contact a dry pocket and have its own water absorbed away by the medium component. Try to keep both the air and medium temperature warm: 70-75°F. Higher temperatures enhance growth, but excessively high temperatures do not allow for production via photosynthesis to keep up with food breakdown in normal cell energy use (respiration). You can buy electric heating pads to put beneath containers holding cuttings to maintain a constant temperature.

Get some air circulation around the cuttings as often as possible. This discourages fungal growth. Place in bright, but not direct light. An east window is fine, but a west window is too warm; a south facing window is too bright and a north facing window is too dim. Indoor florescent or LED lights are the best way to ensure adequate light supply to the cuttings.

One way to provide good environmental conditions for asexual propagation is through the use of a mist bed. This system sprays a fine mist of water over the cuttings once every few minutes, and the time is adjustable. It should only be on during the day, as nighttime operation would keep the medium too wet and encourage rotting. Misting inhibits transpiration and forces the plant to conserve water while it forms new roots. If a mist system is unavailable, one can be imitated in a small propagation tray in the home. Choose an appropriate medium, moisten it, and place it in a tray. Place the tray in a perforated or slitted clear plastic bag. This increases the relative humidity and inhibits water loss by the plant and medium yet allows air circulation.

Tug gently at the cuttings after 2-3 weeks to test for rooting and transplant to individual pots when roots resist your tugs. Dig them out, do not pull them out! Different plants require different rooting times, so do not expect them all to root at the same time. For information on starting plants outdoors, see Chapter 9: "The Vegetable Garden."

Cuttings

Many types of plants, both woody and herbaceous, are frequently propagated by cuttings. A **cutting** is a vegetative plant part which is severed from the parent plant in order to regenerate itself, thereby forming a whole new plant. Take cuttings from healthy, disease-free plants, preferably from the upper part of the plant (this season's growth). Avoid taking cuts from leggy stems, heavily fertilized plants, or plants showing symptoms of moisture stress or nutrient deficiency.

Remove cuttings from the plant with a sharp blade to reduce injury to the parent plant. Dip the cutting tool in rubbing alcohol (70% or higher) or a mixture of one part bleach to nine parts water to prevent transmitting diseases from infected plant parts to healthy ones. Remove flowers and flower buds to allow the cutting to use its energy and stored carbohydrates for root and shoot formation rather than fruit and seed production. To hasten rooting, increase the number of roots, or to obtain uniform rooting, use a rooting hormone, preferably one containing a fungicide. Prevent possible contamination of the entire supply of rooting hormone by putting some in a separate container for dipping cuttings.

Place stem and leaf cuttings in bright, indirect light. Root cuttings can be kept in the dark until new shoots appear. Some additional tips for successful propagation include: cuttings from young plants root better than those from mature plants; lateral shoot cuttings are more successful than terminal shoots; avoid flower buds; take cuttings in the morning and keep them cool and moist until ready to plant; space cuttings so that each will receive adequate light and ventilation; ensure that buds on cuttings are pointed upwards.

Three methods of cuttings, described below, can be used: stem cuttings, leaf cuttings, and root cuttings.

Stem cuttings

Numerous plant species are propagated by stem cuttings. Some can be taken at any time of the year, but stem cuttings of many woody plants must be taken in the fall or in the dormant season. Success with herbaceous plants is generally enhanced when done in the spring; these plants are actively growing then, and more apt to root quickly on their own. There are several different types of stem cuttings depending on the part of the stem needed. At least one node should be below the surface. Although some plants root at internodes, others only root at nodal tissue.

How to: Stem cutting

Tip cuttings: Detach a 2-6 inch piece of stem, including the terminal bud. Make the cut just below a node. Remove leaves that would touch or be below the medium. Cuttings should retain three or four leaves for best rooting. Dip the stem in rooting hormone if desired. Gently tap the end of the cutting to remove excess hormone. To prevent the root hormone from being scraped off, create a hole in the media with a pencil before inserting the cutting into the media. Insert deeply enough into the media for the tip to be able to support itself. Firm medium around stem.

Figure 8-1: Tip and medial cuttings.

Medial cuttings: Make the first cut just above a node, and the second cut just below a node 2 to 6 inches down the stem. Remove the leaves below the bottom node. Prepare and insert the cutting as you would a tip cutting. Be sure to position right side up. Axial buds are always above leaves.

Cane cuttings: Cane cuttings provide an easy way to propagate new plants from overgrown ones, especially houseplants such as *dieffenbachia*, corn plant, Chinese evergreen, and other plants with thick stems. Cut cane-like stems into sections containing one or two eyes, or nodes. Dust ends with fungicide or activated charcoal. Allow to dry several hours. Lay horizontally with about half of the cutting below the media surface, eye facing upward. Cane cuttings are usually potted when roots and new shoots appear but new shoots from *dracaena* and *croton* are often cut off and rerooted in sand.

Figure 8-2: Cane cutting.

Single eye: The eye refers to the bud which emerges at the axil of the leaf at each node. This is used for plants with alternate leaves when space or stock material are limited. Cut the stem about 1/2 inch above and 1/2 inch below a node. Place the cutting horizontally or vertically in the medium.

Figure 8-3: Single eye.

Double eye: This method is used for plants with opposite leaves when space or stock material is limited. Cut the stem about 1/2 inch above and 1/2 inch below the same node. Insert the cutting vertically in the medium with the node just touching the surface.

Figure 8-4: Double eye.

Heel cutting: This method uses stock material with woody stems efficiently. Make a shield-shaped cut about halfway through the wood around a leaf and axial bud. Insert the shield horizontally into the medium.

Figure 8-5: Heel cutting.

Leaf cuttings

Leaf cuttings are used almost exclusively for a few indoor plants. Leaves of most plants will either produce a few roots but no plant, or just decay. Examples of plants that propagate from leaf cuttings include African violets, bush-type peperomias, sansevieria, jade plant, and jelly bean plant.

How to: Leaf cuttings

Whole leaf with petiole: Detach the leaf and up to 1-1/2 inches of petiole. Insert the lower end of the petiole into the medium. One or more new plants will form at the base of the petiole. The leaf may be severed from the new plants when they have their own roots, and the petiole can be reused. (Example: African violet).

Figure 8-6: Whole leaf with petiole.

Whole leaf without petiole: This is used for plants with **sessile leaves** (leaves without petioles). Insert the cutting vertically into the medium. A new plant will form from the axillary bud. The leaf may be removed when the new plant has its own roots. (Example: donkey's tail).

Figure 8-7: Whole leaf without petiole.

Split vein: Detach a leaf from the stock plant. Slit its veins on the lower leaf surface. Lay the cutting, lower side down, on the medium. New plants will form at each cut. If the leaf tends to curl up, hold it in place by covering the margins with the rooting medium. (Example: Rex begonia).

Figure 8-8: Split vein.

Leaf sections: This method is frequently used with snake plant and fibrous rooted begonias. Cut begonia leaves into wedges with at least one vein. Lay leaves flat on the medium. A new plant will arise at the vein. Cut snake plant leaves into 2-inch sections. Consistently make the lower cut slanted and the upper cut straight so you can tell which is the top. Insert the cutting vertically. Roots will form fairly soon, and eventually a new plant will appear at the base of the cutting. Do not allow cuttings to become too moist because they may rot.

Figure 8-9: Leaf sections.

For all leaf cuttings (except for succulents), enclose the potted cuttings in a plastic bag and monitor to make sure the leaf stays in contact with the growing media.

Root cuttings

Root cuttings are usually taken from 2-or-3-year-old plants during their dormant season when they have a large carbohydrate supply. Root cuttings of some species produce new shoots, which then form their own root systems, while root cuttings of other plants develop root systems before producing new shoots.

How to: Root cuttings

Plants with large roots: Make a straight top cut. Make a slanted cut 2-6 inches below the first cut. Store about 3 weeks in moist sawdust, peat moss, or sand at 40ºF. Remove from storage. Insert the cutting vertically with the top approximately level with the surface of the rooting medium. This method is often used outdoors (Example: horseradish).

Figure 8-10: Plants with large roots.

Plants with small roots: Take 1-2 inch sections of roots. Insert the cuttings horizontally about 1/2 inch below the medium surface. This method is usually used indoors or in a hotbed. (Example: bleeding heart).

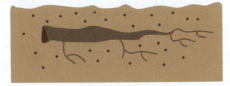

Figure 8-11: Plants with small roots.

Layering

Stems still attached to their parent plants may form roots where they touch a rooting medium. Severed from the parent plant, the rooted stem becomes a new plant. This method of vegetative propagation, called layering, promotes a high success rate because it prevents the water stress and carbohydrate shortage that plague cuttings. Some plants layer themselves naturally, but sometimes plant propagators assist the process. Layering may be enhanced by wounding one side of the stem or by bending it very sharply. The rooting medium should always provide aeration and a constant supply of moisture.

How to: Layering

Tip layering: Dig a hole 3-4 inches deep. Insert the shoot tip and cover it with soil. The tip grows downward first, then bends sharply and grows upward. Roots form at the bend, and the recurved tip becomes a new plant. Remove the tip layer and plant it in the early spring or late fall. Examples: purple and black raspberries, trailing blackberries.

Figure 8-12: Tip layering.

Simple layering: Bend the stem to the ground. Cover part of it with soil, leaving the last 6-12 inches exposed. Bend the tip into a vertical position and stake in place. The sharp bend will often induce rooting, but wounding the lower side of the branch or loosening the bark by twisting the stem may help. Examples: *forsythia*, honeysuckle.

Figure 8-13: Simple layering.

Compound layering: This method works for plants with flexible stems. Bend the stem to the rooting medium as for simple layering, but alternately cover and expose stem sections. Wound the lower side of the stem sections to be covered. Examples: heart-leaf philodendron, pothos.

Mound (stool) layering: Cut the plant back to 1 inch above the ground in the dormant season. Mound soil over the emerging shoots in the spring to enhance their rooting. Examples: gooseberries, apple rootstocks.

Figure 8-14: Compound layering.

Figure 8-15: Mound (stool) layering.

Air layering: Air layering is used to propagate some indoor plants with thick stems, or to rejuvenate them when they become leggy. On monocots, slit the stem just below a node; for dicots, girdle the stem as show in the figure. Pry the slit open with a toothpick. Surround the wound with wet unmilled sphagnum moss. Wrap plastic or foil around the sphagnum moss and tie in place. When roots pervade the moss, cut the plant off below the root ball.

Figure 8-16: Air layering.

Propagation from plant parts can be considered a modification of layering, as the new plants form before they are detached from their parent plants.

Division

Most perennials left in the same place for more than 3 years are likely to be overgrown, overcrowded, have dead or unsightly centers, and need basic fertilizer and soil amendments. The center of the clump will grow poorly, if at all, and the flowers will be sparse. The clump will deplete the fertility of the soil as the plant crowds itself. To divide mature clumps of perennials, select only vigorous side shoots from the outer part of the clump. Discard the center of the clump. Divide the plant into clumps of three to five shoots each. Be careful not to over-divide; too small a clump will not give much color the first year after replanting. Divide perennials when the plants are dormant just before a new season of growth, or in the fall so they can become established before the ground freezes. Stagger plant divisions so the whole garden will not be redone at the same time; good rotation will yield a display of flowers each year. Do not put all the divisions back into the same space that contained the original plant. That would place too many plants in a given area. Give extra plants to friends, plant them elsewhere in the yard, or discard them.

How to: Division

Stolons and runners: A stolon is a horizontal, often fleshy stem that can root, then produce new shoots where it touches the medium. A runner is a slender stem that originates in a leaf axil and grows along the ground or downward from a hanging basket, producing a new plant at its tip. Plants that produce stolons or runners are propagated by severing the new plants from their parent stems. Plantlets at the tips of runners may be rooted while still attached to the parent, or detached and placed in a rooting medium. Examples: strawberry, spider plant.

Figure 8-17: Stolons and runners.

Offsets: Plants with a rosetted stem often reproduce by forming new shoots at their base or in leaf axils. Sever the new shoots from the parent plant after they have developed their own root system. Unrooted offsets of some species may be removed and placed in a rooting medium. Some of these must be cut off, while others may be simply lifted off of the parent stem. Examples: date palm, *haworthia*, bromeliads, many cacti.

Figure 8-18: Offsets.

Bulbs (separation): New bulbs form beside the originally planted bulb. Separate these bulb clumps every 3-5 years for largest blooms and to increase bulb population. Dig up the clump after the leaves have withered. Gently pull the bulbs apart and replant them immediately so their roots can begin to develop. Small, new bulbs may not flower for 2 or 3 years, but large ones should bloom the first year. Examples: tulip, narcissus.

Figure 8-19: Bulbs / separation (tulip bulbs).

Corms (separation): A large new corm forms on top of the old corm, and tiny cormels form around the large corm. After the leaves wither, dig up the corms and allow them to dry in indirect light for 2-3 weeks. Remove the cormels, then gently separate the new corm from the old corm. Dust all new corms with a fungicide and store in a cool place until planting time. Examples: crocus, gladiolus.

Figure 8-20: Corms.

Crowns (separation): Plants with more than one rooted crown may be divided and the crowns planted separately. If the stems are not joined, gently pull the plants apart. If the crowns are united by horizontal stems, cut the stems and roots with a sharp knife to minimize injury. Divisions of some outdoor plants should be dusted with a fungicide before they are replanted. Examples: snake plant, iris, prayer plant, day lilies.

Grafting

Grafting and budding are methods of asexual plant propagation that join plant parts so they will grow as one plant. These techniques are used to propagate cultivars that will not root well as cuttings, whose own root systems are inadequate, to get larger plants faster, or to improve disease resistance. One or more new cultivars (scion) can be added to existing fruit and nut trees by grafting or budding.

The portion of the cultivar that is to be propagated is called the **scion**. It consists of a piece of shoot with dormant buds that will produce the stem and branches. The **rootstock** (see Chapter 10: "Fruits in the Home Garden" for further discussion) provides the new plant's root system and sometimes the lower part of the stem. The **cambium** is a layer of cells located between the wood and bark of a stem from which new tissues originate.

Four conditions must be met for grafting to be successful: the scion and rootstock must be compatible; each must be at the proper physiological stage; the cambial layers of the scion and stock must meet; and the graft union must be kept moist until the wound has healed.

Grafting tools that simplify the process are available commercially.

How to: Grafting

Cleft grafting: Cleft grafting is often used to change the cultivar or top growth of a shoot or a young tree (usually a seedling). It is especially successful if done in the early spring. Collect scion wood 3/8 to 1/2 inch in diameter. Cut the limb or small tree trunk to be reworked perpendicular to its length. Make a 2-inch vertical cut through the center of the previous cut. Be careful not to tear the bark. Keep this cut wedged apart. Cut the lower end of each scion piece into a wedge. Prepare two scion pieces 3-4 inches long. Insert the scions at the outer edges of the cut in the rootstock. Tilt the top of the scion slightly outward and the bottom slightly inward to be sure the cambial layers of the scion and rootstock touch. Remove the wedge propping the slit open and cover all cut surfaces with grafting wax.

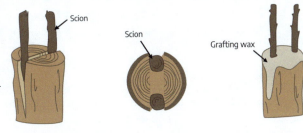

Figure 8-21: Cleft grafting.

Bark grafting: Unlike most grafting methods, bark grafting can be used on large limbs, although these are often infected before the wound can completely heal. Collect scion wood 3/8 to 1/2 inch in diameter when the plant is dormant, and store the wood wrapped in moist paper in a plastic bag in the refrigerator. Saw off the limb or trunk of the rootstock at a right angle to itself. In the spring, when the bark is easy to separate from the wood, make a 1/2-inch diagonal cut on one side of the scion, and a 1-1/2-inch diagonal cut on the other side. Leave two buds above the longer cut. Cut through the bark of the stock, a little wider than the scion. Remove the top third of the bark from this cut. Insert the scion with the longer cut against the wood. Nail the graft in.

Figure 8-22: Bark grafting.

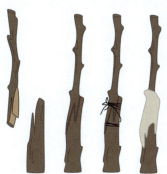

Whip or tongue grafting: This method is often used for material 1/4 to 1/2 inch in diameter. The scion and rootstock are usually of the same diameter, but the scion may be narrower than the stock if the cambium of the scion is aligned with the cambium of the root stock on one side. This strong graft heals quickly and provides excellent cambial contact. Make one 2-1/2-inch long sloping cut at the top of the rootstock and a matching cut on the bottom of the scion. On the cut surface, slice downward into the stock and up into the scion so the pieces will interlock. Fit the pieces together, then tie and wax the union.

Figure 8-23: Whip or tongue grafting.

Care of the graft

Very little success in grafting will be obtained unless proper care is maintained for the following year or two. If a binding material such as strong cord or nursery tape is used on the graft, this must be cut shortly after growth starts to prevent girdling. Rubber budding strips have some advantages over other materials. They expand with growth and usually do not need to be cut, as they deteriorate and break after a short time. It is also an excellent idea to inspect the grafts after 2 or 3 weeks to see if the wax has cracked, and if necessary, rewax the exposed areas. After this, the union will probably be strong enough and no more waxing will be necessary.

Limbs of the old variety which are not selected for grafting should be cut back at the time of grafting. The total leaf surface of the old variety should be gradually reduced as the new one increases until at the end of 1 or 2 years, the new variety has completely taken over. Completely removing all the limbs of the old variety at the time of grafting increases the shock to the tree and causes excessive suckering. Also, the scions may grow too fast, making them susceptible to wind damage. Future maintenance will be necessary to remove any sprouts from rootstock to prevent it crowding out the scion. If using a whip (1 branch) rootstock, remove all of the buds from the rootstock at the time of grafting.

Budding

Budding is the union of one bud and a small piece of bark from the scion with a rootstock. It is especially useful when scion material is limited. It is also faster and forms a stronger union than grafting.

How to: Budding

Patch budding: Plants with thick bark should be patch budded. This is done while the plants are actively growing, so their bark slips easily (that is, it peels up in one even layer exposing the underlying wood). Remove a rectangular piece of bark from the rootstock. Cover this wound with a bud and matching piece of bark from the scion. If the rootstock's bark is thicker than that of the scion, pare it down to meet the thinner bark so that when the union is wrapped the patch will be held firmly in place.

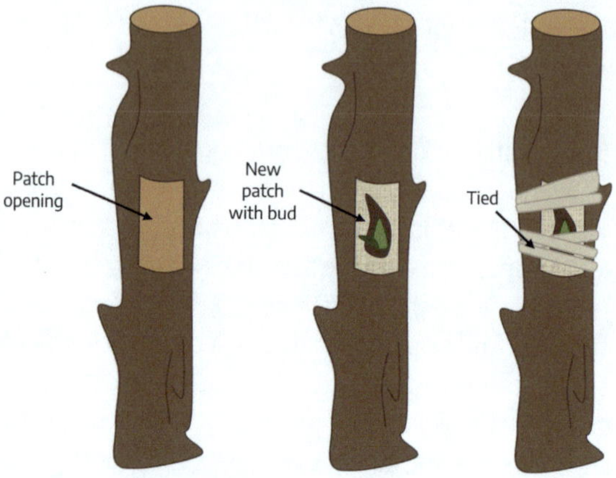

Figure 8-24: Patch budding.

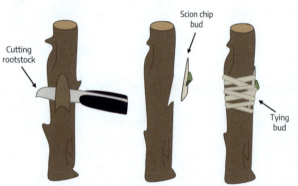

Chip budding: This budding method can be used when the bark is not slipping. Slice downward into the rootstock at a 45 degree angle through 1/4 of the wood. Make a second cut about one inch upward from the first cut. Remove a bud and attending chip of bark and wood from the scion shaped so that it fits the rootstock wound. Fit the bud chip to the stock and wrap the union.

Figure 8-25: Chip budding.

T-budding: This is the most commonly used budding technique. When the bark is slipping, make a vertical cut (same axis as the root stock) through the bark of the rootstock, avoiding any buds on the stock. Make a horizontal cut at the top of the vertical cut (in a T shape) and loosen the bark by twisting the knife at the intersection. Remove a shield-shaped piece of the scion, including a bud, bark, and a thin section of wood. Push the shield under the loosened stock bark. Wrap the union, leaving the bud exposed.

Figure 8-26: T-budding.

Care of buds

Place the bud in the stock in August. Force the bud to develop the following spring by cutting the stock off 3 to 4 inches above the bud. The new shoot may be tied to the resulting stub to prevent damage from the wind. After the shoot has made a strong union with the stock, cut the stub off close to the budded area.

Plants Suited for Asexual Methods of Propagation

Example plants suitable for cuttings:

Stem cuttings:

- Tip – used for almost all house plants except those that don't form stems such as African violet, and those with rigid stems such as *dieffenbachia*
- Medial – same as tip
- Cane – *dieffenbachia*, swiss cheese plant, *aglaonema*
- Single eye – alternate leaf plants such as devil's ivy
- Double eye – opposite leaf plants such as *coleus*
- Heel – *dieffenbachia*

Leaf cuttings:

- Whole leaf with petiole – African violet, *peperomia*, *begonia*
- Without petiole – donkey's tail, jade, ghost plant, *peperomia*
- Split vein – *begonia*
- Leaf sections – *sansevieria*, *begonia*

Root cuttings:

- Large – horseradish
- Small – bleeding heart, geraniums, ming aralia

Example plants suitable for layering:

- Tip – purple and black raspberries, trailing blackberries
- Simple – *forsythia*, honeysuckle, spider plant, most vine-type plants (*philodendron*, grape ivy, devil's ivy, Swedish ivy, etc.)
- Compound – heartleaf philodendron, pothos
- Mound – gooseberries, apple rootstocks
- Air Layering – plants with rigid stems such as *dieffenbachia*, ficus, rubber plant, *aralia*, *croton*

Example plants suitable for division:

- Stolons/Runners – date palm, haworthia, bromeliads, cacti and succulents, flame violet, strawberry begonia, spider plant
- Separation – spider plant, strawberry begonia, bromeliads.
- Bulbs: tulip, *narcissus*, *hyacinth*, *amaryllis*, lilies
- Corm – *crocus*, *gladiolus*, *freesia*.
- Crowns: *sansevieria*, iris, prayer plant, day lilies, Boston fern, cast iron plant, peace lily

Example plants suitable for grafting:

Cacti and succulents, various fruit trees, ornamental trees

Example plants suitable for budding:

Various fruit trees, ornamental trees

Additional Resources

- Plant Propagation with the VCE Master Gardener Program playlist (https://www.youtube.com/watch?v=FMyiS0BenFo&list=PLnWrSBjZVh9cH1uuxWu6Dq85Fwc5-shpv)
- For information on providing supplemental light to seedlings, see The University of Minnesota Extension publication "Light for indoor plants and starting seeds." (https://extension.umn.edu/planting-and-growing-guides/lighting-indoor-plants#types-of-grow-lights-2651610)

Attributions

- Susan Perry (2021 reviser)
- Beth Kirby (2021 reviser)
- Pamela H. Smith, Fairfax County Master Gardener Coordinator (2015 reviser)
- Roger Harris, Professor and Department Head, Department of Horticulture, Virginia Tech (2015 reviewer)
- Diane Relf, Extension Specialist, Horticulture (2009 reviser)

Image Attributions

- Figure 8-1: Tip and medial cuttings. Grey, Kindred. 2022. CC BY-NC-SA 4.0.
- Figure 8-2: Cane cutting. Grey, Kindred. 2022. CC BY-NC-SA 4.0.
- Figure 8-3: Single eye. Grey, Kindred. 2022. CC BY-NC-SA 4.0.
- Figure 8-4: Double eye. Grey, Kindred. 2022. CC BY-NC-SA 4.0.
- Figure 8-5: Heel cutting. Grey, Kindred. 2022. CC BY-NC-SA 4.0.
- Figure 8-6: Whole leaf with petiole. Grey, Kindred. 2022. CC BY-NC-SA 4.0.
- Figure 8-7: Whole leaf without petiole. Grey, Kindred. 2022. CC BY-NC-SA 4.0.
- Figure 8-8: Split vein. Grey, Kindred. 2022. CC BY-NC-SA 4.0.
- Figure 8-9: Leaf sections. Grey, Kindred. 2022. CC BY-NC-SA 4.0.
- Figure 8-10: Plants with large roots. Grey, Kindred. 2022. CC BY-NC-SA 4.0.
- Figure 8-11: Plants with small roots. Grey, Kindred. 2022. CC BY-NC-SA 4.0.
- Figure 8-12: Tip layering. Grey, Kindred. 2022. CC BY-NC-SA 4.0.
- Figure 8-13: Simple layering. Grey, Kindred. 2022. CC BY-NC-SA 4.0.
- Figure 8-14: Compound layering. Grey, Kindred. 2022. CC BY-NC-SA 4.0.
- Figure 8-15: Mound (stool) layering. Grey, Kindred. 2022. CC BY-NC-SA 4.0.
- Figure 8-16: Air layering. Grey, Kindred. 2022. CC BY-NC-SA 4.0.
- Figure 8-17: Stolons and runners. Grey, Kindred. 2022. CC BY-NC-SA 4.0.
- Figure 8-18: Offsets. Grey, Kindred. 2022. CC BY-NC-SA 4.0.
- Figure 8-19: Bulbs / separation (tulip bulbs). Grey, Kindred. 2022. CC BY-NC-SA 4.0.
- Figure 8-20: Corms. Grey, Kindred. 2022. CC BY-NC-SA 4.0.
- Figure 8-21: Cleft grafting. Grey, Kindred. 2022. CC BY-NC-SA 4.0.

- Figure 8-22: Bark grafting. Grey, Kindred. 2022. CC BY-NC-SA 4.0.
- Figure 8-23: Whip or tongue grafting. Grey, Kindred. 2022. CC BY-NC-SA 4.0.
- Figure 8-24: Patch budding. Grey, Kindred. 2022. CC BY-NC-SA 4.0.
- Figure 8-25: Chip budding. Grey, Kindred. 2022. CC BY-NC-SA 4.0.
- Figure 8-26: T-budding. Grey, Kindred. 2022. CC BY-NC-SA 4.0.

CHAPTER 9: THE VEGETABLE GARDEN

Chapter Contents

- Planning the Vegetable Garden
- Soil Preparation
- Selecting Gardening Equipment
- Seed for the Garden
- Transplants for the Garden
- Irrigating the Home Garden
- Fertilizing the Garden
- Weed Control in the Garden
- Vegetable Planting Guide
- Intensive Gardening Methods
- Container Gardening
- Vegetable Gardening in the Fall
- Season Extenders
- Organic Vegetable Gardening
- Additional Resources

Growing your own vegetables can be a rewarding experience. It allows you to engage directly with your food from garden plot to plate and can easily be done on a scale that matches the space that you have available for growing. However, vegetable gardening does not come without challenges. From environmental factors such as water, temperatures, and sunlight, to biotic factors such as insects and diseases, vegetable gardeners have their work cut out for them. With proper planning, regular observation, and careful maintenance, you can keep your garden bountiful for many months. The use of season extenders and careful planning can even allow you to grow throughout the year in Virginia.

Planning the Vegetable Garden

When planning your garden, it is important to ask a few basic questions:

- Who will be doing the gardening work?
- Will the home garden be a group project with family members who will work willingly through the season to a fall harvest, or will you be handling the hoe alone? Remember, a small, weed-free garden will produce more than a large, weedy mess.
- What fruits and vegetables do you and your family like to eat? There is no value in taking up gardening space with vegetables that no one eats. Make a list of your family favorites, ranked in order of preference. This will make a useful guide in deciding how much of each to plant. Successive plantings of certain crops, such as beans, will give a longer harvest period and increase your yield. List recommended varieties and planting dates.
- How do you plan to use the produce from your garden? If you plan to can, freeze, dry, or store it, this will be a factor in planning the size of the garden and in selecting the varieties to grow. Some varieties have much better keeping quality than others. Care should be used in choosing the kinds of plants to grow, making sure the varieties you select are adapted to your area and intended use. It is always advisable to use a crop calendar suited for your area (see VCE publication "Virginia's Home Garden Recommended Planting and Harvest Dates" 426-331).
- How much space is available to be converted into usable garden space?

Vegetable versus Fruit

Vegetables are edible plant parts that do not contain seeds, for example kale, asparagus, carrots, broccoli, and onions. Fruits are the ripened ovaries of a female flower part that contains seeds, and in some cases may only be the seed itself, for example squash, tomatoes, cucumbers, peppers, peas, avocados and many other products of flowering plants. However, through common usage we have come to refer to many fruits as vegetables in our gardens and in the produce section of the grocery store. Classification is often ambiguous and it really depends on whether you are engaged in a botanical or culinary discussion.

Economic Value of Crops

It is difficult to evaluate the economic value of crops grown in the vegetable garden due to the different lengths of time they require for maturity and harvest, the availability of varieties and vegetable types not generally found in the marketplace, and the lack of comparison values for vegetables that are not acceptable by commercial standards (cracked tomatoes, crooked cucumbers, etc.), but which are perfectly usable by the gardener. Nevertheless, several studies have attempted to determine what crops bring the most value per square foot of garden space, partly to aid small-space gardeners in making decisions about what to plant. Of course, if no one in the family likes beets, there is no point in growing them just because they are economically valuable, but this list may help you determine what vegetables to plant and what to buy.

High value crops:

- Tomatoes
- Green bunching onions
- Carrots
- Leaf lettuce
- Cucumbers
- Turnip (greens and roots)
- Peppers
- Summer squash
- Broccoli
- Edible pod peas
- Head lettuce
- Onion storage bulbs
- Swiss chard

Low value crops (Not recommended for small spaces):

- Corn
- Winter squash
- Pumpkins
- Melons

Values above are based on pounds produced per square foot, retail value per pound at harvest time, and length of time in the garden. Miniature varieties or trellising may increase value per square foot.

Planting Guidelines

- Winter is the best time to plan next year's garden and to order the seed.
  Plan the garden on paper first. Draw a map showing the arrangement and spacing of crops. To keep the garden growing all season, make a spring, summer, and fall garden plan.
- Plan the garden and order seeds at least three months earlier. Some plants may be started indoors as early as mid-February.
- In your plan, place tall and trellised crops on the north side of the garden so they won't shade the shorter vegetables.
- Group plants by length of growing period. Plant spring crops together so later crops can be planted in these areas when the early crops mature. Consider length of harvest as well as time to maturity. Place perennial crops to the side of the garden where they will not be disturbed by any tillage that is needed.

Locating the Garden

- Vegetables grow best in a level area with loose, well-drained soil and at least six hours of sun (eight to ten hours is ideal).
- Use contour rows, terraces, or raised beds on sloped or hillside sites to avoid erosion. South-facing slopes are

warmer and less subject to damaging frosts.
- Avoid placing the garden in low spots, at the base of a hill, or at the foot of a slope bordered by a solid fence. Such areas are slow to warm up in the spring, and frost settles in these places since cold air naturally drains into low areas.
- Avoid windy locations; if you must plant in a windy spot, build or grow a windbreak.
- Locate near a good and easily accessible supply of water.
Avoid planting near trees and shrubs; they compete for nutrients and water and may cause excessive shading.
- Sites too near buildings may result in plants not receiving enough sunlight. Observe shading patterns through the growing season, if possible, before starting the garden. If you have a shaded area you wish to use anyway, plant shade-tolerant crops. If needed, increase effective light by providing reflective surfaces around plants.
- Try not to plant vegetables from the same family (peas and beans or squash and pumpkin) in exactly the same location in the garden more often than once in 3 years. Rotation prevents the buildup of insects and disease. Use previous year's plans as guides for rotating crops.
- Avoid locating the garden on a site where buildings with lead paint have stood; lead may be present in toxic amounts. If you are unsure about your chosen location, have the soil tested for lead content, or have tissue analyses done on some leafy vegetables.
- Gardening where sod has long been established, whether converted pastures or lawns, requires a great deal of preparation to eliminate weeds.

Treated Wood in the Vegetable Garden

Some home gardeners have been concerned with the safety of pressure-treated landscape timbers in the garden, specifically when used to build raised bed vegetable gardens. On 12 February 2002, the Environmental Protection Agency (EPA) announced a voluntary decision by the wood preserving industry to phase out the use of wood preservatives that contain arsenic for any wood products destined for consumer use. The phaseout was completed by 31 December 2003. This transition affects virtually all residential uses of wood treated with chromated copper arsenate, also known as CCA, including wood used in play structures, decks, picnic tables, landscaping timbers, residential fencing, patios, and walkways/boardwalks. Since January 2004, the EPA has not allowed CCA products for any of these residential uses.

The EPA has not concluded that there is unreasonable risk to the public from CCA lumber, but believes that any reduction in exposure to arsenic is desirable. More information on CCA lumber can be found here: https://www.epa.gov/ingredients-used-pesticide-products/chromated-arsenicals-cca.

CCA has been replaced with two other formulations in pressure-treated wood – ACQ and copper azole (CA-B). Information on ACQ can be found here: https://www.epa.gov/ingredients-used-pesticide-products/overview-wood-preservative-chemicals.

Soil Preparation

The ideal vegetable garden soil is deep, well-drained, high in organic matter, and has good structure. Proper soil preparation provides the basis for good seed germination and subsequent growth of garden crops. The regular addition of manure, compost, cover crops, and other organic materials can raise the soil nutrient level to a point at which the need for the addition of synthetic fertilizers is greatly reduced.

Soil Testing

For a new garden, check initial soil fertility and pH by having your soil analyzed (a pH reading indicates acidity/alkalinity of soil, where 7 is neutral and lower pH values are more acidic, higher values more alkaline). Once the garden is established, check soil fertility and pH at least once every 3 years. Vegetables vary to some extent in their nutrient and pH requirements, but most garden crops will do well within a soil pH range of 6.2 to 6.8. This is a little below neutral, or slightly acid. If soil pH is too high or low, poor crop growth will result, largely due to the effects of pH on the availability of nutrients to plants. In addition to pH, a soil test will also give you an idea of the relative nutrient level of phosphorus (P) and potassium (K) in the soil.

Soil sample kits are available for checking your soil's pH and may be obtained from your local VCE office. VCE will email results to you with recommendations for adjusting pH and correcting nutrient deficiencies, if any are present. Private companies also do soil testing; these give detailed reports and recommendations in many cases, but may be expensive (3 to 5 times the cost of VCE). For best results, carefully follow the instructions for taking the soil sample.

Adjust nutrient and pH by adding recommended fertilizers and/or lime for raising the pH (or acidifiers if the goal is to lower the soil pH). In new garden spots, remove sod with a spade before tilling. You can use the sod to patch your lawn or put it in a compost pile to decay. Next, plow, spade, or rotary till the soil when soil moisture conditions are right. To test, pick up a handful of soil and squeeze it. If it stays in a ball, it is too wet. If it crumbles freely, it should be about right. Excessively dry soil is powdery and clumpy and may be difficult to work. Take samples at the surface and at a 4- to 6-inch depth in several locations in the garden plot. If soil sticks to a shovel, or if when spading the turned surface is shiny and smooth, it is still too wet. Working soils when excessively wet can destroy soil structure, which may take years to rebuild. Plowing with a tractor when the soil is wet is especially damaging, causing the formation of a compaction layer that will inhibit root growth. Soils with adequate humus levels generally allow more leeway because of their improved structural qualities.

Just prior to planting, break up large clods of soil and rake the bed level. Small-seeded vegetables germinate best in smooth, fine-surfaced soil. Do not pulverize the seedbed soil. This destroys the structure and promotes crusting and erosion problems.

Tilling the Soil

Traditional tilling

The type of equipment used to prepare your garden will depend on the size of the garden, your physical ability, time, and budget. Options include hand-digging with a spade or shovel, tilling with a power rotary tiller, and using a small garden tractor or a full-sized farm tractor. Rotary tilling (rototilling) is sufficient for most home gardens, as long as plant debris accumulation is not out of hand. Rotary tilling mixes the upper layers of soil rather than completely turning the soil over. One possible harmful effect of rototilling is the formation of a compaction layer just beyond the reach of the tines. Use of deep-rooted cover crops or double digging can do much to prevent or alleviate this problem when it exists. Small gardens can be designed using raised beds which may be worked entirely by hand if the area is small enough.

Gardeners often wonder whether to plow/till in the spring or fall. Working the soil in fall has several advantages over the traditional, spring plowing. It allows earlier spring planting, since the basic soil preparation is already done when spring arrives. Turning under large amounts of organic matter is likely to result in better decomposition when done in the fall, since autumn temperatures are higher than those of early spring, and there is more time for the process to take place. Insects, disease organisms, and perennial weeds may be reduced by killing or inactivating them through burial or exposure to harsh winter weather. The physical condition of heavy clay soils may be improved by the alternate freezing and thawing, which breaks up tightly aggregated particles. Also, snow is trapped between the hills of roughly plowed soil, so more moisture is retained than on flat, bare ground. Incorporation of limestone in the fall gives it time to become integrated with the soil and influence spring plant growth.

Fall plowing alone is not recommended for hillside or steep garden plots, since soil is left exposed all winter, subject to erosion when spring rains come. If a winter cover crop is grown to improve soil and prevent erosion, the ground will have to be tilled in the fall to prepare the soil for seed and again in spring to turn under the green manure. Spring plowing is better for sandy soils and those where shallow tilling is practiced. Generally, most gardens must be disked or rotary tilled in the spring to smooth the soil for planting.

No-till or low-till methods

Tilling has become a staple of spring garden preparation for many gardeners. It can be used to prepare a clean seed bed, kill weeds, and warm up the soil for planting. However, in recent years many gardeners have started to focus on low or no-till gardening to help avoid some of the negative impacts regular tilling can cause.

It's important to consider the three indicators of soil health when making decisions regarding tillage in your garden:

- Physical: The physical structure of the soil has an impact on drainage and retention of water, soil erosion, surface crusting and more.
- Biological: The biological properties of soil include all the organisms present in the soil food web, from bacteria and fungi to earworms and plants.
- Chemical: The chemical properties of the soil are the nutrients (both macronutrients and micronutrients), pH, and more.

Tillage of the soil, especially deep tilling practices, can negatively affect the physical and biological properties of the soil. Tilling causes a weakening of the microbial community within the soil. This impacts the soil's ability to hold water, sequester and hold carbon, and hold other important nutrients. Tilling can also increase the potential for erosion and can increase the loss of organic matter in the soil. Untilled soil is rich in both fungi and bacteria, whereas tilled soil disrupts the important fungal community and may not have access to the benefits fungi provide to the garden.

Low and no-till gardening techniques

There are many techniques that can assist with low or no-till gardening. Here are a few steps that you can take in your garden to work toward a low or no-till garden:

Soil coverage: In low-till gardening, the soil should be covered throughout each season. This could be through cover crops, mulched crops, or a layer of mulch (for example straw, grass, chopped leaves) on top of the soil. Mulches from the fall can be left to protect the soil during the winter months.

Leave the roots: Rather than pulling out the entire plant at the end of the season, cut plants at the soil level so their roots remain. The roots remaining in the soil will slowly decompose and add organic matter to your soil.

Spring practices: A broad fork can be used in the spring to add soil amendments, lessen compaction, and prepare the garden for planting. Organic mulches left over from the winter can be pulled back and planted.

Cover crops: The root system of cover crops benefits the soil and the cover crop becomes manure when incorporated into the soil. Cover crops can be planted within plantings or when not growing crops. Learn more about cover crops, including recommendations for cover crops in Virginia, in Chapter 2 "Soils and Nutrient Management."

Weed control

Tilling can kill weeds that have begun to grow. However, this risks bringing dormant weed seeds to the surface as they can remain viable in the soil for many years.

Rather than tilling for weed control, you can kill weeds with black plastic, cardboard, or tarps. This smothering layer should remain on the soil for several months to a year.

The aforementioned practice of soil coverage is also crucial for weed control. Covering the soil will make it more difficult for weed seeds to germinate and grow.

If weeds do germinate and take hold in the garden, pulling by hand or using a hoe or other garden tool will help to control. This should be done before weeds are able to go to seed.

Soil Amendments

Any addition to the soil that improves its physical or chemical condition is considered a soil amendment. Many types of amendments are valuable to the home gardener.

Amendments to change pH and nutrient levels and improve soil quality

Lime, sulfur, and gypsum are common amendments used to change soil pH. The correct soil pH is essential for optimum plant growth. Dolomitic limestone adds calcium and magnesium while also raising soil pH (lowering acidity). Gypsum adds calcium and some sulfur but does not enhance the structure of eastern U.S. clay soils as it does soils in western states.

Agricultural sulfur is used to acidify alkaline soil. The amount to add depends on the current and desired pH, which is one good reason to have garden soil checked every 3 years.

Wood ashes can be used as a soil amendment to raise soil pH. They contain potash (potassium), phosphate, boron, and other elements. Apply twice as much ash as limestone to achieve the similar desired effect. Ashes should not come into contact with germinating seedlings or plant roots as they may cause root burn. Spread in a thin layer over the winter, and incorporate into the soil; check pH yearly if you use wood ashes. Never use coal ashes or large amounts of wood ash (no more than 20 lbs. per 1000 square feet), as toxicity problems may occur.

In special cases, perlite is sometimes added to clays to attempt to improve soil texture. Soil texture is defined as the percents sand, silt, and clay present in a soil. However, these inert materials can be expensive, and extremely large quantities are needed to do any good. Compost, manures, and other amendments usually serve the purpose better and are more economical at improving the structure or way the soil binds together.

Organic matter is a great soil improver for both clay and sandy soils. Good sources of organic matter include manures, leafmold, sawdust, and straw. These materials are decomposed in the soil by soil organisms. Various factors, such as moisture, temperature, and nitrogen availability, determine the rate of decomposition. Adequate water must be present, and warm temperatures will increase the rate at which the microbes work. Proper balance of carbon and nitrogen (C to N ratio) in the material is needed to ensure adequate nutrient availability both to growing plants and decomposition organisms. Adding nitrogen may be necessary if large amounts of undecomposed leaves, straw, sawdust, or other high-carbon substances are used. Nitrogen is used by the soil organisms to make proteins for their own bodies, and if it is not present in sufficient amounts, the microbes have no qualms about stealing the plant's share. Generally, fresh green wastes, such as grass clippings, are higher in nitrogen than dry material.

The use of compost is one way to get around the decomposition problem. Compost is usually made by the gardener from plant and/or animal wastes. Correct composting is an art that can result in a valuable nutrient and humus source for any garden. The basis of the process is the microbial decomposition of mixed, raw, organic materials to a dark, fluffy product resembling rich soil, which is then spread and worked into the garden soil (refer to Chapter 2: "Soils and Nutrient Management" for more information).

Animal manures are commonly used as a garden soil amendment, though care should be taken to avoid food safety concerns related to pathogens like E. coli; see the VCE publication "Food Safety for School and Community Gardens" FST-60P for more information. The value of manure in terms of the nutrients it contains varies. Fresh horse, sheep, rabbit, and poultry manures are quite high in nitrogen and may even burn plants if applied directly to a growing garden. They are best applied in the fall and tilled under. Manure usually has fewer total nutrients than synthetic fertilizers in terms of N, P, and K, but is a valuable soil builder. Unfortunately, manures may be a source of weed seeds; if this is a problem, composting in a hot pile may help. In urban areas, manure may be hard to come by, but country dwellers usually find it plentiful. Be cautious of the source of your manure as manure can sometimes be contaminated by herbicides.

Another source of inexpensive soil improvement that should not be underestimated is the cover crop. Green manures, or cover crops, such as annual rye, ryegrass, and oats, are planted in the garden in the fall for incorporation in the spring. For best results, seed should be sown a month before the first killing frost. In a fall garden, plant cover crops between the rows and in any cleared areas. Cover cropping provides additional organic matter, holds nutrients that might have been lost over the winter, and helps reduce erosion and loss of topsoil. Legume cover crops can increase the amount of nitrogen in the soil and reduce fertilizer needs. A deep-rooted cover crop allowed to grow for a season in problem soil can help break up hardpan and greatly improve tilth. Even home gardeners can benefit from the use of cover crops! See the VCE publication "Virginia Cover Crops Fact Sheet Series No. 2" CSES-121NP for more information. Incorporate green manures at least two weeks before planting vegetables; they should not be allowed to go to seed before incorporation.

The regular addition of manure, compost, cover crops, and other organic materials can raise the soil nutrient level to a point at which addition of synthetic fertilizers is greatly reduced. This comes about not only through the intrinsic fertilizing value of the amendment, but also through the increased action of microorganisms on soil and humus particles; humic acid (and other acids) helps to release previously locked-up nutrients naturally present in the soil, and the extra surface area provided by humus serves as a reserve, holding nutrient elements until they are needed by plants. This highly desirable soil quality does not come about with a single or even several additions of organic material, but rather requires a serious, long-term, soil-building program. Information is widely available in books and magazine articles on this subject.

Remember, your soil is alive and constantly changing. By keeping it fertile and rich, many gardening problems may be diminished. Soil is the base for plant growth, and much attention should be paid to getting and keeping it in the best condition.

Selecting Gardening Equipment

Garden catalogs and stores are full of gardening tools, many highly specialized; some are very useful, others are nice but not necessary, and some are gimmicks. The gardening equipment you need depends on the size of your garden, your age and strength, and whether you want to get the job done in a hurry or prefer to take your time. The minimum equipment needed by most gardeners includes a shovel or spade, a hoe, a rake, and a trowel. A wide selection of styles is available in each of these tools, and the choice is really one of personal preference and price range. You can get the best value by knowing each tool's uses and particular qualities to look for and buying at the end of the gardening season when prices are reduced.

Hand Tools for Cultivating

A garden**shovel** with a pointed blade is lighter and smaller than most other shovels and is well suited for use in the garden. Shovels are earth movers with dish-shaped blades mounted to the handle at an angle. A spade has a flat blade and is designed for cutting rather than lifting or moving soil. Spades are excellent for shaping straight-sided trenches and for edging beds. For general-purpose digging, lifting, and moving, a long-handled shovel is ideal. Both shovels and spades come with long or short handles in standard or D-shaped styles. Choice of handle style will depend on personal preference; long handles offer greater leverage and are less tiring to use in many cases. Short handles are often thicker and stronger than long ones.

A **spading fork** is another useful digging tool. It is ideal for breaking and turning heavy soils and for loosening subsoil layers when double digging a bed. Turning coarse compost, spreading mulches, and digging root crops are other jobs suitable for a spading fork.

A **hoe** is essential in any garden for preparing the seed bed, removing weeds, and breaking up encrusted soil. Several different hoe styles are available. The pointed hoe with a heart-shaped blade is lightweight and useful for opening seed furrows and cultivating between plants. The hula, or action hoe, is a type of scuffle hoe which is very lightweight and maneuverable. Pushing and pulling it just under the soil surface eliminates newly emerging weeds and breaks up any crust on the soil surface. This type of hoe is most easily used on soil which is not compacted, since the blade is relatively thin and lacks the clod-breaking capabilities of a heavier hoe; it is also less effective in cases where weeds have gotten a good start. Other types of scuffle hoes are somewhat more sturdy and are used with a pushing motion rather than pushing and pulling. Probably the most commonly used hoe is the square-bladed hoe, which lends itself well to many garden tasks.

A sturdy **rake** is useful in clearing the garden of rocks and debris. It is also helpful in spreading mulches and smoothing seedbeds. The correct-sized rake for you depends on your size and strength and the uses you intend to put it to. As the number of tines increases, the rake weight also increases; avoid choosing a rake so heavy it will tire you after a short period of use. The length of the rake handle is important too; the tip of the handle should come up to your ear when standing upright. A handle that is too short will make your work harder, causing excess bending and back strain.

Especially in the spring, a **trowel** will be in constant use for those many digging jobs that need not be done with full-sized tools. The trowel is perfect for transplanting seedlings and bulbs or digging shallow-rooted weeds. Small **hand cultivators**, often sold in sets with trowels, are good for weeding in small areas and between closely spaced plants. Another useful, small digging tool is appropriately named a **digger** (or weeder, cultivator, or asparagus knife). This tool is available from most hardware or discount stores inexpensively. It is useful for digging up weeds with long taproots, such as dandelions or Queen Anne's lace, or for prying out Johnson grass rhizomes. It consists of a long (10 to 14 inch), solid-metal rod with a two-pronged blade at one end and a handle at the other. This tool is practically indestructible and well worth the small investment of its price for people with strong hands and arms or extremely loose, friable soil.

Rotary Tiller

The power **rotary tiller** is probably the power tool most commonly purchased by gardeners. Whether or not a gardener needs a rotary tiller depends on the size of the garden, the gardener's capabilities, and the intended uses of the tiller. Renting a tiller or hiring someone to till the garden meets the needs of most gardeners. If a tiller is to be purchased, tiller selection may be based on the nature of the work to be done, the quality of the machine and ease of repair, as well as personal preference. The tiller's engine powers rotating blades, or tines, which can make garden soil loose and fluffy, ready for planting. It can also chop up plant debris and mix it into the soil. Incorporating organic matter and manures into the garden is easily accomplished with a tiller, reducing the tendency to procrastinate this necessary chore. The ability of the tiller to do these jobs effectively is a function of its weight, strength, design, and type of tines, as well as the type of soil. A heavy, powerful tiller is most effective on stony, clay soils, while in a small garden or one with light soil, a smaller tiller is more appropriate. Very lightweight tillers, known as soil blenders, are designed mainly for raised-bed gardening.

Rotary tillers are available with front-mounted or rear-mounted tines. Rear-tined tillers are generally better able to self-propel on all but the rockiest soils. They travel straight and can produce a footprint-free seedbed.

Front-tined tillers are usually light in weight, but may require considerable strength to guide them through the soil. The front-tined tiller may not make as straight a pass as the heavier, rear-tined type, but it is much easier to turn. Due to this increased maneuverability, the front-tined tiller is easy to use in small gardens and in corner areas.

The purchase of a tiller is a major investment. Features to look for include heavy cast-iron, steel plate and tubing, heavy bearings, strong welds used in construction, and easily operable controls. Ask to look at the operator's manual and try to determine how simply a tune-up can be performed; you may save yourself a great deal of trouble and money if you can replace plugs and points yourself. Also consider the locations of service centers and parts dealers. Careful attention to your needs, abilities, and price range is important. Talk to people who have the types of tillers in which you are interested. If possible, borrow or rent various types of machines and send for information before buying. If you are considering the purchase of a rotary tiller, plan to do so well ahead of time so you will not be rushed into a purchase. A good tiller is a long-term investment, so plan carefully before you buy.

Carts/Wheelbarrows

A wheelbarrow or cart is very handy to have in and around the garden area. Select one that is easy to handle when full, with good maneuverability. Durable construction is well worth paying for to ensure a long, useful life. Be sure to choose the size appropriate for your physical abilities and garden needs. A wheelbarrow generally requires more strength and control than do most garden carts, but many of the small carts generally available are made of relatively flimsy metal and, though inexpensive, are not particularly long lasting or suitable for heavy items such as rocks. Again, consider your needs. If you plan to haul only light straw, leaves, sawdust, and such materials, then one of the small carts may be suitable. For heavier jobs, you may need a wheelbarrow; or investigate some of the newer garden carts, especially those with bicycle-size tires, which make easy work of hauling. They are made of heavy plywood and metal, but are well balanced and easy to maneuver. These carts do, however, involve a sizeable investment (up to several hundred dollars) and a large storage space. Therefore, only serious gardeners or those with other uses for such a cart find them economical.

Watering Equipment

Watering is an essential garden job for most gardeners. An adequate water supply makes a big difference in garden yields. Purchase of watering equipment depends on available facilities, water supply, climate, and garden practices. If there is no outdoor spigot near the garden, the expense of having one installed may be greater than the benefits gained except in very drought-prone areas or in the case of a gardener who is fully dependent on the season's produce. Where rainfall is adequate except for a few periods in the summer, it is wise to keep watering equipment simple; a garden hose with a fan-type sprinkler will suffice. In areas where there are extended periods of hot weather without precipitation, the local water supply is likely to be short. Overhead sprinklers are wasteful of water, so in this case, a drip irrigation system may be in order. Drip irrigation puts water right at the roots and doesn't wet plant leaves, helping to prevent disease. Timers are available that allow automatic watering with drip and some other systems. Cultural practices, such as mulching, close plant spacing, shading, cultivar selection, and wide bed planting, will significantly reduce water needs. See Chapter 17: "Water Quality and Conservation" for more information.

Monitoring Equipment

While soil testing products can be purchased for household use, your VCE office can provide reliable, affordable testing through Virginia Tech's Soil Testing Lab. After initially testing the soil for a new garden, testing does not have to be done more frequently than once every 3 years for most gardening purposes. Some gardeners like to monitor the soil quality frequently, though, making a commercial soil test kit a worthwhile purchase. An electronic pH tester is on the market for those who like gadgets.

Soil temperature is critical for many vegetable and food crops. Soil thermometers measure soil temperature and the internal temperature of a compost pile. Seeds planted in soil that is too cold will often rot, and seedlings planted in cold soil will delay growth until the ground temperature gets warmer and will likely result in stunted plants. A soil thermometer will assist the gardener in determining the proper time to plant seeds and seedlings. Optimal soil temperatures for seeds of early vegetables are between 45 and 50°F and 50 to 55°F for seedlings. Soil temperatures for warm weather species should be at least 65°F.

Serious gardeners often invest in various types of equipment that allow them to monitor the microclimate around the garden or indoors. A rain gauge is an inexpensive device that helps the gardener determine if enough rain has fallen for garden plants. A minimum-maximum thermometer is a costly, but often useful, device to measure nightly lows and daytime highs within an area; these are especially valuable in a greenhouse. Light and watering meters can be purchased for indoor plant monitoring.

Seeding and Planting Tools

Depending on the size of your garden and your physical abilities, you may want to consider a row seeder. Seeders with wheels make easy work of sowing long rows of corn or beans or other vegetables. Seeders are available which make a furrow, drop the seeds properly spaced, and close up the furrow behind the seed – all in one pass. They do not perform quite as well on small-seeded crops, and it is not really worth the effort of setting up a seeder for small areas. A hand-held seeder is probably a better choice for this type of work. Broadcast seeders are available for sowing cover crop seeds, such as rye or wheat, but are generally not necessary for the average home gardener since broadcasting is easily done by hand once the proper technique is learned.

Trellises/Cages

Trellises and cages for vining plants save space and keep fruits off the ground, reducing the amount of stooping required for harvest and damage to plants. Look for heavy-duty materials and sturdy design that will stand up to rain, wind, and drying. Wire should be of a heavy gauge, and wood should be treated with non-phytotoxic (i.e., not toxic to plants) materials. Metal parts should be rustproof or at least rust-resistant. If you build your own, you will probably save a considerable amount of money and get better quality for the price.

Harvesting and Processing Equipment

Harvesting equipment varies depending on the size and type of garden, whether or not food is to be stored, and the way in which it is to be processed. Baskets are useful to most gardeners. They may be purchased at garden or farm supply stores or sometimes may be scrounged from local grocery stores or fruit stands. Berry baskets for small fruits, baskets with handles for carrying vegetables, and peck or bushel baskets for storage are all useful. Fruit pickers are nice and easy to use for tall fruit trees. A sharp knife for cutting vegetables off plants is handy and helps prevent plant damage. See the VCE publication "Food Safety for School and Community Gardens" FST-60P (FST-296) for more information.

Purchasing and Maintaining Tools

When purchasing tools, buy for quality rather than quantity. Your tools will be in frequent use throughout the garden season. Cheap tools tend to break or dull easily and may end up making a job unnecessarily difficult and frustrating. Quality tools will last and tend to increase in value with time if well kept. Tools should be lightweight for easy handling, but heavy enough to do the job properly. Metal parts should be of steel, which will stay sharp, keep its shape, and outlast softer metals. Wooden handles may split or splinter; fiberglass handles are more durable.

Keeping a tool clean and sharp will increase its usefulness and lengthen its life. Learn the techniques of sharpening each tool, and practice them frequently. Professional gardeners often carry sharpening stones or files while working and sharpen after every hour or so of use. Clean your tools after each use and oil the blades.

The last and perhaps most important step in tool care is to put tools in their proper places. Tools left in the garden will rust and break and can be a safety hazard. Some gardeners paint handles with a bright color to make their tools easy to spot. And, if each tool has its own place in the storage area, it is simple to determine if tools are missing before closing up for the day.

Before winter sets in, sharpen tools, then coat metal parts lightly with oil and rub wooden handles with boiled linseed oil. Drain power tools of gasoline, and obtain filters, mufflers, and tune-up parts so a fall or late-winter tune-up can get the machine ready for early spring jobs. Have maintenance done, if needed, in the winter, when demand is lowest and you can afford to let the repairer take his or her time.

In fall, any trellises or cages that have been outdoors should be cleaned and stored inside if possible. Traps and other pest control devices should also be stored if the pest season is over. Cold frames and other season extenders should be protected from damage by ice and snow or high winds, and once their job is done, should be repaired if necessary and stored. Tools with wheels, like cultivators, seeders, and carts, should be oiled and stored. With thoughtful selection and care your tools will give many years of service. This extra help in the garden will pay for itself in time.

Seed for the Garden

Choosing and purchasing vegetable seeds are some of the most enjoyable gardening pastimes. Thumbing through colorful catalogs and dreaming of the season's harvest are ways to make winter seem a little warmer. Seed purchased from a dependable seed company will provide a good start toward realizing that vision of bounty. Keep notes about the seeds you purchase, such as their germination qualities, vigor of plants, tendencies toward insects and disease. From this information, you can determine whether one seed company is not meeting your needs, or whether the varieties you have chosen are unsuitable for your area or gardening style. For example, if powdery mildew is a big problem on squash family plants in your area, the next year you may want to look for mildew-resistant varieties.

Saving Seed

Saving your own vegetable seed is another pleasurable activity. It offers a sense of self-sufficiency and can save money. You can maintain a variety that is not available commercially, which helps to perpetuate a broad genetic base of plant materials. Breeders often search for old-time varieties when attempting to improve commercial plants, since the heirloom vegetables (as they are sometimes called) often have disease and pest resistance or cold hardiness. Participation in a seed exchange can be a rewarding experience. You may find unusual varieties available for trade in an exchange that are otherwise hard to find.

There are certain considerations to be kept in mind when saving seed. Seeds from **hybrid** varieties will not produce plants that are the same as the parent plants; therefore, only open-pollinated varieties should be used for home seed production. Some seed dealers have responded to the increasing interest in seed saving by clearly marking open-pollinated varieties in their catalogs. Another consideration in saving seed is the possibility of carrying seed-borne diseases into the next year's crop. Many commercially grown seeds are grown in dry areas unsuitable to fungal, viral, and bacterial diseases that may be present in your region. Take care to control diseases that can be carried in seed. Another weather-related factor is the speed of drying of seeds, which can be adversely affected by frequent rains and/or humidity. Finally, if you've ever saved squash seed during a season in which you had more than one type of squash planted, you have probably seen the weird results that may be obtained from cross pollination! Saving seeds from cross-pollinated crops is not generally recommended for the novice because of problems with selection, requirements for hand pollination and isolation, biennial habits, and genetic variability. Failure to let the seed mature adequately on the plant also leads to nonviable seed. Common, self-pollinated annual plants from which seed may be saved include lettuce, beans, peas, herbs, and tomatoes.

Beans and peas: Allow seed pods to turn brown on the plant. Harvest pods, dry for one to two weeks, shell, then store in a cool (below 50°F), dry environment in a paper bag.

Lettuce seed: Cut off seed stalks when fluffy in appearance, just before all the seeds are completely dried. Seeds will fall off the stalk and be lost if allowed to mature on the plant. Dry the harvested seed stalk further; shake seeds off; then store in a cool, dry environment in an envelope or small glass jar.

Herb seeds: Herbs vary in the way their seeds are produced. In general, allow herb seeds to stay on the plants until they are almost completely dry. Some seed heads, such as dill, will shatter and drop their seeds as soon as they are dry. Watch the early ripening seeds; if they tend to fall off, harvest the other seed heads before they get to that point, leaving several inches of stem attached. Hang several stems upside down, covered with a paper bag to catch falling seed, in a warm, dry place until the drying is complete. Remove seeds from the seed heads and store in envelopes or small glass jars. Some herb seeds (dill, celery, anise, cumin, coriander, and others) are used for flavoring and are ready to use once dry.

Tomato seeds: Pick fruit from desirable plants when ripe. Cut fruit and squeeze out pulp into a container. Add a little water, then let ferment two to four days at room temperature, stirring occasionally. When seeds settle out, pour off pulp and spread seeds thinly to dry thoroughly. Store in an envelope or glass jar in a cool, dry place.

Lost Crops of Africa for Virginia Farmers

Harbans Bhardwaj, Professor, Virginia State University

The need for crop diversification and the development of crop varieties for sustainable food production are important factors for production of adequate and nutritious food for a growing human population worldwide. This is especially true of US agriculture, which depends upon a limited number of crops. The National Research Council of The National Academy of Science has published three books related to the "lost crops of Africa" (grains, vegetables, and fruits) which provide extensive information about new potential crop plants.

Figure 9-1: Egusi watermelon.

There are about 374,000 plant species currently known to science, with about 308,000 being vascular plants and about 295,000 being flowering plants. Out of all known plant species, some 120 are cultivated for human food but just nine of these crops supply over 75 percent of global plant-derived energy intake and of these, only three – wheat, rice and corn – account for more than 50 percent.

The New Crops Program of Virginia State University initiated a project in 2017 with five crops from West Africa: African eggplant, African potato, African rice, Egusi watermelon, and Marama bean. The aim of this project was to address the lack of local production/supply of exotic specialty crops to an increasing population of immigrants and Americans that appreciate different types of cuisine, enhancing income of small farmers via production of specialized crops to support tastes of immigrants, and crop diversification. Imports of exotic crops are currently supplying the market for immigrant needs and the local specialty crop industry is missing the potential improvement in economic, environmental and social sustainability.

All of these crops grew well in Virginia. Thirty-nine lines of African rice planted in May 2019 produced seed when planted without standing water indicating that African rice has potential for production in non-traditional areas. Marama bean grew but did not produce flower or seed. Being a perennial crop, it would need protection from cold in the winter in Virginia. Growth of African potato plants was impressive – both types (rotundifolius and esculentus) produced marketable tubers. Seventeen lines of African eggplant with different colored fruits, transplanted in the field from greenhouse grown seeds, grew well and produced marketable fruits.

Figure 9-2: Potato esculentus.

Twenty-two lines of Egusi watermelon produced several fruits each. These watermelons have bitter flesh but are grown for their seeds that are edible and very nutritious. During 2019 and 2021, several lines of finger millet and pearl millet (additional crops) were successfully produced – these crops were successful even without water in a tunnel. Further work to introduce several African crops to Virginia farmers is continuing.

Saving purchased seed

Properly stored seed remains viable for different lengths of time depending on the type of seed. Be aware that seed companies may store seeds up to the number of years of their viability prior to selling them. See table 9-1 "Viability of saved vegetable seeds." To ensure maximum viability of purchased seed after its package has been opened, remaining seed should be sealed in airtight containers and stored in a cool, dark location. Glass jars with rubber seals, such as baby food jars or canning jars, or tightly sealed plastic bags stored inside jars are good choices. Be sure to label all stored seed with the species name and original package date.

Be sure to label remaining stored seed clearly with permanent (preferably waterproof) ink, indicating the variety and date saved. To test for germination, sprout seeds between moist paper towels; if germination is low, either discard the seed or plant enough extra to give the desired number of plants.

Table 9-1: Viability of vegetable seeds (average number of years seeds may be saved)

Vegetable	Years	Vegetable	Years
Asparagus	3	Leek	2
Bean	3	Lettuce	6
Beet	4	Muskmelon	5
Broccoli	3	Mustard	4
Brussels sprouts	4	Okra	2
Cabbage	4	Onion	1
Carrot	3	Parsley	1
Cauliflower	4	Parsnip	1
Celery	3	Pea	3
Chinese cabbage	3	Pepper	2
Collard	5	Pumpkin	4
Corn, sweet	2	Radish	5
Cress, water	5	Rutabaga	4
Cucumber	5	Spinach	3
Eggplant	4	Squash	4
Endive	5	Tomato	4
Kale	4	Turnip	4
Kohlrabi	3	Watermelon	4

Depth for Planting Vegetable Seeds

The depth to cover seeds when you plant them depends on a number of factors, such as the size of the seed, the type of soil you have, and the season of the year. As a general rule, vegetable and flower seeds should be covered about four to five times their lateral diameter or width (not their length). Most seeds should be planted from 1/4 to 1/2 inch deep. There are exceptions, however, so read the packet directions. Small seeds, such as celery, should be planted only 1/8 inch deep. Vine crops, sweet corn, and beans can be planted 1 inch or deeper. Some seeds require light for germination and should not be covered at all. These instructions apply to seeds planted both inside and out.

Starting Seeds Indoors

To start seeds indoors, it is important to have enough light. More homegrown seedlings are probably lost due to this one factor than to any other. Vegetable seedlings grown under low-light conditions are likely to be leggy and weak, and many will fall over under their own weight after they are 3 to 4 inches tall. If you do not have a sunny room or back porch with a southern exposure, you will probably need supplemental lights. A simple, fluorescent shop light with one warm-white and one cool-white bulb (or with grow lights) will suffice.

It is probably easiest to use a soilless or peat-lite mix to start seedlings, since garden soil contains disease organisms that can be highly destructive to small plants. Soil can be sterilized in the oven by baking it at 200°F until the internal soil temperature is 180°F. It should be held at that temperature for 30 minutes. This is a smelly process, but it works. Garden soil for use in containers should be conditioned with compost and perlite to prevent excess moisture retention and/or shrinkage. A homemade mix of 50% vermiculite and 50% fine sphagnum peat is excellent for starting seeds. Fertilizer at half the normal strength may be added to the mixture. Mix well before using.

Many types of containers can be used to start seeds. Flats or other large containers may be used; plant in rows, and grow seedlings until they have one or two sets of true leaves, then transplant into other containers for growing to the size to transplant outdoors. Seedlings may also be started in pots, old cans, cut-off milk cartons, margarine tubs, egg cartons, or other throwaways. The pop-out trays found at garden centers are easy to use and reusable after cleaning. Peat pots or organic cow pots are nice, especially for large seeds. Sow one or two large seeds directly in each pot.

Table 9-2: Plant production data chart

* indicates transplants not recommended

Crop	Days to Emergence from Seeding	Optimum (degrees F) Germination Soil Temperature Range	Number of Weeks to Grow Transplants
Beans	5-10	65-85	*
Beets	7-10	50-85	*
Broccoli	3-10	50-85	5-7
Cabbage	4-10	50-85	5-7
Carrots	12-18	50-85	*
Cauliflower	4-10	50-85	5-7
Celery	9-21	50-65	10-12
Chard, Swiss	7-10	65-85	*
Corn, Sweet	5-8	65-85	*
Cucumber	6-10	65-85	4 (peat pots)
Eggplant	6-10	65-85	6-9
Lettuce	6-8	50-65	3-5
Melons	6-8	65-85	3-4 (peat pots)
Okra	7-10	65-85	*
Onion	7-10	65-85	8
Parsley	15-21	50-85	8
Peas	6-10	50-65	*
Pepper	9-14	65-85	6-8
Potatoes, Sweet	(slips)	65-85	5-6
Radish	3-6	50-65	*
Spinach	7-12	50-65	*
Squash	4-6	65-85	3-4 (peat pots)
Tomato	6-12	65-85	5-7
Turnip	4-8	50-65	*

Thin to one seedling per pot. Peat pots or organic cow pots may be planted directly in the garden; do not allow the edges of the pot to stick out above the soil since they will act as a wick and moisture will evaporate from this exposed surface. Many seed starting kits are now available and provide everything you will need, but remember that these are used as part of a hobby and not as a way to save money instead of buying plants at a nursery.

Regardless of the type of container chosen, fill it three quarters full with seed-starting mixture and sow the seeds. Cover to the specified depth, and water the mix. It may help to cover the containers with plastic wrap to maintain a steadier moisture level. Seeds and seedlings are extremely sensitive to drying out. They should not be kept soaking wet, however, since this condition is conducive to damping-off, a fungus disease deadly to seedlings. Damping-off can be prevented or diminished by sprinkling milled sphagnum moss, which contains a natural fungicide, on top of the soil.

Another option is to use peat pellets or cubes, which are preformed and require no additional soil mix. The pellets or cubes are soaked until thoroughly wet, then seeds are planted in the holes provided. The whole pellet or cube may then be planted without disturbing the roots. The only disadvantage to this method is the expense.

Starting Seed Outdoors

Many seeds may be sown directly in the garden. If garden soil is quite sandy or is mellow (with a high content of organic matter), seeds may be planted deeper. Young seedlings can emerge quite easily from a sandy or organic soil. If garden soil is heavy with a high silt and/or clay content, however, the seeds should be covered only two to three times their diameter. In such soils, it may be helpful to apply a band of sand, fine compost, or vermiculite, 4 inches wide and 1/4 inch thick, along the row after seeds are planted. This will help retain soil moisture and reduce crusting, making it easier for seedlings to push through the soil surface.

Soil temperature has an effect on the speed of seed germination. In the spring, soil is often cold, and seeds of some plants will rot before they have a chance to sprout. Table 9-2: Plant production data chart gives optimum soil temperatures.

When planting the fall garden in midsummer, the soil will be warm and dry; therefore, cover the seeds six to eight times their diameter. They may need to be watered each day with a sprinkler or a sprinkling can to promote germination. Moisture can also be retained with a shallow mulch or by covering the row with a board until the seeds have sprouted. Shading the area may be helpful to keep the soil cooler for seed germination, especially when planting cool-weather crops in summer. Seed that requires a lower germination temperature may benefit from being kept in the refrigerator for two weeks before planting or from pre-sprouting indoors. Pre-sprouting is a useful technique for planting in cold soils, as well. However, seed must be handled very carefully once sprouted to prevent damaging new root tissue.

Planting Layouts

Row planting

A string stretched between stakes will provide a guide for nice, straight rows, if desired. Use a hoe handle, a special furrow hoe, or a grub hoe to make a furrow of the appropriate depth for the seed being planted. Sow seed thinly; it may help to mix very small seed with coarse sand to distribute the seeds more evenly. Draw soil over the seed, removing stones and large clods. Firming soil so that it is in direct contact with seeds improves uptake of soil moisture by the seed, hastening germination. When plants have grown to 4 to 6 inches tall, thin according to seed packet instructions to provide adequate room for growth.

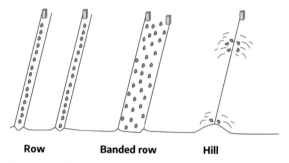

Figure 9-3: Planting techniques.

Wide row or banded planting

Many crops may be sown in wide rows or bands instead of in long, single rows. Crops of spinach, bean, pea, beet, lettuce, and carrot are especially suited to this type of culture. Sow seed evenly over the area, then rake it in, firming soil over the seeds. Thin young plants to allow room for growth.

Hill planting

Larger vegetables, such as melons, squash, sweet corn, and cucumbers, may be planted in hills or groups of seed. Soil is mounded to a foot or so in diameter, at the recommended spacing. Plant four to six seeds per hill, firming the soil well. Thin the seedlings to three to five plants per hill.

Transplants for the Garden

Most gardeners use transplants in the garden at some time or another to give long-season plants a chance to grow to maturity under their preferred weather conditions or just to lengthen the harvest season. Cool-season crops, such as head lettuce, broccoli, and celery, would not have a chance to reach their prime harvest stage in most places in Virginia in spring if not given those extra weeks indoors to get a head start. Tomatoes would certainly have a short harvest period in all but southeastern Virginia if started from seed in the ground, and peppers and eggplants might not produce at all if not grown from transplants.

Due to the amount of time, attention, and need for controlled growing conditions, many gardeners prefer to purchase plants for their gardens. However, for a larger choice in varieties and the control of plant production from seed to harvest, others choose to start their own transplants.

Annual Plant Transplants

Transplants of annual vegetables and flowers should be stocky, healthy, free from disease, and have good roots. They should not be too small or too mature (tomatoes will transplant all right with fruits already on them, but many other plants will drop flowers or fruit after transplanting). Be sure plants have been hardened off so that they will easily adapt to environmental change but not be so hardened that they are woody and yellow, otherwise they will not resume active vigorous growth. Successful transplanting is achieved by interrupting plant growth as little as possible. Younger plants that do not have dense roots growing out of the pot will usually become established fastest.

Have garden soil prepared before transplanting. All additives that require time to break down, such as manure, limestone (if called for in soil test), fertilizer, and green manure, should be incorporated the autumn before planting if at all possible. Well-decayed compost may be added just before planting.

Transplant on a shady day, in late afternoon, or in early evening to prevent wilting. It helps to water the plants several hours before transplanting. When using bare-root plant soak the roots thoroughly an hour or two before setting them out in the garden. They should not be allowed to dry out completely at any time. Handle plants carefully. Avoid disturbing the roots or bruising the stems. Dig a hole large enough to hold the roots of the plants. Set the plants slightly deeper than previously planted and at recommended intervals. Tomatoes are an exception to the rule of how deep to plant; they will develop roots all along the stems, and you can plant deep enough to leave only two or three sets of leaves exposed. Press soil firmly around the roots of transplants. Water the plants once or twice during the next week if there is insufficient rain.

Table 9-3: Ease of transplanting

Easily Survive Transplanting	Require Care in the Operation	Not Successfully Transplanted by Usual Methods
Broccoli	Celery	Bean
Brussels sprouts	Eggplant	Carrot
Cabbage	Melon	Corn, Sweet
Cauliflower	Onion (tends to bolt)	Cucumber (tend to stop growth)
Chard	Pepper	Melon
Chinese cabbage		Okra
Lettuce		Pea
Sweet potato slips		Squash
Tomato		

Perennial Plant Transplants

When buying small fruit plants and perennial crowns, such as asparagus, order early or buy from reliable local outlets. Occasionally stores allow plants to dry out, so watch for this, especially if you are buying sale plants. Select varieties that will do well in your growing conditions. For perennial plants, it will pay to do some research to find out what the major disease and insect pests are and buy resistant varieties. Dormant, bare-root plants, and 1- or 2-year-old crowns are preferred. Look for roots that are full, slightly moist, and have color. Roots that are dry brown or soggy black are indicative of poor storage and will probably not give good results. Check crowns for signs of viable buds. Inspect plants for signs of insects or disease. If you receive plants by mail that are not satisfactory, do not hesitate to send them back.

Once you have the plants, keep the roots moist (but not soaking wet) by misting occasionally, and do not allow them to freeze or be exposed to high temperatures. If it is necessary to keep the crowns for more than a few days, place in cold storage (not freezing) or else heel in a trench of moist soil in a shaded location. Pack soil firmly against roots to eliminate any air pockets.

Transplant crowns according to directions, digging holes large enough to give the roots plenty of room to spread. Remove any discolored or dried out roots. Perennial plants appreciate a dose of compost mixed into the bottom of the hole. Once transplanted, shade the plants if necessary and water when needed. Extra care at the beginning of their growth will result in productive, healthy plants.

Irrigating the Home Garden

Adequate soil moisture is essential for good crop growth. A healthy plant is composed of 75 to 90% water, which is used for the plant's vital functions, including photosynthesis, support (rigidity), and transportation of nutrients and sugars to various parts of the plant. During the first two weeks of growth, plants are becoming established and must have water to build their root systems.

During the growing season of April through September, vegetable crops need enough water each week to wet the soil down 5 to 6 inches. In most soils, this means that about 1 inch of water needs to be applied each week in the form of rainwater, irrigation water, or a combination of both. Keep a rain gauge near the garden or check with the local weather bureau for rainfall amounts, then supplement rainfall with irrigation water, if needed. There are ways, however, to reduce the amount of water you have to add.

During dry periods, one thorough watering each week of 1-2 inches of moisture (65-130 gallons per 100 square feet, or approximately 2/3 gallon per square foot) at one time is usually enough for most soils and will add enough water to soak the soil to a depth of 5-6 inches (this varies with the nature of the soil). Do not water again until the top few inches of soil begin to dry. A trickle irrigation system will be much more efficient in use of water. It uses more frequent or continuous application of water in smaller amounts to prevent soil dryness. If there is any doubt, dig down 6 inches into the soil to check for moisture, but take care not to damage any roots.

Frequent, light watering will only encourage shallow rooting which will cause plants to suffer more quickly during drought periods, especially if mulches are not used. On the other hand, too much water, especially in poorly drained soils can be as damaging to plant growth as too little water. A good rule to remember is to water deeply and infrequently.

For some diseases of vegetable crops, wet foliage provides a favorable environment for disease development. **Overhead watering** (in which water is sprayed down on crops, directly wetting the crop surface) should be conducted so as not to prolong the time leaves are wet from dew (which is usually late evening through 9-10:00 am); therefore, late morning or early evening are the worst times for overhead watering. Watering in the early morning, which is usually the least windy time of day, also helps to decrease evaporation.

Reducing Water Demands

All of the water you apply may not be available to plants, particularly if the soil is a heavy clay. Clay particles hold soil moisture tightly. If, for example, there are 4 1/2 in of water per foot of this type of soil, there may be as little as 1 1/2 in available for plants. A relatively high level of humus in the soil, brought about by the addition and breakdown of organic matter, can improve this proportion to some extent. By causing clay particles to form aggregates or large clumps of groups of particles, humus also adds air spaces to tight clays, allowing moisture to drain to lower levels as a reserve, instead of puddling and running off the top of the soil.

The **water-holding capacity** of sandy soils is also improved by addition of organic matter. Though most soil water in sandy soil is available, it drains so quickly that plants are unable to reach water after even a few days following a rain. Humus in sandy soil gives the water something to cling to until it is needed by plants. Addition of organic matter is the first step in improving the moisture-holding capacity of the soil (see subsequent discussion of reducing water demands).

Mulching is a cultural practice that can significantly decrease the amount of water to be added to the soil. A 2- to 3-inch (6 to 8 inches of loose straw or leaves will compact to 2-3 inches of mulch) organic mulch can reduce water needs by as much as half by reducing evaporation of moisture directly from the soil. Organic mulches themselves hold some water and increase the humidity level around the plant. If they become dry it may be necessary to add an extra 1 or 2 inches of water when overhead watering to soak through the mulch. Plastic mulch also conserves moisture, but may increase soil temperatures dramatically during the summer (to the detriment of some plants and the benefit of others) if not covered by other mulch materials or foliage.

Shading and the use of **windbreaks** are other moisture-conserving techniques. Plants that wilt in very sunny areas can benefit from partial shade during the afternoon in summer. Small plants, in particular, should be protected. Air moving across a plant carries away the moisture on the leaf surfaces, causing the plant to need more water. In very windy areas, the roots often cannot keep up with leaf demands, and plants wilt. Temporary or permanent windbreaks can help tremendously.

During those times when cultural practices simply aren't enough, when rainfall is sparse, and the sun is hot, watering can benefit the garden with higher yields or may save the garden altogether in severe drought years.

By knowing the critical watering periods for selected vegetables, you can reduce the amount of supplemental water you add. This can be important where water supplies are limited. In general, water is most needed during the first few weeks of development, immediately after transplant, and during development of fruits.

Specifically, the critical watering periods for selected vegetables are:

- Asparagus – Spear production, fern development
- Beans – Pod filling
- Broccoli – Head development
- Cabbage – Head development
- Carrot – Seed emergence, root development
- Cauliflower – Head development
- Corn, sweet – Silking, tasseling, ear development
- Cucumber – Flowering, fruit development
- Eggplant – Flowering, fruiting
- Lettuce – Head development; moisture should be constant
- Melons – Flowering, fruit development
- Peas – Pod filling
- Tomato – Flowering, fruiting

In areas prone to repeated drought, look for drought-resistant varieties when buying seed or plants.

Irrigation practices, when properly used, can benefit the garden in many ways:

- Aid in seed emergence
- Reduce soil crusting
- Improve germination
- Reduce wilting and checking of growth in transplants
- Increase fruit size of tomato, cucumber, and melon
- Prevent premature ripening of peas, beans, and sweet corn
- Maintain uniform growth
- Improve the quality and yields of most crops

Irrigation Methods

The home gardener has several options for applying water to plants. Most gardeners either use overhead watering (a watering sprinkler can, a garden hose with a fan nozzle or spray attachment, portable lawn sprinklers), or a drip application (a perforated plastic soaker hose, drip or trickle irrigation, or a semiautomatic drip system). When properly cared for, quality equipment will last for a number of years.

Some basic techniques and principles for overhead watering:

- Adjust the flow or rate of water application to about 1/2 inch per hour. A much faster flow than this will cause runoff, unless the soil has exceptionally good drainage. To determine the rate for a sprinkler, place small tin cans at various places within the sprinkler's reach, and check the level of water in the cans at 15-minute intervals.
- When using the oscillating type of lawn sprinklers, place the sprinkler on a platform higher than the crop to prevent water from being diverted by plant leaves and try to keep the watering pattern even by frequently moving the sprinkler, overlapping about half of each pattern.

Several types of drip or trickle equipment are available. A soaker hose is a fibrous hose that allows water to seep out all along its length at a slow rate. Soaker hoses have a short lifespan and are more expensive than polyethylene drip tubing or drip tape. Drip tubing or drip tape allow water to drip out of small holes spaced along the tubing; a flow regulator usually has to be included with the system so water can reach the end of the hose (rather than spraying out at full force). Special, double-wall type of irrigation hoses help maintain an even flow. Drip tape or tubing should be placed with holes facing up (as recommended by manufacturers) along one side of the crop row or underneath mulch. Finally, there is the emitter-type system, best used for small, raised-bed or container gardens, in which short tubes, or emitters, come off a main water supply hose. Emitters put water right at the roots of the desired plants. This type of system is best used in combination with a coarse mulch or black plastic.

Fertilizing the Garden

The amount of fertilizer to apply to a garden depends on the natural fertility of the soil, the amount of organic matter present, the type of fertilizer used, and the crop being grown. The best way to determine fertilizer needs is to have the soil tested. Soil testing is available through your local VCE office.

Vegetables fall into three main categories according to their fertilizer requirements: heavy feeders, medium feeders, and light feeders. It may be advantageous to group crops in the garden according to their fertilizer requirements to make application easier. (For a complete discussion of fertilizers, refer to Chapter 2 "Soils and Nutrient Management").

Weed Control in the Garden

Most gardeners are well aware that weeds readily grow wherever their seeds are dispersed. Weed seeds are able to remain viable in the soil for years until the environmental conditions become conducive for their growth. Many weeds that would otherwise not be growing in a lawn or natural areas appear to spring up as if by magic when the soil is cultivated. These weeds are competition for intentionally placed plants in our garden and can take up valuable water, nutrients, sunlight, and space if not properly managed.

Beneficial Weeds

Despite the competition they can create for our cultivated species, weeds can also have positive benefits for the garden. Some, such as morning glory and even thistles, have flowers that rival those intentionally planted in flower beds. Some weeds can also provide additional habitat and food sources to beneficial insects gardeners spend time and energy working to encourage.

Wild plants also have other virtues. Parts of some plants are used in natural dyes and other homemade products. Weeds can be a good source of nitrogenous materials for the compost pile if pulled before flowering. Certain soil problems (e.g., deficiencies, pH changes, soil compaction, etc.) can be brought to light by the presence of weed species that thrive under those specific conditions.

Control: Cultivation

Vegetable gardeners hoping to control weed populations and lessen their impact on vegetable development should strive to remove weeds while they are young. There are a number of methods to remove weeds from the garden, from hand pulling to using hand tools or motorized equipment. See the "Selecting Gardening Equipment" section of this chapter for more information on the common tools available for gardeners.

Turning under weeds can add beneficial organic matter to the soil, however, many plants with heavy roots or rhizomes may survive. Hand-pulled weeds, except for rhizomatous grasses, may be laid on top of the soil to dry out after shaking them free of soil and will eventually have the same effect of adding organic matter to the soil. However, if rain is predicted within a day or two, it's better to collect the weeds and add them to the compost pile rather than turning under. Rain may wash soil around the roots allowing weeds to survive. Do not leave weeds that have begun to go to seed. In order to destroy weed seeds in compost, the pile must reach 140 degrees F. Failure to reach this temperature and destroy seeds means viable weed seeds may remain in compost. If not dried up completely, grasses that spread by rhizomes or stolons also present a problem. In these cases it's best to either: let the trash collectors take the weeds, burn the weeds and spread the ashes in the garden (if local ordinances permit), or maintain a "pit" compost pile (where the organic material is actually buried in the soil) for these items, kitchen scraps, and other problematic materials. Gardeners can also work to reduce weed growth by mowing, especially before seed heads are fully formed.

Cultivation is best timed when soil is somewhat moist. Avoid pulling, hoeing, or otherwise cultivating when soil is wet so as not to impact soil structure. Dry soil can also make cultivation more difficult. Planning for this work a day or two after a rain or irrigation will increase the ease of removing weeds in the garden. If you have a choice, remember that the work will be much more pleasant in the cool temperatures of early morning or evening. On hot, summer afternoons, you are likely to fatigue more easily; get a sunburn; or suffer from sun poisoning, sunstroke, or worse. Wear protective clothing if you must work when it's sunny, and stop frequently for rest and water.

Control: Mulching

Mulching is an optional alternative to weeding but requires a reliable source for these materials. Thick layers of organic mulch will not allow most annual weeds to grow. Black plastic can often control weeds with runners that organic mulch can't control. For weed suppression in paths, newspaper or cardboard covered with organic mulch will offer good control. Sawdust, however, is not recommended for use right around plants because of its tendency to crust and because bacteria take nitrogen from the soil, thus from the vegetables, to break down the sawdust.

Control: Close Spacing

Once vegetable plants are established, if they have been planted close enough to each other, they will shade the soil and help to prevent the growth of many weeds. In order to achieve this effect, plants need to be spaced so that leaves of the adjacent plants touch and form a canopy at their mature growth stage.

250 | CHAPTER 9: THE VEGETABLE GARDEN

Control: Cover Crops

Another method of long term weed control is the integration of cover crops into your garden beds. This method can reduce available gardening space, but can be beneficial both for weed control and soil health. Cover crops must be maintained throughout their lifecycle, including mowing, harvesting, or plowing them under at the right time in their growth cycle. These additional steps can be time-consuming and may require specialized tools. See Table 9-5 for more information on using cover crops.

Control: Herbicides

There are herbicides labeled for home vegetable garden use but they should be used sparingly and with caution. Always follow the instructions listed on the label, including what plants it can be used for, application rates, and more. The label is the law and you should not deviate from it. To learn more about pesticide use and safety, please see Chapter 7: "Integrated Pest Management."

Vegetable Planting Guide

Use the VCE publication "Virginia's Home Garden Vegetable Planting Guide" and your USDA zone to determine your last frost date and determine the earliest and latest planting dates for vegetable crops. This is particularly important in making maximum use of garden space by following one crop with another as soon as the first harvest is complete.

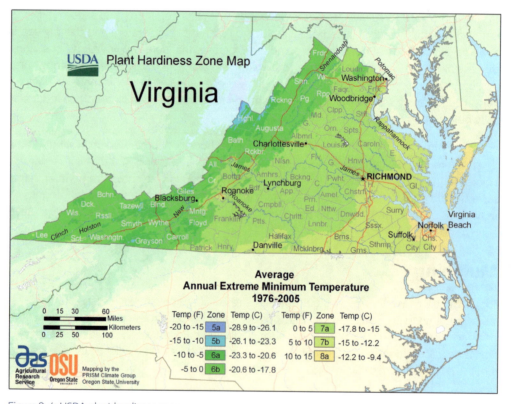

Figure 9-4: USDA plant hardiness zone map.

The Vegetable Planting Guide can be used to determine the approximate proper amount of crop to plant for the desired yield, the amount of seed or transplants required for that amount of crop, and proper spacing between plants in a row. In intensive, raised-bed gardens, use the in-row figures between all plants; i.e., use equidistant spacing between plants. Sow seeds to a depth three to five times the diameter of the seed. For midsummer plantings, sow up to twice this depth.

The planting date for vegetables depends on the hardiness of the particular crop. Most planting directions are based on the average **frost date**. Average frost date refers to the expected dates of the last frost in the spring and the first frost in the fall for a geographic location. The difference between the two average frost dates determines the average number of frost free days for crop production.

Intensive Gardening Methods

The purpose of an intensively grown garden is to harvest the most produce possible from a given space. More traditional gardens consist of long, single rows of vegetables spaced widely apart. Much of the garden area is taken by the space between the rows. An intensive garden reduces wasted space to a minimum. The practice of intensive gardening is not just for those with limited garden space; rather, an intensive garden concentrates work efforts to create an ideal plant environment, giving better yields with less labor.

Though its benefits are many, the intensive garden may not be for everyone. Some people enjoy the sight of long, straight rows in their gardens. Others prefer machine cultivation over hand weeding; though there is often less weeding to do in intensive plantings. Because of fewer pathways and closely spaced plants, the weeding that must be done is usually done by hand or with hand tools. Still other gardeners like to get their gardens planted in a very short period of time and have harvests come in all at once. The intensive ideal is to have something growing in every part of the garden at all times during the growing season.

A good intensive garden requires early, thorough planning to make the best use of time and space in the garden. Interrelationships of plants must be considered before planting, including nutrient needs, shade tolerance, above- and below-ground growth patterns, and preferred growing season. Using the techniques described below, anyone can develop a high-yielding intensive garden. For more information, see the VCE publication "Intensive Gardening Methods" 426-335.

Table 9-4: Vegetable planting guide

Crop	Distance between plants in row	Distance between rows	Intensive spacing distances	Approximate amount of seed/transplants for 10' row	Approximate yield per 10' row	Approximate number of plants per person per planting	Number of plantings spring/summer	Number of plantings fall
Asparagus	12-18"	36-48"	15-18"	10 crowns	3-4 lbs	5-10	1	
Beans, bush	1-3"	24-36"	4-6"	1 oz seed	3-5 lbs	10	4	
Beans, pole	4-12"	36-48"	6-12"	1 oz seed	6-10 lbs	3-5	2	
Beans, lima	3-6"	24-36"	4-6"	1 oz seed	4-6 lbs	4-8	1	
Beets	2-3"	12-18"	2-4"	1/8 oz seed	8-10 lbs	10-20	2	2
Broccoli	12-24"	18-36"	12-18"	10 transplants	4-6 lbs	3-5	2	3
Brussels Sprouts	18-24"	30-36"	15-18"	7 transplants	3-5 lbs	2-5		1
Cabbage	12-18"	18-36"	15-18"	10 transplants	10-25 lbs	4-8	1	2
Chinese Cabbage	4-30"	18-36"	10-12"	10 transplants	20-30 lbs	6-8	1	2
Carrots	thin to 1.5-2"	6-12"	2-3"	1/20 oz seed	7-10 lbs	10-30	1	2

Table 9-4: Vegetable planting guide (continued)

Crop	Distance between plants in row	Distance between rows	Intensive spacing distances	Approximate amount of seed/ transplants for 10' row	Approximate yield per 10' row	Approximate number of plants per person per planting	Number of plantings spring/ summer	Number of plantings fall
Cauliflower	12-24"	24-36"	15-18"	10 transplants	8-10 lbs	3-5	1	2
Chard, Swiss	6-12"	18-30"	6-9"	1/5 oz seed	8-12 lbs	3-5	1	2
Collards, Kale	12-24"	18-36"	12-15", 15-18"	10 transplants	4-8 lbs	3-7	1	2
Cucumbers	12-18"	48-72"	12-18"	10 transplants	8-10 lbs	2-4	3-Feb	
Eggplant	18-24"	30-42"	18-24"	7 transplants	10-12 lbs	1-3	1	
Kohlrabi	4-6"	12-36"	6-9"	30 transplants	4-8 lbs	3-6	1	2
Leeks	4-6"	12-30"	3-6"	1/10 oz seed	5-10 lbs	10-12	1	1
Lettuce, head	6-10"	10-18"	10-12"	20 transplants	2-4 lbs	5-10	3	3
Lettuce, baby salad	0.2-0.4"	6-12"	4-6"	1/4 oz seed	2-4 lbs	10-15 feet of row	2	3
Muskmelons	24-36"	60-90"	18-24"	5 transplants	15-25 lbs	2-3	2	
Mustard	1-2" thin to 6"	18-30"	6-9"	1/10 oz seed	3-6 lbs	5-10	1	2
Okra	12-18"	36-48"	12-18"	15 transplants	5-10 lbs	3-5	2	
Onions (bulbing)	2-4"	12-18"	2-4"	60 transplants	7-10 lbs	20-30	1	
Peas, garden	2-3"	12-30"	2-4"	1/2 oz seed	2-6 lbs	20-30	2	
Peppers	12-24"	30-36"	12-15"	10 transplants	5-18 lbs	3-5	2	
Potatoes	10-18"	24-42"	10-12"	1 lb	10-20 lbs	10	1	
Pumpkins	2-4'	5-8'	24-36"	1/20 oz seed	10-20 lbs	1	1	
Radish	3/4-1"	6-12"	2-3"	1/8 oz seed	3-5 lbs	2 feet of row	2	4
Rutabaga	3-6"	12-30"	4-6"	1/8 oz seed	8-12 lbs	10-20		1
Southern Peas (Cowpeas)	3-4"	24-36"	3-4"	1 oz seed	5-18 lbs	20-30	1	
Sweet Corn	6-12"	24-36"	15-18"	1/2 oz seed	7-10 lbs	15-20	5-Mar	
Spinach	0.5-1" thin to 4"	6-12"	4-6"	1/8 oz seed	4-6 lbs	15	2	2
Squash, summer	18-36"	36-60"	18-24"	1/10 oz seed	20-80 lbs	1-2	3	
Squash, winter	2-4'	3-10'	24-36"	1/10 oz seed	10-80 lbs	1-2	1	
Sweet Potato	9-12"	30-48"		15 slips	8-12 lbs	5	1	
Tomatoes	18-36"	36-50"	18-24"	7 transplants	15-45 lbs	2-4	2	
Turnips	2-3"	12-24"	4-6"	1/8 oz seed	8-12 lbs	10-20	1	1
Watermelons	3-4'	5-10'	18-24"	3 transplants	8-40 lbs	2	2	

The Raised Bed

The raised bed or growing bed is the basic unit of an intensive garden. A system of beds allows the gardener to concentrate soil preparation in small areas, resulting in effective use of soil amendments and creating an ideal environment for vegetable growth. Some people like to use frames for their beds but it is not necessary and traditional cultures throughout the world do not.

Beds are generally 3 to 4 feet wide and as long as desired. The gardener works from either side of the bed, reducing the incidence of compaction between plants caused by walking on the soil.

Figure 9-5: Raised beds.

Soil preparation is the key to successful intensive gardening. To grow so close together, plants must have adequate nutrients and water. Providing extra synthetic fertilizers and irrigation will help, but there is no substitute for deep, fertile soil high in organic matter. Humus-rich soil will hold extra nutrients, and existing elements that are "locked up" in the soil are released by the actions of earthworms, microorganisms, and acids present in a life-filled soil, making them available for plant use.

By their nature, raised beds are a form of wide-bed gardening, a technique by which seeds and transplants are planted in wide bands of several rows or broadcast in a wide strip. In general, the goal is to space plants at equal distances from each other on all sides, such that leaves will touch at maturity. This saves space, and the close plantings reduce moisture loss from surrounding soil.

Vertical Gardening

The use of trellises, nets, strings, cages, or poles to support growing plants constitutes vertical gardening. This technique is especially suited, but not limited, to gardeners with a small garden space. Vining and sprawling plants, such as cucumbers, tomatoes, melons, and pole beans, are obvious candidates for this type of gardening. Some plants entwine themselves onto the support, while others may need to be tied. Remember that a vertical planting will cast a shadow, so beware of shading sun-loving crops, or take advantage of the shade by planting shade-tolerant crops near the vertical ones. Plants grown vertically take

Figure 9-6: Vertical gardens.

up much less space on the ground, and though the yield per plant may be (but is not always) less, the yield per square foot of garden space is much greater. Because vertically growing plants are more exposed, they dry out faster and may need to be watered more frequently than if they were allowed to spread over the ground. This fast drying is also an advantage to those plants susceptible to fungal diseases. A higher rate of fertilization may be needed, and soil should be deep and well-drained to allow roots to extend vertically rather than compete with others at a shallow level.

Interplanting

Growing two or more types of vegetables in the same place at the same time is known as interplanting. Proper planning is essential to obtain high production and increased quality of the crops planted. This technique has been practiced for thousands of years and is gaining widespread support in this country. To successfully plan an interplanted garden, the following factors must be taken into account for each plant: length of the plant's growth period; its growth pattern (tall, short, below or above ground); possible negative effects on other plants (such as the allelopathic effects of sunflowers and Jerusalem artichokes on nearby plants); preferred season; and light, nutrient, and moisture requirements. Interplanting can be accomplished by alternating rows within a bed (plant a row of peppers next to a row of onions), by mixing plants within a row, or by distributing various species throughout the bed. For the beginner, alternating rows may be the easiest to manage at first.

Long-season (slow to mature) and short-season (quick to mature) plants like carrots and radishes, respectively, can be planted at the same time. The radishes are harvested before they begin to crowd the carrots. An example of combining growth patterns is planting smaller plants close to larger plants, radishes at the base of beans or broccoli. Shade tolerant species, like lettuce, spinach, and celery, may be planted in the shadow of taller crops. Heavy feeders, such as cabbage family crops, should be interplanted with less gluttonous plants.

Interplanting may reduce insect and disease problems. Pests are usually fairly crop-specific; that is, they prefer vegetables of one type or family. Mixing families of plants helps to break up large expanses of the pest-preferred crop, helping to contain early pest damage within a small area, thus giving the gardener a little more time to deal with the problem. One disadvantage is that when it does come time to spray for pests, it's hard to be sure that all plants are protected.

Wide Row Planting

Plants are closely spaced in a raised bed or interplanted garden. **Wide row planting** refers to planting in such closely-spaced bands rather than in rows of individual plants. An equidistant spacing pattern calls for plants to be the same distance from each other within the bed; that is, plant so that the center of one plant is the same distance from plants on all sides of it. In beds of more than two rows, this means that the rows should be staggered so that plants in every other row are between the plants in adjacent rows. The distance recommended for plants within the row is the distance from the center of one plant to the center of the next. This results in an efficient use of space and leaves less area to weed and mulch. The close spacing tends to create a nearly solid leaf canopy, acting as a living mulch, decreasing water loss, and keeping down weed problems. However, plants should not be crowded to the point that disease problems arise or competition causes stunting.

Succession and Relay Planting

Succession planting is an excellent way to make the most of an intensive garden. To obtain a succession of crops, plant something new in spots vacated by spent plants. Planting corn after peas is a type of succession. This following of early crops with new ones provides for a gradual change from a spring garden to summer and fall gardens. Cool-season crops (broccoli, lettuce, pea) are followed by warm-season crops (bean, tomato, pepper), and where possible, these may be followed by more cool-season plants or even a winter cover crop. It is extremely important to avoid using members of the same family in succession cropping. For example, do not follow peas with beans. Insects and disease populations from the first crop will still be present, causing greater problems on the next.

Relaying is another common practice, consisting of overlapping plantings of one type of crop. The new planting is made before the old one is removed. For instance, sweet corn may be planted at two-week intervals for a continuous harvest. This requires some care, though; crops planted very early are likely to get a slower start because of low temperatures. In the case of sweet corn, it can be disastrous to have two varieties pollinating at the same time, as the quality of the kernels may be affected. Give early planted corn extra time to get started, for best results. Another way to achieve the same result is to plant, at once, various varieties of the same vegetable; for example, you can plant an early season, a mid-season, and a late-season corn at the same time and have a lengthy harvest.

Planning an Intensive Garden

Begin planning your garden early. In January or February, when the cold days of winter seem never-ending, pull out last year's garden records and dig into the new seed catalogs. As with any garden, you must decide what crops you want to grow based on your own likes and dislikes, as well as how much of each you will need. An account of what cultivars were most successful or tasted best is helpful in making crop choices.

Good gardening practices, such as watering, fertilizing, crop rotation, composting, and sanitation, are especially important in an intensive garden. An intensive garden does require more-detailed planning, but the time saved in working the garden and the increased yields make it well worthwhile.

Starting seeds indoors for transplanting is an important aspect of intensive gardening. To get the most from the garden plot, a new crop should be ready to take the place of the crop being removed. Several weeks may be gained by having 6-inch transplants ready to go into vacated areas. Don't forget to recondition the soil for the new plants.

Container Gardening

If you don't have space for a vegetable garden or if your present site is too small, consider raising fresh, nutritious, homegrown vegetables in containers. A window sill, patio, balcony, or doorstep can provide sufficient space for a productive container garden. Problems with soil-borne diseases, nematodes, or poor soil can also be overcome by switching to container gardening.

Grow vegetables that take up little space, such as carrots, radishes and lettuce, or crops that bear fruits over a period of time, such as tomatoes and peppers, for best use of space and containers. Dwarf or miniature varieties often mature and bear fruit early, but most do not produce as well overall as standard varieties. With increasing interest in container gardening, plant breeders and seed companies are working on vegetables specifically bred for container culture. These varieties are not necessarily miniature or dwarf and may produce as well as standard types if properly maintained.

The amount of sunlight that your container garden spot receives may determine what crops can be grown. Generally, root crops and leaf crops can tolerate partial shade, but vegetables grown for their fruits generally need at least six hours of full, direct sunlight each day and perform better with eight to ten hours. Available light can be increased somewhat by providing reflective materials around the plants (e.g., aluminum foil, white-painted surfaces, marble chips).

Container gardening lends itself to attractive plantscaping. A dull patio area can be brightened by the addition of barrels of cherry tomatoes or a colorful herb mix. Planter boxes with trellises can be used to create a cool, shady place on an apartment balcony. Container gardening presents opportunities for many innovative ideas.

Choosing Containers

There are many possible containers for gardening. Clay, wood, plastic, and metal are some of the suitable materials. Containers for vegetable plants must (1) be big enough to support plants when they are fully grown, (2) hold soil without spilling, (3) have adequate drainage, and (4) never have held products that would be toxic to plants or people. Consider using barrels, cut-off milk and bleach jugs, window boxes, clothes baskets lined with plastic (with drainage holes punched in it), even pieces of drainage pipe or cement block. If you are building a planting box out of wood, you will find redwood and cedar to be the most rot-resistant, but bear in mind that cedar trees are much more plentiful than redwoods. Wood for use around plants should never be treated with creosote or pentachlorophenol (Penta) wood preservatives. Penta is a restricted-use chemical, not available to non-licensed individuals; however, you may still find it on some pretreated woods. Penta and creosote may be toxic to plants as well as harmful to people. The chemicals in pressure-treated wood should not leach out if handled properly.

Figure 9-7: Container garden.

Figure 9-8: Hanging strawberry planter.

Some gardeners have built vertical planters out of wood lattice lined with black plastic, then filled with a light-weight medium; or out of welded wire, shaped into cylinders, lined with sphagnum moss, and filled with soil mix. Depending on the size of your vertical planter, 2-inch diameter perforated, plastic pipes may be needed inside to aid watering.

Whatever type of container you use, be sure that there are holes in the bottom for drainage so plant roots do not stand in water. Most plants need containers at least 6 to 8 inches deep for adequate root growth.

As long as the container meets the basic requirements described above it can be used. The imaginative use of discarded items or construction of attractive patio planters is a very enjoyable aspect of container gardening. For ease of care, dollies or platforms with wheels or casters can be used to move the containers from place to place. This is especially useful for apartment or balcony gardening so that plants can be moved to get maximum use of available space and sunlight and to avoid destruction from particularly nasty weather.

Figure 9-9: Vertical planter made from fabric.

For information about growing vegetables in containers, including spacing and minimum container size, see the VCE publication "Vegetable Gardening in Containers" 426-336 (SPES-255P).

Media for Container Gardens

A fairly lightweight potting mix is needed for container vegetable gardening. Soil straight from the garden usually cannot be used in a container because it may contain too much clay. Clay soil consists of extremely small (microscopic) particles. In a container, the bad qualities of clay are exaggerated. It holds too much moisture when wet, resulting in too little air for the roots, and it pulls away from the sides of the pot when dry. It is also extremely heavy! Container medium must be porous to support plants, because roots require both air and water.

Packaged potting mix available at local garden centers is relatively lightweight and, if of high quality, may make a good container medium. Soilless mixes, such as peatlite mix, are generally too light for container vegetable gardening, not offering enough support to plant roots. If the container is also lightweight, a strong wind can blow plants over, resulting in major damage. Also, soilless mixes are sterile and contain few nutrients, so when fertilizers are added, trace elements must be included. If you wish to use a sterile mix you may add garden soil for weight and better water holding capacity but remember it will introduce insects, weeds, and diseases. For a large container garden, the expense of prepackaged or soilless mixes may be quite high. Try mixing your own with one part peat moss; one part garden loam; one part clean, coarse (builder's) sand or perlite; and a slow-release fertilizer (14-14-14) according to container size. Lime may also be needed to bring the pH to around 6.5. In any case, a soil test is helpful in determining nutrient and pH needs, just as in a large garden.

Planting Container Gardens

Plant container crops at the same time you would if you were planting a regular garden. Fill a clean container to within 1 to 2 inches of the top (depending on the size of the container) with the slightly damp soil mixture. Peat moss in the mix will absorb water and mix much more readily if wetted before putting the mix in the container. Sow the seeds or set transplants according to instructions on the package. Put a label with the name, variety, and date of planting on or in each container. After planting, gently soak the soil with water, being careful not to wash out or displace seeds. Thin seedlings to obtain proper spacing when the plants have two or three true leaves. If cages, stakes, or other supports are needed, provide them when the plants are very small to avoid root damage later.

Watering Container Gardens

Pay particular attention to watering container plants. Because the volume of soil is relatively small, containers can dry out very quickly, especially on a concrete patio in full sun. Watering daily or even twice daily may be necessary. Apply water until it runs out the drainage holes. On an upstairs balcony, this may mean neighbor problems, so make provisions for drainage of water. Large trays filled with coarse marble chips work nicely. However, the pot should never be in direct contact with the drainage water as it will be absorbed and keep the soil too wet. The soil should never be soggy or have water standing on top of it. When the weather is cool, container plants may be subject to root rots if maintained too wet. Clay pots and other porous containers allow additional evaporation from the sides of the pots, and watering must be done more often. Small pots also tend to dry out more quickly than larger ones. If the soil appears to be getting excessively dry (plants wilting every day is one sign), group the containers together so the foliage creates a canopy to help shade the soil and keep it cooler. On a hot patio, you might consider putting containers on pallets or other structures that will allow air movement beneath the pots and prevent direct contact with the cement. Check containers at least once a day and twice on hot, dry, or windy days. Feel the soil to determine whether or not it is damp. Mulching and windbreaks can help reduce water requirements for containers. If you are away a lot, consider an automatic drip emitter irrigation system.

Fertilizing Container Gardens

If you use a soil mix with fertilizer added, then your plants will have enough nutrients for eight to ten weeks. If plants are grown longer than this, add a water-soluble fertilizer at the recommended rate. Repeat every two to three weeks. An occasional dose of fish emulsion or compost will add trace elements to the soil. Do not add more than the recommended rate of any fertilizer, since this may cause fertilizer burn and kill the plants. Container plants do not have the buffer of large volumes of soil and humus to protect them from over-fertilizing or over-liming. Just because a little is good for the plants does not guarantee that a lot will be better.

General Care of Container Gardens

Vegetables grown in containers can be attacked by the various types of insects and diseases that are common to any vegetable garden. Plants should be periodically inspected for the presence of foliage-feeding and fruit-feeding insects as well as the occurrence of diseases. Protect plants from very high heat caused by light reflected from pavement. Move them to a cool spot or shade them during the hottest part of the day. Plants should be moved to a sheltered location during severe rain, hail, or wind storms and for protection from early fall frosts.

Indoor Container Gardening

If you want fresh, homegrown vegetables over the winter, or if you don't have an outdoor space in which you can place containers, it is worth trying some indoor container gardening. Of course, you cannot have a full garden in the house, but a bright, sunny window can be the site for growing fresh food all year. Some small-fruited tomatoes and peppers, several types of lettuce, radishes, and many herbs are among the plants you can include in the indoor garden.

Follow directions given above for preparing pots and for watering and fertilizing. However, note that plants will dry out less quickly indoors and will also grow more slowly, needing less fertilizer. To make watering easy it is wise to set the pots in large trays with 1-2 inches of decorative stones in them. Not only will this eliminate the need to move the plants in order to water them, which may discourage you from watering when you should, but it will also provide humidity, which is a major requirement, especially during winter when the house is warm and dry.

A sunny, south-facing window is a must for indoor vegetable growing. Fruiting vegetables, such as tomatoes and peppers, will also need supplemental light, such as a combination warm-white/cool-white fluorescent light during winter months. Insufficient light will result in tall, spindly plants and failure to flower and set fruit.

The small-fruited varieties of tomatoes, such as Tiny Tim, Small Fry, and Roma (a paste tomato), may be raised quite satisfactorily in the home. They will challenge your gardening ability and supply fruits that can be eaten whole, cooked, or served with salad. The Tiny Tim tomato grows to a height of about 12-15 inches. Small Fry, which is about 3 feet tall, and Roma will need more space and should be located on an enclosed porch or in a sun room. It may also be worth experimenting with varieties developed for hanging baskets. Some of the small-fruited peppers may be grown as indoor plants. Like tomatoes, they require warm, bright conditions to grow well indoors. Fruits will be ready to harvest from peppers and tomatoes about ten weeks after planting.

Whiteflies and aphids may present a problem on indoor tomato and pepper plants. Keep a close watch for these pests so they do not get a good start in your planting. Yellow sticky traps, either purchased or homemade, are effective in trapping whiteflies. Insecticidal soap or other pesticides approved for vegetable plants can be used to control aphids. Fortunately, you will be less likely to experience problems with outdoor pests, such as tomato hornworm, corn earworm (in peppers), and late blight, than you would if plants were outside.

For a quick-growing crop, try radishes. These must be grown very rapidly if they are to be crisp and succulent. Scatter radish seeds on moist soil in a 6-inch pot. Cover with 1/4 inch of soil, and place a piece of glass or plastic wrap over the pot to conserve moisture until the seeds germinate. Carrots are slower, but can be grown in the same way; use the small-rooted varieties, such as Little Finger, for best results indoors.

Experiment with various types of lettuce. Try leaf lettuce and the miniature Tom Thumb butterhead cultivar. Space them according to package directions. Keep lettuce moist and in a very sunny spot.

If light is limited, an old standby for fresh taste and high food value is sprouted seeds. Almost any seeds can be sprouted: corn, barley, alfalfa, lentil, soybean, rye, pea, radish, mung bean, sunflower, etc. Use seeds that have not been treated with pesticides. Use any wide-mouthed container, such as a Mason or mayonnaise jar. Soak seeds overnight, drain, and place in the container. Cover with a double cheesecloth layer held with rubber bands or a sprouting lid. Set the container in a consistently warm spot, and rinse and drain seeds two or three times daily. In three to five days, sprouts will be 1-3 inches long and ready for harvesting.

Herbs

Many herbs are less demanding than vegetable plants, and cooks find it pleasant to be able to snip off a few sprigs of fresh parsley or chop up some chives from the windowsill herb garden. Chives grow like small onions with leaves about 6 inches tall. These plants prefer cool conditions with good light, but will grow quite well on a windowsill in the kitchen. One or two pots of chives will provide leaves for seasoning salads and soups. Plant seeds in a 6-inch pot. The plants should be about 1 inch apart over the entire surface area. It will require about 12 weeks from the time seeds are planted until the first leaves can be cut. For variety, try garlic or Chinese chives, which grow in a similar fashion, but have a mild garlic flavor.

Parsley seeds can be planted directly into 6-inch pots, or young, healthy plants can be transplanted from the garden. One vigorous plant per pot is enough. Standard parsley develops attractive, green, curly leaves about 6 or 8 inches tall. Italian, or flat-leaved, parsley has a slightly stronger flavor and is a favorite for pasta dishes. Leaves can be clipped about 10 to 12 weeks after planting the seeds.

Cilantro, or the leaves of the young coriander plant, can be grown in the windowsill garden. Grow cilantro as you would parsley. Thyme and other herbs will also grow well indoors if given the right conditions.

Vegetable Gardening in the Fall

Planning for a Fall Harvest

By planning and planting a fall vegetable garden it is possible to have fresh vegetables up to and even past the first frosts. At the time when retail vegetable prices are on the rise, you can be reaping large and varied harvests from your still-productive garden site.

Many varieties of vegetables can be planted in midsummer to late summer for fall harvests. Succession plantings of warm-season crops, such as corn and bean, can be harvested until the first killing frost. Cool-season crops, such as kale, turnip, mustard, broccoli, and cabbage, grow well during the cool fall days and withstand light frosts. Timely planting is the key to a successful fall garden. Use the VCE publication "Virginia's Home Garden Vegetable Planting Guide" to determine the appropriate date for planting (this publication has pre-calculated planting dates for fall harvest).

To calculate the time to plant a particular vegetable for the latest harvest in your area, you need to know the average date of the first killing frost and the number of days to maturity for the variety grown. Choose earliest maturing varieties for late plantings. The formula below for determining the number of days to count back from the first frost will help determine when to start your fall garden.

Number of days from seeding or transplanting outdoors to harvest

+

Number of days from seed to transplant if you grow your own

+

Average harvest period

+

Fall Factor (about two weeks)

±

Frost Tender Factor (if applicable); 2 weeks

=

Days to count back from first frost date

The frost tender factor is added only for those crops that are sensitive to frost (corn, beans, cucumber, tomato, squash), as these must mature two weeks before frost in order to produce a reasonable harvest. The fall factor takes into account the slower growth that results from cooler weather and shorter days in the fall and amounts to about two weeks. This time can be reduced two to five days by presprouting seeds. Almost any crop that isn't grown for transplants can benefit from presprouting. Sprout seeds indoors, allowing them to reach a length of up to an inch. Sprouted seeds may be planted deeper than normal to help prevent drying out, and they should be watered well until they break the soil surface. Care should be taken not to break off the sprouts when planting them.

When planting fall crops, prepare the soil by restoring nutrients removed by spring and summer crops. A light layer of compost or aged manure or a small application of a complete fertilizer will boost soil nutrients in preparation for another crop.

Dry soil may make working the soil difficult and inhibit seed germination during the midsummer period. Plant fall vegetables when the soil is moist after a rain, or water the area thoroughly the day before planting. Seeds may be planted in a shallow trench to conserve moisture. Cover the seeds about twice as deeply as you do in the spring. An old-time trick for germinating seeds in midsummer is to plant the seeds, water them well, then place a board over the row until the sprouts just reach the soil surface; at that time, remove the board. An organic mulch on top will help keep the soil cool and moist but should not be deep enough to interfere with germination.

Mulching between rows can also help keep soil cool and decrease soil drying. In severe hot weather, a light, open type of mulch, such as loose straw or pine boughs, may be placed over the seeded row. This must be removed as soon as seedlings are up so they receive full sun. Starting transplants in a shaded cold frame or in a cool indoor area is another possibility.

The fall garden gives you a chance to try again any spring failures you might have encountered. Some crops, in fact, grow well only in the fall in certain areas. Cauliflower and long-season Chinese cabbage are two examples of crops that do not produce well in mountain areas in spring because they cannot reach maturity before the cool weather ends. Protection of vegetable plants during cold periods may extend your season even further. Although in the hot days of summer, the last thing you want to think about is planting more crops to take care of, look ahead to the fall garden. It offers its own satisfaction through prolonged harvest of fresh vegetables, savings in food costs, and the knowledge that you're making full use of your gardening space and season.

Care of Fall Crops

The beginning of fall garden care comes when the weather and the radio station announce the first arrival of frost. Your main concern then should be to harvest all ripe, tender crops. Tomato, summer squash, melon, eggplant, cucumber, pepper, and okra are some of the crops that cannot withstand frost and should be picked immediately. Store the vegetables in a place where they can be held until needed for eating or processing. If the frost warning is mild, predicting no lower than 30°F, try covering tender plants in your garden that still hold an abundance of immature fruit. Baskets, burlap, boxes, blankets, row covers, or buckets help protect them from the frost. Warm days after the frost will still mature some of the fruit as long as the plants have this nightly frost protection. Much will depend on the garden's microclimate. If your spot is low and unsheltered, it is likely to be a frost pocket. Gardens sheltered from winds and on the upper side of a slope are less susceptible to early frost damage.

When using a cold frame to extend the harvest season, be sure to close the top on frosty nights to protect the plants from the cold. When the sun comes out the next morning and the air warms, open the cold frame again; leave it closed if daytime temperatures are low.

Cool-season crops, such as cabbage, cauliflower, broccoli, spinach, and Brussels sprouts, can withstand some cold. In fact, their flavor may be enhanced after a frost. They cannot stay in the garden all winter, but do not need to be picked immediately when frost comes. Kale, spinach, evergreen bunching onion, lettuce, parsley, parsnip, carrots, and salsify are some crops that may survive all winter in the garden. Mulch these overwintering vegetables with 8 inches of mulch to prevent heaving of the soil. Most of these vegetables can be dug or picked as needed throughout the winter or in early spring.

Care of Perennial Vegetables

Prepare perennial vegetables for winter around the time of first frost also. Most will benefit from a topdressing of manure or compost and a layer of mulch, which reduces damage from freezing and thawing of the soil. Dead leaf stalks of perennial vegetables, such as asparagus and rhubarb, should be cut to the ground after their tops are killed by frost, though some people prefer to leave asparagus stalks until late winter to hold snow over the bed. Don't forget strawberry beds. Remove weeds that you let grow when you were too busy last summer. You can transplant some of the runner plants if you have had no disease problems and the plants are vigorous. Carefully dig a good-sized ball of soil with the roots. Mulch the bed well with a light material. Old raspberry canes can be cut back at this time or late in the winter see Chapter 10: "Fruits in the Home Garden."

When tender crops have been harvested and overwintering crops cared for, pull up all stakes and trellises in the garden except those stakes that are clearly marking the sites of overwintering plants. Clean remnants of plant materials and soil from stakes and trellises. Hose them down and allow to dry. Tie stakes in bundles, and stack them so that they won't get lost over the winter. If possible, roll up wire trellises and tie them securely. Store these items inside your attic, barn, or shed in an area where they are out of the way and where rodents and other animals cannot get to them to use as winter nests.

Preparing Soil for Winter

After caring for perennial vegetables, you are ready to prepare the soil for winter. Pull up all dead and unproductive plants, and place this residue on top of the soil to be tilled under or in the compost heap. Remove any diseased or insect infested plant material from the garden that may shelter overwintering stages of disease and insect pests. If this plant material is left in the garden, you are leaving an inoculum of diseases and insects that will begin to reproduce next spring and add to your pest problems.

Clean-up also gives you the chance to add compost to the garden. Compost contains highly nutritious, decomposed plant material and beneficial organisms and is an excellent soil builder. By spreading compost and other wastes on the soil and plowing them in, you are adding nutrients to the soil for next year's crop. The beneficial insects and microorganisms in the compost will help integrate the compost with the soil, and the added humus will improve soil structure.

Don't overlook other excellent sources of organic material available during the fall. Leaves are abundant, and neighbors will usually be glad to give their leaves away. Put some on the garden now, and store some for next year's mulch. Leaves will mat if put on in too thick a layer and will not decompose quickly. You can help leaves break down more easily by running a lawn mower back and forth over the pile. Put the shredded leaves directly onto the garden or compost them.

If you wait until spring to add organic material to the garden, it may not have time to decompose and add its valuable nutrients to the soil by the time you are ready to plant, and you may have to delay planting to a later date. Hot (very fresh) manure can also burn young seedlings. By adding these materials in the fall, you give them plenty of time to decompose and blend into the soil before planting time. If you don't have enough organic material for the entire garden, try to cover those areas that you want especially rich for next summer's crop.

Check with your county recycling center for mulch or compost but keep in mind that it may contain weed seed or disease.

If possible, plow or rotary till in the fall. Turning under vegetation in the fall allows earlier planting in the spring and is especially good for heavy soils, since they are exposed to the freezing and thawing that takes place during the winter. This helps to improve soil structure. If you have a rainy fall or if the garden is steep and subject to erosion, you may decide you'd rather plant a cover crop for winter garden protection. A cover crop decreases erosion of the soil during the winter, adds organic material when it is incorporated in the spring, improves soil tilth and porosity, and adds valuable nutrients. Winter cover crops can be planted as early as August 1, but should not be planted any later than November 1. They should make some growth before hard frost. Where you have fall crops growing, you can sow cover crop seed between rows a month or less before expected harvest. This way, the cover crop gets a good start, but will not interfere with vegetable plant growth.

Prepare the soil for cover crop seed by tilling under plant wastes from the summer. Broadcast the seed, preferably before a rain, and rake it evenly into the soil. Spring planting may be delayed somewhat by the practice of cover cropping, since time must be allowed for the break down of the green manure. If you have crops that need to be planted very early, you may prefer to leave a section of the garden bare or with a **stubble mulch** (a stubble of crop residue left in place for winter).

When time or weather conditions prohibit either tilling or cover cropping, you may wish to let your garden lie under a mulch of compost, plant wastes, or leaves all winter to be plowed or tilled under in the spring. However, if you want to plant early the next spring, a mulch of heavy materials, such as whole leaves, may keep the soil cold long enough to delay planting. In this case, chop them fine enough so they will break down over the winter. The addition of fertilizer high in nitrogen will also help break down organic matter more quickly.

Table 9-5: Cover crops

Type	Legume / Non-legume	Amount to Sow / 100ft (oz.)	When to Sow	When to Turn Under	Effects	Notes
Alfalfa	L	1/2	spring late summer	fall spring	Fixes 150-250lbs N/ac/yr; deep roots break up hard soil, trace elements to surface	Loam, fairly fertile soil; needs warm temps for germination. Lime if pH is low Hardy In mountains sow by Aug 10 Drought tolerant Inoculate

Table 9-5: Cover crops (continued)

Type	Legume / Non-legume	Amount to Sow / 100ft (oz.)	When to Sow	When to Turn Under	Effects	Notes
Barley	N	4	fall spring	spring fall	Adds organic matter, improves soil aggregation	Prefers medium-rich, loam soil Lime if pH is low Not as hardy as rye Tolerates drought
Buckwheat	N	2 1/2	spring summer	summer fall	Mellows soil; rich in potassium	Must leave part of garden in cover crop during season Grows quickly Not hardy
Crimson clover	L	1/3	spring fall	fall spring	Fixes 100-150lbs N/ac/yr	Not reliably hardy Sow before mid-Sept in Piedmont and mountains Not drought tolerant Lime is pH is low White clover is a bit hardier
Fava beans	L	plant 8" apart	early spring late summer	early summer fall	Some types fix 70-100lbs N/ac/yr in as little as 6 weeks Use small seeded rather than large seeded table types	Will grow on many soil types Medium N/ac in drought tolerance Likes cool growing weather Good for mountain areas If planted in early spring can grow late vegetables Inoculate with same bacteria as hairy vetch
Oats	N	4	spring fall	summer spring	Adds organic matter; improves soil aggregation	Needs adequate manganese Not hardy; tolerates low pH
Rye, winter	N	3 1/2	fall	spring	Adds organic matter; improves soil aggregation	Very hardy Can plant until late October
Vetch, hairy	L	2 1/2	early fall	spring	Fixes 80-100lbs N/ac/yr	Inoculate; slow to establish Fairly hardy Till under before it seeds; can become a weed
Wheat, winter	N	4	fall	spring	Adds organic matter; improves soil aggregation	Prefers medium-rich loam soil Lime if pH is low Not as hardy as rye Tolerates drought

Care of Garden Equipment in Fall Gardening

Clean-up of tools and equipment is another important practice related to the garden that should be completed in the fall. Proper clean-up of tools now will leave them in top shape and ready to use when spring comes. Clean, oil, and repair all hand tools. Repaint handles or identification marks that have faded over the summer. Sharpen all blades, and remove any rust. Power tools should be cleaned of all plant material and dirt. Replace worn spark plugs, oil all necessary parts, and sharpen blades. Store all tools in their proper place indoors, never outdoors where they will rust over the winter.

Unless you are lucky enough to live in a warm area where a cold frame will protect vegetables all winter, you will need to clean up the frame when all vegetables have been harvested. Remove all remaining plant material, and spread it on the cold frame soil. Spade the plant refuse and any other organic material into the soil in the cold frame as thoroughly as possible. Do not leave the top on the cold frame over the winter as the cold air or the weight of snow may crack or break the glass. Remove the top, wash it thoroughly, and store it on its side in a protected indoor area where it will not get broken.

Season Extenders

To get the most out of a garden, you can extend the growing season by sheltering plants from cold weather both in early spring and during the fall. Very ambitious gardeners harvest greens and other cool-weather crops all winter by providing the right conditions. There are many ways to lengthen the growing season, and your choice depends on the amount of time and money you want to invest.

Cold Frames and Hot Beds

Cold frames, sun boxes, and hot beds are relatively inexpensive, simple structures providing a favorable environment for growing cool-weather crops in the very early spring, the fall, and even into the winter months.

Figure 9-10: Cold frame.

Hot beds are heated by soil-heating cables; steam-carrying pipes; or fresh, strawy manure buried beneath the rooting zones of the plants. Cold frames and sun boxes have no outside energy requirements, relying on the sun for their source of heat. Heat is collected by these frames when the sun's rays penetrate the sash, made of clear plastic, glass, or fiberglass. The ideal location for a cold frame is a southern or southeastern exposure with a slight slope to ensure good drainage and maximum solar absorption. A sheltered spot with a wall or hedge to the north will provide protection against winter winds. Sinking the frame into the ground somewhat will also provide protection, using the earth for insulation. To simplify use of the frame, consider a walkway to the front, adequate space behind the frame to remove the sash, and perhaps weights to make raising and lowering of glass sashes easier. Some gardeners make their cold frames lightweight enough to be moved from one section of the garden to another.

Another possibility is the Dutch light, which is a large, but portable, greenhouse-like structure that is moved around the garden.

New designs in cold frames include passive solar energy storage. For example, barrels painted black and filled with water absorb heat during the day and release it at night. The solar pod, shown below, is one design that provides for this type of heat storage. Other new cold frames are built with a very high back and a steep glass slope and are well insulated. These may also include movable insulation that is folded up during the day and down at night or during extremely cold weather.

In early spring, a cold frame is useful for hardening-off seedlings that were started indoors or in a greenhouse. This hardening-off period is important as seedlings can suffer serious setbacks if they are moved directly from the warmth and protection of the house to the garden. The cold frame provides a transition period for gradual adjustment to the outdoor weather. It is also possible to start cool-weather crops in the cold frame and either transplant them to the garden or grow them to maturity in the frame.

Spring and summer uses of the cold frame center around plant propagation. Young seedlings of hardy and half-hardy annuals can be started in a frame many weeks before they can be started in the open. The soil in a portion of the bed can be replaced with sand or peat moss or other medium suitable for rooting cuttings and for starting sweet potato slips. Fall is also a good time for sowing some cool-weather crops in frames. If provided with adequate moisture and fertilization, most cool-season crops will continue to grow through early winter in the protected environment of the cold frame. Depending on the harshness of the winter and whether or not additional heating is used, your frame may continue to provide fresh greens, herbs, and root crops throughout the cold winter months.

Figure 9-11: Solar pod.

Growing frames can be built from a variety of materials; wood and cement block are the most common. If you use wood, choose wood that will resist decay, such as a good grade of cypress or cedar. Wood frames are not difficult to build. Kits may also be purchased and easily assembled; some kits even contain automatic ventilation equipment.

There is no standard-sized cold frame. The dimensions of the frame will depend on amount of available space, desired crops, size of available window sash, and permanency of the structure. Do not make the structure too wide for weeding and harvesting; 3-4 feet is about as wide as is convenient to reach across. The sash of the frame should be sloped to the south to allow maximum exposure to the sun's rays.

Insulation may be necessary when a sudden cold snap is expected. A simple method is to throw burlap sacks filled with leaves over the sash on the frame at night to protect against freezing, or bales of straw or hay may be stacked against the frame. Ventilation is most critical in the late winter, early spring, and early fall on clear, sunny days when temperatures rise above 45°F. The sash should be raised partially to prevent the buildup of extreme temperatures inside the frame. Lower or replace the sash each day early enough to conserve some heat for the evening. In summer, extreme heat and intensive sunlight can damage plants. This can be avoided by shading with lath or old bamboo window blinds. Watering should be done early so that plants dry before dark, to help reduce disease problems.

You may convert your cold frame to a hot bed. For a manure-heated bed: dig out to 2 feet deep (deeper to add gravel for increased drainage), add an 18-inch layer of strawy horse manure, and cover with 6 inches of good soil.

Cloches and Hotcaps

Cloches and hotcaps are covers placed over plants to provide a greenhouse-like atmosphere for seeds and small plants in order to get an early start on the season or to extend the fall garden as long as possible. Cloches are set out over individual plants or are made into tunnels for whole rows. They trap solar radiation and moisture evaporating from the soil and plants. The cloche (pronounced klosh) was originally a bell-shaped glass jar set over delicate plants to protect them from the elements. The definition has expanded, however, to include many types of portable structures that shelter plants from drying winds and cold air.

Hotcaps function as miniature greenhouses, trapping the heat from solar radiation. An effective hotcap transmits sufficient solar energy for photosynthesis and for warming the air inside, but not so much that the plant is damaged by overheating. Hotcaps also must retain sufficient heat throughout the night to protect plants against low temperature injury. Hotcap designs vary from wax paper cones to water-filled plastic insulators. All hotcap designs are most effective during sunny weather and have little effect on temperature during cloudy periods. The greatest temperature differences occur during sunny days and clear nights.

Elaborate designs include fiberglass tunnels, special plastic cloches, row covers with slits in them to allow some aeration, and panes of glass connected by specially designed hinges to form a tent. There are a variety of forms on the market now, some work, some don't, and some are easily constructed from materials around the home. Cloches are generally lightweight, portable, and reusable. It is preferable to have a design that can be closed completely at night to prevent frost damage and opened or completely removed during the day for good air circulation. Cloches should be anchored or heavy enough that they don't blow away.

Although expensive, water-filled plastic insulators have been shown to be more effective than other materials and can add several weeks' growth to the early part of the season. Wax paper hotcaps are easy to install and disposable. Plastic jugs may be difficult to secure in the field and can only protect small plants; they do not retain sufficient heat to provide frost protection. They can delay fruit development unless ventilation is provided and can become hot enough to kill plants. For most gardens, simply cover plants overnight if there is a danger of frost. Be sure to remove the covering during the day.

Floating Row Covers

Row covers are a more recent development in extending vegetable production past frost dates. They are simple devices, pieces of material (in spunbonded polyesters) laid over transplants in the field. As the plants grow taller, the material is pushed up by the plants. Row covers retain heat and protect against frost so crops can be planted earlier in the spring and harvested later in the fall. They have demonstrated insect and vertebrate pest protection while also protecting plants from wind damage. Row covers generally provide 4 to 5 degrees of frost protection, so cool-season crops can be planted in air temperatures as low as 28°F. Covers should be removed from the crops when air temperatures beneath the cover reach 80°F. Problems associated with row covers are lower light transmission, as nonwoven materials allow 75 to 80% transmission of light to the crop. The fabric covers can be extended through two seasons if treated with care. If used in conjunction with other season-extending techniques, row covers can mean earlier harvests with greater yields in addition to extended harvests.

Figure 9-12: Growth difference and quality after a freezing event in cilantro grown under low tunnels and open field.

Greenhouses

There is an almost overwhelming selection of greenhouses on the market, and plans for building even more types are available. If you intend to purchase or build a greenhouse, it is wise to investigate the alternatives thoroughly, preferably visiting as many operating home greenhouses as possible. List your needs and wants ahead of time, and determine how you will use your greenhouse. Then compare on that basis. Many companies will send free specifications and descriptions of the greenhouses they offer; look in gardening magazines for their ads. The conservation-minded person may find a solar greenhouse desirable. The initial cost is generally higher for a solar greenhouse than for the simpler, free-standing, uninsulated types, but for maximum use with lower heating bills, one can insulate north and side walls, provide liberal glass area for winter sun catching, and make use of some type of solar radiation storage. When attached to a house, these greenhouses can be used for supplementary household heating, but there is a trade-off between heating the home and growing plants (especially heat-loving ones) in the greenhouse. Some researchers have concluded that a good compromise is to forget winter tomatoes and grow cool-weather crops during the winter in an attached greenhouse. In addition, they may retain excessive amounts of heat from late spring to fall and can make cooling the home more difficult.

Shading

It is not always easy to start seeds or young plants for fall crops in the hot and dry conditions of August. One simple way to provide shade in otherwise exposed conditions is to build a portable shade frame for placing over rows after seeds are sown or transplants are set out. This can be the same type of frame used for starting early seeds, using shade cloth, or lath strips or an old bamboo shade instead of plastic.

Culinary Herbs

Herbs have been used for seasoning, medicine, fragrance, and sorcery for thousands of years. Among the legendary varieties are henbane and mandrake for witches' spells, St. Johnswort for casting out evil, comfrey for healing, and *Alchemilla* sp. (lady's mantle) for gold. Each leaf of the *Alchemilla* sp. gathers a drop of dew during the night; it was believed that if the drops were gathered and used properly, they would facilitate the process of alchemy – the making of gold from base metals. Tarragon, rosemary, and thyme are among the most ancient of seasonings, yet there are few culinary achievements that can top good poultry roasted with these three herbs.

Most herbs can be grown successfully with a minimum of effort. Several are drought-tolerant, some are perennials, and many are resistant to insects and diseases. They are versatile plants, providing flavors for seasoning food and fragrances for room-freshening potpourri. And with their enticing scents, diverse textures, attractive shapes, and countless shades of green and gray, herbs are often used to make a landscape that appeals to the senses of touch and smell as well as sight.

The classic use for herbs in the landscape is the formal garden. Many intricate designs have been drawn and planted using the beauty of herb plants to enhance the pattern of the garden; diamonds, compasses, and knots are among the most popular designs. The knot garden is especially intriguing; herbs with various textures and colors are planted carefully and trimmed neatly to create the appearance of ropes looping over and under each other. The effect is striking, especially when viewed from an upper-story window. Theme gardens are also popular. There are Biblical gardens, scent gardens, tea gardens, witch's gardens, kitchen gardens, and apothecary gardens, to name a few.

Figure 9-13: View of the National Herb Garden.

Site: When selecting a site to plant your herbs, keep in mind that most culinary herbs are native to the Mediterranean region and therefore prefer full sun, good air circulation, and well-drained soil.

Start with a small herb garden that can be easily constructed and maintained, but leave space around it so that you can plan its expansion during the long, cold months of winter. Choose a soil that is fertile and loamy for best results; although many of the herbs will live in poor ground, for the healthiest plants and best harvest, they need good soil to thrive. Most herbs require a soil pH of 6.3 to 6.8 for optimum growth, but lavender prefers a pH of 6.5 to 7.0.

Prepare the soil to a depth of 8 inches. If it is heavy or has poor drainage, amend it with composted organic matter. Raised beds are an excellent solution to this problem. Fill them with a mixture of the heavy soil and the suggested amendments, or use a pre-mixed, soilless potting medium.

Plant perennial herbs in an area that will not be disturbed by tilling. Those that spread by runners, such as the mints, should be given a large, isolated area or must be contained in some fashion (to a depth of 10 to 12 inches) to prevent them from taking over the garden.

Some tender perennials need protection from winter winds. Plant on an eastern exposure, if possible. Evergreen trees and shrubs can be used to break the wind and create a "microclimate" for the herbs. Rocks are often incorporated into the design of herb gardens to provide focal points and windbreaks and to help keep roots cool and moist during the heat of summer.

Propagation: Annual herbs are best started from seed. When starting small seeds indoors, the easiest method is to sow them directly into peat pots filled with seed-starting mix, about six weeks before the last frost date. Cover seed with a thin layer of moist seed-starting mix or milled sphagnum moss. Later, thin the seedlings to four or five per pot. Larger seeds may also be started by this method, then thinned to one plant per pot. Keep the soil surface moist by misting with a spray bottle until the plants are established.

Although many perennial varieties may be started from seed, it is much easier to get plants from your local nursery or a reputable mail-order company. In addition, many culinary herbs, such as tarragon, can only be propagated asexually; seed-grown plants lack the oils that give them flavor. Propagate them from root divisions or cuttings taken in the summer, after new growth has hardened. Allow cuttings to root in a window box or some other suitable container, preferably covered with plastic to maintain high humidity. About 5 inches of clean, coarse sand is a good rooting medium. Keep the sand moist and out of direct sunlight when the plants are young. In 4-6 weeks, move the plants to pots or cold frames for the winter. Transplant all herb plants after danger of severe frost. Control weeds during the growing season to prevent competition for water and nutrients which are needed by your herbs. A light mulch (about 1 inch) will conserve soil moisture and help control weeds.

Most of the herbs that have a mature height under 12 inches may be grown in 6-inch pots as indoor plants. There are many dwarf varieties of the larger herbs that would be appropriate indoors, as well. Basil 'Spicy Globe,' dwarf sage, winter savory, parsley, chives, and varieties of oregano and thyme are some of the best for windowsill culture. When given proper care in a sunny window, they will supply sprigs for culinary use through all seasons. When cooking, use greater quantities of fresh herbs; although they often have better flavor than dried herbs, they are usually not as strong.

Culture: Although many herbs are considered drought-tolerant, some moisture is needed to maintain active growth. For a continual supply of fresh-cut herbs, periodic irrigation during dry periods is needed. As with all plants, a thorough watering with a period of drying is preferred over frequent sprinkling. Annual herbs require a higher level of available soil moisture than most perennial herbs.

Proper nutrient balance is very important. Weak, succulent growth can be caused by over-fertilization, making the plant susceptible to disease and insect pests. Rapid growth also dilutes the concentration of essential oils that impart the distinctive flavor to the culinary herb. Inadequate fertilizer can severely limit new growth, predisposes the plant to insect and disease problems, and increases the susceptibility of tender perennials to winter injury. A light application of fertilizer to perennials in early spring should promote new root and shoot growth and ensure vigor in the new growing season. Generally, adequate herb growth can be achieved with 1/4 to 1/2 the nitrogen recommended for vegetables in your area. Sequential harvests of annual herbs will be facilitated by light applications of fertilizer after each heavy harvest.

The high concentration of essential oils in healthy, actively growing herbs repels most insects. However, aphids and spider mites can be a problem. Aphids seem to be more prevalent in crowded conditions with rapidly growing, succulent plants. Spider mites thrive in dry conditions and can be controlled by spraying the plants with plain water at regular intervals, especially during periods of drought. Since there are very few labeled pesticides for use on herbs, the best defense against pests is preventative cultural management, such as good sanitation, removal of weak or infested growth, and regular pruning.

Periodic, judicious pruning promotes vigorous, sturdy plants that are less susceptible to disease and winter injury. If they are allowed to grow unchecked, some herbs will take on a gangly, unkempt appearance. If you are lavish in your use of herbs, regular harvesting for use in cooking, potpourri, and flower arrangements should keep your herbs sufficiently pruned.

Harvesting: It is best to harvest your herbs in the morning, just after the dew has dried, but before the sun gets hot. The concentration of essential oils is highest at this point. Harvest your herbs for fresh use all season, but for drying, cut just before the plants bloom. This will ensure the maximum concentration of essential oils. When harvesting, cut just above the first joint of tender growth – it takes the plant longer to send out new shoots from woody growth.

Stop making large harvests of the perennial herbs in late summer or fall. This will allow time for new growth to harden and gather carbohydrates in preparation for winter. However, small harvests can be made during most of the fall. Sage flavor may actually be improved by two or three frosts prior to harvest.

If you are interested in saving seed for the next season, choose one or two plants of each variety and allow them to bloom and go to seed. Harvest the seed heads when they change from green to brown or gray, and dry them thoroughly to ensure a good germination rate.

Drying: The best dried herbs are those that have been dried rapidly, but without excessive heat or exposure to sunlight.

When harvesting to dry, it is often necessary to spray the plants with a garden hose the day before cutting to clean dirt and dust off the leaves. The next morning, after the leaves have dried, make your harvest. Remove dead or damaged leaves and make small bunches of the herbs. Tie the stems together and hang them in a temperate, well-ventilated, darkened room that has little dust. Label each bunch, since several of the herbs look similar when dried.

Herbs may also be dried by removing the leaves and spreading them in a single layer on cookie sheets or foil, though it is preferable to use trays made of window screening for maximum air circulation. Again, remember to label the different varieties for accurate identification after drying.

Herb leaves are dry if they crumble into powder when rubbed between your hands. When the drying process seems to be complete, fill a small, glass container with the herb and seal. Put it into a hot oven for about 15 minutes or microwave it (don't use a metal cover!) for about 5 minutes, then check for condensation on the inside of the jar. If there is moisture present, let the rest of the herbs dry some more; if your harvest is not completely dry when stored, it may succumb to molds. If necessary, herbs may be dried on cookie sheets in an oven set for 110°F or less, though there is some loss of essential oils using this method.

When completely dry, store whole leaves in air-tight containers, preferably of dark glass or some material that will not let in light, in a cool to temperate place out of direct sunlight. This will ensure good flavor and color in your seasonings. To conserve essential oils, do not crush the herb until you add it to your cooking.

Table 9-6: Herb culture and use chart

Common Name	Height	Plant Spacing	Cultural Hints	Uses
Basils	20-24"	12"	Grow from seed Sun	Use in anything with tomatoes
Borage	24"	12"	Grow from seed, self-sowing Best in dry, sunny areas	Young leaves used in salads for cucumber flavor
Chervil	10"	3-6"	Sow in early spring Partial shade	Aromatic leaves used in soups and salads
Coriander	24"	18"	Grow from seed Sow in spring in sun or partial shade	Seed and leaves used in food
Dill	24-36"	12"	Grow from seed sown in early spring Sun or partial shade	Feathery foliage and seeds used in flavoring and pickling
Parsley	6"	6"	Grow from seed started in early spring Slow to germinate Sun Biennial	Brings out flavors of other herbs High in vitamin C
Catnip	3-4'	18"	Hardy; sun or shade Grow from seed or by division	Leaves for soothing tea
Chives, Garlic	12"	12"	Little care Divide when over-crowded Grow from seed or by division	Good indoor plant Cut long strands at base; mild onion or garlic flavor
French Tarragon	24"	24"	Sun or semi-shade Grow from cuttings or division	Aromatic seasoning; principal flavor in béarnaise sauce; great with fish or chicken
Lavender	24"	18"	Propagate from cuttings Grow in dry, rocky, sunny locations with plenty of lime in the soil Requires pH 6.5 to 7.2	Use for sachets, potpourri
Lemon Verbena	36"	36"	Tender perennial; propagate from cuttings Sun or partial shade	Strongest lemon scent Used in teas or in potpourri
Lovage	3-4'	30"	Rich, moist soil Grow from seed planted in late summer Sun or partial shade	Of the carrot family; strong celery flavor
Mints	1-3'	18"	Grow from cuttings or division Sun or partial shade	Aromatic; used as flavoring Unusual varieties include orange, blue balsam, ginger, chocolate
Oregano	24"	9"	Grow from seed, cuttings, or division Sun	Flavoring for tomato dishes, pasta
Rosemary	3-6'	12"	Grows in well-drained nonacid soil from cuttings Sun Marginally hardy; plant in protected site	Leaves flavor sauces, poultry, meats, rice, and soups Good for topiary bonsai

Table 9-6: Herb culture and use chart (continued)

Common Name	Height	Plant Spacing	Cultural Hints	Uses
Sage	18"	12"	From seed or cuttings Sun Renew every 3-4 years	Seasoning for meats, especially pork; herb teas
Thyme	8-12"	12"	Light soil, well-drained Renew every 2-3 years Grow from cutting or division Sun	Aromatic foliage for seasoning Varieties include lemon, orange, nutmeg, and wooly

Organic Vegetable Gardening

The term "organic" is used frequently to describe various gardening and landscaping practices as well as numerous products available for sale. There are some misconceptions about just what the term means as well as much misinformation about what constitutes organic gardening. Most often the word "organic" is used to describe a no-pesticide gardening system or a no-chemical system. This is not always the case. The purpose of this section is to define what "organic" means and to describe the practices and principles used in effective organic gardening systems.

Organic Defined

Finding a reliable, consistent definition of organic gardening is a challenge in itself. There are so many perceptions of what is involved in an organic system that finding a general consensus is difficult.

The Merriam-Webster Dictionary defines organic as "Food grown or made without the use of artificial chemicals."

The US Department of Agriculture defines organic products as food or other agricultural products that have been produced through approved methods that integrate cultural, biological, and mechanical practices that foster cycling of resources, promote ecological balance, and conserve biodiversity. Synthetic fertilizers, sewage sludge, irradiation, and genetic engineering are not to be used. (U.S. Department of Agriculture, National Organic Program). More specifics about the program can be found on the National Organic Program Website: https://www.ams.usda.gov/about-ams/programs-offices/national-organic-program.

According to the USDA National Organic Standard Board, organic agriculture:

- Is an ecological production management system that promotes and enhances biodiversity, biological cycles, and soil biological activity;
- Is based on minimal use of off-farm inputs and on management practices that restore, maintain or enhance ecological harmony;
- Has a primary goal of optimizing the health and productivity of interdependent communities of soil life, plants, animals and people.

Certified Organic, USDA: The National Organic Program (NOP) is the federal regulatory framework governing commercial organic agriculture. In Virginia, it is administered by the Virginia Department of Agriculture and Consumer Services (VDACS). Under these regulations, any commercial producer who markets any products as "organic" must first obtain certification to make this claim. This is a long and difficult process that investigates every aspect of production to ensure that all organic guidelines are followed and involves copious recordkeeping and site visits.

Of course, home gardeners wishing to implement organic methods do not need to obtain such certification. Anyone can benefit from the ideas and practices of organic gardening!

Building the Organic Garden Soil

Starting from scratch to build an organic soil is a simple task but it can take time to complete. Depending on the present condition of the soil this task can take months or even years until a satisfactory soil has been developed.

The first step is to know what is there to start with. This means a soil test must be performed to measure fertility and pH levels to determine what adjustments, if any, will need to be made to the soil chemistry. In addition to the traditional soil test, a second level of testing will be needed. At the bottom of the VCE publication "Soil Sample Information Sheet" 452-126 just under the box marked "Routine" there is another box marked "Organic Matter." Both the "Routine" and the "Organic Matter" boxes should be checked. This will provide a sample result that also measures the amount of organic material already in the soil, expressed as a percentage. Remember that the soils are tested based on what types of plants will be produced in that soil so this will need to be determined prior to taking the sample.

The next step is to learn what the plants will need for the soil in an organic gardening system. In most cases the basic needs for nutrients and pH levels will be the same. It is important to remember that the purpose of this sample is to build the soil to support the health and vigor of the plants, not to simply determine how much lime and fertilizer to use.

Next, start building the soil by incorporating organic materials such as compost, manure, crushed limestone, and other materials to bring the soil up to the level needed to support the plants. In many cases the materials can be spread on top of the soil and then worked in, down to a depth that will be slightly below the anticipated root depth for the desired plants. This practice of incorporating organic material into the soil never ends. Organic material improves the soil as it breaks down and therefore becomes depleted. It must be replaced often to continue to achieve the benefits for plant growth. The frequency of adding organic material depends on the soil type and the climate. A simple guideline to use at the beginning is to add it annually then adjust the schedule as needed.

Periodic retesting will be needed to track the progress toward the desired soil composition. Once that level has been achieved the soil will still need to be tested every 3 years to maintain everything at the correct level.

As an aside, it is important to note that under the rules of the USDA Certified Organic program, land must not have man-made fertilizers or synthetic pesticides applied to that property for at least 3 years before the crops and produce can be certified as organic. Organic farms maintain buffers between certified organic fields and conventional production fields. Local conditions and the individual doing the organic certification determine the width of buffers.

Soil Amendments

Compost

Compost is one of the primary soil amendments that organic gardeners rely upon. Some organic gardeners prefer to make their own compost to ensure that only organic materials go into the mix. This helps to avoid accidental introduction of pesticides, contaminants, and other synthetic materials that may come from unknown sources. Safe composting guidelines should always be followed. **Vermicompost** (compost made by worms as they digest plant material) may also used in organic systems.

Manure

Manure is another soil amendment used by organic gardeners but this too needs to be scrutinized. The NOP standard does not permit human sludge from waste treatment plants to be used in organic production. Sludge is composed of whatever people flush down their toilets and pour down their kitchen sinks. Since there is no certainty as to what is in the sludge it should not be used. Animal waste is often used in organic systems, though care should be taken to ensure any chemical residues from the animals' diets are not introduced into your garden. The animal waste should be well composted before it is used. Compost should be applied no earlier than 90 days before harvest if the crop does not touch the ground, or no earlier than 120 days before harvest if the crop touches the ground. Manure must be incorporated into soil.

Compost and manure should not be the only component of an organic fertility program. Some crops will require additions of concentrated natural amendments such as blood meal, bone meal, or potassium sulphate.

A soil test will point to a need for additional fertilizer or other products to provide the correct soil chemistry for the type of plants being grown.

Organic Materials Review Institute

The Organic Materials Review Institute (OMRI) (https://www.omri.org/) is an independent nonprofit that reviews materials and certifies them as meeting organic standards. Products with an OMRI label are sold in many stores. OMRI products may be used in Certified Organic production and processing of foods, feeds, and pesticides. In the example given earlier, the crushed limestone may have an OMRI label and the pelleted limestone may not. If the manufacturer of the pelleted limestone wanted to have an OMRI label on their product, they then could apply to OMRI to certify that their product is produced in a sustainable way that complies with OMRI and Certified Organic standards. OMRI may ask them to change a product or a process in order to be able to put the OMRI label on their product. The company producing the pelleted limestone would pay a fee to OMRI. Once the changes had been made, the pelleted limestone could then have an OMRI label, and a consumer would know it was produced in a sustainable way and a farmer or grower could use that product and keep their farm's Organic Certification.

Organic Cultural Practices

Garden crop failures may be caused by poor soil, poor plant selection, poor plant placement, watering or feeding practices, or ecosystem-level problems. All of these can be corrected by using better cultural practices in the garden.

In an organic gardening system, there are no quick fixes to plant health problems. Traditional gardening methods can utilize synthetic fertilizers and pesticides to correct problems quickly, but these options may not be available to the organic gardener.

Many garden and landscape pests can be prevented by maintaining plant health, and the organic gardener takes a proactive approach to managing plant health. Healthy plants can use their own internal defenses to repel insects and to prevent disease pathogens from becoming established in the various plant tissues. Plants that are weak and/or unhealthy will attract pest problems; therefore it is important to follow an effective strategy in establishing healthy plants and monitoring plant health to keep the impact from plant pests to a minimum.

The cultural best management practices outlined below can prevent problems from occurring in the first place. Such practices are found in both conventional gardening, as well as organic gardening, and should not be viewed as exclusive to one or the other.

Plant selection: Select plants appropriate for your site and location. Plants should be known to thrive in the soil moisture and sunlight conditions for the planting site (for example, don't plan to plant tomatoes in a shady vegetable bed). If you struggle with a particular disease problem, consider planting varieties resistant to that problem. Use a soil test to determine if the present soils are adequate for the plants desired or if soil amendments will be needed.

When selecting plants, inspect each one carefully. Look for any evidence of unwanted insects such as egg masses, cocoons, or the insects themselves. Also look for signs or symptoms of diseases such as dark spots on foliage, odd growths on the stems, open wounds, or evidence of rot. Reject any plants that seem to be "off-color," wilted, or simply do not appear to be healthy.

Resistant cultivars: The horticulture community works to create new varieties and cultivars of favorite plants that are resistant to troublesome pest problems. These resistant varieties and cultivars are developed through traditional breeding programs where many plants with diverse genetics are crossbred and offspring that show resistance to disease or pests (or have other favorable qualities) are selected and marketed.

This process can produce hybrid varieties (labeled as F1). Seeds saved from hybrid plants will not produce "true" when planted the following year.

When selecting new plants for the garden, try to select from these new varieties as much as possible to avoid the use of pesticides.

Soil management: Healthy plants have healthy root systems. One key to a healthy root system is healthy soil. Manage the soil to optimize its benefits for the specific plants that will be grown. This is normally done with amendments such as compost and lime to improve structure, drainage, moisture holding ability, and pH. Use a soil test to determine what amendments are necessary! Cover crops such as grains and legumes are used to protect the soil when there is no crop present, and these can be incorporated into the soil to add nutrients and organic matter or can be mowed and left in place to serve as an organic stubble mulch.

Water Management: Many plant health issues arise from improper use of water. Too little or too much water can both lead to planting failures, plant diseases, and plant stress that will attract insect pests. Learn what the moisture requirements are for the plants being grown and then manage the water available to those plants. Remember that the soil structure influences the water available to the plants' roots and incorporate this knowledge into the irrigation schedule.

Irrigation: Irrigating in the early morning will not only reduce evaporative moisture lost, it will also reduce the chances of foliar diseases in the garden. Watering in the morning will allow the leaves to dry more quickly as the weather warms up. Watering in the evening will allow the foliage to stay wet for a longer period of time, which may help in the development of disease pathogens.

Try to avoid wetting the foliage when irrigating. The water must go into the soil to be taken up by the plants' roots. Keeping the foliage dry will help to prevent many diseases such as Septoria leaf spot and early blight on tomatoes.

Proper planting practices: Always be sure to plant at the right time of year and under the right conditions. Follow guidelines for correct planting such as depth and spacing. When planting seedlings, pay close attention to the roots as this is the only time they will receive much attention. Planting properly will help to get the plants off to a good start and will increase the chances of better plant health throughout the life of the plant.

Plant spacing: Proper spacing of new plants is critical to their health. Planting too close will reduce air circulation between plants and can lead to intense below ground competition for growing space among the roots. Both of these can place the plants under stress. Be certain to learn the proper spacing between plants. It is okay to plant wider than recommended, but it is not okay to plant closer together (unless an intensive gardening method, such as raised beds, is being used). For perennial plants the spacing should be based on the mature size of the plants.

Plant location: The garden needs to be planned to take full advantage of the growing conditions available. Rows and individual plants should be arranged to take advantage of prevailing winds, direction of sunlight, and movement of water both above and below ground. Tall plants should be sited so they do not interfere with the sunlight requirements of smaller plants.

Vegetable interplanting: Over centuries of gardening, humans have learned a lot about how plants interact with each other and their environments. For example, many people have observed that some plants will grow and produce better if in close proximity with certain other plants. Some plants can attract pollinators better if they work together, some plants will attract insect predators to aid in pest prevention, and some plants repel some types of insect pests. These plants are known as companion plants.

One example of this is the Diohe'ko or "three sisters" method developed by the Seneca Nation of western New York. This system involves grouping beans, squash, and corn in hills together so that the plants can provide mutual benefits to each other. A second example of this is the practice of planting marigolds near garden vegetables. The marigolds can help to attract pollinators and will also repel insect pests and soil nematodes.

Another aspect to this practice is that certain plants may be antagonistic to one another. Instead of helping each other to grow better, they will actually prevent each other from reaching optimal growth.

There are excellent intercropping charts available through Extension agencies at various universities (although you will find these charts have not been updated to reflect the intercropping term, and will instead call this practice "companion planting"). One outstanding example is the Washington State University publication "Cool Season Planting Chart for Companion, Interplanting, and Square Foot Gardening."

Mulch in the organic garden: Research has proven the benefits to be gained from the use of mulch in a garden. For the organic gardener this just means that organic mulches should be used. Organic mulch can be pine needles, shredded bark, ground leaves, or other organically derived products that can be placed around the plants without harming them.

The benefits from mulch are simple. Mulch will trap moisture by blocking direct sunlight from the soil thereby keeping more moisture in the soil for plant roots. Mulch will also keep the soil it covers cooler on hot summer days reducing stress on the plants. During the winter, mulch can be used to insulate perennial vegetables like asparagus or rhubarb.

Organic mulch has one more advantage. It can be tilled into the soil at the end of the growing season to add to the organic composition of the soil.

Additional Resources

- Organic Materials Review Institute (OMRI) https://www.omri.org/
- Baker, N. T. and Capel P. D. (2011). "Environmental Factors That Influence the Location of Crop Agriculture in the Conterminous United States." USGS National Water-Quality Assessment Program. https://pubs.usgs.gov/sir/2011/5108/pdf/SIR2011_5108.pdf

References

- "No-Till or Low-Till Gardening Methods" section adapted from "Low and No Till Gardening," by Nate Bernitz (2020) University of New Hampshire.
- "Weed Control in the Garden" section adapted from "Weed Control," Dalhousie University.
- "Organic Gardening Practices" section adapted from "Cultural Practices," ibiblio.
- Lomas, J. (1991). Sprinkler irrigation and plant disease under semi-arid climatic conditions. EPPO Bulletin, 21: 365-370. https://doi.org/10.1111/j.1365-2338.1991.tb01263.x
- Ludy, R. L., M. L. Powelson, and D. D. Hemphill Jr. (1997). "Effect of Sprinkler Irrigation on Bacterial Soft Rot and Yield of Broccoli" Plant Disease 81:6, 614-618. https://doi.org/10.1094/PDIS.1997.81.6.614
- Teeluck, M., and B. G. Sutton. "Discharge characteristics of a porous pipe microirrigation lateral." Agricultural water management 38.2 (1998): 123-134.

Attributions

- Margaret Brown, Arlington Extension Master Gardener (2021 reviser)
- Jim Revell, Bedford Extension Master Gardener (2021 reviser)
- Stuart Sutphin, Extension Agent, Agriculture and Natural Resources (2015 reviser)
- Cathryn Kloetzli, Extension Agent, Agriculture and Natural Resources (2015 reviser)
- Leonard Githinji, Assistant Professor, Virginia State University & Extension Specialist, Sustainable & Urban Agriculture (2015 reviewer)
- Diane Relf, Extension Specialist, Consumer Horticulture (2009 reviser)

Image Attributions

- Figure 9-1: Egusi watermelon. Bhardwaj, Harbans. Virginia State University. 2021. CC BY-NC-SA 4.0.
- Figure 9-2: Potato esculentus. Bhardwaj, Harbans. Virginia State University. 2021. CC BY-NC-SA 4.0.
- Figure 9-3: Planting techniques. Grey, Kindred. 2022. CC BY-NC-SA 4.0.

- Figure 9-4: USDA plant hardiness zone map. USDA. 2012. Public domain. https://planthardiness.ars.usda.gov/.
- Figure 9-5: Raised beds. "High raised beds in organic vegetable garden." Local Food Initiative. 2016. Flickr. CC BY 2.0
- Figure 9-6: Vertical gardens. Includes "Pea Trellis – Square Foot Garden" by Calder, Dale. 2010. Flickr. CC BY-NC-SA 2.0 and Cattle panel. Johnson, Devon. 2022. CC BY-NC-SA 4.0.
- Figure 9-7: Container garden. "Herb garden." Dave Cooksey. 2008. Flickr. CC BY-NC-SA 2.0.
- Figure 9-8: Hanging strawberry planter. "Strawberries" Sheryl Westleigh. 2011. Flickr. CC BY-NC-ND 2.0
- Figure 9-9: Vertical planter. "vertical-garden." wiccahwang. 2011. Flickr. CC BY 2.0.
- Figure 9-10: Cold frame. Virginia Cooperative Extension. From "Season Extenders" 2009. CC BY-NC-SA 4.0.
- Figure 9-11: Solar pod. Virginia Cooperative Extension. From "Season Extenders" 2009. CC BY-NC-SA 4.0.
- Figure 9-12: Row covers. Virginia Cooperative Extension. From "Low Tunnels in Vegetable Crops: Beyond Season Extension" 2018. CC BY-NC-SA 4.0.
- Figure 9-13: View of the National Herb Garden. USDA Agricultural Research Service Photo by Keith Weller. 2016. Public domain.

CHAPTER 10: FRUITS IN THE HOME GARDEN

Chapter Contents:

- Planning a Tree Fruit Planting
- Buying Trees
- Planting Fruit Trees
- Fruit Tree Management
- Pest Management for Fruit Trees
- Planning the Small Fruit Garden
- Blueberries
- Caneberries
- Grapes
- Strawberries
- Additional Resources

Success with a fruit planting depends upon how well it is planned and how well carried out the plans are. Proper attention must be given to insect and disease control, pruning, fertilization, soil management, and other necessary practices. Small fruits offer advantages over fruit trees for home culture in that they require a minimum amount of space for the quantity of fruit produced. Small fruits are also quicker to bear fruit after planting than trees and pest control typically is often less intensive. When planning for your fruit garden, plant only what you can care for properly. It is better to have a small, well-attended planting than a large, neglected one.

Planning a Tree Fruit Planting

It is desirable to locate the fruit planting as close to your home as possible. Where space is limited, fruit trees may be set in almost any location suitable for ornamental plants. Consider the mature size of the tree when designing the planting. Dwarf fruit trees fit nicely in ornamental plantings as well as orchards. They come into bearing earlier than standard-sized trees, occupy less space, and can be more easily pruned and sprayed with equipment normally available to the average gardener. Most nurseries carry dwarf and semi-dwarf apple trees of all varieties. Dwarf pear, peach, and cherry trees of a few varieties are offered by some nurseries, but are not recommended because trees may not survive more than five years due to disease and incompatibility problems.

Spacing and Size of Planting

How far apart must the trees be set? This is an important factor and, to a large extent, it influences selection of site and varieties. The table below shows the minimum desirable distances between fruit trees in home orchards. They can be set farther apart if space allows but, for best results, should not be set closer than the minimums indicated. To maintain a bearing surface low enough for necessary pest control, and to maintain uniform bloom throughout the tree, trees should not be crowded.

Space, site, family size, available time, and pollination requirements determine the size of the planting. Choose fruits based on family preference, adaptability, and available space. Never attempt to plant more than you can care for properly.

Table 10-1: Space requirement, yield, bearing age, and life expectancy of tree fruits

Fruit	Minimum Distance Between Plants (feet)	Approximate Yield per Plant (bushels)	Bearing Age (years)	Life Expectancy (years)
Apple - seedling root	30	8	6 to 10	35 to 45
Apple - semidwarf	18	4	4 to 6	30 to 35
Apple - dwarf	8	2	2 to 3	30 to 35
Pear - standard	25	3	5 to 8	35 to 45
Pear - dwarf	12	0.5	3 to 4	15 to 20
Peach	20	4	3 to 4	15 to 20
Plum	20	2	4 to 5	15 to 20
Quince	15	1	5 to 6	30 to 40
Cherry - sour	18	60 qt.	4 to 5	15 to 20
Cherry - sweet	25	75 qt.	5 to 7	20 to 30

Site Selection

The importance of selecting the best site possible for fruit planting cannot be overemphasized. Good air drainage is essential. Cold air, like water, flows downhill. For this reason, fruit buds on plants set in a low spot are more likely to be killed by frost than those on a slope. Frost pockets; low, wet spots; and locations exposed to strong, prevailing winds must be avoided. South-facing slopes encourage early bud development and can sometimes result in frost damage. Select late-blooming varieties for this location.

Deep, well-drained soil of moderate fertility should be selected. A fertile, sandy loam or sandy clay loam is suitable for most tree fruits. Adequate water drainage is the most important soil characteristic. Poor fertility may easily be improved by proper fertilization and cultural practices, but improving soil with poor internal drainage is difficult and expensive. Moderately fertile soil is desirable; deep, well-drained soil is vital.

Variety Selection

Give special attention to the selection of varieties. They must be adapted to your soil and climatic conditions. If possible, without sacrificing too much yield or quality, select varieties with the fewest insect and disease problems.
Several varieties of the same kind of fruit maturing at different times may be planted to prolong the harvest season. Consider the value of certain varieties for special uses, such as freezing, canning, and preserving. Some varieties may be purchased in season from commercial growers more economically than you can grow them yourself.

Cross-pollination is necessary for satisfactory fruit set in many tree fruits. Select varieties that are cross-fruitful and that have overlapping bloom dates. To be certain of adequate cross-pollination, plant at least three varieties of apples. Don't confine your selections to Winesap and Stayman; These varieties will not cross-pollinate. Golden Delicious is used by many commercial growers as a pollinizer for other varieties of apples in their orchards. Ornamental crabapples can also be used as a pollinizer for all apple varieties.

CHAPTER 10: FRUITS IN THE HOME GARDEN | 277

Some suggested varieties for the home fruit garden

Varieties are listed in order of ripening

1 – Principal uses: c – cooking; d – dessert; f – freezing.

2 – In Eastern Virginia mildew, blight, brown rot, bacteriosis, fruit cracking, and poor color can be serious problems due to climatic conditions, and these varieties are difficult to grow.

Apples

- Lodi – 1c, 2
- Jerseymac – 1c, d, 2
- Ginger Gold – 1c, d
- Paulared – 1c, d, 2
- Gala – 1d, 2
- Grimes Golden – 1c, d, 2
- Jonathan (red strain) – 1c, d, 2
- Golden Delicious – 1c, d
- Delicious (red strain) – 1c, d, 2
- Idared – 1c, d, 2
- Winesap – 1c, d, 2
- Stayman (red strain) – 1c, d, 2
- Rome Beauty (red strain) – 1c, d, 2
- Fuji – 1c, d, 2
- Granny Smith – 1c, d, 2
- Cripps Pink (Pink Lady) – 1c, d, 2

Scab-immune apples

- Pristine – 1c, d, 2
- Williams Pride – 1d, 2
- Redfree – 1d, 2
- Dayton – 1c, d, 2
- Crimson Crisp – 1d, 2
- Scarlet O'Hara – 1d, 2
- Jonafree – 1d, 2
- Liberty – 1d, 2
- Sundance – 1c, d, 2
- Enterprise – 1c, 2
- Goldrush – 1c, 2

Cherries (sweet) – 2

- Napoleon (Royal Anne) – 1c, d
- Vernon – 1c, d
- Ulster – 1c, d
- Hedelfingen – 1c, d
- Windsor – 1c, d
- Hudson – 1c, d

Cherries (sour)

- Montmorency – 1c, f

Pears

- Harrow Delight – 1c, d
- Moonglow – 1c, d
- Harvest Queen – 1c, d
- Maxine – 1c, d
- Seckel – 1c, d
- Orient – 1c
- Kieffer – 1c

Plums (European)

- Earliblue – 1c, d
- Blue Bell – 1c, d
- Stanley – 1c, d
- Shropshire (Damson) – 1c

Plums (Japanese)

- Early Golden – 1c, d
- Methley – 1c, d
- Shiro – 1c, d

Nectarines

- Redgold – 1d
- Flavortop – 1d
- Fantasia – 1d

Peaches

- Jerseydawn – 1d
- Redhaven – 1c, d, f
- Loring – 1c, d, f
- Redkist – 1c, d, f
- Earnies Choice – 1c, d, f
- Cresthaven – 1c, d, f
- Biscoe – 1c, d, f
- Encore – 1c, d, f
- White Hale – 1d
- Carolina Belle – 1d
- Summer Pearl – 1d
- Raritan Rose – 1d

Some fruit trees should be planted in pairs to encourage proper pollination. At least two of the recommended pear, plum, and sweet cherry varieties should be planted. In general Japanese and European plums are not effective as pollinizers for each other; two varieties of the same type should be planted. Windsor is a good pollinating sweet cherry variety. Sour cherries cannot be used to pollinate sweet cherries because they are different species.

All of the sour cherry, peach, and nectarine varieties listed are sufficiently self-fruitful to set satisfactory crops with their own pollen.

Apricots present a unique challenge to Virginia growers. The buds of currently available varieties respond to the first warm days of early spring and are usually killed by frost or low temperature after bloom. Unless protection can be provided, a crop can be expected no more frequently than once every 3-5 years.

Apple Rootstocks

Apples, like other tree fruits, will not produce trees with the same characteristics from seed. If you plant a seed from a Red Delicious apple, the fruit would likely be small, unattractive, and of poor quality. Therefore, fruit trees are propagated vegetatively by either budding or grafting scion wood of the desired cultivar on a rootstock. The rootstock and scion variety maintain their respective genetic identities, but are joined at the graft union and function as a unit.

Traditionally, apple trees have been propagated on rootstocks from apple seeds. More recently, increasing use is being made of vegetatively propagated or clonal rootstocks which have inherent advantages over seedlings. Three major considerations in rootstock selection are:

Size control

Most apple trees available are grafted onto clonal rootstocks for tree size control. By proper selection of rootstock, one can determine mature tree size. For example, the same variety of apple will produce a 16- to 18-foot tree on the rootstock Malling Merton (MM)111, down to a dwarf tree of 7 to 8 feet or less on Malling (M)9 or M.27 rootstock. Intermediate sizes can be attained by other rootstocks, such as M.26 and M.7. Some apple trees offered to consumers may be labelled as dwarf trees, but the buyer does not know the rootstock or how dwarfing it may be. However, there are nurseries willing to offer selected scion/rootstock combinations to home fruit growers. Some of the earlier rootstocks such as M.9 and M.26 were susceptible to diseases, such as fireblight. The newer "Geneva-series" rootstocks are more resistant to fireblight and collar rot and these are suggested for planting if available. The relative sizes of trees on the various rootstocks are shown below. Another rootstock Budagovsky.9, "Bud.9" produces trees similar in size to M.9, G.11 and G.41 is also resistant to fireblight.

Precocity

Precocity is the ability of rootstocks to induce fruitfulness. Precocity is measured in apple rootstocks by observing the length of time from planting to when the cultivar produces flowers. Trees on seedling rootstocks usually do not begin fruiting until they are 7 to 8 years old. Trees on M.9, G.11, G.41 or Bud.9 rootstock will often produce crops in 2-3 years. Other rootstocks are intermediate in this regard. Usually, the more dwarfing the rootstock, the earlier the tree will bear fruit.

Stability

A major consideration in selecting apple rootstocks is the degree of anchorage provided. For example, trees on M.9, M.27, G.11, G.41, G.65 and Bud.9 rootstock are very small, but because of brittle roots, must be provided some type of support. This can consist of a post, a trellis, or other means of holding the tree upright. The semi-dwarfing M.7 rootstock may require support for the first few years, but some varieties can grow without support. The more vigorous MM.111 rootstock does not require support and is thus like a seedling. More detailed information on selecting apple rootstock, see the VCE publication "Tree Fruit in the Home Garden" 426-841 (SPES-259P).

Buying Trees

Obtain the best nursery stock available. Buy only from reputable nurseries that guarantee their plants to be true to name, of high quality, and packed and shipped correctly. Beware of bargains. High prices do not necessarily mean high quality, but good nursery stock is not cheap.

Usually, 1-year-old trees are preferred. A common mistake made by many gardeners is to select oversized or ready-to-bear nursery trees. Experience has shown that younger trees bear almost as soon, are easier to keep alive, and develop into more healthy, vigorous trees. The older trees cost nurseries more to grow and are sold for higher prices, but are usually worth less than younger trees.

For peaches, nectarines, and apricots, a 4-foot tree, ½-inch in diameter, is considered the ideal size for planting. Vigorous, 4- to 7-foot, 1-year-old whips about 3/4-inch in diameter are preferred for apples. Pears, quince, plums, cherries, and apples may be planted as 1- or 2-year-old trees. Either will be satisfactory as long as the trees have attained sufficient size and have good root systems.

When purchasing apple trees on dwarfing rootstock, be sure to specify the rootstock desired. There are several possibilities for planting: M.9, G.935 and Bud.9 trees and smaller are very dwarfing, have rather weak root systems, and must have mechanical support; M.7 and G.30 trees, which produce trees 70 to 80% as large as a mature tree from seedling may require early support for most varieties; and MM.111EMLA (virus free) which produces a tree 80 to 90% of the size of a mature tree from seedling, does not require support, and is nearly problem-free except for its large size.

Planting Fruit Trees

Time of Planting

Virginia climatic conditions are such that good results can be obtained regardless of whether the trees are planted in fall or early spring. Planting about a month after the first killing frost in the fall or about a month before bloom in the spring is generally recommended. The important things to remember are that trees should be dormant and the soil should have proper moisture content.

Handling Nursery Stock

Fruit trees are usually purchased as containerized plants from local nurseries and garden centers or as bare root trees from mail order companies. Both types of trees can give good results. Mail order companies usually offer a larger selection of varieties.

Mail order trees should be inspected upon arrival to make sure the roots and packing material are moist. If trees cannot be planted immediately, they can be stored in the original packing for a week or two in an unheated basement or garage. Do not expose to freezing temperatures which may damage roots, or high temperatures which may induce bud break. Check the roots frequently and moisten if necessary. In the absence of a cool storage place, trees can be heeled in carefully in a trench of moist soil in a shaded location. It is a good idea to soak the roots in a bucket of water for a few hours before planting.

Planting the Trees

Thoroughly prepare the soil where fruit trees are to be planted.. If the places selected for trees are in a lawn, it is best to remove the turf and spade the soil deeply over an area of several square feet where each tree is to stand.

Dig the hole a little deeper and wider than necessary to accommodate the roots, leaving the soil loose in the bottom of the hole.

Prune the roots of young trees only where necessary to remove broken and damaged shoots or to head back some that are excessively long. Should a tree be so badly scarred or damaged that there is doubt of its survival, it is wise to discard it.

Set the tree at approximately the same depth it grew in the nursery. Never set it so deep that the union of the scion and rootstock is below ground level when the hole is filled.

Then begin filling the hole with topsoil, shaking the tree gently to filter the soil among the roots. Tamp the soil firmly and thoroughly with your foot or a well-padded stick. The addition of water when the hole is about 3/4 full will aid in settling the soil around the roots and increase chances for the tree's survival. After the water has completely soaked in, finish filling the hole, leaving the soil loose on top.

Fruit Tree Management

Cultural Practices

Young fruit trees should be mulched or cultivated until they begin to bear. Weeds must be eliminated so they will not compete for available moisture and fertilizer. Cultivation must be shallow to avoid injury to roots near the surface. The cultivated or mulched area should extend a little beyond the spread of the branches.

There are several concerns with the use of mulch around fruit trees. Both organic and inorganic mulch (e.g., black plastic) provide habitats for voles. Organic forms of mulch also release nitrogen throughout the season, which affects the grower's ability to control when and how much nitrogen is available. Fertility of established trees can be managed with mulch, and fertilizer is often not needed and can cause a reduction in fruit load.

Fertilize young trees three times. Apply fertilizer about two weeks after planting, and again six and ten weeks after planting. Apply 0.3 pounds of actual nitrogen each time (i.e., 1/3 pound 10-10-10, 0.2 pound nitrate of soda, or 0.1 pound ammonium nitrate).

Temporary nitrogen deficiency may occur when mulch material low in nitrogen begins to decay. This can be overcome by the addition of nitrogen fertilizer. Usually about ¼ pound of ammonium nitrate, ½ lb. of nitrate of soda or 2 pounds of 10-10-10 to each 100 square feet of mulched area will be enough.

The use of black polyethylene plastic as a mulch has given good results.

Holes may be punched in the plastic to allow moisture penetration. Although it does not decay and add humus to the soil, neither does it cause a temporary nitrogen shortage.

When trees are planted in rows, the area between the rows may be allowed to grow in sod or used for interplanting with low-growing vegetables or strawberries. Another option for inter-row planting is clover, which is easily managed and provides an organic source of nitrogen. There is no objection to this practice in the home orchard, provided ample plant nutrients and moisture are available for proper development of the fruit trees. Under sod culture, frequent, close mowing during the growing season is desirable. This reduces competition for necessary moisture and plant nutrients and also aids in disease and insect control.

Fruit trees, especially those on dwarfing rootstock, are becoming prominent in landscape designs. Under lawn culture, fruit trees can be given more attention than is usually convenient under other systems of culture. Equipment and materials for watering, pruning, spraying, and other cultural practices are essentially the same as those required for ornamental plantings. It is a good practice to cultivate lightly for the first year or two or until the tree has become firmly established. Lawn grass, if kept closely clipped, may be allowed to grow around the base of the tree in the third year, but fertilizer should be applied at twice the usual rate.

Chemicals for weed control should be used with extreme caution in the home garden. Careless use can result in severe injury to fruit trees and nearby ornamental plantings. See your Extension agent for latest weed control recommendations.

Fertilization

Before planting, test your soil pH. If your soil is acid, it should be limed to adjust the pH to a level between 6.0 and 6.5. As a rule, no fertilizer is recommended or needed at planting time. After the young tree becomes established and growth begins, apply nitrate fertilizer in a circle around the tree, about 8-10 inches from the trunk. Usually fruit trees show no increased growth or fruitfulness from the use of any nutrient element except nitrogen. Other elements are used by the tree; however, only in special cases are they deficient in the soil. Deficiencies are more likely to occur on light, sandy soils. Because there are many soil types and varying levels of natural fertility, it is difficult to make one fertilizer recommendation that will apply equally well in all areas.

A rule of thumb practiced in many commercial apple orchards is to apply about ¼ pound of a 16% nitrogen fertilizer, or its equivalent, for each year of the tree's age from planting. For peach orchards, the amount of fertilizer should be doubled.

Avoid over-fertilization with either organic or inorganic materials. Excessive vegetative growth will result, usually accompanied by delayed fruiting and possible winter injury. Where poor growth results after the use of nitrogen only, other elements may be needed. Contact your local Extension agent for fertilizer recommendations specific to your locality.

Fertilizer may be applied either after the leaves have fallen or in early spring, about 3 or 4 weeks before active growth begins. On light, sandy soils, it is best to delay application until early spring. When trees are grown in a lawn area, delay fertilizing the lawn until after trees are dormant to avoid late-summer growth on the trees. The usual method of application is to scatter fertilizer evenly under the tree, starting about 2 feet from the trunk and extending to just beyond the tips of the branches.

Terminal growth and general vigor of the individual tree should be observed closely. Where growth the past year was short, increase the amount of fertilizer slightly. If growth was excessive, reduce the amount or withhold it entirely. Remember that both pear and quince are highly susceptible to fire blight, and excessive growth will make this disease more prevalent.

Mature, bearing trees of peach, nectarine, and sweet cherry should produce an average of 10-15 inches of new growth annually. From vigorous, young, nonbearing trees, about twice that amount can be expected. In general, 8-10 inches of terminal growth is considered adequate for mature, bearing apple, pear, quince, plum, and sour cherry trees. About twice that amount is sufficient for young, nonbearing trees.

Pruning

The general purpose of pruning fruit trees is to regulate growth, improve fruit size and quality, control tree size, and reduce production costs. Pruning is necessary to shape the trees for convenience of culture and for repair of damage.

Most pruning is done during the dormant season, preferably just before active growth begins in the spring. At this time, pruning wounds heal faster, flower buds can be easily recognized, and injury from low winter temperature is avoided. Summer pruning may be done to help train young trees to the desired shape, remove water sprouts and other undesirable growth, and maintain smaller tree size. It should be remembered, however, that all pruning has a dwarfing effect. For maximum yield of high-quality fruit, prune only as necessary to establish a tree with a strong framework capable of supporting heavy crops annually without damage and to maintain a tree sufficiently open to allow penetration of sunlight, air, and spray material for good fruit development and pest control.

Although pruning procedures vary according to the type, age, and variety, all newly planted fruit trees should be pruned in the spring before growth starts. This is necessary to stimulate lateral bud development from which to select good scaffold limbs. For a discussion of the proper pruning techniques to use on different fruit trees, see Chapter 14: Pruning.

Thinning

Quite frequently, peach and apple trees set many more fruit than they can mature to a desirable size. By thinning or removing excess fruit, this difficulty can be overcome. Thinning not only allows for an increase in size of the remaining fruit on the tree, but also improves fruit color and quality, reduces limb breakage, and promotes general tree vigor. Thinning helps maintain regular, annual bearing in certain apple varieties, such as Golden Delicious, Yellow Transparent, and York

Imperial, that otherwise have a tendency to bear heavy crops every other year. Another benefit from thinning fruits is that it permits more thorough spraying or dusting for effective disease and insect control.

The sooner peach trees are thinned after bloom, the earlier ripening will occur and the larger the fruits at harvest. Fruit size will not greatly increased by thinning if it is delayed until after the pits begin to harden (60 days after bloom).

It is generally recommended that peaches be spaced 6-8 inches apart on a branch. When thinning by hand, grasp the stem or branch firmly between your thumb and forefinger and pull the fruit off with a quick motion of the second and third fingers. Small fruited varieties on trees that are pruned lightly should be thinned to a spacing of 8-10 inches between fruit.

Many growers use the pole method of thinning peaches. A 4- or 5-foot section of bamboo or other light wood is used. A piece of 3/4-inch garden or spray hose about 15 inches long is forced tightly onto the end of the pole, leaving 8-10 inches of the hose extending beyond the end of the pole. A snug fit is necessary so the hose will remain in place while being used. Many modifications of this tool are used. One of the most common is a 30-inch section of plastic pipe, 1 inch in diameter. Remove peaches by striking the limbs about 18 inches from their tips with the flexible part of the hose, using sharp, firm blows. This dislodges any loosely attached fruits. With a little practice, you should be able to remove individual fruits by this method. Remove small and insect-injured fruit and retain the largest fruit.

Figure 10-1: Vase.

Apples should be thinned as soon as possible after the fruit has set. If full benefits are to be obtained, thinning should be completed within 20 to 25 days after full bloom. In hand-thinning apples, use the same general technique used in hand-thinning peaches. A distance of 6-10 inches between fruits is recommended. With varieties of Delicious apples, where greater size of individual fruits is important, the greater spacing is preferred. The center apple of a cluster is usually the largest and the best apple to leave.

Thinning plums usually is limited to the large, Japanese varieties. The primary concern here is to facilitate insect and disease control. Plums are usually thinned by hand to about 4 inches apart.

Pest Management for Fruit Trees

Figure 10-2: Central leader.

Voles may cause serious damage to the fruit planting. They chew off the bark at ground level or below and often completely girdle a tree, causing it to die. Most of this damage takes place during winter. Keep mulch pulled away from the base of the tree, and examine it frequently for the presence of voles. In many home and commercial plantings, voles are controlled by placing poison bait in their runways. These poisons and complete directions on how to use them may be obtained from many spray material dealers. Voles may also be controlled by trapping. This can be successful where only a few trees are involved.

Rabbits are responsible for the loss of thousands of young fruit trees each year. Perhaps the most satisfactory method of preventing rabbit damage is the use of a mechanical guard. Galvanized screen or "hardware cloth" with a ¼-inch mesh is frequently used. A roll 36 inches wide may be cut lengthwise, forming two 18-inch strips. By cutting these strips into pieces, 14 inches long, guards 14 by 18 inches are obtained. Roll or bend the strip around the trunk of the tree so the long side is up and down the trunk and the edges overlap. Twist a small wire loosely about the center to prevent the strip from unrolling. Push the lower edges well into the ground. This metal guard will last indefinitely and can be left in place all year, but do not allow weeds to grow inside the guard.

Tar paper, building paper, sheets of magazines, and aluminum foil can also be used in a similar manner, but must be removed in the early spring to prevent damage to the tree. Perforated plastic guards are available, but are not recommended because they do not allow enough air movement around the tree. However, there are plastic meshes, like the metal ones, that are acceptable.

Other methods of rabbit control have been successful. Ordinary whitewash has given good results in some instances. A repellent wash recommended by the USDA, containing equal parts of fish oil, concentrated lime sulfur, and water, is used by some commercial growers. Also, rabbit repellents under various trade names are available. All these materials may be applied with a paint brush, from the ground up into the scaffold limbs.

Tree Fruit Spraying

To successfully manage significant insect or disease problems, it is necessary to follow a spray program. Information on the use of chemicals for such a program is available from your Extension office. If growing organically, a spray program is still necessary. Your Extension office can provide organic alternatives.

To be successful with your spray program, spray at the proper time and do it thoroughly. Leave no portion of the tree unsprayed. To make the job easier and to ensure adequate coverage, thin out excessive growth and remove all dead and weak wood. Cut old trees back to 20 feet or less, if possible. Train younger trees so they reach a height of no more than 18 feet.

Semi-dwarf and dwarf trees should be considered when making your planting. Their small size makes the task of spraying easier. Early maturing varieties are less likely to be seriously affected by insects and diseases than late-maturing varieties because of the shorter growing season. This factor should not be overlooked in the selection of varieties.

Sanitation

Adopt good orchard sanitation practices. The destruction of places that harbor insects and diseases plays a large part in the control program. Conditions that encourage voles should also be eliminated.

These are some practices to include in an orchard sanitation program:

- Collect and burn debris.
- Remove and destroy all dropped fruit.
- Rake and burn apple and cherry leaves.
- Scrape loose bark from trunks, crotches, and main limbs of apple trees.
- Prune out and destroy all dead or diseased limbs, branches, and twigs.

Apple Varieties of Yesteryear

Arkansas Black Twig, Baldwin, Fall Cheese, Miliam, and Roxbury Russet are apple varieties not found in the modern supermarket, yet in the opinion of some apple connoisseurs, the dessert quality of these and other old-time apple varieties is superior to that of most of those in popular demand today.

Most of the old varieties are no longer grown because they had serious cultural problems such as poor storage, disease, bitterpit, alternate bearing, and nonuniform ripening. Many of the old varieties lost favor with the commercial grower because of low productivity, lack of attractiveness, susceptibility to the ravages of insects and diseases, and poor storage and shipping quality. Before growing an old variety, you should taste the fruit and talk to experts to determine the problems you are likely to have.

There is increasing interest in growing old fruit varieties. Individuals, historical organizations, and government-supported institutions are getting involved. Some commercial nurseries now propagate one or more of the better-known varieties, and there are several that specialize in antique fruit varieties of all types. North American

Fruit Explorers, a nonprofit association of fruit gardening enthusiasts, actively promotes the culture of old fruit varieties. It is a valuable source for anyone interested in locating information on sources of bud wood, characteristics of varieties, and successful cultural practices.

Among the old-time apple favorites available from private and commercial sources are some that have occupied a prominent place in Virginia history. Perhaps the most widely known is the Albemarle Pippin. Although seldom found in the orchards of Virginia, it is of some importance in western states under the name Yellow Newtown. Still found in some of the old orchards on both the eastern and western slopes of the Blue Ridge are such varieties as Arkansas Black Twig, Baldwin, Ben Davis, Esopus Spitzenburg, Fallawater, Gano, Golden Russet, Gravenstein, Grimes Golden, Horse Apple, King David, Lady Apple, Limber Twig, Lowery, Maiden Blush, Milam, Mother Apple, Northern Spy, Roxbury Russet, Smokehouse, Virginia Beauty, Winter Banana, and Wolf River. Many of the less well-known but equally good varieties, such as Bellflower, Father Abraham, Fall Cheese, and Winter Cheese, may be found in private collections and at renovated historical sites.

Figure 10-3: Roxbury Russet apple specimen watercolor from 1912.

Whether from a sense of nostalgia, a desire to preserve some of our history, or pride in having an antique to display, many of the old apple varieties have been saved from extinction. Some have already been around for centuries; hopefully, they can survive a few more. They are too good to lose.

Table 10-2: Space requirement, yield, bearing age, and life expectancy of small fruits

* per parent plant grown in the matted row system

Fruit	Minimum Distance Between Rows (feet)	Minimum Distance Between Plants (feet)	Approximate Yield per Plant (lbs.)	Average Bearing Age (years)	Life Expectancy (years)
Blackberry (erect)	10	5	5-10	1	5-12
Blackberry (trailing)	8	6	5-10	1	5-12
Blueberry	6	5	4-6	3	20-30
Grape (American)	8	6	10	3	20-30
Grape (hybrids)	8	5	10	3	20-30
Grape (muscadine)	8	10	15	3	20-30
Raspberry (red)	8	3	3-5	1	5-12
Raspberry (black)	8	4	3-5	1	5-12
Raspberry (purple)	8	4	3-5	1	5-12
Strawberry (June bearing and day neutral)	3	1	1-2*	1	1-2
Strawberry (ever bearer)	3	1	3/4 - 1	3-Jan	2

Planning the Small Fruit Garden

As a general rule, plant selection and production area in a home garden should be limited to what you can properly care for. It is better to have a well-tended, small planting area rather than a neglected, large one. Small fruits offer certain advantages over fruit trees for home culture in that small fruits require less space for the amount of fruit produced, and bear one or two years after planting. Success with small fruit planting will depend on the attention given to all phases of production including crop and variety selection, site selection, soil management, fertilization, pruning, and pest management.

Table 10-3: Suggested varieties for the home small fruit planting

Blueberries: Rabbiteye and southern highbush varieties are suitable for southern and Central Virginia; northern highbush varieties are suitable for Northern Virginia and the mountains.
Raspberries: Killarney and Nova are floricane-bearing raspberries not suitable for southern or Central Virginia.
Strawberries: Camarosa and Sweet Charlie are suitable only for the Coastal Plains and Piedmont regions of the state.

Crop	Variety	Type	Fruit size	Yield/plant (lbs)	Flavor
Blueberry	Brightwell	Rabbiteye	Medium	5	Good
Blueberry	Duke	Northern Highbush	Medium	2-3	Very good
Blueberry	Legacy	Northern Highbush	Medium	5	Very good
Blueberry	O'Neal	Southern Highbush	Medium	2-3	Very good
Blueberry	Powderblue	Rabbiteye	Medium	5	Good
Blueberry	Premier	Rabbiteye	Medium	5	Good
Blueberry	Suziblue	Southern Highbush	Very large	2-3	Excellent
Blackberry	Chester	Floricane	Medium	10-15	Good
Blackberry	Kiowa	Floricane	Very large	10-15	Excellent
Blackberry	Natchez	Floricane	Very large	5-10	Good
Blackberry	Navaho	Floricane	Medium	5-10	Excellent
Blackberry	Ouachita	Floricane	Medium	5-10	Very good
Blackberry	Prim-Ark® 45	Primocane	Large	10-15	Very good
Blackberry	Prim-Ark® Freedom	Primocane	Very large	10-15	Very good
Raspberry	Caroline	Primocane	Medium	3-5	Excellent
Raspberry	Heritage	Primocane	Medium	5	Good
Raspberry	Himbo Top	Primocane	Large	3-5	Very good
Raspberry	Joan J	Primocane	Medium	3-5	Excellent
Raspberry	Josephine	Primocane	Large	3-5	Excellent
Raspberry	Killarneye	Floricane	Medium	3	Good
Raspberry	Novae	Floricane	Medium	3	Excellent
Strawberry	Earliglow	Early Season	Medium	0.5-0.8	Excellent
Strawberry	Camarosa	Mid-season	Medium	0.8-2	Good
Strawberry	Camino Real	Early Season to Mid-season	Large	1-2	Very good
Strawberry	Chandler	Mid-season	Medium	1-1.5	Good
Strawberry	Flavorfest	Mid-season to Late-season	Medium	0.8-1.5	Very good
Strawberry	Sweet Charlieh	Early Season	Small	0.5-0.8	Excellent

Table 10-4: Suggested varieties of grapes for home planting

* These grape varieties must be grafted to a rootstock to ensure adequate vigor and tolerance to root-feeding phylloxera.

Grape use	Variety	Type	Fruit Color	Flower Type
Table use	Concord	Seeded	Blue/black	
Table use	Delaware	Seeded	Red	
Table use	Himrod	Seedless	Golden-yellow	
Table use	Mars	Seedless	Black	
Table use	Niagara	Seeded	White/green	
Table use	Seneca	Seeded	White/yellow	
Table use	Steuben	Seeded	Blue/black	
Table use	Sunbelt	Seeded	Blue/black	
Wine	Chambourcin*		Red	
Wine	Chardonel*		White	
Wine	Norton		Red	
Wine	Traminette		White	
Wine	Vidal Blanc*		White	
Muscadine	Carlos		Bronze	Perfect
Muscadine	Magnolia		Bronze	Perfect
Muscadine	Nesbitt		Black	Perfect
Muscadine	Scuppernong		Greenish bronze	Female

Site Selection

Locate your small fruit planting in full sun, as part of, or near the vegetable garden. Select a site that is free from frost pockets, low/wet spots, and exposure to strong prevailing winds. Blueberries should be planted far enough from the roots of trees, to avoid competition for moisture and nutrients. Blueberries may be planted to form a dense hedge, or used in a foundation planting around the home. Where space is a limited, small fruits could also be integrated with ornamental plants. Caneberries grow best on leveled lands. Grapes and raspberries may be planted on a trellis, or a fence along a property line.

Soils

Small fruits thrive in a fertile, sandy loam soil, rich in organic matter, but they will give good returns on the average garden soil under adequate fertilization and good cultural practices. Incorporation of additional organic matter before planting is desirable. Small fruits are best planted on raised beds 8-12 inches high and 2-4 feet across. Drip irrigation is highly recommended.

For best results, small fruit plants should be set no closer than the minimums indicated in Table 10-2. Overcrowding frequently results in weak plants and low yields. It also makes insect and disease control more difficult.

Special attention should be given to variety selection. Varieties must be adapted to your soil and climatic conditions. If possible, without sacrificing too much yield or quality, select varieties with the least insect and disease problems.

Ordering Plants

Obtain the best nursery stock available. Buy certified plants from a reputable nursery. Place your order early, as soon as you decide what you want. Specify variety, size, grade of plants desired, and the preferred time of shipment. It is best to have the plants arrive at the time you are ready to set them out. Unless you specify otherwise, some nurseries will only send plant material at the proper time to be planted in your area.

When your order arrives, unpack the bundles and inspect the plants. The roots should be moist and have a bright, fresh appearance. Shriveled roots indicate that the plants have been allowed to freeze or dry-out in storage or transit. Such plants seldom survive. Water root system lightly only if they are very dry.

If the plants cannot be set immediately, they should be kept either in cold storage or heeled-in to soil. Wrap them in a garbage bag or other material that will prevent them from drying out, and store them at a temperature just above freezing. Strawberry plants in small quantities may be held in the refrigerator for a few days. If refrigerated storage is not available, remove the plants from the bundle and heel them in carefully in a trench of moist soil in a shaded location. Pack the soil firmly around the roots to eliminate all air pockets and to prevent the roots from drying out.

Establishing and Maintaining the Planting

There is probably nothing that causes more disappointment and failure in small fruit plantings than the lack of careful preparation and attention to detail, at the time the plantings are established. Prepare the soil properly, set the plants carefully, and generally create conditions favorable for new growth. Detailed suggestions for the establishment of each of the small fruits follows. These suggestions should be closely followed for best results.

Once the planting has been established, future success will depend on the care it is given. If the planting is to be productive and long-lived, it must be properly fertilized. Competition from weeds or other plants must be avoided. Insects and diseases must be controlled, and the plants must be properly pruned. Study the maintenance suggestions for each of the small fruit crops, and plan to care for the planting properly. To do otherwise, will probably result in disappointment and wasted effort.

Blueberries

There are three types of blueberries that can be grown in home gardens in Virginia: rabbiteye, southern highbush, and northern highbush. Although they may be grown in any area where native blueberries, azaleas, mountain laurel, or rhododendrons do well, they have a better flavor when grown where nights are cool during the ripening season. They are very exacting in soil and moisture requirements. Berries should be picked as soon as they ripen, to minimize infestation of fruits with spotted wing drosophila.

Figure 10-4: Rabbiteye blueberries.

Rabbiteye and southern highbush type blueberries are best suited for climates where summers are generally hotter. These varieties have low winter chilling requirements. "Chilling" is a measure of accumulated hours of temperatures below 45°F in the dormant season. In general, the chilling requirement or rabbiteye and southern high bush type are 250-600 hours, and for northern highbush requirement is 800-1000 hours. Therefore, when buying blueberry plants for your garden, make sure to ask whether you are buying rabbiteye, southern, or northern highbush type.

Variety Selection

To provide adequate cross-pollination and to increase chances for a good crop of fruit, two or more varieties that bloom at the same time should be planted. The following varieties suggested below for planting, ripen over a six- to eight-week period, beginning in early June and continuing through July. Most are vigorous and productive under good growing conditions and produce berries of large size and good quality.

Rabbiteye varieties

Alapaha, Climax, Premier, Titan, and Vernon are early season varieties. Brightwell, Powderblue and Tifblue are mid-season varieties. Centurion and Ochlokonee are late season varieties. In central and southern Virginia, planting early, mid, and late season Rabbiteye varieties will allow you to harvest fruits during the July-August months.

Titan is a new variety. It is the largest fruited rabbiteye variety that has been developed to date. Vernon also has large berries. Alapaha and Ochlockonee have medium sized berries with good eating quality and less pronounced seeds than other Rabbiteye varieties.

Southern highbush varieties

Most of the southern highbush varieties blooms early in the season and may be damaged by frosts in late spring. Southern highbush varieties are recommended for central and southern Virginia. Suziblue, Palmetto and O'Neal are early season varieties. Suziblue has very large fruit and it has excellent flavor. Palmetto is a medium sized berry and it has an outstanding flavor. O'Neal is a popular variety with medium size and very good flavor fruit. Camellia, Jubilee and Magnolia are mid-season southern highbush. Camellia has a very large size fruit. Jubilee and Magnolia are smaller fruited varieties with good plant vigor. Bird and deer feeding may be a problem with southern highbush varieties.

Northern highbush varieties

Northern highbush blueberries are self-fertile; however, larger and earlier ripening berries result if several varieties are planted for cross-pollination. In Virginia, the northern highbush varieties should be planted in northern Virginia and in the mountain region with adequate soil conditions.

Duke, Earliblue, Patriot and Spartan are early season northern highbush varieties. Duke is a popular variety with medium size fruit and very good flavor. Earliblue produces very early in the season, it is not a heavy a producer. Patriot is a heavy producer with very large berry size. Spartan has large berry size and good flavor.

Bluecrop, Blueray and Legacy are mid-season northern high bush blueberries. Bluecrop, although lacking in vigor, is very hardy and drought-resistant. The fruits are medium sized. Blueray is very hardy, and productive, and is recommended for planting. The fruit is large, dark blue, flavorful. Legacy is a highly adaptable variety, slower in production in the first few years, however, yields can be very high once the plants become established.

Elliott and Jersey are late season northern highbush varieties. Elliott has a good, mild flavor when fully ripe (if not fully ripe the flavor will be very tart). It is winter hardy and bears firm, medium sized fruits. Jersey, one of the leading commercial varieties, is also a favorite in the home garden. The plants are vigorous and hardy, producing heavy crops of medium, dark berries of good quality. Since these are picked fully ripe, they are also more susceptible to damage caused by spotted winged drosophila.

Establishing the Blueberry Planting

Soils: Blueberries are shallow-rooted plants and must either be irrigated, heavily mulched, or planted in a soil with a high water table. Adequate drainage must be provided, because they cannot tolerate saturated soils. High water table in clay soils promote root rot diseases. Raised beds with drip irrigation are preferable. They grow best in porous, moist, sandy soils, high in organic matter, with a pH range of 4.2 to 5.2. Have the soil tested, and if the pH is not in the 4.2 to 5.2 range, work such materials as peat moss, pine needles, pine bark, or sulfur into the area where the plants are to be set. This should be done six months to a year before planting. To acidify sandy soils, sulfur is recommended at the rate of 0.75 pound per 100 square feet for each full point the soil tests above pH 4.5. On heavier soils use 1.5-2 pounds. Once proper soil pH is established, it can be maintained through the annual use of an acid fertilizer, such as ammonium sulfate or cottonseed meal. pH of the soil should be tested every three years.

Planting: Vigorous, two-year-old plants about 15 inches high are recommended for planting. Set in early spring about 3 or 4 weeks before the average date of the last frost. For rabbiteye varieties, plant every 4-5 feet in row, and 10 feet between rows. For northern and southern high bush verities, plant 3-4 feet in row, and 6-8 feet between rows.

Give the roots plenty of room. Where the plants are to be set, dig the holes wider than and as deep as necessary to accommodate the root systems. It is not necessary to incorporate organic matter or other soil amendments into the backfill soil. Trim off diseased and damaged portions of the top and roots, and set the plants at the same depth that they grew in the nursery. Spread the roots out, and carefully firm the soil over them. Water thoroughly after planting.

Maintaining the Blueberry Planting

Soil Management: Mulching is the preferred soil management practice in the blueberry planting. The entire area around and between the plants should be mulched. Hardwood or softwood bark and sawdust, applied to a depth of 4 or 5 inches is recommended. Many growers use a combination mulch – a layer of leaves on the bottom, with 2-3 inches of sawdust on top. Renewed annually, this heavy mulch retains moisture, keeps the soil cool, and adds needed organic matter. If soil pH is an issue, make sure to mulch with pine bark or apply sulfur on top of mulch. Mulches provide a relatively warm environment, and can attract voles particularly during winter season. In areas where voles are a problem, mulch application should be less thick and be applied more frequently. Control through trapping and chemical baiting may be needed.

Fertilization: No fertilizer should be applied at planting time, and usually none is needed during the first growing season. On poor soils, however, the application of 2 ounces of ammonium sulfate around each plant about the first of June is beneficial.

Ammonium sulfate, at the rate of 2 ounces per plant, should be spread in a circle around each plant, about 6-8 inches from its base, just before the buds begin to swell the second spring. Increase the amount each succeeding spring by one ounce, until each mature bush is receiving a total of eight ounces annually. Cottonseed meal has proven to be an excellent fertilizer for blueberries and is used by many home gardeners. It supplies the needed nutrients and helps maintain an acid soil. Use it at the rate of one half pound per plant. Where sawdust is used as a mulch, it will be necessary to apply additional nitrogen to prevent a deficiency as the sawdust decays. Usually about 0.75 pound of ammonium sulfate for each bushel of sawdust is sufficient.

Pruning: Until the end of the third growing season, pruning consists mainly of the removal of low spreading canes, and dead and broken branches. As the bushes come into bearing, regular annual pruning will be necessary. This may be done any time from leaf fall until before growth begins in the spring. A mature blueberry plant should produce three to five new canes per year. During pruning, clean out old, dead wood, and keep three best one-year-old canes. Locate the oldest canes and prune out one of every six existing canes; cut as close to the ground as possible. A mature blueberry bush should have ten to fifteen canes: two to three canes each of one-, two-, three-, four-, and five year old canes.

Pest Control: Birds are by far the greatest pests in the blueberry planting. Covering the bushes with wire cages, plastic netting, or loosely woven cotton fabric cloth (tobacco cloth), is perhaps the best method of control. Aluminum pie tins have been used successfully. They are suspended by a string or wire above the bushes, such that they twist and turn in the breeze and keep the birds away. Spotted wing drosophila will lay eggs on ripe or ripening fruits, and infestation on fruits can be minimized by picking fruits as soon as they are ripe.

Harvesting the Blueberry Planting

Some varieties of blueberry will bear the second year after planting. Full production is reached in about six years, with a yield of 4-6 quarts per plant, depending on vigor and the amount of pruning. Blueberries hang on the bushes well and are not as perishable as blackberries or raspberries. Picking is usually necessary only once every five to seven days, more frequently if bird pressure is high. Blueberries will keep for several weeks in cold storage.

Caneberries

Both raspberries and blackberries (often, commonly referred to as **caneberries** or brambles) will usually yield a moderate crop of fruit the second year after planting, and a full crop the third season. With good management, it is possible for gardeners to extend the productive life of well-maintained plantings beyond 10 years.

Variety Selection

For blackberry and raspberry, there are two fruiting types: **primocane** and **floricane**. Primocane type raspberry and blackberry bear fruits on the first year cane (shoot) which are ready for harvest in late summer. After harvest, if the cane is pruned at the point below where it produced fruit in the first year, the lower part of the cane will produce another crop (second harvest) next summer after the cane is exposed to chilling during the winter months. Therefore, the primocane fruiting blackberry and raspberry varieties can produce two crops (harvests) each year. The second crop is usually ready for harvest in Central Virginia in first week of June. It is important to prune and remove canes after the second harvest, and allow the new canes to grow.

Of the many varieties of blackberries and raspberries available, few have proven totally satisfactory for growing under Virginia conditions. Only top-quality, virus-free, one-year-old plants of the best varieties should be planted.

Blackberry varieties

Of interest to home owners would be the thornless blackberry varieties that would allow children and adults to pick berries without the concern of being scratched on the skin. However, there are some very tasty and productive thorny blackberry varieties. Some popular blackberry varieties include:

Figure 10-5: Blackberries.

- Chester is a thornless, late bearing, semi-erect variety, high in yields with a medium fruit size. The variety is resistant to cane blight.
- Kiowa is a thorny, early-season, blackberry variety that bears the world's biggest blackberry fruit. Kiowa blooms earlier and longer than other blackberry varieties. The berry ripens in early June.
- Navaho is a thornless, erect, mid to late season blackberry, that produces better quality fruits when trellised. The fruit shape is conic, the berry size is medium, but very firm, and the flavor is excellent.
- Natchez is a thornless, early bearing variety that produces large fruit that ripens in early June. When fully ripened, it is very sweet and tasty. Natchez is a semi-erect variety and needs trellising for improved production and better fruit quality.
- Prime-Ark® 45 is thorny primocane variety that produces firm berries, free of molds and diseases. Berries are large in size, with good flavor, and are suitable for long distance shipping.
- Prime-Ark® Freedom is the world's first thornless primocane, released in 2013. This is an erect type, producing very large fruits, and has a good flavor. The fruit is harvested in the fall and is good for fresh consumption. As a primocane type blackberry, the Prim Ark® Freedom can produce two crops per year.

Dewberries and boysenberries are also included under blackberries. Dewberry is a trailing form of blackberry, and boysenberry is a hybrid of loganberry (*Rubus loganobaccus*) and various blackberries and raspberries. The boysenberry plant is easily winter killed and should be planted only in areas of mild winters. Plants are extremely vigorous and productive and the berries are large and flavorful when fully ripe. Thornless boysenberries are also available. Recommended varieties of dewberry and boysenberry include:

- Lucretia dewberry, best of the trailing blackberries, is relatively winter hardy, vigorous, and productive. The fruits are very large, often 1.5 inches long, shiny, sweet flavor berry.
- Lavaca, a seedling of the boysenberry, is superior to its parent in production, size, and resistance to cold and disease. The fruit is also firmer, less acidic, and of slightly better quality.

Raspberry varieties

Raspberry types are based on berry color: red, black, and purple. Chances for success with raspberry plantings are better if the plantings are located in the cooler mountain sections of the state. Fruit production and quality can be improved if trellises are used when planting raspberry.

Red raspberries have generally been more successful in the warmer areas of the state than have the other types.

- Caroline is an early primocane bearing variety. The conical fruit is medium sized, firm, and has excellent flavor. The variety has medium vigor and good disease resistance.
- Heritage is primocane bearing variety. Fruit of Heritage is medium sized, firm, and of good quality. This variety is resistant to most diseases, but is susceptible to late leaf rust.
- Himbo Top is a primocane raspberry variety, with high tolerance to Phytophthora root rot disease. This variety produces a large, firm, conic fruit, bright red in color, with very good flavor.
- Joan J is a very productive, spine free, primocane bearing variety. Fruit is very firm, glossy, and dark red in color used for fresh consumption.
- Jaclyn is the earliest of the primocane bearing varieties. Fruits are dark red, large, and have an excellent flavor. Used primarily for fresh consumption.
- Josephine is a primocane bearing variety that has an upright, vigorous plant. Berries are dark red in color, large, have excellent flavor, and long shelf life. Plant is resistant to potato leaf hopper.
- Killarney is a high yielding, floricane bearing variety. Fruit is medium-sized, bright colored, but is soft in warm weather. This is a hardy cultivar and suitable for colder climates. Susceptible to mildew and anthracnose. Good flavor and freezing quality.
- Latham is a standard, floricane bearing variety. Plants of this variety are vigorous, with few spines, moderately productive, and susceptible to fire blight and powdery mildew. The berries are small in size and soft. The flavor is somewhat tart.
- Nova is mid-season, floricane bearing variety. Fruits are somewhat acidic in taste. Considered to have better than average shelf life. Plants are hardy and resistant to cane diseases and late leaf rust, but are susceptible to cane botrytis.

Black raspberries are very susceptible to viral diseases and are readily infected when grown near red varieties carrying a virus. Plants of red and black raspberries should be separated by at least 700 feet.

- Cumberland, a floricane bearing variety, ripens about one week later than New Logan. Cumberland has long been a favored variety due to its attractive, firm berries with fair flavor. The plants are vigorous and productive, but not particularly cold hardy.
- Jewel, a floricane bearing variety, has firm, glossy, large and flavorful fruits. Plants are vigorous, cold hardy, upright, and resistant to most diseases. Jewel is a high yielding variety.
- New Logan yields heavy crops of good quality, large, glossy-black fruits. Plants hold up well during drought, and are relatively tolerant to mosaic and other raspberry diseases.
- Purple raspberries are a hybrid of the red and black types. The fruits have a purple color and are usually larger than the parent varieties. They are tarter in taste compared to either the reds or black raspberries, and are best used in jams, jellies, and pies. They are excellent for quick freezing. Plants are less hardy than the parents, but are vigorous, and very productive.
- Brandywine is the best purple raspberry available. It ripens later than most red or black varieties. The fruit is large, firm, and quite tart, but of good quality. This variety is resistant to most diseases, but is susceptible to crown gall. Royalty, has a delicious sweet flavor, soft fruit, and high productivity. It is excellent for fresh use, and for jam and jelly.
- Royalty is resistant to mosaic-transmitting aphids and raspberry fruit worm. Canes have thorns.

Establishing the Caneberry Planting

Soil: Caneberries grow best in deep, sandy loam soils, rich in organic matter. Ideal soil should have a pH of 6.0 to 6.5, and be well drained to a depth of at least 3 feet. Caneberries are sensitive to excess waterlogging, and even temporary water accumulation can weaken canes, hinder plant growth, and increase incidences of diseases, particularly root rots. Therefore they are best grown on raised beds.

Planting: Caneberries should be planted late in fall, or early in the spring, about four weeks before the average date of the last frost. Work the soil as for garden vegetables, particularly where the plants are to be set. When planting in rows, allow at least 8 feet between rows to facilitate cultivation. Red and purple raspberries may be set 3 feet apart within the row; set erect and semi-erect blackberries plants 5 feet apart. Black raspberry rows should be no less than 4-5 feet apart, and trailing blackberry rows no less than 6 feet apart.

Set the plants at about the same depth they grew in the nursery. The crown should be at least 2 inches below the soil line. Spread out the roots, and firm the soil carefully around them. Do not allow the roots to dry out. Most caneberry fruits come with a portion of the old cane attached. This serves as a handle in setting the plants. Soon after new growth begins, the handle can be cut off at the surface of the ground and destroyed, as a safeguard against possible anthracnose infection.

Maintaining the Caneberry Planting

Soil Management: Caneberries grow best in soils containing three percent or more organic matter. Organic matter in soil can be maintained using a permanent mulch. Mulch should be applied soon after setting the plants, and maintained throughout the life of the planting by replenishing annually, or as needed. Hardwood or softwood bark should be applied at least 5 or 6 inches in depth. If mulch material is unavailable, or if cultivation seems necessary, keep the cultivation very shallow to avoid disturbing the roots, and repeat cultivation often as necessary, to control weeds until the beginning of harvest.

Fertilization: If materials low in nitrogen are used, it may be necessary to add sufficient nitrogenous fertilizer to prevent a temporary deficiency as the mulch begins to decay. Usually about 0.5 pound nitrate of soda, or 0.75 pound of 10-10-10, for each 100 square feet of mulched area will be enough. On fertile soils, or where good mulch is maintained, it is usually unnecessary to make an application of fertilizer in the caneberry planting. Additional fertilizer should be added after soil test has been done, and on basis of recommendations. If growth is poor, addition of 2-3 pounds of ammonium nitrate to each 100 feet of row, when growth begins in the spring, will be beneficial. Adjustments to fertilizer grades and amount should be made based on plant growth and soil type. However, do not over fertilize, because it may result in too much vegetative growth, burning of foliage, yield loss, injury to roots, a decrease in fruit quality, and an increase in disease.

Training and Pruning: Trailing and erect-growing blackberries and black and purple raspberries need some kind of support. They may be grown on a trellis, trained along a fence, or tied to stakes. Other caneberries may either be trained to supports, or with more severe pruning, grown as upright, self-supporting plants. Red raspberries sucker so are frequently grown in hedgerows. On vigorous sites some type of minimal containment trellising may be needed in some seasons.

A simple trellis, used in many home gardens, consists of two wires stretched at 3 and 5 foot levels between posts set 15 to 20 feet apart. Fruiting canes are tied to these wires in the spring. The erect varieties are tied where the canes cross the wires. Canes of trailing varieties are tied horizontally along the wires, or fanned out from the ground and tied where they cross each wire.

Where stakes are used for support, they are driven into the ground about one foot from each plant, and allowed to extend 4 or 5 feet above the ground. Canes are tied to the stake at a point about midway between the ground and the tips of the canes, and again near the ends of the canes.

Caneberry plants are biennial in nature; the crowns are perennial. New canes grow from buds at the crown each year. The new shoots called 'primocanes' will produce vegetative growth the first season, go through a dormant winter season, and then are referred to as 'floricanes' the second year. Primocane bearing varieties produce fruit on first year canes (shoots). The base of these primocanes will survive, while the top portion of the cane will die off after fruiting.

Dormant pruning is usually delayed until danger of severe cold has passed, and accomplished before the buds begin to swell in spring. Dormant pruning consists of the removal of all dead, weak, diseased, and severely damaged canes, and the selection and pruning of the fruiting canes for the coming season. At the dormant pruning, thin each plant until only 4 or 5 of the best canes remain. Where possible, fruiting canes 0.5 inch or more in diameter are selected. Cut the lateral branches of the black raspberry to 9-12 inches long; those of the purple raspberry to 12-15 inches long and the blackberry to 15-18 inches long. At the dormant pruning, where supports are used, head the canes to 4 or 5 feet in height. Canes grown without support should be headed to 3 feet. All dead and weak canes should be removed after harvest or at the dormant pruning. They should be thinned to seven or eight of the best canes per hill, cut to about 5 feet in length, and tied to either a stake or trellis.

Summer top pruning stimulates lateral branching. Summer top pruning consists of removing the top 3-4 inches of the new shoots by snapping them off with the fingers, or cutting them with shears or a knife. Where trained to supports, let them grow 6-8 inches taller than the support before topping. Blackberry plants should be summer-top pruned when the young shoots (primocanes) are about 5 feet tall. For, black raspberries and purple raspberries summer-topping should be done when young shoots are about 3-4 feet tall. To prevent the planting from becoming too thick and reducing yields, it may be necessary to remove excess sucker plants as they appear. This can be done either with a hoe or by hand. In the hedgerow type of culture, leave only 3 or 4 shoots per running foot of row. Grown in hills, 4-5 new shoots may be allowed to develop in each hill.

Primocane bearing red raspberries should not be summer-topped, as this will reduce potential of canes to bear fruits in summer. Canes of primocane bearing varieties are handled in the same manner as the others during the dormant season. At the dormant pruning, where the hill system of culture is used, thin until only five to seven of the best canes remain per hill.

If the plants are grown in hedgerows, keep the width of the rows to 18 inches or less and remove all plants outside the row areas. Thin the canes within the hedgerows to 6-8 inches apart, saving the best canes.

Where the canes are supported either by a trellis or stakes, cut the canes back to a convenient height for berry picking, usually about 5 feet. Grown as upright, self-supporting plants without use of trellises or stakes, the canes should be cut back to about 3 feet in height whether in hills or in hedgerows. Any lateral branches should be cut to about 10 inches in length.

Grapes

Grapes of some type can be grown almost anywhere. Careful selection of cultivated varieties compatible with local soil and climatic conditions has led to successful production in home gardens and commercial vineyards.

Variety Selection

Table grapes

Grape varieties should be selected for their intended use. Some seeded varieties such as Concord or Niagara may be used either for fresh table consumption, home juice or jelly production, or for wine production, but most varieties were developed or selected for a specific use. The following varieties are generally classified by intended use and have fared reasonably well over a wide geographic area of Virginia, with certain noted qualifications. All American, hybrid and *Vitis vinifera* grapes are self-fertile, meaning that a different pollinizer is not required for them to adequately set fruit.

Figure 10-6: Muscadine grapes.

- Concord is by far the most widely planted blue-black grape. The good-quality fruit ripens unevenly in the hotter areas of the state. A similar variety called 'Sunbelt' was developed in Arkansas to ripen more uniformly in hot climates. Concord is an excellent and versatile variety for the home gardener! The vines are vigorous and productive and, except for black rot, they are relatively disease tolerant.
- Delaware is a high-quality, red grape ripening about one week before Concord. Quite susceptible to downy mildew, this variety produces clusters and berries that are rather small and vines that grow slowly. Delaware has an unusually good balance of sweetness and acidity. It yields fine-quality white wines and is often used in blends for sparkling wine.
- Himrod, a golden-yellow grape, has good flavor and is considered seedless, although vestigial seeds can be present. Hardy, vigorous, and productive, it has been superior to its sister seedling, Interlaken, in areas where both have been grown.
- Mars has medium-sized, seedless, blue-black berries of the slip-skin type, and is sweet and enjoyable. It is a cold-hardy plant with high resistance to black rot, powdery mildew, and downy mildew.
- Niagara has green-white berries and is used in wine and as a table grape. It is the most widely planted white American grape in the United States and is used extensively for white juice.
- Seneca, an early season yellow grape, is noted for its good flavor and tender pulp. It holds well on the vine and will keep in cold storage for about two months after harvest. Vine vigor and productivity are only moderate, and this variety is quite susceptible to black rot and powdery mildew.
- Steuben is a blue-black variety ripening about one week after Concord. The berries are medium in size with a sweet, spicy flavor. They keep well in storage. The vines are hardy, vigorous, and productive. Steuben makes a very nice wine in addition to its use as a table grape.

Wine grapes

American and hybrid varieties

- Chambourcin is a black grape that produces a red wine often compared to Merlot. Although Chambourcin can be grown on its own roots, graft to a rootstock, such as C-3309, 101-14, or 420-A, for best performance.
- Chardonel is a mid-season, white wine grape. It is productive and generally more disease resistant than one of its parents, Chardonnay. Chardonel must be purchased from a grapevine nursery as a grafted grapevine. We recommend any commonly used rootstock variety, such as C-3309, 101-14, or 420-A.
- Norton is a late ripening American type wine grape hybrid of *Vitis aestivalis*. Norton is a black grape with small clusters and small berries. The fruit can be very acidic and vines should be trained to a high wire cordon, affording excellent fruit exposure to help reduce fruit acidity.
- Traminette is a mid-season white wine grape with good productivity and partial resistance to several fungal diseases. It produces a wine with some of the spicy, rose-like characteristics similar to one of its parents, Gewürztraminer.
- Vidal Blanc is a mid- to late-season, white wine grape. It is moderately susceptible to downy mildew and powdery mildew, as well as aerial phylloxera. Vidal should be purchased from a grapevine nursery as a grafted grapevine. We recommend any commonly used rootstock variety, such as C-3309, 101-14, or 420-A.

Vitis vinifera varieties

Vitis vinifera grape varieties are the most important and the most abundant grapes grown globally for wine and raisin production. They are, however, difficult to grow in the backyard situation. Vinifera varieties are extremely susceptible to many diseases; most are susceptible to winter cold injury below 5 F, and all vinifera varieties must be grafted to rootstocks tolerant of grape phylloxera. If you choose to grow vinifera grape varieties, pay particular attention to the disease management described under "Pest Management" below.

Cabernet franc is a black grape that produces fine red wine. Vines are vigorous and more cold hardy than other black vinifera types.

Chardonnay, considered by many to be superior to all other varieties for dry white wine, is only moderate in hardiness, vigor, and productivity. It is a medium-sized, white grape in a compact cluster ripening 3-5 days ahead of Concord. Vines are extremely sensitive to fungal diseases such as powdery mildew, downy mildew, and black rot.

Muscadine grape varieties

In areas where it is adapted, the muscadine grape is a favorite for home plantings. It is highly desirable for juice, jam, and jelly, and some varieties are cultivated for the unusual style of the wine. Muscadine grapes are cold-tender and should not be planted where temperatures fall below 5 F. In Virginia, plant only in USDA cold hardiness zones 7b or greater.

Many muscadine varieties have imperfect flowers and require pollination from either male or perfect-flowered varieties. Of those suggested for planting, Carlos, Magnolia, and Nesbitt are perfect-flowered and will supply adequate pollination for female-flowered varieties such as Scuppernong.

- Carlos, a 1970 introduction from North Carolina, is a perfect-flowered bronze variety, ripening with Scuppernong and similar in size and flavor. It makes excellent white wine and is relatively cold hardy, disease resistant, and productive. It is recommended for both commercial and home garden plantings.
- Magnolia is a perfect-flowered, bronze variety of large size and very high quality. The vine is vigorous and very productive.
- Nesbitt is a large, black, perfect-flowered variety from North Carolina. Fruit ripens over a three-week period and vines are relatively cold-hardy.
- Scuppernong, a name commonly applied to all bronze-skinned muscadine grapes, is the oldest and best-known variety. Berry clusters are usually small and shatter badly, but the grape quality is good, and it has a very distinctive flavor. As a female flowered variety, Scuppernong would require a pollinator variety that blooms at roughly the same time.

Establishing the Grape Planting

Site and soil essentials

Grapes should be planted where they have benefit of the sun for most of the day. They are deep-rooted plants, frequently penetrating to a depth of 6 to 8 feet under good soil conditions. Most grapes require 160 or more frost-free days to ripen the crop, so the site should be relatively high to surrounding topography to allow cold air drainage, and the general climate of the area should afford at least 160 frost free days. Good air movement aids disease management. Avoid use of volatile herbicides, such as those that contain 2,4-D or dicamba, in the vicinity of the grape planting, as grapevines can be severely damaged by drift from such herbicides.

Grapevines grow best on well drained, sandy loam soils with 2-5 percent organic matter and moderate fertility. Sandy or heavy clay soils may be used, however, if provisions are made for adequate fertilization, moisture, and soil drainage. Grapes are tolerant of a wide range of soil acidity, but prefer a 6.0 to 6.8 pH range.

Planting grapes

Dormant grapevines are usually set in early spring, at or slightly before the average date of the last frost. Vigorous, one-year-old plants are preferred. Allow plenty of room between plants within a given row; at least 5 feet for the American bunch varieties and 8 feet or more for the vigorous-growing muscadine type. Trim the roots to about 6 inches in length to encourage formation of feeder roots near the trunk. Where the vines are to be set, dig the holes large enough so the roots can be spread without crowding and the plants can be set at about the same depth that they were grown in the nursery. For grafted vines, use care in firming the soil around set vines to ensure that the graft union remains about 3 inches above the final, settled soil line. Prune the planted vine to a single cane, and head it back to two buds, after buds have broken and all risk of frost has passed.

Maintaining the Grape Planting

Soil management for grapes

Mulching is the preferred soil management practice in home grape planting as mulch will suppress weeds and conserve soil moisture. Hardwood or softwood bark mulch to a depth of 4-6 inches is recommended. There have been cases where mice have girdled vines with mulch up to the trunk, so it is best to keep some space between the trunk and mulch through the winter.

Although grapes are deep-rooted plants, they do not compete well with weeds and grass, especially shortly after planting. If mulch material is unavailable, some cultivation should be done. Cultivation should be shallow and only as necessary to eliminate undesired vegetation.

Fertilization of grapes

Like all fruit plants, grapes usually require nitrogen fertilization. Except in sandy soils, this element may be the only one needed in the fertilization program. In the home garden, 2 ounces of calcium nitrate (15.5 percent N) per vine should be applied after growth begins in the spring. Spread the fertilizer in a circle around the plant, 10-12 inches from the trunk. Repeat the application about six weeks later. Repeat this fertilization at the same timing and rates in the second and third seasons. A blended fertilizer, such as 10-10-10, applied at 3 ounces per vine may be substituted where phosphorus and potassium are also needed.

Fertilizer applications to mature, bearing vines should be based on the growth and vigor of the plant. If the average cane growth is only 3 feet or less, additional nitrogen may be needed. Where proper pruning is practiced and competition from weeds and grass is kept to a minimum, however, it is doubtful that you will need to go beyond the amount recommended for a three-year-old vine.

Training and pruning grapes

Much attention is given to the training and pruning of grapes. To be most productive, they must be trained to a definite system and pruned rather severely. There are several training systems used. Two that are commonly used are the vertical trellis and the overhead arbor. Both of these are satisfactory in the home planting if kept well pruned.

Of the many variations of the vertical trellis, the single trunk, four-arm Kniffin system is the most popular. Posts are set 15 to 20 feet apart and extend 5 feet above the ground. Two wires are stretched between the posts, the lower being about 2.5 feet above the ground and the upper at the top of the posts. Set between the posts, the vine is trained to a single trunk with four semipermanent arms, each cut back to 6-10 inches in length. One arm is trained in each direction on the lower wire.

During annual winter pruning, one cane is saved from those that grew from near the base of each arm the previous summer. This cane is cut back to about ten buds. The fruit in the coming season is borne on shoots developing from those buds. Select another cane from each arm, preferably one that grew near the trunk, and cut it back to a short stub having two buds. This is a renewal spur. It should grow vigorously in the spring and be the new fruiting cane selected the following winter. All other growth on the vine should be removed. This leaves four fruiting canes, one on each arm with eight to ten buds each, and four renewal spurs, one on each arm cut back to two buds each.

The same training and pruning techniques may be effectively used in training grapes to an arbor system. Arbors are generally overhead structures occasionally used in home plantings to add a decorative feature to the garden or lawn. Many variations can be found by browsing the Web. The principal difference between trellises and arbors is that the wires supporting the grapevine arms are placed overhead and parallel with each other on the arbor instead of vertically on trellis posts. Overhead wires or wooden frames are usually placed 6-7 feet above the ground, well within reach.

If an arm dies or for any reason needs to be replaced, choose the largest cane that has grown from the trunk near the base of the dead arm and train it to the trellis wire. To renew the trunk, train a strong shoot from the base of the old trunk to the trellis as though it was the cane of a new vine. Establish the arms in the same manner as for a new vine, and cut off the old trunk.

A high-wire cordon training system can be used with varieties such as Norton that have trailing or procumbent shoot growth habits. The top wire of the trellis is placed about 6 feet above the ground. Trunks are trained up to this wire and then horizontally extended along the top wire to which they are loosely tied. These horizontal trunk extensions are termed "cordons" and are annually pruned to short, two- to four-node "spurs" derived from the previous season's canes. It is important to train or comb the current growing season's shoots downward from the cordons if using a high-wire system.

Pruning may be done at any time after the vines become dormant. In areas where there is danger of winter injury, pruning should be delayed until early spring. Vines pruned very late may bleed excessively, but there is no evidence that this is injurious.

Pest management in grapes

Grapes and grapevines are subject to diseases and insect pests. Certain varieties, such as Norton, as well as most muscadine varieties, are relatively resistant to common fungal diseases. On the other hand, all of the *Vitis vinifera* varieties and many of the hybrid grape varieties are either moderately or highly susceptible to one or more fungal diseases, including black rot, downy mildew, and powdery mildew. Chief insect pests include Japanese beetles and grape berry moth. If acceptable to the grower, a fungicide spray program will likely be minimally required for American and hybrid grapes, and mandatory for *Vitis vinifera* varieties to avoid crop loss to these diseases. Japanese beetle and grape berry moth infestations vary from year to year and may or may not require insecticide sprays. For further information on chemical pest control, please consult the VCE Pest Management Guide. In addition to potential disease and insect threats, ripe grapes are attractive to birds, deer, and raccoons. Bird netting can be used to exclude birds, but must be applied to the planting soon after grapes begin to acquire color and ripen. Vertebrate pests such as deer and raccoons can be excluded with woven wire, electric fencing, or combinations of fencing small enough to exclude raccoons and tall enough (8-10 feet) to discourage deer.

Harvesting the Grape Planting

For best quality, bunch grapes should be fully ripe when harvested. They will not improve in sugar content or flavor after being removed from the vine. Most varieties should be used immediately because they do not keep well after ripening. Cut the clusters off with a knife or shears to avoid bruising the fruit and damaging the vine.

Muscadine grapes grow either singly or in small, loose clusters. Some varieties may be shaken off easily when ripe, others have to be handpicked. The grapes should be used soon after harvesting, since their storage life is relatively short.

Strawberries

Strawberries are the most widely cultivated small fruit in America. They are the favorite of many for pies, jams, jellies, preserves, and for eating fresh. Strawberries are adaptable to a greater range of soil and climatic conditions, and are well suited to the home garden, (where supplemental watering is readily accessible).

Figure 10-7: Strawberry.

Variety Selection

Strawberry varieties vary in their adaptability to soil and climatic conditions and can be classified into short-day or June bearing types, and day-neutral or everbearing types. The short-day strawberries will initiate flower buds when days are shorter than 14 hours or when temperatures are below 60 F. Most of the varieties that fruit solely in May-June are short day varieties, with flower buds initiated from late August to early November, however the short days in spring (March) will also initiate flower buds. Day-neutral varieties will initiate crown growth and flower buds throughout the season except when temperatures are very high (above 86 F). These varieties will bear fruits in

May-June somewhat yielding lower than short-day varieties. Day-neutral varieties will yield a second crop in midsummer at most locations, and a third heaviest crop in late summer and early fall. The varieties suggested for planting in Virginia have been selected on the basis of plant vigor, productivity, and quality of the fruit. Virus-free plants of the varieties are available and should be purchased. To keep disease pressure low, it is recommended to replace strawberries each year, and plant new berries at a different location in the garden than previous year.

Short-day or June bearing varieties:

- Camino Real has a compact growth habit, and a darker fruit color compared to Camarosa. Fruit is attractive and conical in shape. The variety is suitable for both fresh market and processing, and is resistant to Verticillium wilt, and root and crown rots.
- Camarosa is a widely grown cultivar in the world. It has good disease profile resistance but is susceptible to verticillium wilt. Fruit is large, firm, and holds well in the rain. The fruit tastes better when it is picked past its glossy red stage.
- Chandler is another variety popular throughout the world and is greatly adaptable to the eastern United States. Fruit is medium to large in size, with medium firmness. Chandler has good taste, is high yielding, and is suitable for fresh consumption and processing. This variety is susceptible to diseases, but harvests over a long period.
- Delmarvel is productive on a variety of different soil types. It is an attractive large sized berry, with good aroma and flavor. Plants are disease resistant except for Rhizoctonia, but exhibit good winter hardiness.
- Earliglow is a variety noted for its superior dessert quality and disease resistance. The medium-large berries are very attractive, with a glossy appearance and deep-red color. It is one of the best for eating fresh, as a frozen product, and in jams and jellies. The plants are very vigorous and productive; however, they bloom early and are subject to frost injury, and late berries are small in size.
- Flavorfest is a mid to late-season variety, with a sweet tasting berry, and a medium size fruit. This variety is resistant to anthracnose disease.
- Sweet Charlie is a winter tender variety with overall lower yields for the season. This variety has a small fruit size. It is grown for its early bearing capacity, excellent flavor, and sweet taste. The plants are susceptible to Phytophthora.
- Lateglow was developed for its production of late-season fruit and good disease resistance. Its berries are very large, symmetrical, and attractive. It is a good dessert variety, can be eaten fresh, or frozen.

Day-neutral or everbearing varieties:

- Albion has a relatively open plant canopy. It is resistant to wilts and rots, and is one of the most widely grown varieties in northern California. Berries are cone shaped, with a dark red hue, and sweet flavor. The variety is good for fresh consumption and processing.
- San Andreas has good disease resistance. This variety produces high quality fruit, has an outstanding flavor, and an exceptional appearance. Fruits are medium to large in size, and symmetrical/conic in shape. Fruit color is slightly lighter than Albion. This variety is suitable for fresh market, processing, and home gardens.

Establishing the Strawberry Planting

Soil

Although strawberries grow best in a fertile, sandy loam soil, with a pH of 5.9 to 6.5, they may be successfully grown in any good garden soil that is well drained and well supplied with organic matter. Soil for strawberries should be thoroughly prepared for planting, loose, and free of lumps. Raised beds are preferable.

Strawberries may be used as a border for a flowerbed, or as a ground cover. Avoid planting early varieties on south-facing slopes and be sure to select a site where tomatoes, potatoes, or eggplants have not been grown. These crops often carry verticillium wilt which lives in the soil for many years, and some strawberry varieties are very susceptible to this disease. Strawberries bloom very early in the spring, and the blossoms are easily killed by frost. In areas where late frosts are a hazard, try to select a site for your planting that is slightly higher than surrounding areas. Do not set strawberries in soil that has recently been under sod. A land that was under crop cultivation for a prior year or two, may have soil better prepared for strawberries, and will assist in controlling weeds and white grubs, both of which are troublesome in strawberry plantings. Where grubs and ants are a problem, chemical control may be necessary.

Planting strawberries

Virus-free plugs should be set out in late fall or dormant crowns in early spring- about three or four weeks before the average date of the last frost. Plants should be placed no less than 12 inches apart in rows that are 2-3 feet apart. Take care to set each plant so the base of the bud is at soil level. Spread the roots out, and firm the soil carefully around them to prevent air pockets which allow them to dry out.

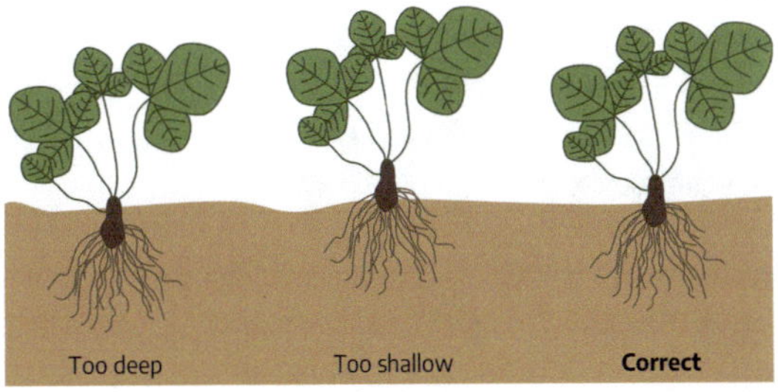

Maintaining the Strawberry Planting

Figure 10-8: Strawberry planting depths. Left is too deep, center is too shallow, right is correct.

Soil management

Cultivation for weed control in strawberries should begin soon after planting, and continue at approximately 2-3 week intervals throughout the first growing season. Cultivation must be shallow to prevent root injury. Hoe as often as necessary, to remove grass and weeds growing between the plants.

In colder areas, home garden strawberry plantings should be winter mulched. Any organic material free of weed seeds makes acceptable mulch. Hay, straw, and pine needles are most frequently used. Mulch should be applied 2-4 inches deep over and around the plants after the first freezing weather in the fall when the soil is below 50 F (usually around mid-December). This protects them from injury due to freezing, and heaving of the soil during the winter. After the danger of frost is over in the spring, about half the mulch should be raked off the plants into the area between the rows. Mulch left around the plants will help keep the berries clean, conserve moisture, reduce diseases, and check weed growth.

Fertilization of strawberries

Broadcast 4 pounds of 10-10-10 fertilizer per 100 linear ft of row, 2-3 weeks before planting. If leaves appear light green in color after three to four weeks of transplanting, side dress with 1.5 pounds of ammonium nitrate per 100 ft. of row. The limited shallow root systems will not initially benefit from fertilizer placed in the row middles. In coastal plains in late January or February, apply 0.75 pound of ammonium nitrate. In spring, choose a fertilizer grade with higher P and K and apply one-half pound of nitrogen per 100 ft of row.

Production system

There are two popular training systems used in strawberry production. Modifications of these systems can be found.

In the hill system or plasticulture system, plants are spaced 12-16 inches apart in a single or staggered double row. All runners are removed as soon as they appear, and the plants are encouraged to multiply in large crowns. This system is desired by many because the planting is easier to cultivate and harvest, and produces larger, better berries than other systems. However, many plants are required and the initial cost of the planting is high. Black plastic mulch is particularly effective with this training system, but requires drip irrigation lines for optimum performance. This "plasticulture" system is currently popular with commercial growers.

Under the matted-row system, used by many home gardeners, runner plants are allowed to set freely in all directions. The original plants should be set 18-24 inches apart in the row. Keeping the width of the plant bed narrow (16-18 inches), results in a good grade of fruit that is easy to pick. During the planting season, all flower stems on the plants should be removed as soon as they appear. This strengthens the plants and allows early and vigorous runner production. Early-formed runner plants bear the best fruit the following year.

Renovation of strawberry bed

If your strawberry planting is in a vigorous condition, it may be retained for fruiting the second year. However, allowing a planting to fruit more than 2 years often results in smaller berries and weak plants. If retaining plants, remove the mulch and clip the tops of the plants to within 1 inch of the crowns with a scythe or mower soon after harvest (mid-July). If insects and foliage diseases are prevalent, move the leaves and mulch material out of the planting, and burn them. Apply a quickly soluble nitrogen fertilizer such as ammonium nitrate (NH_4NO_3) at 0.25 to 0.5 pound, or 1-2 pounds of 10-10-10 per 100 feet of row, to encourage vigorous top growth. Any good garden fertilizer supplying an equivalent amount of nitrogen may be used if desired.

Some plant thinning may be needed, particularly in the matted-row system. Thin plants (remove oldest) to 6-8 inches apart after new foliage appears. Keep the planting free of weed throughout the summer, irrigating when necessary during the dry season, to keep the plants growing vigorously. Fertilize again in the early fall as recommended for the first year, and renew the mulch after freezing weather begins.

Pest control

Birds are one of the biggest pests in the strawberry planting. It may be necessary to cover the plants with plastic netting to keep the crop from being eaten before the berries are ripe enough to harvest. Aluminum pie tins or used metallic compact discs (CD's), suspended by a string or wire above the plants in such manner that they twist and turn in the breeze, may be successful in keeping birds away.

Culture of everbearing varieties

Irrigation is particularly important for everbearing varieties because the late-summer/early fall crop ripens during a period when soil moisture is usually quite low. Soil preparation and fertilizer requirements before planting are the same as for regular varieties. Best yields are obtained from everbearing varieties if they are set in early spring in the hill system about one foot apart, cultivated for the first 10 days to 2 weeks, then mulched to a depth of 1-2 inches with sawdust. As the sawdust decays, the development of a nitrogen deficiency could occur. It can be quickly overcome with the application of one pound of 10-10-10 to each 100 square feet of mulched area.

Remove runners as soon as they appear, to encourage the plants to multiply in large crowns. Blossom clusters should be removed until the plants have become firmly established and are growing vigorously, usually about the first of August. Berries will begin to ripen about a month later, and plants will continue to bear fruit until frost, if weed growth is kept down and adequate moisture is supplied. Allow the plants to bear fruit for the spring and fall crops the second year, then replant the following spring.

Harvesting the planting

In the home garden, strawberries should be allowed to develop an overall red color and become fully ripened before harvesting. Sometimes the tops (sun exposed) are red but the bottoms are still white and not ready for harvest. It is at the fully ripe stage that the sugar content is highest and the flavor is best. It may be necessary to harvest every day during the peak of the season, especially in warm periods.

Harvest the berries carefully by the stems just above the caps to prevent bruising. Pick all that are ripe. Ripe fruits when left unpicked on the plant, increase infestation of strawberry sap beetle and spotted wing drosophila. Ripe strawberries may be held for a day or two in a refrigerator.

Strawberry growing in pyramids and barrels

In a garden where space is extremely limited or where the gardener wishes to use the strawberry planting as a novelty or decorative feature, the strawberry pyramid or the strawberry barrel can be useful and interesting. Pyramids may be square or round. The frames for a square pyramid can be constructed out of landscaping wood. A suggested soil mixture for the pyramid is two parts good garden soil, one part peat, and one part sand.

In preparing a strawberry barrel, 1-inch diameter holes are made in the sides of the barrel at approximately 8-inch spacing. As the barrel is filled with successive layers of soil, strawberry plants are carefully inserted through the holes, so that the roots are held firmly in contact with the soil. A porous tile inserted down the middle of the barrel will facilitate water reaching all of the plants (see diagram). Though the strawberry barrel may be a successful novelty, yields of fruit will be smaller than those in open field culture, and much more attention to planting, watering, and winter protection are required.

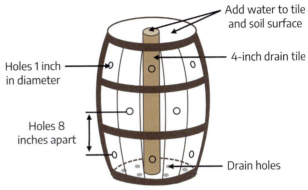

Damage to the strawberry plants growing under normal cultural conditions can be expected if they are not protected from extreme cold during the winter. Owing to the fact that plants growing in a pyramid or barrel are elevated above normal ground level and therefore are highly exposed, additional winter damage can be expected to roots, crowns, and fruit buds. Consequently, care must be taken to provide adequate winter protection. Pyramids can be mulched with 6-8 inches of straw after the soil is frozen. In the coldest part of the state, strawberries in barrels will survive better if protected with burlap covering. In cold winters, enclose straw in the burlap for added insulation. However, even with careful mulching, some plant injury can be expected during severe winters.

Figure 10-9: Barrel planter.

Figure 10-10: Pyramid culture.

List of material necessary for a 72-inch wide, 5 level, square-sided pyramid where each ascending level is 12 inches less in width:

- 4 boards 6' long and 6" wide
- 4 boards 5' long and 6" wide
- 4 boards 4' long and 6" wide
- 4 boards 3' long and 6" wide
- 10 feet of 2" x 2" for corners
- 1 pound of 6 penny galvanized nails

Additional Resources

- "Freeze damage depends on tree fruit stage of development" Michigan State University: https://www.canr.msu.edu/news/freeze_damage_depends_on_tree_fruit_stage_of_development
- "Picture Table of Critical Spring Temperatures for Tree Fruit Bud Development Stages" Michigan State University: https://www.canr.msu.edu/resources/picture-table-critical-spring-temperatures-for-tree-fruit-bud-development-stages
- "Growth Stages of Blueberries" Michigan State University: https://www.canr.msu.edu/blueberries/growing_blueberries/growth-stages

Attributions

Adapted from "Small Fruit In the Home Garden" 426-840 (SPES-399P) by Jayesh B. Samtani, Assistant Professor and Small Fruit Extension Specialist, Hampton Roads Agricultural Research and Extension Center; Reza Rafie, Extension Specialist, Horticulture, Virginia State University; Tony K. Wolf, Professor, Viticulture, Alson H. Smith Jr. Agricultural Research and Extension Center

- Michael Cole, Norfolk Extension Master Gardener (2021 reviser)
- Meagan Shelley, Bedford Extension Master Gardener (2021 reviser)
- Dan Nortman, Extension Agent, Agriculture and Natural Resources (2015 reviser)
- Jayesh B. Samtani, Small Fruit Production Specialist, Hampton Roads AREC, (2015 reviewer)
- Reza Rafie, Extension Specialist, Horticulture, Virginia State University (2015 reviewer)
- Tony K. Wolf, Professor of Viticulture, Alson H. Smith Jr. AREC, (2015 reviewer)
- Keith S. Yoder, Extension Specialist, Tree Fruit Pathology (2015 reviewer)
- Rich Marini, Extension Specialist, Tree Fruits (2009 reviser)
- Jerry Williams, Associate Professor, Horticulture – Small Fruits (2009 reviser)

Image Attributions

- Figure 10-1: Vase: Grey, Kindred. 2022. CC BY-NC-SA 4.0. Includes grass by Milena Zanotelli from Noun Project (Noun Project license).
- Figure 10-2: Central leader: Grey, Kindred. 2022. CC BY-NC-SA 4.0. Includes grass by Milena Zanotelli from Noun Project (Noun Project license).
- Figure 10-3: Roxbury Russet. U.S. Department of Agriculture Pomological Watercolor Collection. Rare and Special Collections, National Agricultural Library, Beltsville, MD 20705.
- Figure 10-4: Blueberries. "Blueberry 4." by UGA CAES/Extension. 2008. Flickr. CC BY-NC 2.0.
- Figure 10-5: Blackberries. Johnson, Devon. 2022. CC BY-NC-SA 4.0.
- Figure 10-6: Grapes. "Muscadines" by UGA CAES/Extension. 2016. Flickr. CC BY-NC 2.0.
- Figure 10-7: Strawberries. Johnson, Devon. 2022. CC BY-NC-SA 4.0.
- Figure 10-8: Strawberry planting depths. Left is too deep, center is too shallow, right is correct. Grey, Kindred. 2022. CC BY-NC-SA 4.0.
- Figure 10-9: Barrel planter. Grey, Kindred. 2022. CC BY-NC-SA 4.0.
- Figure 10-10: Pyramid culture. Grey, Kindred. 2022. CC BY-NC-SA 4.0.

CHAPTER 11: LAWNS

Chapter Contents:

- Establishing a Lawn
- Renovating an Old Lawn
- Recommended Turfgrass Varieties for Virginia
- Purchasing Quality Seed
- Purchasing Quality Sod
- Annual Lawn Maintenance
- Additional Resources

Grasses that are used for lawns are commonly referred to as turfgrasses. They are durable perennial grasses that can be mowed to a short height to form a uniform, compact, and soft groundcover. They are somewhat tolerant of foot traffic and ideal for sports fields such as golf courses, recreation areas like parks, or residential areas for children's playgrounds or entertainment.

Producing quality lawns in Virginia can be challenging. Virginia is located within the turfgrass transition zone and its cold winters and hot dry summers are not favorable for establishing or maintaining lawns in an easy, affordable, and environmentally friendly way. However, with proper cultural practices, a healthy lawn can be established and maintained.

Establishing a Lawn

Turf may be established from seed, sprigs, plugs, or sod. The method used depends on the type of grass desired, the environmental and soil conditions, time constraints, and financial considerations. These factors are discussed more in the section on Seed versus Sod. The same basic requirements for lime, fertilizer, and seedbed preparation apply for both seeding and vegetative establishment. After the new lawn is established and growing well, begin a good, comprehensive maintenance program to keep it healthy and attractive.

Soil Test

The first step in establishing a new lawn is to have the soil tested. Test results will determine which basic nutrients are available in the soil, and will allow recommendations to be made for liming and fertilization. Forms and sample boxes, along with instructions for obtaining good samples, are available from your Extension office. Samples should be taken from several areas in the lawn. Samples from areas that have similar soil types should be combined into one sample. For most yards, one combined sample is adequate. Large yards with widely varied conditions may require more samples. There is no need to submit more samples than you are willing to individually treat, if turf areas do not exceed 5 acres.

Pre-Plant Weed Control

Observe the topsoil or lawn area to be planted and determine if there are weeds present that should be controlled prior to planting. Grassy weeds that are particularly troublesome in lawns of Kentucky bluegrass, perennial ryegrass, or fine fescues are dallisgrass, quackgrass, tall fescue, orchardgrass, and bermudagrass. These weeds can be controlled prior to planting by properly applying a non-selective herbicide such as glyphosate.

Controlling troublesome perennial broadleaf weeds prior to establishment can be beneficial. Refer to the most current version of the VCE Pest Management Guide for recommendations on chemical controls and timings specific to individual species.

Pre-plant weed control needs to account for the wait time between when a chemical control is applied and when the area can be seeded to prevent residual herbicide damage to newly planted turf. Refer to product labels for the appropriate wait time.

Pre-Plant Installation of Irrigation and Drainage

If irrigation systems or drainage tiles are necessary, they should be installed prior to topsoil application in order to avoid contamination of topsoil with subsoil. Stockpiling of topsoil is advisable if considerable subsoil grading is necessary.

Soil Preparation

Remove building debris and other trash from the lawn area during all stages of construction. Such material causes mowing hazards and blocks root system development. Rotting wood is often the host for troublesome "fairy ring" diseases which are difficult to control. The subgrade should be sloped away from the house, and the area should be allowed to settle for 2 or 3 weeks before seeding or sodding. Several wetting and drying cycles will aid settling and help you locate low spots in the lawn which should be filled. Topsoil depth after settling should be a minimum of 6 to 8 inches. Therefore, 8 to 10 inches of loose topsoil should be called for in the establishment specifications.

Lime

Soils in most areas of Virginia are acid, and lime recommendations will be made from the soil test to raise the soil pH to 6.5, as based on Virginia Tech Soil Testing Lab recommendations. Lime rates are based on the target pH and the buffer index from the soil analysis. The lime should be tilled into the soil to a minimum depth of 4 to 6 inches. If soil tests indicate low available magnesium levels, dolomitic limestone should be used. Otherwise, use ground agricultural limestone.

Have soil tested

The soil analysis will determine lime and fertilizer needs. The soil should be tested at least a month before the lawn establishment is started.

When to Establish

Seed will germinate only under proper conditions. There are certain periods each year when temperature, moisture, and day length are most favorable for establishing turfgrass. In general, early fall seeding of cool-season grasses is much preferred over spring seeding to allow maximum establishment and growth before the turf's first full summer. Early spring seedings may also bring good results if moisture is adequate, but it is likely the lawn will need supplemental irrigation to survive the first summer. In Northern Virginia and the areas of Western Virginia at lower elevations, the best seeding dates are mid-to-late March for spring seeding, and the last week of August to mid-September for fall seeding. It may be possible to get good results as late as the middle of October for fall seeding. At higher elevations (greater than 1200 feet) in Western Virginia, the best seeding dates are April and early May in the spring and mid-August to mid-September in the fall. In southern and southeastern Virginia, February 15 to March 30 is the best period to plant for spring warm-season grasses. In the fall, September 15 to October 15 is most suitable for cool-season grasses. Sod of **Kentucky bluegrass** and **tall fescue** can be installed throughout the year except in mid-winter when the ground is frozen. When extreme heat and drought conditions exist in summer, sodding operations should be delayed. If done under drought conditions, the turf must be kept moist and cool.

Improved strains of warm-season grasses such as **zoysiagrass**, **bermudagrass**, **centipedegrass**, (possible use from Southside through the southern coastal plain of Virginia) and **St. Augustinegrass** (used on the coast in Southeast Virginia) which are normally sprigged, plugged, or sodded, should be established during May after the soil is warm. There also are improved-quality, cold-tolerant seeded bermudagrasses and zoysiagrasses now commercially available. May and June plantings will have the greatest chance of surviving the first winter, especially for seeded establishments. These grasses have been successfully planted as late as July; however, late summer plantings are not recommended because there is not sufficient time for proper root and rhizome establishment before cold weather.

Seed versus Sod

A quality lawn containing the recommended mixtures of grass varieties and species can be established with either seed or **sod** (the upper layer of soil with grass growing, often harvested and rolled). Both seed and sod of recommended varieties are available, and the soil preparation for the two methods does not differ. The latest recommendations for top performing turfgrass varieties in Virginia can be found on the Extension publication site.

Initially, seed is less expensive than sod. However, soil erosion potential and heavy weed pressure are both more likely with seeded establishments than with sod. If reseeding of certain areas or even an entire lawn is necessary, the overall expense may be less with sod. Also, because of the time required for seed to germinate and become well-rooted in the soil, there is often excessive potential for erosion. Sodding practically eliminates such problems, a consideration which may be especially important on steep hills or banks

Sodding provides an immediately pleasing turf that is quickly functional and will compete with viable weed seed already present in the soil. When using seed, an intensive weed control program may be necessary to reduce weed competition.

Seed establishment is only recommended in the early fall or early spring, whereas sod may be established in nearly any season if moisture is available.

Seeding and Mulching

A well-prepared seedbed is essential for the establishment of turfgrasses. The seedbed should be tilled to a depth of 6 inches if possible, with lime (if needed), compost and fertilizer worked into the soil prior to seeding. Tilling 1-2 inches of compost into the soil improves soil structure and helps the turf establish more quickly. Prepare a smooth, firm seedbed, then divide the seed and sow in two directions, perpendicular to each other. If low rates of seed are being sown (typical with smaller-seeded grasses like Kentucky bluegrass, bermudagrass, or zoysiagrass), mixing the seed with a dry carrier such as sand, calcined clay, or a granular organic fertilizer will aid in gaining uniform coverage. Cover the seed by raking lightly and rolling. Avoid a completely smooth surface that promotes the washing of the seed. A finished seedbed should have shallow, uniform depressions (rows) about 1/2 inch deep and 1-2 inches apart, such as those made by a corrugated roller. Uniformly mulch the area with straw or other suitable material so that approximately 50% to 75% of the soil surface is covered. This is normally accomplished by spreading 1 bale of straw per 1000 square feet. This amount of mulch would simply be chopped up with the mower the first few times the new lawn is mowed. Heavier rates of mulch that might shade the turf should be removed when the seedlings are about 2 inches tall, being careful not to remove the young, recently rooted seedlings.

Sodding

Figure 11-1: Pile of freshly cut sod in field.

Soil preparation should be similar to that described for seeding. Take care not to disturb the prepared soil with deep footprints or wheel tracks. These depressions restrict root development and give an uneven appearance to the installed sod. During hot summer days, the soil should be dampened just prior to laying the sod. This avoids placing the turf roots in contact with an excessively dry and hot soil. Premium quality, certified sod is easier to transport and install than inferior grades. Such sod is light, does not tear apart easily, and quickly generates a root system into the prepared soil. Before ordering or obtaining sod, be sure you are prepared to install it. Sod is perishable, and should not remain on the pallet or stack longer than 36 hours. The presence of mildew and distinct yellowing of the leaves is usually evidence of reduced turf vigor.

To reduce the need for short pieces when installing sod, it is generally best to establish a straight line lengthwise through the lawn area. Working from the edge of a sidewalk or driveway is a logical starting point. The sod pieces are then staggered as when laying bricks. A sharpened masonry trowel is very handy for cutting pieces, forcing the sod tight, and leveling small depressions. Immediately after the sod is laid, it should be rolled and kept very moist until it is well-rooted in the soil.

Plugging and Sprigging

The highest quality cultivars of the zoysiagrass, bermudagrass, and St. Augustinegrass must be vegetatively established using either **plugs** or **sprigs**. Plugs are small squares/circles of sod grown in a tray. Sprigs are the stems from shredded sod. Sprigs should include leaves, a stolon, and roots.

The soil should be prepared as described for seeding or sodding. Rooted plugs of zoysiagrass are commonly available, and are 1 to 2 inches in diameter with 1 to 2 inches of soil attached. St. Augustinegrass usually requires 4 inch diameter plugs. The plugs should be fitted tightly into pre-cut holes and tamped firmly into place. Plugs are normally planted on 6- to 12-inch centers. Planting plugs on 6-inch centers requires 4000 plugs per 1000 square feet. On 12-inch centers, only 1000 plugs are required per 1000 square feet.

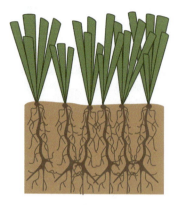

Figure 11-2: Plug.

Sprigs can be broadcast over a previously disked area and covered lightly with soil by disking again. They can also be planted in shallow depressed rows on 6 to 12 inch centers, then covered with soil. In either case, the sprig should root at the nodes. Sprigs can be purchased as sod and then shredded, or can often be purchased by the bushel. Generally, one bushel of sprigs is produced from shredding one square yard of sod. Sprigging rates for bermudagrass and zoysiagrass range from 7 to 10 bushels per 1000 square feet.

Post-Planting Irrigation

New seedings and spriggings require intensive irrigation to ensure successful establishment. Seedings require light and frequent watering to ensure that the seed and surface of the soil are constantly moist. Plan to keep the soil moist for 30 days following planting. During hot days this may necessitate 3 or 4 light waterings during the day to provide adequate moisture for rapid and successful germination. If the soil dries out during the germination or sprigging process, the plant material is likely to die. Areas sodded and plugged also require intensive irrigation initially. However, frequent light watering is only required until the sod or plug is rooted. Once sod or plugs are rooted, irrigation applied every second or third day, wetting the soil to a 6-inch depth, is adequate. As a rule of thumb, once the lawn requires mowing, it is time to change the irrigation strategy to a 'deep and infrequent' approach.

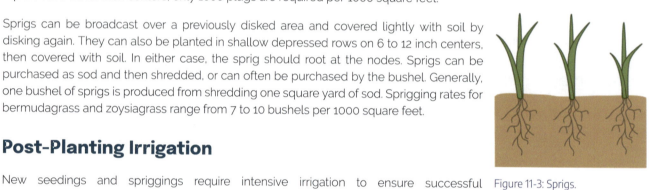

Figure 11-3: Sprigs.

Renovating an Old Lawn

A lawn of less than satisfactory appearance but fair condition may be renovated without having to be completely tilled. Advantages of renovation include less expense and mess, since minimum tilling of the soil is required. The lawn will be able to take light traffic during the renovation period. Some conditions reduce the chances of successful renovation. If the soil is extremely compacted, has a pH below 5.2, very low soil phosphorus availability, or the grade is very uneven, complete re-establishment with plowing or disking may be a better choice.

Determine Cause of Poor Quality

Lawns usually require renovation because of one or more of the following reasons: poor soil chemical and/or physical properties, poor fertilization practices, inadequate drainage, excessive traffic, poor selection of grass variety or species, weed invasion, compaction, drought, insect or disease damage, or excessive shade.

Have Soil Tested

The soil analysis will determine lime and fertilizer needs. The soil should be tested at least a month before the lawn renovation is started. Simply put – don't guess, soil test!

Control Weeds and Undesirable Grasses

If possible, control perennial grass weeds such as tall fescue (in warm-season turf), bermudagrass (in zoysia and cool-season turf), nimblewill, and quackgrass prior to the soil preparation process. Glyphosate, applied in accordance with label directions, will control most perennial grassy weeds. Begin treatment with glyphosate 30 to 45 days prior to renovation to provide the opportunity for re-treatment if regrowth occurs. Perennial broadleaf weeds can be controlled either prior to renovation or after the new seed has been mowed two times. If controlling broadleaf weeds prior to renovation, pay attention to any planting restrictions that might be indicated on the label. In most situations, apply the broadleaf weed control at least 30 days prior to soil disruption and seeding.

One very important weed competitor that is a serious problem with spring plantings is crabgrass. Standard preemergent (PRE) herbicides for crabgrass control will also control any grasses that are planted from seed, so there must be a very well defined plan of when grasses will be planted and how one is going to manage the weeds. The VCE Pest Management Guide should always be the resource to consult for the latest information on these pesticides. Two very popular herbicides that fit crabgrass control programs for most (not all) grass establishments from seed are mesotrione and quinclorac. Consult the PMG for the rates and timing of their applications in order to optimize grass establishment and crabgrass control.

Dethatch and/or Aerify if Necessary

Thatch is an organic mat of stems that forms between the mineral soil and the turfgrass canopy. It is primarily comprised of rhizomes (below-ground stems), stolons (above-ground stems), or seedheads. Grasses that don't spread by lateral stems typically do not produce a lot of thatch. Due to the high cellulose content of grass, thatch is slow to decay and forms a hydrophobic mat between the soil and grass leaves. Thatch layers greater than ½ inch in thickness will eventually cause a decline in turfgrass performance and will make renovations using seed very difficult..Use a vertical mower or dethatching machine(many rental businesses will have these machines available) to remove thatch (if it is a problem). Even if the existing lawn is not thatch, these machines are great renovation tools because they promote good seed to soil contact.. Seed planted on top of the thatch layer is largely wasted since thatch is a hydrophobic layer of undecomposed organic matter that is not conducive to root establishment.. Aerification with a coring aerifier (often called a 'plugger') helps prepare a lawn for renovation by inoculating the thatch with soil, reducing compaction, and creating moisture collecting holes in the soil. Dethatching after aerification helps bust the cores and provide a better seedbed by promoting more soil to seed contact.

Apply Lime and Fertilizer

Consult soil test recommendations.

Sow the Seed

Renovated lawns can be drill-seeded and/or broadcast-seeded. Drill seeding provides the best seed-soil contact and the highest germination rate. Drill seeding alone generally leaves a "row effect," which can be masked by also broadcast seeding. The best method involves drill seeding in two perpendicular directions and then broadcast seeding. Lightly rake or drag the area after seeding.

Water Frequently

Water lightly and frequently every day until the seed has germinated and developed a 2- to 4-inch root system. Then water less frequently but more deeply to keep the soil moist.

New Lawn Maintenance

Begin mowing the new lawn when the 1/3rd rule applies. This mowing rule of thumb says to never remove more than 1/3rd of the leaf blade during any mowing event. For instance, if the desired maintenance cutting height of a new tall fescue stand is 2 inches, cut the grass when it reaches 3 inches tall. Be sure that the lawn mower blade is sharp. A dull mower tends to pull grass seedlings out of the ground. Try to minimize traffic on the new lawn until it is mature. Broadleaf weed control may be necessary. Do not apply broadleaf weed control to new lawns until they have been mowed three or more times (often indicated on the herbicide label). Begin a good, comprehensive fertilization program based on the recommendations in Extension publications.

Healthy Virginia Lawns: Grassroots in Chesterfield

By Seth Guy, Environmental Educator, Virginia Cooperative Extension, Chesterfield

You can help improve Virginia's waterways starting in your own backyard! Growing turf in Central Virginia can prove difficult as we live in what is considered a transition zone for turfgrasses. This means that the climate can be hostile towards both cool-season grasses and warm-season grasses. This can lead to the excess use of fertilizers trying to maintain a beautiful lawn. Using excess fertilizers not only becomes expensive, it can also be detrimental to our waterways.

Chesterfield Extension Master Gardeners' Grass Roots, a Virginia Healthy Lawns program, is an excellent source of assistance for Chesterfield homeowners to determine just what their lawn needs to be as healthy as possible. Master Gardeners support the program, providing information about soil acidity, why the pH matters, when to fertilize your grass and how to minimize a property's impact on Swift Creek Reservoir and James River, which helps to continue the improvement of the Chesapeake Bay watershed. It all starts with a soil test, a measurement of the customer's lawn area, and a survey of the condition of the grass and the presence of weeds. For a small fee, a Master Gardener team will perform these tasks and send a soil sample from your lawn to Waypoint Analytical's soil lab for analysis to determine the best course of action.

Over the past 16 years since the start of Grass Roots, Chesterfield Master Gardeners have helped more than 6,000 residents adopt the lawn care practices of Virginia Healthy Lawns. This has resulted in beautiful healthy turf for the customers and a reduction of excess nutrients reaching the local watersheds.

Recommended Turfgrass Varieties for Virginia

The Maryland – Virginia Turfgrass Variety Recommendation Work Group meets each spring to consider the previous year's data from the Virginia and Maryland National Turfgrass Evaluation Program trials and to formulate these recommendations. To qualify for this recommended list, turfgrass varieties: 1) must be available as certified seed, or in the case of vegetative varieties, as certified sprigs or sod; 2) must be tested at sites in both Virginia and Maryland; and 3) must perform well, relative to other varieties, for a minimum of two years to make the list as a "promising" variety and for three years to make the recommended category. All test locations in Virginia and Maryland are considered in making these recommendations.

Table 11-1: Temperature ranges (°F)

Function	Warm-Season Turfgrasses	Cool-Season Turfgrasses
Ideal Shoot Growth	80-95°	60-75°
Ideal Root Growth	75-85°	50-65°
Upper Limit Shoot Growth	120°	90°
Upper Limit Root Growth	110°	77°
Lower Limit Shoot Growth	65°	40°
Lower Limit Root Growth	50°	33°

Table 11-2: Turfgrass characteristics

Type of grass	Common Bermuda	Hybrid Bermuda	St. Augustine	Fescue	Zoysiagrass	Centipedegrass
Leaf Texture	Medium	Fine	Coarse	Fine - Coarse	Fine - Medium	Medium - Coarse
Shade Tolerance	Low	Low - Medium	Low	High	High	Medium - High
Cold Tolerance	Low - High	Low - High	Low	High	High	Medium - High
Heat Tolerance	High	High	High	Medium	High	High
Drought Tolerance	High	High	Medium	Medium	High	Medium
Wear Tolerance	Very Good	Excellent	Poor	Good	Excellent	Poor
Salinity Tolerance	Good	Good	Good	Fine	Good	Poor
Fertility Requirements (Nitrogen)	Medium - High	Low	Medium - High	Medium	Medium	Very Low
Mowing Height (Inches)	1	1	3	3	1	2
Optimum Soil pH Range	6.0 - 7.0	6.0 - 7.0	6.5 - 7.5	5.5 - 6.5	6.0 - 7.0	5.0 - 6.0

Table compiled by Randy Jackson, Unit Director. Funding provided by ES-USDA project #91-EWQI-1-9034 Chesapeake Bay Residential Watershed Water Quality Management

The Virginia Crop Improvement Association (VCIA) will accept the turfgrass mixtures listed in the current "Virginia Turfgrass Variety Recommendations" publication, which can be found by searching "Turfgrass Variety Recommendations" on the Extension publications website (https://www.pubs.ext.vt.edu/). All seed or vegetative material must be certified and meet minimum quality standards prescribed by the VCIA. Varieties can be considered for removal from these lists due to declining performance or insufficient recent data relative to other varieties. Varieties can also be considered for removal from these lists due to seed availability problems and/or due to seed quality problems. Varieties specific to certain locations in the state due to temperature extremes etc. will also be denoted on the list.

Many seeding specifications (for municipalities, counties, state and governmental agencies, landscape architects, and professional organizations) state that varieties used for turfgrass establishment must come from this list, and that blends or mixtures follow the guidelines for certified sod production. Specifications for state highway seeding are now developed from this list, but their specifications may require some species and/or varieties not normally recommended for uses other than roadside seeding. Seed availability may vary between turf seed suppliers.

Turfgrass varieties fall into two basic categories: cool-season and warm-season. Cool-season grasses, such as Kentucky bluegrass, tall fescue, fine-leaf fescue and perennial ryegrass, have a long growing season in most areas of Virginia and provide green winter color. Warm-season grasses, such as zoysiagrass, bermudagrass, centipedegrass, and St. Augustinegrass go dormant after the first hard frost and stay brown through the winter months. Zoysiagrass greens up around mid-May in northern Virginia. While the winter color of the warm-season grasses may make them less desirable, maintenance costs are somewhat reduced since water requirements are less and the shorter growing season requires fewer mowings per year.

The following recommendations are developed from research conducted in Virginia and Maryland. Turf and seed specialists from the University of Maryland, the United States Department of Agriculture, the Virginia Department of Agriculture and Consumer Services, and Virginia Tech concur in making these recommendations.

Kentucky Bluegrass

Best suited to areas in and west of the Blue Ridge Mountains and north of Richmond, **Kentucky bluegrass** provides lush, blue-green, fine-bladed lawns. It is a fairly aggressive creeper having an extensive rhizome system. This makes it a desirable cool-season grass for heavily trafficked turfs. In the transition zone, bluegrass lawns may require irrigation in the summer to keep from going into summer dormancy. It does not perform well in heavy shade or on poor soil. Kentucky bluegrass is best suited to a well-drained soil and moderate to high levels of sunlight and management. It can be established from seed or sod.

While classified as Kentucky bluegrasses, there are a number of hybrid bluegrasses (crosses between Kentucky bluegrass and Texas bluegrass) now commercially available. These grasses have similar maintenance requirements to standard Kentucky bluegrasses, but appear to be better suited in the warmer climates of Virginia than standard bluegrasses.

Blends of Kentucky bluegrass varieties are recommended in Virginia, as it is thought they are more likely to provide good quality turf over a wide variety of management and environmental situations. There are two categories of blends.

When seeding a mixture of Category I (recommended) seed, individual varieties should make up no less than 10 percent nor more than 35 percent of the total mixture by weight. Category II seed (promising) includes Kentucky bluegrass varieties that can be blended for use in special situations. They can be mixed with Category I varieties at the rate of 10 to 35 percent. Perennial ryegrass is mixed at the rate of 10 to 15 percent by weight with bluegrass in erosion control situations.

Where erosion is a concern or seedings are being made outside of recommended dates, the addition of Virginia Tech recommended, certified perennial ryegrass varieties to the Kentucky bluegrass mixture at 3 pounds per 1000 square feet (10% to 15% on a weight basis) is recommended.

Categories I and II Seeding Rates: 1.5 to 2.5 lbs per 1000 square feet.

Tall Fescue

Tall fescue is a fine to moderate coarse-textured turfgrass which is tolerant of a wide range of soil types and climatic conditions. It provides very good quality turf under low to moderate management levels and can be established from seed or sod.

Tall fescue does not have the recuperative potential of Kentucky bluegrass since it does not spread by rhizomes (rhizomatous tall fescues are in their early stages of development, but lateral growth rates are still not comparable to those of bluegrass at this time). Therefore, infrequent overseeding may be necessary to maintain desirable turf density in tall fescue lawns.

The fine-bladed turf-type tall fescues dominate the home lawn market in this area. The leaf texture is now so fine that they are commonly mixed with Kentucky bluegrass in sod production. A 90% tall fescue/10% Kentucky bluegrass mixture, whether planted as seed or sod, provides increased recuperative potential and may be advantageous where traffic is expected.

Seeding rate: 4 to 6 pounds per 1000 square feet of tall fescue blends, 3-4 pounds per 1000 square feet for standard mixtures (90-95% tall fescue plus 5-10% Kentucky bluegrass).

Creeping Red, Hard, and Chewing Fescues

These grasses are known collectively as the **fine-leaf fescues**. As a group of grasses, they exhibit the best tolerance of shade, drought, low-nitrogen, and acid soil. These cool-season grasses require the least intensive maintenance of any of the grasses adapted to Virginia. They perform best in shady lawns in mixtures with shade-tolerant Kentucky bluegrasses as noted earlier. They are excellent choices for reduced input turfgrass areas such as highway rights of way, cemeteries, etc. They have very poor tolerance of intensive traffic or poorly drained soils. Choices in seed are quite limited for all species of fine-leaf fescues. Seed is more limited for fine fescues than any other turfgrass in this area, but for the first time, there is now fine-fescue sod available from a limited number of growers in the state. Seeding Rate: 3 to 5 lbs. per 1000 square feet.

Perennial Ryegrasses

Perennial ryegrass is a fine-medium textured grass that mixes well with Kentucky bluegrass. Some strengths of the perennial ryegrasses are their quick germination and establishment rate, good traffic bearing characteristics as a mature turf, and early spring green-up. They blend well with Kentucky bluegrasses to provide quick erosion control. However, they tend to be susceptible to disease in hot weather and exhibit poor heat and drought tolerance. At present in Virginia, monostands of perennial ryegrass are not capable of providing the level of season-long quality normally associated with a good Kentucky bluegrass mixture without fungicide support. They are best utilized in mixtures with Kentucky bluegrass (5-10% by weight), as noted earlier. Perennial ryegrass is only currently recommended in monostands on heavy traffic areas such as athletic fields where the benefits of rapid germination from seed and traffic tolerance as a mature turf are valued. Variety recommendations are listed with the Kentucky bluegrass recommendations. For standard seedings of perennial ryegrass, use 3-5 pounds per 1000 square feet. Perennial ryegrass also has one additional use for lawns and that is as a winter overseeding component, primarily on bermudagrass lawns. The ryegrass is introduced to the lawn in the early fall for winter color and growth. Typical winter overseeding levels are 5-10 lbs per 1000 square feet for lawns. Remember that the ryegrass will be a competitor with the bermudagrass next spring and will cause a delay in spring greening of the bermudagrass. It is not recommended to oversee any of the other warm-season grasses.

Zoysiagrass

Zoysiagrass is a warm-season grass of fine to medium texture that turns brown with the first hard frost in the fall and greens up about mid-May. Zoysiagrass as a whole has the best cold tolerance of the warm-season grasses used in Virginia, particularly the wider-leaf varieties that are *Z. japonica* species. Finer textured zoysias of the *Z. matrella* species are now used throughout Virginia, but they are not generally considered to be as cold hardy as the *Z. japonica* varieties. It spreads by both rhizomes and stolons, but is a very slow creeper. It is well-suited for lawn use in Virginia and has a low fertility and irrigation requirement. It does well in full sun and has moderate shade tolerance. Its density as a mature turf precludes much weed control and when managed properly, it has very few disease and insect problems as well. The grass has a slow recuperative potential and, therefore, is not recommended for heavily trafficked lawns or athletic fields. It can be established from sod, plugs, or sprigs and with recent developments, a few improved varieties can be established from seed. However, its rate of establishment is extremely slow regardless of the establishment method. Zoysia plugs planted on 12-inch centers will normally require two or three growing seasons to provide full cover. If established from seed, 2-3 lbs of pure live seed per 1000 square feet are recommended, anticipating it will take a full growing season to gain coverage from a mid-spring/early summer planting.

Planting Rate: 2-inch diameter plugs on 6- to 12- inch centers or sprigs broadcast at 7 to 10 bushels per 1000 square feet will require 2 to 3 growing seasons for 100% cover. Planting Dates: May 1 to July 15.

Bermudagrass

Bermudagrass is a fine-bladed, warm-season grass that aggressively creeps by both rhizomes and stolons. Bermudagrass has exceptional drought tolerance and its aggressive growth habit and tolerance to mowing heights of as low as ½ inch make it a great grass for athletic fields and golf course fairways. Its use as a lawn is best suited to the warmest areas of Virginia, but recent releases in cold-hardy varieties (both seeded and vegetative) have expanded the possibility of it being used anywhere in the state. Hybrid bermudagrass can be established by sod, sprigs, or plugs. Two-inch diameter plugs of bermudagrass planted on 12-inch centers will normally provide 95% to 100% cover in one growing season. Seeded bermudagrasses are established at 0.5 to 1 pound of pure live seed per 1000 square feet. Sprigging Rate: 7 to 10 bushels per 1000 square feet. Moderate winter damage can be expected on bermudagrasses once every 6 or 7 years in Virginia.

Centipedegrass

Centipedegrass is a coarse-textured stoloniferous warm-season grass that is adapted in southern Virginia from Martinsville to the coast. It is the lowest maintenance, highest density warm-season grass available. Centipedegrass is established primarily from seed, but sod is available (most coming from farms in the Carolinas). It has a characteristic yellow-green color and prefers acidic soil conditions. Its shade tolerance is moderate and it has very poor traffic tolerance. It is an excellent low-input turf for the warmest climates of Virginia. Centipedegrass is established at levels of ¼ to ½ pound of pure live seed per 1000 square feet.

St. Augustinegrass

St. Augustinegrass is a coarse-textured stoloniferous warm-season grass that has the best shade tolerance of this category. It is grown almost exclusively on the coast of Virginia where the climate is moderated by the ocean and does not persist in any area that has extreme winters. St. Augustinegrass is a very aggressive creeper that has the highest pest pressure (insect and disease) of any of the warm-season grasses. Its use in far southeastern Virginia will primarily focus on shaded lawns and general purpose turfs. St. Augustinegrass can be established by plugs or by sod.

Grass Choices for Virginia Beach

The eastern part of Virginia (zones 7b to 8a) is best suited for warm-season grasses though the predominant lawn grass continues to be the cool-season tall fescue.

Warm-season grasses have the potential for winterkill during extreme winters, they will be dormant (i.e. no green color) 4-5 months out of the year, some are serious weed problems (bermudagrass, aka wiregrass), and not all varieties can be established from seed. However, warm-season grasses typically require 30% less water and have much lower pest pressures than cool-season turfgrasses, so an argument can be made that warm-season lawns can actually be quite 'enviromentally friendly' when properly selected and maintained.

Warm-season grass choices for Virginia Beach include: Bermudagrass, Centipedegrass, St. Augustine, Zoysiagrass. A cool-season option is tall fescue.

Purchasing Quality Seed

The purchase of lawn seed is a long-term investment, as the seed you buy will influence your success in developing a beautiful lawn. It is not possible to evaluate the quality of seed by looking at it. Information that will help you make a wise choice is printed on the seed packages.

There are differences in lawn seed, and it pays to compare. The price you pay for seed will represent only a small portion of the total cost of planting, fertilizing, mowing, etc. Don't let low cost be the only factor you consider when purchasing lawn seed. Choose those varieties that have been tested and proven to be the best for your area of Virginia.

Virginia has a seed label law that is basically a truth-in-labeling law. The label on the package must include an analysis of the seed it contains. This analysis enables the purchaser to determine the kind of seed contained in the package, estimate how well it should perform, and compare its cost-effectiveness with other brands.

Example Seed Label:

Kind: Kentucky bluegrass
Variety: Super-Duper
Pure Seed: 98%
Germination: 85%
Inert Matter: 1%
Date of Test: (month and year)
Other Crop Seed: 0.7%
Lot# – 1A
Weed Seed: 0.3%
Noxious Weeds: 120 Annual Bluegrass per pound
John Doe Seed Co., Richmond, VA

- Germination – The percentage of viable (live) seed. The date of test should be within the last 12 months.
- Pure Seed – The percentage (by weight) that is actually seed of the crop specified.
- Inert Matter – The percentage (by weight) of chaff, dirt, trash, and anything that is not seed.
- Weed Seeds – The percentage (by weight) of all weed seeds in the sample and the number of noxious weed seeds present. If possible, avoid seed lots with noxious weeds.
- Other Crop Seeds – The percentage (by weight) of crop seed other than the crop specified. For example, in tall fescue, this includes orchardgrass and ryegrass. In Kentucky bluegrass, it can include bentgrass, ryegrass, tall fescue, or perennial ryegrass contaminants.

Cost Effectiveness

When considering seed lots of similar quality, compare the amount of pure live seed (PLS) in the package. The only thing you really want to pay for is seed that will grow. To determine the amount of PLS, look at the analysis on the label, multiply the germination percentage by the percentage of pure seed, and then multiply by 100 to get the percentage pure live seed.

Calculating pure living seed example

Germination: = 85%
Purity: = 98%
0.85 x 0.98 = 0.833
0.833 x 100 = 83.3% pure live seed (PLS)

To obtain the cost per pound of PLS, divide the price per pound by the PLS. If the seed costs $2.25 per lb, then 2.25 ÷ 0.833 = $2.70, the actual cost per pound of pure live seed.

Similarly, when it comes to planting rates, use the PLS value. If the recommendation is to plant 2 lbs of pure live seed per 1000 square feet, and the PLS is 83.3, then one needs 2 ÷ 0.833 = 2.4 lbs of seed from the package per 1000 square foot.

Quality

Certified seed is a guarantee from the seller that you will get the kind and variety of lawn seed named on the label. Buying certified seed is a good practice. If the seed is certified, a blue certification label will be attached to the seed package.

The Virginia and Maryland Cooperative Extension Services have worked with the U.S. Department of Agriculture, seed nurseries, and the Virginia Crop Improvement Association to develop a program that helps purchasers recognize quality lawn seed. In both states, special labels are placed on packages containing seed that meets very high standards of purity, germination, and freedom from weed and other crop seed. Seed in a package that carries one of these labels is certified and recommended for use in both states.

Purchasing Quality Sod

There are several types of sod being grown in Virginia. The basic types are Kentucky bluegrass blends, tall fescue-Kentucky bluegrass mixtures, bermudagrass, and zoysiagrass. Each of these types of sod is best suited to particular uses and geographic areas of Virginia. Some sod producers grow sod in the Virginia Crop Improvement Association (VCIA) certified sod program, which means that the sod produced must meet established standards of quality.

VCIA-certified sod is high-quality and meets rigid standards which require preplanting field inspections, prescribed varieties and mixtures, periodic production inspections, and a final preharvest inspection. This program provides the consumer with guaranteed standards of quality. Sod in the VCIA program which cannot quite meet program VCIA-certified standards may be classified as VCIA approved sod and sold at a lower price than sod in the certified category which meets all VCIA standards. VCIA-certified sod can be identified by its label. High quality sod is also available outside the VCIA certified sod program, but it is not graded by standards and quality and can only be ensured by pre purchase inspection. The following four products comprise 98% of Virginia's sod market: Kentucky bluegrass blends, Tall fescue or tall fescue-Kentucky bluegrass mixtures, Bermudagrass, Zoysiagrass.

Annual Lawn Maintenance

The wide variety of microclimates and soil types make it difficult to formulate a uniform program for lawn maintenance in Virginia. The basic factors required for maintaining a lawn are discussed; however, the recommendations may need to be modified for your particular location. As mentioned earlier, the first thing to do is have the soil tested.

In addition to considering the genetic potential of the turfgrass in your lawn, important factors in maintaining high turfgrass quality include an annual program of mowing, fertilization, weed control, irrigation, and leaf management. In addition to these, the following cultural practices may be necessary in some years: dethatching, pH adjustment, aeration, disease control, and insect control. In order for these maintenance practices to be fully effective, their timing is of utmost importance. Please refer to the respective cool-season or warm-season calendar for the optimum timing of main maintenance practices.

Maintenance Calendar for Cool-Season Turfgrasses in Virginia 430-523 (SPES-162P)

- **Seeding (initial establishment and renovation):** Preferred timing August-October, second best timing March-May
- **N Fertilization:** Preferred timing August-October, second best timing March-May and November-December
- **PRE herbicides:** Preferred timing March-April (targeting summer annual weeds) or August-September (targeting annual bluegrass and winter annual broadleaves)
- **POST herbicides:** Preferred timing March-June or August-November (weeds must be actively growing to achieve control with postemergence herbicides)
- **Cultivation/dethatching:** Preferred timing September-November, second best timing March-April

Maintenance Calendar for Warm-Season Turfgrasses in Virginia 430-522 (SPES-161P)

- **Planting (initial establishment and renovation)**: Preferred timing May-June, second best timing July
- **N Fertilization**: Preferred timing April-August, second best timing mid-February-mid-March
- **PRE herbicides**: Preferred timing March-April (targeting summer annual weeds) or August-September (targeting annual bluegrass and winter annual broadleaves)
- **POST herbicides:** Preferred timing March-October, second best timing December-mid-February (weeds must be actively growing to achieve control with postemergence herbicides)
- **Disease concerns:** May-July, September-October
- **Insect concerns:** July-early-August
- **Winter overseeding:** Preferred timing August-early-October
- **Cultivation/dethatching:** Preferred timing May-early-June, second best timing late-June

Genetic Potential

The potential for a lawn to provide a quality surface is very dependent upon the varieties of grass in the lawn. New, improved varieties are being released each year. Periodic infusion of improved varieties will increase the chances of producing a high-quality lawn. The best maintenance program is not likely to overcome the limitations of inferior turfgrasses in the stand.

Mowing

Mowing grass is one of the most time-consuming practices in turfgrass management, and yet the total impact of mowing management is seldom considered. To appreciate the true impact of mowing on turfgrass, it is necessary to understand the physical, environmental, and physiological effects of mowing on the turfgrass community.

The most obvious physical effect of mowing is the decrease in leaf surface area of the grass plants. The grass plant's leaves are the site of photosynthesis, and any decrease in leaf surface area proportionately decreases the plant's ability to produce the carbohydrates essential for root, shoot, rhizome, and stolon growth. If more than 1/3 of the grass vegetation is removed during mowing, root growth is temporarily slowed by the plant's inability to produce carbohydrates at the previous rate. Carbohydrates can be pulled out of reserve to enhance extensive root, rhizome, and stolon development. However, carbohydrate reserves can be called upon to these structures only a limited number of times while the grass plant is recuperating from the shock of a severe mowing. We need to think of mowing primarily as a carbohydrate-depleting management factor. Improper mowing habits can weaken the plant as the mowing season progresses, reducing its recuperative potential and predisposing it to insect, disease, and drought susceptibility. It has been shown that severe defoliation of the grass plant has extreme effects upon root growth. For example, in cases where 50% of the existing Kentucky bluegrass foliage was removed by mowing, only 35% of the roots were producing growth 33 days after mowing.

Wound hormones are produced every time grass is cut. These compounds along with phenol oxidase enzymes are involved in wound-healing. The production of compounds involved in healing mowing wounds occurs at the expense of food reserves. If you are cutting grass with a dull mower, you are creating severe wounds that require more wound healing compounds and therefore more use of stored food reserves. Be sure to keep your mower blades sharp! Continuous use of dull mowers depletes the plant of stored reserves necessary for survival during the stress-filled months of July and August. Eventually the plant's ability to heal the mowing wound is impaired by a lack of food reserves, and the open wound becomes a site of fungal entry leading to serious disease problems. Every unit of plant energy that must be utilized to heal dull mower wounds is simply one less unit that will be available for healing during periods of stress.

Nothing is more mismanaged in lawns than their cutting height. Lowering the mowing height beyond those for which a grass is adapted severely disrupts the environmental and competitive forces that exist in the turfgrass community. In a mixed community of turfgrass plants, some plants will become less competitive as the mowing height is lowered. It is essential to realize that lowering mowing heights to 1 inch or less decreases the amount of leaf area intercepting sunlight. Lower mowing heights increase the number of plants per unit area for some grasses (for instance, some bermudagrass varieties), but it is highly likely that the individual plants in the crowded community become weaker, and for such types of mowing, specialized mowing equipment (i.e. reel mowers) are required. Weaker plants require more intensive management to be able to withstand periods of stress. Suboptimal mowing heights in Kentucky bluegrass and tall fescue often lead to increased weed populations of annual bluegrass and crabgrass. The table below shows recommended mowing heights for turfgrasses commonly used. The lowest ranges of these heights should only be used during the most optimal growing periods of the year (e.g. summer for bermudagrass or zoysiagrass, late summer/early fall and early to mid-spring for tall fescue or Kentucky bluegrass). Mowing at these lower ranges during optimal growing periods can actually improve turfgrass density. However, it is very prudent to begin raising the cutting height of a respective grass 4-6 weeks before the onset of a predictable environmental stress period such as summer or winter. As a rule, raise the cutting height of cool-season grasses in mid-May and raise the cutting height of warm-season grasses in early September so that the grasses are better prepared to survive the coming environmental stress period.

Table 11-3: Turfgrass mowing heights for lawns (inches)

Heights of 1 inch or lower are best achieved with a reel mower

Type of grass	height
Kentucky bluegrass	1.5-2.5
Tall fescue	3-4
Creeping red fescues	2-3
Perennial ryegrass	1.5-2.5
Bermudagrass	0.5-2
Zoysiagrass	0.75-2
Centipedegrass	1-2.5
St. Augustinegrass	3-4

Selecting higher mowing heights for cool-season grasses helps to maximize the amount of food being produced by photosynthesis. Higher mowing heights will reduce stress levels on the turf and, at the same time, increase the likelihood of the grass surviving drought, since root development potential is increased by the higher mowing height.

Frequency of mowing can have severe effects on turfgrass communities. Excessive mowing frequency reduces total shoot yield, rooting, rhizome production, and food reserves. Mowing frequency should be determined by seasonal growth demands, and should be often enough that no more than 1/3 of the existing green foliage is removed by any one mowing.

Collecting clippings on home lawns is not advised. There is no significant benefit to the lawn derived from the collection of clippings if the lawn is being mowed with the proper frequency. Clippings are not a major contributor to thatch buildup. They do provide significant amounts of nutrition to the lawn as they decompose. Three years of returning clippings to a lawn has been shown to increase the growth rate 38% over lawns where clippings were not returned. In addition, earthworm populations increase where clippings are returned, improving aeration and water infiltration.

In summary, mowing is the most frequently necessary maintenance practice in the production of a good lawn. For good results, mow as high as is reasonable for the desired appearance and use of the turf, use a sharp blade, and don't mow more often than necessary – but do mow often enough so that plant height is being reduced by not more than 1/3 each time. A final thought – keep the clippings on the lawn to utilize this 'free fertilizer' and protect water quality that can be endangered from clippings that enter storm water drains.

Fertilization

The time table for fertilizing cool-season grasses is completely different from that of warm-season grasses. Warm-season grasses go dormant during the time when the cool-season grasses make the most effective use of fertilizer for root growth and development.

Late-fall fertilization is essential in the maintenance of quality cool-season grasses. The advantages of late-fall fertilization observed in research and field observation are increased density, increased root growth, decreased spring mowing, improved fall-to-spring color, decreased weed problems, increased drought tolerance, and decreased summer disease activity. The amounts of fertilizer to apply and the time periods when they should be applied are critical.

The ideal lawn fertilization program provides the nutrition that maximizes the chances of producing a quality lawn. Temperature and moisture vary greatly and affect turfgrass growth. Therefore, nutritional needs vary from month to month. Excessive stimulation of growth from nitrogen fertilizers can be more detrimental than no fertilization at all. The source of nitrogen in fertilizers influences nitrogen availability to the turfgrass plant. There are two types of nitrogen sources: quickly available and slowly available. Quickly available materials are water-soluble and can be immediately utilized by the plant. Slowly available nitrogen sources release their nitrogen over extended periods of time and, therefore, can be applied less frequently and at higher rates than the quickly available nitrogen sources.

The numbers on the fertilizer bag (such as 10-10-10 or 46-0-0) indicate the percent of Nitrogen (N), Phosphate (P_2O_5), and potash (K_2O) in the fertilizer. If your soil test indicates low or medium levels of phosphorus or potassium, complete fertilizers (those containing nitrogen, phosphorous, and potassium) should be used. If high levels of phosphorous and potassium are present in the soil, then fertilizers supplying only nitrogen will be adequate.

Fertilizers can provide nitrogen to plants immediately or over an extended period of time. The amount that can be safely applied at one time depends upon the availability of the nitrogen. The portion of the nitrogen that is slowly available is listed on the fertilizer bag as Water Insoluble Nitrogen (WIN). For example, a 20-10-10 fertilizer with 5% WIN actually provides 5/20 or 1/4 of its nitrogen in the slowly available form. A 50 lb. bag of this material would provide 10 lbs. of total Nitrogen (.20 X 50 = 10 lbs.) of which 2.5 lbs. (.05 X 50 = 2.5) would be slowly available (WIN).

A fertilizer label will provide the following information

Guaranteed Analysis

- Total Nitrogen 16%
- Water Insoluble Nitrogen (WIN) 5.6%
- Available Phosphoric Acid (P_2O_5) 4%
- Soluble Potash (K_2O) 8%

The above percentages are relative to the total fertilizer by weight. To find the percentage of WIN relative to the total nitrogen, perform the following calculation:

5.6/16 x 100 = 35%

WIN may also be listed in the asterisked fine print of a water soluble source. For Example:

Guaranteed Analysis

- Total Nitrogen 35%
    - 35.0% Urea Nitrogen*
- Soluble Potash (K_2O) 8%
  *Contains 12% Slowly Available Nitrogen from coated Urea

Note: In this case, total nitrogen percentage (35%) is relative to the total fertilizer by weight, and the urea nitrogen percentage (35%) is relative to the total nitrogen. The slowly available nitrogen percentage (12%) is relative to the total fetilizer (35 x 35/100 = 12.25).

Nitrogen Fertilization of Cool-Season Grasses

Table 11-4: Program I

Nitrogen fertilization of cool-season grasses using predominantly quickly-available nitrogen fertilizers (less than 15% slowly-available nitrogen or WIN)

Nitrogen Application by Month (lbs N/1000 sq ft)

Quality Desired	Sept.	Oct.	Nov.	May 15 to June 15
Low	0.7	0.7	0	0
Medium	0.7	0.7	0.7	0
High	0.7	0.7	0.7	0-0.5

Table 11-5: Program II

Nitrogen fertilization of cool-season grasses using predominantly slowly-available fertilizers (15% or more slowly-available nitrogen or WIN)

Nitrogen Application by Month (lbs N/1000 sq ft)

Quality Desired	Sept.	Oct.	Nov.	May 15 to June 15
Low	0.9	0.6	0	0
Medium	0.9	0.9	0-0.2	0
High	0.9	0.9	0.9	0-0.5

Important Comments about Programs I and II:

- Fine fescues perform best at 1-2 lbs of nitrogen per 1000 sq ft per year.
- Applications in successive months should be at least 30 days apart and deliver no more than 0.7 lb of N per 1000 square feet per active growing month.
- Natural organic and activated sewage sludge products should be applied early in the August 15 to September 15 and the October 1 to November 1 application periods to maximize their effect since they release N due to microbial activity.
- Up to 0.7 lb of nitrogen in Program I and up to 0.9 lb of nitrogen in Program II may be applied per 1000 sq ft in the May 15 to June 15 period if nitrogen was not applied the previous fall or to help a new lawn get better established.

Nitrogen Fertilization of Warm-Season Grasses

Table 11-6: Program III

Nitrogen fertilization of warm-season grasses using predominantly quickly-available nitrogen fertilizers (less than 15% slowly-available nitrogen or WIN)

Nitrogen Application by Month (lbs N/1000 sq ft)

Quality Desired	April	May	June	July/August
Low	0.9	0.9	0	0
Medium	0.9	0.9	0.9	0
High	0.9	0.9	0.9	0.9

Table 11-7: Program IV

Nitrogen fertilization of warm-season grasses using predominantly slowly-available nitrogen (15% or more slowly-available nitrogen or WIN)

Nitrogen Application by Month (lbs N/1000 sq ft)

Quality Desired	April	May	June	July/August
Low	1	1	0	0
Medium	1	1	1	0
High	1	1	1	1

Important Comments about Programs III and IV:

- If overseeded for winter color, add 1/2 to 1 lb of readily available nitrogen per 1000 sq ft in Sept./Oct. and/or Nov.
- Applications in successive months should be approximately four weeks apart.
- Centipedegrass and mature zoysiagrass perform best at 1 to 2 lbs of nitrogen per 1000 sq ft per year.
- Improved winter hardiness on bermudagrass will result from the application of potassium in late August or September.

If no WIN is listed on the fertilizer label, assume that it is all water-soluble or quickly available nitrogen, unless the fertilizer label indicates that it contains sulfur-coated urea. Sulfur-coated urea fertilizers provide slowly available nitrogen, but the fertilizer label does not list it as WIN. If the fertilizer contains sulfur-coated urea, include that portion as water insoluble nitrogen when determining the portion of the fertilizer that is slowly available.

Statements on a fertilizer bag such as "contains 50% organic fertilizer" do not mean that the fertilizer is 50% slowly available. It is impossible to calculate the amount of WIN from this information. For example, Urea (46-0-0) which contains carbon, hydrogen, oxygen, and nitrogen, is in fact an "organic" fertilizer, yet it contains no slow release nitrogen.

Weed Control

Weeds in the landscape are considered as a sub-category of pests. As such, Integrated Pest Management (IPM) applies equally to weeds. For more information on IPM, see Chapter 7 "Integrated Pest Management and Pesticide Safety"

Weed control can be minimized by good mowing and fertilization management, since this makes grass more capable of competing with weeds. If chemical control should be necessary, care should be taken to apply chemicals at the time of year when they will be most effective. Follow label directions closely and never exceed recommended rates. Improper application of weed control chemicals can result in damage to desirable grasses, ornamental plantings, and the environment.

There are two basic groups of weeds: broadleaf weeds and weedy grasses. Broadleaf weeds consist of the familiar dandelions, chickweed, clover, ground ivy, wild onions, oxalis, plantain, and anything which is not classed as a grass. Examples of weedy grasses are nimblewill, quackgrass, crabgrass, and goosegrass. Of course, even what is a desirable turfgrass for some can be a serious weed for others (e.g. bermudagrass in tall fescue, creeping bentgrass in Kentucky bluegrass). Control for each of the two groups varies.

There are good selective herbicides available for broadleaf weed control. In general, broadleaf weeds respond best to weed killers when they are most actively growing and/or in the seedling stage. This is usually in early to mid fall and mid to late spring. When equally effective, fall applications are preferable because fewer ornamental and garden plants are in an active state of growth. Applications of high rates of weed killer during hot, dry conditions may brown desirable grasses. Annual weedy grasses such as crabgrass, foxtail, and goosegrass are controlled with preemergence herbicides that are applied in the spring, prior to germination. Pesticide recommendations for control of specific broadleaf and grassy weeds are contained in the VCE Pest Management Guide.

Control of perennial weedy grass such as common bermudagrass, nimblewill, and quackgrass is more difficult because selective herbicides that have activity generally can not control the weed in single applications. Therefore, persistence in weed treatment is required and in some instances spot spraying, physical removal, or total kill of existing lawns may be necessary. Pesticide options for controlling perennial weedy grass are available in the VCE Pest Management Guide.

Sedges are often called 'nutgrass' but they are not in the grass family. They can easily be identified by their triangular stem. Sedges can be controlled with use of herbicides that specifically target sedges. These herbicides do not damage mature turfgrass. Sedges are warm-season in nature and there are both annual and perennial biotypes. They are best controlled soon after their emergence in early-mid summer.

Control of mosses is usually done through cultural means. Improving surface drainage, reducing soil compaction, improving soil fertility and adjusting the pH can improve the ability of turf to outcompete moss. While some selective pruning can increase exposure to sunlight, lack of sunlight is often the main reason for moss to out complete turf in soil that has improved to otherwise favor turf. In this case, alternative ground covers are a better option than turf.

Weed Identification

Virginia Tech's Weed Identification website is a very comprehensive weed identification tool: Virginia Tech Weed ID website (https://weedid.cals.vt.edu/). Additional resources for weed identification include: VCE publication "Identification of Virginia's Noxious Weeds" SPES-244NP

Virginia Cooperative Extension also offers weed identification services through its Weed ID clinic. For more information on weeds, see the current VCE Pest Management Guide.

Irrigation

Lawns can use an inch or more of water per week in hot, dry weather. If rainfall does not provide this much water and soil moisture reservoirs are depleted, irrigation will be necessary to keep the lawn green. The lawn should be watered when the soil begins to dry out but before the grass actually wilts. At that stage, areas of the lawn will begin to change color, displaying a blue-gray or smoky tinge. Also, loss of resilience can be observed; footprints will make a long-lasting imprint instead of bouncing right back. Alternate wetting and drying periods are normal and beneficial to developing balanced microbial activity in soils. Ideally, the lawn should be watered shortly after the development of the blue-grey cast noted above.

Cool-season grasses usually go semi-dormant in the hottest part of the summer, returning to full vigor in cooler fall weather. If you want to keep the lawn green through the summer, regular deep watering will be necessary. If the lawn does go dormant (turns brown), let it stay that way until it naturally greens up again. Too many fluctuations between dormancy and active growth can weaken the lawn.

Light sprinkling of the surface is actually more harmful than not watering at all, since this encourages root development near the surface and increases crabgrass germination. This limited root system will require more frequent waterings and will necessitate keeping the surface wet, which is ideal for weeds and diseases. Watering should be an "all or nothing" type of commitment. If you water, do it consistently and deeply. If you don't intend to be consistent, it is better not to water at all and to allow the grass to go dormant until natural conditions bring it back. Encouraging deep root growth by irrigating infrequently, but heavily, will maximize water use efficiency and turfgrass quality.

The best time to water a lawn is in the early morning. Evaporation is minimized and water-use efficiency is better than during midday. Early evening or night watering is not encouraged because it leaves the blades and thatch wet at night. This maximizes the potential for disease activity.

Dethatching

In addition to regular maintenance factors already discussed, in some years it may be necessary to remove thatch from lawns with thatch-forming grasses. Thatch is the tightly interwoven layer of living and dead stems, leaves, and roots that exists between the green blades of grass and the soil surface. This layer of decomposing organic matter accumulates on the soil surface in an innocuous fashion. During the early stages of thatch development, when it measures less than 0.5 inch in thickness, it can actually be beneficial to the grass. Thin layers of thatch can increase wear tolerance of turf by providing better dissipation of compaction forces, reducing weed populations by providing hostile conditions for germination, reducing water evaporation by blocking sunlight and air exchange with the soil surface, and insulating crown tissue, protecting it from frost and traffic damage. Thatch problems are inevitable with certain grasses under intensive turfgrass management programs unless thatch reduction principles are built into the program. The single cause of thatch buildup is the fact that the accumulation rate of dead organic matter and stems on the soil surface is greater than the decomposition rate. There are many reasons for this imbalance between rate of accumulation and decomposition. Some of the factors involved include excessively high nitrogen levels, the type of turfgrass, excessive irrigation, mowing management, chemical use, and soil type.

The effect of excessive thatch buildup upon turfgrass quality is subtle but deadly. This layer of undecomposed organic matter is capable of altering pest populations, moisture relations, nutrient utilization patterns, soil temperatures, and other climatic and biotic factors.

For all intents and purposes, thatch is not caused by leaf clippings. Recycle clippings to the lawn to take advantage of their nutrient composition.

The moist microclimate created by the thatch layer favors fungal invasion and allows pathogenic microorganisms to live and sporulate. The probability of insect pathogens surviving the winter is increased by the insulating effect of thatch. Soil-borne fungus and insect pathogens often escape control methods due to the inability of applied pesticides to penetrate the thatch layer. The thatch layer prevents adequate water infiltration, causing reduced root growth and increased potential for wilt damage. When thatch layers are kept moist, roots tend to develop in this zone, and crown regions of the individual turfgrass plants tend to be elevated in the thatch. This elevation of the crown region away from the soil leads to increased exposure to temperature extremes and a greater probability of stress-related damage. Interception of lime and fertilizer applications by thatch layers produces erratic fertilizer response. In some cases, the microorganisms tie up the applied nitrogen, rendering it unavailable to the turfgrass plants.

Preventive thatch management involves turfgrass selection, modification of nutrition, cultivation, mowing, and irrigation practices. Kentucky bluegrass, creeping red fescue, bermudagrass, zoysiagrass, and St. Augustinegrass are all prone to thatch development under intensive management because they produce lateral stems. Tall fescue and perennial ryegrass, bunch type-grasses, are low thatch producers and if they do produce thatch, then they are being mismanaged in terms of N fertilization.

Figure 11-4 shows a block of turf with thatch, mat, and soil layers in profile. Note that the crown of the grass plant is elevated into the thatch layer. The mat is the layer of decomposing thatch which is becoming integrated into the soil. There is no simple method of controlling thatch development. Preventive programs for thatch reduction should be built into the maintenance program. Curative programs involving the labor-intensive process of dethatching may also be required at times.

The pH of the thatch layer appears to be more important to thatch decomposition than soil pH. Researchers have shown that light annual applications of lime (20 to 25 lbs. per 1000 square feet) may be beneficial in speeding the thatch decomposition rate. Moderate use of nitrogen with more frequent small applications appears to decrease thatch buildup. Aerification and topdressing of turfgrass speeds up thatch decomposition by returning microbes into the thatch layer and improving the environment for their maximum activity. Aerobic microorganisms involved in the thatch decomposition benefit from improved oxygen levels as much as the turfgrass. Earthworm castings serve to inoculate the thatch layer with microorganisms and soil to improve moisture retention in the thatch layer, thus increasing microbial activity.

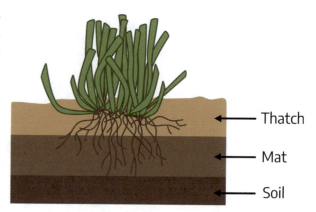

Figure 11-4: Thatch buildup and decomposition mat.

If the thatch layer in your lawn is more than 2 inches thick, dethatching and/or aeration will be beneficial. Timing of these is critical, and is best done during periods when the plants can recover from the treatment. Warm-season grasses should be dethatched in early to mid-summer. Kentucky bluegrass and other cool-season grass lawns should be dethatched in early fall or early spring. Spring **verticutting** can lead to excessive crabgrass invasion if improperly timed. Vertical mowers and aerifiers can be rented. Dethatchers physically remove thatch and deposit it on the surface of the lawn. This material should then be raked up and removed. If overseeding is planned, it is good to do this in conjunction with the verticutting or aerating process, since the grooves cut in the soil will provide good soil contact for the new seed.

pH Adjustment

Soils in Virginia are typically acid, and from time to time it may be necessary to add lime in order to keep the soil pH near 6.2. Soil test results will tell how much lime should be applied.

Aeration

If soil is heavy or compacted, or thatch buildup is a problem, aeration may be necessary. Roots need oxygen as well as water and nutrients. Compacted soil restricts the absorption of water and does not allow the soil to exchange oxygen with the atmosphere.

Aeration is best done by a machine which forces hollow metal tubes into the ground and brings up small cores of soil which are left laying on the surface. The soil should be moist, not too wet or too dry, when this is done. Simply punching holes with a spiked roller may improve water retention, but this practice also increases compaction in the soil. Reinoculation of thatch layers with soil and microbes through the aeration process is beneficial in helping to create an environment conducive to thatch decomposition. Another great soil improvement strategy to tie together with core aeration is a surface application of compost. As little as ¼ inch depth of compost one to two times per year is an important way to improve soil physical and chemical properties and reduce fertilizer, water, and pesticide water inputs for the turf over time.

Disease Control

Proper management will greatly reduce a lawn's susceptibility to disease. Disease damage may be difficult to identify, since many of the symptoms may also be caused by improper management or by environmental factors such as competition from tree roots. Nearly all lawn diseases are caused by fungi, and fungicides can be applied to prevent and control them.

Disease or sickness in turfgrasses, as in other plants, develops from an interaction between a susceptible plant, a disease-producing organism (usually a fungus), and an environment favorable for the disease-causing organism to attack. Scientists who work with turfgrass diseases sometimes use a disease triangle to illustrate the concept of disease. The three sides of the **disease triangle** represent three factors that interact to produce turfgrass disease: the disease causer, the susceptible grass, and a favorable environment (Figure 11-5). Three factors interact to cause turfgrass disease; therefore we must observe all three factors to gather information for diagnosis of the problem, and we can change any or all of these three factors to combat the disease.

The first step in turfgrass disease management is the identification of the problem. Disease management strategies that are effective against one disease may have no effect on or may even worsen another disease.

The three factors (grass, disease-causer, and environment) provide the sources of information for diagnosis (Figure 11-6). The environment during the onset of the disease is one source of diagnostic information. For example, what were the temperature, the light intensity, and the moisture conditions just prior to and during disease development? The nature of the disease site is also important. Air and water drainage, soil conditions, sun/shade, slope, and nearness of other plantings or buildings may all be important in development of turfgrass diseases. Prior chemical applications to the site, including pesticides and fertilizers, may be contributive. Heavy thatch accumulation and poor mowing practices that stress the turf may trigger or amplify certain disease problems in turf areas.

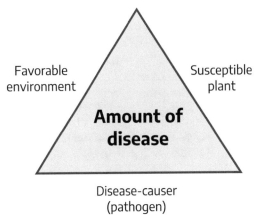

Figure 11-5: Disease triangle.

The nature of the symptoms on the grass is a very important source of diagnostic information. Two kinds of symptoms should be looked for in diseased turfgrass areas- symptoms on the stand, and symptoms on individual plants. A home lawn, an athletic field, and a golf green or fairway are all examples of turf stands. Symptoms on the stand are the appearance and the visible patterns of the disease on the planting. These are extremely important in turfgrass disease diagnosis because different diseases appear differently on turf stands. The visible differences in pattern are often critical factors in identifying particular diseases. Diseases can appear on the turf stand as spots, patches, rings, circles, or may be unpatterned. Certain diseases never appear as rings, while others always appear as rings. Symptoms to look for on individual plants include leaf spots, leaf blight, wilt, stunt, yellowing, and root discoloration or rot. Leaf spots can be very good diagnostic clues because the leaf spots of diseases are usually unique in shape, color, and size. Leaf blighting is different from these unique leaf spots because leaf blighting is rot on the leaf that has no definite form. Leaf blighting can be any size or shape and may involve the entire leaf.

Certain life stages of turfgrass disease-causers can be seen without magnification. The fungi that cause most turfgrass diseases are microscopic. But in stripe smut, powdery mildew, and rust diseases, that spores of the causal fungi pile up in such numbers that they become visible as black, white, or orange powder on grass leaves. In red thread disease, the fungus sticks together and forms the pink or red antler-like threads that typify the disease. When the causal fungus can be seen, its appearance is often the most important clue for diagnosis.

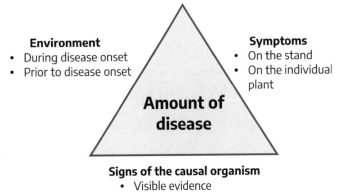

Figure 11-6: Diagnosis triangle.

Because the three components of disease development combine to influence the onset of turfgrass disease, the task of disease management on turfgrasses involves manipulation of these three – the environment, the grass, and/or the disease-causing organism – to favor the grass and inhibit the causal fungus.

The environment can be altered in many ways. The ones chosen depend on the disease to be managed. Water manipulation can be a valuable tool in disease management. Effective strategies to reduce free water include morning irrigation, removal of dew, and reduction in amount and/or frequency of irrigation. Other management strategies may involve some forms of improved air and water drainage, improved soil conditions by aeration, thatch reduction, manipulation of light conditions, regulation of fertilization levels, and implementation of proper mowing practices.

When establishing new turf areas or when renovating disease-damaged turf, it is important to select grasses that are resistant to diseases known to be common in the area or that have damaged the existing stand. Disease resistant grasses can be seeded to minimize turf loss from disease. Disease severity can often be reduced by appropriate changes in the grass that is being grown. It is a bad practice to replant that same grass that has been killed by the same disease year after year, if there is another option. In selecting grasses for turf establishment or renovation, it is preferable, where possible, to use mixtures of different grasses or blends of different varieties rather than seeding a single kind of grass. The seeding of mixtures or blends produces a diverse population of grass plants. Such turf is usually more likely to survive stress caused by disease. Diversity in plantings almost always increases odds of survival.

The causal organism may be attacked by applying chemicals that will either kill the organism or keep it from growing. Again, it is important to have identified the causal organism correctly, so that an appropriate fungicide can be selected. Arbitrary selection and application of fungicides without knowledge of the disease can do as much harm as good. Using the wrong fungicide wastes money, and may increase the amount of disease or produce other undesirable side effects.

Planning an effective disease management program involves not only "spraying something," but selecting cost effective and environmentally sound disease control strategies. The financial, environmental, and aesthetic costs of disease management strategies must be considered. Good, common sense approaches to disease management should employ all available disease management strategies.

The Virginia Tech Disease Diagnostic Lab provides identification services for samples that are handled through local Virginia Cooperative Extension offices.

Insect Control

There are naturally many different types of insects present in a lawn. Most of these are not harmful to the grass. Control for insects is not necessary unless the pest population builds up enough to cause visible damage to the lawn.

Close examination on hands and knees is the best way to identify insect pests in a damaged lawn. You may be able to see the insect in action. If you think you have an insect problem, your local Extension Office can help in identifying the pest and suggesting recommended control measures.

The most common above-ground insect pests in Virginia lawns are chinch bugs and sod webworms which feed on grass leaves and stems. Below ground, the most common pests are white grub larvae which feed on roots.

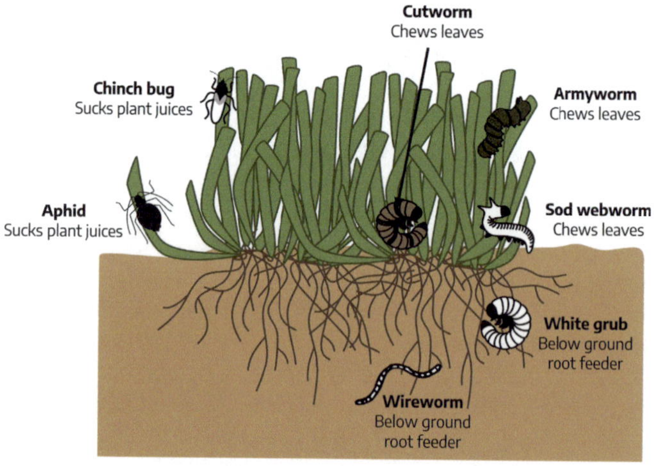

Figure 11-7: Lawn insects above and below ground. Certain insects (wireworm, white grub) feed on roots while others (cutworm, army worm) chew leaves or suck plant juices (chinch bug, aphid).

Chinch Bugs are small, white and black insects that suck sap from grass, producing yellow and then brown patches. To test for chinch bugs, cut both ends off of a large tin can, push one end into the soil, and fill the can with water. Chinch bugs will float to the surface if present.

Sod Webworms are the larval or caterpillar stage of several species of Lepidoptera. Adults are commonly seen flying in jerky, short flights as you walk through the grass. Caterpillars do the damage, feeding on the grass blades at night. Sod webworms prefer well-managed lawns. Damage appears as small brown areas in the grass.

White Grubs are the larval or grub stage of several species of beetles and chafers. Typically cream-colored with a brown head and a dark area at the posterior end, white grubs feed on roots, causing brown areas in the lawn. Usually turf can be rolled back like a rug to reveal white grubs.

Additional Resources

- Identification of Virginia's Noxious Weeds SPES-244NP
- VCE Pest Management Guide
- Virginia Crop Improvement Association (VCIA): http://www.virginiacrop.org/
- Virginia Tech Soil Testing Lab: https://www.soiltest.vt.edu/
- VCE Turf and Garden Tips podcast: https://ext.vt.edu/lawn-garden/turfandgardentips.html

Attributions

- JC Gardner, Portsmouth Extension Master Gardener (2021 reviser)
- Khosro Aminpour, Albemarle/Charlottesville Extension Master Gardener (2021 reviser)
- Mike Goatley, Jr., Extension Specialist, Turfgrass (2015 reviser)
- Thomas P. Kuhar, Professor, Department of Entomology (2015 reviser)

Image Attributions

- Figure 11-1: Pile of freshly cut sod in field. "Sod used for landscaping" by Bob Nichols for USDA from Flickr. 2013. CC BY-SA 2.0
- Figure 11-2: Plug. Grey, Kindred. 2022. CC BY-NC-SA 4.0.
- Figure 11-3: Sprigs. Grey, Kindred. 2022. CC BY-NC-SA 4.0.
- Figure 11-4: Thatch buildup and decomposition mat. Grey, Kindred. 2022. CC BY-NC-SA 4.0.
- Figure 11-5: Disease triangle. Grey, Kindred. 2022. CC BY-NC-SA 4.0.
- Figure 11-6: Diagnosis triangle. Grey, Kindred. 2022. CC BY-NC-SA 4.0.
- Figure 11-7: Lawn insects above and below ground. Grey, Kindred. 2022. CC BY-NC-SA 4.0. Includes aphid by Phạm Thanh Lộc from Noun Project, worm by Sean Maldjian from Noun Project, and Caterpillar by Kevin from Noun Project (all Noun Project license).

CHAPTER 12: INDOOR PLANTS

Chapter Contents:

- Purchasing an Indoor Plant
- Factors Affecting Plant Growth Indoors
- Growing Media
- Containers
- Repotting
- Training and Grooming
- Common Indoor Plant Pests
- Care of Specific Plants
- Terrariums and Dish Gardens
- Plant Lists
- Additional Resources

This chapter is designed to familiarize you with the basic aspects of indoor plant care rather than attempting to acquaint you with specific cultural requirements of the more than 250 common plants available for indoor growth. Indoor plant gardeners need to carefully select plants that can best withstand the conditions of a specific indoor location, as home and office locations are often challenging environments for plants to thrive.

Purchasing an Indoor Plant

When purchasing a plant, consider the environmental conditions of where it will live, such as light, temperature, humidity, and ventilation. Select plants that are sturdy, clean, well-potted, and shapely. Plants which have new flower and leaf buds along with young growth are usually of superior quality.

Choose plants with healthy foliage. Check the undersides of the foliage and the axils of leaves for signs of insects or disease.

Avoid plants which have yellow or chlorotic leaves, brown leaf margins, wilted foliage, spots or blotches, or spindly growth. In addition, avoid those with torn leaves and those which have been treated with "leaf shines," which add an unnatural polish to the leaves.

Remember that it is easier to purchase a plant which requires the same environmental conditions your residence has than to alter the environment of your home to suit the plants.

Transporting House Plants

When transporting plants, remember that heat or cold weather can cause damage to the plants. In the summer, avoid leaving the vehicle shut because temperatures will rise and destroy the plant in a short period of time. The plant can be burned by the sun shining on it even though the air conditioner is on and it's comfortable in the vehicle. Shade the plant from direct sun while it is in the vehicle.

Transporting a tropical indoor plant in very low temperatures can kill or severely damage plants. During the winter, you may need to wrap plants with newspaper or paper bags, place in the front of the vehicle, and turn on the heater. In most vehicles, the trunk or covered truck bed is too cold to carry plants safely during winter.

On an extended trip, make special arrangements so that plants will not be frozen or damaged by cold weather. Many foliage plants will be damaged considerably if the temperature drops below 50°F, so maintain as warm a temperature as possible around these plants when transporting them from one location to another. Never allow wind to blow across them from open car windows.

Acclimatization

Tropical plants grown in full sun have leaves (sun leaves) which are structurally different from the leaves of plants grown in shade (shade leaves). Sun leaves have fewer chloroplasts, and thus less chlorophyll. Their chloroplasts are located deep inside the leaves and the leaves are thick, small, and large in number. Shade leaves have greater numbers of chloroplasts and thus more chlorophyll, are thin, large, and few in number. When plants are grown in strong light, they develop sun leaves which are photosynthetically very inefficient. If these same plants are placed in low light, they must either remake existing sun leaves or drop their sun leaves and grow a new set of shade leaves which are photosynthetically more efficient. To reduce the shock which occurs when a plant with sun leaves is placed in shade, gradually reduce the light levels it is exposed to. This process is called acclimatization. The gardener should acclimatize plants when placing them outdoors in summer by gradually increasing light intensities, and reverse the process before plants are brought indoors in the fall. For newly purchased plants grown in high-light conditions, acclimatize them by initially locating them in a high-light (southern exposure) area of your home and gradually moving them to their permanent, darker location over a period of 4 to 8 weeks.

Factors Affecting Plant Growth Indoors

Light, water, temperature, humidity, ventilation, fertilization, and soil are chief factors affecting plant growth, and any one of these factors in incorrect quantity will prevent proper plant growth indoors.

Light

Light is probably the most essential factor for indoor plant growth because they use this energy source to photosynthesize. When examining light levels for tropical plants, consider three aspects of light: intensity, duration, and quality.

Light intensity influences the manufacture of plant food, stem length, leaf color, and flowering. A geranium grown in low light tends to be spindly and the leaves light green in color. A similar plant grown in very bright light would tend to be shorter, better branched, and have larger, dark green leaves. Indoor plants can be classified according to their light needs by high, medium, and low light requirements. The intensity of light a plant receives indoors depends upon the nearness of the light source to the plant (light intensity decreases rapidly when moved away from the source of light). The direction the windows in your home face will affect the intensity of natural sunlight that plants receive. Southern exposures have the most intense light, eastern and western exposures receive about 60% of the intensity of southern exposures, and northern exposures receive 20% of a southern exposure. A southern exposure is the warmest, a western exposure is warmer than eastern as it receives the warm afternoon sun, and a northern exposure is the coolest. Other factors which can influence the intensity of light penetrating a window are the presence of curtains, trees outside the window, weather, seasons of the year, shade from other buildings, and the cleanliness of the window. Reflective (light-colored) surfaces inside the home/office will increase the intensity of light available to plants. Dark surfaces will decrease light intensity. Excessive dust on leaves can decrease light intensity reaching the leaves.

Day-length or duration of light received by plants is also of some importance, but generally only to those plants which are photosensitive. Poinsettia, kalanchoe, and Christmas cactus bud and flower only when day-length is short (11 hours of daylight or less). Most flowering indoor plants are indifferent to day-length. More information on this topic can be found in the "Environmental Factors Affecting Plant Growth" section in Chapter 1: Botany.

Low light intensity can be compensated by increasing the time (duration) the plant is exposed to light, as long as the plant is not sensitive to day-length in its flowering response. Increased hours of lighting allow the plant to make sufficient food to survive and/or grow. However, plants require some period of darkness to develop properly, and thus should be illuminated for no more than 16 hours. Excessive light is as harmful as too little light. When a plant gets too much direct light, the leaves become pale, sometimes burn, turn brown, and die. Therefore, during the summer months, protect plants from too much direct sunlight.

Light quality is the third aspect that should be taken into consideration with indoor plants. **Light quality** refers to the spectral distribution of light, or the number of different colored photons emitted by the light source (for example, blues, reds, greens). Additional lighting may be supplied by either incandescent or fluorescent lights. Incandescent lights produce a great deal of heat and are not very efficient users of electricity. If artificial lights are to be used as the only source of light for growing plants, the quality of light (wavelength) must be considered. For photosynthesis, plants require mostly blues and reds, but for flowering, infrared light is also needed. Incandescent lights produce mostly red and some infrared light, but are very low in blues. Fluorescent lights vary according to the phosphorus used by the manufacturer. Cool-white lights produce mostly blue light, and are low in red light. Foliage plants grow well under cool-white fluorescent lights, which are also cool enough to position quite close to plants. Blooming plants require extra infrared light which can be supplied by incandescent lights or special horticultural-type (fluorescent or LED) lights.

Water

Overwatering and underwatering account for a large percentage of tropical plant losses. The most common question gardeners ask is, "How often should I water my plants?" There is not a good answer to this question. Some plants like drier conditions than others. Differences in potting medium and environment influence water needs. Watering as soon as the soil crust dries can result in overwatering.

Figure 12-1: Black root root on a potted plant. Root rot can be caused by over watering.

Plant roots are usually in the bottom 2/3 of the pot, so do not water until the bottom 2/3 starts to dry out slightly. You can't tell this by looking at the plant. By the time the plant wilts or changes color due to lack of water, it has been damaged and will be less vigorous. You have to feel the soil. For a 6-inch pot, stick your index finger about 2 inches into the soil (approximately to the second joint of your finger). If the soil feels damp, don't water. Keep repeating the test until the soil is barely moist at the 2-inch depth. For smaller pots, 1 inch into the soil is the proper depth to measure.

Water the pot until water runs out of the bottom. This serves two purposes. First, it washes out all the excess salts (fertilizer residue). Second, it guarantees that the bottom 2/3 of the pot, which contains most of the roots, receives sufficient water. However, don't let the pot sit in the water that runs out. After a thorough watering, wait until the soil dries at the 2-inch depth before watering again. If the soil has become excessively dry and pulled away from the sides of the pot, it will be necessary to soak the container in the sink or other container until the soil is fully rehydrated and expanded. When testing for watering, pay attention to the soil. If your finger can't penetrate 2 inches deep, the plant either needs a more porous soil mix or the plant is becoming root-bound.

Be aware of the temperature of the water. Cold water can stun or damage some tropical plants. Warm or room temperature water is best.

Temperature

Most house plants tolerate normal temperature fluctuations. In general, indoor foliage plants grow best between 70 and 80°F during the day and from 60 to 68°F at night. Most flowering indoor plants prefer the same daytime range but grow best at nighttime temperatures from 55 to 60°F. The lower night temperature induces physiological recovery from moisture loss, intensifies flower color, and prolongs flower life. Excessively low or high temperatures may cause plant failures, stop growth, or cause spindly appearance and foliage damage or drop. A cooler temperature at night is actually more desirable for plant growth than higher temperatures. A good rule of thumb is to keep the night temperature 10 to 15° lower then the day temperature. When purchasing a new plant, check the label or do research on ideal temperature conditions. Some plants prefer cooler temperatures, while some need warm temperatures.

Humidity

Atmospheric humidity is expressed as a percentage of the moisture saturation of air. When humidity is too low, brown tips and margins may appear on tropical plant leaves. To provide increased humidity, attach a humidifier to the heating or ventilating system in the home, or place gravel trays (in which an even water level is maintained) under the plant containers. This will increase the relative humidity in the vicinity of the containers. As the moisture around the pebbles evaporates, the relative humidity is raised. Make sure the bottom of the pot does not come in contact with the water in the pebble tray, as it could soak up too much water and damage the plant roots.

Another way to raise humidity is to group plants close together. Some people spray a fine mist on the foliage, however, this is of doubtful effectiveness for total humidity modification unless repeated frequently throughout the day. Time this so that the plants will be dry by night. This lessens the chance of disease, since cool dampness at night provides an ideal environment for disease.

Fertilization

Indoor plants, like most other plants, need fertilizers containing three major plant food elements: nitrogen (N), phosphorus (P), and potassium (K). They are available in many different combinations and under a multitude of brand names. Each brand should be analyzed on the label, indicating specifically how much water-soluble elemental nitrogen, phosphate, or potash is available in every pound of the product. The three numbers on a package of fertilizer, such as 20-5-20, indicate the percentages (by weight) of nitrogen, phosphorus, and potassium, respectively, in the fertilizer product. Commercial fertilizers used for indoor plants are sold in granular, crystalline, liquid, or tablet forms. Each should be used according to instructions on the package label. Frequency of fertilizer application varies somewhat with the vigor of growth and age of each plant. Some need it every 2 weeks, while others will flower well for several months without needing any supplement. As a general rule, fertilize every 2 weeks from March to September. During the winter months, no fertilizer is needed because reduced light and temperature result in reduced growth. Fertilizing at this time could be detrimental to some plants.

Soluble Salts

Reduced growth, brown leaf-tips, dropping of lower leaves, small new growth, dead root-tips, and wilting are all signs of high **soluble salts**. These salts will accumulate on top of the soil forming a yellow to white crust. A ring of salt deposits may be formed around the pot at the soil line or around the drainage hole. Salts will also build up on the outside of clay pots, but is generally not harmful.

Soluble salts are minerals dissolved in water. Fertilizer dissolved in water becomes a soluble salt. When water evaporates from the soil, the minerals or salts stay behind. As the salts in the soil become more and more concentrated, plants find it harder and harder to take up water. If salts build to an extremely high level, water can be taken out of the root-tips, causing them to die.

High soluble salts damage the roots directly, and because the plant is weakened, it is more susceptible to attack from insects and diseases. One of the most common problems associated with high salt levels is root rot.

The best way to prevent soluble salt injury is to stop the salts from building up. Water correctly. When you water, allow some water to drain through, and then empty the drip plate. Water equal to 1/10 the volume of the pot should drain through each time you water. Do not allow the pot to sit in the water! If you allow the drained water to be absorbed by the soil, the salts that were washed out are taken back into the soil. Salts can be reabsorbed through the drainage hole or directly through a clay pot.

Plants should be leached every 4 to 6 months. Leach a plant before fertilizing so that the fertilizer does not wash away. Water the soil thoroughly as usual. Then, after about five minutes, water again, letting excess water flow out the bottom drain holes. The first watering dissolves the fertilizer salts. The second washes the salt out of the soil. If a layer of salts has formed a crust on top of the soil, you should remove the salt crust before you begin to leach. Do not remove more than 1/4 inch of soil. It is best not to add more soil to the top of the pot. If the soluble salt level is extremely high or the pot has no drainage, repot the plant.

The level of salts that will cause injury varies with the type of plant and how it is being grown. A plant grown in the home may be injured by salts at concentrations of 200 ppm. The same plant growing in a greenhouse, where the light and drainage are good, will grow with salts at 10 times that level, or 2000 ppm. Some nurseries and plant shops leach plants to remove excess salts before the plant is sold. Consider leaching newly purchased plants the first time you water them.

Growing Media

The potting soil or medium in which a plant grows, must be of good quality. It should be porous for root aeration and drainage, but also capable of water and nutrient retention. Most commercially prepared mixes are termed soil-less, which means they contain no soil. High-quality artificial mixes generally contain slow-release fertilizers, which take care of a plant's nutritional requirements for several months. You can also prepare your own soil-less mix.

Preparing Soil-less Mixes

Soil-less mixtures can be prepared with a minimum of difficulty. Most mixes contain a combination of organic matter, such as peat moss or ground pine bark, and an inorganic material, like washed sand, vermiculite, or perlite. Materials commonly used for indoor plants are the peat-lite mixtures, consisting of peat moss and either vermiculite or perlite. The following are the most common media components.

Peat moss is readily available baled or bagged; sphagnum peat moss is recommended. Such materials as Michigan peat, peat humus, and native peat are usually too decomposed to provide necessary structural and drainage characteristics. Most sphagnum peat moss is acid in reaction with a pH ranging from 4.0 to 5.0. It usually has a very low fertility level. Sphagnum peat moss is mined, creating concerns about environmental damage, while **coconut coir** is readily renewable and environmentally friendlier than peat moss. Coir is a pH-neutral, non-hydrophobic soil amendment that aerates and improves water retention of soil.

Figure 12-2: Sphagnum peat moss.

Vermiculite is a sterile, lightweight, mica product. When mica is heated to approximately 1800°F, its plate-like structure expands. Vermiculite will hold large quantities of air, water, and nutrients needed for plant growth. Its pH is usually in the 6.5 to 7.2 range. Vermiculite is available in four particle sizes. For horticultural mixes, sizes 2 or 3 are generally used. If at all possible, the larger-sized particles should be used, since they give much better soil aeration. Vermiculite is available under a variety of trade names. Vermiculite collapses with time and loses its positive characteristics.

Perlite is a sterile material produced by heating volcanic rock to approximately 1800°F. The result is a very lightweight, porous material that is white in color. Its principal value in soil mixtures is aeration. It does not hold water and nutrients as well as vermiculite. The pH is usually between 7.0 and 7.5. Perlite can cause fluoride burn on some foliage plants, usually on the tips of the leaves. The burn progresses from the tip up into the leaf. Fluoride burns can be prevented by adding 1 1/2 times the recommended amount of lime when mixing the soil. Artificial mixtures are usually very low in trace or minor elements, therefore, it is important to use a fertilizer that contains these trace elements. A good formula for artificial mix (makes 3 bushels of media) follows.

- 1 bushel shredded coconut coir or peat moss
- 2 bushels perlite or vermiculite
- 1/2 cup finely ground agricultural lime
- 1/3 cup 20% superphosphate
- 1/2 cup 8-8-8 or similar analysis mixed fertilizer
- 1 level teaspoon chelated iron

Soil Mixes for Specific Plants

Soils must have the most efficient composition for the type of plant to be grown. We can divide indoor plant soils into four distinct groups, according to the type of plant to which they are most suited.

Artificial soil mixes work well but a mixture with soil could be used. Any soil containing garden loam should be pasteurized. This can be done easily at home. Spread the soil on a cookie tray and bake it at 180°F for 30 minutes. Do not heat it longer than 30 minutes, and be aware that it will smell unpleasant while baking.

Foliage Plants: This soil should be moderately rich, have a good base of clay loam, and hold moisture and fertility adequately. It must be a crumbly, well-textured soil. It is generally made up of one part of good garden loam, one part of clean sand or perlite, and half to one part of either peat moss, compost, leaf mold, or vermiculite. Mixing about 1 teaspoon of superphosphate with each quart of mixed potting soil is desirable and encourages good root growth after repotting. If the garden soil is alkaline, sphagnum peat moss will have enough acid reaction to neutralize the mixture. This soil is used for all foliage plants and some flowering plants that do not prefer a rich soil.

Flowering House Plants: This soil is often referred to as humus soil because it contains about 50% humus-rich materials or similar ingredients. It is important that the soil does not become so rich that it is soggy after watering. Two parts of sphagnum, or one part sphagnum and one part vermiculite, are added to one part garden loam and one part clean sand. Also add 1 teaspoon of superphosphate per quart of soil mixture. This soil is generally used for African violets, gloxinias, begonias, calla lilies, and other tropical flowering plants.

Cacti and Succulents: This soil does not need any humus material. It is composed of equal parts of sand, garden soil, and vermiculite or perlite. It is preferred for cacti and other fleshy leaved, desert-type succulents.

Orchids: Fir-tree bark or Osmunda fiber is generally used in glazed or plastic pots. The container should be large enough so that new growth is 1-2 inches from the rim of container. Broken clay pieces can make up the lower inch in the container.

Containers

There are many types of containers from which to choose. A good container should be large enough to provide room for soil and roots, have sufficient room above the soil line for proper watering, provide bottom drainage, and be attractive without competing with the plant it holds. Containers may be made from ceramics, plastic, fiberglass, wood, aluminum, copper, brass, and many other materials.

Clay and Ceramic Containers

Unglazed and glazed porous clay pots with drainage holes are widely used. Ornate containers are often nothing but an outer shell to cover the plain clay or plastic pot. Clay pots absorb and lose moisture through their walls. Frequently the greatest accumulation of roots is next to the walls of the clay pot because moisture and nutrients accumulate in the clay pores. Although easily broken, clay pots provide excellent aeration for plant roots and are considered by some to be the healthiest type of container for a plant.

Ceramic pots are usually glazed on the outside, sometimes also on the inside. They are frequently designed without drainage holes. This necessitates careful watering practices and does not allow for leaching. Small novelty containers have little room for soil and roots and are largely ornamental. They should be avoided. It should be noted that putting pot chips, clay pot shards or gravel in the bottom of a pot does not improve soil drainage; they only provide a small space beneath the soil where some excess water can drain inside the pot.

Plastic and Fiberglass Containers

Plastic and fiberglass containers are usually quite light and easy to handle. They have become popular in recent years because they are relatively inexpensive and often quite attractive in shape and color. Plastic pots are easy to sterilize or clean for reuse, and because they are not porous, they need less frequent watering and tend to accumulate fewer salts.

Repotting

Actively growing indoor plants need repotting from time to time. This occurs very rarely with some slower-growing plants, more frequently with others. Foliage plants require repotting when their roots have filled the pot and are growing out the bottom holes. It is useful to know that certain species actually prefer to be pot-bound, such as African violets, aloe, and jade plant.

When repotting becomes necessary, it should be done without delay. The pot selected for repotting should be no more than 2 inches larger in diameter than the plant's current pot, should have at least one drainage hole, may be either clay, ceramic, or plastic, and must be clean. Wash soluble salts from clay pots with water and a scrub brush, and wash all pots in a solution of 1 part liquid bleach to 9 parts water.

Figure 12-3: This pot-bound plant is in need of repotting.

Potting media should be coarse enough to allow good drainage, yet have sufficient water retention capabilities. Most plants are removed easily from their pot if the pot is held upside-down while knocking the lip of the container sharply upon the edge of a table. Hold your hand over the soil, straddling the plant between the fore and middle fingers while knocking it out of its present container. Do not pull the plant out of the container.

Potting media should be moistened before repotting begins. To repot, place soil in bottom of pot. If the plant has become root-bound it will be necessary to cut and unwind any roots that circle the plant, otherwise the roots will never develop normally. If the old soil surface has accumulated salts, the top inch should be removed. Set the rootball in the middle of the new soil. Fill soil around the sides between the rootball and pot. Do not add soil above the original level on the rootball, unless the roots are exposed or it has been necessary to remove some of the surface soil. Do not pack the soil as this decreases aeration. To firm or settle it, tap the pot on a level surface or gently press the soil with your fingers. After watering and settling, the soil level should be sufficiently below the level of the pot to leave an inch or more headroom.

Headroom is the space between the soil level and the top of the pot that allows for watering a plant. A properly potted plant has enough headroom to allow water to wash through the soil to thoroughly moisten it.

Large indoor trees may require assistance to safely remove the plant from the pot. It should not be pulled out by the trunk or branches. It is easier to remove if the soil is moist. If the tree is root bound or has roots growing through the drain hole, the pot may have to be broken to avoid damaging the roots. It is often best to repot a large plant outdoors in warm weather.

Figure 12-4: Steps in repotting a plant include carefully removing the plant from old container, breaking up root ball, planting into a pot a few inches larger than the current pot, setting the plant in the new pot and adding media around the sides and bottom, and watering and settling the soil.

Training and Grooming

Pinching is the removal of 1 inch or less of new stem and leaf growth, just above a node. This leaves the plant attractive and stimulates new growth. It can be a one-time or continuous activity, depending on the needs of the plant. If a plant should be kept compact but well-filled out, frequent pinching will achieve this.

Pruning is a similar activity. Pruning includes removal of other than terminal shoot tips. Sometimes an entire branch or section of a plant should be removed for the sake of appearance.

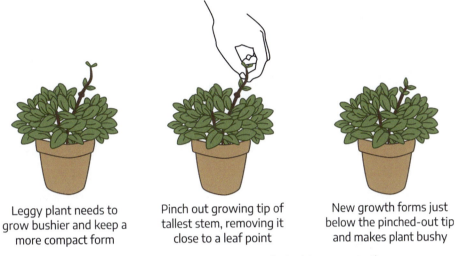

Leggy plant needs to grow bushier and keep a more compact form

Pinch out growing tip of tallest stem, removing it close to a leaf point

New growth forms just below the pinched-out tip and makes plant bushy

Figure 12-5: Pinching plants leaves them more attractive and stimulates new growth.

Disbudding is another related care activity. Certain flower buds are removed either to obtain larger blooms from a few choice buds or to prevent flowering of a very young plant (or recently rooted cutting) that should not bear the physical drain of flowering early.

Ivies and hoya, as well as philodendron and syngonium, can be easily trained on trellises.

It is important to keep plants clean and neat. It not only improves the appearance of plants but reduces the incidence of insects and disease problems. Remove all spent flowers, dying leaves, and dead branches. Keep leaves dust-free by washing plants with warm water and mild soap (cover pot to prevent soap from entering the soil). Dust can clog stomata and reduce respiration. If tips of leaves become brown and dry, trim them off neatly with sharp scissors.

Common Indoor Plant Pests

Indoor plants may still be exposed to potential plant pests. It is important to inspect for pests prior to purchasing plants to ensure that you are buying a healthy plant and to prevent possible infestation of any other indoor plants you may have at home. It is also important to inspect plants that you may have kept outside during the summer months. Here we will describe some of the common indoor plant pests you may see and different pest control options. Please remember to read any pesticide labels to assure you are using the appropriate product for your plant, pest, and environment.

Table 12-1: Common Indoor Plant Pests

Pest	Description	Mechanical Control Options	Chemical Control Options
Mealybugs	Soft-bodied insects with a white, waxy, cotton-like covering; suck sap from plant phloem; prefer tight crevices (between touching leaves, crotches of branches, on pots and tools)	Remove heavily infested leaves/branches	Insecticidal soaps are NOT effective; rubbing alcohol via cotton swab or spray
Aphids	Small, piercing-sucking insects that feed on plant juices; can be green, orange, red, black, etc.; molt ~4x leaving behind white sheds of exoskeleton that are easier to notice	Remove heavily infested leaves/branches; squish by hand; wash off with water	Insecticidal soap labeled for indoor plant use
Spider Mites	Extremely small arthropods- usually require a lens with 10X magnification; damage is more noticeable than the mites; stippling of leaves, loss of color, webbing	Wash off leaves with water	Insecticidal soap or a miticide labeled for indoor plant use (multiple treatments are usually needed); discard heavily infested plants
Scale	Small, armored insect from 1/16 to 1/8 in in diameter; attach to plants to feed; most do not move as adults; crawler stage is best time to control chemically	Remove heavily infested leaves/branches; physical removal with fingernail, brush, cotton swab	Horticultural oil or insecticidal soap labeled for indoor plant use (multiple treatments are usually needed)
Thrips	Small, slender insects about 1/16th inches long; 2 pair of fringed wings; mouthparts used for rasping leaf surface giving a stippled effect; frass commonly noticed before the insect; commonly found on flowers	Yellow/blue sticky traps	Insecticidal soap or neem oil labeled for indoor plant use
Whitefly	Small, white, gnat-like insect that hold their wings roof-life over their body; both larvae and adults have sucking mouthparts; feed on leaves; resembles aphid damage; common on hibiscus, poinsettia, tomatoes, etc.	Yellow sticky traps	Insecticidal soap or neem oil labeled for indoor plant use; discard heavily infested plants
Fungus Gnats	Small, black flies with larvae that feed on decaying matter in the soil; usually introduced from infested potting soil; can cause root damage if populations are extremely high; not a huge threat to plant health, but more of a nuisance	Yellow sticky traps; potato slices stuck into the soil (larvae will eat into the slice); discard slice (with the larvae) after a couple of days	Bacillus thuringiensis, subspecies israelensis applied to the soil (for larvae only)

Troubleshooting Indoor Plant Problems

Do your plants look unhealthy? Are you unsure of what might be the cause of your plant's condition? Below, we provide some signs of common indoor plant problems unrelated to plant disease and the potential treatments for these issues.

Table 12-2: Troubleshooting Common Indoor Plant Problems

Problem	Symptoms	Treatment
Overwatering	Lower leaves curl and wilt Mushy stems and rot Wet soil Yellow falling leaves	Water less frequently Use pots with drainage holes Do not allow water to sit in water for more than 30 minutes Repot in fresh soil
Underwatering	Tips of leaves brown Wilting Crispy leaves Leaf drop Yellowing leaves Dry soil	Water! Water until water drains from the bottom of the pot Submerge pot in water for 5 minutes; drain off excess

Table 12-2: Troubleshooting Common Indoor Plant Problems (continued)

Problem	Symptoms	Treatment
Light	Too little light: - Spindly stems, leggy plants - Small leaves - Loss of color in leaves Too much light: - Old leaves curling - Brown margins - Brown spots on leaves	Too little light: - Move to a better lit area - Supplement with artificial light Too much light: - Mover further away from light source - Provide shade

Care of Specific Plants

There are a number of wonderful house plants currently available for gardeners of all skill levels. When making the decision what plant is best for your space, choose plants that fit the light duration, light intensity, and temperature levels your house can provide. You should also consider growing what you enjoy having in your home, house plants are as much about beauty and enjoyment as they are about the health benefits they provide. Indoor plants can be a wonderful addition to any room and with the diversity of plants available through local plant nurseries and online, you will certainly be able to find a plant that fits your needs. The following are a few of the broad categories of houseplants that you may encounter:

Bulbous Plants

Just like bulbs are planted outside for beautiful seasonal blooms, they can also be grown indoors. The constant temperatures and control over the environment allows for varieties to be grown that may not survive many outdoor conditions. Bulbous plants are generally grown for their beautiful blooms.

Figure 12-6: Amaryllis.

Additional information can be found here: VCE Publication "Forcing Flower Bulbs for Indoor Bloom" HORT-67NP, Cornell Extension publication "Bulbous Plants for Indoor Bloom" (http://chemung.cce.cornell.edu/resources/bulbous-plants-for-indoor-bloom) and University of Minnesota Extension "Growing bulbs indoors" (https://extension.umn.edu/planting-and-growing-guides/growing-bulbs-indoors).

Trailing and Climbing

Trailing and climbing plants can add a wonderful dimension to any indoor plant collection. They can be trained to grow on different support structures within the home or as set in the pot where they are planted. There are many varieties of climbing and trailing plants, so ensure that you know what your specific plant needs to thrive in an indoor environment. For example, some ivies are able to thrive under fluorescent lights in an office environment, where other vining plants may not be able to do so successfully. Trailing and climbing indoors plants are often grown for their foliage and shape.

Additional information on ivy: Clemson Cooperative Extension "Growing English Ivy Indoors" (https://hgic.clemson.edu/factsheet/growing-english-ivy-indoors/).

Ferns

There are a number of ferns that can successfully grow indoors under the correct conditions. Humidity, temperature, and light are all important factors for ferns and a fern that doesn't receive exactly what it needs will not grow well in its indoor setting. Fiddlehead and staghorn ferns are two popular varieties that can add a great deal of interest to the home. Additional information on ferns: University of Georgia Cooperative Extension "Growing Ferns" (https://extension.uga.edu/publications/detail.html?number=B737&title=Growing%20Ferns).

Flowering Plants

Bringing beautiful blooms inside can be a rewarding experience and there are many flowering plants well adapted to growing indoors. As with other types of plants, be sure to understand the requirements for your plant. Some may need periods of darkness, cool temperatures, additional artificial light, or more in order to bloom indoors. However, when those needs are met you are granted with a colorful and exciting addition to your home!

Additional information on specific flowering plants can be found here: University of Missouri Extension "Care of Flowering Potted Plants" (https://extension.missouri.edu/publications/g6511).

Foliage Plants

Many indoor plants are grown solely for their interesting leaves. Whether you'd like to grow plants for unique colors, shapes, sizes, or patterns, there are indoor foliage plants that will fit your interests.

For more on easy to grow foliage plants: New Hampshire Extension "Which foliage houseplants are easiest to grow?" (https://extension.unh.edu/blog/2019/12/which-foliage-houseplants-are-easiest-grow).

Succulents

A succulent describes a type of plant that stores water in its stems and leaves. There are hundreds of plants that fall into this category of all shapes, colors, and sizes. Succulents can be hardy and able to survive outdoors in colder climates, or soft. Soft succulents are those that need consistent temperatures and are the ones that thrive in indoor environments when properly maintained. Succulents require regular watering once the soil has dried and should be placed in bright direct or indirect sunlight. Cacti are one large category of succulents often available for indoor growing.

More information here: Iowa State University Extension and Outreach "Care of Succulents Indoors" (https://hortnews.extension.iastate.edu/2021/12/care-succulents-indoors).

Trees and Tree-Like Plants

Indoor trees and plants that have been trained to take a tree-like form can add a lot to an indoor space. Not only can some citrus fruits grow indoors, sharing their fruits for your kitchen, but they also offer the height and mass that many indoor plants aren't able to offer. A tree can fully fill a space and adds interest to a room.

For information on growing citrus indoors: University of Minnesota Extension "Growing Citrus Indoors" (https://extension.umn.edu/house-plants/growing-citrus-indoors).

Indoor Plants and Toxicity for Pets

By Marion Ehrich and Dennis Blodgett, Virginia Maryland College of Veterinary Medicine, Virginia Tech

Family pets can be poisoned by a number of different toxic plants found inside the home or outside in the home garden. Lists are long, for example the ASPCA (American Society for Prevention of Cruelty to Animals) Animal Poison Control Center lists over 400 plants that can be toxic to dogs and cats. A full list of these toxic plants is available from the ASPCA: https://www.aspca.org/pet-care/animal-poison-control/toxic-and-non-toxic-plants. Another good source of information is your local veterinarian.

Veterinarians and other health professionals are often called about poisonous plants because plant poisonings are on rule-out lists for many different pet disorders. Most plant poisonings are not life-threatening, but anything eaten, even non-toxic plants, can cause gastrointestinal disturbances such as vomiting. Dogs are notorious for indiscriminate eating. Cats are more fastidious, but may ingest toxic houseplants and end up with minor to life threatening clinical signs. Certain common houseplants belonging to the *Araceae* family can release insoluble calcium oxalate crystals. These include dieffenbachia, philodendron, pothos (pictured), in addition to Calla lily and Peace lily. These crystals cause mouth and gastrointestinal irritation almost immediately, can be painful, and can last from hours to days. Contact with a local veterinarian should be considered.

Figure 12-7: Dieffenbachia can release insoluble calcium oxalate crystals when ingested.

Terrariums and Dish Gardens

Terrariums

A terrarium is a "miniature garden" in which plants are often contained within a tightly closed glass or clear plastic vessel, usually with a moveable top and requiring very little attention. Because such containers are kept closed most of the time, air inside stays at high humidity, similar to a greenhouse. This is an ideal environment for a variety of houseplants. Condensate eventually forms on the inside of the container and is returned to the medium as water, which may preclude the addition of water for several weeks. Overwatering is one of the most common problems in terrarium care – medium should be kept moist, not wet. If conditions inside become too moist, the top should be removed to evaporate excess water. A standard medium, along with a sand and/or gravel base for drainage and charcoal to absorb unpleasant odors are commonly used. Fertilizer applications are made only to sustain plants and when in use should be in soluble dilute form. The terrarium should be placed in bright, but not direct sunlight at average room temperatures.

Figure 12-8: Terrarium.

Dish Gardens

Desert dish gardens can be made by planting various arid type cacti and other succulents together in a decorative dish container. Open, shallow dishes are the best choices for containers. Choose the soil based on the type of plant being grown.

Figure 12-9: Dish garden.

Table 12-3: Light requirements for selected indoor plants

Plant (common name)	Direct Light	Bright Light	Average Light	Low Light
Areca palm	x	x		
Asparagus - Sprengeri	x	x		
Asparagus - Meyeri	x	x		
Aloe vera		x	x	
Boston fern		x	x	
Burro's tail	x	x		
Chinese evergreen		x	x	x
Coleus	x	x		
Corn plant		x	x	
Croton		x	x	
Devil's ivy	x	x	x	
Dieffenbachia	x	x	x	
Fiddleleaf fig		x	x	
False aralia		x	x	
German ivy - green		x	x	
German ivy - variegated		x	x	
Gold dust dracaena		x	x	
Grape ivy		x	x	
Heartleaf philodendron		x	x	x
Jade plant	x	x		
Japanese aralia		x	x	
Kangaroo ivy		x	x	
Maidenhair fern			x	x
Moses-in-the-cradle		x	x	
Norfolk island pine		x		
Parlor palm		x	x	x
Peperomia		x	x	
Piggyback		x	x	
Ponytail palm	x	x		
Rubber plant	x	x		
Schefflera	x	x	x	
Snake plant	x	x	x	x
Spider plant		x	x	
Spiderwort	x	x	x	
Strawberry begonia		x		
Swedish ivy	x	x	x	
Tahitian bridal veil	x	x	x	
Velvet plant	x	x		
Weeping fig		x		

Plant Lists

Cool Temperature Plants

Grow best at 50-60 °F during the day and 45-55 °F at night

- Azalea
- Cacti and succulents[1,2] (only during winter rest periods)
- Camellia
- Cast-iron plant[2]
- Chrysanthemum
- Citrus (grapefruit, lemon, orange)
- Creeping fig
- Daffodil, Narcissus
- Easter lily[2]
- Euonymus japonica (Spindle tree)
- Ivy[2]
- Hyacinth
- Hydrangea
- Japanese aralia
- Jasmine
- Jerusalem cherry
- Miniature rose
- Mock orange
- Norfolk Island pine
- Persian violet
- Primrose
- Tulip
- Tree ivy
- Wandering Jew
- White calla lily
- Zephyr lily

Key for temperature lists:

[1] Will also do well at high temperatures

[2] Will also do well at medium temperatures

[3] Will also do well at cool temperatures

Medium Temperature Plants

Grow best at 60-65 °F during the day and 55-60 °F at night

- Amaryllis
- Asparagus fern
- Avocado
- Baby's tear
- Begonia
- Bird's nest fern
- Bromeliads[3]
- Bush violet
- Cacti and Succulents[1,3]
- Cast-iron plant[1]
- Christmas cactus
- Citrus
- Coleus
- Crown of thorns[3]
- Earth star[3]
- Easter lily[1]
- English ivy[1]
- German ivy
- Gold-dust tree
- Hibiscus
- Kangaroo vine[3]
- Living stones[3]
- Palms
- Panda plant
- Peperomia
- Piggyback plant
- Pilea
- Podcarpus
- Purple passion fruit
- Schefflera
- Shamrock plant
- Snake plant[3]
- Staghorn fern[3]
- Strawberry begonia
- Wax plant

High Temperature Plants

Grow best at 70-80 °F during the day and 64-70 °F at night

- African violets
- Bromeliads
- Cacti and Succulents[2,3]
- Caladium calathea (Peacock plant)
- Chinese evergreen
- Coconut palm
- Copperleaf
- Cordyline
- Croton
- Crown of thorns[2]
- Dracena
- Earth star[2]
- False Aralia
- Ficus
- Flame violet
- Geranium
- Golden pothos
- Hen and chicks
- Impatiens
- Kangaroo vine[2]
- Living stones[2]
- Peace lily
- Philodendron
- Prayer plant
- Purple velvet plant[2]
- Sensitive plant
- Snake plant
- Staghorn fern[2]
- Swiss cheese plant
- Screw pine

Plants for Specific Indoor Gardening Uses

Plants that will grow in water

- *Aglaonema modestum* Chinese Evergreen
- *Crassula arborescens* Jade Plant
- *Dieffenbachia* (all varieties)
- *Hedera helix* English ivy
- *Hemigraphis colorata*
- *Hoya carnosa* Wax plant
- *Monstera deliciosa* Cutleaf Philodendron
- *Pellionia pulchra* Satin Pellionia
- *Philodendron cordatum* Philodendrons
- *Philodendron micans* (all climbing types)
- *Piper nigrum* Black Pepper
- *Piper ornatum* Celebes Pepper
- *Scindapsus aureus* Devil's Ivy
- *Scindapsus pictus* Painted Devil's Ivy
- *Stephanotis floribunda* Stephanotis
- *Syngonium podophyllum* Arrowhead, Syngonian
- *Tradescantia* (all varieties)

Plants that withstand adverse house conditions

- *Aglaonema modestum* Chinese Evergreen
- *Anthurium aemulum* Climbing Anthurium
- *Aspidistra elatior* Iron Plant
- *Chamaedorea elegans* 'bellas' Dwarf Parlor Palm
- *Cissus rhombifolia* Grape Ivy
- *Crassula arborescens* Jade Plant
- *Dieffenbachia amoena*
- *Dracaena fragrans* Massangeana Dracaena
- *Euphorbia mili* Crown of Thorns
- *Ficus elastica* Indian Rubber Tree
- *Ficus benjamina* 'Exotica' Java Fig
- *Hemigraphis colorata* Hemigraphis
- *Howeia belmoreana* Kentia Palm
- *Pandanus veitchii* Screw pine
- *Peperomia obtusifolia* Peperomia
- *Philodendron cordatum* Philodendron
- *Sansevieria trifasciata* Snakeplant
- *Sansevieria laurentii* Goldenstripe
- *Sansevieria zeylanica* Sansevieria
- *Scindapsus aureus* Devil's Ivy
- *Syngonium podophyllum* Arrowhead, Syngonium

Plants well-suited as large container decorative specimens

- *Acanthus mollis* Artists Acanthus
- *Acanthus montanus* Mountain Acanthus
- *Alocasia cuprea* Giant Caladium
- *Alsophila australis* Australian Tree Fern
- *Codiaeum pictum* Croton
- *Dieffenbachia amoena* Spotted Dumbcane
- *Fatshedra lizei* Botanical Wonder
- *Fatsia japonica* Japan Fatsia
- *Ficus eburnea* Ivory Fig
- *Ficus elastica* 'variegata' Variegated India Rubber
- *Ficus lyrata* Fiddleleaf Fig
- *Monstera deliciosa* Cutleaf Philodendron
- *Pandanus veitchii* Screwpine
- *Philodendron elongatum* Philodendron
- *Philodendron giganteum* Giant Philodendron
- *Philodendron x mandaianum* Philodendron
- *Philodendron panduraeforme* Philodendron
- *Philodendron selloum* Philodendron
- *Philodendron wendlandii* Philodendron
- *Polyscias paniculata* 'variegata' Jagged-leaf Aralia
- *Schefflera digitata* Schefflera
- *Strelitzia reginae* Bird of Paradise

Plants that perform well under average home conditions

- *Acanthus montanus* Mountain Acanthus
- *Aechmea calyculata* Bromeliad
- *Aechmea orlandiana* Bromeliad
- *Asparagus sprengeri* Sprenger Asparagus
- *Araucaria heterophylla* Norfolk Island Pine
- *Begonia aconitifolia* Begonia
- *Begonia ulmifolia* Elm-leaved Begonia
- *Beloperone guttata* Shrimp plant
- *Caladium bicolor* Fancy-leaved Caladium
- *Cissus antarctica* Kangaroo Vine
- *Cissus rhombifolia* Grape Ivy
- *Cordyline australis* Grass Palm
- *Cyrptanthus acaulis* Earth Star
- *Cyrtomium falcatum* Holly Fern
- *Dieffenbachia x bausei*
- *Dieffenbachia picta*
- *Euphorbia milii* Crown of Thorns
- *Fatsia japonica* Japanese Fatsia
- *Fatshedera lizei* Bush Ivy
- *Ficus benghalensis* Banyan Fig
- *Ficus eburnea* Ivory Fig
- *Ficus religiosa* Bo-tree Fig
- *Grevillea robusta* Silky Oak
- *Hedera helix* (all varieties) English Ivy
- *Pedilanthus tithymaloides* Slipper or Red Bird Flower
- *Peperomia clusiaefolia* Peperomia
- *Peperomia crassifolia* Peperomia
- *Peperomia obtusifolia* Variegated' Variegated Peperomia
- *Peperomia sandersii* Watermelon Peperomia
- *Pereskia aculeata* Lemon Vine
- *Philodendron cordatum* Heartleaf Philodendron
- *Philodendron* 'dubia' Philodendron
- *Philodendron giganteum* Giant Philodendron
- *Philodendron imbe* Imbe philodendron
- *Philodendron x mandaianum* Philodendron
- *Philodendron panduraeforme* Panda Plant
- *Philodendron erubescens* Redleaf Philodendron
- *Philodendron selloum* Philodendron
- *Philodendron tripartitum* Trileaf Philodendron
- *Philodendron wendlandii* Philodendron
- *Pilea involucrata* Artillary Plant
- *Piper nigrum* Black Pepper
- *Piper ornatum* Celebes Pepper
- *Polyscias balfouriana* Balfour Aralia
- *Polyscias filicifolia* Fernleaf Aralia
- *Polyscias paniculata* 'Variegata' Jagged-leaf Aralia
- *Rhoeo spathacea* Moses-in-the-cradle

- *Sansevieria trifaciata* 'Hahni' Hahn's Sansevieria
- *Sansevieria parva* Parva Sansevieria
- *Sansevieria subspicata* Rededge Sansevieria
- *Saxifraga sarmentosa* Strawberry geranium
- *Schismatoglottis picta* Painted Tongue
- *Scindapsus aureus* Devils Toy Pathos
- *Spathiphyllum* 'Clevelandii' Spathiphyllum
- *Syngonium podophylum* 'Emerald Gem' Variegated Arrowhead
- *Tradescantia* (all varieties)

Low, creeping plants for groundcovers in interior plant boxes

- *Episcia cupreata* Episcia
- *Ficus pumila* Creeping Fig
- *Ficus radicans* Climbing Fig
- *Fittonia verschafeltii* Silver Fittonia
- *Hedera helix* 'Hahns' Hahn's English Ivy
- *Hemigraphis colorata* Hemigraphis
- *Pellionia daveauana* Pellionia
- *Pellionia pulchra* Pellionia
- *Philodendron cordatum* Heartleaf Philodendron
- *Pilea nummulariifolia* Creeping Artillery Plant
- *Saxifraga sarmentosa* Strawberry Begonia
- *Scindapsus aureus* Devil's Ivy
- *Tradescantia* (all varieties)
- *Vinca major* 'variegata' Variegated Vinca

Vines and trailing plants for totem poles and trained plants

- *Anthurium almulum* Climbing Anthurium
- *Cissus antarctica* Kangaroo Vine
- *Cissus discolor* Begonia Cissus
- *Cissus rhombifolia* Grape Ivy
- *Clerodendrum* Balfouri Glorybower
- *Ficus pumila* Creeping Fig
- *Vanilla fragrans* 'Marginata' Vanilla

Plants suitable for hanging baskets

- *Achimenes grandiflora* Bigpurple Achimenes
- *Aeschynanthus parasiticus* Lobecup Basketvine
- *Aeschynanthus parasiticus* 'Black Pagoda' Black Pagoda Basketvine
- *Aeschynanthus radicans* Lobbs Basketvine, Lipstick plant
- *Aeschynanthus pulcher* Scarlet Basketvine
- *Asarina erubescens* Creeping Gloxinia
- *Asparagus plumosus* Fern Asparagus
- *Asparagus sprengeri* Sprengeri Fern
- *Begonia* 'Elsie M. Frey' Elsie M. Frey Begonia
- *Begonia x hiemalis* Winter Flowering Begonias
- *Callisia elegans* Striped Inch plant
- *Ceropegia woodii* String of Hearts, Rosary Vine
- *Chlorophytum bichetii* St. Bernard's Lily
- *Chlorophytum comosum* 'Variegatum' Green Lily
- *Chrysanthemum morifolium* 'Anna' Daisy Cascade
- *Chrysanthemum morifolium* 'Jane Harte' Daisy Cascade
- *Cissus quadrangula* Winged Treevine
- *Codonanthe crassifolia* Central American, Bellflower
- *Coleus rehneltianus* 'Trailing Queen' Trailing Coleus
- *Columnea x banksii* Goldfish Vine
- *Columnea microphylla* Small-leaved Goldfish Vine
- *Commelina communis* aurea-striata Variegated Widows Tear
- *Cyanotis kewensis* Teddy Bear Plant
- *Cyanotis somaliensis* Pussy Ear
- *Cymbalaria muralis* Kenilworth Ivy
- *Davallia fejeensis* 'plumosa' Rabbit's Foot Fern
- *Episcia cupreata* 'Amazon' Amazon Flame Violet
- *Episcia cupreata* 'Chocolate Soldier' Carpet Plant
- *Episcia cupreata* Ember Lace Episcia
- *Episcia cupreata* 'Emerald Queen' Emerald Queen Episcia
- *Episcia cupreata* 'Silver Sheen' Silver Sheen Episcia
- *Episcia dianthiflora* Lace Flower Vine
- *Episcia* 'Moss Agate' Panama Episcia
- *Erythrorhipsalis pilocarpa* Bristletufted twig cactus
- *Euphorbia mammillaris* Corncob Plant
- *Fittonia verschaffeltii* Mosaic Plant
- *Fittonia verschaffeltii* Silvernerve Fittonia
- *Fittonia verschaffeltii* var. Pearcei Snake Skin Plant
- *Fuchsia* 'Jubilee' Jubilee Fuchsia
- *Fuchsia* 'Swingtime' Swingtime Fuchsia
- *Hatiora salicornioides* Drunkard's Dream
- *Hedera helix* 'Hahns Variegated' Variegated Hahn's English Ivy
- *Hedera helix* 'Ivalace' Ivalace English Ivy
- *Hemigraphis colorata* Red Ivy
- *Hemigraphis* Exotica Waffle Plant
- *Hoya australis* Porcelain Flower
- *Hoya bella* Miniature Wax Plant
- *Hoya carnosa* 'Compacta' Compact Wax Plant
- *Hoya carnosa* 'Exotica' Exotic Wax Plant
- *Hoya carnosa* 'Krinkle Curl' Hindu Rope Plant
- *Hoya carnosa* 'Tri-color' Variegated Wax Plant
- *Hoya imperialis* Honey Plant
- *Hoya keysi* Pubescent Wax Plant
- *Hoya longifolia shepherdii* Shepherd's Wax Plant
- *Hoya motoskei* Spotted Wax Plant
- *Hoya purpureo-fusca* Silver Pink Wax Plant
- *Hypocyrta nummularia* Miniature Pouch Flower
- *Hylocereus undatus* Nightblooming Cereus
- *Ipomoea batatas* Blackleaf Sweet Potato
- *Kalanchoe gastonis-bonnieri* Life Plant
- *Kalanchoe manginii* Mangin Kalanchoe
- *Kalanchoe pubescens* Jinglebells Kalanchoe
- *Kalanchoe uniflora* Miniature Kalanchoe
- *Mammillaria elongata* Lace Mammillaria
- *Nephrolepis exaltata bostoniensis* Boston Fern
- *Nephrolepis exaltata* 'Rooseveltii' Tall Featherfern
- *Pelargonium x frangrans* Scented Geranium
- *Pellonia daveauana* Trailing Watermelon Vine
- *Pellonia pulchra* Satin Pellonia
- *Peperomia acuminata* Mexico Pepperface
- *Peperomia cubensis* Cuban Pepperface
- *Peperomia glabella* 'Variegata' Variegated Waxprivet Peperomia

- *Peristrophe hyssopifolia* 'Aurea-Variegata' Marble-leaf
- *Philodendron micans* Velvet-leaf Vine
- *Philodendron oxycardium* Heart-leaf Philodendron
- *Pilea nummulariifolia* Creeping Charley
- *Platycerium alcicorne* Elkhorn Fern
- *Plectranthus coleoides* 'Marginatus' Candle Plant
- *Plectranthus oertendahli* Prostrate Coleus
- *Plectranthus purpuratus* Moth King
- *Plectranthus tomentosus* Succulent Coleus
- *Polypodium aureum* Hare's Foot Fern
- *Portulacaria afra* 'Variegata' Rainbow Bush
- *Rhipsalis capilliformis* Treechair Rhipsalis
- *Rhipsalis cassutha* Mistletoe Rhipsalis
- *Rhipsalis houlletiana* Snowdrop Cactus
- *Rhipsalis paradoxa* China Rhipsalis
- *Rhipsalis pentaptera* Fivewing Rhipsalis
- *Rhipsalis trigona* Triangle Rhipsalis
- *Ruellia makoyana* Monkey Plant
- *Schlumbergera bridgesii* Christmas Cactus
- *Schlumbergera gaertneri* Easter Cactus
- *Scindapsus aureus* Devil's Ivy
- *Sedum morganianum* Burro Tail
- *Senecio herreianus* Green Marblevine
- *Setcreasea purpurea* Purple Heart
- *Stapelia gigantea* Giant Toadplant
- *Stenotaphrum secundatum* 'Variegatum' Variegated St. Augustine Grass
- *Streptocarpus saxorum* False African Violet
- *Tradescantia albiflora* 'Albovittata' Giant White Inch
- *Tradescantia sillamontana* White Velvet, White Gossamer

Plants suitable for desert dish gardens

- *Adromischus* Calico hearts, Leopard spots
- *Aloe*
- *Astrophytum myriostigma* Bishop's cap
- *Cephalocereus nobilis* Cylinder cactus
- *Cereus peruvianus* 'Monstrosus' Curiosity plant
- *Crassula* Jade plant
- *Crassula lycopodioides* Toy cypress, Watch chain
- *Crassula rupestris* Rosary Vine
- *Echeveria derenbergi* Painted lady
- *Echeveria elegans* Mexican snowball
- *Echeveria secunda* var. glauca Hens and chickens
- *Echinocactus Grusonii* Golden barrel cactus
- *Echinocereus pectinatus* var. neomexicanua Rainbow cactus
- *Echinocereus reichenbachii* Lace cactus
- *Echinocereus micromeris* Button cactus
- *Euphorbia lactea* cristata Crested euphorbia, Frilled fan
- *Faucaria tigrina* Tiger jaws
- *Gasteria liliputana* Miniature gasteria, Miniature ox tongue
- *Haworthia* Pearl plant, Wart plant
- *Haworthia fasciata* Zebra haworthia
- *Haworthia margaritifera* Pearl plant
- *Lithops* species Living stones
- *Mammillaria bocasana* Powder puff cactus
- *Mammillaria elongata* Golden star cactus
- *Mammillaria fragilis* Thimble cactus
- *Opuntia erectoclada* Dominoes, Pincushion cactus
- *Opuntia microdasys* Bunny ears
- *Opuntia vilis* Dwarf tree oputia
- *Portulacaria afra* Elephant bush
- *Portulacaria afra* variegata Rainbow bush
- *Rebutia kupperiana* Scarlet crown cactus
- *Rebutia minuscula* Red crown cactus
- *Sedum* Stonecrop
- *Sedum acre* Golden carpet, Gold moss
- *Sedum adolphi* Golden sedum
- *Sedum dasyphyllum* Golden glow
- *Sedum lineare* Carpet Sedum
- *Sedum morganianum* Burro's tail
- *Sedum multiceps* Miniature Joshua tree
- *Sedum pachyphyllum* Jelly beans
- *Sedum x rubrotinctum* Christmas cheer
- *Stahlii* Coral beads

Plants suitable for tropical terrariums

- *Aglaonema commutatum* Chinese evergreen
- *Begonia boweri* Miniature begonias
- *Chamaedorea elegans* Neanthe bella, Parlor palm
- *Cissus antarctica* 'Minima' Dwarf kangaroo ivy
- *Coffea arabica* Arabian coffee plant
- *Cordyline terminalis* minima 'Baby Ti' Dwarf ti plant
- *Cryptanthus bivittatus* minor Dwarf rose-stripe earth star
- *Dizgygotheca elegantissima* False aralia
- *Dracaena sanderana* Belgian evergreen
- *Dracaena surculosa* Gold dust dracaena
- *Ficus diversifolia* Mistletoe fig
- *Ficus pumila* 'Minima' Dwarf creeping fig
- *Fittonia verschaffeltii* Mosaic plant
- *Maranta leuconeura* kerchoveana Prayer plant
- *Nephrolepis exaltata* cvs. Boston fern
- *Peperomia sandersii* Watermelon peperomia
- *Pilea cadierei* 'Minima' Aluminum plant
- *Pilea depressa* Miniature pilea
- *Pilea microphylla* Artillary plant
- *Pilea nummulariifolia* Creeping Charlie
- *Pteris* species Brake ferns, Table ferns
- *Saintpaulia* cultivars Miniature African violets
- *Selaginella* Club moss, Moss fern
- *Selaginella kraussiana* Creeping club moss
- *Selaginella emmeliana* Sweat plant
- *Sinningia pusilla* (and other miniature cultivars) Miniature gloxinias
- *Syngonium* Arrowhead vine, Nephthytis

Additional Resources

- Colorado State PlantTalk information for growing many common houseplants: https://planttalk.colostate.edu/topics/houseplants/
- "Forcing Flower Bulbs for Indoor Bloom" HORT-67NP: https://www.pubs.ext.vt.edu/HORT/HORT-76/HORT-76.html
- ASPA houseplant toxicity information: https://www.aspca.org/pet-care/animal-poison-control/toxic-and-non-toxic-plants
- University of Connecticut "Safe and Toxic houseplants": https://homegarden.cahnr.uconn.edu/factsheets/houseplants-safe-and-toxic-varieties/

Attributions

- Courtney Soria, Loudoun County Extension Master Gardener (2021 reviser)
- Nancy Butler, Hanover Extension Master Gardener (2021 reviser)
- Melanie Smith, Hanover Extension Master Gardener (2021 reviser)
- Meredith Hoggatt, Extension Agent, Agriculture and Natural Resources (Author of "Common Indoor Plant Pests," 2022)
- Lisa Sanderson, Extension Agent, Agriculture and Natural Resources (2015 reviser)
- Megan Tierney, Extension Agent, Agriculture and Natural Resources (2015 reviser)
- Stephanie Huckestein, Education and Outreach Coordinator, Hahn Horticulture Garden, Virginia Tech (2015 reviewer)
- Diane Relf, Extension Specialist, Horticulture (2009 reviser)

Image Attributions

- Figure 12-1: Black root rot. Image 5427727 by Cheryl Kaiser, University of Kentucky, Bugwood.org. CC BY-NC 3.0 US
- Figure 12-2: Peat moss. Johnson, Devon. 2022. CC BY-NC-SA 4.0.
- Figure 12-3: Pot bound plant. Reed, Kathleen. 2022. CC BY-NC-SA 4.0.
- Figure 12-4: Steps in repotting. Reed, Kathleen and Johnson, Devon. 2022. CC BY-NC-SA 4.0.
- Figure 12-5: Pinching plants leaves them more attractive and stimulates new growth. Grey, Kindred. 2022. CC BY-NC-SA 4.0.
- Figure 12-6: Amaryllis. "Amaryllis." 2013. Hige, Aka. Flickr. CC By-SA 2.0.
- Figure 12-7: Dieffenbachia. "Dieffenbachia houseplant" Aj West. 2017. Wikimedia. CC BY-NC-SA 4.0.
- Figure 12-8: Terrarium. "Succulent Plant Terrarium." Fraxinus.ornus. 2013. Wikimedia. CC BY-SA 4.0.
- Figure 12-9: Dish Garden. "Succulent Dish Garden – Lisa Greene, AAF, AIFD, PFCI." 2012. Flower Factor. Flickr. CC BY-NC 2.0.

CHAPTER 13: WOODY LANDSCAPE PLANTS

Chapter Contents:

- What is a Woody Plant?
- Species Diversity and Monoculture
- Hardiness
- Growth Rate
- Functions of Woody Plants
- Choice of Nursery Stock
- Right Plant for the Right Place and Right Function
- Invasive Plants
- Challenge
- Additional Resources

The knowledge of woody landscape plants is essential for anyone in the realm of landscape horticulture. Woody plants can be found in polished urban settings and in relatively untouched natural areas. With knowledge of these plants, you will be able to properly design and manage landscapes, as well as to diagnose and solve landscape plant-related problems.

The information presented in this chapter is designed to prepare you for most tasks and issues that you will encounter in dealing with the use of woody plants. Knowledge of fundamental plant aspects such as hardiness and plant biology are key to using and managing woody plants in a landscape.

This chapter will not delve into the identification of woody plants. However, knowing how to identify at least the most commonly used woody landscape species is a great asset to anyone dealing with these plants. A very scholarly and thorough treatment relative to the identification and use of woody plants is the *Manual of Woody Landscape Plants* by Michael A. Dirr (6th edition, 2009, Stipes Publishing). This text is an excellent reference and is often considered the "bible" of woody plants.

Figure 13-1: Plants can grow very large because of the ability of their roots and stems to increase in girth, or to undergo secondary growth. Most of the tissue produced by secondary growth is secondary xylem, or wood, which conducts water and minerals and provides strength to the roots and stems.

The goal of this chapter is to provide you with the fundamental woody plant information to understand the basics of woody plant biology relative to landscape applications, and how to appropriately select and manage woody species in the landscape. Some details such as pruning, fertilization, and soil aspects will only be superficially addressed in this chapter since this information is covered in depth in other chapters.

What is a Woody Plant?

Woody plants are perennial (life span ranges from decades to centuries, or in some cases millennia) in which the shoot (above ground portion of the plant) persists during plant dormancy (usually late-autumn to early-spring). For example, an oak tree (*Quercus* spp.) has a trunk that persists for 12 months, year after year. In contrast, the shoot system of an herbaceous perennial, such as a hosta (*Hosta* spp.), dies to the ground each fall but the root system persists year after year. Because the shoot system of an herbaceous perennial dies at the end of each growing season, no yearly increase in stem/trunk diameter occurs as it does in woody plants. Woody plants are described as trees, shrubs, groundcovers, and vines. Technically, wood is composed of xylem tissue, mostly dead lignified vascular cells that transport water from the roots to the trunk, stems, leaves, flowers, and fruit. Wood also serves as the structural support system for plant parts.

As with most issues, there are shades of gray. For example, nandina (also called heavenly bamboo; *Nandina domestica*) is a shrub. However, in the northern part of its adaptable range (USDA Plant Hardiness Zone 6), the shoot system can be killed by low winter temperatures. However, this species will usually produce a new set of shoots (top portion of a plant) the following spring from the root system. Thus, nandina, while typically considered a woody plant, in some years and locations can grow as an herbaceous perennial due to weather-related conditions. We will cover plant hardiness in detail in a future section.

Woody Plant Botany

In many plants, growth in a given tissue ceases when mature. In woody plants, roots and stems continue to increase in diameter in regions that are no longer elongating, thus increasing the girth of the plant. This increase in girth is called **secondary growth.**

At the start of each growing season, woody plants resume primary growth, adding additional secondary tissues through growth of two lateral meristems: the vascular cambium and the cork cambium.

The **vascular cambium** is the main growing tissue of stems and roots in most plants. It produces the secondary xylem and secondary phloem. In temperate regions, the vascular cambium is dormant during winter and is reactivated in the spring when the plant's buds begin to expand and resume growth. During reactivation, the cambial cells take up water, expand, and begin to divide. New growth layers, or increments, of secondary xylem and secondary phloem are laid down during the growing season.

The **cork cambium** falls outside the vascular cambium and is responsible for growth that replaces the epidermis in stems and roots. It is a layer of bark. **Bark** is a nontechnical term that refers to all the tissues outside the vascular cambium, including the periderm.

Gymnosperms, woody magnoliids (woody flowering plants that are neither monocots or dicots), and woody dicots undergo secondary growth and are called "woody plants." Herbaceous plants are plants with shoots that undergo little or no secondary growth (Evert and Eichhorn, 2012).

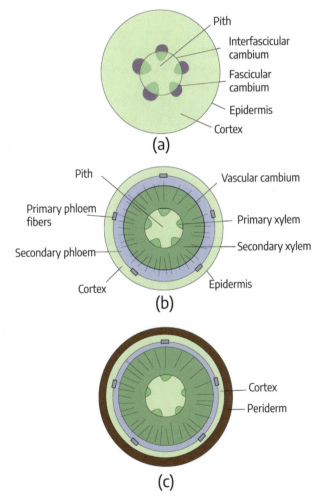

Figure 13-2: Diagram of secondary growth in woody stem. (a) Shows the origin of the vascular cambium. (b) After formation of some secondary xylem and secondary phloem. (c) At the end of the first year's growth; showing the effect of secondary growth including formation of the periderm.

Woody plants can be categorized in several different ways. Three categories, organized by growth habit and foliage type, are:

- **Deciduous trees**, shrubs, groundcovers, and vines (**angiosperms** that lose their leaves in the fall)
- **Broadleaf evergreen** trees, shrubs, groundcovers, and vines (angiosperm species that retain foliage throughout the year)
- **Conifers** (**gymnosperms**, mostly evergreen but there are notable deciduous species, that have needle, scale-like, or awl-like foliage)

Note: angiosperm species have true flowers. Gymnosperms bear naked seeds in cones and modified cones.

Plant Sex

Woody species can be categorized relative to the sex of flowers they produce. If a species produces plants with both male and female flower parts on them (either both sexes in a single flower or separate male and female flowers on the same plant), then that species is termed **monoecious** (literal translation: "one house"). The majority of woody species are monoecious. If a species produces

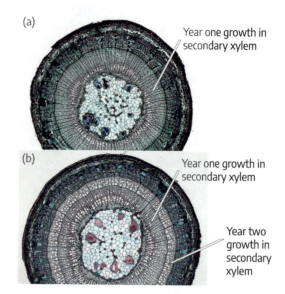

Figure 13-3: Cross section of a a woody dicot stem after (a) one year of growth and (b) after two years of growth. A second ring of growth in the secondary xylem is visible after two years. Each year of growth produces a new ring.

plants with either only male or only female flowers, then that species is termed **dioecious** (literal translation: "two houses"). Dioecious species require both male and female plants in close proximity to produce fruit/seed. *Ilex verticillata* (winterberry), a dioecious species, is a popular woody landscape species due to its abundance of showy fruit, and a male plant must be nearby to fertilize (pollinate) female plants for fruit production. If one has a dioecious plant and it has not set fruit, then it may be a male (fruitless by design), or it may be a female with no male in the vicinity. In some cases, a female will produce fruit without sexual fertilization, and this is termed parthenocarpy. There are several popular landscape taxa that are parthenocarpic such as *Ilex* ×'Nellie R. Stevens' and *Ilex cornuta* 'Burfordii'.

Woody Plant Sizes and Growth Habits

Woody plants are characterized by their height and growth habits. Size characterizations are somewhat arbitrary designations, however, they are useful categories for landscape design and plant selection.

Trees have single or multiple trunks (usually three or less). Mature trees sizes are:

- Small trees: 15-25 feet tall
- Medium trees: 25-50 feet tall
- Large trees: 50 feet tall

From a functional perspective, small trees can be distinguished from medium and large trees. Medium and large trees are generally not differentiated in landscape use since they are both used in areas that require larger scales or in larger areas. Small trees can be used in relatively small areas or anywhere the scale of the surroundings requires or can accommodate a tree less than 25 feet tall (e.g., courtyard and small residential landscape property). A careful determination of the available volume of space and proximity to other landscape or residential features will dictate the appropriate tree size for an area.

Shrubs typically have multiple trunks (usually more than three). Mature shrub sizes are:

- Small shrubs ≤ 5 feet tall – also considered as a groundcover when less than 3 feet tall
- Medium shrubs > 5-9 feet tall
- Large shrubs > 9 feet tall

As with tree sizes, shrub size should be used to match the existing volume of landscape space to be occupied by plants.

The distinction between a small tree and a large shrub is somewhat arbitrary. Many species, such as cornelian cherry dogwood (*Cornus mas*) for example, can be considered a large shrub or a small tree depending on how it is pruned. An unpruned multi-stem cornelian cherry dogwood is shrub-like, however, if one removes the lower branches and some of the multiple trunks, it will look like a small tree. Thus, plant size and category classifications are open to interpretation and affected by pruning.

Groundcovers generally have a horizontal growth habit and are less than 3 feet tall.

Vines, due to their relatively supple young stems, are shrubs that are unable to sustain an upright habit unless they grow on an upright structure. Many vine species can grow as tall as the structure they cling to. In the absence of a structure, a vine will grow on the ground in a prostrate or mound fashion.

Vines have three modes of attachment. They adhere to a structure by:

1. Twining (stems wind around a structure or matrix, e.g. Japanese wisteria *Wisteria floribunda*)
2. Rootlets (stems have adventitious roots that attach to a structure, e.g. English ivy *Hedera helix*)
3. Tendrils (modified stems leaves, or **petioles** that attach to a structure by twining or holdfasts, e.g. Virginia creeper *Parthenocissus quinquefolia*).

Figure 13-4: Examples of different sized trees: A small tree, American Hornbeam Carpinus caroliniana; A midsize tree, Yellowwood, Cladrastis kentuckea; Two choices of large tree: Deodar Cedar Cedrus deodara (left) and Southern Magnolia Magnolia grandiflora (right).

Vines with rootlets and tendrils (with holdfasts) can grow up a wall (or other vertical surface) since rootlets and tendrils adhere firmly to a surface. Vines that twine will not grow on a wall unless there is a lattice or some other matrix for it to cling to. All vine types can grow up trees regardless of climbing mode.

Factors affecting plant size

Plant size is affected by a plant's genetics and the environment. In terms of the environment, available resources such as water, light, and nutrients, as well as site-related conditions (e.g., soil, climate, competition, pest pressure, and human impacts) greatly influence plant growth. Also remember that within a population of any plant species, there will be a great amount of variability in plant characteristics such as height, width, leaf size, and flower, and fruit characteristics due to genetics. In terms of mature height, one may find individuals that are much taller or shorter than the average individual. Thus, ascribing a plant size, e.g., small tree or medium tree, to particular species is less than precise. For example, American hornbeam (*Carpinus caroliniana*) is generally categorized as a small tree with a mature height of 20-30 feet tall. Our definition of a small tree is 15-25 feet tall, so one can see that occasionally this species can be classified as a medium tree. There are American hornbeams that are 65 feet tall; by definition such a tree would fall into the large tree category. Such atypical plants may be growing in an ideal site and/or may have the genetic capacity for taller than average height.

Plant size and landscape use

Woody plant size is a very important aspect because one of the most common landscape design/plant installation mistakes is to design/install a species that will grow outside its intended volume of space. Pruning, while a necessary component of tree care, is a generally an ineffective remedy for this mistake (since size-limiting pruning will need to be continually repeated); additionally, it is also time consuming, costly, and creates plant debris which then creates debris disposal issues. In some cases, pruning is not a viable option since the required pruning will significantly distort the tree/shrub form. Trees placed too close to a structure can pose a significant liability when they mature, since limbs/trunks have the potential to fall and damage a structure during snow, ice, or wind storms. Tree pruning/removal is very expensive; so, one must be very careful in designing/placing trees next to structures.

Species Diversity and Monoculture

Species diversity is the use of many varied taxa (family, genus, species) within an "area", where an area may range from a residential site to municipal or larger sites. Species diversity implies that a landscape (garden size to much larger areas) is composed of a mix of species from a wide range of genera and plant families. Species diversity guards against a disproportionate loss of landscape plants in the event of an insult such as a pest attack (e.g., insect, mite, fungus, or virus) or some damaging environmental event (e.g., drought; excessive rain, wind, or snow; ice storm; or atypically high/low temperatures).

The overuse of any plant taxa (i.e., cultivar, species, genus, or family) in a landscape is regarded as a monoculture. There are no research-based values (number and type of taxa per unit land) for determining a monoculture, and "overuse" is a matter of degree. A classic example of monoculture was the American elm (*Ulmus americana*). By the 1930s there were tens of millions of American elm trees planted in North America. The American elm was widely planted as a street tree since it was fast growing, tolerated urban conditions, and had a beautiful vase shape. In 1930, Dutch elm disease, a fungus spread by a beetle, was introduced into the U.S. The disease has killed most of the native and planted American elms and only a very small fraction of American elms have survived this disease. While there are no scientifically determined values for the relative number of plant taxa in a landscape to have a diversified landscape, a landscape should have a sufficient number of plant species in several plant families and genera to ensure genetic diversity. Tree inventories are especially helpful to determine the family and species composition of a landscape/area.

Hardiness

Hardiness refers to a plant's ability to withstand low winter temperatures and remain aesthetically pleasing. Plant hardiness is an especially important concept to understand because lack of this understanding can result in some very costly plant use mistakes.

USDA Plant Hardiness Zone Map

The USDA Plant Hardiness zone map divides the country into different 10-degree F zones based on average annual minimum winter temperature. Zone 1a is the coldest and zone 13b is the warmest, with Virginia ranging from 8a to 5a. Zones in the current map (2012 version) are based on 1976–2005 weather data and are calculated by averaging the lowest daily winter temperatures for a given location during this time period. Zones do not represent the coldest it will ever be in an area.

Each woody landscape species has a designated hardiness rating. These ratings may vary depending on the source of the plant information. Redbud (*Cercis canadensis*) has a plant hardiness rating of zone 4 to 9 (often designated by 4 – 9). The first part of this rating (the number 4) refers to the lowest temperatures this species can tolerate (zone 4; -20 to -30° F). The second part (the number 9) refers to the highest temperatures that this species can tolerate. Thus, one can successfully grow redbuds from zone 4 through 9. The hardiness rating of Fraser fir (*Abies fraseri*) is 4 to 7, and will perform poorly in zone 8 (and even in zone 7b) due to this fir's lack of heat tolerance (and other heat-related aspects).

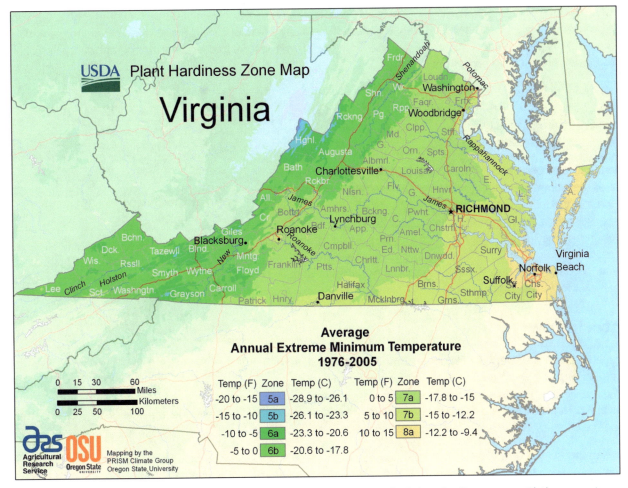

Figure 13-5: USDA plant hardiness zone map for Virginia: This map shows the state divided into hardiness zones, with the warmest zones 8a in Norfolk, Virginia Beach, and the Eastern Shore and the coldest zones in Highland County. Most of the state falls into zones 6a and 6b in the west to 7b in the east. View an interactive version of this map here: https://planthardiness.ars.usda.gov/

Of course, the USDA Hardiness Plant Zone designations are a guide and not an exact tool to rate plant temperature response since plant hardiness is a complicated phenomenon. Factors that are involved with the hardiness of a particular species are the prevailing weather conditions for a particular year, and how well established a plant is (penetration of roots from root ball into surrounding soil). Plants that are not well established will be much less hardy then an established plant. In terms of weather, the minimum temperatures and how long these temperatures persist, and how the onset of cold weather proceeds can affect a species' tolerance to low temperatures. In some years, woody species have been damaged when there is a mild fall that is followed by uncharacteristically low temperatures. In this case, the plants did not gradually acclimate to low temperatures, and did not achieve the necessary degree of hardiness. Late spring frosts are also damaging to some species, so in addition to the minimum temperature, the manner in which low temperatures prevail has a major influence on plant hardiness. Soil moisture conditions will also affect winter hardiness. In a relatively dry fall and winter, foliage of evergreens (conifers and broadleaved) will experience significant leaf damage. Excessive soil moisture can also negatively impact plant hardiness. Again, plant hardiness is not only related to low temperatures, but is the result of interacting factors.

Provenance

We already noted that the hardiness range of redbud (*Cercis canadensis*) is zone 4-9. In terms of a natural population, we can expect that redbuds, and most other woody plants, in the most northern parts of its population will have the genes to tolerate zone 4 winters (-20 to -30° F). Redbuds, and most other woody species, from the southern portion of its hardiness range will have genes to tolerate the relatively high summer heat of the southern U.S. Seed collected from the southern part of the redbud population may not have the genes to tolerate the minimum winter temperatures in zone 4. Conversely, plants from zone 4 will most likely not have the genes to tolerate the heat of zone 9. Thus, when procuring plant material, the source of the plant material may be an important consideration. The term to describe the geographical source of plants (and other entities) is called **provenance**.

The Virginia Department of Forestry (DOF) grows seedlings sourced from Virginia trees and shrubs, which can be ordered seasonally through the DOF Buy Virginia Trees website (https://www.buyvatrees.com/).

A plant native to one part of Virginia may not be native to other parts of the commonwealth. For example, Sweet Bay Magnolia (*Magnolia virginiana*) is native to the eastern parts of Virginia, but not the western parts. On the other hand, Carolina hemlock (*Tsuga caroliniana*) is native only to the western-central part of the commonwealth. To look up whether a particular species is native to your county, use the Digital Atlas of the Virginia Flora (http://www.vaplantatlas.org/).

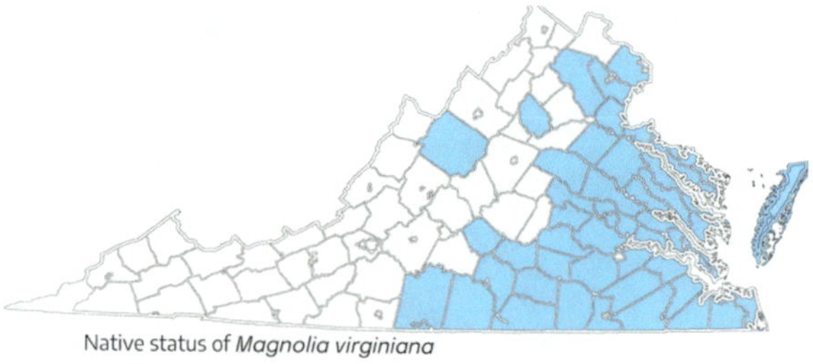

Historic Lows

Remember that the USDA Plant Hardiness Zone Map is based on average annual minimum temperatures and were calculated by averaging minimum annual temperature collected over the 29 years that data were recorded. Since the low temperature for any one zone is an average, the possibility exists that the low temperature for any one winter may be lower than the zone indicates.

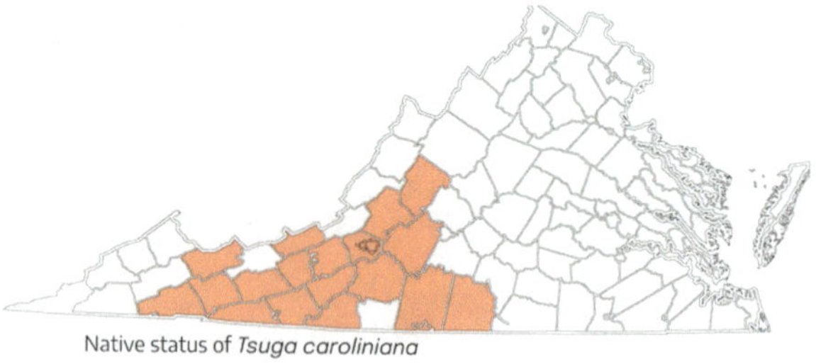

Figure: 13-6: Comparison of native range of two different Virginia species. Range is shown as shaded counties.

For example, Blacksburg, Virginia is in zone 6b; the USDA Plant Hardiness Zone Map notes that the average minimum temperature range for zone 6b is 0 to -5° F. In fact, the record low for Blacksburg is -18° F (January, 1985). Several zone 6b woody species (and most zone 7a plants planted on a gamble) were killed in January 1985. Thus, knowledge of the historical low temperatures for a particular area you are landscaping is important to ensure that woody species are selected to survive the extreme low temperatures. This is especially important if you are planting numerous individuals of one species. Keep in mind that the use of hardiness zone ratings is a guide and not an exact science.

Hardiness of Plant Parts

Not all plant parts are equally hardy. The root system is the least hardy portion of the entire woody plant. Since roots are insulated by the soil (winter root zone soil temperatures are generally warmer than ambient air temperatures), root zone temperatures are usually not a consideration for landscape plants. However, if one is overwintering container-grown woody plants without protection, as in the case of a roof-top garden, then low temperatures and root hardiness should be taken into consideration.

The temperature that roots will tolerate is species specific. For example, roots of flowering dogwood (*Cornus florida*) are killed at 20° F, whereas roots of white spruce (*Picea glauca*) are killed at -10° F. There is a rule of thumb for unprotected container-grown plants that prescribes that one must select a species with a hardiness zone rating that is two zones lower than the zone you are in for the roots to tolerate the low winter temperatures. Thus, one should select a zone 4 species to survive as a container-grown plant in zone 6. Nursery growers in many parts of Virginia overwinter container-grown plants by covering plants in plastic blankets or in plastic-covered hoop houses; such coverings trap ground heat and maintain root zone temperatures above the ambient outside temperatures. There are websites that list root killing temperatures for many woody plant species.

The above ground portion of a woody plant, the shoot system (leaves and stems), gradually acclimates to lower temperatures in the fall with the onset of low temperatures and progressively short periods of daylight. Parts of the shoot system vary in their low temperature tolerance. Woody plant flower buds are usually less winter hardy than vegetative buds (produce leaves and stems) and stems. Thus, low winter temperatures may injure or kill flower buds, but not affect vegetative bud and stems. A classic example of this phenomenon occurs in bigleaf hydrangea (*Hydrangea macrophylla*). Listed as a zone 6 to 9 species, bigleaf hydrangea flower production in zone 6 is commonly less than in zone 7 because typical zone 6 winter temperatures kill the flowers buds which were produced in the summer prior to the year they flower. Unless the minimum winter temperatures are relatively high in zone 6, very few if any bigleaf hydrangea flower buds will survive the winter; even stems are commonly killed in typical zone 6 winters. In response to this zone 6 flowering problem with bigleaf hydrangea, cultivars of *Hydrangea macrophylla* have been selected that flower on new wood (to be discussed) and will flower in the summer even after a low temperature winter.

Microclimate

In any county, city, neighborhood, or area around a house/structure there may be areas that have minimum and maximum temperatures that are atypical for that area's designated hardiness zone. Slope, altitude, compass orientation, proximity to water or a building, the amount of pavement and buildings, overhead canopies such as trees and arbors are some of the aspects that will influence temperature. Zones of atypical high or low temperatures are called **microclimates**. Knowledge of these microclimates will influence how you choose species according to hardiness zones for these areas. For example, since cold air is heavier than warm air, cold air moves down a slope, and air at the bottom of the slope would be colder than the temperature of air at top of the slope. Knowing microclimates that are warmer than your zone (such as a protected location on the south side of a house or under an arbor), will allow you to successfully grow a species that is not typically hardy in your zone.

Growth Rate

Woody Plant Growth Rate Categories

Woody plants are categorized into three growth rate categories. These are:

- Slow: less than or equal to 12 inches per year
- Moderate: 13-24 inches per year
- Fast: greater than or equal to 25 inches per year

Woody plant growth rate is an aspect that impacts: 1) maintenance, 2) placement/spacing of plants, and 3) how slowly or quickly a plant will fill its intended space in the landscape. Most species have a moderate growth. A fast-growth rate can be an asset if one is planting a row of small plants for a privacy hedge, or can be a liability if one has to prune to control plant size or density. As noted for plant size, growth rate is not only dictated by plant genetics, but also by available resources such as water, light, and nutrients, as well as site-related conditions (e.g., soil, climate, competition, pest pressure, and human impacts).

Conifer Growth Rates

Conifers are best described by their growth rate and NOT by a mature size since mature size designations are generally not accurate. The American Conifer Society database (https://conifersociety.org/conifers/) has published the following categories, growth rates, and approximate size (height and/or width) of conifers.

Table 13-1: Conifer growth rates

Category	Growth per year (inches)	Approximate size at 10 years (feet)
Miniature	<1	<1
Dwarf	1-6	1-6
Intermediate	6-12	6-15
Large	>12	>15

A dwarf conifer, usually a cultivar of a conifer species, has a slower growth rate than the species. Dwarf conifers are valuable components of a woody plant palette since they offer numerous options of using plants with a variety of sizes, forms, textures, and colors in space-restricted landscapes.

Functions of Woody Plants

Woody plants serve aesthetic, architectural, and environmental functions. They also serve specific landscape-related functions.

Aesthetic Functions

Woody plants can have attractive foliage, flowers, fruits, bark, and/or form throughout the year. Because woody plant shoots (stems/trunks) persist in the dormant season, in contrast to most herbaceous plants, characteristics such as branch/trunk structure (form/habit), bark, fruit, and foliage in the case of evergreens (broadleaf and conifers) serve to beautify the landscape when plants are dormant.

The visual characteristics of plants, size, form, color, and texture, are like paints on an artist's palette. Thus, as an artist selects different colored paints to compose a picture, one who selects woody species for a landscape design does so by choosing plant sizes, forms, colors, and textures as manifested by trunk/ branch configuration, bark, foliage, flowers, and fruit characteristics. There are limitless combinations of size, form, color, and textures that will make a landscape attractive for 365 days a year. Because plants are ever-changing throughout seasons and years, the landscape "picture" is dynamic as well.

Plant size and form has a very large impact on where a plant can be grown and how it is used in the landscape. Plant size, as previously discussed, will impact where a species can be placed in the landscape. Large trees, by virtue of their mass, are visually dominant structures in the landscape. Most trees and shrubs have an oval or round form. Some trees can have a weeping or **pendulous** form (branches hang down), a **fastigiate** form (narrow oval), or a **columnar** form (column-like). Some deciduous trees and many conifers (especially in their youth) have a conical or pyramidal form. Tree form also influences how one perceives the landscape. In general, round and oval forms have a neutral effect on the eye; conical, fastigiate, and columnar forms bring the eye skyward; pendulous forms bring the eye to the ground plane.

Other sensory aspects are involved in woody plant selection such as smell (flowers), taste (fruit), and movement (leaves fluttering, flower petals falling).

Architectural Functions

Woody plants serve important architectural functions in the landscape. Woody plants give a landscape structure, and are likened to the backbone of landscape. Trees, shrubs, and groundcovers serve as the ceilings, walls, and floors of outdoor spaces. They also serve to frame views and create outdoor rooms. In addition, woody plants can be pruned and trained to create structures such as walls, doorways, and architectural focal points such as topiaries.

Environmental Functions

Woody plants have numerous significant effects on the landscape environment. While expounding on these effects is not the focus of this chapter, there are a few noted effects that you should know. The shade of deciduous trees that are mainly placed on the southeast and southwest side of a structure can cool structures in hot months. Trees for shade are generally not placed directly on the south side of a house since the sun is at a very high position in the sky at midday, the time at which the sun is due south of a structure. The sun's high position means that a shade tree would have to be very close to a structure to provide shade, and this close placement would be a potential hazard in the event the tree fell on the house. Evergreen trees/shrubs placed on the northwest side of a structure can prevent heat loss from a structure in cold months by acting as a wind break.

Figure 13-7: Japanese Elms, Zelkova serrata shading a city street in Richmond.

Woody plants also reduce noise, pollution, runoff, and soil erosion. Trees reduce air pollution by trapping particulate matter in their leafy canopies and by absorbing noxious pollution into their leaves. The particulate matter is eventually washed away with rain. Absorbed pollutants are incorporated into the soil after leaf fall where they are broken down by microbes. These actions reduce human health problems related to air pollution. Tree canopies also intercept large amounts of rain, reducing the amount of runoff that is discharged into streams and rivers and extending the time that a watershed has to absorb rainfall. This reduces flooding and erosion.

As trees grow they accumulate biomass that absorbs carbon and nutrients, locking them into a biological cycle that keeps them out of the atmosphere and hydrosphere. The storage of carbon reduces the greenhouse effect that is linked to problems of global climate change. Absorbed nutrients stay out of water bodies where they would otherwise harm fish and other aquatic species.

In summer, trees ameliorate climate by transpiring water from their leaves, which has a cooling effect on the atmosphere. At night, when the earth radiates heat back into space, temperatures often drop to the cooling or dew point, when water vapor, some of which is produced by trees during the daytime, condenses. This releases latent heat back into the atmosphere. When groups of trees intercept sunlight and use it for photosynthesis, they shade roads, buildings, and other structures, and they help reduce energy consumption.

Woody plants serve as wildlife habitats, and can produce food for households (e.g., blueberries, apples, and figs). Of course, trees and shrubs have a marked social effect on humans as noted by their presence and effects in parks, botanical gardens, cemeteries, urban green spaces, and natural areas. Benefits to society are harder to quantify, but that does not mean they are less important than the ecological services that trees provide. Societal benefits include increased job satisfaction, faster recovery time for hospital patients, and improved child development (see VCE publication "Value, Benefits, and Costs of Urban Trees" 420-181).

To calculate individual tree benefit estimates or view tree canopy estimates for your area, go the U.S Forest Service's iTree calculator website (https://www.itreetools.org/).

Specific Landscape Uses of Plants

In addition to the previously mentioned architectural and environmental functions, plants are used in the landscape for numerous functions related to various landscape design reasons. These uses are overlapping and are not exclusive to each other. For example, a hedge can function as a border and a barrier. These are the main specific landscape uses of plants:

- **Accent plant**(s): a plant or plants that are used to add emphasis, draw attention to, or compliment another plant, structure, art work, or any other landscape feature.
- **Barrier**: a row (linear or curvilinear) of plants that separates one area from another and impedes movement (e.g., human, pets)
- **Border**: a row (linear or curvilinear) of plants that separates one area from another
- **Foundation plant**(s): Use of species or more than one species (usually evergreen) to 1) hide the view of an

undesirable sight such as the foundation of a house, or 2) give a structure or landscape element a "base" to avoid the stark transition of the ground with the structure.
- **Hedge**: a living fence to separate areas either for barrier or border functions
- **Massing/Grouping**: use of many plants, usually of a single or two species, to 1) collectively emphasize the features of the species (e.g., form flowers, fall foliage color), 2) to give a natural appearance, 3) create a border or barrier
- **Screen**: plants used to screen a view/object or to provide privacy.
- **Specimen plant:** a plant that is featured by itself (or with smaller plants around it) to act as a focal point in the landscape. A specimen plant has sufficiently notable characteristics (e.g., size, form, color, and texture via trunks/stems, foliage, flowers, and fruit) that warrant its use as a focal point. A plant may be a focal plant 12 months a year, such as a Japanese maple in a courtyard, or for part of a year such as in the case of a conifer amongst deciduous plants; the conifer will be most evident and have a strong visual impact in winter months when deciduous trees are leafless.

Choice of Nursery Stock

Most woody plants purchased at garden centers are sold either as container-grown plants or as balled-and-burlapped, commonly called B&B, plants.

The Virginia Department of Forestry (DOF) grows seedlings for Virginia landowners, which can be ordered seasonally through the DOF Buy Virginia Trees website (https://www.buyvatrees.com/). These seedlings are suited for Virginia soils and climate.

Container-Grown Plants

Most shrubs, groundcovers, vines, and young trees are produced and sold in plastic containers with a pine bark-based potting soil. The advantages of container-grown plants are:

- Have 100% of an intact root system
- Convenient to transport
- Relatively light weight

There are two disadvantages of container-grown plants:

- The pine bark potting soil only holds about a one to two day water supply for the plant
- Plants can become root bound

Relative to the water reservoir capacity of the pine bark, a container-grown plant must be watered daily or every other day (depending on plant water use and weather conditions) during the growing season (or until the root system has grown into the surrounding soil and can support itself without supplemental irrigation). A way to avoid this frequent irrigation of container-grown plants is to plant them in the fall when plant water needs are greatly reduced. Of course, most landscape plants, newly planted or established, will need some degree of irrigation during drought periods.

If a container-grown plant has become root bound (solid mass of circling roots on the perimeter of the root ball), then the plant has stayed in that container too long. This is an undesirable situation since roots of most species cannot escape this circular entanglement. In some cases, roots can be pried, teased, or cut from the root ball to encourage growth into the surrounding soil.

Balled-and-Burlapped Plants

Balled-and-burlapped plants are grown in the field. They are then machine-dug and lifted out of the soil. The somewhat round root ball is then covered with burlap (and sometimes with a wire cage) to keep the root ball intact. While some balled-and-burlapped plants are sold in retail garden centers, most of these plants are used in the landscape contracting trade and are planted by landscape contracting company personnel.

Figure 13-8: Balled-and-burlapped plants (center) surrounded by container grown plants.

Advantages of balled-and-burlapped plants are:

- A less intense production system compared to container-grown plants
- Root system is surrounded by mineral soil that retains water for long periods and when planted requires irrigation only about once a week
- Relatively large trees are available via the balled-and-burlapped system

Disadvantages of a balled-and-burlapped plant are:

- Approximately 80+ % of the root system is removed
- Plants take three years to recover from root severance
- Root balls are very heavy; transporting and planting are relatively labor intensive compared to transporting and planting container-grown plants

Regardless of woody plant growing/harvesting system (container versus balled-and-burlapped), adequate irrigation of recently transplanted plants is extremely important for plant survival. In both systems, one should apply enough water to wet the root ball and very little of the surrounding soil; most mineral soils are very moisture retentive. Applying excessive irrigation (an amount to wet root ball and surrounding soil) can keep the soil around the root ball too wet and this can discourage root growth into the soil; this is especially true for soils with a relatively high clay content.

Bare Root Plants

Bare root plants are perennials that are dug up and sold without soil around the roots, during their dormant season. They are often small and young. Many plants purchased online are shipped bare root because the lack of soil makes them lighter and easier to ship. Strawberries, asparagus, fruit trees, and ornamental trees/shrubs are all commonly sold as bare root plants.

Once in your care, bare root plants should not be allowed to dry out. If you do not plant them immediately, they should be stored in a cool location but kept away from extreme cold. Cut off any dead roots and branches before planting. Most bare root plants should be soaked in water before planting. Your plant should come with instructions for soaking and planting. Spread remaining roots out evenly in the hole and gently pack soil around them. Bare root trees may need to be staked the first year.

After planting, bare root plants will begin to grow again. You should see shoots or other signs of growth relatively quickly after planting. A bare root plant that does not grow the first year is dead.

Right Plant for the Right Place and Right Function

One of the biggest challenges dealing with woody plants is to determine the appropriate species for a landscape. The inappropriate selection of woody plants has major consequences such as:

- Increased cost, time, and effort in woody plant maintenance
- Potential hazards from trees/tree parts falling on people, property, and structures
- Potential hazards from species with thorns or poisonous plant parts

- Incurring major costs of removing trees that pose hazards, are prone to storm or pest damage, or are not suited to the landscape

Steps to Select the Right Plant for the Right Place and Function

There are four steps to choose the right plant for the right place. Following these steps will help you create a beautiful, functional, and environmentally sound landscape.

1. **What are the functions and themes of the areas of your landscape?**

    For example, lawn for recreation, shady area with arbor for relaxation, sunny area for vegetable garden, beds next to a house for foundation plants, and beds near property border for privacy planting. These functional aspects will dictate whether trees, shrubs, groundcovers, or vines are needed. You should also consider the theme of your landscape. Is your area to be more natural or more formal? Formal landscapes usually have a linear and/or modular design and utilize species with a distinct symmetry (or are pruned to be symmetrical). Conversely, natural landscapes tend to have curvilinear design and utilize species that are less symmetrical.

    One must take into consideration the mature size of trees for four reasons. 1) Trees will ultimately occupy a much larger volume than the initial planting and thus may grow into areas occupied by other plants or structures. 2) Trees will cast a considerable amount of shade to the south, southeast, and southwest, which may impact plants that require a full or near full sun exposure such as lawns and conifers. 3) As trees grow the amount of leaf and other plant part litter (e.g., pollen, flowers, fruit, and stems) greatly increases, hence maintenance greatly increases as well. 4) Tree roots can extend a considerable distance beyond the edge of the tree's canopy and can invade nearby septic or drainage systems. Tree roots will also very effectively compete with other plants for soil water and can render a soil quite dry. Once each area of the landscape has a designated function then proceed to the next step.

2. **What are the functions of the woody plants to be placed in the functional areas of your landscape?**

    Determine the specific aesthetic, architectural, environmental, and landscape functions (these topics covered earlier in the chapter) of the trees, shrubs, groundcovers, and vines to be placed in each area and proceed to the next step.

3. **What are the existing environmental conditions?**

    Important aspects to determine are:

    - Soil texture, pH, and nutrient content
    - Soil moisture aspects/slopes and low areas
    - Sun and shade areas
    - Wind paths
    - USDA Plant Hardiness Zone
    - Prevalence of deer and other vegetation-destroying animals
    - Existing plant species
    - Access to irrigation
    - Existing and future hardscapes, utility conduits and septic systems, warm air vents

    Assessing these conditions will allow you to select the species that are suitable for the site to be landscaped.

4. **Combine information from steps 1, 2, and 3 to design the landscape and to choose the appropriate trees, shrubs, groundcovers, and vines according to the site conditions.**

    Woody plants vary greatly in terms of their size, form, texture, and color. They also vary greatly in their growth rate; soil, water, light requirements/tolerances; hardiness/high temperature; pest susceptibility; messiness; and invasiveness. Thus, examination and determination of the step 3 environmental aspects (site conditions) will dictate the species that should be selected for a particular landscape site. Step 2 will dictate the plant category (tree, shrub, groundcover, and vine) choices.

Invasive Plants

According to the Virginia Department of Conservation and Recreation (DCR), **invasive plants** are "species intentionally or accidentally introduced by human activity into a region in which they did not evolve and cause harm to natural resources, economic activity or humans" ("Invasive Plant Species"). DCR ranks invasive species according to their potential harm, however this list does not have any regulatory authority, so species included on this list may still be sold at nurseries.

Plants deemed "noxious weeds" are subject to regulation. The Virginia Noxious Weeds list is maintained by the Board of Agriculture and Consumer Services (BACS). The Noxious Weed List is available here: https://law.lis.virginia.gov/admincode/title2/agency5/chapter317/section20/

Every four years, an "Invasive Species Management Plan" (http://www.invasivespeciesva.org/document/virginia-invasive-species-mananagement-plan-2018-final.pdf) is prepared by the Invasive Species Advisory Committee. This plan describes the current regulatory landscape of invasive species management in Virginia and offers opportunities for improvement.

See also the VCE publication "Invasive Plants – A Horticultural Perspective" 426-080

Challenge

This chapter has covered the different types and functions of woody plants, but it can only begin a broad learning process. Trees, shrubs and the like form the study backbone of the local flora and support the local fauna; but the species mix will vary wildly from place to place. Simply reading about the glories of oak trees in general does not tell you whether a live oak or chestnut oak is better suited to where you are. The next, really important step is to get to know the woody plants that have the most importance in the local area. Go on guided tree walks, invest in a plant-ID app, or just get up close and observe the woody plants around you through the seasons. Take care to note the interactions with those plants: a short list to start: insects, birds, mammals, other plants, stormwater patters, and people.

Additional Resources

- VCE Master Gardener Tree Steward Manual: https://pressbooks.lib.vt.edu/treesteward/
- VCE publication "Value, Benefits, and Costs of Urban Trees" 420-181
- U.S Forest Service's iTree calculator website: https://www.itreetools.org/
- Noxious Weed List: https://law.lis.virginia.gov/admincode/title2/agency5/chapter317/section20/
- "Invasive Plants – A Horticultural Perspective" 426-080

Books:

- Dirr, Michael, A. (2009.) *Manual of Woody Landscape Plants*, 6th edition. Stipes Publishing.

References

"Invasive Plant Species of Virginia." Virginia Department of Conservation and Recreation. https://www.dcr.virginia.gov/natural-heritage/invspinfo

Evert, Ray F. and Eichhorn, Susan E. *Raven Biology of Plants*. 2012. W. H. Freeman.

Attributions

Prepared by Alex X. Niemiera, Professor, Department of Horticulture (2015)

- Carol King, Hampton Extension Master Gardener (2021 reviewer)

Image Attributions

- Figure 13-1: Plants can grow very large. Johnson, Devon. 2022. CC BY-NC-SA 4.0.
- Figure 13-2: Diagram of secondary growth in woody stem. Johnson, Devon. 2022. CC BY-NC-SA 4.0. Adapted from "Figure 26-6" in *Raven Biology of Plants*. 2012. by Eichhorn, Susan E., and Evert, Ray F. Originally from W. Troll. 1937. *Vergleichende Morphologie der Hoheren Pflanzen*, vol. 1, pt. 1, Verlage von Gebru ̈ der Borntraeger, Berlin.
- Figure 13-3: Cross section of woody dicot stem. Johnson, Devon. 2022. CC BY-NC-SA 4.0. Includes "Woody Dicot Stem: Two Year Tilia" and "Woody Dicot Stem: One Year Tilia" Berkshire Community College Bioscience Image Library form Flickr. 2014. Public Domain.
- Figure 13-4: Examples of different sized trees. Carol King. 2022. CC BY-NC-SA 4.0.
- Figure 13-5: USDA plant hardiness zone map. USDA. 2012. Public domain. https://planthardiness.ars.usda.gov/.
- Figure 13-6: Comparison of native range of two different Virginia species. Johnson, Devon. 2022. CC BY-NC-SA 4.0. Includes "Map of Virginia Counties and Independent Cities.svg" by Dbenbenn. 2009. Wikimedia. CC BY-SA 3.0. Data from Digital Atlas of the Virginia Flora.
- Figure 13-7: Japanese Elms, *Zelkova serrata* shading a city street in Richmond. Carol King. 2022. CC BY-NC-SA 4.0.
- Figure 13-8: Balled-and-burlapped plants (center) surrounded by container grown plants. Johnson, Devon. 2022. CC BY-NC-SA 4.0.

CHAPTER 14: PRUNING

Chapter Contents:

- Reasons for Pruning
- Pruning Tools
- Pruning Techniques
- Controlling Size
- Maintaining or Improving Plant Health
- Reducing the Risk of Personal Injury or Property Damage
- Training the Plant
- Improving the Quality of Plants, Flowers, and Ornamental Features
- Pruning for Fruit
- Training and Pruning Small Fruit
- Additional Resources

To prune or not to prune? This is a question that gardeners often face. Most feel they ought to, but are not sure why or how. Pruning is a routine and necessary practice for the orchard, is regularly done in the rose garden, but is often rather haphazard elsewhere in the landscape. Landscape pruning for some species is sometimes only brought to mind when a shrub or tree begins to encroach on neighboring property, a path, or a building. However, proper pruning should be a regular part of woody plant maintenance.

This chapter explains the reasons for pruning, the proper techniques and tools to use, and when various types of plants should be pruned.

Pruning is the deliberate removal of plant tissue, living and dead, to achieve specific objectives in plant care and landscape management. Training of young woody plants to avoid future structural issues is a subset of this topic, though again with specific reasons related to the plants in question. Many plants do not need pruning often or even at all, especially if they are well chosen for their planting sites. There are specialized tools and techniques which are meant to reduce the stress on the pruned plant and improve the chance of achieving the desired result.

Reasons for Pruning

Before pruning any plant, the wise gardener will first ask several questions: What is the plant? How does it fit into its setting? Why am I considering pruning this plant? Generally, the reasons for pruning can be organized into these categories:

- Controlling the plant size
- Maintaining or improving plant structure and health
- Reducing the risk of personal injury and property damage
- Training the plant
- Improving the quality of flowers and ornamental features
- Managing fruit production

Pruning Tools

Pruning shears are good for branches up to 3/4-inch in diameter. Attempting to cut larger branches risks making a poor cut and/or ruining the shears. There are two blade or cut styles of hand shears: **bypass pruners** (with two blades that cut like scissors) and anvil cut. In the **anvil style**, a sharpened blade cuts against a broad, flat plate. In the scissor style, a thin, sharp blade slides closely past a thicker blade. Bypass pruners generally make cleaner, closer cuts. When buying pruners, test the pruners in your hand to make sure you can hold them comfortably. If they are too large or small, too heavy or too hard to squeeze, try another style or brand – there is a wide variety of pruning tools available. If you have trouble using pruning tools, there may be special equipment available to suit you. For example, ratchet pruners are useful if your grip is not strong because they can be closed easily with very little pressure.

Figure 14-1: Pruning tools.

Lopping shears have long handles and are operated with both hands. Even the cheapest can cut 1/2-inch diameter material. The better ones can slice through branches of 2 inches or more, depending on species and condition (e.g., pin oak is tougher than linden, and dead wood is tougher – until decay sets in – than live wood). Lopping shears are also available with telescoping handles (to extend reach) and ratchet mechanisms.

Pole pruners have a cutter with a hooked blade above and a cutting blade beneath. The cutter is on a pole and is operated by a cord or chain pulled downward. Fully extended, they can be used to reach branches 12 feet or more above the ground. The poles can either be in sections that fit together or telescoping. Wooden poles are heavy. Aluminum poles are light but can conduct electricity if they touch an overhead wire. Fiberglass or some type of plastic compound is probably the best option. Use of pole pruners can be dangerous, as material cut overhead can fall on the operator (unless it hangs up in other branches); exercise caution and wear head and eye protection. Poles can be fitted with saws. Obtaining an accurate pruning cut with a pole saw is very difficult. Consider employing a professional to make those cuts that you cannot easily reach with from the ground.

Hedge shears have long, flat blades and relatively short handles, one for each hand. Heavy-duty shears, with one blade serrated, are good for difficult jobs. Power hedge shears are also available. The most common for home use are electric models. Although these are less physically demanding, they often result in ragged and improperly placed cuts that are entry points for insects and disease, especially if they are kept sharp.

There are many makes and models of pruning saws. Fineness of cutting edge is measured in points (teeth per inch). An 8-point saw is for delicate, close work on small shrubs and trees. Average saws are about 6 points, while 4-1/2-point saws are for fairly thick cuts. A fixed-blade saw with a protective scabbard is safe and easy to use. Look for a folding saw with a locking mechanism. Blades can be either straight or curved. Many prefer a curved blade that cuts on the draw stroke. A double-edged saw has fine teeth on one side, coarse on the other; these can do significant damage to surrounding branches and may be difficult to use in densely branched plants. Bow saws are good where no obstruction exists for a foot or more above the area to be cut.

Chain saws come in a variety of sizes, both gas and electric. Chain saws are used to remove large limbs or entire trees and cannot make fine, close cuts. Chain saws should be used only with appropriate safety gear by people who fully understand their operation and handling for pruning. Improper or careless handling can do significant damage to trees and people in a very short time. Therefore, the use of chain saws is best left to professionals.

Care of Tools

Clean and oil tools regularly. Thoroughly remove all plant residue, disinfect if needed, and wipe an oily cloth on blades and other surfaces after each use. Keep cutting edges sharp and don't use them to cut wire. Several passes with a good file or oil-stone will usually suffice for hand pruners, loppers, and shears. Saws probably need to be sharpened by a professional or have the blades replaced. Wooden handles should be painted, varnished, or regularly treated with linseed oil. Don't twist or strain pruners or loppers. Keep the branch to be cut as deeply in the jaws and near the pivot as possible.

Pruning Techniques

There are two basic types of pruning cuts: **heading cuts** and **thinning cuts**. Heading cuts reduce the height or width of a plant by cutting back lateral branches and removing terminal buds. Heading cuts may stimulate growth of buds closest to the cut. Heading cuts are not the same as topping cuts. Topping cuts are made indiscriminately in internode areas; heading cuts are made at nodal areas either above side branches or buds.

> **Topping cuts** should not be made to trees because they reduce the tree's food-making capacity, stimulate undesirable water-sprout growth; leave large wounds that are more vulnerable to insect attack and fungal decay; create a hazard as weakened shrubs are more prone to wind and storm breakage; injure bark and increase harmful sun exposure on trunk and branches; and disfigure trees leaving ugly stubs, conspicuous pruning cuts, and a broom-like branch growth habit which replaces the tree's natural beauty and form. Topping trees reduces their real estate value by 20 to 100%. For more information, see the VCE publication "Stop Topping Trees!" 430-458

Thinning cuts, also called reduction cuts, remove branches at their points of origin or attachment. When you prune a branch back to another branch or prune a branch from the trunk, you are thinning. Thinning cuts stimulate growth throughout the tree, rather than in single branches as do heading cuts.

Twigs and Small Branches

When pruning twigs and small branches, always cut back to a vigorous bud or an intersecting branch. This location is called a node, and there is a concentration of meristem cells here that will help to seal the pruning wound faster. When cutting back to a bud, choose a bud that is pointing in the direction you wish the new growth to take. Be sure not to leave a stub over the bud or cut too close to the bud. Be sure to make branch collar cuts as described under "Branch Removal" later in this chapter.

When cutting back to a side (lateral) branch, choose a branch that forms an angle of no more than 45 degrees with the branch to be removed. Also, the branch that you cut back to should have a diameter at least a third that of the branch to be removed.

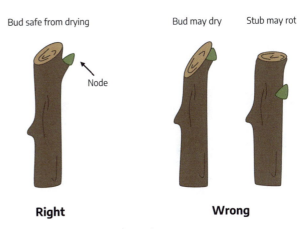

Figure 14-2: Proper pruning angle.

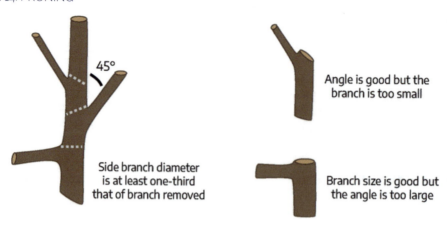

Figure 14-3: Pruning angle diagrams.

Branch Removal

All branches with discernible "branch collars" should be removed outside the collar, not flush with the trunk. The **branch collar** is the swollen area that forms around the base of a branch, often appearing a bit swollen. If you wound the branch collar, you compromise the zone protecting the rest of the tree (the trunk and roots) from decay. The collar area contains a chemically protective zone. In the natural decay of a dead branch, when the decay advancing downward meets the internal protected zone, an area of very strong wood meets an area of very weak wood. The branch then falls away at this point, leaving a small zone of decayed wood within the collar. The decay is designed to stop in the collar. When the collar is removed or compromised, the protective zone is removed or compromised, causing a serious trunk wound. Wood-decay fungi can then easily infest the trunk. Even if the pruned branch is living, removal of the collar at the base still causes injury to the tree. If the collar is not evident, find the **branch bark ridge** (a prominent ridge of raised bark that forms within the branch crotch) extending down the trunk on both sides at an angle. The angle formed by this ridge and the trunk can be used to estimate the location of the branch collar (labeled B in Figure 14-4).

The total amount of live plant tissue removed in one pruning season should generally be limited to one quarter the mass of the tree or shrub. This practice allows the plant to support its recovery from the stress of pruning. It should be noted that different species and individual plants will vary in their tolerance for pruning. This is one of the reasons why it is important to know the plant to be pruned before starting. A significant exception to the one-quarter guideline is rejuvenation pruning, when the objective is to give a plant in poor condition a chance to start over.

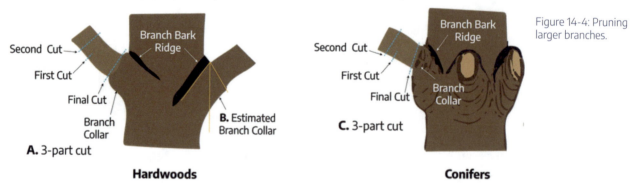

Figure 14-4: Pruning larger branches.

When cutting branches too large or too heavy to support with one hand while removing with pruners, use a 3-part cut to prevent the limb from falling before it's fully cut and tearing bark away from the tree. A 3-part cut is accomplished by first making an undercut; that is, sawing the bottom of the branch 6 to 12 inches out from the trunk and about 1/3 of the way through the branch. Next, make a second cut from the top, about 3 inches further out from the undercut, until the branch falls away. The resulting stub can then be cut back at the collar of the branch, labeled A and C in Figure 14-4. If there is danger of the branch damaging other limbs below or objects on the ground, it must be properly roped and supported, then carefully lowered to the ground after the second cut by a professional arborist.

Don't coat pruning cuts with tree paint or wound dressing; these products actually inhibit the tree's ability to seal the pruning wound. Some tests have suggested that wound dressings are beneficial when pruning trees that are susceptible to canker or systemic disease (oak wilt and Dutch elm disease). Tree paint won't prevent decay, promote wound closure, or prevent disease-carrying insects from entering tree wounds. The best way to prevent oak wilt and Dutch elm disease is to avoid pruning oaks and elms in May and June when insects are more active.

Controlling Size

This is often the worst reason for pruning and unfortunately one of the most common. Generally it is hard on the plant and creates unnecessary yard waste. Over time, poor planning results in trees and shrubs which grow to sizes that exceed the space allowed for them. Where space is limited, regular pruning becomes necessary to keep plants in bounds and may impact survival. It is best to reduce labor, select plants that will not exceed the allotted space when mature. Regular pruning is necessary on formal hedges to maintain a uniform growth rate. For hedges, labor and yard waste can be reduced by choosing small or slow-growing plants and allowing them to grow in a more natural form, rather than keeping them tightly pruned. If a formal garden design relies on clipped shrubs or trees, plant selection should focus on those that will tolerate frequent pruning, such as boxwood or yew.

Maintaining or Improving Plant Health

Pruning can be a useful tool in maintaining plant health. For example, diseased tissue and the reproductive structures of pathogens can be removed from a plant to minimize spread of disease. Pruning can improve light and air circulation which can suppress certain diseases and insects. Pruning low-growing branches from a plant can reduce plant/soil contact which can affect the spread of some soil-borne diseases.

When pruning to maintain plant health, first consider sanitation, which includes the elimination of dead, dying, or diseased wood. Any dying branch or stub can be the entry point or build-up chamber for insects or disease that could spread to other parts of the tree. When removing diseased wood such as a fungal canker or fire blight, it is important that the cut be made in healthy wood beyond the point of infection. Do not prune during wet weather as disease inoculum is easily spread by water. Carefully dispose of diseased wood in the trash or by burning. Do not put it in a household compost pile or place by the curb for municipal recycle pick up as both of these processes lead to spread of inoculum. Disinfect your tools between plants, or between cuts on the same plant when disease is present. Tools should either be sprayed with the sanitizer and allowed to air dry or dipped in the sanitizer for the recommended length of time. Some readily available sanitizers include ethanol (70% or greater), sodium hypochlorite (a 1:14 solution of 8.25% household bleach), and Lysol Brand Concentrate Disinfectant.

The development of a sound framework through proper thinning will help prevent disease and loss of vigor while maintaining or improving form. To avoid future problems, remove crossing branches that rub or interfere with each other. Even evergreen shrubs usually will benefit from an occasional thinning of foliage. This thinning will allow penetration of light and air throughout the shrub.

Broadleaf Trees

Maintenance pruning of broadleaf trees is intended to preserve or improve the structure of the trees, enabling them to withstand stresses from wind and weather. Pruning should be looked at as a planned program over time rather than a one-time intervention. Maintenance pruning includes removing dead or diseased branches as soon as they are noticed. Water sprouts and suckers are two types of vigorous shoot growth generally considered undesirable and should be removed except on over mature trees which may form water sprouts for photosynthesis reserves (extra food production). Water sprouts occur along branches, often at pruning sites. Suckers grow from the trunk or roots. Both are rapid vegetative growths with weak attachments to the root of the tree, some trees are prone to such growths; in others they can be an indication of decline or stress.

Corrective pruning may also be required. Corrective pruning removes damaged wood and eliminates rubbing branches. When a tree's leader is lost due to storm damage or disease, replace it by splinting an upper lateral on the highest scaffold to a vertical position. Prune all laterals immediately below the new leader. Use wood or flexible wire splints, removing them after one growing season.

Pruning at different seasons triggers different responses. Late winter or early spring, before bud break, is a good time to prune many species because callus tissue forms rapidly and food production is unaffected. However, sap from the tree may be cosmetically undesirable. When pruning flowering trees, try not to cut off flower buds. Some trees, such as cherry, plum, and crab apple, form buds on old wood. Others, such as crape myrtle, bloom on new wood. Summer pruning tends to suppress growth of both suckers and foliage. Late summer or early fall pruning causes vigorous regrowth, which in some species may not harden off by winter, leading to possible cold damage. Whenever unexpected damage from vandalism or bad weather occurs, prune immediately.

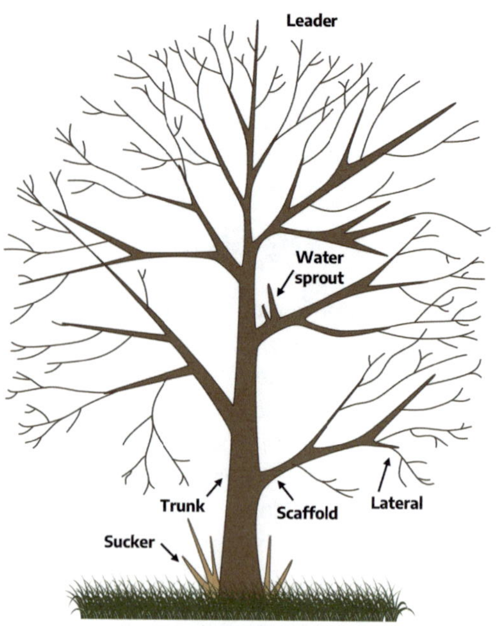

Figure 14-5: Tree diagram.

Rejuvenation of broadleaf trees

Some broadleaf trees will regrow from fresh stumps with healthy roots. Hollies and crape myrtles are two examples. If such trees are damaged in storms or otherwise lose major trunks, then they can be regrown from new shoots, with training as for young trees. Rejuvenation can also be a useful tactic when a large shrub or small tree is in decline due to neglect. Once the underlying cause of the neglect is corrected (more light, more water, improving the soil with compost, etc.), then the tree or shrub can be cut back drastically to shock the plant into new growth. Typically this is done by cutting out a third of the plant each year over a period of three years. However, if the alternative is to remove the plant now, then a complete cut to the ground may be worth trying.

Conifers

Conifers generally need less pruning than broadleaf trees. Because conifers have dominant leaders, young trees rarely require training-type pruning. If a young tree has two leaders, prune one out to prevent multiple leader development. Selective branch removal is generally unnecessary as evergreens tend to have wide angles of attachment to the trunk.

Conifers are grouped on the basis of their branch arrangement. Spruces, firs, and some pines (white pine) have whorled branches that form a circular pattern around the growing tip. The annual growth of a whorl-branched conifer is determined by the number of shoots that are pre-formed in the buds. Whorl-branched conifers usually have only one flush of growth each year in which these preformed shoots expand into stems that form the next whorl. The second group of evergreens are those with a random branching habit. Yew, arborvitae, cedar, false cypress, and juniper are all random-branched species.

Corrective pruning for conifers consists mainly of removal of dead, diseased, or damaged branches. Allow evergreen trees to grow in their natural form. Don't prune into the inactive center (where no needles or leaves are attached) of whorl-branched conifers because new branches won't form to conceal the stub, in most conifers. When a tree's leader is lost due to storm damage, train a replacement leader as described for broadleaf trees.

Most conifer pruning is done for corrective reasons, so seasonal timing is usually not as important as it is for deciduous species. Pruning during dormancy is the most common practice and will result in a vigorous burst of spring growth. Pines and other whorl-branched conifers become denser if new growing tips ("candles") are pinched in half as they expand in the spring. Use your fingers or shears to remove part of the candle. Prune random-branched conifers in early spring when new growth will cover the pruning wounds. Maintenance pruning of random-branched conifers is done in summer to keep plants within a desired size range. Whenever possible, avoid pruning conifers in late summer and early fall. Pruning at this time can stimulate new growth that may not harden off before winter, and thus may be damaged or killed by the cold.

Norfolk Master Gardener Crape Myrtle Pruning

By Paulette Crawford, Extension Master Gardener, Norfolk

There are about 48,000 Crape Myrtle trees along the city streets in Norfolk, Virginia. These are city trees, mostly planted on the verge throughout the entire city. Crape myrtles thrive in the Norfolk area. They are heat and drought tolerant and are known as the tree of 100-day blooms. Crape myrtles are resilient and require little maintenance, however, crape myrtles are prone to producing canes or suckers. These suckers can be a nuisance, but they pose no problem for the tree. Suckers can grow quite large when not pruned, and this can be unsightly and even become an obstruction.

In 2015 Norfolk Extension Master Gardeners launched the Crape Myrtle Pruning (CMP) project, a partnership with the Norfolk City Forester's office. Together, EMGs and the City Forester identify areas that have a concentration of crape myrtles with significant sucker growth. The City Forester provides tools, safety equipment and initial training to Master Gardeners to ensure they are taught the proper way to prune and the limited pruning allowed for city trees as well as proper safety precautions. This has provided an opportunity for Master Gardeners to work within their community alongside volunteers teaching them proper pruning techniques. EMGs host community prune events throughout the year because minor pruning can be performed at any time.

Master Gardeners lead small groups of community volunteers during each CMP event and educate the volunteers on proper pruning methods and the importance of proper tree pruning. They also cover Norfolk's rules regarding care and maintenance of trees on city property and appropriate tree pruning safety precautions. While most of their minor pruning focuses on suckers, they also remove small branches. EMG volunteers are restricted by Norfolk rules, which require them to have both feet on the ground, only prune what can easily be reached, and use only hand tools. Volunteers learn the importance of using appropriate tools (hand pruners, lopping shears, and hand saws) and the proper way to use each tool.

While it is ideal to prune in winter when plants are dormant and branch structure is visible, suckers can be removed any time. Corrective pruning can be performed when problems are detected such as crossing, dead or damaged branches, as well as low hanging branches overhead. Community volunteers learn by hands-on pruning lessons. Then they take what they have learned and apply it to trees in their own landscape, and they understand the limited pruning they can perform on city trees adjacent to their property. In the process, this improves the city and residential landscapes.

From time to time EMGs encounter trees which offer on-the-spot learning in the field. For example, crape myrtle bark scale is identified and discussed with the volunteers and then reported to the City Forester. A frequent topic of interest is the practice of "topping" or severely cutting back branches also known as "crape murder." Volunteers take the time to discuss why this is improper and the risks and problems it can create for the tree. For more information on crape myrtle bark scale, see the VCE Publication "Crapemyrtle Bark Scale" ENTO-465NP (https://www.pubs.ext.vt.edu/content/pubs_ext_vt_edu/en/ENTO/ento-465/ento-465.html).

EMGs are also invited to civic leagues and other groups to discuss their project and the care and maintenance of crape myrtles.

Figure 14-6: Crape myrtle before (left) and after Norfolk EMGs pruned (right).

Pruning Shrubs: Growth Habit

Understanding the natural 'habit' or shape of shrubs should guide pruning decisions. All shoots grow outward from their tips. Whenever tips are removed, lower buds are stimulated to grow. Buds are located at nodes, where leaves are attached to twigs and branches. Buds may occur singly or in groups.

Shrubs have mounding, cane, or tree-like growth habits. Those with **mounding habits**, such as evergreen azalea and spirea, generally have soft, flexible stems, small leaves, and are often used in mass plantings. Shrubs with **cane habits** include forsythia and nandina. These shrubs spread by sending up erect new branches, called canes, from their base. **Tree-like shrubs** have woodier, finely divided branches and can be pruned as a single-trunk or multi-stemmed trees. Witch hazel is an example.

Pruning mounding shrubs

The pruning recommended for most mounding shrubs consists of maintenance pruning, gradual rejuvenation, and extensive rejuvenation pruning. This is required to keep them healthy and in scale with their surroundings. Older shrubs often grow out of proportion with their surroundings, and may have large amounts of unproductive wood. Two rejuvenation techniques are used to restore old shrubs, provided they still have sufficient vigor and are growing in a favorable location. Maintenance pruning practices should begin at the time of planting or after rejuvenation of older shrubs. Always remove dead, diseased, or broken branches first.

Proper method of pruning a crape myrtle

This plant, pictured before pruning, needs to have all weak and dead stems removed.

Same shrub after removal of weak and interfering wood and base sucker growth.

Results of proper pruning are graceful, vigorous growth with distinctive shape.

Improper method of pruning a crape myrtle

Cutting at the dotted line is the usual course taken by those who prune shrubs.

The same plant after a bad pruning, as indicated above. The sucker growth remains.

Results: the lovely natural shape of the shrub is lost, and bloom will be sparse.

Figure 14-7: Proper (left) and improper (right) methods of pruning.

Pruning cane-like shrubs

To reduce height of shrubs with a cane habit, first remove the tallest canes by cutting or sawing them out near ground level. Then, thin out any canes crowding the center, as well as those growing in an unwanted or unruly direction. For height maintenance of mounding-type shrubs, prune only the longest branches. Make thinning cuts well inside the shrub mass where they won't be visible. This method reduces mounding shrubs by up to 1/3 their size without sacrificing their shape.

Pruning tree-like shrubs

Shrubs with a tree-like habit are the most difficult to shorten. After removing any rubbing branches, prune to open up the center of the shrub. Keep the crown open and maximize light penetration by careful use of thinning cuts. Prune branches that touch the ground and suckers originating from the roots. Wait until the very end of the job to make any heading cuts. Tree-like shrubs can usually tolerate removal of 1/8 to 1/4 of their branches.

Rejuvenation Pruning of Shrubs

Some older shrubs will recover and regain beauty if rejuvenated by removal of old wood by one of the following methods.

Gradual rejuvenation removes growth gradually. The first year, remove 1/3 of the oldest, unproductive branches. New, productive stems should quickly replace the old wood. The next year, take 1/2 of the lingering old stems. Finally, in the third year, prune out the remainder of the old branches. Thus, all the branches should be less than 4 years old. This method takes longer to complete, but the shrub stays more attractive throughout the rejuvenation period. Renewal pruning is the term used for a continual maintenance system of annually removing 1/3 of the oldest growth throughout the life of the shrub. Forsythia will respond to this type of renewal pruning as an ongoing procedure to maintain its health and vigor.

Before — After

Figure 14-8: Gradual rejuvenation

Extensive rejuvenation involves complete removal of the entire plant 6-10 inches above the ground. Use heavy lopping shears and a pruning saw. Remove half of the new canes that develop by mid-summer, and head back some of the remaining canes. When using a heading cut, be sure to prune to outward-pointing buds so that the inner portion does not become too dense. Shrubs that tolerate extensive rejuvenation are abelia, honeysuckle, hydrangea, lilac, mallow, rose-of-sharon, spirea, and St. John's wort (hypericum).

Pruning Evergreen Shrubs

For most evergreen shrubs, thinning is the most desirable procedure. Some evergreens can be sheared when a stiff, formal appearance is desired; however, they will still need to be thinned occasionally. Late season shearing can stimulate new growth that may not be properly acclimated for cold winter temperatures, resulting in plant injury. Both evergreen and deciduous shrubs grown for foliage should be pruned in late winter before new growth starts. Minor corrective pruning can be done at any time.

Pruning Hedges

Hedges consist of plants set in a row so as to merge into a solid, linear mass. They have served gardeners for centuries as screens, fences, walls, and edgings.

A well-shaped hedge is no accident. It must be trained from the beginning. The establishment of a deciduous hedge begins with the selection of nursery stock. Choose young trees or shrubs that are 1 to 2 feet high, preferably multiple-stemmed. When planting, cut the plants back to 6 or 8 inches. This will induce low branching. Late in the first season or before bud-break in the next season, prune off half of the new growth. In the following year, again trim off half the new growth to encourage branching.

In the third year, start shaping. Hedges are often shaped with flat tops and vertical sides. This unnatural shaping is seldom successful. The best shape, as far as the plant is concerned, is a natural form – rounded or slightly pointed top with sides slanting to a wide base. After plants have been pruned initially to induce low branching, the low branching will be maintained by trimming the top narrower than the bottom, so that sunlight can reach all of the leaves on the plant.

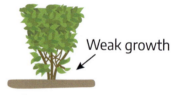

Figure 14-9: Pruning hedges.

Rounded or peaked tops aid shedding snow, which may break branches if not removed. Before shaping, some thought should be given to the shape of the untrimmed plant. For example, naturally conical arborvitae does particularly well in a Gothic arch shape. Common buckthorn, a spreading plant, is more easily shaped to a Roman arch.

Trim to the desired shape before the hedge grows to the desired size. Never allow the plants to grow untrimmed to the final height before shearing; by that time it will be too late to get maximum branching at the base. After the hedge has reached the dimensions desired, trim closely in order to keep it within bounds.

Evergreen nursery stock for hedging need not be as small as deciduous material, and should not be cut back when planted. Trim lightly after a year or two. Start shaping as the individual plants merge into a continuous hedge. Do not trim too closely, because many needle-bearing evergreens do not easily generate new growth from old wood.

These questions often arise: "How often should this hedge be trimmed?" and "When should I trim?" Answers depend to some extent on how formal an appearance is desired. In general, trim before the growth exceeds 1 foot. Hedges of slow-growing plants, such as boxwood, need trimming sooner. Excessive untrimmed growth will kill leaves beneath and also pull the hedge out of shape. This is especially true with weak-stemmed shrubs. In the mountain areas of Virginia, yews and other evergreens may need shearing only once annually, and then not before July; in milder areas, two or even three shearings may be necessary. Deciduous material should be trimmed earlier than July, but after the spring flush of new growth, and will often need to be trimmed once or twice more. Frequency depends on the kind of shrub, season, and degree of neatness desired.

Broad flat top with snow accumulation | Straight lines | Peaked and rounded tops | Rounded forms following nature's tendency

Figure 14-10: Hedge shapes.

What can be done with a large, overgrown, bare-bottomed, and misshapen hedge? If it is deciduous, the answer is fairly simple. In the spring, before leaves appear, prune to one foot below the desired height. Then trim carefully for the next few years to give it the shape and fullness desired. Occasionally, hedge plants may have declined too much to recover from this treatment; replacing them may be necessary.

Rejuvenating evergreen hedges is more difficult. As a rule, evergreens cannot stand the severe pruning described above. Arborvitae and yew are exceptions; other evergreen hedges may have to be replaced.

What tools should be used to trim hedges? The traditional pair of scissor-action hedge shears is still the best all-round tool. It will cut cleaner and more closely than electric trimmers, which often break and tear twigs. Hand shears can be used on any type of hedge, while electric trimmers do poorly on large-leaved and wiry-twigged varieties, and sometimes jam on thick twigs. Hand shears are also quieter and safer, less likely to gouge the hedge or the operator. Hand pruners are useful for removing a few stray branches. Larger branches can be removed with loppers and/or a pruning saw.

It should be pointed out that shearing of hedges consists of cuts which stimulate a dense canopy or shell of foliage that encourages diseases in the interior of the hedge and increases the amount of yard waste produced. Where possible, natural unsheared hedges should be used.

Root Pruning

A tree growing in the woods or landscape for several years develops a wide-spreading root system. The area in a 3-foot radius of the trunk of the tree more than five to ten years old contains very few of the small feeding roots essential to gathering nourishment for the tree. As a consequence, if the tree were to be dug and moved, as much as 90-95% of the necessary feeding roots would be cut off in the balling operation. This is the reason many nurseries root-prune trees and shrubs: to force them to grow a large number of small feeding roots near the base of the plant which are moved in the balling operation and aid in establishment after transplanting.

To make it possible to safely dig and move small trees or shrubs, such trees should be root-pruned a year or so before they are moved. In the spring, sever half the roots by forcing a sharp spade into the soil around the plant alternately leaving a shovel width of untouched soil between cuts. The circle of cuts should be smaller than the size of the ball that will eventually be dug. In the fall, sever the other half of the roots, thus cutting all the roots that are at a depth of a foot or less. The tree can then be moved the following spring. Recent research indicates that most of the new roots grow from the cut root end. Therefore, a root ball 4 to 6 inches larger than the root-pruned area must be dug to get the newly developed roots.

Root pruning is also used to force a vigorously growing fruit tree or wisteria vine into bloom. Using a spade to cut the roots early in the spring, as explained above, is all that is sometimes necessary to force a tree, shrub, or vine into bloom the following year. This takes advantage of a plant's natural reaction to stress or wounding: propagation beginning with flowering.

Pruning Vines and Ground Covers

Pruning ornamental vines is similar to pruning shrubs. Flowering vines are pruned according to flower production; those that flower on new wood are pruned before new growth begins, those that flower on previous season's growth are pruned immediately after flowering. Vines that are grown for foliage are pruned to control growth and direction. Timing is less critical than for flowering vines. Keep flowering vines from setting seed that will be spread by birds.

Ground cover plants require very little pruning. Dead or damaged stems should be removed whenever observed. Some trailing ground covers, such as English ivy, may need pruning to prevent encroachment to natural areas, on lawn areas, or other plants. With liriope, a grass-like ground cover, appearance is improved by annual pruning. Before new leaves are an inch tall, remove the dead leaves from the previous year. For large liriope plantings, a lawn mower set to cut above the new leaf tips will speed this early spring job.

Invasive plant cuttings, such as English Ivy should be burned or discarded as trash. Do not compost or otherwise discard.

Reducing the Risk of Personal Injury or Property Damage

One of the more important reasons for pruning is to keep landscape plants from injuring the people and structures in those landscapes. Often, the problem is trees overhanging houses, paths, playgrounds, and roads. Utility line pruning is a professional specialty of its own, reflecting the importance of managing trees around power lines. People who have a responsibility for trees should consider the possibility that those trees could drop limbs or obstruct traffic. Proper pruning can prevent such situations if undertaken early enough. Even better, informed selection and training of trees can avoid this discussion altogether.

Shrubs can also crowd paths or whip into walkers' faces. Often such shrubs are of the mounding variety, such as beautyberry. If relocation is not feasible, then a regular pruning schedule may be necessary to reduce risk.

Certified arborists with special training can identify the level of risk posed by tree condition, situation, and potential for harm. For example, a large diseased branch hanging over a playground generally warrants immediate attention, while a distressed tree in an open field with no traffic under it may best be allowed to stand as a habitat for wildlife.

Training the Plant

Training Trees

The first pruning of young trees and shrubs consists of removing broken, crossing, and pest-infested branches. This is best done at the time of transplanting. Additional pruning should not be done until the next year.

The old rule of pruning away 1/3 of the top growth at transplanting to compensate for root loss is not recommended. Research proves that excessive pruning at transplanting is detrimental to plant establishment.

It is easier to shape branches with hand pruners when trees are young than to prune larger branches later. As a rule, the central leader of a tree should not be pruned unless a leader is not wanted, as is the case with some naturally low-branched trees or where multiple-stemmed plants are desired. Trees with a central leader such as linden, sweet gum, or pin oak may need little or no pruning except to eliminate branches competing with the central leader; these should be shortened or removed. Train main scaffold branches (those that form the structure of the canopy) to produce stronger and more vigorous trees.

The height of the lowest branch can be from a few inches above the ground (for screening or windbreaks) to 8+ feet above the ground near a path or patio and 14 feet or more beside a street. Some branches below the lowest permanent scaffold branches should be left for three to four years after planting, then removed over the next two to three years. These temporary branches protect young bark from sun scald, add strength to the trunk, and help produce food for the growing tree.

For greatest strength, branches selected for permanent scaffolds should have a wide angle of attachment with the trunk. Branch angles of less than 30 degrees from the main trunk ("V" shaped crotch) result in a higher percentage of breakage, while those between 60 and 70 degrees have a very small breakage rate. The breakage on "V" crotches is caused by the inclusions of bark within the crotch as the tree grows. This prevents the development of strong connective tissue.

Vertical branch spacing and radial branch distribution are important. Major scaffold branches of trees that will grow to large shade trees should be spaced at least 10 to 12 inches apart vertically. Closely spaced scaffolds will have fewer lateral branches. The result will be long, thin branches with poor structural strength. Good radial spacing prevents one limb from overshadowing another and, therefore, reduces competition for light and nutrients. Over several years, remove or prune shoots that are too low, too close, or too vigorous in relation to the leader and scaffold branches. Total amount of foliage removed in any one year should be limited to about one-quarter, not including dead tissue and suckers. **Suckers** are vigorous shoots **growing from the trunk or roots.**

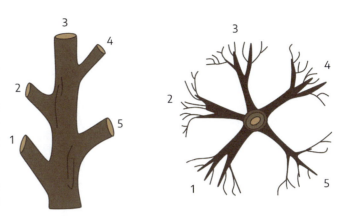

Figure 14-11: Vertical and radial arrangement of scaffold branches.

Training Shrubs

Shrubs require little, if any, pruning at transplanting. Occasionally, branches may have been damaged in transit, and these should be removed at the time of planting.

Training for Special Effects

Specialized training techniques such as bonsai, topiary, and espalier require special pruning techniques. Bonsai is an art form that stems from ancient oriental culture, originating in China and developed by the Japanese. Bonsai techniques severely dwarf trees through careful pruning of both roots and shoots over many years. Bonsai strives to create a miniature tree that is shaped to create the illusion of age. Topiary uses special pruning and training techniques to create unusually shaped shrubs, vines, and trees. Typical topiary forms include spiral, turret and tiered globe shapes. Animals are also popular topiary forms. Topiary requires a long-term commitment to gradual pruning to achieve and maintain the desired shape and a suitable pruning-tolerant plant choice. Espalier is a technique that trains a tree to a flat surface in a decorative pattern. It is commonly used for fruit trees as it allows the production of high quality fruit in a relatively small space.

Improving the Quality of Plants, Flowers, and Ornamental Features

The more flowers and fruit a plant produces, the smaller they become, as can be seen on an unpruned rose bush or fruit tree. Pruning reduces the amount of wood and so diverts energy into the production of larger, though possibly fewer, flowers and/or fruit. Most flowering shrubs will bloom either on 1-year old growth or on new growth. Properly timed pruning will increase the production of wood that will bear flowers.

Some deciduous shrubs have colored barks which are especially delightful in winter. The best color is produced on young stems; the greatest stem length and most intense color result from hard pruning

When the shrub to be pruned is grown for its flowers, the pruning must be timed to minimize disruption of the blooming. Spring flowering shrubs bloom on last season's growth and should be pruned soon after they bloom. This allows for vigorous growth during the summer, which will provide flower buds for the following year.

Flowering and Pruning of "Old Wood" and "New Wood" Species

A **bud** is a small package of partially preformed tissue which becomes leaves/stems or flowers. In some cases, buds contain partially preformed flower tissue (flower bud), and usually have a different appearance than a vegetative bud, a bud that contains partially preformed leaf and stem tissue. Some buds contain both floral and vegetative tissues. The time of year that flower buds are produced on woody plants will dictate the time of pruning, thus it is important to know whether a species flowers on "old wood" or "new wood."

The majority of woody plants flower on "old wood" during the spring or early summer. This means that the flower buds of spring or early summer-flowering species were produced on stems in the year prior to flowering. For example, rhododendrons (*Rhododendron* spp.) that flower in spring produced their flower buds about 10 months earlier in the summer of the prior year. Therefore, prune spring-flowering shrubs right after they finish flowering; pruning spring flowering shrubs in the summer, fall, winter, or early spring removes flower buds and results in a poor or lack of flower display the following spring.

In general, spring-flowering and early summer species flower on one-year-old stems; thus, flowering occurs on the outermost portions of the plant. Some shrub species, such as lilacs (*Syringa vulgaris*) and forsythia (*Forsythia ×intermedia*), require the removal of the larger, older stems on an annual basis to encourage the production of younger, flowering wood. Removing older branches results in the growth of new stems that produce more flowers compared to the amount of flowers produced on large, old stems.

Table 14-1: Examples of shrubs and small trees that bloom on last season's growth

Scientific Name	Common Name
Cercis chinensis	Chinese redbud
Chaenomeles japonica	Japanese Quince
Chionathus virginicus	Fringe tree
Deutzia species	Spring-Flowering deutzias
Exochorda racemosa	Pearlbush
Forsythia species	Forsythia
Kerria japonica	Kerria
Lonicera species	Honeysuckle
Magnolia stellata	Star magnolia
Philadelphus species	Mockorange species
Pieris species	Pieris species
Rhondodendron species	Azaleas and Rhododendron
Rosa species	Rambling rose species
Spiraea species	Early white spirea species
Syringa species	Lilac species
Tamarix parviflora	Small-flowred tamarix
Viburnum species	Viburnums
Weigela florida	Old-fashioned weigela

Summer-flowering species produce their flower buds on "new wood". This means that the flower buds of summer-flowering species were produced on stems during the spring/summer in the same year that the plant bears flowers. For example, crape myrtles (*Lagerstroemia* spp.) that flower in the summer produced their flower buds a month or two prior to flowering. Plants that flower on new wood can be pruned late in the growing season (after they finish flowering, during the fall, winter, and early spring since the stems removed during these times will not have any preformed flower buds on them).

Most shrubs that bloom after June usually do so from buds which are formed the same spring. Such shrubs should be pruned in late winter to promote vigorous growth in the spring.

Table 14-2: Examples of shrubs and small trees that bloom on current season's growth

Scientific Name	Common Name
Abelia x grandiflora	Glossy abelia
Buddleia davidii or globosa	Butterfly bush
Callicarpa japonica	Japanese beauty bush
Clethra alnifolia	Summer sweet
Hibiscus syriacus	Shrubs althea
Hydrangea arborescens	Hills of Snow
Hydrangea paniculata	Pegee Hydrangea
Hypericum species	Saint John's wort
Lagerstroemia indica	Crape Myrtle
Rosa species	Bush rose
Spiraea bumalda	Anthony Waterer Spirea
Spirea japonica	Mikado Spirea
Symphoricarpos species	Snowberry
Tamarix hispida	Kashgar
Tamarix odessana	Odessa
Vitex agnus-castus	Chaste tree

The general pruning procedure, illustrated above for crape myrtle, applies to many other large shrubs and small trees of similar structure.

Pruning Roses

All roses need some type of pruning. If roses are not pruned for a number of years, plants deteriorate in appearance, often develop more than the usual disease and insect problems, and the flowers become smaller and smaller.

Hybrid Tea, Grandiflora, and Floribunda roses require annual pruning in the spring, after winter protection has been removed. As a guideline, follow the old saying that roses are pruned when the forsythia blooms. If rosebushes are pruned too early, injury from repeated frost may make a second pruning necessary.

The only tools necessary are sharp hand pruners and gloves. If the rose collection is large, a small saw and loppers will also help. Loppers are used to cut out large dead canes.

Remove branches that are dead, damaged, diseased, thin, weak, growing inward, and branches that cross or interfere with other branches. Proper pruning encourages new growth from the base, making the plant healthy and attractive and resulting in larger blossoms. Cut at least 1 inch below damaged areas. Remove all weak shoots. If two branches rub or are close enough that they will do so soon, remove one. On old, heavy bushes, cut out one or two of the oldest canes each year.

Cut back the remaining canes. The height to which a rose should be cut will vary depending upon the normal habit of the particular cultivar. The average pruning height for Floribundas and Hybrid Teas is between 12 and 18 inches, but taller growing Hybrids and most Grandifloras may be left at 2 feet. Make cuts at 45-degree angles above a strong outer bud. Aim the cut upward from the inner side of the bush to push growth outward and promote healthy shoots and quality flowers.

Other types of roses have special pruning needs:

A **rose standard**, or tree rose, is a Hybrid Tea, Grandiflora, or Floribunda budded at the top of a tall trunk. Prune tree roses as you do Hybrid Teas, cutting the branches to within 6 to 10 inches of the base of the crown in order to encourage rounded, compact, vigorous new growth.

Miniature roses are 6 to 12 inches high with tiny blooms and foliage. Miniature roses do not need special pruning. Just cut out dead growth and remove the hips.

Old-fashioned **rambler roses** have clusters of flowers, each usually less than 2 inches across. They often produce canes 10 to 15 feet long in one season. Ramblers produce best on year-old wood, so that this year's choice blooms come on last year's growth. Prune immediately after flowering. Remove some of the large, old canes. Tie new canes to a support for the next year.

Large-flowering **climbing roses** have flowers more than 2 inches across, borne on wood that is 2 or more years old. Canes are larger and sturdier than those of ramblers. Many flower just once in June, but some, called ever-blooming climbers, flower more or less continuously. This group should be pruned in autumn, any time before cold weather sets in. First cut out dead and diseased canes. After this, remove 1 or 2 of the oldest canes each season to make room for new canes. The laterals, or side shoots, are shortened 3 to 6 inches after flowering. If the plant is strong, keep 5 to 8 main canes, which should be tied to the trellis, fence, wall, or other support. If it is not strong, leave fewer canes.

Pruning for Fruit

The general purpose of pruning fruit trees is to regulate growth, improve fruit size and quality, and reduce production costs. Pruning is necessary to shape trees for convenience of culture and repair of damage.

Most pruning is done during the dormant season, preferably just before active growth begins in the spring. At this time, pruning wounds heal quickly, flower buds can be easily recognized, and injury from low winter temperature is avoided. Summer pruning may be done to help train trees to the desired form and maintain small tree size. It should be remembered, however, that all pruning has a dwarfing effect. For maximum yield of high quality fruit, prune only as necessary to establish a tree with a strong framework capable of supporting heavy crops annually without damage and to maintain a tree sufficiently open to allow penetration of sunlight, air, and spray material for good fruit development and pest control.

Apple Trees

The objectives of training, directing, or modifying growth into a desired form include early fruit production, development of an optimum tree structure for supporting future crops, and producing quality fruit. These objectives can be met by maintaining a proper balance between vegetative and potential fruiting wood. Excess shoot growth will delay the onset of fruiting. However, excess pruning of young, nonbearing trees will also delay the beginning of fruit production in the life of that tree. Training should be emphasized in the development of trees, with pruning used as a tool in the training process to redirect limbs, stimulate branching when desired, or to remove growth that is in an undesirable location. Pruning should not be used to invigorate growth in an attempt to compensate for poor fertilization, poor weed control, or drought conditions.

Future pruning of an apple tree is greatly affected by early training. Much of the pruning of young, bearing trees is the result of errors made in training in the early life of the tree. Thus, it is imperative that training begin early.

A delay for the first 3 to 4 years will result in a poorly-developed, weak tree. Correction of such a problem, usually with heavy pruning, will only further delay and decrease fruit production.

Limb spreading

An integral part of a tree-training program is limb-spreading. Limb orientation affects vigor in various ways. An upright or vertical limb produces the longest shoots near the apex and tends to exhibit high vegetative vigor. As limbs are oriented away from vertical, they exhibit reduced vigor of shoots near the apex, more uniform branching along the shoot, and favor development of fruiting spurs. Fruits hang along the limb and are less prone to rub. A limb orientation around 60 degrees from vertical is desired.

Horizontal orientation of limbs results in the development of vigorous **watersprouts** along the upper surface of the limb, at the expense of potential fruiting spurs.

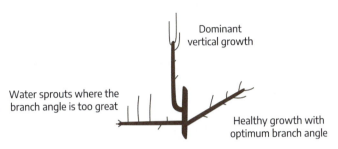
Figure 14-12: Limb orientation.

Thus, correct limb-spreading (near 60 degrees from vertical) can be used to develop a proper balance between vegetative and fruiting growth. Steel wire about 1/8" thick or wooden strips with finishing nails in each end are inserted between the selected scaffold limb and the main trunk of the tree. Limb-spreading should begin early, as many cultivars, such as Red Delicious (particularly spur-types), naturally develop narrow crotch angles. If these narrow crotch angles are not widened (greater than 35 degrees), a situation can quickly develop in which bark is trapped between the trunk and scaffold (bark inclusion). This bark inclusion prevents layers of annual wood from growing together and creates the potential for splitting. If these narrow crotch angles with bark inclusions are allowed to develop, later attempts at limb-spreading may result in splitting of the crotch.

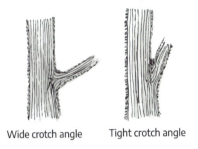
Figure 14-13: Limb angles.

Two objectives exist for limb-spreading: 1) development of a strong, wide crotch angle (greater than 35 degrees) free of bark inclusion and 2) limb orientation at 60 degrees from vertical to balance vegetative and fruiting growth. To derive the benefits of limb-spreading, the crotch must be physically strong, to undergo spreading without splitting.

Poor pruning practices are not a wise substitute for proper limb-spreading in the training of upright scaffolds. Improper pruning cuts will not change the crotch angle, improve limb position, or aid in the control of vegetative vigor. Scaffolds should be spread and lower laterals removed if necessary.

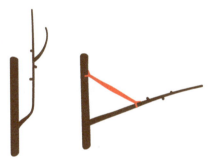
Figure 14-14: Using a spreader to widen crotch angle.

Pruning schedule for apple trees

Scaffold selection for spacing

Scaffold selection can begin in the early summer, especially on cultivars developing narrow crotch angles. Shoots developing below the lowest desired scaffold should be removed. Generally, in the first year, 4 to 6 good scaffolds can be selected that are evenly distributed and not directly above one another.

The vertical spacing between scaffolds can vary from 3 inches to 12 inches depending on the ultimate size of the tree. Limbs with crotch angles less than 35 degrees should be spread or removed. Hardwood toothpicks and clothespins can be used if training is done in early summer while shoots are soft. Short pieces of #9 wire can also be used. Shoots undesirably located can be completely removed at this time.

At planting

Trees must be pruned at planting. Pruning forces the growth of laterals from which future scaffolds will be selected. Head trees to a height of 30 to 35 inches. If feathered (branched) trees are planted, they should be headed to a strong bud to stimulate growth of the central leader. Feathers desirably located can be retained as scaffolds and should be headed by a third. Undesirable feathers should be removed.

First year dormant season

Select shoots to be retained as scaffolds if this was not done earlier. Spread selected scaffolds before any pruning is done. Spreading changes the shape of the tree and may influence pruning decisions. Remove only branches with narrow crotches or branches that are too low. The central leader should be headed to maintain dominance and induce branching. This is done 3 to 5 inches above the point where the next tier of scaffolds is desired. Refrain from heading scaffolds unless they need to be shortened or stiffened. Generally a year-old shoot naturally branches in the season after development. Spreading that scaffold will encourage uniform branching. However, a scaffold will often exhibit excess vigor and upset the balance of the tree.

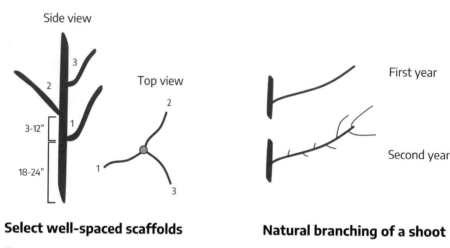

Figure 14-15: Training of apple trees.

Second growing season

Limbs not previously trained can be easily spread early in the growing season when wood is flexible. Fruit developing on the central leader should be removed to prevent the leader from bending. Retain all branches with wide crotch angles.

Second year dormant season

Some of the scaffolds that were selected and spread in the first year may turn up and resume vertical growth. Longer spreaders can be used to spread the limbs back to the desired orientation. The smaller spreaders can be moved further up into the tree. Again, scaffolds should be spread before pruning. The central leader should be headed again to maintain vigor and stimulate branching. Typically, only one or two pruning cuts are required the second winter.

Succeeding years

Continue training and pruning following the previously discussed principles of central leader dominance and proper scaffold selection and training. Scaffolds should be maintained in a 60 degree orientation. A conical tree shape should be maintained. Thus, the upper scaffold should be shorter than the scaffold below it. After the third year, upper scaffolds can be shortened with the use of thinning cuts to remove shoots at the junction with a lateral scaffold or trunk. Thinning cuts are less invigorating than heading cuts, improve light penetration, and can redirect the limb. Remove crossing branches and vigorous watersprouts. Shoots growing up into the tree should be removed. Weak water sprouts can be spread to induce fruiting.

Shorten limbs with thinning cuts

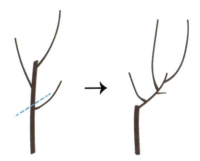
Prune to lateral to maintain height

Figure 14-16: Reducing length.

Once the desired tree height is reached, the tree can be maintained by annually cutting back to a weak lateral on the central leader. This will maintain vigor in the top center of the tree while maintaining desired tree height. In the top half of the tree, remove branches with a diameter half the diameter of the trunk at the point of attachment.

Bearing apple trees

When pruning is underway, older, bearing trees should be pruned first. Young, nonbearing apple trees and stone fruits should not be pruned until after February 1 to minimize chances of winter injury.

The balance between vegetative and fruiting growth is influenced by the crop load, fertilization, and pruning. Fruiting may be poor because vigor is too high or too low. Low vigor can be the result of inadequate fertilization, no pruning, excessive cropping, or shading of fruiting wood. Good fruiting wood requires moderate vigor and exposure to good light levels.

Light is the source of energy that produces the crop. Bearing wood that is shaded is low in vigor and produces small, poorly colored fruits. Good light exposure is necessary for the development of flower buds as well as optimum size, color, and sugar content of the fruit. Studies have shown that a typical tree canopy is composed of different layers or zones in respect to light exposure. As shown below, an outside zone of leaves and fruit receives a high proportion of direct light and light levels above those required for good growth and fruiting; a second zone receives adequate light exposure; and a third, inner zone receives inadequate light exposure and is unproductive.

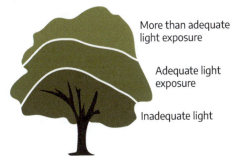
Figure 14-17: Sources of light.

The relative proportion of these zones in a tree is influenced by tree size and shape. As tree size increases, the percentage of the tree that is shaded and unproductive (third zone) increases. Trees that have wide tops and narrow bottoms also have a high percentage of shaded areas in the tree canopy. Trees should be cone-shaped, or larger at the bottom than the top, to maximize adequate light exposure.

Good light exposure in the tree canopy can also be maintained by a good pruning program. Ideally, pruning should remove unproductive wood and develop a uniform distribution of vigor and light exposure throughout the tree. Proper pruning can also help to maintain desired tree size and shape.

Pruning should be done on a regular basis, and consists of moderate cuts made throughout the tree to distribute vigor and provide good light penetration. Heading cuts should only be used where branching is desired or in areas where vigor is low. Drooping or low-hanging branches should be removed or pruned to a lateral that is positioned above horizontal. Remove crossing, dead, or damaged limbs. Watersprouts should be removed unless one is needed for the development of new bearing surface. Watersprouts can be easily removed by hand as they develop in the summer.

Without regular annual pruning, trees often become overly thick, and irregular bearing may occur. Spray penetration is reduced, and problems such as scale may develop in the dense areas of the tree. With this type of tree, make many thinning cuts throughout the tree with emphasis on the upper, outer portions of the tree. This will open up areas into the tree canopy as well as reestablish good tree shape.

Avoid heading cuts to outward-growing limbs unless necessary. Such cuts result in weak limbs and an umbrella shape that creates a sucker problem. Remove no more than 2 large limbs per year. If large amounts of pruning are required, it should be spread over a 2 to 3 year period. In addition, such pruning should be preceded and followed for 1 to 2 years by a reduction or elimination of nitrogen application depending on soil type, variety, and grower experience.

The excess vigor that can result from severe pruning can decrease fruit quality. The effect is much the same as from excessive nitrogen application and may include excessively large, poorly colored, soft apples which will not store well. Vegetative growth competes with fruit for calcium; thus, under conditions of excessive vigor, **cork spot** may develop.

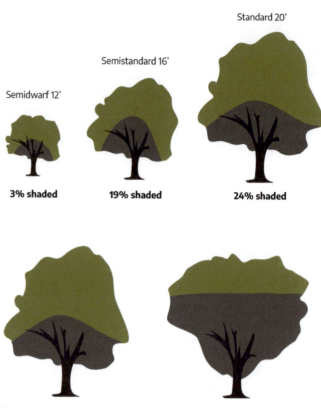

Figure 14-18: Tree shape and light exposure.

Hedging and topping should only be used to maintain tree size when trees are at or near desired size. Such pruning is often used in an attempt to reduce tree size. Misuse can result in a disruption of vigor and loss of yield which may take several years to control. Hedging and topping (mainly heading cuts), especially of one-year shoots, induce masses of shoots close to the plane where cutting takes place. This localized invigoration of shoots can shade and weaken inner areas of the tree.

Pruning Other Fruit Trees

Pear

Pear trees are trained along the same general lines as those recommended for apples. Heading back is undesirable because of the tendency of the tree to throw out soft terminal shoots, which are highly susceptible to fire blight. It is best to limit pruning to thinning-out cuts.

Cherry

Sweet cherry trees are trained to the modified leader system recommended for the apple. Special attention should be given to the selection of scaffold limbs because sweet cherry is subject to winter injury and splitting at the point where the limbs join the main stem of the tree. It is essential that the crotch angles be as wide as possible to ensure a strong framework.

A sour cherry tree with no strong branches at the time of planting should be headed to about 24 inches above the ground. Selection of laterals can be made at the beginning of the second year's growth. If it has some good laterals when planted, remove branches lower than 16 inches from the ground. Select about three permanent lateral or scaffold limbs along the leader, 4 to 6 inches apart and not directly over one another. Do not head them back, since this tends to stunt terminal growth.

In the following years, select side branches from the leader until there is a total of 5 or 6 scaffold limbs well distributed above the lowest branch along 3 or 4 feet of the main stem. The leader is then usually modified by cutting to an outward-growing lateral. After fruiting begins, pruning consists mainly of thinning out excessive and crowded growth each year to allow sunlight to filter through the tree.

Plum

The plum may also be pruned in a manner similar to the apple. European and prune types generally develop into well-shaped trees, even if little pruning is done. Thinning out excessive growth constitutes the bulk of pruning after heading back to 30 to 36 inches at the time of planting. Varieties of the Japanese type are usually a little more vigorous, and may need some heading back as well as thinning of excessive growth after they come into bearing.

Peach

Peach trees are usually trained to the open-center system. Newly planted trees should be headed to about 30 inches in height, just above a lateral branch or bud. If the tree is branched when it comes from the nursery, select 3 or 4 laterals that are well-spaced up and around the trunk for the permanent scaffold limbs. The lowest limb should be about 15 inches and the highest about 30 inches from the ground. Cut these back to two buds each, and remove all other laterals.

If no desirable laterals are available, head the tree to the desired height and cut out all side branches to one bud. A number of shoots will develop during the season, from which you can select scaffold limbs. Selection can be made during the summer or delayed until just before growth begins the second season.

Once the scaffold system of the young peach tree is established, fairly heavy pruning is required to develop a low spreading tree. Remove all strong, upright shoots growing in the center of the tree, and lightly head back terminal growth on the scaffold limbs to outward-growing laterals. This aids in the development of an open-center tree.

As fruit is borne on wood of the previous year's growth, it is necessary that the peach be pruned annually to stimulate new growth and maintain production near the main body of the tree. Pruning of the mature peach tree consists mainly of moderate thinning and heading back to outward-growing laterals to keep the tree low and spreading. A height of 8 or 9 feet is usually preferred.

Pruning Fruit Trees Summary

When pruning fruit trees for best production, remember these basic concepts:

Pruning invigorates and results in rapid growth close to the pruning cut. Pruning reduces the number of shoots, so remaining shoots are stimulated. However, total shoot growth and size of the limb is reduced. Pruning always reduces yield.

Two types of pruning cuts are heading back and thinning out. Heading is cutting off part of a shoot or branch to stimulate branching and stiffen the limb. Thinning cuts remove the entire shoot or branch at its junction with a lateral, scaffold, or trunk. Thinning cuts are less invigorating, improve light penetration, and can redirect the limb.

Figure 14-19: Heading and thinning.

Limb position affects vigor and fruitfulness. Vertical or upright branches, typical in the tops of trees, produce the longest shoots near the end of the limb and tend to be excessively vigorous and not very fruitful. Fruit are often of poor quality and subject to limb rub. Limbs growing slightly above horizontal are more apt to develop a uniform distribution of vigor and fruitfulness. Light distribution tends to be even, and because fruit hang along the branch, they are less prone to limb rub. Limbs growing below horizontal tend to develop suckers along the upper surface. Excess sucker growth will result in shading. Hangers, or limbs developing on the underside of branches or scaffolds, are heavily shaded and low in vigor. Fruit developing on such wood is of poor size and color.

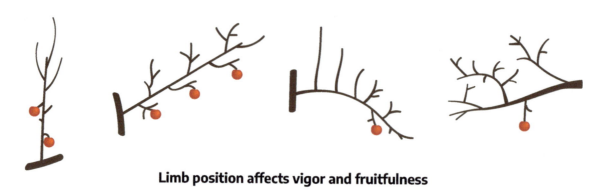

Figure 14-20: Limb position affects vigor and fruitfulness.

Invigoration from pruning is, in part, a nitrogen response. Pruning alters the balance between the tree top and root system. Removal of part of the top increases the amount of nitrogen available for the remaining growing points. Thus, a pruning program should be developed along with a good fertilization program. Severe pruning and/or excess fertilization can disrupt the vigor of the tree and decrease fruiting.

Special Training Systems for Fruit Trees

Numerous training systems, based on the art of espalier, which originated in France and Italy about 400 years ago, have been devised. Some are quite elaborate, requiring considerable time and patience as well as detailed knowledge of the plant's growth characteristics. The easiest espalier system is the horizontal cordon. Apples, pears, and plums adapt well to this system. The trees are usually supported by a wall, fence, or wire trellis. Training to the four-tier cordon or four-wire trellis is relatively easy.

An espalier system can serve to separate yard areas and to provide an effective way of producing a large volume of high quality fruit in a limited area. Trees trained in this fashion should be grafted on dwarfing rootstock. Otherwise, they tend to grow too large and are difficult to hold within bounds.
A simple, four-wire trellis may be constructed by setting 8-foot posts 2 feet in the ground, spacing them 12 feet apart, and running wires through the posts at heights of 18, 36, 54, and 72 inches. Plant two unbranched whips of the desired variety 6 feet apart between each two posts.

Before growth begins in the spring, cut off the whip just above the first bud, below the point where the whip crosses the lowest wire. Usually three or more shoots will develop near the point of the cut. Retain the uppermost shoot and develop it as the central leader. The other two can be developed into main scaffold branches to be trained along the lower wire, one on each side of the central stem. Remove all other growth. The two shoots selected for scaffold limbs should be loosely tied to the wire as soon as they are 10-12 inches long. Twine, plastic chain link ties, or other suitable material may be used. Tie the shoots so that they are nearly horizontal. This reduces vegetative vigor and induces flower bud formation. If the end of the shoot is tied below the horizontal, however, new growth at the end will stop, and vigorous shoots will develop along the upper side. At the end of the first season, the lateral branches on the lower wire should be established and the central leader should have grown above the second wire.

During the dormant pruning at the end of the first winter, cut the central leader off at a bud just below the second wire. Repeat the process of the previous spring by developing two scaffold branches to tie to the second wire and allow the central leader to grow above the third wire.

This process is repeated during the next two seasons, at which time a total of eight scaffolds, four on each side of the tree, should be firmly established. The leaders should be bent to form one of the scaffolds, rather than being cut off at the top wire.

By the end of the fourth season, the trees should be in heavy production. All pruning is then done during the spring and summer months. After new growth in the spring is about 2 inches long, cut it off, and remove about 1/4 of the previous season's growth. Terminals of the scaffold are left untouched.

About the first of August, or as soon as new growth reaches 10-12 inches in length, cut it back to two or three buds. Repeat about a month later, if necessary. This encourages fruit bud formation and prevents excessive vigorous growth.

Training and Pruning Small Fruit

Grapes

For grapes to be most productive, they must be trained to a definite system and pruned rather severely. There are several training systems used. The two most common are the vertical trellis and the overhead arbor. Both of these are satisfactory in the home planting if kept well-pruned.

Of the many variations of the vertical trellis, the single-trunk, four-arm, Kniffin system is the most popular. Posts are set 15 to 20 feet apart and extend 5 feet above the ground. Two wires are stretched between the posts, the lower being about 2 1/2 feet above the ground, and the upper at the top of the posts. The vine is set between the posts and trained to a single trunk with four semi-permanent arms, each cut back to 6 to 10 inches in length. One arm is trained in each direction on the lower wire.

During annual winter pruning, one cane is saved from those that grew from near the base of each arm the previous summer. This cane is cut back to about ten buds. The fruit in the coming season is borne on shoots developing from those buds. Select another cane from each arm, preferably one that grew near the trunk, and cut it back to a short stub having two buds. This is a renewal spur. It should grow

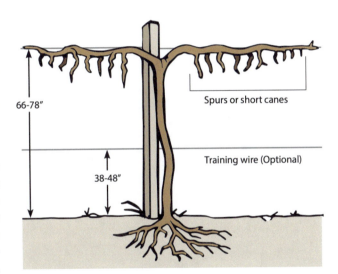

Figure 14-21: High-wire, cordon-trained system for grapevines. Cordons are semi-permanent, horizontal extensions of the trunk(s). Cordon length will depend on in-row vine spacing; the cordon of one vine should extend almost to the cordons of the adjacent vines in the row. Cordons are pruned to short canes or spurs of one to four nodes in length. Total node number should not exceed about five nodes per linear feet of row. Thus, for vines spaced 7 feet apart in the row, total retained nodes should not exceed 35.

vigorously in the spring and be the new fruiting cane selected the following winter. All other growth on the vine should be removed. This leaves four fruiting canes, one on each arm, with eight to ten buds each, and four renewal spurs, one on each arm, cut back to two buds each.

The same training and pruning techniques may be effectively used in training grapes to the arbor system. The only difference is that the wires supporting the arms are placed overhead and parallel with each other instead of in a horizontal position. Overhead wires are usually placed 6 to 7 feet above the ground.

If an arm dies or for any reason needs to be replaced, choose the largest cane that has grown from the trunk near the base of the dead arm and train it to the trellis wire. To renew the trunk, train a strong shoot from the base of the old trunk to the trellis as though it were the cane of a new vine. Establish the arms in the same manner as for a new vine, and cut off the old trunk.

Pruning may be done anytime after the vines become dormant. In areas and on varieties where there is danger of winter injury, pruning should be delayed until late winter or early spring. Vines pruned very late may bleed excessively, but there is no evidence that this is permanently injurious.

Stages in training the young vine to the single trunk, four-arm Kniffin system:

1. After pruning the first winter. The single cane is cut back and tied to the lower wire. If the cane has grown less than 3' during the first summer, it should be cut back to two buds.
2. After pruning the second winter. Two new canes of four or five buds each are tied on the bottom wire. A third new cane is tied up to the top of the wire and cut off.
3. After pruning the third winter. Three of the arms (A) and fruiting canes (B) have been formed. A cane (C) with four or five buds is left to establish the fourth arm.
4. A fully formed vine after pruning the fourth winter. The arms (A) should be shorter than those shown. The vine consists of a single, permanent trunk, four semi-permanent fruiting arms (F), and four renewal spurs (S), with two new buds on each.

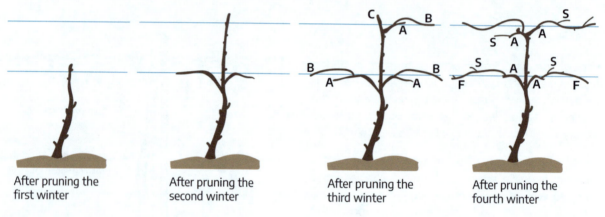

Figure 14-22: Single trunk, four-arm Kniffin training system.

Blueberries

Until the end of the third growing season, pruning consists mainly of removing low spreading canes and dead and broken branches. As the bushes come into bearing, regular annual pruning will be necessary. This may be done any time from leaf fall until growth begins in the spring. Select six to eight of the most vigorous, upright-growing canes for fruiting wood and remove all others.

After about 5 or 6 years, the canes begin to lose vigor and fruit production is reduced. At the dormant pruning, remove the older canes of declining vigor and replace with strong, vigorous new shoots that grew from the base of the bush the previous season. Keep the number of fruiting canes to six or eight and remove the rest. Head back excessive terminal growth to a convenient berry-picking height.

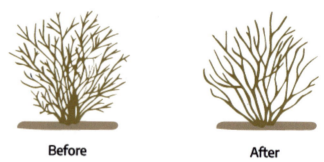

Figure 14-23: Left, unpruned blueberry plant. Right, after pruning, a mature blueberry bush should have 10 to 15 canes.

Brambles

Trailing blackberries need some form of support. They may be grown on a trellis, trained along a fence, or tied to stakes. Other brambles may either be trained to supports or, with more severe pruning, grown as upright, self-supporting plants. Red raspberries and erect-growing blackberries are frequently grown in hedgerows.

Figure 14-24: Left, an unpruned blackberry plant. Right, once plants are dormant, only retain four to five of the best canes.

A simple trellis, used in many home gardens, consists of two wires stretched at 3 and 5 foot levels between posts set 15 to 20 feet apart. Fruiting canes are tied to these wires in the spring. The erect varieties are tied where the canes cross the wires. Canes of trailing varieties are tied horizontally along the wires or fanned out from the ground and tied where they cross each wire.

Where stakes are used for support, they are driven into the ground about 1 foot from each plant and allowed to extend 4 or 5 feet above the ground. Canes are tied to the stake at a point about midway between the ground and the tips of the canes, and again near the ends of the canes.

Canes of bramble fruits are biennial in nature; the crowns and roots are perennial. New shoots grow from buds at the crown each year. Late in the summer, the new canes develop lateral branches with fruit buds on them. Early in the second season, fruit-bearing shoots grow from these buds. After fruiting, the old canes wither and die, and new shoots spring up from the crowns.

These fruiting canes may be removed any time after harvest. They should be cut off close to the base of the plant, removed from the planting, and destroyed. As a sanitation practice, some growers do this immediately after harvest. Most, however, wait until the dormant pruning.

The dormant pruning is usually delayed until danger of severe cold is past and accomplished before the buds begin to swell. It consists of the removal of all dead, weak, and severely damaged canes, and the selection and pruning of the fruiting canes for the coming season. Where possible, fruiting canes 1/2-inch or more in diameter are selected.

Figure 14-25: For plants grown in hedgerows, thin canes to 6 to 8 inches. The figure shows, left, before thinning, and right, after thinning.

Black raspberries should be topped in the summer when the young shoots are about 24 inches high; purple raspberries, when about 30 inches high. Summer-topping consists of removing the top 3 to 4 inches of the new shoots by snapping them off with the fingers or cutting them with shears or a knife. Where trained to supports, let them grow 6 to 8 inches taller before topping.

At the dormant pruning, thin each plant until only four or five of the best canes remain. Cut the lateral branches of the black raspberry to 9 to 12 inches long; those of the purple raspberry to 12 to 15 inches long.

The following comments concerning red raspberries do not apply to the Heritage variety, which is an everbearing type.

Red raspberries should not be summer-topped. Canes of everbearing varieties are handled in the same manner as those of ordinary varieties. At the dormant pruning, where the hill system of culture is used, thin until only seven or eight of the best canes remain per hill.

If the plants are grown in hedgerows, keep the width of the rows to 18 inches or less, and remove all plants outside the row areas. Thin the canes within the hedgerows to 6 to 8 inches apart, saving the best canes.

Where the canes are supported either by a trellis or stakes, cut the canes back to a convenient height for berry-picking, usually 4 or 5 feet. Grown as upright, self-supporting plants, whether in hills or in hedgerows, the canes should be cut back to about 3 feet in height. Any lateral branches should be cut to about 10 inches in length.

New shoots of erect blackberries should be summer-topped when they are 30 to 36 inches high. To prevent the planting from becoming too thick and reducing yields, it may be necessary to remove excess sucker plants as they appear. This can be done either with a hoe or by hand. In the hedgerow type of culture, leave only three or four shoots per running foot of row. When grown in hills, four to five new shoots may be allowed to develop in each hill.

At the dormant pruning, where supports are used, head the canes to 4 to 5 feet in height. Canes grown without support should be headed to 3 feet. Cut lateral branches back to 15 or 18 inches long.

Trailing blackberries require little pruning. All dead and weak canes should be removed after harvest or at the dormant pruning. They should be thinned to seven or eight of the best canes per hill, cut to about 5 feet in length, and tied to either a stake or trellis.

Figure 14-26: Primocane-fruiting raspberry with second-year canes and new canes.

Currants and Gooseberries

Currants and gooseberries typically form bushes with many branches arising near the ground level. Pruning may be done any time during the dormant period and consists primarily of thinning out excess stems.

Except for the removal of weak, broken, or prostrate stems, very little pruning is done until the plants are 4 years old. The mature bush should have three or four stems each of 1-, 2-, and 3-year-old wood. The actual number should be determined by the vigor of the bush. Heading back is done only to reduce the height of extra long, 1-year-old shoots.

Remove all wood over 3 years old. Cut off the damaged and low prostrate stems, retaining only the most vigorous of the 2- and 3-year-old shoots. Head back young shoots that are too long.

In Virginia, European black currants are prohibited (see Administrative Code 2VAC5-450-40. European black currant plants). European black currants may harbor white pine blister rust, a non-native fungus that affects white pines. The fungus needs two hosts to complete its lifecycle: white pine and most commonly, a currant or gooseberry plant (*Ribes ssp.*).

Figure 14-27: Pruning currants.

Figure 14-28: Pruning gooseberries.

Additional Resources

- Pruning (and other fruit maintenance) videos from the University of Maine Extension: https://extension.umaine.edu/highmoor/videos/

Attributions

- Carol King, Hampton Extension Master Gardener (2021 reviser)
- John Freeborn, Assistant State Master Gardener Coordinator (2015 reviser)
- Dan Nortman, Extension Agent, Agriculture and Natural Resources (2015 reviser)
- Stuart Sutphin, Extension Agent, Agriculture and Natural Resources (2015 reviser)
- Susan Day, Associate Professor, Department of Horticulture (2015 reviewer)
- Adam K. Downing, Extension Agent, Natural Resources, Certified Arborist (2009 reviser)

Image Attributions

- Figure 14-1: Pruning tools. Johnson, Devon. 2022. CC BY-NC-SA 4.0. Includes: Bypass secateurs by KoS on Wikimedia. 2006. Public domain; Bypass pruners and hardwood cuttings.jpg by Gmihail at Serbian Wikipedia. 2006. CC BY-SA 3.0 RS; A chainsaw being used on a small board by kalleerna on Wikimedia. 2009. CC BY-SA 3.0; Trois scies à bûches by Taveneaux, transferred from fr.wikipedia to Commons. 2006. Public domain. Pruning saw, pole saw, lopping shears, and hedge trimmers by Johnson, Devon. 2022. CC BY-NC-SA 4.0.
- Figure 14-2: Proper pruning angle. Grey, Kindred. 2022. CC BY-NC-SA 4.0.
- Figure 14-3: Pruning angle diagrams. Grey, Kindred. 2022. CC BY-NC-SA 4.0.
- Figure 14-4: Pruning larger branches. Johnson, Devon. 2022. CC BY-NC-SA 4.0.
- Figure 14-5: Tree diagram. Grey, Kindred. 2022. CC BY-NC-SA 4.0. Includes grass by Milena Zanotelli from Noun Project (Noun Project license).
- Figure 14-6: Crape myrtle before (left) and after Norfolk EMGs pruned (right). Gowen, Marilyn. 2021. CC BY-NC-SA 4.0.
- Figure 14-7: Proper (left) and improper (right) methods of pruning. Grey, Kindred. 2022. CC BY-NC-SA 4.0. Includes grass by Milena Zanotelli from Noun Project (Noun Project license).
- Figure 14-8: Gradual rejuvenation. Grey, Kindred. 2022. CC BY-NC-SA 4.0. Includes grass by Milena Zanotelli from Noun Project (Noun Project license).
- Figure 14-9: Pruning hedges. Johnson, Devon. 2022. CC BY-NC-SA 4.0.
- Figure 14-10: Hedge shapes. Johnson, Devon. 2022. CC BY-NC-SA 4.0.
- Figure 14-11: Vertical and radial arrangement of scaffold branches. Grey, Kindred. 2022. CC BY-NC-SA 4.0.
- Figure 14-12: Limb orientation. Grey, Kindred. 2022. CC BY-NC-SA 4.0.
- Figure 14-13: Limb angles. Carol King. Extension Master Gardener Tree Steward Handbook. 2021. CC BY-NC-SA 4.0.
- Figure 14-14: Using a spreader to widen crotch angle. Johnson, Devon. 2022. CC BY-NC-SA 4.0.
- Figure 14-15: Training of apple trees. Grey, Kindred. 2022. CC BY-NC-SA 4.0.
- Figure 14-16: Reducing length. Johnson, Devon. 2022. CC BY-NC-SA 4.0.
- Figure 14-17: Sources of light. Johnson, Devon. 2022. CC BY-NC-SA 4.0.
- Figure 14-18: Tree shape and light exposure. Johnson, Devon. 2022. CC BY-NC-SA 4.0.
- Figure 14-19: Heading and thinning. Johnson, Devon. 2022. CC BY-NC-SA 4.0.
- Figure 14-20: Limb positions affects vigor and fruitfulness. Johnson, Devon. 2022. CC BY-NC-SA 4.0.
- Figure 14-21: High-wire, cordon-trained system for grapevines. Virginia Cooperative Extension. Small Fruit in the Home Garden. 2022. CC BY-NC-SA 4.0.

- Figure 14-22: Single trunk, four-arm Kniffin training system. Johnson, Devon. 2022. CC BY-NC-SA 4.0. Adapted from four-arm Kniffin training in Virginia Cooperative Extension. Small Fruit in the Home Garden. 2022. CC BY-NC-SA 4.0.
- Figure 14-23: Left, unpruned blueberry plant. Right, after pruning, a mature blueberry bush should have 10 to 15 canes. Johnson, Devon. 2022. CC BY-NC-SA 4.0.
- Figure 14-24: Left, an unpruned blackberry plant. Right, once plants are dormant, only retain four to five of the best canes. Johnson, Devon. 2022. CC BY-NC-SA 4.0.
- Figure 14-25: For plants grown in hedgerows, thin canes to 6 to 8 inches. The figure shows, left, before thinning, and right, after thinning. Johnson, Devon. 2022. CC BY-NC-SA 4.0.
- Figure 14-26: Primocane-fruiting raspberry with second-year canes and new canes. High-wire, cordon-trained system for grapevines. Virginia Cooperative Extension. Small Fruit in the Home Garden. 2022. CC BY-NC-SA 4.0.
- Figure 14-27: Pruning currants. Johnson, Devon. 2022. CC BY-NC-SA 4.0.
- Figure 14-28: Pruning gooseberries. Johnson, Devon. 2022. CC BY-NC-SA 4.0.

CHAPTER 15: HERBACEOUS LANDSCAPE PLANTS

Chapter Contents:

- Annuals
- Perennials
- Biennials
- Tropicals
- Geophytes
- Pond and Bog Plants
- Ornamental Grasses
- Ferns (Pterophytes)
- Succulents
- Planning the Herbaceous Border
- Containers and Hanging Baskets
- Additional Resources

This chapter covers ornamental herbaceous plants in the context of the landscape – whether planted in the ground or used in containers and hanging baskets. Herbaceous plants can add color, texture, and interest to any landscape at any scale.

Figure 15-1: This property has a large lawn, shrubs, trees, but no herbaceous plants: boring!

Figure 15-2: This property has lawn, shrubs, trees, and lots of herbaceous plants, creating an interesting and layered landscape.

Throughout this chapter, think about the possibilities for expanding areas with herbaceous plants within your own garden and also how to recommend these plants and practices to others – part of your role as an Extension Master Gardener (EMG). Note this is written in context of the mid-Atlantic region.

An herbaceous plant is any vascular plant that isn't woody, or a plant with woody stems that die back to the ground in the winter. Let's break that huge quantity of species down into something a bit more useful. Herbaceous garden plants can be divided up by life cycle and/or physiology.

Annuals

Annuals are not as straightforward as you might think. A "true" **annual** is something you can plant seeds of in the spring; it then flowers and sets seed (if not a sterile hybrid) before the growing season ends. Think "sunflower" (*Helianthus annuus*). However, we use the term "annual" for a lot of species that are actually perennial in their native environment – wherever that may be – they're just not cold-hardy in your particular location. Nurseries, garden centers, and landscapers will often lump these together under the term "color." Another term is **bedding plants**, which encompass a wide variety of non-hardy, seasonal things like annuals, tropicals, herbs, vegetable transplants, etc. There are warm-season and cool-season annuals as well as those that do better is sun or shade. A vast palette of flower and foliage colors await the creative gardener – so many fun things for beds, hanging baskets and containers! We'll talk more about annuals throughout this chapter.

Figure 15-3: Coleus are available in an array of colors and leaf shapes, perfect for sun or shade.

Perennials

Perennials simply live for more than one growing season. Trees and shrubs are perennial. Orchids growing in southeast Asia are perennial. For our purposes, "perennial" means "herbaceous perennial," and will refer to herbaceous plants that can tolerate freezing temperatures – a "hardy perennial."

Most perennials die back to roots/crown each winter but some species may remain evergreen or semi-evergreen, depending on location. Most **temperate** perennials (those native to moderate temperature regions without extreme cold or a tropical climate) also require a certain amount of cold, in both temperature and duration, to survive and rebloom. The higher the USDA hardiness zone, (i.e., zone 9 or 10) the fewer the number of temperate perennials that perform well. Classic perennials include *Hosta* spp., daylily (*Hemerocallis* spp.), purple coneflower (*Echinacea* spp.), etc.

Figure 15-4: The best perennials, such as this native perennial sunflower (*Helianthus divaricatus*) provide color, beauty, and pollen and / or nectar for bees, butterflies, and other pollinators.

Recommendations for perennials suitable for Virginia are available in the following publications:

- VCE Publication "Selecting Plants for Virginia Landscapes: Showy Flowering Shrubs" HORT-84P
- VCE Publication "Edible Landscape Species: Shrubs, Vines, Groundcovers" SPES-317P
- VCE Publication "For the Birds, Butterflies & Hummingbirds: Creating Inviting Habitats" HORT-59NP
- VCE Publication "Selecting Landscape Plants: Groundcovers" 426-609
- VCE Publication "Problem-free Shrubs for Virginia Landscapes" 450-236
- Plant Virginia Natives Regional Plant Guides (https://www.plantvirginianatives.org/)

Is This Perennial Hardy or Not?

The United States Department of Agriculture's Agricultural Research Service (ARS) Plant Hardiness Zone Map (https://planthardiness.ars.usda.gov/) divides the U.S. into 13 zones according to the average of lowest minimum temperatures recorded for a 30-year period. Each of the 13 zones is further split into "a" (cooler) and " b" (warmer). The current version of this map is based on 1976–2005 weather data, and it was updated in 2012 with GIS data, providing much more detailed information and revealing microclimates. The new map is online only, and is searchable by zip code or one can browse through and zoom in on a specific region or state.

The commonwealth of Virginia has a wide range of hardiness zones, due to our "sea-to-mountains" topography. Virginia Beach has the same hardiness zone (8a, 10 to 15 F) that stretches down the coast of the Carolinas and across central Georgia and Alabama. The piedmont region is zone 7: 7b east and south of Richmond and 7a west across central VA. As the elevation increases, the hardiness zone gets lower. The Blue Ridge and Allegheny mountains are mostly Zone 6b or 6a, with a few spots of 5b at the highest elevations. While *Canna* spp. and elephant ears (*Colocasia* spp.) may be reliably perennial in Suffolk, they probably will not survive the winter in Winchester.

These zones are referenced in gardening books, plant catalogs, and on plant tags and labels in order to help gardeners select plants appropriate to their growing area. Again, these zones are defined as "average annual extreme minimum temperature." For example, in Zone 6b, -5 to 0°F, it may not reach that low every year, though it could drop even lower. Keep in mind that cold hardiness is only one of many factors to impact herbaceous plant performance. Proper temperature acclimation, amount of light, soil moisture (too much or too little can be problematic), humidity, and heat tolerance all determine whether your plants thrive or not.

Biennials

Biennials possess a unique herbaceous lifecycle–vegetative growth occurs the first year. The next year the plants flower and set seed. The cold of winter in between serves to **vernalize** (cool the plants in order to encourage flowering) the plants, triggering the reproductive phase. For some plants, the vegetative phase is desired – herbs and leafy vegetables such as parsley, spinach, and lettuce. The flowering stage is called "bolting." Ornamentals such as some, but not all, of the foxgloves (*Digitalis*) and hollyhocks (*Alcea*) produce flowers during the second growing season, so planning ahead is required if growing them from seed. If happy with the garden site and situation, many biennials will freely reseed around.

Beyond classifications based on life cycle (annual, perennial, and biennial) , there are plenty of other herbaceous plant categories as well.

Tropicals

Tropicals are plants that lend a lush, exotic touch to the garden. For example, tropicals include broad or lush foliage from species we associate with tropical climates such as banana (*Musa* and *Ensete*), elephant ears (*Colocasia, Alocasia*), bamboo (*Phyllostachys* and many others), *Canna* and many more.

There are a few hardy species in each of these genera; however, most will not survive beyond Zone 8 or 9. The upside is they all grow rapidly if treated well (plenty of water and fertilizer), making a wonder show for the season. Bananas and elephant ears can be lifted and overwintered as house plants, or allowed to get "frosted" – the foliage knocked back by frost/freeze. Then you can cut back the tops, lift the roots or tubers, and store in a cool garage or basement. Plant into beds or containers after the threat of frost has passed in the spring. For more information on hardy tropicals, see the VCE publication "Cold-Hardy Topicals for Virginia Landscapes" 3005-1446.

Figure 15-5: Tropicals.

Geophytes

Geophytes are herbaceous plants with underground storage organs, rather than fibrous root systems. Often lumped together under the generic term "bulbs," these storage organs can also be corms, tubers, rhizomes, or other structures. These organs contain reserves of carbohydrates, nutrients, and water. Geophytes typically undergo a dieback or "dormancy" period, which varies depending on season of bloom.

Knowing when geophytes bloom is key to knowing when to plant them. Many summer-blooming geophytes, such as *Dahlia* and hybrid *Gladiolus* are not cold hardy and should be planted in late spring after all danger of freezing has passed.

Spring-blooming geophytes include those icons of spring: Crocus, tulip (*Tulipa*), and daffodils (*Narcissus*). Spring bloomers are generally cold-hardy perennials and are purchased and planted mid to late autumn. Just like holiday décor, spring bulbs are starting to show up in stores earlier and earlier – even in August. Do not plant until the weather is reliably cool and the soil temperature is below 50 degrees F. Never store purchased bulbs in the fridge – many veggies and fruit give off ethylene, which will damage the developing flower.

Types of Geophytes

Figure 15-6: Daffodils grow in attractive clusters.

Bulbs: The bulb itself is made of modified leaves or scales, with a compressed stem and a basal plate where roots emerge, like an onion. Once the flower has **senesced** (petals dropped off), the foliage persists for several weeks and then eventually declines, turning yellow or brown. This next bit of advice goes for ALL hardy geophytes: if you want the bulb to flower again next year, leave the foliage in place for as long as you can stand it. The photosynthetic process taking place in the leaves is putting critical carbohydrates back into the storage organ. Once the foliage is no longer visible, the bulb is not dormant! **Flower primordia** (the small buds at the end of stems from which flowers develop) are forming throughout the summer and autumn.

Corms: Storage structure is a modified stem with a basal plate – described as "solid bulbs." Spring blooming (hardy) corms include *Crocus*. The summer bloomers include *Gladiolus*, *Freesia*, and *Ixia*.

Tubers: Thickened underground stem with no basal plate. Tubers such as *Caladium* have "eyes," meristematic tissue from which roots and shoots emerge, like potatoes that have been in the bin too long.

Tuberous roots: Thickened root tissue. Growth arises from buds at the top (crown) of the root mass. A piece of the crown must be included in any divisions. Includes *Dahlia*, *Anemone* x *coronaria*, and *Ranunculus*.

Rhizomes: Modified stems that grow horizontally at or below the soil surface. Rhizomatous perennials include German (bearded) Iris (*Iris germanica*), lily-of-the-valley (*Convallaria majalis*), *Calla*, and *Oxalis*.

Enlarged hypocotyl: Sounds painful, but the storage organ is simply the swollen portion of the stem below the cotyledon and above the roots. *Cyclamen* and *Gloxinia* are examples.

Pond and Bog Plants

Creating an ornamental pond, container water garden, or bog opens the door to another unique suite of herbaceous plants. Pond plants are not only beautiful, they are essential to a healthy pond, in that they take up excess nutrients such as nitrogen and phosphorus (both excreted by fish and created as organic matter such as leaves break down), provide shade to keep water temperatures down in summer, and help hide fish from predators. A naturally-maintained water garden attracts and nurtures wildlife of all kinds, from salamanders to birds, bees to mammals.

Pond Plants Categories

Floating plants (free-floating): These plants have buoyant leaves–no rooting situation is required. The floating roots excel at absorbing excess nutrients. Two popular species are water lettuce (*Pistia stratioites*) and water hyacinth (*Eichornia crassipes*).

Though considered invasive in the deep South and tropics, neither are freeze tolerant. Because they do not overwinter, they are not a problem here.

Submerged plants: These plants root into the gravel and remain under water, providing valuable oxygenation to the water as well as a great shelter for fish and other critters. Canadian water weed (*Elodea canadensis*) and ribbon grass (*Vallisneria americana*) are both native and cold-hardy additions to a Virginia pond.

Floating foliage, rooted to pond bottom (or containers): Leaves floating on or held at the surface keep water cool and the shade provided reduces algae growth. Two of our most iconic aquatic plants – water lily (*Nymphaea*) and lotus (*Nelumbo*) fall into this category. Cold-hardy and tropical varieties are available of both.

Marginal plants or "emergent": These are the plants that thrive in shallow water, from a few inches up to 1'. These can be grown either rooted into a gravel substrate or in containers placed in several inches of water. There are many, many species, several of which are native to the Southern U.S., such as alligator flag (*Thalia dealbata*), pickerel weed (*Pontedaria cordata*), and cattails (*Typha latifolia*).

Figure 15-7: *Thalia* adds vertical interest to any water feature.

Bog Plants

Bog plants are a bit different – they require consistently moist soil but cannot tolerate standing water for long periods of time. Full sun and low soil pH (amended with peat) are also necessary for a successful bog garden. Pitcher plants (*Sarracenia*) are fascinating and easy to grow, once the site needs have been met. Look for cold-hardy species such as *S. purpurea* and *S. flava*.

Proper maintenance of pond plants is important to the health of the pond. Nearly all are deciduous, so once cold temperatures have knocked back the above-surface foliage and flowers, the dead plant material needs to be removed immediately. Organic matter that falls to the bottom of the pond not only forms a layer of glop, but decomposes with the help of bacteria that also use up valuable oxygen. Timely removal of leaves and other debris is essential to a healthy water garden.

Figure 15-8: Pitcher Plants (*Sarroenia*) can be grown in containers as well as bogs.

Ornamental Grasses

As a landscape plant category, ornamental grasses includes "true" grasses, that is, members of the Poaceae family, as well as grass-like plants such as rushes (*Juncaceae*) and sedges (*Cyperaceae*). Turf-type grasses are not included. How do we distinguish among these? True grasses are monocots, with round but hollow stems (called "culms"), and parallel veins in the leaves. There is such a wide range, but one example is little bluestem (*Schizachyrium scoparium*). **Rushes** also have round (and frequently unbranched) stems, but are filled with pith and not hollow. **Sedges** bear triangular stems – hence the old plant id tip: "rushes are round and sedges have edges." Rushes and sedges prefer moist soil. Many grasses are very drought tolerant.

Most ornamental grasses are hardy perennials, but a few are not hardy and should be used as annuals. The most popular non-hardy grass is purple fountain grass (*Pennisetum* x *advena* 'Purpureum' and additional cultivars).

There are a vast number of perennial grasses, sedges, etc. for USDA Zones 5-8. Ornamental grasses can provide three to four seasons of interest: foliage color and texture for spring and summer, blooms in summer or fall, fall foliage color, and winter structure. Add to the list of positives "deer resistant" and "drought tolerant" for most species. Knowing the growth habit of a species is important when deciding where to plant – many are clumping (caespitose), but a few are either stoloniferous or rhizomatous runners. When planting, allow sufficient space – a good rule of thumb for many is to space plants as wide as they are tall. An exception would be an extremely narrow/vertical grass such as feather reed grass. Several wonderful native species have extensive root systems, for example, switchgrass (*Panicum virgatum*) roots can extend several feet below the soil surface. Take this into account when deciding where to plant; after a few years, relocation can become difficult.

Figure 15-9: Muhly grass is an attractive addition to a border garden.

Once planted and established, the only maintenance required for true grasses is to cut back the previous year's growth in early spring before the new growth gets going. A 6-12 inch "crew cut" made with shears or a string weeder works well for most.

Unlike most true grasses that require at least six to eight hours of full sun each day, there are many shade-tolerant sedges – a textural boost to the shade garden. Most *Carex* are evergreen or semi-evergreen and rather slow growing. Do not cut them back annually, only trim out dead foliage.

Ferns (Pterophytes)

Ferns are herbaceous but non-flowering. They have a completely different reproductive physiology, which is fascinating but beyond the scope of this chapter. Hardy ferns are indispensable in the shady or partially-shaded garden. Ferns are deer-resistant and the ultimate "mixer" – adding wonderful texture and no-fuss foliage. Green goes with everything, and in the case of Japanese painted fern (*Athyrium nipponicum* 'Pictum'), silver and burgundy does as well. Mix ferns in with *Hosta*, *Heuchera*, *Carex*, and other shade perennials to form a shady tapestry of color. There are a wide array of perennial ferns available, from the petite deer fern to majestic cinnamon ferns.

Most do best with reasonably moist soil but can tolerate short periods of drought. Most are deciduous, but our native Christmas fern (*Polystichum acrostichoides*) is evergreen. Simply cut back dead or tattered fronds in the winter and early spring, before the fiddleheads arise in spring. Note some ferns are slow to emerge in spring, so be patient! This works to your advantage in filling in gaps left by ephemeral shade perennials such as Virginia bluebells (*Mertensia virginica*) and bleeding hearts (*Lamprocapnos spectabilis*).

Figure 15-10: *Carex oshimensis* "Evergold" adds wonderful texture and color to the shade garden and is evergreen in the warmer parts of Virginia.

Figure 15-11: The fresh, bright green fronds of ostrich fern blends well with other shade perennials.

Succulents

Succulents are another broad group. Some are hardy (*Sedum* and *Sempervivum* species), but many are not (jade plant, *Crassula argentea*). The popularity of succulents as non-demanding, low water use container and patio plants has soared over the past few years. Sedums form the primary matrix for green roof plantings. Fleshy stems and "leaves," thick waxy cuticle, and other adaptations allow succulents to survive very dry conditions. Many succulents are in the Crassulaceae family, and have the capacity for CAM – crassulacean acid metabolism. In a nutshell, this is a water-saving strategy that allows stomates to close during the day when hot and dry, thus conserving water, and open at night for gas exchange. Succulents are extremely low maintenance and terrific for containers, patio gardens, or sunny windowsill plants. Most will suffer if overwatered. Use a light hand, especially during cool and cold weather.

Adapting the Garden for Therapeutic Benefits

By Phyllis Turner, Extension Master Gardener, Bedford

Research has shown that gardening is a great activity to improve and maintain both physical and emotional well-being. However, a bit of creativity may be needed to adapt the garden to meet the needs of the gardener. The gardens at Bedford Nursing Home, developed by Bedford Extension Master Gardeners, exemplify the many benefits of a therapeutic garden. Enjoyment of home-grown fruits, veggies, and flowers is an added bonus to the nursing home residents.

Developed in 2008, the therapeutic garden project provides horticulture-related activities each month for residents living at a long-term care facility. When weather permits, activities are held outside and utilize several types of raised beds and containers: a low raised bed with trellis and bean pole, a deep raised bed that allows the gardener to be seated on the side of the garden, an elevated bed that accommodates gardening either standing or sitting in a chair. When weather keeps residents indoors, horticulture-related activities include workshops such as making potpourri from dried plants, seed and acorn art, and holiday decorations. Discussions about propagating plants, birds in the garden, pollinator gardens, and insects in the garden are more examples of activities.

Figure 15-12: Linda Esser, Bedford Extension Master Gardener Pruning the thornless blackberries at the therapeutic garden.

> All activities include both therapeutic and educational objectives. Some of the benefits that residents get from the project include: a connection with the environment, reversal of dependency, improvement of self-esteem, positive mental state, impact on a living thing, anchor in reality, and improvement in communications.
>
> A picture says more than words about the self-esteem a resident gets from harvesting their own peanuts not to mention the satisfaction of Extension Master Gardeners sharing their love of gardening! It's a win-win for everyone.
>
> Bedford Nursing Home is a full partner in this project and provides financial support for the garden. This is important for the success of the program.

Planning the Herbaceous Border

Much of the excitement of creating a herbaceous border or mixed border (herbaceous combined with woody plants) lies in endless options of plant shapes, sizes, colors, and textures. In form, placement, and selection of plants, the contemporary border follows few rigid rules and allows fullest expression of the gardener's taste.

The first step in planning the material for an all-season, mixed border is to select key plants for line, mass, color, and dependability. Line is the silhouette or outline of a plant, color is the tint or tone of any color on the color wheel, mass is its shape or denseness, and dependability refers to its ability to remain attractive with a minimum of problems. There are literally hundreds of gardening websites, blogs, Pinterest pages, books, videos, and catalogs for reference.

Figure 15-13: Masses of Joe-Pye weed, *Heliopsis* spp., and grasses make an impact.

The most attractive herbaceous or mixed borders are those which are located in front of some sort of background, such as a fence, shrubbery, or a structure. In some cases, taller ornamental grasses or masses of large perennials such as blue false indigo (*Baptisia australis*) may serve a dual purpose as both citizens in the border and as background plants.

A general rule is to avoid a ruler-straight front edge, unless the garden is very spacious or formal. A gentle to boldly sweeping curve, easily laid out with a garden hose, is best even along a fence. The border can taper as it recedes from the main viewing point if an effect of distance is desired. The deeper the curve, the slower the eye moves and the greater will be the visual enjoyment. A border outlined with bricks or flat stones set flush with the soil may be better than a steeply cut lawn edge which must be trimmed after mowing.

Even the advanced gardener finds it advantageous to plan a border to scale on graph paper. The hardest task, organizing the selection of plants, will be simplified if only two main mass forms are considered: drifts and clumps. Drifts are elongated groupings of a plant that flow through sections of the border. Clumps consist of circular groupings of a variety, or a single large plant such as a peony (*Paeonia* spp.). The length of drifts and the diameter of clumps, as well as their heights, should be varied for best effect, and the dimensions should always be in proportion to the overall size of the border.

Figure 15-14: One of everything ("flower confetti") rarely produces desirable results!

Establish plants in groups large enough to form masses of color or texture. As a rule, five to seven plants will create the desired effect. A large peony or grass will be of sufficient size to be attractive, but a random collection of different small to medium sized plants will present a disorganized, checkerboard appearance. Each group of flowers should have an irregular shape. These masses of color and texture should blend into a pleasing, natural pattern of color harmony, instead of rows, blocks, or other symmetrical designs (except in a formal garden).

Flower borders may be of any width, depending on the space available. In a small yard the bed may be only 2 or 3 feet wide. In a spacious location, the border planting may have a width of 6 or 8 feet. If the border is quite deep, a pathway of stepping stones may be helpful as a means of working among the flowers without compacting the soil.

Tall flowers should be selected for the back part of the bed, with medium-height species in the middle, and smaller varieties along the front as edging plants. This is very easily done because the height of all varieties is stated in seed catalogs. Plants along the front edge of the bed should be located far enough back to allow easy mowing of the lawn.

Plant height is best limited to 2/3 the width of the border, e.g., no plants taller than 4 feet in a border 6 feet wide. Height lines should be broken up by letting some tall plants extend into the medium height groups, with a few recessed clumps or drifts leading the eye back into the border. This gives a more natural effect than a step profile. Try to vary heights, but in general keep taller plants in the back and shorter ones toward the front.

Figure 15-15: Any open space invites weeds! Keep that in mind for the very front border as well.

The distance between plants in a flower border depends on the form of the individual plants and the effect which is desired in the landscape. Allow adequate space between plants but just to a point. Plants will grow; gardens are dynamic entities! If they become overcrowded, just remove the excess (and share with your friends).

The enormous color range in perennials, plus their easy relocation if disharmony occurs, gives the gardener great latitude in choosing and combining colors. A border in tones of the same color can be effective, several closely related colors may be used, or the border may be made wildly exuberant with a vast variety of hues in one or more seasons. (Hues are modifications of color such as orange-red.) The objective is a balanced composition in every season, with no section being at any time too heavily weighted with one color, and the bloom distributed so that it always makes a pleasing pattern through the bed.

Many gardening books give excellent lists of compatible colors; these plus a garden notebook and camera are invaluable for planning and revising color schemes. For real floral artistry, it is perhaps more important to consider intensity, which is the vividness of a color, rather than hue. For example, light tones placed near dark ones, or contrasting palest tones with the most intense, can give new interest and life to the border. Also consider location and color. White is especially good near patios because it shows up well in the evening or dusk hours when patios are often in use. Some colors are suitable only as dramatic accents: deep, pure red clashes with almost anything (unless softened by dark green foliage), yet properly used it evokes strength and depth. White flowers and gray foliage are indispensable as separators of conflicting colors. Red, orange, and yellow are warm colors. Blue, green, and violet are cool colors.

Even in a small border, single plants of different varieties should not be used as it gives a jumbled look. Do not set in precise rows but in groups, as they might grow in nature. Allow enough space for each group to grow comfortably. Pick a few plant combinations and let these be the basis of your planting. Replicating these groupings down the length of the border guides the eye. Repetition is pleasing to a point, but don't overdo any one plant. Do not confine yourself to material that blooms all at one time and aim for a steady succession of color.

Figure 15-16: Warm, rosy pinks and purples work well together.

As gardeners become adept at producing color harmony and combinations in the border, they become more aware of the roles played by plant forms and foliage. Good foliage is obviously vital in plants with short blooming periods. Consider how much of the plant foliage will be usable and whether it is a positive or negative attribute. Some plants practically disappear when their blooming season is over (i.e., oriental poppy (*Papaver*) and bleeding heart), but others stay presentable even when not in flower. Plants with distinctive forms, color, and foliage — airy and delicate, or strong and solid — are wonderfully useful for creating interest. Shrubs with burgundy, maroon, or gold foliage, ornamental grasses, and even handsome-foliaged vegetables like chard and kale can be used for effect.

The most logical way to choose plants is first by location, second by period of bloom, then by height and width, and finally by color. Location takes into account the amount of sun or shade and water required. This information is easy to find in books or on the internet.

A last bit of advice: don't be afraid to be bold, even if it results in some mistakes. Flowers are easy to move, change, or take out altogether. There is no need to be conservative or confined. Most herbaceous plants are fast growers and can be transplanted at almost any time to help create the desired effect.

Table 15-1: Made in the shade (or part shade)

A simple, three-season (or four-season, depending on severity of winter) garden of non-fussy, easy-care hardy perennials.

Scientific name	Common name	Relative height	Description	Other notes
Asarum canadense	Deciduous ginger	Low	Wonderful native groundcover with iridescent, kidney shaped leaves. Forms large colonies where happy.	Native
Begonia grandis	Perennial begonia	Low to medium	Bold paisley-shaped leaves with reddish undersides and stems, soft pink blooms mid-summer through frost.	Late to emerge, so don't forget it's there! Non-native.
Eurybia divaricata	White wood aster	Low	Clouds of white aster flowers in late summer and early fall, when little else is blooming in the shaded.	Native, low growing
Helleborus x *hybridus*	Hellebore, Lenten rose	Medium	Earliest of spring flowers (late winter in warm areas). Cream to lavender to deep purple. Leathery evergreen foliage.	Non-native. Great early pollen source for bees. Extremely deer-resistant.
Hosta species and hybrids	Hosta, plantain lily	Low to medium	It's all about the foliage. So many gorgeous cultivars to choose from – gold to blue-green to variegated.	Non-native. Unfortunately delicious to deer and rabbits.
Polygonatum odoratum 'Variegatum'	Variegated Solomon's Seal	Medium	Cream and green foliage graces arching stems. White bell-shaped flowers dangle from leaf nodes in spring. Great yellow fall color.	Non-native but a must-have plant.
Matteuccia struthiopteris	Ostrich fern	Medium to tall	Vase –shaped clumps of broad, feathery fronds. Wonderful texture and height. Spreads by rhizomes to form new clumps – easy to remove (and share with friends!) if need be.	Native across most of the N. hemisphere. Deer-resistant.
Stylophorum diphyllum	Celandine poppy	Medium	Spring bloom with bright yellow poppy flowers and interesting foliage. Reseeds around where happy.	Native

Table 15-2: Sure things for sun

Some flowers, some foliage, all easy and wonderful

Scientific name	Common name	Relative height	Description	Other notes
Amsonia hubrichtii	Blue star	Medium	Thin foliage forms perfect mounds. Light blue flowers in spring, terrific texture in summer, then stunning gold to bronze fall color.	Native to OK + AR. Give it a year or two to reach full size. Deer-resistant.
Asclepias tuberosa	Orange milkweed	Low	Bright orange umbels in summer are beloved by butterflies and avoided by deer.	Native. Late to emerge, don't move once established (tap root).
Calamagrostis x *acutiflora* 'Karl Foerster'	Feather reed grass	Medium to tall	The vertical form of stems and plumes makes exclamation points throughout the garden. Does not spread. Early summer blooms.	Non-native. Cut back in early spring for a fresh flush of growth.
Echinacea species and hybrids	Purple cone flower	Medium	Some of the older E. purpurea and E. tennesseensis cultivars are tougher and longer-lived than the fancy new hybrids.	U.S. Native. Tolerates most soils. Attracts bees and butterflies.
Eutrochium purpureum, E. maculatum, and *E. dubium* (previously *Eupatorium* genus)	Joe-Pye weed	Tall	Large umbels of silvery-pink to pale purple flower heads, interesting foliage on tall, strong stems. Try compact cultivars such as 'Little Joe' and 'Phantom' for the smaller garden.	Native. Brings bees and butterflies. Tolerant of wet soils.
Sporobolus heterolepis	Prairie dropseed	Low to medium	The fine foliage forms graceful mounds, accented by sprays of flowers in late summer. Drought and clay tolerant.	U.S. Native. Deer-resistant.
Symphyotrichum oblongifolium	Aromatic aster	Medium	Shrubby habit, smothered with lavender flowers throughout fall; often last option for bees and other pollinators	Native. Deer-resistant.

Containers and Hanging Baskets

Gone are the days of "monoculture" hanging baskets of impatiens or begonias. Mixed baskets and containers present an opportunity to combine foliage and flowers into portable works of art. Tropicals, perennials, annuals, and grasses can all co-exist in the same vessel. Though there are very few rules for containers and baskets, here's a few tips for success:

- Confirm that the plants are compatible for the same environmental conditions, mainly light level (sun versus shade) and water (drought tolerant, needs consistently moist soil, etc.).
- Use the largest container or basket possible for the space and your budget. All those 4" containers of annuals are going to grow throughout the season, so give them some space to flourish. Big containers and big (14" diameter or larger) baskets make wonderful focal points for patios, decks, and borders.
- Add some controlled-release fertilizer to the media when filling the container or basket, and be sure to top-dress with a bit more fertilizer later in the summer. Frequent watering will leach nutrients out rapidly, resulting in chlorotic (yellowing) foliage and reduced blooms and vigor.
- When picking out plants for containers, look for three components: thriller, filler, and spiller. This bit of wisdom works like a charm. Pick a strong vertical component – grasses, *Canna* spp., elephant ears, or anything else with a bold upright habit. Add something to fill around the bare soil at the base – coleus (*Solenostemon scutellerioides*) is ideal but so are dozens of other goodies. Plants that spill from the container soften the edges and complete the picture – chartreuse or maroon ornamental sweet potato (*Ipomoea batatas*), a cascading petunia, or myriad other options work well.

Additional Resources

Books:

- Matlack, K., Matlack, C., and Matlack J. (2009). *Container Gardening: 250 Design Ideas & Step-by-step Techniques*. Taunton.
- **Perennials:** Armitage, A. M. (2008). *Herbaceous Perennial Plants: A Treatise on Their Identification, Culture, and Garden Attributes*. Stipes.
- **Perennials:** DiSabato-Aust, T. (2007). *The Well-tended Perennial Garden: Planting & Pruning Techniques*. Timber.
- **Ferns:** Olsen, S. (2007). *Encyclopedia of Garden Ferns*. Timber.
- **Pond Plants:** Speichert, C. G. and Speichert, S. (2008). *Timber Press Pocket Guide to Water Garden Plants*. Timber.
- **Succulents:** Baldwin, D.L. (2013). *Succulents Simplified: Growing, Designing, and Crafting with 100 Easy-care Varieties*. Timber.
- **Ornamental Grasses:** Darke, R. (2007). *The Encyclopedia of Grasses for Livable Landscapes*. Timber.
- **Ornamental Grasses:** Darke, R. (1999). *The Color Encyclopedia of Ornamental Grasses: Sedges, Rushes, Restios, Cat-tails, and Selected Bamboos*. Timber.
- **Ornamental Grasses:** Greenlee, J., Holt, S. (2009). *The American Meadow Garden: Creating a Natural Alternative to the Traditional Lawn*. Timber.
- **Geophytes:** Bryan, J. E. (2005). *Timber Press Pocket Guide to Bulbs*. Timber.

Attributions

- Stacey Morgan Smith, Extension Master Gardener (2022 reviser)
- Elaine Mills, Extension Master Gardener, Arlington/Alexandria (2022 reviser)
- Holly L. Scoggins, Associate Professor, Horticulture (2015 reviser)
- Diane Relf, Extension Specialist, Horticulture (2009 reviser)

Image Attributions

- Figure 15-1: Lawn, shrubs, trees, but no herbaceous plants: boring! *Master Gardener Training Handbook*, Virginia Cooperative Extension, 2018. CC BY-NC-SA 4.0.
- Figure 15-2: Much better! *Master Gardener Training Handbook*, Virginia Cooperative Extension, 2018. CC BY-NC-SA 4.0.
- Figure 15-3: Coleus are available in an array of colors and leaf shapes, perfect for sun or shade. *Master Gardener Training Handbook*, Virginia Cooperative Extension, 2018. CC BY-NC-SA 4.0.
- Figure 15-4: The best perennials, such as this native perennial sunflower (*Helianthus divarioatus*) provide color, beauty, and pollen and / or nectar for bees, butterflies, and other pollinators. *Master Gardener Training Handbook*, Virginia Cooperative Extension, 2018. CC BY-NC-SA 4.0.
- Figure 15-5: Tropicals. *Master Gardener Training Handbook*, Virginia Cooperative Extension, 2018. CC BY-NC-SA 4.0.
- Figure 15-6: Daffodils. *Master Gardener Training Handbook*, Virginia Cooperative Extension, 2018. CC BY-NC-SA 4.0.
- Figure 15-7: *Thalia* adds vertical interest to any water feature. *Master Gardener Training Handbook*, Virginia Cooperative Extension, 2018. CC BY-NC-SA 4.0.
- Figure 15-8: Pitcher Plants (*Sarroenia*) can be grown in containers as well as bogs. *Master Gardener Training Handbook*, Virginia Cooperative Extension, 2018. CC BY-NC-SA 4.0.
- Figure 15-9: Muhly grass. Kennedy, Ken on Flickr. CC BY-SA 2.0
- Figure 15-10: Carex oshimensis "Evergold" adds wonderful texture and color to the shade garden and is evergreen in the warmer parts of Virginia. *Master Gardener Training Handbook*, Virginia Cooperative Extension, 2018. CC BY-NC-SA 4.0.

- Figure 15-11: The fresh, bright green fronds of ostrich fern blends well with other shade perennials. *Master Gardener Training Handbook*, Virginia Cooperative Extension, 2018. CC BY-NC-SA 4.0.
- Figure 15-12: Linda Esser, Bedford Extension Master Gardener Pruning the thornless blackberries at the therapeutic garden. Turner, Phyllis. 2022. CC BY-NC-SA 4.0.
- Figure 15-13: Masses of Joe-Pye weed, Heliopsis, and grasses make an impact. *Master Gardener Training Handbook*, Virginia Cooperative Extension, 2018. CC BY-NC-SA 4.0.
- Figure 15-14: One of everything ("flower confetti") rarely produces desirable results! *Master Gardener Training Handbook*, Virginia Cooperative Extension, 2018. CC BY-NC-SA 4.0.
- Figure 15-15: Any open space invites weeds! Keep that in mind for the very front border as well. *Master Gardener Training Handbook*, Virginia Cooperative Extension, 2018. CC BY-NC-SA 4.0.
- Figure 15-16: Warm, rosy pinks and purples work well together. *Master Gardener Training Handbook*, Virginia Cooperative Extension, 2018. CC BY-NC-SA 4.0.

CHAPTER 16: LANDSCAPE DESIGN

Chapter Contents:

- Plans and Maps
- Site Analysis
- User Analysis
- Elements and Principles of Design
- Sustainability
- Planting Design (Plan)
- Energy Conservation through Landscaping
- Maintenance
- Themes
- Additional Resources

Landscape design is the process of planning and organizing the natural and man-made parts of the landscape into an aesthetic, functional, and environmentally sustainable space. This can apply to the whole landscape or an area within the landscape.

Landscape design can help to balance people's wants and needs with the environment and natural resource protection and preservation. Landscape design can affect site aesthetics, use and functionality, property value, water quality, wildlife, and long term management. Informed, thoughtful and creative planning and design can integrate the human and environmental factors for a positive impact at the individual residence level; which collectively impacts the larger community and watershed.

Why is it important? People's wants and needs must be balanced with the environment and natural resource protection and preservation. Landscape design can affect site aesthetics, use and functionality, property value, water quality, wildlife, and long term management. Informed, thoughtful and creative planning and design can integrate the human and environmental factors for a positive impact at the individual residence level, which collectively impacts the larger community and watershed levels.

- What does a successful landscape design involve
- Gathering information and creating a plan to make the best use of the space
- The most of a site's natural features and advantages
- Balancing human impact, the environment and long term sustainability of the design
- Utilizing materials and plants that best ft the site and the design

Plans and Maps

The planning process is the most important part of landscape design, but unfortunately it is often neglected. An overall plan should be developed so that when any landscape work is done, it will be part of the whole picture. Usually it takes several years to implement a landscape plan. Construction and plantings are completed as weather and finances and other resources allow. Many plantings also need time to mature to create the desired effect. The overall landscape plan should include goals, timeline, budget, a list of resources and contacts, and various site maps and information. The smaller the house, site, and budget, the greater the need for an overall plan, because every square foot of space and every dollar must produce maximum results.

Prepare a scale base map of the site using one of the following techniques.

- Use landscape design software or use graph paper and let one square equal so many feet
- Have a friend help hold and read a tape measure or use a measuring wheel
- Record all measurements clearly on the map

Draw the site to scale:

- Using a ruler, let 1 inch equal 8 feet for a small site, and 16 feet for a large site
- Using an engineer's or architect's scale, let 1 inch equal 10 feet for a small site, or 20 feet for a large site

A base map should include the following: (make 5-6 copies of this map and don't write on the original)

- Property lines, easements, or setbacks
- North point
- House, garage, other buildings or structures
- Scale used
- Location of septic tank or sewer lines
- Walks and driveways
- Doors, windows, porches, and location of specific rooms
- Fire hydrants, meters, utility lines, water spigots, HVAC unit, telephone poles, and lines

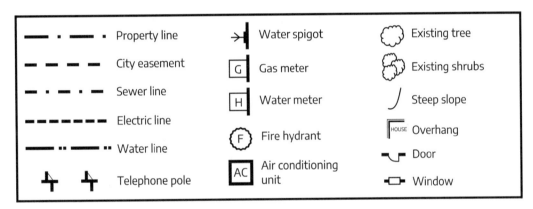

Figure 16-1: Suggested symbols for plans and maps.

Site Analysis

This involves gathering additional information about the site that could impact the design. Spend time (10-15 minutes) in different parts of the site at different times of the day just observing. Use one copy of the base map to add items from the list below. These are reminders of unique site features to incorporate into the design or challenges that need to be addressed in the design.

- Rock outcroppings, slopes, erosion, compacted or poor soil areas
- Path of stormwater runoff. Use arrows to show the direction of surface water flow onto the site, across the site, off the site, and any low or constantly wet areas
- Setbacks, easements or streams (shorelines) that might have special restrictions/limitations
- Desirable and undesirable features of the site and adjoining property (noise, smells, traffic)
- Views – good and bad views from windows, porches, decks, and different parts of the site
- Prevailing wind direction
- Light coming from security lights, street lights, neighbors
- Areas that need privacy screening
- Access to equipment that may need maintenance (such as septic or propane tanks and well pumps)

On another copy of the base map add the plant information. Existing healthy plants are a valuable resource that can be incorporated into the design. Make extra copies of this map as the plant information will change as the design develops.

- The cold hardiness and heat tolerance zones for the site
- The location of existing trees, shrubs, turf and other plants
- Microclimates (dry shade, wet soils, tree root competition, etc.)
- Locations for specific plants (e.g., 8' privacy hedge, small flowering tree, wildlife habitat, etc.)
- Create a companion list to this map identifying the plants on this map, noting their condition, and thoughts on keeping or removing them and any maintenance needed
- Create a list of favorite or desired plants that might be included in the design
- If you can't identify the existing plants or need suggestions for new plants, create a list of resources to help like the Extension office, nearby botanical gardens or arboretums, and websites

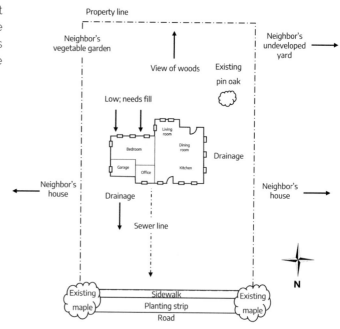

Figure 16-2: Map example showing front of property bordering sidewalk with planting strip and road, existing trees, and other important features such as drainage direction and low spot in back.

An understanding of the water, soil, and climate conditions of a site is essential for plant selection and establishment and a successful design.

Water Factors

Water is critical to a successful landscape design. How much water is available will determine:

- The plants used in the design
- Whether an irrigation system is needed and what type to establish and maintain plants
- Whether to include natural or man-made water features in the design
- Whether there are drainage or erosion issues that need to be addressed in the design

During and after a rain, observe how water moves onto, across, and off the site. Look for soil splashed on windows or outside walls, water pathways, erosion, tree roots or rocks becoming exposed, small rills or gullies beginning to show, locations where water collects or where water stands. These areas may need to be addressed in the design through plantings or drainage techniques. See Chapter 17: "Water Quality and Conservation" for more information.

Soil Factors

See Chapter 2: "Soils and Nutrient Management" for more information.

Drainage

Drainage can vary a great deal from one area to another, even if the site is relatively flat. During and after a rain, note any locations where water collects, is slow to drain, or stands for more than 24 hours. These areas may need to be addressed in the design through plantings or drainage techniques. A percolation or "perk" test may be needed in any location where water stands to determine the infiltration or percolation rate. More information on perk tests can be found online.

Soil Texture

To determine texture, send a soil sample to a lab and request a textural analysis. Traditional soil survey maps can only be used on undisturbed sites. This disqualifies most urban and suburban sites, as they are significantly disturbed during development. Soil (sometimes called fill) is often hauled away from or onto a developed site and can be very different from the existing site soil. Soil texture can affect many site design and maintenance decisions including: plant selection, stormwater management, choice of irrigation method, and amount of irrigation, and stability for structures.

Soil pH and Fertility

Send soil samples to a lab for analysis. A soil sample should be collected from each different area (e.g., front lawn, back lawn, wooded area, flower bed, vegetable garden, or any problem area). Soil pH and fertility can vary over short distances and can be influenced by paved areas and foundations (these often raise pH), past gardening practices, fill hauled onto a site, and drainage issues. Soil tests provide a base line of information that could impact the design decisions like plant selection, plant location, and any site preparation including soil amendments like organic matter, lime, or fertilizer. Soil tests should be done every 3 years.

Topography

Changes in elevation can add interest and variety to a landscape. Natural variations should be considered an asset, and artificial ones should be minimized. For example, a hilly wooded site lends itself to an informal or natural design, with large areas left in a natural state. And, while grading of terraces or retaining walls might be necessary to facilitate construction or control water drainage, they should be kept to a minimum and designed to detract as little as possible from the natural terrain while accommodating vehicle and pedestrian traffic on the site. A particular challenge is creating topography for a water feature (i.e., a waterfall to a pond) in generally flat areas. If the feature isn't integrated into the overall site design and topography, it looks like it landed from outer space!

Compaction

Areas with heavy foot traffic, where cars are or have been parked, or where there has been any construction activity, are likely to be compacted. Test soil compaction by forcing a shovel or other tool into the ground when soil is moderately moist. In healthy soil it should be fairly easy to push the tool into the ground, provided you do not hit any stones or large roots. Soil may be uniformly compacted, or there may be a hard layer, known as a hardpan, 6-18 inches under the topsoil that can restrict root growth and drainage. Because few plants will thrive in heavily compacted soil, aeration and/or amendments may be needed. Compacted areas should be noted on the site analysis map and addressed as part of the site preparation plan before implementing the design.

Climate and Microclimate

Climate includes sun, shade, all forms of precipitation, wind, and temperature. All these affect the way a house should be placed on a site, how the land is used, and what is planted. In planning the landscape, utilize the advantages of climate and microclimates. In protected microclimates, grow plants that might not normally survive or thrive in that growing zone, or use the microclimate to extend the growing season. Microclimates also create opportunities for diversity and adding unique plants to the landscape. In warm climates, enlarge the outdoor living area. In cold climates, plant so that the winter scene is enjoyed from the inside.

Cold Hardiness and Heat Tolerance

Cold hardiness and heat tolerance zone numbers help determine if a plant species will tolerate the temperature averages and extremes of a site. Refer to the USDA Hardiness Zone Map (https://planthardiness.ars.usda.gov/) to determine the zones for a specific site. Other climate factors, such as rainfall, snow cover, soil types, winds, elevation and pollution should also be considered, as these may affect plant survival.

Sun and Shade Patterns

People respond differently to sun and shade, so it's important to study the amount and location of each at a site. Note daily and seasonal patterns and those areas that are heavily shaded or are exposed to late afternoon sun. The sun is highest and shadows are shortest in the summer. Take into account planned and existing structures and plantings. Sun for a minimum of 6 hours a day during the growing season is generally adequate for vegetables and other plants requiring "full sun," although 8 to 10 hours will result in significantly better growth and yield.

As the sun moves from east to west, it travels in the southern sky casting shadows to the north side of houses, structures, and trees.

Plan future shade from tree plantings carefully in order to keep sunny areas for lawns and gardens, and summer shade for the house and patio/deck. Place trees off the corners (rather than the sides) of the house where they will accent the house but not block views and air circulation. Remember to plan and plant for the mature size of the tree(s). Consider possible shade from trees and houses on neighbors' property also.

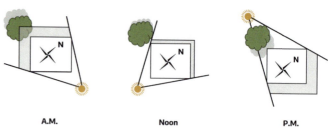

Figure 16-3: Daily shade pattern.

A number of tools and apps are now available to help gardeners estimate the amount of sun a site receives. The iTree program (https://www.itreetools.org/) can help you estimate the shade value of individual trees.

Site specific temperature

Note exposed surfaces that reflect or give off heat, such as patios and driveways. These can greatly increase air temperatures around them making the area hotter during the day and radiating back heat overnight. Identify wind patterns and areas protected from or exposed to cold winter winds or drying summer winds. Note any low areas where cold air might settle and injure marginally hardy plants. Northern exposures receive the least light, and therefore are the coolest. The east and west receive more light; western exposures are warmer than eastern because they receive afternoon light. The southern exposure receives the most light and tends to be the warmest. These factors can create microclimates that will affect plant selection and survival.

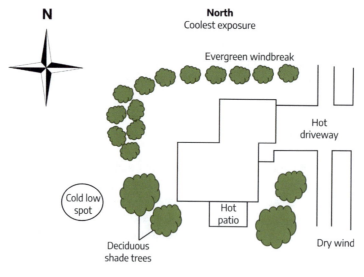

Figure 16-4: Exposures: This property faces east with a south-facing patio that gets hot. In the north of the property, a wind break blocks cold winds.

User Analysis

A landscape design should balance people's wants and needs with the environment and natural resource protection and preservation. A user analysis is essential to creating a design that will keep the balance while changing over time as the user's needs and lifestyle changes or as the users change. A user analysis should include: the people who will use it, their habits, actions, needs, desires, physical abilities, and economic abilities. A re-evaluation should occur when the user or situation changes. A successful landscape should change and mature with the user. For example: a plan for a young family would include inexpensive plantings and open areas in which children and pets can play. As a family reaches its middle years, more extensive and expensive plantings can be incorporated. The children's play area can transition into other functions. For example, the sand box can become a water garden. With the approach of retirement years, the landscape should become lower maintenance. Mature trees and shrubs will carry the landscape theme, high-labor areas such as flower beds can be minimized. Ramps may replace steps.

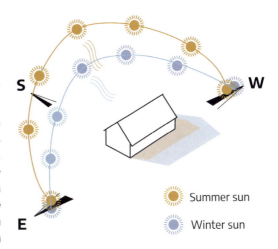

Figure 16-5: Winter and summer sun direction.

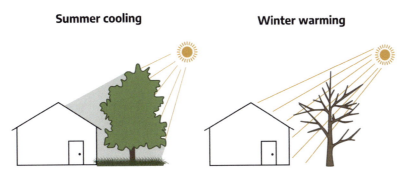

Figure 16-6: Energy efficient tree placement where a deciduous tree's foliage blocks sun in the summer and loses leaves in winter, allowing sun to reach the house.

Use Areas

Public, private, and service areas can usually be easily defined in residential landscapes. The final design of these areas should reflect the user's priorities, aesthetics and functional requirements.

Public – is the part of the site that passersby and visitors view and that the user sees every time they come or go from the site. It is generally in front of the house and is attractively maintained to compliment the house and give a welcoming appearance.

Private – is generally behind the house and is for the user's activities such as entertaining, family activities, and pets. It is usually screened from public and/or neighbors views and has easy access from the house.

Service – is usually to the side of the house. It is the utility, work, or production area and it often connects the public and private areas. This area can be screened off and is for storage, work, garbage and recycling, oil tank, air conditioning unit, sheds, vehicle parking, wood storage, compost pile, etc.

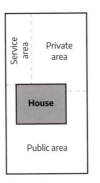 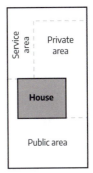 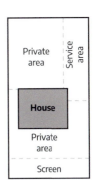

Figure 16-7: Landscape area examples.

Traffic Flow

Think about different arrangements of these areas in relation to rooms in the house, user activities, views, and traffic flow. Draw the three general areas on one copy of the site map. Then within these large areas, draw smaller areas for specific functions or activities. Consider what is happening in each of the areas, time of day the area is being used, the frequency of use of each area and the traffic flow to, from, and through each area. Add lines to show vehicle and foot traffic patterns from area to area and from the house to each area. Different colors or line thicknesses can denote more frequently used walkways or vehicle routes. Don't forget to create a legend to show what each color or line means. Consider whether the walkways should be formal or informal to fit into the overall design. Also note which walkways need to be wider, need lighting, or need heavy duty surfacing materials. For example, a wider walkway with an even surface is more formal and better for a front entrance, where garbage and recycling cans need to be wheeled, or for children, the elderly, high heels, and wheelchairs.

A narrower walkway with mulch or stepping stones is informal and can be used to meander through a garden area or across a turf area that is frequently mowed, or where there is infrequent activity or access. Heavy duty surfacing materials are needed for driveways, especially if there are turns for side parking areas or to pull into a garage. Consider using permeable paving materials for walkways and driveways for better water infiltration and reduced runoff. Also consider that driveways can serve additional functions such as a basketball court, tricycle riding area, or chalk art canvas.

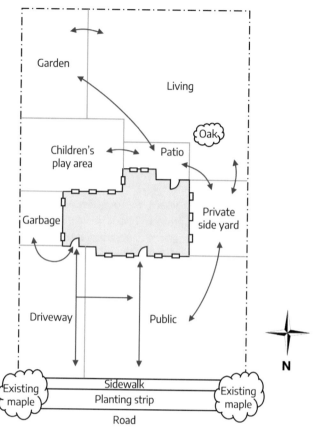

Figure 16-8: Traffic flow around a yard showing the paths people walk between landscape features.

Space Transitions and Dividers

Different areas of the landscape need to flow into each other and sometimes they need to be delineated, separated, or protected by fencing or screening.

- Transitions are the connecting links between spaces. For example: between the house and the landscape, between the front yard and backyard, between the service and private areas. Transitions should be composed of characteristics that are found in both of like common colors, textures, forms, plants, paving, or other materials.
- Dividers define or give privacy to spaces, create the background for outdoor activities, protect the landscape and house from prevailing winds or sun, and provide security. Dividers can be made up of fences, walls, plants as hedges, or plants as borders.

Elements and Principles of Design

The site and user analyses gather essential information that is incorporated into the landscape design. Each design is a unique creation. While there are no set rules, landscape designs are based on certain elements and principles. Keep the horizontal and vertical aspects of the site in mind when developing a design as landscapes are three-dimensional.

Scale

Scale refers to the size relationship or proportion between different parts of a landscape. This could be between buildings and plants, plants and plants, or plants and people. Scale can change over time as plants grow, so design using the mature size (height and spread) of the plants. This is especially important when locating trees and shrubs near a building. Plants that grow large may overwhelm a small building or small plants around a large building can be similarly out of scale. When a landscape is out of scale, it appears uninviting and awkward like something is missing or not in the right place.

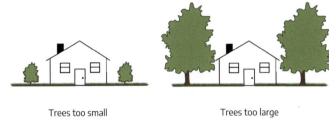

Figure 16-9: Tree out of scale with house.

Balance

Balance in landscaping refers to an aesthetically pleasing integration of elements. It is a sense of one part being of equal visual weight or mass to another. There are two types of balance — symmetrical and asymmetrical. Symmetrical balance is formal. It has an obvious axis with everything on one side duplicated or mirrored on the other side. Asymmetrical balance is more informal, and is achieved by using different objects on both sides of a less obvious axis. For example, when there is a large existing tree or shrub, a grouping or cluster of smaller plants is used to counterbalance it. Balance may also be achieved through the use of color and texture. Whichever type of balance is used in the design, the result is the same; there is equal visual weight or mass on each side of the axis.

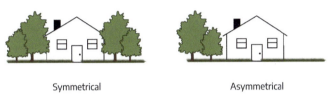

Figure 16-10: Landscape balance.

Unity (Harmony or Simplicity)

Unity is grouping or arranging different parts of the design to appear as a single unit. Repetition of shapes, lines or colors creates unity. The design should look like everything belongs together and be aesthetically pleasing from every view. Groundcovers and turf unify a landscape by connecting different spaces. Repetition of the same plants in sweeps or groupings creates unity. A landscape with too many different plants, accessories (sculpture, yard ornaments, etc.), colors, shapes or textures in a limited area lacks unity. The landscape is chaotic, confusing, and disordered. The viewer doesn't know where to look or go. A landscape with unity complements the house, draws the eye and the traffic flow in a specific direction, and presents an overall theme, tone, and order to the space.

Rhythm

Rhythm is even repetition, and it directs the eye in the landscape through continuity and flow. Rhythm is repetition of color, line, shape, or texture in regular measures and in a definite direction. Some examples are: several of the same plant planted exactly the same distance apart in a bed, the same curves repeated along a walkway or bed edges, the same paver pattern repeated every 3 steps in the walkway.

Accent (Focal Point)

An **accent** or focal point is something that deliberately stands out from the overall landscape. It gives the eye a place to rest. Without them, landscapes can appear monotonous or dull. Both the public and private areas of a landscape should have an accent. If those areas are divided into smaller areas, then each space should have one. Usually there is only one accent per space. Accents can be: sculpture, specimen plants, garden accessories, a water feature, boulders, the front door, or the house itself.

More Than Just a Pretty Space

Scott Douglas, Director Hahn Horticulture Garden, Virginia Tech

As landscape designers, our first goal is to create beautiful spaces, but what if you want more from your design? We can all go beyond visual beauty by creating aesthetic landscapes that also serve a purpose. Your design could also support pollinators, provide habitat for wildlife, grow food for nearby residents, improve water quality (rain gardens), or any combination of those purposes.

Figure 16-11: Conceptual image of a productive highway corridor that includes pollinator support, stormwater management and solar power production.

At the residential level, every gardener can support pollinators by planting a wide variety of blooming plants (including a lot of native plants) to extend the bloom period as long as possible. In order to maximize your bloom period, start by focusing on the extremes with early spring bloomers (bulbs and spring ephemerals) and late fall bloomers (asters and Russian sage). Once you have those bookends established, you can shift your attention to filling in between them with your favorite summer flowers.

Keep in mind that your plantings can evolve as the growing season progresses. If you underplant perennial plantings with bulbs and spring ephemerals, you can create multiple flushes of color in your beds. For example, daffodils and hyacinths can create a beautiful spring display and once they start dying back, the coneflowers, black-eyed susans, and other summer bloomers can take over and hide the dying foliage of the early bloomers.

As the size of the property you are designing increases, the greater the overall impact can be. Most office parks and corporate campuses have massive swaths of turf that could be transformed into meadows or large-scale rain gardens. Many college campuses have underutilized outdoor spaces that could serve similar purposes. At the national scale, our highway and interstate systems feature thousands of acres of highly managed turf along the shoulders and medians that could be converted into productive landscapes. Imagine if the interstate near you was a lush landscape of native grasses and wildflowers!

While this all sounds very euphoric, there are some challenges to designing beyond the typical landscapes that we see today. All landscapes require maintenance, even something as "wild" and "native" as a meadow planting. A meadow garden will require long-term maintenance by people with strong horticultural knowledge, way beyond what is required for the "mow-blow-go" landscapes that we are accustomed to seeing these days. Maintenance staff will need strong plant identification skills so they can determine which plants should stay and which plants need to be removed. Invasive weeds will continually assault these landscapes, with their seeds being blown in or deposited by birds and other animals. Once these invasive plants establish themselves, they will self-seed and slowly take over the planting. It will be a continual battle to keep the weeds at bay.

There is so much opportunity in the landscape and every landscape can serve a purpose beyond just aesthetics. What purpose will yours serve?

Sustainability

Sustainable landscaping can also be called low maintenance, green, environmentally friendly, or conservation landscaping. The following sustainable concepts and practices should be kept in mind as a landscape design is developed. All the practices can't be used in every landscape, but even incorporating a few will make the landscape healthier, more resilient, and less maintenance intensive.

Sustainable Concepts

- **Biological diversity** – using many different plant species promotes beneficial insects, provides food and habitat for animals, and reduces pest and weather impacts.
- **Resource conservation** – using existing topography, water, plants, and views in the design reduces costs and disturbance to the environment, using locally sourced plants, construction, and other materials saves transportation costs and supports the local economy.
- **Long term planning** – planning for mature plant sizes and the long-term look and use of the landscape reduces labor and costs by minimizing plant crowding and maintenance.
- **Low impact / input** – disturbing the site as little as possible and using healthy, site appropriate plants reduce maintenance and pesticide and fertilizer use.
- **Water conservation** – grouping plants with similar water needs, using rain sensors, rain chains, rain barrels, and rain gardens/swales to collect and manage runoff, help to conserve valuable water resources.

Sustainable practices include:

- Rain chains and barrels
- Rain sensors
- Landscaped swales
- Permeable paving
- Ground covers and mulches
- Compost
- Canopy layering
- Passive solar heating/cooling
- Plant diversity
- Plant selection and spacing
- Plant grouping based on water
- Drip irrigation and watering bags
- Aeration
- Long term planning
- Correct planting
- Minimal site disturbance
- Grasscycling
- Recycled products
- Low input lawn
- Reduced or no fertilizers
- Zero or as needed pesticides
- Solar lights
- Soil testing
- Storm drain protection
- Use native plants
- Minimal deadheading

Construction Materials

Landscape design is not synonymous with plants. Often there are structures (pergolas, gazebos, fences, sheds, decks, arbors, benches, etc.) and hardscape (walls, walkways, steps, terraces, patios, outdoor kitchens, fire pits, lighting, etc.) included in a design. Careful consideration should be given to the construction materials and their use in order to create the desired design aesthetic. A wide variety of products are available, and many factors influence the choices.

Considerations:

- The specific look or effect being created
- Budget – may need to do it in phases
- Do it yourself or hire someone
- Timeline for the project(s) and best time of year to do it
- Natural, synthetic, or recycled products
- Source location – local, non-local, on-line
- Availability of the product
- Shipping/hauling/delivery expenses
- Durability and weather resistance

CHAPTER 16: LANDSCAPE DESIGN

- Space to store materials and supplies (e.g., piles of stone or pallets of pavers)
- Security of stored materials (from vandalism or theft)
- Access for delivery or transportation of materials to specific construction site (e.g., delivered in the front driveway, but need to transport to the back yard for use)
- Any property restrictions (e.g., colors, fence height/style, historic, easements, etc.)

Planting Design (Plan)

On a fresh copy of the site base map, mark where plants are needed for:

- Separating areas
- Screening undesirable views or privacy
- Providing shade or windbreaks
- Accent (e.g., specimen plant or to complement the house)
- User activities (e.g., turf for play, herbs and vegetables, plant collections, butterfly, cutting or rain garden, erosion control, pet area, seasonal interest, etc.)
- Specific conditions (e.g., dry shade, hot and dry southwest exposure)

Figure 16-12: Plan example: School Garden Design Concept created by U.S. Forest Service landscape architect Matt Arnn.

Review the site analysis maps and information and the user analysis information to determine what plants are needed where on the site. Think about individual plants and groups of plants that will meet the desires of the user(s), serve a purpose (functionality), tie the various areas together into a unified plan (aesthetics), and be environmentally sustainable. Keep in mind that landscapes are dynamic. Plants grow and change over time. Consider successional planting. For example, planting annuals or perennials between the shrubs until they mature or planting a sun loving groundcover under the newly planted small tree, to be changed to a shade loving groundcover in several years when the tree canopy widens).

Different symbols should be used to indicate the different types of trees, shrubs, groups, and groundcovers. Create a legend and label each symbol or use these examples. Add symbols for the hardscape later. A first draft of a planting design might just be different sizes of circles in the general locations. As the design comes together, the next drafts should use the different symbols for specific types of plants. The symbols should be drawn to scale (plant or group width) in order to see how many of a plant are needed or will fit into the actual space. Examples of common symbols are below. More complicated symbols can be found on-line. All of this can be done without knowing the exact plants. For example, an evergreen hedge is needed for privacy on the east side of the site or a deciduous tree is needed on the southwest corner of the house, or a butterfly garden is located off the patio in a sunny area.

As the planting design becomes more detailed, exact plants can be specified. Sometimes there may only be a certain amount of space available at a site location and that will determine which exact plant is used (e.g., only 6' width for a hedge). Sometimes the user already knows exactly which plant(s) they want and that is incorporated into the design (e.g., a 15' wide weeping Japanese maple accent plant or a 60' wide chestnut oak for shade). Sometimes research to find the exact plant for a location or purpose is needed. In that case, make a list of the specifications to help narrow down the plant choices.

Plant choice specifications:

- Height – low, medium, tall
- Form – spreading, upright, arching, globe

- Purpose – shade, background hedge, screen, accent, mass
- Seasonal Interest – fruit, flowers, foliage, bark, fragrance
- Type – annual, perennial, woody, herbaceous, evergreen, deciduous, tree, shrub, bulb
- Maintenance – pests, pruning, debris (leaves, berries, cones)
- Cultural Needs – shade, sunlight, moisture requirements, hardiness zone

Add a planting key to the planting design to list the exact plants as they are selected. Keep a "backup" list of second and third choices in case the first plant choice isn't available. The planting design may need to be implemented in phases if there are time, availability, or budget constraints. For example, bed areas can be defined, prepared, and mulched during the summer but planted in the fall; large trees, which are expensive, can be planted first and the other plants when the budget allows; or the area around the patio can be planted but the back of the yard can wait until later. Numerous resources are easily available to help with plant selection. A good place to start is at the local Extension office, nearby botanical or public gardens, or with local garden groups, clubs, or societies.

Using native plants is becoming the norm rather than the exception. While there are many reasons and benefits to using native plants, the design rule should always be put the right plant in the right place. The Virginia Department of Conservation and Recreation and the Virginia Native Plant Society are good resources for more information on native plants.

Benefits of using native plants:

- Increase landscape biodiversity, sustainability, and resilience
- Reduce maintenance and chemical (fertilizer and pesticide) inputs
- Provide food and habitat for beneficial insects and wildlife
- Support the local ecology
- Provide a sense of place (e.g., palm tree in Florida, cactus in Arizona)
- Manage erosion and stormwater
- Prevent invasive plants
- Provide beauty
- Improve soil, water, and air quality

Considerations for using native plants:

- Make sure the plant is native to the area (plants native to other parts of the United States may not do well in Virginia)
- Do not dig native plants from the wild and transplant into a landscape (unless they are being rescued)
- Urban/developed sites often don't have the specific growing conditions needed (soil, water, sun/shade exposure)
- A native plant just may not be the best choice for a particular location or design need
- Native plants can sometimes be difficult to find, transplant, and establish
- Native plants may not be as "ornamental" or aesthetically pleasing as non-natives
- Many native species are too large in size for smaller landscapes
- Some native species are aggressive spreaders or seeders and can be a maintenance headache or invasive
- There is often controversy about what exactly is native (i.e., before a certain historical time, are cultivars or varieties of a native species is truly "native")

Energy Conservation through Landscaping

A well designed landscape can significantly reduce home heating and cooling cost; making the home and budget more comfortable while conserving energy and helping the environment.

- **Deciduous trees** (those that shed their leaves) planted on the west sides of a house cast shade on the house keeping it cooler which reduces air conditioning costs. In the winter when the leaves fall off, the sun warms the house reducing heating costs. This is especially effective on houses with brick, concrete, or dark colored walls. Remember to account for the mature size of the tree canopy and don't plant it too close to the house. Branches that extend over the room can drop debris that can stain shingle and clog gutters. Also don't plant a tree if it will block any solar panels

on the house.
- Collectively, tree and shrub canopies cool the air through transpiration; thus conserving energy.
- If trees can't be used to shade the house, then partial shading can be accomplished with shrubs. Plant them far enough away from the foundation so that the mature canopy edge reaches 1' from the house. This creates shade and an insulation space, but keeps the branches from rubbing the house or causing mold or mildew problems and provides access space.
- Using trees, shrubs or a trellis or fence to shade the air conditioning unit reduces the air temperature around the unit which make it more efficient. Again, this reduces costs and energy use, and can also increase the life expectancy of the unit.
- Evergreen trees planted on the north side of the house block cold winter winds which reduces the amount of heating required in the winter.
- Trees can also be planted to influence wind movement around and through a house. The idea isn't to reduce winds (as they can help cool the house), but to influence the wind's circulation patterns. This is appropriate for times of the year when temperatures are mild and air conditioning is not needed or when there is no air conditioning. Determine the prevailing wind direction, then plant trees along that pathway to act as a funnel for breezes into the windows, thereby maximizing natural cooling. If there are existing trees, then prune up the low branches to allow the breezes to pass through to the house. If air conditioning is used frequently, then directing winds with tree position can actually increase air conditioning use and thus cost.
- Light-colored construction materials in the landscape (for roofs, fences, decks, and patios) reflect light and don't absorb as much heat; keeping the house and surrounding living areas cooler. Planting a green roof on the house acts as insulation. Inside temperatures are more even and heating and cooling costs are reduced. Green roofs also significantly lengthen the life expectancy of a roof and reduce stormwater runoff. For more information on conserving energy with the landscape see VCE Publication "Conserving energy with the landscape" 426-712.

Maintenance

Landscape maintenance should be assessed in the user analysis and accounted for in the design process. The level of maintenance (low, moderate, high) is subjective and totally dependent on the user. Someone who enjoys working in the yard, may consider pruning, raking leaves, mowing or pulling weeds low or moderate maintenance. Someone who wants a well maintained landscape but can't or doesn't like to do those tasks would probably consider a landscape requiring them high maintenance. Realize that all landscapes need maintenance. New landscapes or recently renovated areas in a landscape will need more as plants get established. Mature or more naturalized landscapes should require less maintenance unless renovation or invasive species control is needed. Landscapes that have more spaces, are more elaborate, are large, are formal, or are heavily used often need more maintenance. A low-maintenance plan is the goal of most homeowners, and that can be achieved through thoughtful design, careful planning, and smart plant choices.

Practices for cost efficiency and lower maintenance:

- Keep the overall design simple.
- Decide which tasks the user can/will do and which will be hired out.
- Have a small lawn area or none at all.
- Avoid sharp angles, tight corners, and irregular areas that are hard to mow.
- Layer plant canopies (tree, shrub, groundcover) for habitat for beneficial insects and birds.
- Use groundcovers or natural mulches to reduce weeds and conserve water.
- Use permeable paving in heavily traveled areas to reduce compaction and runoff.
- Provide mowing strips of brick or concrete to edge flower beds and shrub borders.
- Use fences or walls instead of clipped formal hedges for screening.
  Use fewer annuals and more trees, shrubs, perennials and bulbs for color.
- Use annuals in small amounts for accent in highly visible areas.
  Select plants well adapted to the site conditions, with pest resistance (including any turf).
- Do not have an irrigation system.
- Group plants with similar water requirements.
- Use plants that have low debris (pine cones, leaves, fruit, sap, etc.)

- Avoid aggressive plants (spread quickly or seed prolifically)
- Scout frequently to catch any problems early.

Themes

A theme is an idea or concept. There are as many themes for landscapes as there are gardeners and designers. An entire landscape can be designed around one theme, or the design can incorporate several themes. Theme can be based on particular historic periods, location, plant species, colors, architectural or gardening styles, hobbies, etc.

Examples of garden themes:

- Rose or bulb
- Butterfly or pollinator
- Water or bog
- Topiary
- Rain garden
- Medicinal
- Herb or vegetable
- Seaside
- Tropical Fragrance or texture
- English cottage
- Winter interest
- Native plant
- Mediation
- Evening or night
- Cut flower
- Edible landscape
- Rock or xeriscape
- Japanese
- Wildlife habitat
- Sculpture

Additional Resources

- VCE Publication "Problem Free Trees for Virginia Landscapes" 450-236 (PPWS-69P)
- VCE Publication "Trees for Problem Landscape Sites — Air Pollution" 430-022 (HORT-123P)
- VCE Publication "Rain Garden Plants" 426-043 (SPES-57P)
- VCE Publication "Backyard Wildlife Habitats" 426-070
- VCE Publication "The Effect of Landscape Plants on Perceived Home Value" 426-087
- VCE Publication "Planning the Flower Border" 426-202
- VCE Publication "Patriotic Gardens: How to Plant a Red, White, and Blue Garden" 426-210 (HORT-185)
- VCE Publication "What About Landscaping and Energy Efficiency?" BSE-145(BSE-334NP)
- VCE Publication "Selecting Landscape Plants: Flowering Trees" 426-611 (SPES-321P)
- VCE Publication "Selecting Landscape Plants: Boxwoods" 426-603 (HORT-290P)
- VCE Publication "Selecting Landscape Plants: Ground Covers" 426-609
- VCE Publication "Selecting Landscape Plants: Shade Trees" 426-610

- VCE Publication "Selecting Landscape Plants: Flowering Trees" 426-611
- VCE Publication "Selecting Plants for Virginia Landscapes: Edible Landscape Species – Trees" SPES-316
- VCE Publication Energy series: "What about Landscaping and Energy Efficiency?" BSE-145NP
- VCE Publication "Creating a Water-wise Landscape" 426-713
- VCE Publication "Landscaping for Less in the Landfill" 426-716
- VCE Publication "Selecting Turfgrass" 426-719
- VCE Publication "Mulching for a Healthy Landscape" 426-724
- VCE Publication "Tree Fruit in the Home Garden" 426-841
- VCE Publication "Virginia Firescapes: Firewise Landscaping for Woodland Homes" 430-300
- VCE Publication "Problem-free Shrubs for Virginia Landscapes" 450-236
- VCE Publication "Problem-free Trees for Virginia Landscapes" 450-237
- VCE Publication "Introduction to Cold-Hardy Tropicals for Virginia Landscapes" 3005-1446
- VCE Publication "Virginia Turfgrass Variety Recommendations" CSES-17NP
- VCE Publication "A Lawn To Dye For – How to Create a Perfect Lawn: Choosing The Right Grass" CSES-41NP
- VCE Publication "For the Birds, Butterflies & Hummingbirds: Creating Inviting Habitats" HORT-59NP
- VCE Publication "Selecting Plants for Virginia Landscapes: Showy Flowering Shrubs" HORT-84P
- VCE Publication "Selecting Plants for Virginia Landscapes: Edible Landscapes" SPES-317
- Landscape for Life: https://landscapeforlife.colostate.edu/
- US National Arboretum: https://usna.usda.gov/
- VA Dept. of Conservation & Recreation (native plants): https://www.dcr.virginia.gov/natural-heritage/nativeplants
- State Arboretum of Virginia: https://blandy.virginia.edu/content/state-arboretum-virginia

Books

- The Plant Growth Planner, Caroline Boisset, ISBN 0-13-681230-9
- The Principles of Gardening, Hugh Johnson, ISBN 0-671-50805-9
- Taylor's Guide to Gardening in the South, ISBN 0-395-59681-5
- The New York/Mid Atlantic Garden's Book of Lists, ISBN 0-87833-261-8
- Best Plants for Hampton Roads A Landscape & Garden Companion, ISBN 0-9726455-0-0
- Bringing Nature Home, ISBN 978-0-88192-992-8
- The Living Landscape, ISBN 978-1-60469-408-6
- Sustainable Landscaping for Dummies, ISBN 978-0-470-41149-0
- Conservation Landscaping Guidelines, ISBN 978-1-49362-497-3
- The Essential Garden Design Workbook: Second Edition, ISBN 978-0-88192-975-1

Attributions

- Sabrina Morelli, Arlington Extension Master Gardener (2021 reviser)
- Laurie J. Fox, Horticulture Associate, Horticulture Department, Hampton Road AREC (2015 reviser)

Image Attributions

- Figure 16-1: Suggested symbols for plans and maps. Grey, Kindred. 2022. CC BY-NC-SA 4.0.
- Figure 16-2: Map example. Grey, Kindred. 2022. CC BY-NC-SA 4.0. Includes Simple compass rose by Brosen (modification by Howcheng) from WikimediaCommons CC BY 3.0.
- Figure 16-3: Daily shade pattern. Grey, Kindred. 2022. CC BY-NC-SA 4.0. Includes Simple compass rose by Brosen (modification by Howcheng) from WikimediaCommons CC BY 3.0 and sun by andainul muttaqin from Noun Project (Noun Project license).

CHAPTER 16: LANDSCAPE DESIGN | 415

- Figure 16-4: Exposures. Grey, Kindred. 2022. CC BY-NC-SA 4.0. Includes Simple compass rose by Brosen (modification by Howcheng) from WikimediaCommons CC BY 3.0
- Figure 16-5: Winter and summer sun direction. Grey, Kindred. 2022. CC BY-NC-SA 4.0. Includes Simple compass rose by Brosen (modification by Howcheng) from WikimediaCommons CC BY 3.0 and sun by andainul muttaqin from Noun Project (Noun Project license).
- Figure 16-6: Energy efficient tree placement. Grey, Kindred. 2022. CC BY-NC-SA 4.0. Includes sun by andainul muttaqin from Noun Project (Noun Project license).
- Figure 16-7: Landscape area examples. Grey, Kindred. 2022. CC BY-NC-SA 4.0.
- Figure 16-8: Traffic flow. Grey, Kindred. 2022. CC BY-NC-SA 4.0. Includes Simple compass rose by Brosen (modification by Howcheng) from WikimediaCommons CC BY 3.0.
- Figure 16-9: Tree out of scale with house. Grey, Kindred. 2022. CC BY-NC-SA 4.0.
- Figure 16-10: Landscape balance. Grey, Kindred. 2022. CC BY-NC-SA 4.0.
- Figure 16-11: Conceptual image of a productive highway corridor. Douglas, Scott. 2021. CC BY-NC-SA 4.0.
- Figure 16-12: Plan example. "110310_DM_LSC_0127." Arnn, Matt. U. S. Department of Agriculture. 2011. Flickr. CC BY-ND 2.0

CHAPTER 17: WATER QUALITY AND CONSERVATION

Chapter Contents:

- Watersheds
- Surface, Ground, and Storm Waters
- Water Pollution
- Water Quality Standards
- State Regulatory Information
- Water-Wise Landscaping
- Stormwater Best Management Practices (BMPs)
- Additional Resources

Water is a priceless limited resource and should be treated as such. The earth's population continues to grow rapidly, and as weather patterns and climate continue to change, there is increased demand for and stress on water supplies. Water shortages are becoming more frequent and severe, and water use restrictions are now permanent in many parts of the world and across the United States. Regulations governing water quality protection and water quantity conservation are more numerous and stringent than ever before. For these reasons, it is everyone's responsibility to be a good steward of this essential, invaluable and finite resource.

Watersheds

What Is a Watershed?

A **watershed** is an area of land that drains to a lake, river, **wetland**, or other waterway. When **precipitation** occurs, water travels over forest, agricultural, or urban/suburban land areas before entering a waterway. Water can also travel into underground **aquifers** on its way to larger bodies of water. Together, land and water make up a watershed system. Watersheds can be any size. For example, the Chesapeake Bay Watershed drains upstream land from a 64,000 square mile area in six states. Local watersheds drain much smaller areas, perhaps only a few acres in size.

Figure 17-1: Watershed.

Virginia Watersheds

Everyone lives in a watershed, and Virginia has nine major watersheds with numerous sub-watersheds. Virginia's watersheds ultimately drain into three main bodies of water. Nearly two-thirds of Virginia drains into the Chesapeake Bay. Southeastern and south-central Virginia drain into the Albemarle Sound in North Carolina. Rivers in Southwest Virginia flow to the Mississippi River and then to the Gulf of Mexico.

CHAPTER 17: WATER QUALITY AND CONSERVATION | 417

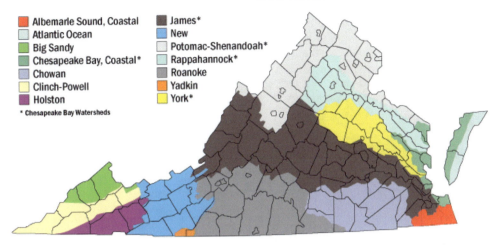

Figure 17-2: Virginia watershed boundaries. Courtesy of Virginia Department of Conservation and Recreation.

Why Are Watersheds Important?

Healthy watersheds are a vital component of a healthy environment. Watersheds act as a filter for **runoff** that occurs from precipitation and snowmelt, providing clean water for drinking, **irrigation**, and industry. Recreation and leisure are important components of watersheds, with many possibilities in Virginia for boating, fishing, and swimming. Watersheds also support a variety of plant and wildlife communities. Scientists and community leaders recognize the best way to protect our water resources is to understand and manage them on a watershed basis. Human activities as well as natural events that occur in a watershed can significantly affect water quality and quantity.

Water Cycle

Earth's water is always cycling; constantly moving and changing states between liquid, vapor, and ice. The water cycle, also known as the hydrologic cycle, describes the continuous movement of water on, above, and below the surface of the Earth. Development negatively impacts the water cycle by 1) stripping plant cover, and 2) replacing it with impervious surfaces (roofs, roads and parking lots) that prevent **infiltration** of precipitation. The result is the generation of high volumes of runoff from urban development that causes **erosion** and **flooding** downstream.

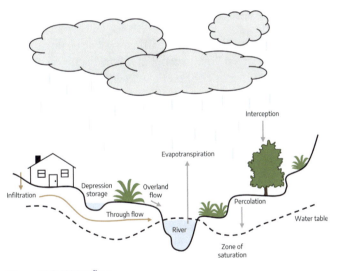

Figure 17-3: Water flow.

Surface, Ground, and Storm Waters

Surface, ground, and storm waters are often viewed and treated as separate entities, but they are part of an interconnected system where each impacts the other and humans impact them all. Depletion of surface and ground water sources is caused by over-use. Flooding, erosion and reduced **groundwater** recharge are caused by development (impervious surfaces). Water **pollution** is caused by carelessness, irresponsible behavior, and a lack of understanding that water is a finite resource critical to our survival.

Surface Water

Surface water is water on the earth's surface or that has not penetrated much below the ground such as in a stream, river, lake, wetland, reservoir, stormwater pond, or ocean.

Surface water is replenished by precipitation, and is lost through **evaporation**, infiltration into the ground where it becomes ground water, and use by plants or by man.

Groundwater

Groundwater is water located beneath earth's surface, held underground in the soil and in pores and crevices in rock (aquifer).

Wells are holes or shafts sunk into the earth to obtain water. One in five Virginians, or nearly 1.7 million people, rely on private water supplies such as wells, springs, and cisterns for their household water (Virginia Cooperative Extension 2015). In the U.S., all water systems (with the exception of a few private wells) are regulated under the Safe Drinking Water Act, which requires routine water testing and treatment. However, people with private water supplies are responsible for all aspects of system management, including water testing, interpreting test results, and addressing problems. Through the Virginia Household Water Quality Program, Virginia Cooperative Extension provides access to affordable and confidential water testing, interpretation of results, and education about system care and dealing with problems. Testing includes total coliform and E. coli bacteria, nitrate, lead, copper, arsenic, pH, hardness, sulfate, fluoride, iron, manganese, sodium, and total dissolved solids. For more information about the Virginia Household Water Quality Program and wells and springs in Virginia, visit the Biological Systems Engineering well water testing website (https://www.wellwater.bse.vt.edu/).

Stormwater

Stormwater is water that originates during precipitation events and snow/ice melt. Stormwater can soak into the soil (infiltrate), be held on the surface and evaporate, or run off into surface water bodies. Storm events are measured by their duration, depth, and intensity.

- **Duration** (hours): Length of time over which rainfall (storm event) occurs.
- **Depth** (inches): Total amount of rainfall occurring during the storm duration.
- **Intensity** (inches per hour): Depth divided by the duration.

Infiltration allows the stormwater to be filtered and eventually will flow into streams and rivers or help to replenish aquifers. The more frequent and intense storms and flooding events caused by our changing climate increases stormwater runoff. Increased stormwater runoff can cause new pollution problems or make existing pollution problems worse. This runoff can increase levels of **sediments**, nutrients, and other **pollutants** in local waterways, causing water quality challenges.

These intense rainfall and flooding events can overwhelm stormwater management systems put in place by municipalities. These municipal systems can get backed up and cause localized flooding or increased runoff of **contaminants** into local waterways. Cities may also see challenges with their wastewater drainage systems, which can be overwhelmed by large rain events and lead to sewer overflows into waterways.

Urban watersheds face additional challenges due to the impact that development has on how water travels and increased impervious surfaces throughout these areas. Urban areas will most commonly have reduced infiltration of water to the soil and a higher runoff volume. Urban municipalities install management systems to help provide efficient **drainage** and prevent damage to public and private property, streets, streams, and other waterways.

Water Pollution

Pollution can refer to either contaminants themselves or to the act of contaminating water bodies (surface and ground) when pollutants are discharged (directly or indirectly) into them without treatment to remove harmful compounds.

Pollutants include:

- Nutrients (primarily nitrogen and phosphorus)
- Sediment
- Pathogens (disease causing microorganisms)
- Petroleum products and fuel
- Detergents and solvents
- Pharmaceuticals
- Heavy metals
- Pesticides
- Manufacturing and industrial waste
- Sewage and fecal matter
- Leaves, trash and other debris

Water pollution affects the entire ecosystem. The effect can be acute (one time immediate effect) or cumulative (building up over time). Sometimes the pollution can be cleaned up or inactivated quickly, but most of the time the recovery process is lengthy.

Groundwater and surface water are interconnected parts of the water cycle and both can be contaminated through a variety of mechanisms. When precipitation falls, part of that water is absorbed by plant canopies, part evaporates, part runs off into surface water bodies, and part soaks into the ground. Water that soaks into the ground is held in the soil, taken up by plants or it infiltrates deeper into the soil. The water that reaches the saturated zone (**water table**) is known as recharge water, and it is needed to resupply groundwater that is continually being brought to the surface through natural springs, wells, plant use, and other means. Pollutants flow with the water either horizontally on the surface or vertically into the ground. When water infiltrates the soil and carries a pollutant with it, it's called **leaching**.

Water Contamination Mechanisms

- Pollutants in the air fall to the ground with precipitation (atmospheric deposition)
- A pollutant is deliberately discharged into the water
- A pollutant is accidentally discharged into the water
- A pollutant is moved by runoff
- A pollutant attaches to sediment which is then moved by runoff
- Surface water leaches a pollutant into the groundwater
- Contaminated groundwater is pumped into a surface water body

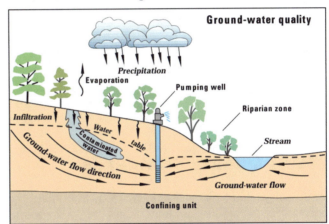

Figure 17-4: Various pathways by which contaminants can reach the groundwater.

Water Pollution Categories

Point source pollution comes from a single source, typically a spill, a discharge pipe, or an illegal dump of chemicals.

Nonpoint source pollution comes from a large land area, not from one specific location or source; typically from daily and land use activities, collected and concentrated through runoff

Water quality programs, which include both regulatory, voluntary and grant programs, have significantly reduced point source pollution in the United States. Because non-point source pollution is wide spread and is the result of many different activities, it is much more difficult to regulate and reduce.

Examples of Pollution Include:

- Accumulation of sediment from erosion flowing into the Chesapeake Bay, destroying submerged aquatic vegetation and associated habitat, which then can lead to "dead zones" from lack of oxygen in the water.
- Excess fertilizer in runoff from landscapes creating algae blooms in stormwater retention ponds.
- Raking or blowing leaves or dumping chemicals into a storm drain.
- A pesticide gets into a surface water body and kills fish as a result of not following label directions.
- A pesticide tank accidentally overturns and pesticides leach through the soil and contaminate groundwater.
- Dog waste that is not "scooped" up washes into the water and swimming areas are closed because of high levels of pathogens

Persistence and solubility determine the contamination potential of a chemical.

Persistence

Persistence is the amount of time a chemical remains active before it is degraded or broken down into harmless components. Persistence is measured in a "half-life" which is the amount of time it takes for one-half the original amount of a chemical to be degraded. Chemicals that have a long half-life remain active for a longer periods of time.

Solubility

The ease with which a chemical dissolves and mixes with water is called solubility.

A chemical with a long half-life and high solubility would have the greatest potential for water contamination. Conversely, a chemical with a short half-life and low solubility would not be chemically active as long and would have a reduced risk of water contamination.

Contaminants are inactivated in many ways. They can be diluted by surface water until they are below a harmful level. They can be broken down into harmless components by sunlight (photodecomposition) or by microorganisms (biological degradation) or through chemical reactions (natural or manmade). Contaminants can change form through volatilization and move into the atmosphere. Finally, they can be absorbed into the plant where they are used, broken down or stored, or they can attach to soil particles or organic matter (**adsorption**).

Water Quality Standards

Water quality can be evaluated using many standards, including: color, odor, dissolved oxygen content, nutrient levels, aquatic life, pathogens, **turbidity**, salinity, pH, chlorophyll, sediment, and many more. Standards are used to assess water quality for purposes such as drinking, swimming, irrigation, wildlife and aquatic life health, and food safety (fish and shellfish). Water quality in undisturbed healthy ecosystems is measured and documented using different standards, then water quality in disturbed ecosystems is measured and compared. Standards provide the basis for the regulations governing water quality and the measure of water quality improvement or decline over time.

The Virginia Department of Environmental Quality (DEQ) extensively tests Virginia's rivers, lakes and tidal waters for pollutants. More than 130 pollutants are monitored annually to determine whether the waters can be used for swimming, fishing and drinking. Waters that do not meet standards are reported to the citizens of Virginia and the U.S. Environmental Protection Agency in the Virginia Water Quality Assessment 305(b)/303(d) Integrated Report.

DEQ has developed a list of impaired waters since 1992 that includes segments of streams, lakes and estuaries that exhibit violations of water quality standards. The report details the pollutant responsible for the violations, and the suspected cause and source of the pollutant. Since 1998, DEQ has developed plans, with public input, to restore and maintain the water quality for the impaired waters. Within these plans are "total maximum daily loads," or TMDLs. TMDL is a term that represents the total pollutant a water body can assimilate and still meet standards. For example, the Chesapeake Bay TMDL is based on nutrient (nitrogen and phosphorus) and sediment standards.

Water Conservation and Protection

How can residential landscapes be smartly designed and used for water conservation and protection? How can small simple practices by individuals have a significant and positive impact on water quality? How can we ensure the state's surface and ground water resources are high quality and plentiful and still have attractive lawns and landscapes? The answer is a balance between awareness and action. First there has to be an understanding of the value of water, how the water cycle works, and that water is everyone's business. Then everyone has to do something. Collectively, many small actions by individuals lead to powerful results. There are really only two main water quality issues to focus on:

- Water misuse and waste
- Stormwater management

Statistics

- The average American family uses 320 gallons of water per day
- About 30% of those 320 gallons is devoted to outdoor uses
- More than 50% of that outdoor water is used for watering lawns and gardens
- As much as 50% of water used for irrigation is wasted due to evaporation, wind, or runoff caused by inefficient irrigation methods and systems

Source: *WaterSense program, EPA: https://19january2017snapshot.epa.gov/www3/watersense/pubs/outdoor.html*

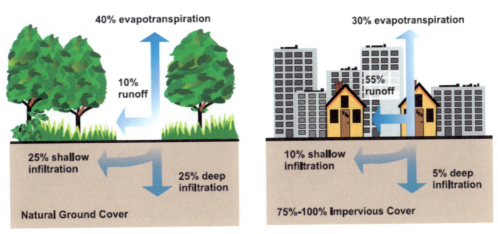

Figure 17-5: Increasing impervious surface in a watershed increases runoff and decreases infiltration and evaporation.

Virginia's average annual rainfall is 38-49 inches depending on the city and region (coastal, piedmont or mountain) of the state (National Centers for Environmental Education, 2022). While the rainfall is generally distributed fairly evenly throughout the year, distinct wet and dry periods do occur. Storm events are increasing in magnitude and dry periods are becoming longer, possibly due to climate change. With human population comes development and associated impervious surfaces, which replaces the natural vegetation and soil filtering system of the watershed. More development generates more runoff. When water runs across impervious surfaces, pollutants (from the list above) are collected and carried into storm drains. Runoff water does not go to a treatment facility; instead, storm drains deliver the polluted water directly into waterways and water bodies. Runoff is the biggest contributor to non-point source pollution. The three important runoff components to manage are: volume, velocity or flow rate, and pollutants.

State Regulatory Information

Virginia is in EPA Region 3 (Mid-Atlantic) which also includes Delaware, District of Columbia, Maryland, Pennsylvania, and West Virginia.

Chesapeake Bay Total Maximum Daily Load (TMDL): TMDL is a historic and comprehensive "pollution diet" that involves all the states in EPA Region 3 plus a part of New York state. A TMDL is used to determine the maximum amount of pollution a water body can assimilate without violating water quality standards. The Bay TMDL includes pollution from permitted point sources (waste water), and nonpoint and natural sources (landscapes, wildlife, etc.). The TMDL, the largest ever developed by EPA (encompassing a 64,000-square-mile watershed), identifies the necessary pollution reductions from major sources of nitrogen, phosphorus and sediment. The TMDL was established in 2010 with rigorous accountability measures to initiate sweeping actions to restore clean water in the Chesapeake Bay and the region's streams, creeks and rivers. It is based on watershed implementation plans (WIPs) for reducing pollution going into the bay prepared by the 6 states and the District of Columbia; submitted to and approved by EPA. Specifically, the TMDL sets Bay watershed limits of 185.9 million pounds of nitrogen, 12.5 million pounds of phosphorus and 6.45 billion pounds of sediment per year – a 25% reduction in nitrogen, 24% reduction in phosphorus and 20% reduction in sediment.

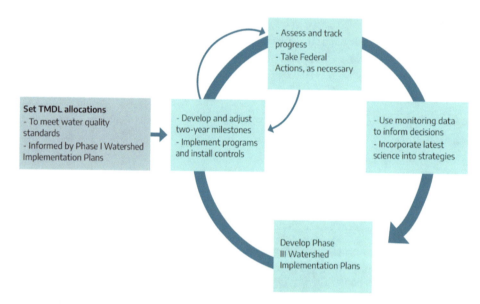

Figure 17-6: Ensuring results: The EPA's plan for maintaining TMDL standards.

In 2012, the jurisdictions submitted Phase II implementation plans designed to strengthen the initial cleanup strategies and reflect the involvement of local partners. They also submitted a set of two-year milestones outlining near-term restoration commitments. The Bay TMDL is a key part of an accountability framework to ensure that all pollution control measures needed to fully restore the Bay and its tidal rivers are in place by 2025, with practices in place by 2017 to meet 60% of the necessary pollution reductions. For more information, visit the EPA's Chesapeake Bay TMDL website (https://www.epa.gov/chesapeake-bay-tmdl).

State Water Control Board: The board is one of three regulatory boards (Air Pollution Control Board, State Water Control Board and Waste Management Board) that is composed of Virginia citizens appointed by the Governor. The board is responsible for adopting many of Virginia's environmental regulations including state mandates on water quality in the Clean Water Act and the Code of Virginia. The board reports to the Virginia General Assembly.

The State Water Control Law (Code of Virginia): The law requires the Board to establish standards of water quality and to modify, amend or cancel any such standards or policies every three years. It also requires the Board to hold public hearings periodically for the purpose of reviewing the water quality standards. The Virginia State Water Control Law incorporates the Chesapeake Bay Preservation Act, Erosion and Sediment Control Law, Virginia Stormwater Management Act, and General Permit for Discharges of Stormwater from Construction Activities.

Virginia Antidegradation Policy: Virginia's antidegradation policy protects water quality at three levels or "tiers." Tier 1 specifies that existing instream water uses and the level of water quality to protect the existing uses shall be maintained and protected. This means that, as a minimum, all waters should meet adopted water quality standards. Tier 2 protects water that is better than specified water quality standards. Only in limited circumstances may water quality be lowered in these waters. Tier 3 are exceptional waters where no new, additional or increased discharge of sewage, industrial wastes or other pollution are allowed. These waters must be specifically listed in the regulation.

Virginia Water Quality Standards: These standards are part of the State Water Control Law. They consist of statements that describe water quality requirements. They also contain numeric limits for specific physical, chemical, biological or radiological characteristics of water. These statements and numeric limits describe water quality necessary to meet and maintain uses such as swimming and other water-based recreation, public water supply, and the propagation and growth of aquatic life. Standards include general and specific descriptions, because not all requirements for water quality protection can be quantified or numerically defined. The standards are adjusted constantly to reflect changes in law, technology and information available to the Water Board and DEQ.

Virginia Department of Environmental Quality (DEQ): DEQ administers Virginia's laws and the regulations approved by the State Water Control Board through two Divisions (Water Permitting and Water Planning) with the goals of improving and protecting Virginia's streams, rivers, bays, wetlands and ground water for aquatic life, human health and other beneficial water uses.

Water-Wise Landscaping

Start with a site analysis. Then use that information to develop a management plan which incorporates water conserving and protection best management practices (BMPs) that meet the site and user goals and that conserve and protect water resources. The plan can be set up as a one year monthly check or reminder list. It can also include long term planning. For example: researching and selecting trees is done in the spring or summer and purchasing and planting in the fall when they are dormant and do not need as much irrigation to get established; the driveway is badly cracked, so it will be replaced with permeable pavers in 2 years.

Calculate the size of the property. Multiply the length x width to get the total square feet. Then add up the square feet of all the impervious surfaces (roofs of the house and outbuildings, driveway, sidewalks, patio, etc.). Rainfall runs off of these surfaces. Divide the impervious surface number by the property size to get the percent (%) of the property that generates runoff. This calculation assumes that there is 100 % runoff from the impervious surfaces. There is no right or wrong answer, but the higher the %, the more important water management is for the property.

Example:

Property size: 80' x 136' = 10,880 square feet (about 1/4 acre)

Imperious surfaces:

- House roof 60' x 80' = 4,800 square feet
- Driveway 12' x 50' = 600 square feet
- Patio 15' x 20' = 300 square feet
- Sidewalks 3' x 50' = 150 square feet

Total = 5,850 square feet

5,850 square feet / 10,880 square feet = 54% impervious

In this example, rainfall runs off of over half of the property. If 45 inches of rain fell in one year, that would be 84,997 thousand gallons of runoff; enough to fill 1,214 standard bathtubs! The U.S. Geological Survey has a rainfall calculator (https://water.usgs.gov/edu/activity-howmuchrain.html).

Conduct a water quality site analysis. Use the chart on the site analysis form at the end of the chapter to evaluate the landscape practices that impact water quality. This information might come from landscape design documents or a walk around the property. Put a check in the plus column if the practice is existing or being done and a check in the minus column if it is not. Use the comments section to note whether a practice in the plus column could be improved. As with the % impervious number, there is no right or wrong answer. This chart is simply a tool to evaluate what practices could be done better or added to the landscape to improve water management.

Runoff calculation tool: The U.S. Environmental Protection Agency has an advanced stormwater calculator (https://swcweb.epa.gov/stormwatercalculator/) that allows you to enter information about your site and generate estimated yearly runoff, maximum runoff, and more.

Irrigation

Irrigation is the application of water to land. Irrigation systems can be expensive to install and require maintenance. Remember to call MISS UTILITY at 811 before digging to install a system. Take the time to design an efficient adaptable system based on the landscape design, user lifestyle and vegetation.

Overhead irrigation

- Also called high flow, spray or sprinkler irrigation
- Can include rigid pipe, fixed risers, irrigation heads (spray, rotor, and impact)
- Applies water over top of plants simulating rainfall
- Uses a higher volume of water than drip irrigation
- Has a higher potential than drip irrigation for waste from runoff and evaporation
- Problems include: broken line or heads, uneven coverage,
- Can be operated by a controller
- Needs to be checked periodically for problems

Drip irrigation

- Also called low flow or volume, micro, and trickle irrigation
- Can include soaker hoses, flexible tubing, drip lines or emitters, micro spray
- Applies water to the plant root zone with less volume, evaporation, and runoff
- Problems include: clogged emitters, lines chewed by wildlife, may require a pressure reducer and filter, tripping hazard
- Can be operated by a controller
- Needs to be checked regularly for problems

Trees and shrubs really only need irrigation long enough to get established. Watering bags or a temporary drip system is suitable for those areas. Annuals, perennials, vegetables, and lawns require more and consistent water. Consider reducing the amount of annuals and lawn in the landscape to conserve water as they require the most. Use irrigation heads that spray the exact amount of water exactly where it needs to go and not on impervious surfaces like sidewalks or driveways. Parts of the landscape may need to be re-designed to eliminate unusual shaped spaces that are difficult to irrigate. Sprayer heads or heights may need to be adjusted as plants grow. Set the irrigation timer for watering early in the morning and only 1-2 times a week. The general recommendation is for 1 inch of water per week during the growing season. Early and infrequent deep watering grows a healthier plant. The foliage is not wet frequently or for long periods of time which reduces diseases. Roots grow strong and deep, and there is very little runoff or loss from evaporation with the hotter temperatures later in the day. Perennials and vegetables often do better with a drip system. Water is used more efficiently than with an overhead spray system, and again, disease problems are reduced. Irrigation systems should have a connected rain sensor so it doesn't come on when it is raining. The system timer should be set in the fall for less or no irrigation because plants are dormant and natural rainfall is usually adequate. The system should also be inspected annually for leaks, breaks, broken heads or heads that aren't spraying the correct pattern or amount of water. All these maintenance chores insure the system runs efficiently, reducing waste and especially cost if city water is being used. There are many internet sites with information on designing irrigation systems and on efficient sprayer heads.

How to calibrate an overhead irrigation system

- Use 4-6 rain gauges or straight-sided cans (soup, coffee). If using cans, make sure all are the same shape and size.
- Place the rain gauges or cans in a scattered pattern in the area being irrigated
- Run the irrigation system for 15 minutes
- Measure the amount of water in each gauge or can to the nearest 1/8-inch
- If the amounts in each container are NOT close to the same amount, check for leaks and adjust the spray heads for more even coverage. Repeat steps above.
- If the amounts in each container are close to the same amount, then add the amounts together and divide by the number of containers to get the average depth of water collected.
- Multiply the average depth of water times four to determine the irrigation rate in inches per hour.
- Use the chart to determine the amount of time to run the irrigation system to apply the desired amount of water

Table 17-1: Time in minutes required to apply water at a given irrigation rate

Inches of water applied	0.5" inches of water applied/hour	1" inches of water applied/hour	1.5" inches of water applied/hour	2" inches of water applied/hour
0.5"	60 minutes	30 minutes	20 minutes	15 minutes
0.75"	90 minutes	45 minutes	30 minutes	23 minutes
1"	120 minutes	60 minutes	40 minutes	30 minutes

If runoff occurs before the irrigation cycle is finished, then the timer should be reset for a split application: irrigate for half the time, wait 2-4 hours then irrigate the rest of the time remaining. Do this in the morning before daytime temperatures and sunlight cause evaporation.

Stormwater Best Management Practices (BMPs)

Stormwater BMPs can be used individually or connected together to manage runoff. For example, a downspout can be disconnected from the storm drain so that it runs into a rain barrel or into swale which then connects to a rain garden. A combination of BMPs is frequently used to manage water quality on a site. They can be designed as part of the site development or retrofitted into the site over time.

Remember, the three important runoff components to manage are: volume, velocity, and pollutants. Reduce the volume, slow the velocity, and remove the pollutants.

Healthy Soil

A healthy soil acts like a sponge and filter; soaking up stormwater and filtering it as it infiltrates and percolates through the layers into the ground water. Soil texture, organic matter content and pH all affect the movement of pollutants through the soil. Water infiltrates sandy soils quickly and clay soils more slowly. Water should not stand for more than 4 days after a storm, ideally 2 days or less as mosquitos can go from egg to adult in standing water at 7 days. Aeration and incorporation or spreading organic matter on top of the soil (especially in lawn areas) will improve drainage. Soils with a higher organic matter content filter pollutants more effectively. Organic matter promotes healthy microbial populations, which break down pollutants, and many pollutants will adsorb to organic matter particles and become inactivated. Organic matter also provides nutrients to plants which means less fertilizer is needed. A soil test should be done every 3 years to make sure there are adequate nutrients available for plants and to prevent over fertilization. Soil pH can affect the movement of chemicals, especially fertilizers, through the soil by influencing their availability to plants. In very acidic or very alkaline soils, some nutrients can become unavailable to plants and then may be leached into the ground water. Bare areas should be covered with mulch or vegetation to prevent erosion. Steep slopes should be planted or terraced to prevent erosion. A healthy soil grows healthy plants, which require fewer nutrients and less pest management thus reducing the potential for pollution from fertilizers and pesticides.

Healthy Plants

Select plants that are adapted to the site and environmental conditions and plant them correctly, so the roots establish quickly and they require less or no irrigation (after establishment). Use pest resistant plants and scout regularly to catch any pest problems early. Use cultural, biological or mechanical control methods and the least toxic insecticides and fungicides to treat when necessary. This is integrated pest management (IPM), and it significantly reduces the amount of chemicals used and thus the potential for water pollution from them. When pesticides (insecticides, fungicides, herbicides) are necessary, use the product least toxic to the applicator and environment. Read the entire label and follow application instructions carefully. Do not apply pesticides right before an irrigation cycle or rain event as they usually need time to dry. If they wash off, they could have off-target effects on other parts of the landscape or the aquatic ecosystem. Plants should be grouped by their water needs (hydrozones) so that irrigation is used only where necessary and efficiently. For example, impatiens should not be planted next to cactus. Use large trees, understory trees, shrubs and lower growing plants to create canopy layers. Canopies intercept rainfall, absorbing some of it and slowing the rest down so it is more likely to soak in than run off when it reaches the ground. Use a mulching mower and leave the grass clippings on the lawn. This is a free and natural source of nutrients and organic matter which keeps the grass healthier and reduces the need for fertilizer. Mowing the lawn at the correct height keeps the grass from thinning, which prevents weeds and reduces the need for herbicides. A healthy dense lawn reduces runoff and erosion.

Nutrient Management

Nutrient management in the landscape is an important BMP. When fertilizer is spread on impervious surfaces or too much is applied, plants can't utilize it and it becomes a pollutant that either runs off or leaches into the ground water. A soil test is recommended every three years and is the only way to tell what is already there and what is needed. Fertilizer should be applied when: plants are young or newly planted, plants are stressed (from insects, disease, drought, storm or construction damage), or plants are actively growing. Fertilizers vary tremendously in solubility and persistence. A water soluble fertilizer dissolves quickly so all the nutrients are available at one time. Slow release fertilizers are formulated so that the nutrients are inside a capsule. The capsule wall degrades over time releasing the nutrients at a slow steady rate. Slow release fertilizers can last from 3 to 18 months. Synthetic fertilizers generally have higher nutrient values than organic fertilizers, so it takes more organic product to get the same application rate. Incorporating fertilizer into a planting bed or hole and using slow release or organic fertilizers reduces the potential for pollution by putting the nutrients at the root zone where they are easily accessible and less likely to run off or leach. Pet waste is a pollutant source that is frequently overlooked. Excrement contains not only nutrients, but pathogens as well. If it is not collected and disposed of properly, runoff carries it into waters used for drinking and swimming where it can cause health problems.

Runoff

Runoff can collect a wide variety of pollutants and carry them long distances and into natural water bodies. Runoff volume and velocity can cause water levels to rise quickly and forcefully, resulting in erosion of stream and pond banks and sediment transport. In addition to the above practices, runoff volume, velocity and pollutants can be addressed by harvesting or by using other BMPs that spread out and slow down the water; giving it a chance to infiltrate, evaporate or have pollutants removed before moving into natural water bodies. (Reference VCE pubs in resources list for more detailed information on these practices).

Rain Barrels

Rain barrels or cisterns are an old practice used to collect/harvest rainwater from roofs for later use. Roofs are used because the water running off a roof generally has fewer pollutants than water running off roads, parking lots and landscapes. One inch of rain falling on a 1000 square foot roof generates 623 gallons of runoff. Be sure to calculate the runoff volume when sizing a cistern or deciding how many rain barrels are needed. Rain barrels can be connected to each other in order to store more water, but always have an overflow plan. Remember that roofs are often slanted or sectioned to run into different downspouts. Stored water should be used or treated before 7 days to prevent mosquitos. The systems should be inspected regularly for debris or sediment buildup and cracked or leaky parts or connections. Water from rain barrels can be used for irrigating plants, washing cars and pets, and filling bird baths and water gardens. Many cities and environmental groups sell or offer make-your-own rain barrel workshops. Rain barrels vary in size, shape and color but generally hold 40-50 gallons and cost $70-$150. Larger more complex systems can cost hundreds to thousands of dollars. Rebates, water bill credits or other incentives are often available for people who install rain harvesting systems in an effort to reduce the volume of stormwater going into aging and over-burdened drainage systems.

Figure 17-7: Rain barrel fed directly by downspout with overflow hose.

From the Rooftops to the Roots – An Integrated Approach to Harvesting Rain Water

By Shawn Jadrnicek, Extension Agent, Virginia Cooperative Extension, Roanoke

Rain barrel water rarely finds its way into the landscape. After collecting all those drops of precious rain, the barrels often stand idle like industrial ornaments in the yard. Their slow flow of gravity-fed trickling water combined with the expense and complexity of installing a pump, filter, and irrigation system, prevents rain barrels from following through with their intended purpose. We encountered this problem at a farm where a 1,500-gallon tank was installed without provisions for using the stored water. During every rain event, the full tank would overflow and wash out an adjacent gravel road.

To solve the problem, we connected the tank to a water garden pond positioned on the south side of the building. The pond was strategically located to reflect sunlight into the adjacent building in the winter, but not in the summer. Since water gardens lose a lot of water to evaporation, we attached a flexible and inexpensive one-half inch poly line to the tank drain and used a float valve to connect the line to the pond. Float valves are similar to the valves in your toilet — the flushing lowers the water level and the float valve engages to refill the tank. As water evaporated from the pond, the float valve allowed gravity to push water from the tank into the pond. A much cheaper method than refilling with city water to keep the water garden full.

Once the water flowed from the tank into the pond, it was used and stored as needed. We placed soil on top of the pond liner, which not only protected the liner but also wicked water out of the pond. The constant wicking action, like an oil candle wick pulling oil out of a vase, drew water out of the pond to irrigate nearby plants. We also drained water from the pond into adjacent rain gardens. Just opening the drain during dry times helped irrigate the rain garden plants. Finally, we rerouted any overflow back into the pond. Rather than an overflowing tank washing gravel away, our new system allowed the tank to overflow into the pond and the pond to overflow into the rain gardens.

Figure 17-8: Turkey Nest pond after construction. The pond serves to capture rainfall and prevent erosion from an overflowing cistern.

Because the pond created various microclimates, we added edible plants such as *Tradescantia virginiana*, *Apios Americana*, *Yucca filamentosa*, *Sagittaria sagittifolia* and *Opuntia ellisiana* and ornamentals such as *Iris virginiana* around its edge. The fish-free pond sustained a wide variety of amphibians which wandered out into the landscape to eat pests and entertained us late into the night with their harmonious symphony.

A **swale** is a shallow and wide channel that moves water slowly from point A to point B allowing it to infiltrate or evaporate along the way, unlike a ditch; which is narrow and deep and moves water quickly from point A to point B. Swales are generally less than 12 inches deep and have vegetation growing in them. They require permeable soil, little space, grading for water flow, and maintenance to keep the vegetative cover dense and trash and debris cleaned out. Swales act like shock absorbers by reducing the initial volume and velocity of runoff flow. See the following VCE publications for more on swales: "Best Management Practice Fact Sheet 11: Wet Swale" 426-130 (BSE-279P), "Best Management Practice Fact Sheet 10: Dry Swale" 426-129 (BSE-278P), and "Stormwater Management for Homeowners Fact Sheet 4: Grass Swales" SPES-12P.

Rain Gardens

Figure 17-9: Swales capture water and move it from point A to point B.

A **rain garden** (bioretention) is a shallow landscaped depression that filters polluted stormwater before it evaporates, evapo-transpires through the plants, or percolates through the soil into the groundwater. Basically, imagine a landscaped puddle. A rain garden has three planting zones (high, middle, and low), with low being wettest the longest. Runoff should move out of the rain garden within four days. If drainage is poor, then aeration or an underdrain or dry well can be used to improve water infiltration. At least 5% of the impervious area should drain into the rain garden to make it worth doing cost and labor wise. The depth of a rain garden is approximately 6 inches. Usually they are dug and graded deeper, 12-24 inches, because organic matter is added, plant root balls displace soil, and mulch is added to the top; which all raise the level. The gardens can be placed at any point along the runoff pathway. One large rain garden or several small ones connected together can be used depending on the available space and landscape design. Always plan for an overflow event. Many rain garden plant lists recommend using natives. Plants should be spaced so that the canopies touch and provide a solid cover to prevent weeds. They generally establish quickly and need to be divided about every 3 years. Mulch should be added sparingly after the establishment period, because adding it every year will raise the level and the garden will not hold enough water to be effective. After establishment, maintenance is minimal and mainly involves removing invasive weeds, tree seedlings, trash, and debris. The most comprehensive resource for residential or small-scale rain gardens in Virginia is the Rain Gardens Technical Guide from the Virginia Department of Forestry. Larger rain gardens that are used for commercial sites are typically engineered and often include underdrains if underlying soils have low **infiltration rates**. These larger rain gardens are known as "bioretention systems."

Cross Section of a Typical Rain Garden

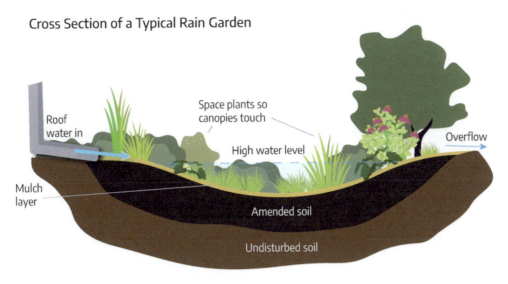

Figure 17-10: Rain garden.

What size should the rain garden be?

To calculate the area needed for a rain garden, divide the number of square feet of impervious surface draining into it by 20. (This calculation assumes all surfaces are 100% impervious)

$$\frac{600 \text{square feet (driveway)} + 2000 \text{square feet (half the roof)}}{20} = 130 \text{square feet (size of rain garden)}$$

Buffer Zones

A buffer zone (**riparian** buffer) is an area of vegetation adjacent to a body of water. It functions similar to a rain garden with high, medium, and low planting zones.

Buffers:

- Slow down and spread out runoff
- Filter sediment, nutrients, and pollutants
- Stabilize the shoreline and prevent erosion
- Provide food and habitat for wildlife
- Add visual and species diversity
- Help moderate flooding

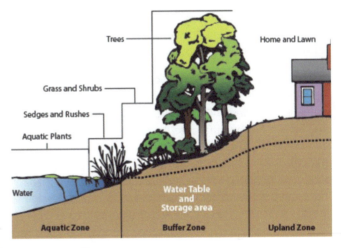

Figure 17-11: Buffers.

Buffer zones are unique for each location, and can be formally landscaped, naturalized, or anywhere in between. Buffer width can range from as little as 5 feet to over 100 feet. No formal design is required. They can be easily created in residential or commercial landscapes along fresh or brackish/salt water. A combination of woody and herbaceous plants is recommended. Most buffer zones are low maintenance. Buffer zones have the biggest impact on improving water quality for the least amount of money, effort, and long term maintenance.

Rooftop or Downspout Disconnect

Rooftop or downspout disconnect and rain chains are practices that slow runoff velocity. Sometimes downspouts connect directly into a pipe that runs into the storm drain. Disconnecting the downspout from the pipe and redirecting the runoff into a swale, a rain garden or into the landscape treats pollutants at the beginning of the runoff pathway and prevents erosion and stream blow out from high volumes and velocities of runoff. In some cases, rain chains can be used in addition to or instead of down spouts. They slow the velocity of the runoff and can be connected from the gutter to a swale, a rain barrel or a rain garden. These practices can be used on any residential or small commercial building as long as the site can handle the volume of runoff and it is directed away from the building foundation. Rain chains and extension pipes for downspouts are inexpensive. Maintenance involves keeping the gutters clear of debris to prevent clogging the downspout or rain chain.

Permeable Paving

Permeable paving includes pervious concrete, porous asphalt and interlocking concrete pavers. Stormwater infiltrates into pores in the concrete and asphalt or into joints between the pavers instead of running off. These products are most suited for low-traffic-load and parking areas, and for pedestrian traffic areas. They are also used on certain highways to prevent hydroplaning. These pavements consist of several layers, including the pervious top layer and underlying layers of gravel or stone that create a stormwater storage reservoir. The pavement depth and materials are determined by the amount of runoff storage needed and by amount of traffic. Permeable pavements provide stormwater management through temporary storage of runoff which then infiltrates or through an underdrain (necessary if soil is not permeable), and discharges to a stormwater drain. Permeable paving can remove sediments, nutrients, and some metals; however, sediment clogs the pores of these systems. Periodic vacuuming of the surface is necessary to remove sediments and keep the system functioning. These systems can be expensive.

Stormwater Ponds

Stormwater ponds can be either wet (retention) or dry (detention). Runoff comes into the pond through storm drains and culverts. This interrupts the runoff pathway which slows the velocity and reduces the volume of runoff from impervious surfaces flowing into natural waterways. The water is stored temporarily while pollutants are removed through settling and biological uptake. Sediments settle to the bottom and vegetation and aquatic organisms filter or break down pollutants over time. A wet pond holds water all the time. When a storm happens, polluted runoff comes into the pond and pushes the clean water out of the pond through an outflow or overflow pipe into natural waterways. Because they retain water for a longer time, wet ponds typically are able to remove more pollutants. Wet ponds should have buffers around the perimeter to stabilize the bank, prevent erosion, and filter runoff coming over land instead of through pipes. The average life expectancy for a wet pond is 15-20 years before it needs to be dredged out so it will continue to hold the desired volume of runoff and not cause flooding.

Dredging is very expensive (approximately $100,000 per quarter acre based on the amount of sediment removed, disposal costs, and permits/fees). Maintaining a buffer around the pond to prevent bank erosion and keeping trash and debris out of the storm drains and the pond extend the life of the pond. A dry pond is designed to hold water for a short period of time before allowing the water to discharge to a nearby stream. Between rain events, a dry pond looks like a large, grassy low area. When it rains, the pond fills with water and holds it for 48-72 hours to allow sediment and pollutants to settle out. Because they detain water for a brief time before allowing it to flow out, dry ponds are also called detention ponds. Dry ponds are generally more common, less expensive to install, require less maintenance and may involve less liability for the communities around them. However, they are also the least efficient pond for removal of pollutants. Most stormwater ponds are on commercial or municipal property or are in community "common areas" that are maintained by homeowner associations, civic leagues or property management companies.

Green Roofs

Green roofs (living or vegetated roofs) slow and filter stormwater on top of buildings at the very beginning of the runoff pathway. The system components include plants, a light weight growing media, drainage layer, and a waterproof liner to cover the roof structure. It is much easier to design a green roof for a new building than to retrofit an existing building because of the weight load. In addition to stormwater management, green roofs insulate the building, extend the roof life, and lower urban air temperatures. Green roofs are either intensive (thicker and heavier, supporting a wider variety of plants and requiring more maintenance) or extensive (shallow, lighter, and requiring minimal maintenance). There are many green roof designs and systems available. Periodic irrigation and invasive plant removal is required for all of them.

Floating Treatment Wetlands

Floating treatment wetlands (FTWs) are manmade ecosystems that mimic natural wetlands. FTWs are created using floating rafts that support plants grown hydroponically. The rafts float on a wet pond water surface and are either anchored to the bottom or the shore. They improve water quality by filtering, consuming, or breaking down pollutants from the water. FTWs should be located adjacent to the shoreline or where inflow pipes deliver polluted runoff into the pond so they will intercept the most polluted runoff. FTWs located near the shoreline also attenuate wave action and reduce undercutting and bank/shoreline erosion. Designs are available for making FTWs or manufactured ones can be purchased. Cost ranges from $1-$24 per square foot.

Advantages of FTWs include:

- Can be sized to fit into almost any pond or lake
- Enhance the pollutant-removal effectiveness of existing stormwater wet ponds
- Provides a sustainable pollutant-removal system and wildlife habitat
- Can tolerate water-level fluctuations, and improves aesthetics

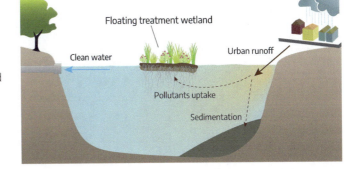

Figure 17-12: Floating treatment wetland.

FTW maintenance includes:

- Removing invasive plants
- Keeping the anchoring system secure
- Harvesting the vegetation for maximum nutrient removal rates

Storm Drain Protection

Storm drain protection/cleaning is a simple but effective runoff management practice. A storm drain is a system to carry runoff from impervious surfaces such as streets, parking lots, sidewalks, and roofs to a stormwater pond or natural water body. Do not rake or blow grass clippings or leaves into a storm drain or dump oil or any other chemicals down it. Keep branches, trash and other debris out of it. If the drain gets clogged, it will cause flooding. When a drain is in the landscape, plant low growing evergreen plants around it to slow and filter runoff before it goes into the drain. The plants also keep trash, grass clippings and mulch from washing into the drain.

Subsurface Drainage

Subsurface drainage might be needed if runoff does not drain through soils in a timely manner. This type of drainage is sometimes used underneath rain gardens. The 2 most common types of subsurface drainage are French drains (under drain, drain tile) and dry wells. A French drain is a trench filled with gravel or containing a perforated pipe that redirects surface water and groundwater away from an area. French drains are primarily used to prevent ground and surface water from penetrating or damaging building foundations. They can also be used to distribute water, such as a septic drain field or behind retaining walls to relieve ground water pressure. A dry well (infiltration basin) is an underground structure that collects runoff and allows it to seep into the ground to recharge groundwater. Water flows into a dry well either through gravity or pipes. Dry wells can be manufactured devices with perforated sides and bottom or a pit filled with gravel or rock covered by landscape fabric to prevent sediment from clogging the pores. Dry wells are usually buried completely, so that they do not take up any land area. For example, the dry wells for a parking lot's storm drains are usually buried below the same parking lot.

Additional Resources

Buffers

- Chesapeake Bay Program: https://www.chesapeakebay.net/
- Virginia Dept. Conservation & Recreation: https://www.dcr.virginia.gov/
- Virginia Institute of Marine Science: https://www.vims.edu/

Rain Gardens

- Virginia Department of Forestry Rain Gardens Technical Guide: https://dof.virginia.gov/wp-content/uploads/Rain-Gardens-Technical-Guide_pub.pdf
- Low Impact Design Center Rain Garden Design Templates: https://lowimpactdevelopment.org/resources/publications/
- Soak Up the Rain information from U.S. EPA: https://www.epa.gov/soakuptherain/soak-rain-rain-gardens

Rainfall calculation tool

- Rainfall calculator: https://www.calctool.org/other/rainfall-volume
- National Stormwater Calculator: https://www.epa.gov/water-research/national-stormwater-calculator

VCE Publications

- Best Management Practice Fact Sheet 1: Rooftop Disconnect 426-120
- Best Management Practice Fact Sheet 5: Vegetated Roofs 426-124
- Best Management Practice Fact Sheet 6: Rainwater Harvesting 426-125
- Best Management Practice Fact Sheet 7: Permeable Paving 426-126
- Best Management Practice Fact Sheet 10: Dry Swales 426-129
- Best Management Practice Fact Sheet 11: Wet Swale 426-130
- Best Management Practice Fact Sheet 14: Wet Ponds 426-133
- Creating a Water-Wise Landscape 426-713
- Home Landscape Practices to Protect Water Quality 426-723
- How to Plan for and Plant Streamside Conservation Buffers with Native Fruit and Nut Trees and Woody Floral Shrubs ANR-69P
- Innovative Best Management Fact Sheet No. 1: Floating Treatment Wetlands BSE-76P
- Irrigating the Home Garden 426-322
- Pest Management for Water Quality 426-615
- Reducing Erosion and Runoff 426-722
- Residential Stormwater: Put It in Its Place Decreasing Runoff and Increasing Stormwater Infiltration 426-046
- Urban Stormwater Terms and Definitions 426-119
- Understanding the Science Behind Riparian Forest Buffers 420-151

References

- "Stormwater" section adapted from "Design Manual Chapter 2 – Stormwater Table of Contents" (2013). Iowa Statewide Urban Design and Specifications. https://intrans.iastate.edu/app/uploads/sites/15/2018/09/Chapter_02-2017.pdf; and "Climate Adaptation and Stormwater Runoff" (2022). Climate Change Adaptation Resource Center, U.S. EPA. https://www.epa.gov/arc-x/climate-adaptation-and-stormwater-runoff
- National Centers for Environmental Education. (2022). "U.S. Monthly Climate Normals (1981-2010)." https://www.ncei.noaa.gov/access/metadata/landing-page/bin/iso?id=gov.noaa.ncdc:C00822
- Virginia Cooperative Extension. (2015). "Impact: Virginia Household Water Quality Program." https://vtechworks.lib.vt.edu/handle/10919/80593
- WaterSense. (2017). "Outdoor Water Use in the United States." https://19january2017snapshot.epa.gov/www3/watersense/pubs/outdoor.html

Attributions

Prepared by Susan D. Day, Research Associate, Horticulture

- Shawn Jadrnicek, Extension Agent, Agriculture and Natural Resources (2021 reviser)
- Laurie J. Fox, Horticulture Associate, Horticulture Department, Hampton Road AREC (2015 reviser)

Image Attributions

- Figure 17-1: Watershed. Grey, Kindred. 2022. CC BY-NC-SA 4.0.
- Figure 17-2: Virginia watersheds. Virginia Department of Conservation and Recreation.
- Figure 17-3: Water flow. Grey, Kindred. 2022. CC BY-NC-SA 4.0.
- Figure 17-4: Various pathways by which contaminants can reach the groundwater. "Pesticides in groundwater can eventually contaminate well water" USGS, Water Science School. 2019. Public Domain.
- Figure 17-5: Increasing impervious surface in a watershed increases runoff and decreases infiltration and evaporation. U.S. Environmental Protection Agency, Washington, D.C. (2003). Wikipedia. Public Domain.
- Figure 17-6: Ensuring results. Johnson, Devon. 2022. CC BY-NC-SA 4.0. Adapted from "Ensuring Results in the Chesapeake Bay." EPA.
- Figure 17-7: Rain barrels. Johnson, Devon. 2022. CC BY-NC-SA 4.0.
- Figure 17-8: Turkey Nest pond after construction. Photo by Shawn Jadrnicek, author of *The Bio-Integrated Farm: A Revolutionary Permaculture-Based System Using Greenhouses, Ponds, Compost Piles, Aquaponics, Chickens, and More.* 2022. CC BY-NC-SA 4.0.
- Figure 17-9: Swale. Johnson, Devon. 2022. CC BY-NC-SA 4.0.
- Figure 17-10: Rain garden. Johnson, Devon. 2022. CC BY-NC-SA 4.0. Adapted from Toronto Region Conservation Authority: Complete Guide to Building a Rain Garden, 8-14-18.
- Figure 17-11: Buffers. "Stormwater Management for Homeowners Fact Sheet 6: Buffers" Virginia Cooperative Extension. CC BY-NC-SA 4.0.
- Figure 17-12: Floating treatment wetland. Johnson, Devon. 2022. CC BY-NC-SA 4.0. Adapted from "Figure 1" Wisconsin State Legislature: Legislative update 9-17-19.

CHAPTER 18: HABITAT GARDENING FOR WILDLIFE

Chapter Contents:

- Habitat Loss and Declining Wildlife Populations
- Habitat Principles
- Conservation Landscaping and Habitat Gardening
- Selected Habitat Gardens that Sustain Wildlife Diversity
- Troubleshooting Wildlife Conflicts
- Additional Resources

Landscaping for wildlife is both an art and a science. Whether we use plants creatively as a form of artistic expression or we design the landscape as merely a utilitarian space, we can sustain the biodiversity around us by planning our gardens with an ecological function in mind. When we plan our surroundings in a way that supports complex interactions between plants and animals, we become more fully connected to nature ourselves.

Habitat gardening is an enjoyable way to more fully appreciate nature while improving the available food, water, and cover for birds, amphibians, mammals, and other wild creatures in our landscape. Applying the principles of good vegetative structure and horizontal layering as we add plants to the landscape will provide wildlife with beneficial food sources as well as much needed cover from predators, winter winds, and summer sun. Nest boxes, water features, brush piles and other amenities will enhance the habitat's value and can be planned as attractive focal points in the garden.

However, as one assesses the existing habitat and makes choices about what plants and amenities to add, care must be taken in the placement of those enhancements, in order to minimize the possibility of attracting "unwelcome" wildlife species. There are no "nuisance wildlife" species; rather, we create the conditions in our landscape that attract wildlife, and sometimes our unwitting choices set the stage for certain wildlife species to become a problem. Therefore, we must plan the habitat garden in a way that balances our need for aesthetics and beauty with the reality of how wildlife will likely use the space as we've designed it.

Habitat Loss and Declining Wildlife Populations

The decline of wildlife species is occurring at an alarming, accelerated rate. The Virginia Department of Wildlife Resources (DWR) maintains a Wildlife Action Plan (published 2015) which identifies 925 species of greatest concern, classified into four groups or 'tiers' that describe varying degrees of population declines attributed to habitat loss. Of these, 290 species or 31% are insects, which are an essential part of aquatic and terrestrial food webs.

Habitat loss is caused by many factors. The most obvious is development and fragmentation of forest, meadow and wetland habitats, as we continue to grow the economy by building commercial and residential sites. This development brings with it a host of factors that adversely impact the remaining or surrounding habitats, and these factors include but are not limited to a prevalence of impervious surfaces that contribute to increased erosion and runoff, which carries chemicals and sediments with it, and the extensive use of lawn and other non-native plants in the landscape for ornamentation. There are adverse impacts occurring in the more rural or agricultural areas, including the routine use of herbicides and pesticides and farming practices that remove hedgerows and large expanses of vegetation in order to maximize production. In addition, as more land disturbance occurs across all these areas—urban, suburban and rural—we've seen a connected proliferation of invasive exotic plant species that compete with native plant communities.

Table 18-1: Wildlife groups and numbers

Wildlife Groups in Virginia (Total Species in Parentheses)	Number of Species of Greatest Conservation Need
Mammals (96)	24
Birds (390)	96
Fishes (210)	97
Reptiles (62)	28
Amphibians (82)	32
Mussels	61
Aquatic Crustaceans	61
Aquatic Insects	148
Terrestrial Insects	142
Other Aquatic Invertabrates	34
Other Terrestrial Invertabrates	202
Total species of greatest concern	925

Except regularly nesting sea turtle species, list does not include marine wildlife.

The additive effect of all these factors or pressures on the environment is an overall reduction in the quantity and quality of aquatic and terrestrial habitats, which is the single most important reason that wildlife populations are in decline, across multiple genera and species. The 2015 revised edition of the Wildlife Action Plan therefore places even greater emphasis on habitat conservation by providing summaries of priority actions that local Planning District Commissions can apply on a regional scale.

What can Master Gardener volunteers do at the local level to support the Wildlife Action Plan? Master Gardeners are in a unique position to influence the trajectory of habitat loss by increasing public understanding of this issue. Oftentimes, homeowners and landowners are either completely unaware of or only vaguely familiar with the connection between their landscape practices and the effects of those practices on habitat quality. Continued emphasis in our education outreach programs about good conservation landscaping practices is essential for raising awareness. If we provide consistent, clear messages and simple guidance about how to improve or restore habitat in our communities, then the resulting actions by the public should help to slow—and ultimately, one hopes, to reverse—the trend of declining wildlife species. Conservation begins at home and in the neighborhood, and habitat gardening is a good first step to restoring and sustaining biodiversity.

Habitat Principles

What Wildlife Needs: Vegetative (Biotic) Components

In order to understand fully what wildlife needs, we must begin with plants. Each plant species in a given geographic area has a total number of individual plants that make up a population, and the collection of plant populations found in that area form an assemblage known as the **plant community**. A diverse, healthy plant community provides multiple ecological services, such as interception of rainfall, which helps to recharge the groundwater and reduce flooding and erosion. Plant communities also contribute to nutrient cycling, oxygen exchange and carbon sequestration processes. Perhaps one of the most crucial functions of a plant community, in addition to these many benefits, is the life-sustaining support it provides to an associated community of wildlife species. The plant community provides organic matter for a variety of organisms, such as bacteria and fungi, and the plants also provide food and cover for wildlife, including birds, mammals, reptiles, amphibians and insects.

Plant and animal communities live and interact together in varying compositions and in distinct, often complementary relationships to each other. These biologically diverse communities, when combined together with the other non-living (abiotic) elements of the surrounding environment, such as soil, water and sunlight, form a functional system of continuous energy exchange called an **ecosystem**. Forests, wetlands and prairies are examples of ecosystems that contain thousands of plant and animal populations that interact with each other in the context of other landscape components.

Together, these interdependent populations of plants and animals make up countless communities within ecosystems, which give an area its species richness and genetic diversity. **Biodiversity** refers to the variety of genes, species and ecosystems in the aggregate, across the larger landscape.

A **habitat** is the area within an ecosystem where an animal is able to secure the food, water, cover and space it needs to survive and reproduce. Every wildlife species has specific habitat requirements; but because there are often overlaps of habitat features within a system, there are usually multiple wildlife species that can live in a given habitat. Salamanders, for example, require moist soil and rich organic matter that can be found in forest, riverine, and wetland ecosystems. Each of those ecosystems contain multiple habitat components—the tree canopy, boggy low areas, rocky outcrops, etc.—and other wildlife species like frogs and birds will be found in association with the habitats in those ecosystems, too. This means that if we want to restore and sustain biodiversity in the landscape around our home or on our property, we simply need to "put back" an assemblage of many of the plant species and other elements that would naturally have occurred there, and arrange the plants and those elements in such a way that many wildlife species will be able to take advantage of them and meet their needs for survival.

Habitat gardens are therefore most successful when they support a broad diversity of wildlife species, and the easiest way to achieve wildlife diversity is to choose a variety of plant species that most closely mimic the vegetative structure of a natural system. Plants are the living or biotic component of the landscape, and vegetative or vertical structure refers to layers of plants that provide a level of complexity and functionality in their arrangement such that they sustain a broad array of wildlife species.

Mulch layer

For example, on the ground plane of an eastern deciduous forest, the first component is the mulch layer, which forms a humus blanket that maintains soil temperature and can protect the ground from erosion. The mulch layer is critical for the decomposition process and supports many insects such as sow bugs, beetles and millipedes. These insects then become food for predatory insects such as centipedes and also serve to feed other wildlife, such as spiders, salamanders, toads, lizards, turtles, small mammals and birds. As the leaf litter and woody debris are broken down through the chewing and shredding of

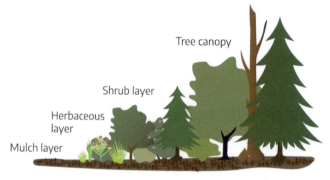

Figure 18-1: Mulch, herbaceous plants, shrubs and small trees, and large trees compose different layers in a forest ecosystem.

insects, along with the associated decay that's wrought by fungi and bacteria, nutrients are released back into the soil, where plants can take them up again. This continuous recycling of organic matter and replenishment of soil is a most valuable aspect of the mulch layer. Therefore, one of the very first steps in establishing a habitat garden is to retain the leaf litter in the landscape, so as to support a rich assortment of organisms that will form the foundation for a complex food web.

Herbaceous layer

The next layer in our forest example is the herbaceous layer. These are plants with green, mostly non-woody stems, and they include species that form the groundcover layer. Groundcovers are plants that creep along the mulch or grow in clumps or masses and provide a protective covering for the soil below. Foamflower (*Tiarella*), wild ginger, striped wintergreen (*Chimaphila maculata*), sundrops, woodland phlox, columbine, and bluebells (*Mertensia virginica*) are some wildflowers or "forbs" we might see in the forest setting. In addition to these groundcover plants, the herbaceous layer may also contain a variety of ferns as well as vines, such as crossvine (*Bignonia capreolata*), pipevine (*Isotrema macrophyllum*), trumpet vine (*Campsis radicans*), and Virginia creeper (*Parthenocissus quinquefolia*). Of special note is that groundcovers in nature are typically much taller than the two to three inches in height we're accustomed to seeing in a conventional lawn. Hence, the herbaceous layer in a productive habitat garden is not likely to be a short carpet but rather a diverse composition of plants of varying heights that simply cover the ground.

Shrub layer

Standing above the herbaceous layer but below the taller trees is the shrub layer or "sub-canopy" layer. This layer is comprised of flowering shrubs that grow in a wide range of sizes, from as small as 2 feet for huckleberry or lowbush blueberry, to medium heights of 6-12 feet for deerberry (*Vaccinium stamineum*), spicebush (*Lindera benzoin*), and viburnums, and as tall as 15 or 20 feet for American hazelnut (*Corylus americana*), witch hazel, and rhododendrons.

Tree canopy layer

Overhead is the canopy formed by the tallest plants, the tree layer. Some trees are small, only 20 to 35 feet in height, such as pagoda dogwood (*Cornus alternifolia*), paw paw (*Asimina triloba*), and redbud (*Cercis canadensis*). Others grow within a range of 30 to 60 feet in height, such as serviceberry (*Amelanchier canadensis*), flowering dogwood (*Cornus florida*), and American holly (*Ilex opaca*). The largest trees, such as oaks and hickories, can attain heights of 80 to 100 feet.

Since most of our built landscapes are typically missing one or more vegetative layers, we can easily support more wildlife species by taking our cues from nature and choosing a palette of plants appropriate for our particular site conditions. For example, if the landscape is primarily wide open lawn, which is devoid of vegetative layers and diversity, we could bring life back to the scene by emulating a meadow habitat made up of sun-loving native grasses and flowers. If our landscape has some tree cover but little else, we could add a shrub layer and herbaceous ground covers. A very wet, boggy area in the yard that's difficult to mow and maintain could be transformed into a mini-wetland, with the addition of common elderberry and buttonbush to make up the shrub layer, and moisture-loving plants like Joe pyeweed (*Eutrochium purpureum*), cardinal flower (*Lobelia cardinalis*), and swamp milkweed (*Asclepias incarnata*) to form an herbaceous layer.

Horizontal and vertical structure layer

Another habitat principle we can apply in our landscape planning is horizontal structure. Over the course of time, plant species within a given community will naturally change, if there are no interventions such as mowing, grazing or burning. Each stage of change occurs in succession after the one before it, and this process of succession is why a plant community that starts out as a meadow will gradually be replaced with woody species and eventually become a forest in the final stage. The arrangement and interspersion of these different successional stages in proximity to each other is what provides horizontal structure. We can use basic gardening and maintenance methods to improve horizontal structure by encouraging the growth of particular vegetative types that will mimic different successional stages, which in turn will support different wildlife species. For example, if we stop mowing an area, we can allow woody shrubs and trees to gradually take over and provide a forest-type habitat. If, on the other hand, we already have a woodland and want to attract wildlife species that require grasses and other flowering herbaceous plants, we can create an opening in the canopy and plant perennials and grasses, then keep the successional changes in check by mowing every two to three years, which will prevent woody vegetation from becoming re-established there.

We can also enhance the places where two habitat types come together, referred to as an **edge**. This transition zone is made up of plants from each of the habitats juxtaposed to each other and therefore contains wildlife species from both habitats as well. The greater the number and variety of plant species along an edge, the higher the abundance of wildlife found there. In a landscape setting, we can maximize this edge effect by increasing the number of plant species in the space between where two different vegetative types occur. For example, where a lawn abuts a stand of trees, we can add a shrub layer alongside the trees, to soften the edge. We could even take the edge one step further by adding a layer of herbaceous flowering plants next to the shrub layer. Hence, even a very small space like a townhouse yard can greatly increase its habitat potential by simply adding layers that improve both vertical and horizontal structure.

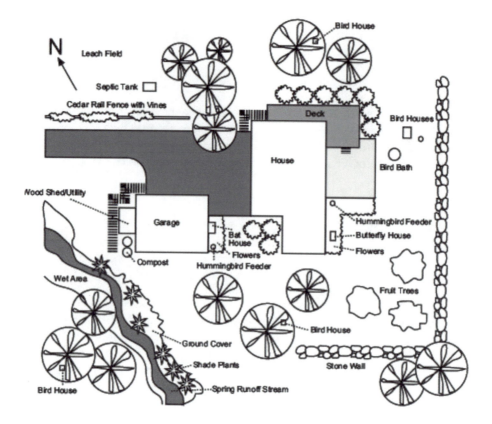

Figure 18-2: Habitat diagram.

Habitat structure: Adding layers of plants to the landscape is a very effective way of increasing available food and cover for wildlife. Flowering perennials form an herbaceous groundcover next to shrubs and small trees of varying heights and texture. Placement of a shrub border is ideal along an edge where the grouping will be adjacent to taller trees. Look for places throughout the property to increase vertical structure, such as along fences, property lines, walkways and driveways. Shrub beds can also be situated in the middle of a lawn to create a habitat island. Arrange the plants in large clusters or groupings, which will maximize the depth of the bed and the interior structure for greater cover, rather than installing a single row of plants.

Similarly, the edges of small creeks and streams that run through the landscape can be enhanced or protected with vegetation. An edge of shrubs and trees planted along a waterway will provide a sheltering buffer for wildlife from human activity, and the roots of the plants will hold the soil and filter runoff that enters the stream – thus improving the aquatic habitat within the stream, too.

Choosing Plants for Wildlife: Interrelationships and Biodiversity

Now that we know how to put a habitat together—arrange it in layers, with lots of structure and diversity—the next step is deciding which plants to use. There's an important case to be made for selecting native plants for wildlife whenever possible.

What's a native plant? According to the Virginia Department of Conservation and Recreation, "Native species are those that occur in the region in which they evolved. Plants evolve over geologic time in response to physical and biotic processes characteristic of a region: the climate, soils, timing of rainfall, drought, and frost; and interactions with the other species inhabiting the local community."

Mounting scientific evidence indicates a strong correlation between the use of native plants in the landscape and insect biodiversity.

According to researchers Desirée L. Narango, Douglas W. Tallamy, and Peter P. Marra, "Over 90% of herbivorous insects specialize on one or a few native plant lineages—thus, ecosystems dominated by nonnative plants are characterized by reduced insect diversity, abundance, and biomass. Given that the majority of terrestrial birds rely on insects as a primary food source for reproduction and survival, the persistence of insectivorous bird populations is inextricably linked to insect conservation," (2018). The choice of plants we make in our landscape not only impacts the biodiversity of insect populations but also multiple bird populations as well. Further, Tallamy and other scientists have found that not all native plants are equally productive. Some plant species support far greater biomass or numbers of organisms than others. For example, native plants in the *Lobelia* genus (such as cardinal flower) only support four species of Lepidoptera (butterflies, moths and skippers), while plants in the *Carex* genus (the sedges) support 36 species of *Lepidoptera*.

As gardeners, then, we have a wide range of choices before us when selecting plants for habitat improvement. The initial decisions we make for habitat gardening will likely be the same as for any other project, based on three primary factors: 1) how we plan to use the site; 2) the current site conditions; and 3) what plant species are most appropriate for those site conditions and the geographic region we live in. Budget is typically a fourth factor. Although it's true that the more native plant species we use, the better the wildlife diversity will be, it's important to find the right balance to suit our specific site, which is an individual choice that will depend on our own particular needs. Ultimately, the degree to which one is able to improve habitat and sustain wildlife will be unique to each situation and dependent on individual preference.

In addition, there are many other reasons to use native plants besides the benefit of providing food and cover for wildlife. Whenever we choose "the right plant for the right place," we ensure a more successful outcome, especially if we select those best adapted for drought—or water-tolerance. And although native plants are not maintenance free—contrary to popular opinion—they can substantially decrease long-term maintenance requirements over time, once established. In general, native plant landscapes use less water, help reduce energy costs, and can increase property value because of their intrinsic aesthetic appeal.

Goochland-Powhatan Extension Master Gardener Habitat Demonstration Garden

By Linda Toler, Extension Master Gardener, Goochland-Powhatan

In 2021, Extension Master Gardener volunteers from the Goochland-Powhatan Master Gardener Association (GPMGA) initiated a project called "HOPE from the Garden" (HOPE stands for Helping Our Planet Endure) to encourage gardeners to adopt practices that will help keep the land healthy and support the life that depends on it, keep local waters clean and plentiful, and keep the air clean and unpolluted.

The initiative focuses on these areas:

- Building and maintaining a healthy soil.
- Minimizing the use of pesticides.
- Reducing lawn areas.
- Incorporating native plants into our landscapes and eliminating invasive plants.

Figure 18-3: Extension Master Gardeners build a lasagna garden.

- Providing healthy wildlife habitats.
- Conserving water.
- Managing stormwater runoff.
- Adopting gardening practices that contribute to clean air.

Some of the specific recommendations within each area are "no-brainers," while others like no-till gardening and reducing lawn areas, may require a change in thinking for some gardeners. Some may ask, "is it even possible to have an attractive landscape that adopts these practices?"

Goochland-Powhatan Extension Master Gardeners believe the answer is "yes." And so, in late Fall 2022, a team of GPMGA volunteers began installation of a "HOPE Garden" in a large, sunny, lawn area in front of the county building housing the Goochland County Extension Office and others.

The main practices illustrated by the garden are:

- Conversion of a lawn area into an ecologically beneficial garden using no-till gardening techniques.
- Design of an attractive garden of native plants that provides value to wildlife.
- Maintaining a garden without the use of synthetic fertilizers and pesticides and gasoline-powered equipment.

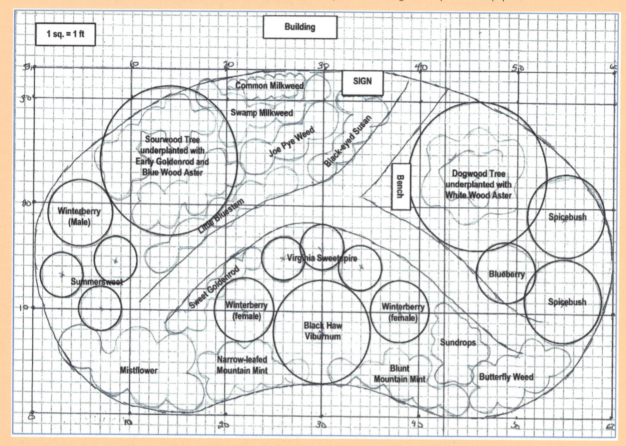

Figure 18-4: HOPE Garden design.

In Fall 2022, garden installation began using a no-till, "lasagna garden" approach. Plentiful fall leaves and grass clippings were layered over sheets of cardboard, wet down, and left to break down over the winter months.

Plant installation began the following spring. Plants selected for the garden are native to Virginia's Capital Region, are attractive in the home landscape, and most importantly, support the invertebrates, birds, and mammals that are so important to our local ecosystems. For example, the native dogwood (Cornus florida) included in the design is the larval host for 115 native caterpillar species. The design includes trees, shrubs, and perennials selected to provide garden interest throughout the year. Each plant was selected for the teaching opportunities it presents. Other features to support wildlife will be added as the garden evolves.

The garden is laid out with pathways for up-close viewing of the plants and their "visitors." Educational signage describing the plants and their benefits to our native ecosystem are planned as are educational events and activities for homeowners and children.

The "HOPE Garden" is a new project that will evolve over time. The volunteers are excited about providing a forum for presenting the positive benefits of converting part of a lawn area into an attractive native plant garden that will help support our native wildlife.

To initiate a project like this in your community, find a location that has visibility in the community, get buy-in from key stakeholders, decide what you want to teach with the garden, and line up a team of hard-working volunteers who are committed to the project and sharing the concepts with the community.

Conservation Landscaping and Habitat Gardening

Conservation landscaping refers to landscape principles that apply best practices for conserving water, soil, and existing native plant communities. The Chesapeake Conservation Landscaping Council has developed simple guidelines that can help homeowners, landowners, landscape professionals and municipal decision-makers take action to improve the health of the Chesapeake Bay watershed. However, these guidelines can certainly be applied to other areas of the state that are outside the Bay watershed, because conservation practices help improve environmental quality no matter where we live.

The "Eight Essential Elements" are useful for making informed landscape choices. A conservation landscape:

1. Is designed to benefit the environment and function efficiently and aesthetically for human use and well-being;
2. Uses locally native plants that are appropriate for site conditions;
3. Institutes a management plan for the removal of existing invasive plants and the prevention of future nonnative plant invasions;
4. Provides habitat for wildlife;
5. Promotes healthy air quality and minimizes air pollution;
6. Conserves and cleans water;
7. Promotes healthy soils;
8. Is managed to conserve energy, reduce waste, and eliminate or minimize the use of pesticides and fertilizers.

Conservation landscaping is therefore a systematic approach that integrates the use of native plants and wildlife habitat into our built environment while simultaneously reducing the need for mowing or for using fertilizers, pesticides, herbicides, water and fossil fuels. With this approach, plants are selected not just for their ornamental appeal but for their function in providing the highest habitat value for the site, in order to sustain multiple wildlife species. There's much less emphasis on using turfgrass as the predominant cover type, because turfgrass supports very little biodiversity. Instead, the principles apply greater emphasis on replacing lawn with assemblages of native plants that would be found locally in the natural environment. In essence, a conservation landscape sustains life and conserves resources in a way that traditional landscaping often does not. Yet, conservation landscapes can provide as much—and many would say they provide more—beauty and aesthetic appeal to the human eye.

After the vegetative components have been chosen and the various layers of plants have become established, it's time to look around the landscape and strategically fill in any remaining spaces with additional structural components that will augment the available habitat for wildlife. These are the non-living or abiotic elements of the landscape. The most commonly used structural components include brush piles and rock piles, snags (dead trees), nest boxes, areas with bare soil, and water features.

Table 18-2: Examples of Conventional Landscaping Practices that Reduce or Increase Habitat Value

Examples of Conventional Landscaping Practices that Reduce Habitat Value	Examples of Conservation Landscaping Practices that Increase Habitat Value
Select plants primarily for their perceived decorative value, unusual physical characteristics, or rapid growth habits that will quickly and easily fill in a site, regardless of where the plant species originated.	Select plants primarily for their utility to wildlife, water quality and ecosystem processes, in order to emulate native plant habitats that would be found naturally in the local region and are most appropriate for the given site conditions. Avoid selecting non-native "alien" or "exotic" invasive plant species known to be problematic in the environment, and control these plants if they enter the landscape, in order to reduce the likelihood of their competition with native plant communities.
Maximize lawn as a predominant feature of the landscape.	Minimize lawn by using it artistically where needed, for its specific functional value, such as for a pathway, or for certain recreational activities, or to frame a view or provide an intentional edge around a planted bed.
Routinely apply fertilizer and pesticides to optimize plant growth.	Use native plant species that are well-adapted to local soils, climate and insect predation, thereby reducing or eliminating the need for fertilizers or pesticides, which can run off the site during a rain event and have harmful effects on water quality and aquatic wildlife species.
Rake-up and bag-up leaves in autumn, and dispose of in the landfill. Remove and dispose of all downed twigs, branches and other woody debris.	Keep leaves on site by shredding and/or composting them, and use the material for mulch and/or as an organic amendment to ornamental planting beds, which will enrich the soil and provide a sustainable food source for insects and other wildlife. Keep downed twigs and branches on site by chipping them and composting the material or using it for mulch, or cut the larger branches into manageable sizes that can be used to create brush piles for wildlife cover.
Remove all dead vegetation from flowering plants in the fall.	Allow dead vegetation to remain on site throughout winter (until late February/early March), which will provide cover for dormant insects or their eggs, and places for birds to feed and seek protection from harsh weather. Design the landscape such that plant species are strategically chosen and placed to provide interesting structural elements in winter dormancy, and therefore greater visual and aesthetic interest throughout the season.
Mow all the vegetation along a creek or stream, down to the water's edge.	Maintain at least a 35 foot buffer of plants such as shrubs and trees along waterways, which will filter runoff from the surrounding land, will shade the water, and will keep the soil from eroding the banks, thereby protecting aquatic wildlife species that cannot tolerate extremes of water temperature and that need clean water to thrive.

Brush Piles and Rock Piles

Brush piles and rock piles provide places for wildlife to seek shelter from the elements of rain, wind and snow over the course of a year. The "nooks and crannies" afford cool, dark areas to hide from the summer sun, or a protected spot to nestle down and retain warmth against the winter's chill. Temperature extremes aside, these simple constructed piles of easily found materials also provide valuable escape cover from predators, as well as places for wildlife to raise young. Rabbits, raccoons, mice, chipmunks, box turtles, lizards, snakes, insect-eating birds are just some of the many other animals that seek out these protected areas from time to time, either to rest, find food, overwinter or lay their eggs. Depending on how big the pile is, some species may create a burrow or nest underneath the pile to live on a more permanent basis.

The limiting factor for brush piles and rock piles, of course, will be the size of the yard, as these piles are best suited to fairly large size lots (at least an acre), with plenty of space. It's also important to locate the pile well away from buildings and vegetable gardens, in order to minimize the likelihood of attracting wildlife such as groundhogs or skunks, which might decide to seek alternative shelter under the foundation of a nearby house or shed. Very small yards, such as a courtyard or a town house lot, are not conducive to making a pile at all.

Rock piles can be placed on the edges of the property near existing vegetation, or behind a shrub bed or adjacent to a stand of trees—wherever the rocks will blend in with the surrounding landscape to look natural and not too contrived. A rock pile can also benefit frogs and other aquatic organisms when stacked loosely among the vegetation next to a creek or a pond, or partially submerged at the water's edge, at least a foot below the water's surface.

To build the pile, choose rocks or old bricks and blocks of various sizes and shapes, ranging from potato size to soccer ball size for the home landscape setting, or larger sizes in the more rural, spacious setting. Arrange the rocks unevenly, with open spaces between them, to fill an area at least five or six feet wide and one or two feet deep. Don't worry about being too artistic with rock placement. Wildlife doesn't care how pretty it looks; they just want a place to hide when the time comes. Consider planting a ground cover around the edges of the rock, or a vine that will grow over it, to provide additional protection. No need to mow there anymore!

Figure 18-5: Rock pile habitat with large opening on bottom to allow amphibians to enter.

Similarly, a brush pile is loosely constructed with lots of open spaces between the branches, which will make it easier for a wren to fly in or a rabbit to run under when threatened. Although a brush pile can be messy and built as big and wide as you like, avoid dumping a big pile of debris on the ground, which is a practice more suited to starting a compost heap. Rather, build the foundation of the brush pile in the manner of a miniature log cabin, starting with stumps or small logs, depending on what you have on hand, and criss-cross these in a couple of stacks until you have a firm base, preferably on level ground. Then stand large tree limbs up against the base, stacked against it, with the butt ends of the branches on the ground, and the thinner, lighter tips pointing up above. This will form a somewhat pyramidal-looking structure that you can continue to add smaller branches to, until most of the interior is no longer visible, but with plenty of empty voids remaining throughout the stack. Place the greatest number of branches on the side of the pile that faces the prevailing winds, to ensure additional protection from summer thunderstorms and winter winds.

Effective brush piles are quite large. In a rural landscape or on a very large lot, they should be at least 12 to 15 feet in diameter and at least five or six feet tall. However, this may not be practical for a smaller suburban lot. A smaller pile, such as six to eight feet wide and four to five feet tall, may be more appropriate for a residential setting and should still be adequate for many wildlife species to use.

Snags

Another structural component that some would say is "worth its weight in gold" for wildlife is a dead tree or snag. Dead trees provide a cornucopia of benefits, because the decaying material is host to innumerable insects and their larvae that chew their way through the wood or otherwise feed beneath the bark. Approximately 30 percent of native bee species use abandoned beetle tunnels in dead trees as a nesting site to lay their eggs. This abundance of burrowing insects, grubs and eggs provide an invaluable protein source for dozens of bird and mammal species. Woodpeckers make their homes in dead trees, too, and the holes they leave behind in the trunk and the branches provide places for bluebirds, chickadees, nuthatches, tree swallows, screech owls, titmice, opossums, tree squirrels, bats, raccoons and other cavity-seekers to raise their young. Snags provide open perches for hawks to hunt from, and when dead trees are located near a water body, kingfishers, flycatchers and herons can hunt from these perches as well. Other birds use snags as a convenient post to sing from when proclaiming their territory. Dead trees also provide a refuge for birds and hibernating mammals in winter, when fewer resources for cover may be available in other parts of the landscape. In a pond environment, a fallen tree in the water can provide excellent habitat structure for fish and other aquatic species.

The astonishing array of wildlife species that rely on dead trees—and on decomposing logs and branches on the ground—cannot be overstated. Therefore, whenever possible, leave dead trees standing. If a dying or dead tree poses a threat to a walkway, driveway or building, the tree can be taken down and left on the ground to decompose naturally and become an interesting if not unusual focal point, especially if it's used as a backdrop for planting flowers and ferns around it. Or, sections of the tree can be cut up and used to make a brush pile, as described earlier. Either way, retaining dead trees and woody material on site will greatly enhance the habitat value for wildlife and also recycle nutrients back into the soil.

Nest Boxes

Birds

Where no dead or dying trees are present, the next best thing is to put up nest boxes for cavity-seekers. Nest boxes provide vital homes for birds and small mammals such as flying squirrels to bear and raise their young, and each species that uses them has different requirements for the box dimensions, including the overall size of the box, the diameter of its opening, and the depth of the cavity within.

Figure 18-6: Eastern bluebird house.

There are several considerations for constructing a bird house. Use untreated wood and select rough-cut lumber that's a minimum of ¾- inch thick (one inch is better). Cedar is a good choice, if available, because of its durability. The box should provide for adequate ventilation near the top, for heat to escape, and holes in the bottom for drainage, if water gets in. The roof of the box should overhang the front, to keep rain from entering, and the box should also have a provision for opening up the side or the top to clean out the contents at the end of the breeding season. Roughen the inside of the front part of the box, or attach a small piece of hardware cloth to it, to make it easier for young birds to climb out when it's time for them to fledge; do not paint the inside of the box. Also, do not attach a perch to the outside of the box, which merely provides an easier foothold for predators and encourages other non-native birds like starlings and house sparrows to attempt to enter.

To install a bird house, place it on a free-standing post or pole, well away from trees, which are the domain of the black rat snake. Secure a conical or stovepipe-type baffle to the post or pole beneath the box, in order to discourage raccoons, snakes and other predators. Do not use grease on the pole, as this is an unreliable method for deterrence and may sicken animals which ingest it. Be sure the front of the box is directed away from the prevailing winds, but face the box towards a distant tree where young birds can land when they leave the nest.

Table 18-3: Examples of Common Nest Box Dimensions

Various sources may recommend different dimensions. More detailed specifications for constructing nest boxes are available from the Cornell Lab of Ornithology.

Bird Species	Diameter of Entrance Hole (inches)	Depth of Cavity (inches) - from bottom of hole to the floor of the box	Floor of Cavity (inches x inches)	Height of Box Above the Ground (feet)	Comments
Eastern Bluebird	1.5	6.5	5 x 5	5-15	Place in open areas away from buildings and spaced 100 feet apart
Carolina Chickadee	1.125	8	4 x 4	5-15	Place in area with mature hardwoods
Northern Flicker	2.5	16-18	7 x 7	8-10	Fill box with sawdust
House Wren	1	6-8	4-6	5-10	This species will fill the nest box with sticks

Bats

Bat houses are constructed very differently than bird houses. A bat house has no floor on the bottom, because bats fly in and out from below, and the interior of the box is made up of several narrow partitions, conducive to the bats hanging between the baffles. The species that most commonly use bat houses in the mid-Atlantic region are the little brown bat and the big brown bat; females of these species congregate in nursery colonies in the summertime and may use boxes to raise their young. However, success with bat houses is mixed and seems to depend on many variables, such as the numbers of partitions within the box and the width between them; or how much sun the box receives (it should be painted a dark color to absorb sunlight, because bats need warm temperatures); or how far above the ground the box is mounted (typically 12 to 20 feet).

Boxes placed in proximity to a natural water source, such as a pond, lake, stream or river, are often said to have the greatest success of use, because bats frequent aquatic areas where insect numbers are typically high. Place bat houses on the side of a building away from nighttime lights, and orient the box towards the southeast for maximum exposure to sunlight in the early morning. Instructions for building a bat house are available online, here is one example from the U.S. Forest Service: "Building a Bat House."

Bees

Another type of nesting house is one that can be made for orchard mason bees, which seek out holes or tunnels in plant stems to build brood cells in which to lay their eggs. Make the bee nest house from plants that have hollow stems, such as reed grass or teasel. If there happens to be a stand of invasive bamboo available, select narrow stems approximately half inch or less in diameter and cut them into five or six inch lengths. Then hollow out about three and a half inches on the end of each stem, leaving part of the tube closed. Gather about 10 to 15 of these pieces, tie them into a bundle with the closed ends together, and hang the bundle horizontally from a tree or building about three to six feet off the ground, in a sunny area with the holes facing east or southeast, and sheltered from the elements.

Figure 18-7: Bat houses have no floor to allow bats to enter/exit from the bottom.Figure 18-5: Bat houses have no floor to allow bats to enter/exit from the bottom.

Or, make a "bee block" by drilling a series of holes between 3/32 and 3/8 inch in diameter, about ¾ inch apart on center, into an untreated (preservative free) block of wood, or into an old log or stump. Do not drill all the way through but rather only three to four inches deep, for holes less than ¼ inch diameter, or five to six inches deep for holes larger than ¼ inch.

Areas with Bare Soil

Bare soil is often an overlooked element in the landscape that can be useful for some wildlife species. Songbirds will appreciate an occasional dust bath where bare soil is available, in order to control mites and other external parasites on their skin or in their feathers. Birds also ingest bits of grit and coarse sand, which help to grind up food such as hard seeds in the bird's gizzard. A simple way of providing the dust they need is to scrape away the vegetation from a two to three foot diameter patch of ground and allow it to dry out.

Areas of bare ground are also extremely important to bees, because almost 70 percent of North America's 4,000 native bee species nest in the ground. These are solitary-nesting bees, which means that individual females seek out their own nest site to tunnel into the ground. Since the soil surface should be bare in order to provide bees the access they need to dig, a good rule of thumb is to clear small patches of bare ground in a sunny, open space, up to a few feet across, and pat the areas firmly to compact the surface. Different locations will attract different bee species; therefore try clearing patches on both flat ground and on slopes, particularly those that are facing south.

Bare ground can also be supplemented with sand pits for bees. Find a sunny spot, dig a hole in the ground about two-feet deep, and fill it with a mix of sand and loam that will provide good drainage.

Water Features

Another structural element that's essential to any habitat garden is the presence of water, which can be provided in many ways. Bird baths are perhaps the easiest and can be purchased in a variety of shapes and sizes. Choose a bird bath with a shallow basin that has gradually sloping sides and is no more than two or three inches deep. Put one or two fist-sized stones into the water where birds can land, and place the bird bath several feet away from a shrub or tree, so that birds can easily seek cover if needed. To extend the season for year-round bird use, install a small heating element that will keep the water from freezing in winter.

An even simpler way of creating a bird bath is to turn the lid of an old trash can upside-down and nestle it within a plant border, or use a large, plastic plant dish the same way. Regardless of size or type, replenish all bird baths with fresh water every few days throughout the summer, to keep mosquitoes from breeding there.

Creating small mud puddles for insects is another method of providing water. Butterflies in particular use wet patches of soil (or wet manure) to obtain minerals, and this "puddling" behavior is commonly seen along the muddy edges of roads after a rain storm. To replicate a small mud puddle, fill a shallow cake pan with a mixture of sand and soil, fill it with water, and place it in a sunny area near a flower bed.

There may also be opportunities in the landscape to capture and divert a portion of the rainwater that falls and to collect it in a shallow depression to create a mini-wetland. Unlike a true rain garden, which is constructed several feet deep with permeable soil and is designed to hold water for no more than four days, the mini-wetland is only about 12 to 15 inches deep and is lined with a layer of clay at the bottom to hold the water for a longer time. The depression is filled with a soil mixture that contains mostly loamy organic matter and a bit of clay, then it's planted with species that are adapted for periodic inundation—hence the habitat. Locate this water feature in a low-lying area where water already naturally collects.

Or, construct the mini-wetland approximately 10 feet away from a building where it will receive some of the water from a downspout, with the aid of a shallow, planted swale that directs the water from the downspout to the area below. One can also connect a flexible plastic pipe to the downspout and bury it in the ground, with the end of the pipe daylighting directly into the clay-lined depression. However, be sure there's enough slope between the building and the water feature, so that the pipe doesn't back up during a heavy downpour.

These examples are simple ways of providing water for terrestrial wildlife species to use for drinking or bathing. A water garden or frog pond provides a larger habitat for aquatic species to live and breed in and is discussed in the section below, "Water Garden for Frogs, Salamanders, and Other Aquatic Species."

Table 18-4: Selected native shrubs for wildlife habitats

Source: USDA-NRCS (2014). Field Office Technical Guide, Section 2, Plant Establishment Guide. [NOTE: This shrub list is excerpted and adapted from a much larger database.]

Common Name	Scientific Name	Height (feet) at 20 years	Not Preferred by Deer	Fruit / Seed Abundance	Value to Pollinating Insects	Bloom Period	Shade Tolerance	Anaerobic (wet) Soil	Drought Tolerance
Highbush Blueberry	Vaccinium corymbosus	6		High	High	Spring	Tolerant	Medium	Medium
Buttonbush	Cephalanthus occidentalis	15		Medium	High	Summer	Tolerant	High	Medium
Eastern Red Cedar (evergreen)	Juniperus virginiana	20	x	Medium	High	Late Spring	Intermediate	Low	High
Black Chokeberry	Photinia melanocarpa	15	x	Medium	Moderate	Spring	Tolerant	Medium	Medium
Red Chokeberry	Photinia pyrifolia	5	x	Medium	Moderate	Mid Spring	Intolerant	Medium	Low
Coralberry	Symphoricarpos orbiculatus	2	x	High	Low	Mid Spring	Intermediate	None	Medium
Southern Crabapple	Malus angustifolia	30	x	High	High	Mid Spring	Intolerant	Low	Medium
Flowering Dogwood	Cornus florida	20		Medium	Low	Early Spring	Tolerant	None	Low
American Black Elderberry	Sambucus nigra, ssp. canadensis	7	x	High	Moderate	Spring	Intolerant	Low	Medium

Table 18-4: Selected native shrubs for wildlife habitats (continued)

Common Name	Scientific Name	Height (feet) at 20 years	Not Preferred by Deer	Fruit / Seed Abundance	Value to Pollinating Insects	Bloom Period	Shade Tolerance	Anaerobic (wet) Soil	Drought Tolerance
White Fringetree	Chionanthus virinicus	20		High	Low	Mid Spring	Tolerant	Low	Medium
Cockspur Hawthorn	Crataegus crus-galli	30		High	High	Late Spring	Intolerant	None	High
American Holly (evergreen)	Ilex opaca	20	X	Low	High	Mid Spring	Tolerant	Low	Medium
Winterberry Holly	Ilix verticillata	6	X	High	High	Late Spring	Intermediate	High	Low
Indigobush	Amorpha fruticosa	6	X	High	High	Late Spring	Intolerant	None	Medium
Common Ninebark	Physocarpus opulifolius	10		High	Moderate	Late Spring	Intolerate	None	High
Pawpaw	Asimina triloba	25	X	Medium	Low	Mid Spring	Tolerant	Low	Low
American Plum	Prunus americana	24	X	Medium	Moderate	Mid Spring	Intolerant	Medium	High
Chickasaw Plum	Prunus angustifolia	12	X	Medium	Moderate	Early Spring	Intolerant	None	None
Eastern Redbud	Cercis canadensis	25		Medium	High	Spring	Tolerant	None	High
Swamp Rose	Rosa palustris	8		Medium	Moderate	Spring	Intolerant	High	Low
Canada Serviceberry	Amelanchier canadensis	20	X	High	Moderate	Mid Spring	Intermediate	Medium	Low
Northern Spicebush	Lindera benzoin	12	X	Low	High	Mid Spring	Intermediate	Medium	Low
Strawberrybush	Euonymus americanus	8		Medium	Low	Late Spring	Intolerant	Low	None
Smooth Sumac	Rhus glabra	12		High	Moderate	Mid Spring	Intolerant	Low	Medium
Winged Sumac	Rhus copallinum	8		High	Moderate	Mid Spring	Intolerant	Medium	Medium
Eastern Sweetshrub	Calycanthus floridus	7	X	Medium	Low	Summer	Intolerant	Low	Low
Blackhaw Viburnum	Viburnum prunifolium	16	X	Medium	Moderate	Spring	Tolerant	None	Medium
Southern Arrowwood Viburnum	Viburnum dentatum var. dentatum	15	X	Medium	Moderate	Early Spring	Intermediate	None	Low
Silky Willow	Salix serricea	12		Medium	High	Mid Spring	Intermediate	High	Low

Selected Habitat Gardens that Sustain Wildlife Diversity

Habitat Garden for Butterflies and Other Pollinators

One of the most popular, visually-rich landscaped habitats is a garden designed specifically to support pollinators. Pollinators are wildlife species that move pollen from the flowers of male plants to the flowers of female plants of the same species, when the pollinator travels from flower to flower in search of nectar, pollen or other insects to eat. Pollinators include hummingbirds, butterflies, moths, bees, wasps, beetles, flies and some species of bats. Their role is to help fertilize female plants and enable the plants to produce seeds, nuts or other fruit. These animals are therefore critical for ecological function. Without pollinator services, plants would not be able to survive reproductively, because over 85% of flowering plants require an animal—usually an insect—to move pollen (Ollerton et al., 2011), and over 25% of the global diets of birds and mammals are comprised of pollinator-produced fruits and seeds (Adamson 2016). Our agricultural industry is also heavily reliant on pollinators to produce the high yielding crops we've come to expect in food production. "In 2009, it was estimated that honey bees contributed USD 11.68 billion to agriculture in the U.S." (Calderone, 2012). In Virginia, bees are attributed with supporting $23 million of the apple industry (McBryde, 2016).

Restoring a site by replacing lawn with pollinator habitat can transform the landscape, because as the new plants become established and begin blooming, insects of all types very quickly descend on the flowers, seemingly from out of nowhere. To plan a pollinator garden, as with any other kind of habitat garden, it's helpful to remember that each group of organisms has different requirements. When we attempt to select plants for butterflies, we need to think of butterflies as if they're "two animals in one," because of their metamorphic life cycle. A butterfly start outs as an egg, develops into a caterpillar that must eat leaves, and then after several stages and successive molts, it forms a chrysalis and develops into an adult, which must get its energy from flower nectar. Hence, to be successful, a butterfly garden must include host plants for the larvae and nectar plants for the adults. For example, the larvae of monarchs need milkweed leaves, while the adults can forage among numerous nectar-producing plants. If the only plants we select for a garden are the ones that simply provide a colorful bed of blooms, then we will have missed half the equation, and the overall habitat value for butterflies will be lower as a result.

A tremendous number of butterfly species rely heavily on tree species as host plants. For example, black cherry trees support swallowtails, painted ladies and luna moths, and black locust trees support sulphurs and skippers. Elm is the host plant for mourning cloak butterflies, willow is the host for tiger swallowtail, and hackberry tree for question marks. Based on the work of Narango et al. 2020, and Tallamy 2007, the following list of 20 woody plant genera includes trees and shrubs ranked by their value for supporting Lepidoptera (the classification of butterflies, moths and skippers). The list is based on an exhaustive search of the scientific literature about host plant ecology. Below are the top 10 tree genera for supporting Lepidoptera:

Ten most valuable woody native plant genera for supporting lepidoptera:

- *Quercus* (oaks) support 534 species of Lepidoptera
- *Prunus* (cherries) 456 species
- *Salix* (willows) 456 species
- *Betula* (birches) 413 species
- *Populus* (poplars) 368 species
- *Malus* (crabapples) 311 species
- *Vaccinium* (blueberries) 288 species
- *Acer* (maples) 285 species
- *Ulmus* (elms) 213 species
- *Pinus* (pines) 203 species

Most valuable ornamental native perennial plant genera for supporting lepidoptera:

- *Solidago* (goldenrods) support 115 species of Lepidoptera
- *Aster* (asters) 112 species
- *Helianthus* (sunflowers) 73 species
- *Eupatorium* (pyeweeds, boneset) 42 species
- *Ipomoea* (morning glories) 39 species
- *Carex* (sedges) 36 species
- *Lonicera* (honeysuckles) 36 species
- *Lupinus* (lupines) 33 species
- *Viola* (violets) 29 species
- *Geranium* (geraniums) 23 species
- *Rudbeckia* (coneflowers) 17 species

These data clearly indicate that butterfly species—indeed, whole populations of butterfly species—are dependent on hundreds of species of trees, shrubs and perennial flowers. We would therefore do well to select several trees, shrubs and flowering plants from the above groups when planning our pollinator garden, knowing that when we do, we'll have all our bases covered, because the myriad connections between all those groups will ensure a high likelihood of a biodiverse habitat.

In addition to Tallamy's work, other scientists are also conducting field research to further document the association between pollinators and specific plant species. In Pennsylvania, for example, Connie Schmotzer at Penn State Extension devised a series of "Pollinator Trials," in part to evaluate "the level of insect attractiveness of various perennial plant species or cultivars." The study monitored "88 pollinator-rewarding herbaceous perennial plants," to see how many and what type of insect pollinators would seek them out. Below is a synopsis of some of the study results:

Best Plants for Pollinator Visitor Diversity (ranked in order of preference, out of 88) (Schmotzer and Ellis, 2014):

- Clustered Mountain mint (*Pycnanthemum muticum*)
- Coastal Plain Joe Pyeweed (*Eupatoriadephus dubius*)
- Stiff Goldenrod (*Solidago rigida*)
- Swamp Milkweed (*Asclepias incarnata*)
- Gray Goldenrod (*Solidago nemoralis*)
- Rattlesnake Master (*Eryngium yuccifolium*)
- Flat Topped Aster (*Doellingeria umbellata*)
- Spotted Joe Pyeweed (*Eupatoriadelphus maculatus* 'Bartered Bride')

Best Plants for Sheer Number of Bee and Syrphid [Fly] Visitors (Schmotzer 2013) (Numbers indicate the mean number of bees/syrphids observed per plot in 2 minutes):

- Clustered Mountain mint (*Pycnanthemum muticum*): 19 bees/syrphids
- Gray Goldenrod (*Solidago nemoralis*): 14 bees/syrphids
- Pink Tickseed (*Coreopsis rosea*): 14 bees/syrphids
- Lance-Leaved Coreopsis (*Coreopsis lanceolata*): 13 bees/syrphids
- Spotted Joe Pyeweed (*Eupatoriadelphus maculatus* 'Bartered Bride'): 12 bees/syrphids
- Rattlesnake Master (*Eryngium yuccifolium*): 12 bees/syrphids

Best Plants for Attracting Butterflies (Schmotzer 2013) (Numbers indicate the mean number of butterflies/skippers observed per plot in 2 minutes:

- Coastal Plain Joe Pyeweed (*Eupatoriadephus dubius*): 17 butterflies/skippers
- Blue Mistflower (*Conoclinium coelestinum*): 5 butterflies/skippers
- Showy Aster (*Eurybia spectabilis*): 4 butterflies/skippers
- Sweet Joe Pyeweed (*Eutrochium purpureum* subsp. *maculatum* 'Gateway'): 3 butterflies/skippers
- Dwarf Blazing Star (*Liatris microcephala*): 3 butterflies/skippers

As one can see, certain plants are like powerhouses when it comes to supporting pollinators. Therefore, all one needs to do to have a highly productive pollinator habitat is to start with the above top genera [goldenrods (*Solidago*); milkweed (*Asclepias*); tickseed (*Coreopsis*); mountain mint (*Pycnanthemum*); pyeweed (*Eupatorium* or *Eutrochium*); asters (*Eurybia*); mistflower (*Conoclinium*); and blazing star (*Liatris*)], and then look at the Virginia regional native plant list for the garden area in question, in order to determine the particular species of goldenrod, milkweed, tickseed, pyeweed, or aster. that would be most suitable for the given site conditions.

Moreover, not only do these represent a broad spectrum of species and flowering types, they also bloom at different times throughout the season, which adds a temporal dimension to the association of insects that will frequent the plants. For example, peak bloom time for mountain mint is mid-June to mid-July; for swamp milkweed, mid-July to mid-August; and for pyeweed, mid-August to early September. This means if we select a variety of plants across flowering times, in addition to selecting across genera, we can magnify the habitat benefits even more. A good rule of thumb is to "provide blooming plants from early spring to fall, with at least three species of flower in bloom each season" [Xerces Pollinator Conservation Fact Sheet].

In addition to the genera listed above, other excellent pollinator plants include those in the coneflower (*Rudbeckia*), beardtongue (*Penstemon*), phlox (*Phlox*), bergamot (*Monarda*), and ironweed (*Vernonia*) genera. Flowering perennials such as these, combined with native warm-season grasses to form meadows in large open settings, will provide early successional habitat that benefits many bird species as well. Some native warm-season grasses suitable for dry, sunny meadows are the following: big bluestem (*Andropogon gerardii*), little bluestem (*Andropogon scoparius* or *Schizachyrium scoparium*), Indiangrass (*Sorghastrum nutans*), and switchgrass (*Panicum virgatum*).

Looked at another way, if landscape diversity is currently low in the built-environment around us, and if we add more forestal and meadow-like components (i.e., a diversity of shrubs, trees, grasses, and flowering perennials), then we'll be supporting the butterfly species that are associated with each of those vegetation types.

An established pollinator habitat garden or meadow should be allowed to stand throughout the dormant months in fall and winter to provide winter cover. Mowing a pollinator garden is rarely necessary, and typically this practice is reserved for larger landscapes where the predominant vegetative type is native warm-season grasses, which are either burned or mowed only once every three years, to keep the thatch on the ground from becoming too thick. There's a fairly short window of time for mowing or burning these rural fields, usually between mid-February to mid-March, which is at the end of winter, when insects have been dormant in the dead vegetation, but before birds begin nesting in the spring.

Here are some additional pollinator habitat tips from the Xerces Society:

- "Avoid pollen-less cultivars and double-petaled varieties of ornamental flowers."
- Butterflies need warmth in order to fly; therefore plant pollinator habitats in open, sunny areas.
- Shelter pollinator habitats from the wind with some type of cover, such as groups of shrubs or hedgerows, trees, or a nearby wall or fence.
- Include some tall grasses in the habitat, allow the grass to remain overwinter, and conserve dead leaves and sticks in small piles. Caterpillars will use the grasses and brush piles to seek safety to build a chrysalis.
- Avoid cleaning out leaves and garden debris in the weeks leading up to the first severe cold spells of winter, because butterflies overwinter (hibernate) in the debris, either as eggs, larvae, pupae or even adults, depending on the species.
- Do not use insecticides in or near the garden, especially neonicotinoids, which "are systemic chemicals absorbed by plants and dispersed through plant tissues, including pollen and nectar."

Butterfly Species Associated with Forest, Field, and Forest/Field Intergrade (Maria Van Dyke, Native Bee Research Lab, Dept. Entomology, Cornell University):

Forest:

- Zebra Swallowtail
- Easter Tiger Swallowtail
- Spicebush Swallowtail
- Pipevine Swallowtail
- Common Blue
- Question Mark
- Eastern Comma
- Mourning Cloak
- Red Spotted Purple

Field:

- Black Swallowtail
- Cabbage White
- Clouded Sulphur
- Orange Sulphur
- American Copper
- Eastern Tailed Blue
- Great Spangled Fritillary
- Meadow Fritillary
- Pearl Crescent

- Red Admiral
- Common Buckeye
- Hackberry Emperor
- Tawny Emperor
- Northern Pearly Eye

Forest/Field Intergrade:

- Monarch
- Common Wood Nymph
- Red-Banded Hairstreak

Bird Garden

In earlier sections of this chapter we describe the importance of enhancing layers of vegetative structure within the landscape to support a biodiverse assemblage of plant and animal communities, and here we revisit that theme again in the context of providing good habitat for birds. The most effective way to design a garden space that will become a home for many bird species is to grow lush shrub borders and hedgerows replete with fruits and seeds; to plant trees for an overhead canopy; and to fill the landscape between those two layers with pollinator habitat that will attract the insects and spiders that birds feed on for protein. These vegetative elements—the herbaceous flowering layer, the shrub layer and the canopy layer—along with other structural elements like brush piles, nest boxes and water features, will ensure an abundance of bird species throughout the seasons.

Birds need plenty of space to establish a territory, engage in courtship, build a nest, raise and feed their young, and move about in the landscape to find food and cover. The choice of shrub species and how they're arranged in relation to the surrounding trees and other elements will provide varying degrees of food and cover depending on the time of year. During the growing season in spring and summer, deciduous plants are full of leaves that provide shade and protection, but in winter, birds will need the cover of evergreens such as eastern redcedar (*Juniperus virginiana*), bayberry (*Morella pennsylvanica*), American holly (*Ilex opaca*), and Virginia pine (*Pinus virginiana*).

In spring, the new growth on trees like oaks, cherry, and poplar are a magnet for insects, and migratory neotropical birds such as orioles, warblers, tanagers, and vireos will utilize the canopy to glean insects from the leaves and branches. As late spring gives way to summer and birds begin breeding, they turn their attention to berry-producing shrubs and other mast (fruits and seeds), as more food becomes available.

Birds will also use hedgerows as a protective corridor to get from one area to another throughout the year. Shrubby thickets made up of species such as blackberries (*Rubus*), sumac (*Rhus*), chokeberry (*Aronia*), dogwood (*Cornus*) and viburnums (*Viburnum*) provide excellent cover and mast for catbirds, mockingbirds, thrashers, robins and many others.

The advancing progression of fruit ripening over the seasons ensures there's always plenty of food available from spring to fall, and many berries and seeds are persistent through the winter. Therefore, prune trees and shrubs in late winter, after the majority of fruits and seeds have been eaten, and before nesting season begins.

In large landscape settings, a good size shrub bed is a large circle of 15 to 30 feet in diameter, with a variety of species planted at least eight feet apart. This many plants results in a deep mass of leaves and branches, where birds can nest or easily dart in and out of when threatened. Alternatively, select one species to fill an entire plant bed, for example five inkberry (*Ilex glabra*) in one bed, or five American beautyberry (*Callicarpa americana*), or five New Jersey tea (*Ceanothus americanus*). In smaller landscapes with less room, plant clusters of just three shrubs instead. Mainly the goal is to group plants together as much as possible, rather than singly, here and there.

Every once in a while we hear folks complain that "all the quail and rabbits are gone," and they claim it's because "there's too many hawks." But the reality is that the decline of small mammals and birds is because too many landowners—in cities and in rural areas—are "cleaning out" fencerows, hedgerows, and ditches. There's a definite need to educate the public about the value in letting hedgerows and fencerows stay a little more wild with blackberries, greenbrier, grape vine, and Virginia creeper, in order to preserve habitat for the small mammals and birds that the hawks feed on, whether one lives on a tiny urban lot or on a large rural farm. "Gardening for birds" is so rewarding that it shouldn't be limited to foundation plantings but extended throughout the landscape.

One other special consideration is the ruby-throated hummingbird, which is a joy to see in any habitat setting, and a bird garden would seem incomplete without these jewels on the wing. As pollinators, they're especially keen on the nectar of tubular-shaped flowers, but they will also use a few other flower types selectively. If the landscape doesn't already include a pollinator patch with some of the following plant species in it, choose at least a few from the plant list below, based on the region of the state it's in, and the growing conditions of the site:

Plant list for ruby-throated hummingbird:

- Wild Columbine (*Aquilegia Canadensis*)
- Oxeye Sunflower (*Heliopsis helianthoides*)
- Coral Bells (*Heuchera americana*)
- Jewelweed (*Impatiens capensis* or *I. biflora*)
- Seashore Mallow (*Kosteletzkya virginica*)
- Cardinal Flower (*Lobelia cardinalis*)
- Great Blue Lobelia (*Lobelia siphilitica*)
- Virginia Bluebells (*Mertensia virginica*)
- Horsemint or Wild Bergamot (*Monarda bradburiana* or *M. fistulosa*)
- Beebalm (*Monarda didyma*)
- Sundrops (*Oenothera perennis*)
- Narrow-Leaved Sundrops (*Oenothera fruticosa*)
- Foxglove Beardtongue (*Penstemon digitalis*)
- Lyre-Leaf Sage (*Salvia lyrata*)
- Buttonbush (*Cephalanthus occidentalis*)—SHRUB
- Yellow Poplar or Tuliptree (*Liriodendron tulipifera*)—TREE
- Trumpetvine or Trumpet Creeper (*Campsis radicans*)—VINE
- Crossvine (*Bignonia capreolata*)—VINE
- Trumpet or Coral Honeysuckle (*Lonicera sempervirens*)—VINE
- Carolina jasmine or jessamine (*Gelsemium sempervirens*)—VINE

Water Garden for Frogs, Salamanders and Other Aquatic Species

The most effective habitat for supporting frogs, salamanders and other aquatic species is an in-ground wildlife pool that mimics a natural pond or wetland system. There are many options for providing ground-level water features, ranging from small and inexpensive to large and elaborate. Pre-fabricated liners are available at many garden centers and offer a convenient way to get a water source into the landscape quickly. These are often shaped like bathtubs and are available in different dimensions. Most are about three feet deep and made of thick, durable plastic or fiberglass, with built-in, shallow shelves for placement of potted aquatic plants. To install a pre-fabricated liner, dig a proportionate hole to accommodate its shape and size, and make sure the liner is level once it's in the ground. Remember to call Miss Utility before digging.

Alternatively, one can dig a water garden by hand and create a custom-made shape that's tailored to the specific site, as big or as small as practical. Locate the garden where it can be seen from a porch or window, and in a level area where there will be at least three to five hours of sunlight per day, with plants shading the water the rest of the day, because most aquatic organisms such as tadpoles need shade protection from temperature extremes.

Dig the deepest area 36 inches, then create shallower edges in concentric circles around this, to make ledges of different heights, such as 24 inches deep, 14 inches deep, and eight or 10 inches deep. The biggest challenge will be to level the sides with each other. Remove any rocks, roots, sticks or other sharp objects from the hole as it's being dug.

A hand-dug water garden will require two flexible plastic (PVC) liners and two geotextile pads that are at least eight ounces in weight each. The size of the liners and pads should be larger than the total size of the pond (for example, a 30 foot diameter pond would need liners 40 x 40 feet). An ideal size is about 18-20 feet long by 12-15 feet wide, but do some research first to see what size pond liners are actually available on the market. Be sure to buy a liner specifically designed for aquatic gardens, and at least 30-45 mil thick, rather than an ordinary tarp or liner from a hardware store, because the typical home improvement products are usually too thin, and are often pre-treated with a fungicide or algicide.

The installation is assembled like a giant sandwich: start with a two-inch layer of sand on the bottom, or use one geo-textile pad; next lay one of the PVC liners over the sand or pad; then lay another geo-textile pad down; and finish with the second PVC liner. The padded underlayment will help protect the water feature from tree roots and small burrowing animals that might tunnel underneath; some folks use old carpeting for this purpose.

Once the plastic layers are installed, use large rocks to hold the liner down in the middle, as well as along the ledges and around the upper edge. Small logs can also be used for edging around the top. If the pond is large, provide shallow, muddy areas, and also flat rocks in the open, where amphibians can bask in the sun. Fill the pond with non-chlorinated water (or wait several days for the chlorine in treated water to dissipate), and check the level during the driest part of the summer, to see if water may need to be added from time to time. To prevent a terrestrial animal like a bird or a chipmunk from falling in and not being able to escape, place a small branch or log in the pond that an animal can use to climb out.

After all the rocks are in place, the next step is to choose the plants. Just as we use layers of plants in a terrestrial habitat for wildlife diversity, use layers in the water garden to achieve the same effect. Ideally the pond will have enough plants to cover from one half to two-thirds of the surface area of the water. Select native aquatic plants suited to the different levels within the pond. Emergent plants root in the bottom, and their stems and leaves grow upright, out of the water. This is the area where salamanders and frogs spawn and lay their eggs. The matrix of plant roots and stems will provide a good micro-habitat for breeding, as well as multiple places for tadpoles and other organisms to feed and to hide. Floating plants root in the bottom, and their leaves float on the water's surface. Submergent plants grow completely underwater.

To achieve the best plant diversity, bring a list with you to the aquatic garden center to make the selection (see chart at the end of this section, "Native Plants for Moist Sites or Aquatic Habitats"). Choose plants that are adapted for each of the pond layers (emergent, floating and submergent), as well as plants to place around the edge that will hang over the water and provide additional cover. Avoid using cattails from a local farm pond, because cattails are very aggressive and will fill a pond quickly and choke out other vegetation.

One other consideration is whether or not to consider a recirculating pump or an aerator. The benefits of an aerator are that it provides water movement, keeps the water's oxygen content high, and minimizes algae build-up. Some amphibians prefer to live and breed in quiet water, while others only live and breed in moving water.

Therefore, if the pond is large enough and designed with different shelves for layers of varying depths, you can provide both types of micro-habitats (i.e., shallow, quiet water, and deeper water with a current) to support a broader range of species. If a pump or aerator will be used, have an electrician install a GFCI (ground-fault protected) outlet in the vicinity of the pond, during the digging stages.

However, if the pond is very small (less than 10 feet in diameter) and is filled with plants, the species that use the water garden will most likely be those that primarily associate with vernal or temporary pools. In this case, the abundance of diverse plants should support enough insect diversity to ensure there will be numerous predaceous insects as well as frogs eating any mosquito larvae, and a pump may not be necessary.

"Mosquito dunks" are not generally recommended for use in a frog pond. These pellets contain spores of bacteria known as Bti, a subspecies of the familiar *Bacillus thuringiensis* (Bt) that is widely used to control grasshoppers, caterpillars and other insects. Bti targets larvae within the suborder Nematocera, which includes mosquitoes; however, there may be larger, ecosystem effects to using Bti in ponds intended for wildlife (Brühl et. al., 2020). As the water garden becomes established with a full complement of diverse plants, many predatory, carnivorous aquatic invertebrates will move into the habitat, such as copepods, water bugs, diving beetles, and dragonfly and damselfly nymphs. These insects and their larvae all feed on mosquito larvae, as do frogs and salamanders.

Perhaps the most important recommendation for providing a safe haven for frogs and salamanders is: do NOT add fish. Fish prey on tadpoles; fish body wastes increase nitrogen in the water and can cause a nutrient imbalance; and goldfish and koi are non-native. Likewise, it is not recommended to purchase tadpoles or snails, as their genetic source cannot be fully confirmed, and releasing organisms from other areas into a new site can introduce pathogens to the environment that may be detrimental to the health of local aquatic populations.

A healthy aquatic habitat will gradually reach an equilibrium as various organisms become established. Over time, though, the pond is bound to gradually fill in with sediment from fallen leaves, and the amount of total water will gradually decrease as the plants' roots fill in and take over. Therefore, every two to three years in late winter (late February), remove any excessive amounts of decaying material or sediment, being careful to scoop out any newts, salamanders or frogs among the material, and temporarily hold them in a bucket, until the job is completed and they can be returned to the water.

Table 18-5: Native Plants for Moist Sites or Aquatic Habitats

Trees should be planted near a water feature or in a buffer along the edge of a creek. Ferns and grasses should be planted next to a water feature. Herbaceous flowering plants should be planted next to a water feature up to the water's edge. Sedges should be planted at the water's edge or in the water up to 1 foot deep. Emergent flowering plants grow in 1-2 feet of water. Floating plants grow in 2-8 feet of water. **Click "next" to see more table rows**

Plant Type	Common Name	Scientific Name	Approx. Height of Plant (ft)
Tree	Green Ash	*Fraxinus pennsylvanica*	50
Tree	Sweetbay Magnolia	*Magnolia virginiana*	20-60
Tree	River Birch	*Betula nigra*	45
Tree	Northern Red Oak	*Quercus rubra*	100
Tree	Red Mulberry	*Morus rubra*	35
Tree	Black Willow	*Salix nigra*	40
Small Tree/Shrub	Red Buckeye	*Aesculus pavia*	20
Small Tree/Shrub	American Elderberry	*Sambucus canadensis*	10
Small Tree/Shrub	American Beautyberry	*Callicarpa americana*	10
Small Tree/Shrub	Southern Bayberry	*Myrica cerifera*	8-20
Shrub	Highbush Blueberry	*Vaccinium corymbosum*	10
Shrub	Possumhaw	*Viburnum nudum*	10
Shrub	Red Osier Dogwood	*Cornus sericea*	10
Shrub	Sweetshrub	*Calycanthus floridus*	10
Shrub	Buttonbush	*Cephalanthus occidentalis*	10
Shrub	Silky Dogwood	*Cornus amomum*	7
Shrub	Virginia Sweetspire	*Itea virginica*	3-6
Shrub	Inkberry	*vIlex glabra*	
Fern	Chain Fern	*Woodwardia areolata*	2
Fern	Lady Fern	*Athyrium filix-femina*	2-3
Fern	Maidenhair Fern	*Adiantum pedatum*	1-2
Fern	Cinnamon Fern	*Osmunda cinnamomea*	3
Fern	Royal Fern	*Osmunda regalis*	3-5
Fern	Sensitive Fern	*Onoclea sensibilis*	1-2
Grass	Inland/River Sea Oats	*Chasmanthium latifolium*	2-4
Grass	Eastern Gammagrass	*Tripsacum dactyloides*	4-6
Grass	Bushy Bluestem	*Andropogon glomeratus*	3-5
Grass	Switchgrass	*Panicum virgatum*	4-6
Herbaceous Flowering Plant	Cardinal Flower	*Lobelia cardinalis*	3-5
Herbaceous Flowering Plant	Swamp Milkweed	*Asclepias incarnata*	5-6

Table 18-5: Native Plants for Moist Sites or Aquatic Habitats (continued)

Plant Type	Common Name	Scientific Name	Approx. Height of Plant (ft)
Herbaceous Flowering Plant	New York Ironweed	*Vernonia noveboracensis*	4-6
Herbaceous Flowering Plant	Blue Vervain	*Verbena hastata*	4-6
Herbaceous Flowering Plant	Joe Pyeweed	*Eupatorium purpureum*	4-6
Herbaceous Flowering Plant	Common Boneset	*Eupatorium perfoliatum*	3-4
Herbaceous Flowering Plant	Blue Mistflower	*Eupatorium coelestinum*	3
Herbaceous Flowering Plant	Blazing Star	*Liatris spicata*	4
Herbaceous Flowering Plant	Turtlehead	*Chelone glabra*	2-4
Herbaceous Flowering Plant	New York Aster	*Symphotricum novi-belgii*	1-3
Herbaceous Flowering Plant	Northern Blue Flag	*Iris versicolor*	2-4
Herbaceous Flowering Plant	Southern Blue Flag	*Iris virginica*	2-3
Sedge	Tussock Sedge	*Carex stricta*	2-4
Sedge	Fox Sedge	*Carex vulpinoidea*	3
Sedge	Shallow Sedge	*Carex lurida*	3
Emergent Flowering Plants	Arrowhead	*Sagittaria lancifolia*	2-3
Emergent Flowering Plants	Pickerelweed	*Pontedaria cordata*	2-3
Emergent Flowering Plants	Soft Rush	*Juncus effusesv*	3
Floating Plants	American White Waterlily	*Nymphaea odorata*	NA
Floating Plants	Yellow Pond Lily	*Nuphar lutea*	NA
Floating Plants	Illinois Pondweed	*Potamogeton illinoensis*	NA
Floating Plants	Longleaf Pondweed	*Potamogeton nodosus*	NA
Floating Plants	Frogbit	*Limnobium spongia*	NA
Submerged Plant	Eel Grass	*Vallisneria americana*	
Submerged Plant	Canadian Waterweed	*Anacharis Canadensis*	
Submerged Plant	Coon's Tail	*Ceratophyllum demersum*	
Iris	Northern Blue Flag	*Iris versicolor*	2-4
Iris	Southern Blue Flag	*Iris virginica*	2-3

Troubleshooting Wildlife Conflicts

The adaptability of wildlife to our urban and suburban built environments is one of the leading causes of wildlife and human conflicts. As we've cleared the land for residences and commerce, and changed the landscape by adding a wider variety of ornamental plantings, the result has been that opportunistic wildlife species like deer, raccoons, and opossums have made themselves right at home among our gardens, in our attics, and under our sheds. In some cases, the developed landscapes of today support even more of certain species than in historical times, such as deer, because habitat fragmentation caused by development has resulted in greater interspersion, increased availability of desirable landscape plants, and less hunting pressure than in bygone years.

Feeding Wildlife

Another primary reason for many of the wildlife conflicts encountered is that people just can't seem to keep themselves from feeding wildlife, whether deliberately or unwittingly. Each time a person feeds an animal, whether their love is birds or deer or squirrels, it naturally brings the animals closer to us, not further away, regardless of what species the animal is. Hence a bird feeder attracts a bear; dog food attracts a skunk; salt licks and apples attract deer; and kitchen scraps thrown in the yard, or a trash can with yesterday's leftovers attracts a raccoon.

Also, feeding wildlife can be problematic for the animals themselves, because bringing animals together artificially increases their numbers and makes it more likely they'll spread diseases to each other. Their behavior may also be altered, and they can become more aggressive towards each other or even towards people, because they gradually lose their fear of humans. Oftentimes when there's an escalating problem in a neighborhood—for example where deer are eating every dogwood and azalea in sight—it's attributed to someone who's been feeding deer. The very first step to resolving this type of problem would be to simply stop feeding. It's also important to remember that state regulations govern the feeding of deer. According to the DWR 2022-2023 Virginia Hunting and Trapping Regulations, "Department regulation makes it illegal to place, distribute, or allow the placement of food, minerals, salt, carrion, trash, or similar substances to feed or attract the following:"

Deer and Elk:

- Attractants prohibited September 1 through the first Saturday in January, statewide.
- Attractants prohibited during any open deer or elk season, statewide
- Attractants prohibited year round in Buchanan, Dickenson, and Wise counties as well as those counties listed which are associated with the management of chronic wasting disease (CWD) in Virginia.

Bears: Attractants prohibited year round, statewide.

All species: It is illegal to feed any wild animal when the feeding results in property damage, endangers people or wildlife, or creates a public health concern.

In addition, if a bird feeder is attracting a bear, the feeder must be taken down immediately, or the homeowner will be in violation of a regulation that prohibits the feeding of bears at any time.

The DWR regulations also state the following: "The Department does not encourage the feeding of wildlife at any time of the year. Feeding restrictions help control the transmission of diseases, wildlife conflicts, littering concerns, and enforcement issues about hunting with bait."

Therefore, some basic pointers about feeding: 1) Do not throw large piles of old bread and kitchen scraps in the yard—this will attract crows, starlings, grackles, vultures, skunks, raccoons and opossums. 2) Do not feed apples and corn to deer and squirrels—this will only encourage them to keep coming back, and their numbers will increase until a conflict arises. It will be much harder to get rid of them later. 3) Do not put cat food or dog food out for wildlife. Avoid using a pet door in a garage for feeding pets, which may encourage wildlife to come into the building. 4) Keep charcoal grills and gas grills clean of grease and other food residue. 5) Take bird feeders down in the summertime, to avoid attracting bears, and because natural food sources are plentiful during the growing season. 6) Use specially-designed trash cans to exclude raccoons and bears; use clamps to tighten trash can lids.

Evaluating a Wildlife Conflict

The process for evaluating and dealing with wildlife conflicts is fairly straightforward. First, determine exactly which species is causing the damage or problem, rather than making assumptions. Just because there's a hole in the cedar soffit under the eaves doesn't necessarily mean a woodpecker made it. Second, once you know what species is involved, find out specific details about its life history and habits, in order to understand more about what the animal likely wants, or why it's doing what it's doing. The third step is to determine the various options available and start with the one that's least toxic or least invasive. These non-chemical, non-lethal options may include changing the habitat to make it less desirable to the animal, or implementing some sort of prevention or exclusion method that will deter the animal from causing the same problem again. The last step is to use chemical and/or lethal means, only if none of the previous options have worked. In some circumstances, more than one option may be necessary to fully address or eliminate the problem.

In the recommendations below, there are several references made to trapping wildlife, but it is not meant to imply that any animal can be trapped and transported somewhere else and released. It is illegal in the state of Virginia to trap and *relocate* any animal to another area.

In the event that a situation presents itself where trapping will be necessary to address a wildlife conflict, consider contacting a licensed trapper who lives in your area and may be willing to assist you with the endeavor. A list of licensed trappers can be found on the DWR website.

Also, several laws and regulations are quoted below, but this is by no means a comprehensive list. If you have any questions about legalities or conflict issues, the most practical and easiest thing to do is to call the DWR Wildlife Conflict Helpline Toll Free Number 1-855-571-9003, 8:00 a.m.-4:30 p.m. Monday through Friday.

Legal Definition of "Nuisance Species"

While there may be many wildlife species we personally consider problematic, there are laws and regulations in the Code of Virginia that provide legal guidance on what actually constitutes a nuisance species. Per regulation, "the following animals: house mouse; Norway rat; black rat; coyote; groundhog; nutria; feral hog; European starling; English sparrow; mute swan; and pigeon (rock dove) are designated as nuisance species and may be taken at any time by use of a firearm or other weapon (unless prohibited by local ordinances), and on some public lands during certain time periods."

According to the Code of Virginia 29.1-100, nuisance species means "those species designated as such by regulations of the Board [as listed above], and those species found committing or about to commit depredation upon ornamental or shade trees, agricultural crops, wildlife, livestock or other property, or when concentrated in numbers and manners as to constitute a health hazard or other nuisance. However, the term nuisance does not include (i) animals designated as endangered or threatened…(ii) animals classified as game [bear, deer, rabbit, squirrel, bobcat, red fox, gray fox, raccoon] or fur-bearing animals [opossum, weasels (long-tailed and least weasels), striped skunk, spotted skunk, river otter, mink, beaver, muskrat] and (iii) those species protected by state or federal law [all songbirds, woodpeckers, hawks, vultures, waterfowl etc. under the federal Migratory Bird Treaty Act, and many other species under the federal Endangered Species Act]."

This means that if a woodpecker is banging on your siding, you are not authorized to harm, harass or "take" (kill) it, even though it definitely is a nuisance!

By law, the only people authorized to harm, harass or "take" (kill) nuisance species as defined above are DWR personnel, Federal personnel with wildlife responsibilities, Animal Control Officers, Commercial Nuisance Animal Permittees, licensed hunters, licensed trappers, and landowners (under certain conditions).

When a Commercial Nuisance Animal Permittee receives a complaint from a private citizen, the Permittee is authorized to: 1) capture or remove wildlife from a building or dwelling and release the animal upon the "curtilage" of the building [the fenced-in ground and buildings immediately surrounding a house or dwelling]; 2) capture and temporarily possess injured, sick or orphaned wildlife for transport to Wildlife Rehabilitation Permittees; 3) capture and temporarily possess and transport wildlife for dispatch (killed); 4) capture wildlife for immediate dispatch; 5) immediately dispatch wildlife. Commercial Nuisance Animal Permittees are not authorized to capture, possess, transport or dispatch: 1) companion animals, including dogs and cats, whether owned or feral; 2) state or federal threatened or endangered species; 3) federally protected migratory bird species; 4) black bears; 5) white-tailed deer; 6) wild turkey. They are also NOT authorized to relocate (release) any live animals, except for squirrels trapped from areas where discharge of firearms is prohibited and when permission is obtained from the landowner where the squirrel is being released.

Control Options

For specific control recommendations for each of the animals listed below, please refer to the VCE Pest Management Guide (PMG), Home Grounds and Animals, section 8: "Other Animals: Vertebrates as Pests." All pesticide (bait, repellent, and rodenticide) recommendations must come from this VCE publication 456-018.

Deer

Too many deer in a forested area can cause overbrowsing to the extent that available habitat is severely compromised for some wildlife species that rely on understory food and cover to survive. However, the effects vary among species. On the one hand, ground-nesting birds such as ovenbirds and shrub-nesting birds like buntings may be adversely affected from overbrowsing, whereas other species like cardinals and nuthatches are not influenced. In addition to the problems posed to other wildlife by overbrowsing, an overabundance of deer can result in the spread of more invasive plants throughout the ecosystem and substantially reduce understory regeneration of oaks and other trees.

Deer are opportunistic, and in a residential setting, if deer are hungry enough and presented with enough easily accessible ornamental plants, they'll selectively pick and choose the plants best suited to their needs at that particular point in time. There are excellent publications available online (such as Managing Deer Damage in Maryland, Bulletin 354) which contain strategic guidelines and plant lists for minimizing deer damage for different land uses. For example, a Christmas tree grower can use repellents to protect new tree seedlings until they're tall enough to be out of reach of deer, whereas repellents are not cost-effective for an agricultural operator of a large nursery, orchard or vegetable farm. A homeowner may select a plant off the recommended list for their landscape bed (Kays 2003), but may subsequently find that deer will eat the plant anyway. Unfortunately, these kinds of "Resistance" lists are not consistently reliable, because deer will browse on plants for a variety of reasons: the health of the individual animal, the quality of the surrounding habitat, the amount of other available food in the area, the time of year, whether or not the animal is lactating. Hence, deer may always eat hostas in one neighborhood, but in another part of the state, deer may rarely eat hostas.

The take-away point is that the plants do not "resist" or "deter" anything. Rather, it's the deer that's in control. Whether or not a deer eats certain plants will depend on how desirable that plant is, how hungry the deer is, and so on. Eating or not eating is a behavior that's up to the deer, not the plant. If a plant smells bad and has waxy, unpleasant leaves, a deer can walk away and eat something else. However, just because a deer walked away one time doesn't mean that another deer won't come along later and eat that plant in one big chomp. According to DWR Deer Biologist Nelson Lafon, "It's a myth that you can deter deer by only using certain plants." Therefore, be wary of nurseries that make claims about a plant's deterrence properties.

Whether or not a planted bed is browsed by deer can also depend on where the plants are located. In general, deer are less likely to browse right up against a house or where dogs or people frequently move about—but here, too, there are always exceptions, if a deer is hungry, persistent or bold enough.

The best option in a home landscape is exclusion of plants using plastic fencing, or woven wire or chain link at least eight feet and preferably 10 feet tall around vegetable gardens and other small planted beds. Use tree protectors around young seedlings to cover the vulnerable bark, and use a cage made of woven wire to protect specimen plants.

For very large areas, electric fencing eight to 10 feet tall works best. There's another fencing design for rural properties that's been promoted by Cooperative Extension for many years, which entails setting the fence at an angle such that deer are said to be less likely to jump over it.

For smaller scale home gardens, try using a modified electric fence with aluminum foil "tents" or wrappers that attach to the wires and are rubbed with peanut butter. A deer is attracted to the peanut butter and receives a shock when its nose touches the foil that conducts the current. This results in aversive conditioning, which deters the deer from coming back to the same area again, at least for a while.

Some homeowners have had success with installing two parallel 4-foot-high fences approximately 3 feet apart from each other. Apparently the panels are too close together for deer to feel comfortable jumping over.

Commercial, chemical repellents can be applied to target plants as a deterrent, but they must be applied at the beginning of the growing season before deer begin browsing on the plants, and they should preferably be applied to so-called deer-resistant species, to maximize potential effect. However, the chemicals may gradually break down over time or get washed off in rain events, and they must therefore be re-applied regularly to maintain effectiveness. There are over a dozen commercially available chemical repellent products, which contain a variety of ingredients that either emit a foul odor which deer find offensive, such as putrefied egg-based compounds, garlic, fish meal, or coyote urine, or various plant compounds like capsaicin (hot pepper) or other chemicals that are distasteful or injurious to the palate.

When everything else fails, get a dog that will chase deer out of the yard!

Bear

Black bears occur throughout most of Virginia, and as development increases, it becomes increasingly likely that people will encounter bear in residential areas. However, in this part of the bear's range, they do not exhibit predatory behavior, and it is extremely unlikely that a bear will attack or harm a human, unless the animal is provoked or feels threatened. As described in the "Feeding Wildlife" section above, one of the primary reasons bear are attracted to human development is because of an available food source. At least 30% of complaints about bear are attributed to the presence of bird feeders, and 50% of complaints are associated with storage of garbage. A much smaller percentage (less than 10%) is related to agricultural food sources such as apiaries, orchards, other crops, and livestock feed.

According to Virginia state law: "It shall be unlawful for any person as defined in §1-230 (Code of Virginia) to place, distribute, or allow the placement of food, minerals, carrion, trash, or similar substances to feed or attract bear. Nor, upon notification by department [DWR] personnel, shall any person continue to place, distribute, or allow the placement of any food, mineral, carrion, trash, or similar substances for any purpose, if placement of these materials results in the presence of bear."

The simplest way to prevent bear encounters is to monitor bird feeders and other food sources outside the home to ensure that bear and other wild mammals are not being attracted. If it becomes apparent that a bear is using a feeder or frequenting a garbage can, or if bear are known to have been sighted in the area, remove all feeders and other open food sources immediately. A good rule of thumb is to take down bird feeders between April 1 and December 1 to prevent problems from occurring.

If a bear is sighted, keep your distance and allow the bear to leave the area. The goal is to keep a bear from feeling comfortable around residential areas, and if there's no food source available, the bear will likely just move through the area and continue on its way. If a bear is sighted in a tree, keep dogs and other pets away, so the bear will leave.

Vole

Voles are herbivores that eat bulbs and roots. They make tunnels near the surface of the sod as they travel from tree to tree to eat roots and strip the bark; they do NOT make mounds. A common vole deterrent is a bait-station ground trap that can be installed above or below ground. To confirm whether or not voles are indeed the ones eating bulbs, use an apple bait test: place the bait near the runway on the surface of the turf, and cover the bait with a bucket, then weight the bucket down with a brick to keep other animals out. Later inspect the bait to see if the apple has been chewed by a vole. Other methods include placing a mouse trap on the ground perpendicular to the runway, then baiting it and covering it as described above.

Other methods of deterring voles: 1) use only a thin layer of mulch around trees, and pull the mulch away from the trunk; 2) avoid killing snakes, which are a primary predator of voles and other small mammals. Owls and hawks are also predators of voles; 3) before planting bulbs, enclose them in a small wire basket, or place a layer of gravel or sharp shale bits ('Perma Till') in the hole when planting, to surround and protect the bulb.

Mole

Moles are insectivores that prey on worms, grubs, and other insects or larvae; they do NOT eat flower bulbs, contrary to popular opinion. Moles tunnel just below the soil surface and leave mounds as they go; they can dig up to 150 feet of new tunnels a day, and their action helps to aerate the soil. It is said they can consume their body weight in food daily, which makes them an important predator of problematic grubs such as Japanese beetle larvae. Moles, like any other wildlife species, have a specific role in the environment, and the first level of dealing with them is tolerance of their activities. Allow moles to continue feeding on the grubs in the soil and consider it a service. If tunneling becomes problematic, try collapsing the tunnels by walking over them, which may also prevent mice and voles from using them as easy runways, or use an underground barrier or baffle to edge around plant beds. When all other options are exhausted, use a mole trap to kill, or use baits. For specific bait recommendations, please see VCE publication 456-018.

Raccoon

Raccoons are wily creatures that can cause all kinds of damage, and they can carry rabies. Raccoons get into chimneys and attics, they get into barns and livestock feed stores or grain, they damage agricultural crops such as corn fields, they get into trash cans and dumpsters. To manage: 1) make sure the chimney has a properly fitted and secure chimney cap; 2) close off any holes under the eaves or other openings where raccoons could get in; 3) remove or secure food sources; 4) if a raccoon is already in a building or attic, try harassment with a loud radio tuned to a talk station; or bright lights.

The legal provision for raccoon damage management, according to the Code of Virginia 29.1-517 Fur Bearing Animals: "When muskrats or raccoons are damaging crops or dams, the owner of the premises may kill them or have them killed under a permit obtained from the Conservation Police Officer [of the Virginia Department of Wildlife Resources]." Under Regulation 4-VAC 15-210-51 Open Season for Trapping-generally: "November 15 through last day in February… except there shall be a continuous open season to trap raccoon within the incorporated limits of any city or town in the Commonwealth and in the counties of Arlington, Chesterfield, Fairfax, Henrico, James City, Loudoun, Prince William, Spotsylvania, Stafford, Roanoke and York."

The above Code and Regulation indicate that if you live in a city or town or one of the counties listed, you can live trap a problem raccoon and release it outside (then seal up any entrances where it was able to get in). If you don't live in one of those areas, and the raccoon is causing conflict that doesn't involve crops or a dam, and you've tried all other options, then hire a professional (Commercial Nuisance Animal Permittee).

Another alternative is to find a licensed trapper who lives in your area and is willing to assist you with the endeavor. A list of licensed trappers can be found on the DWR website.

Rabbit

Use chemical repellents similar to those used for deer, to discourage feeding on plant leaves and shoots. Plant a species like onions, which rabbits do not prefer, in between other plants that are more desirable. Fence the garden with two-foot high hardware cloth (wire mesh) or chicken wire, and extend it at least five inches below the ground, all around the bed. Individual plants or vulnerable seedlings can be covered with a basket.

See also the legal provision for trapping rabbits and squirrels under the "Squirrel" section, below.

Squirrel

Squirrels can wreak havoc in a variety of ways. They can chew their way through the sill of a window, or chew a hole under the eaves to make an entrance and get into an attic. To keep them away from buildings, trim any overhanging tree branches to keep limbs well-away from the roof; staple hardware cloth over any openings under the eaves, or seal them over with a board or piece of metal flashing.

If a squirrel gets inside the house, place a loud radio tuned to a talk station near the room, and/or bright lights to scare them to leave. A "Hav-a-Heart" trap may be available from a local Animal Control Office to live trap the squirrel and release it directly outside, next to the building.

Around bird feeders, squirrels will chew the edges of the feeder if it's made of wood. Many advertised "squirrel-proof" feeders are available on the market, with various designs, such as one that slides a metal baffle over the seed hopper to close it off when a squirrel stands on the edge, or a feeder that has a battery-operated sensor, which spins the feeder to throw the squirrel off. Despite their intended outcome, these feeders may not always work, because squirrels eventually seem to outwit the baffle device, and squirrels have been know to continue to attempt to climb onto the 'spin-feeder' until the feeder's batteries run out. In most cases it's usually best to take feeders down for a time, until the squirrel loses interest and moves on to something else.

The legal provision for squirrel damage management, according to the Code of Virginia 29.1-516 Game Animals: "Landowners, resident members of hunt clubs and tenants (with written permission of landowner) may kill rabbits or squirrels for their own use during the closed season."

Also—Code of Virginia 29.1-530 Open and Closed Season for Trapping, Bag Limits, etc.: "a landowner or his agent may trap and dispose of, except by sale, squirrels causing a nuisance on his property at any time in any area where the use of firearms for such purpose is prohibited by law or local ordinance."

Skunk

Skunks are nocturnal, secretive, solitary and opportunistic. They prey on insects and will eat grasshoppers, crickets and also mice. They may knock over and empty the contents of trashcans; dig up lawns in search of grubs or insect nests; and like raccoons, they can carry rabies. To manage for skunks: 1) use a locking trash can to secure waste; 2) do not leave pet food outside; 3) remove brush and cover away from the foundation of dwellings or other buildings; 4) use a chemical treatment for the grubs in the lawn if their numbers exceed six per square foot; 5) if a skunk is in the crawl space under a building or has burrowed a hole under a shed, lay a board at the entrance as a ramp to try to encourage the skunk to come out; 6) when you're sure the skunk is no longer underneath a building, tightly secure hardware cloth (wire mesh) along the edge of the building foundation to cover any burrow entrance or other opening; 7) use a covered bait trap that's designed to capture a skunk and protect others from being sprayed. Lay a towel or blanket over the trap as an added precaution.

Per Regulation 4VAC15-220-10 Continuous Open Season for Taking of Striped Skunks: "It shall be lawful to take striped skunks (Mephitis mephitis) at any time." And—Regulation 4 VAC 15-220-20 Taking of Spotted Skunks: "A landowner or tenant may take [kill], on his own land or land under his control, spotted skunks (*Spilogale putorius*) committing or about to commit depredation. However the pelt of the spotted skunk may not be sold."

Opossum

Opossums are also nocturnal. Since they're primarily tree-dwellers, they're inclined to enter attics without an invitation. As omnivores, they're also opportunistic when seeking food sources and will get into storage areas or outbuildings where bird seed or dog food is kept. To manage for opossum: 1) remove or secure food sources; 2) use hardware cloth or other screening or exclusion method to protect foundation openings; 3) repair eaves and areas under the roof overhang to keep animals out; and 4) trap as needed.

Since Opossum is legally defined as a furbearer species, the following are applicable regulations for trapping:

- 29.1-517 Fur-Bearing Animals: "A landowner may shoot fur-bearing animals except muskrats or raccoons upon his own land during closed season."
- 29.1-530 Open and Closed Season for Trapping, Bag Limits, etc: "A landowner may trap fur-bearing animals, except beaver, muskrat and raccoons, upon his own land during closed season."
- Regulation 4 VAC 15-210-51 Open Season for Trapping – generally: "November 15 through last day in February, except there shall be a continuous open season to trap opossum within the incorporated limits of any city or town in the Commonwealth and in the counties of Arlington, Chesterfield, Fairfax, Henrico, James City, Loudoun, Prince William, Spotsylvania, Stafford, Roanoke and York."

Groundhog

Groundhogs dig large burrows and can do damage beneath the foundation of a building. Their burrows can be 25 to 30 feet long and from two to five feet deep, and they usually have two entrances. Groundhogs also feed on agricultural crops and may damage fruit trees in orchards. Here it's important to remove fallen fruit as quickly as possible, to avoid attracting groundhogs to the free bounty.

The best measure for keeping groundhogs out of a structure is preventive maintenance, by ensuring that garages, porches, decks, sheds and other outbuildings do not have openings for access that will invite a groundhog's curiosity to explore and dig deeper.

In the garden, use a fence at least three feet high to keep groundhogs out, and extend the bottom of the fence under the ground at least one or two feet, as they may try to burrow underneath it.

Woodpecker

During the early spring, male woodpeckers establish their territory and attract a mate by pounding on dead trees and logs. If sufficient dead trees are not available, a woodpecker may decide that the hollow sound made by rapping on the siding of a house is just as good. In this scenario, one can try hanging reflective or noisy items from the building near where the bird has been striking, such as old CD's, plastic grocery bags, rattling pie tins, or shiny metal flashing cut into strips.

Another possibility is that there may be some insect damage taking place underneath the siding or under the eaves that has attracted the woodpecker. Since woodpeckers are closely associated with dead trees and have a specialized tongue that's adapted for pulling grubs out of wood, these birds spend a lot of time climbing up and down trees listening for the sound of chewing insects beneath the bark, which are a clear signal that food is at hand. Therefore, if scare tactics have not worked in discouraging the woodpecker from leaving the building, it's possible that there's some decay beneath the fascia board. Check for water-damaged wood, which is often an indicator of rot, and replace any damaged material.

Also, stack firewood and lumber at least 10-20 feet away from the house, to avoid insect damage from carpenter ants, termites, borers, and powder post beetles, which might attract woodpeckers as well.

Woodpeckers are protected by the Migratory Bird Treaty Act and may not be harmed, harassed or "taken" at any time.

Bat

Bats are very small and can squeeze between very narrow cracks and crevices underneath boards or eaves. Therefore, to reduce the likelihood of bats entering an attic space or getting into the walls, practice diligent preventative maintenance and make repairs as soon as damage is observed. It's especially important to do this before the breeding season, when nursery colonies will be looking for places to roost to raise their young. At the end of the breeding season, bats will look for shelter to hibernate over winter. Some simple practices for maintenance or repair: 1) Attach ¼ inch steel mesh (hardware cloth) to the inside of gable vents; 2) patch any holes fist size or larger with new siding, paneling, sheet metal, or plywood and paint; 3) Stuff smaller holes with steel wool or copper wool, and then cover with caulk.

If a bat does get into the house, don't panic but try to contain it in one room. Turn off all the lights and open all the windows, and continue watching the bat until you see it leave. If the bat appears to be resting quietly, try to trap it in a plastic container, and then release it outside.

If bats are living in the attic, turn on a loud radio and use bright lights as a deterrence. Another technique is to sit outside the building on a lawn chair at dusk and watch the house from the outside, to see how bats are getting in and out of the structure. Have a ladder and tools and materials ready. When darkness falls, the bats will leave the building en masse, which should provide an opportunity to make repairs and block access to their return. However, in the months of May through August, there may be young bats that stay behind when the adults come out to feed, and it's imperative there are no bats still present within the structure before sealing up the holes.

Sometimes placing a bat house on the wall near the opening where bats have been going in and out may entice them to use the bat house instead. However, if these methods are not successful and a large number of bats is still the structure, seek professional assistance.

Bats are a non-game species and cannot be harmed or taken at any time. There are three federally endangered species of bats in Virginia. Therefore, before implementing a control technique that may cause harm, seek assistance in determining what species of bat is in question.

Snake

Despite people's fears, snakes are rather benign and will usually try to get away when they see anyone approaching. There are 32 snake species in Virginia, and only 3 are venomous. The most common venomous snake seen across the state is the copperhead, which may frequent firewood piles or other areas with protective cover. Snakes that eat rodents are beneficial!

Figure 18-8: Virginia's venomous snakes include northern copperhead, *Agkistrodon contortrix mokasen*, eastern cottonmouth snake, *Agkistrodon p. piscivorus*, and timber rattlesnake, *Crotalus horridus*.

The preventative for snakes is to keep the building maintained and seal up any small cracks, tears, or other openings around windows, doors and under the eaves. Eastern rat snakes are tree climbers and may get inside an attic space. Snakes may also find their way into a basement or crawl space. If a snake gets in, use a towel or small blanket to place over the snake and then secure it to release it outdoors.

Canada goose

One goose produces a pound of manure every day. That's a lot of organic matter that can pollute ponds, lakes and other waterways. Feeding geese only makes the problem worse, because it encourages them to congregate, and the concentration of nitrogen and urea from their droppings will kill fish and other wildlife in the pond water and can also cause an algae bloom. The wisest rule of thumb is not to feed geese at all.

To manage goose conflict, use scare tactics such as reflective tape; noise makers such as horns and whistles; and predator replicas. There's also a bright yellow, inflatable plastic ball with a red eyeball on it that is sometimes used. Inflate the ball and hang it from a tree limb near the water, so it's easily visible to the geese. It's said that they apparently perceive the yellow ball and eye as a predator or something to be avoided. In large areas, such as around a lake in a big subdivision, a dog can be employed to chase geese and keep them from landing. This is most effective if initiated early in the season, when geese are flying over looking for places to land and a safe site to begin nest-building.

Geese prefer wide open lawns and fields, and another effective way to deter them is to leave a wide buffer of grasses, shrubs and other vegetation around the perimeter of the lake or pond. Geese usually approach land from the water's side, and if the bank is full of vegetation, they will not come up on land in that location. Therefore avoid mowing down to the water's edge wherever possible. If a view of the water is desired, carefully select a few small areas between trees or shrubs ,where a few branches can be strategically removed to open a small 'window' to the water, in lieu of cutting out entire shrubs or mowing all the vegetation. Retaining a buffer will be more beneficial to aquatic organisms that live in the water or at the water's edge, too. If there's currently no vegetated buffer to work with, set up a temporary fence or other barrier such as rocks at the very edge of the water along the entire length of the bank, to discourage geese from walking up onto land from the water side.

If geese have already become well established and are nesting, another technique that field biologists use is called "egg addling." This is a mechanical method whereby the eggs in the nest are rapidly shaken in order to break up the contents within, so they won't hatch. Although the adults may still not leave, the method ensures that the goose population at that location will not grow any larger.

In some municipalities a special goose hunt may be organized to reduce their numbers. To inquire how to set this up, contact a DWR Waterfowl Biologist or a Conservation Police Officer.

Additional Resources

General Habitat Information

- *Habitat at Home©*, by Carol Heiser. Virginia Department of Wildlife Resources Habitat Partners© Program.
- Backyard Wildlife Habitats 426-070
- *Bringing Nature Home: How You Can Sustain Wildlife with Native Plants*, by Doug Tallamy. 2009. TimberPress.
- *The Living Landscape: Designing for Beauty and Biodiversity in the Home Garden*, by Darke and Tallamy. 2014. Timber Press.
- Wildlife Habitat Evaluation Program Manual. 2011. 4-H and FFA.
- *The Woods in Your Backyard: Learning to Create and Enhance Natural Areas Around Your Home*, by Kays, Drohan, Downing and Finley. 2006. Natural Resource, Agriculture and Engineering Service, Cooperative Extension.
- Wild Ones: Landscaping with Native Plants. 4th edition. 2004. Chicago State University.
- Conservation Landscaping Guidelines: The Eight Essential Elements of Conservation Landscaping. 2013. Chesapeake Conservation Landscaping Council
- Elizabeth River Project online resources.
- *The Bat House Builder's Handbook*, by Tuttle and Kiser. 2013. University of Texas Press.

Native Plant Resources

- Native Plants for Wildlife Habitat and Conservation Landscaping: Chesapeake Bay Watershed, by Slattery, Reshetiloff and Zwicker. 2003.
- Native Plants for Conservation, Restoration and Landscaping (VA Department of Conservation and Recreation, Natural Heritage Division): Plant lists for physiographic regions of the state (Coastal, Piedmont and Mountain), with a key indicating relative value of plants to wildlife. Also includes a link to a list of Virginia invasive plant species. http://www.dcr.virginia.gov/natural_heritage/nativeplants.shtml
- Regional Native Plant Guides are available (such as Eastern Shore, Northern Neck, Northern Virginia) at VA Coastal Zone Management Program, www.deq.virginia.gov/Programs/CoastalZoneManagement/CZMIssuesInitiatives/NativePlants.aspx
- Digital Atlas of Virginia Flora www.vaplantatlas.org Use the Atlas to see which plants are actually native in your own County.
- Three complete listings of native "Herbaceous Plants," "Shrubs" and "Trees" are available online at http://blogs.lt.vt.edu/mastergardener/app-nativeplants-wildlife/, which are used with permission from the USDA-NRCS (2014) Field Office Technical Guide, Section 2, Plant Establishment Guide.

Gardening for Butterflies and Other Pollinators

- U.S. Fish and Wildlife Service Pollinators web site http://www.fws.gov/pollinators/pollinatorpages/yourhelp.html
- Numerous excellent publications are available from the Xerces Society for Invertebrate Conservation at www.xerces.org , as follows:
- –Attracting Native Pollinators: Protecting North America's Bees and Butterflies, by Mader, Shepherd, Vaughan and Black; 2011;

Xerces Society; 380 pgs.
- –XERCES "Invertebrate Conservation" FACT SHEETS (http://www.xerces.org/fact-sheets/)
- Pollinator Plants [for] Mid-Atlantic Region http://www.xerces.org/pollinator-conservation/plant-lists/
- Conserving Bumble Bees: Guidelines for Creating and Managing Habitat for America's Declining Pollinators, by Hatfield, Jepsen, Mader, Black and Shepherd, 2012. http://ncagr.gov/spcap/bee/documents/ConservingBumbleBees.pdf
- Pollinator Trial Results, by Schmotzer; 2013; Penn State Extension; 2 pg. Fact Sheet. http://extension.psu.edu/plants/master-gardener/counties/lancaster/pollinator-friendly-garden-certification/2013-pollinator-trial-results
- Attracting Pollinators to Your Garden Using Native Plants, by Reel; U.S. Forest Service; 16 pg. color booklet, excellent for the general public http://www.fs.fed.us/wildflowers/pollinators/documents/AttractingPollinatorsEasternUS_V1.pdf
- Urban and Suburban Meadows, by Zimmerman; 2010; Matrix Media Press; 272 pgs. Step-by-step guidelines for evaluating, designing, preparing and planting a site.

Gardening for Birds

- Bird Gardening Book: The Complete Guide to Creating a Bird-Friendly Habitat in Your Backyard, by Stokes; 1998; Little, Brown & Co. 95 pgs.
- Hummingbird Gardens: Turning Your Yard into Hummingbird Heaven, edited by Marinelli and Hanson; 2000; Handbook # 163, Brooklyn Botanic Garden Inc.; 111 pgs.
- Attracting Birds, Butterflies and Other Backyard Wildlife, by Mizejewski; 2010 edition; National Wildlife Federation; 128 pgs.
- Web Page – How to Attract Birds to Your Garden, National Wildlife Federation http://www.nwf.org/How-to-Help/Garden-for-Wildlife/Gardening-Tips/How-to-Attract-Birds-to-Your-Garden.aspx
- Cornell Lab of Ornithology http://www.birds.cornell.edu/Page.aspx?pid=1478 [see also Nest Watch: All About Bird Houses http://nestwatch.org/learn/all-about-birdhouses/]
- Woodworking for Wildlife: Homes for Birds and Animals, 3rd edition, by Henderson; 2010; Minnesota Department of Natural Resources; 164 pgs.

Gardening for Aquatic Wildlife

- Backyard Ponds: Guidelines for Creating and Managing Habitat for Dragonflies and Damselflies, by Mazzacano, Paulson and Abbott; 2014; Migratory Dragonfly Partnership; 22 pgs. www.migratorydragonflypartnership.org
- How to Create a Frog Pond (Emerging Wildlife Conservation Leaders); Amphibian Ark; 17 pgs. http://www.amphibianark.org/pdf/Husbandry/How%20to%20Create%20a%20Frog%20Pond.pdf
- Pond-Building Guide (contains sections on "Characteristics of Amphibian Friendly Ponds" and "Mosquito Control"); 2015; 5 pgs. http://www.treewalkers.org/pond-building-guide/
- A Guide to Creating Vernal Ponds: All the Information You Need to Build and Maintain an Ephemeral Wetland, by Biebighauser; 2002; USDA Forest Service and Izaak Walton League; 36 pgs. http://herpcenter.ipfw.edu/outreach/vernalponds/vernalpondguide.pdf or http://www.watershedconnect.com/documents/science_management_interventions_wetlands
- Habitat Management Guidelines for Amphibians and Reptiles of the Southeastern United States [Technical Publication HMG-2], by Bailey, Holmes, Buhlmann and Mitchell; 2006; PARC (Partners in Amphibian and Reptile Conservation); 88 pgs.
- http://www.privatelandownernetwork.org/pdfs/seHabitatManagementGuide.pdf or https://separc.files.wordpress.com/2013/04/se-hmg.pdf

Wildlife Conflicts

- WILDLIFE CONFLICT HELPLINE Toll Free Number 1-855-571-9003, 8:00 a.m.-4:30 p.m. Monday through Friday (VA Department of Wildlife Resources).
- VA Department of Wildlife Resources—FACT SHEETS on 20 wildlife species available on web site, How to Prevent or Resolve Conflict with Wildlife. http://www.dgif.virginia.gov/wildlife/problems/
- ARTICLES for the general public: When Wildlife Overstays its Welcome, and Feeding Wildlife: Food for Thought—

- www.dgif.virginia.gov/habitat
- Wildlife Damage Control FACT SHEETS available on Beavers, Black Bears, Canada Goose, Moles, and Snakes, from VA Cooperative Extension https://pubs.ext.vt.edu/category/wildlife.html
- Snakes of Virginia, VA Department of Wildlife Resources [Booklet available for $4.95 through e-Store at www.dgif.virginia.gov]
- A Guide to the Bats of Virginia, Special Publication No. 5, by Reynolds and Fernald; 2015; VA Department of Wildlife Resources; 40 pgs. Includes information about how to handle bats in homes or buildings. [Booklet available for purchase through e-Store at www.dgif.virginia.gov]
- DEER RESISTANT PLANTS: "Deer Resistant Plants," North Carolina Cooperative Extension, Urban Horticulture Fact Sheet 15; 8 pgs; http://pender.ces.ncsu.edu/files/library/71/Deer%20Resistant%20Plants.pdf
- Resistance of Ornamentals to Deer Damage, Fact Sheet # 655; 2003; Maryland Cooperative Extension; 8 pgs. http://s130859622.onlinehome.us/ocg/wp-content/uploads/2011/06/DeerResistantOrnamentals.pdf
- Deer: A Garden Pest [Hort 62NP], by Hussey; 2013; VA Cooperative Extension; 4 pg. Fact Sheet. http://www.pubs.ext.vt.edu/HORT/HORT-62/HORT-62-PDF.pdf
- REPELLENTS: "White-Tailed Deer," [Wildlife Damage Management Fact Sheet Series], by Curtis and Sullivan; 2001; Cornell Cooperative Extension; 6 pgs. http://wildlifecontrol.info/pubs/Documents/Deer/Deer_factsheet.pdf
- Managing Deer Damage in Maryland [Bulletin 354], by Kays; 2003; Maryland Cooperative Extension; 40 pgs. Excellent guidelines that can be applied to Virginia, not just Maryland! http://extension.umd.edu/sites/default/files/_docs/programs/woodland-steward/EB354_ManagingDeerDamage.pdf
- Deer Proofing Your Yard and Garden, 2nd Edition, by Hart; 2005; Storey Publishing; 208 pgs.
- Squirrel Wars: Backyard Wildlife Battles and How to Win Them, by Harrison; 2000; Willow Creek Press; 176 pgs.

References

- Adamson, N. L. (2016). "Pollinators in our Communities." https://www.nacdnet.org/wp-content/uploads/2016/06/Xerces-Society-NRCS-NC-Compressed.pdf
- Brühl, C. A., Després, L., Frör, O., Patil, C. D., Poulin, B., Tetreau, G., & Allgeier, S. (2020). Environmental and socioeconomic effects of mosquito control in europe using the biocide bacillus thuringiensis subsp. israelensis (bti). *Science of the Total Environment, 724*.
- Calderone N.W. (2012). "Insect pollinated crops, insect pollinators and US agriculture: Trend analysis of aggregate data for the period 1992–2009." *PLoS ONE. 2012;7*:e37235. doi: 10.1371/journal.pone.0037235.
- "General Information & Hunting Regulations." (2022). Virginia Department of Wildlife Resources. https://dwr.virginia.gov/hunting/regulations/general/
- Hennessy, C. and **Hild, K. (2021).** "Are Virginia opossums really ecological traps for ticks? Groundtruthing laboratory observations?"*Ticks and Tickborne Diseases 12, 5. https://pubmed.ncbi.nlm.nih.gov/34298355/*
- "How many species of native bees are in the United States?" U.S. Geological Survey. https://www.usgs.gov/faqs/how-many-species-native-bees-are-united-states
- Kays, Jonathan S. (2021). "Managing Deer Damage in Maryland (EB-354)." University of Maryland Extension. https://extension.umd.edu/resource/managing-deer-damage-maryland-eb-354
- Kays, Jonathan S., Bartlett, Michael V., and Curtis, Lisa. (2003). "Resistance of Ornamentals to Deer Damage, Fact Sheet # 655." Maryland Cooperative Extension. http://s130859622.onlinehome.us/ocg/wp-content/uploads/2011/06/DeerResistantOrnamentals.pdf
- McBryde, J. (2016). "Virginia Honeybees are all the Buzz" *FarmFlavor*. https://farmflavor.com/virginia/virginia-farm-to-table/all-the-buzz/
- Narango, D. L., Tallamy, D.W., and Marra, P.P. (2018). "Nonnative plants reduce population growth of an insectivorous bird." *Proceedings of the National Academy of Sciences 115* (45), p 11549-11554.
- Narango, D.L., Tallamy, D.W. & Shropshire, K.J. (2020). "Few keystone plant genera support the majority of Lepidoptera species." *Nat Commun* 11,5751. https://doi.org/10.1038/s41467-020-19565-4
- Ollerton, Winfree and Tarrant. (2011). "How Many Flowering Plants are Pollinated by Animals?" *Oikos, 120*, 3.

https://www.ncbi.nlm.nih.gov/pmc/articles/PMC8396518/
- Schmotzer, C. and Ellis, K. (2014). "Bees, Bugs & Blooms." Maryland Native Plant Society. https://www.mdflora.org/Resources/Documents/Handouts/Bees,%20Bugs,%20Blooms,%20top%20plant%20picks,%20MGPSU-1.PDF
- Tallamy, D.W. (2007). *Bringing Nature Home.* Timber Press.

Attributions

Written by Carol A. Heiser, Education Section Manager and Habitat Education Coordinator, VA Department of Game and Inland Fisheries (2015)

- Revised by Nancy Brooks (2021)

Image Attributions

- Figure 18-1: Mulch, herbaceous plants. Johnson, Devon. 2022. CC BY-NC-SA 4.0.
- Figure 18-2: Habitat diagram. Virginia Cooperative Extension. 2020. From "Backyard Wildlife Habitats" 426-070 (SPES-247P)
- Figure 18-3: Extension Master Gardeners build a lasagna garden. Toler, Linda. 2022. CC BY-NC-SA 4.0.
- Figure 18-4: Hope Garden design. Toler, Linda. 2022. CC BY-NC-SA 4.0.
- Figure 18-5: Rock garden. Johnson, Devon. 2022. CC BY-NC-SA 4.0. Includes "Frog green amphibian animal nature." 2017. Josethestoryteller on Pixabay. Adapted from "Living With Wildlife" Figure 3. by Jenifer Rees. Washington Department of Fish and Wildlife.
- Figure 18-6: Eastern bluebird house. Johnson, Devon. 2022. CC BY-NC-SA 4.0.
- Figure 18-7: Bat box. "Bat box in Jamaica Bay Wildlife Refuge." 2017. Rhododendrites. Wikimedia. CC BY-SA 4.0
- Figure 18-8: Virginia's poisonous snakes, Johnson Devon. 2022. Includes "Virginia Living Museum in Newport News, Va." 2016. Chesapeake Bay Program. Flickr. CC BY-NC 2.0, "8125." 2005. Centers for Disease Control. Public Domain. "8162." 2005. Centers for Disease Control. Public Domain.

CHAPTER 19: VIRGINIA NATIVE PLANTS

Chapter Contents

- 8 Reasons to Plant Native Plants
- Virginia's History of Native Plants
- What is a Native Plant?
- Native Plants Outside of Academia
- Natives: Why Now?
- The Flora of Virginia
- Choosing Native Plants to Match Your Site
- Going Native, but to What Degree?
- Why Are Native Plants Important?
- Virginia Invasives: 8 More Reasons to Plant Native Plants
- Additional Resources

If you're becoming an Extension Master Gardener, you almost certainly are aware of native plants. If you've feasted your eyes on the fall foliage on the Skyline Drive, gasped at the beauty of the white trilliums and other spring ephemerals at the G. Richard Thompson Wildlife Management Area in Fauquier, Warren, and Clarke counties, walked the Nancy Larrick Crosby Native Plant Trail at Blandy Experimental Farm at the State Arboretum of Virginia in Boyce, or spent time any of the many national and state parks and forests and natural area preserves, you have hit upon some prime viewing area for plants native to Virginia.

Chances are, you also know what sets native plants apart. You know they are part of Virginia's history, its cultural and natural heritage, and its native ecology. You understand that those special plant-viewing sites are set aside in response to an array of threats to Virginia native plants and habitats, and it wouldn't be surprising if you wanted to make sure you had natives in your own garden or landscape.

Using natives doesn't only incorporate the wonder of having them around us. In selecting natives for spaces and places and in ensuring before purchase that their needs will be met at the place planned, you make a biological connection with and a commitment to the plants, natural communities, interactions, and ecology. It truly is conservation in action, whatever the degree of "going native." In light of habitat destruction and the climate crisis, when you use native plants, you help meet the needs of native animals, from insects and other invertebrates to birds, amphibians, reptiles, and mammals. You provide habitat and can help reconnect natural lands that have been severed from one another as humans have cleared land for myriad purposes. In using native plants, you can replace or repair some of what has been lost or damaged and help it look great at the same time. As you envision a bright future for native plants, you feel the momentum of this change and that you are on the cusp of a time when even larger commercial nurseries will prominently label and display native plants, getting them to a larger, more aware market.

Before you select plants, explore the meaning of **native plant**. Learn about the study of Virginia natives, how to find out what is native to Virginia and specific counties, and which plants might best suit your own piece of Virginia.

8 Reasons to Plant Native Plants

1. They're beautiful and can often be substituted for nonnative standbys.

Native plants are beautiful and can give the effects wanted in home gardens, yards, or landscapes, or in those of a client or project leader. The design can be as formal or as natural as desired, as long as the plants' needs are met, just as is done with the nonnative plants commonly used. The slightly fragrant wild azalea, or pinxterflower (*Rhododendron periclymenoides*), is a great choice for the azalea slot in the moister parts of a yard, and it's native to all but Virginia's four westernmost counties.

Figure 19-1: Pinxter azalea, *Rhododendron periclymenoides*.

2. They're adapted to the native climate.

It may be self-evident, but it's still worth pointing out that native plants evolved in the places to which they are native, so they're better adapted to those conditions, such as rainfall and temperature, than are many garden-variety nonnatives, requiring less watering and other subsidies.

Figure 19-2: Eastern prickly pear cactus, *Opuntia humifusa*, is Virginia's only native cactus.

3. They provide food and habitat for native animals with which they evolved.

Oak trees (*Quercus* spp.) are the main host of the oak treehopper, *Platycotis vitata*, a true bug. While the treehopper relies on the oak, birds and insectivorous insects prey on the leafhoppers. Therefore oak trees support the ecosystem, providing food for leafhoppers which in turn provide food for our native bird population.

Figure 19-3: Nymphs of the oak tree hopper, *Platycotis vitata*, cluster on a branch.

Figure 19-4: Wild turkeys do best in a mixed-hardwood forest.

4. They're part of Virginia's natural heritage.

The wild turkey —first runner-up for national bird—has come back from dangerously low populations little more than a decade ago. Not so strictly allied to a type of plant as is the oak treehopper, turkeys do best in a mixed-hardwood forest that promises lots of acorns, nuts, and fruits, with some younger trees and shrubs for cover.

5. They can bridge fragments of natural habitats.

Natives are the choice for restoring sites such as salt marshes and areas disturbed by construction. When used in the yard, they aren't just landscaping; they're helping heal over natural habitats fragmented by the usual human activities of home and road building and achieving a larger contiguous expanse that appeals more to native animals. If you need to replace a fallen nonnative tree, consider planting a white oak (*Quercus alba*), native to every Virginia county. Oaks provide habitat and food for many, many animals, from herbivores to birds feeding nestlings to acorn-eaters.

Figure 19-5: White oak, *Quercus alba*, is native to every Virginia county.

Figure 19-6: Extension Master Gardeners work together to teach the public about horticulture.

6. They introduce us to a new set of like-minded folks.

Native plants bring together like-minded people interested in horticulture and the environment. There are many ways to get involved, including joining groups like the Extension Master Gardener program or Master Naturalists, which offer programming and volunteer opportunities to expand awareness of and access to Virginia native plants. Attend meetings, programs, workshops, native-plant sales, and field trips. Learn from one other!

Figure 19-7: Native plants evolved to grow in our native soils, making them a natural choice for your landscape.

7. They fit in with organic and thrifty gardening.

In growing native plants, gardeners use few if any pesticides and chemical fertilizers. If plants are matched to the right sites, water is rarely needed after the first season as the plants get established. Native plants that replace traditional lawns require no mowing, resulting in less noise, less exhaust, and less runoff. That helps everybody, from our neighbors to the pollinators and other inhabitants of the ecosystem.

8. They reconnect gardening with ecology.

You know almost innately not to plant tender, water-loving plants in full sun on gravel and not to plant annual sunflowers in a secluded, shady nook in your yard. Natives have needs too, and one must consider what kind of habitats a site provides, such as moisture, sunlight, and soil, to pick plants that are a good fit for such spots. Forcing them to try to make do in a less than ideal place is rarely successful without a lot of constant care. If you're planting the white wood aster (*Eurybia divaricata*), the ecology's in the name: give it a semi-shady to shady, maybe woodsy, spot for best results.

Virginia's History of Native Plants

Figure 19-8: White wood aster, *Eurybia divaricata*, is native to many Virginia counties (though not the easternmost areas of the commonwealth).

Virginians have always been aware of native plants. Indigenous peoples knew them inside and out, relying on them for food, medicine, textiles, utensils, weapons, tools, and construction. English colonists arrived at Jamestown in 1607 and, the next year, were sending back home samples of the pitch and tar extracted from the stately longleaf pine (*Pinus palustris*) they encountered as they explored the northern reaches of its range. These products proved vital in waterproofing ships' timbers, and the wood was perfect for house building.

Colonists paid attention to plants, giving them Anglicized names, while also learning the names the Indigenous peoples used:

> "[...] American Indians had been observing and using Virginia plants for thousands of years before European settlers arrived, and their contributions to modern plant knowledge came down to us embedded not only in herbal remedies and plant lore but also in plant names of Indian origin like Hickory, Chinquapin, and Pipsissewa. And it was with information gleaned from American Indians that European explorers enriched their first descriptions of Virginia plants" (Hugo and Ware 2012).

The richness of the plant life in the Virginia colony appealed to naturalists, who began painstakingly studying them. They collected and preserved them by pressing and drying, keeping track of where they had been growing, describing habitats and habits in detail. Naming and inventorying these plants helped the Crown evaluate what resources the colony's flora offered.

Figure 19-9: Spotted wintergreen, *Chimaphila maculata*, is native to every Virginia county.

The plants of an area make up its flora, and the animals make up its fauna. A published compendium of information on those plants is also called a flora. Virginia had the first "flora" for the so-called New World. Based on the plant collections and descriptions of John Clayton, clerk of Gloucester County, the two-volume *Flora Virginica* was first published in 1739 and 1742. Carolus Linnaeus, who developed the binomial system of nomenclature, provided publication and naming assistance. Typical of books of science and learning at the time, *Flora Virginica* was written primarily in Latin, with just a single illustration: a map of what Clayton had explored in the colony, clearly based on Captain John Smith's well-known map. A second edition, combining the two volumes of the first, was published in 1762. Other than some regional floras and plant lists, *Flora Virginica* would remain our only flora until the publication of *Flora of Virginia* (Weakley et al. 2012) in 2012, exactly 250 years later.

What is a Native Plant?

Flora of Virginia defines **native plant** as a species that was growing in Virginia at the time of European contact. Nonnatives are those that have been introduced, on purpose or inadvertently, since then and have become naturalized here; they manage to reproduce and persist in the wild without the help of humans.

The Virginia Department of Conservation's Natural Heritage Program defines native plants as:

> "[...] those that occur in the region in which they evolved. Plants evolve over geologic time in response to physical and biotic processes characteristic of a region: the climate, soils, timing of rainfall, drought, and frost; and interactions with the other species inhabiting the local community. Thus, native plants possess certain traits that make them uniquely adapted to local conditions, providing a practical and ecologically valuable alternative for landscaping, conservation, and restoration projects, and as livestock forage. In addition, native plants can match the finest cultivated plants in beauty, while often surpassing nonnatives in ruggedness and resistance to drought, insects and disease." (2022)

The idea that native plants are "natural" is inescapable, yet it is not always easy to determine whether a species is native to a spot. It is incorrect, or at least not too meaningful, to say that a plant is native to the United States, to the East, or even to Virginia, because many species are much more localized, spotty, or even spatially disjunct in their distribution. Some species are native in one county but have been introduced to and thus are nonnative in another county. For others, nativity cannot be verified. Of the 3,348 species or infraspecific taxa covered in the December 2020 major update to the Flora of Virginia App, only about 79% (2,648) are native to Virginia, while 753 are nonnative (and the others not known). Fortunately, county-by-county maps are available showing present knowledge of nativity or nonnativity for each Virginia species that grows in the wild.

As we garden with native plants, we may be conscientious about planting only those species that are deemed native to the county we'll be planting in. For this reason, we need to know whether a plant is, or is not, native to that site. This requires a little research using existing tools.

Case Study: Southern Magnolia, Nonnative? How Occurrence and Nativity are Documented

The iconic southern magnolia is not native to Virginia. *Magnolia grandiflora* is widely seen in the state, and you may feel that the grandeur and perfume of this lovely evergreen tree, celebrated in book, film, and song, is almost intrinsic to life. Though some sources say it's native in the extreme southeastern corner of Virginia, the Flora of Virginia (Weakley et al. 2012, 2020) and the Digital Atlas of the Virginia Flora (Virginia Botanical Associates 2022) do not. In the Flora, if an asterisk precedes a species' name, it denotes a nonnative. The possibility that the southern magnolia is native to Virginia is tenuous at best, and voucher specimens are known for only a few counties, and those trees had escaped from cultivation.

Figure 19-10: Beautiful, but not a Virginia native: *Magnolia grandiflora*.

A **voucher specimen** is a specimen of a species that depicts clearly its most important physical characteristics and structures. This helps in identifying specimens collected by others and in other regions. It's a type of study specimen and so has been collected, identified, and preserved by careful drying, and mounted on a standard herbarium sheet of archival paper with a label presenting the details of its collection: collector, date, exact location, and habitat. Once such a specimen has been accessioned by a qualified **herbarium** (an organized and catalogued collection of such specimens, usually at a university or a museum) it is known as a voucher specimen of the plant.

Some native magnolias

Virginia has some spectacular native magnolias. Here are four, with photographs and range maps adapted from those of the Digital Atlas of the Virginia Flora. Green shading means that a voucher specimen exists for the species and that the species is native to that county (in the Digital Atlas, red dots are used for this purpose).

Cucumber-tree, *Magnolia acuminata*

Figure 19-11: Cucumber-tree, *Magnolia acuminata* range covers the western half of Virginia.

Fraser magnolia, *M. fraseri*

Figure 19-12: Fraser magnolia, *M. fraseri* range covers the western panhandle of Virginia and Highland County.

Umbrella magnolia, *M. tripetala*

Figure 19-13: Umbrella magnolia, *M. tripetala* range covers the western panhandle, west-central Virginia, and some of the eastern-most counties.

Sweetbay, *M. virginiana*

Figure 19-14: Sweetbay, M. virginiana range covers the eastern half of Virginia.

Nativity and Distribution by County: Range Maps

Maps showing county occurrence and nativity of species are provided and updated regularly by the Virginia Botanical Associates, which manages the Digital Atlas of the Virginia Flora. Each dot in a county indicates that a voucher specimen exists for the species from that county and, by its color, whether the species is native. Updates take into account new vouchers.

- If there is no dot in a county, the species hasn't been documented for that county, native or not.
- If a species has a red dot in a county, it is native there; and
- If a species has a blue dot in a county, it is naturalized (defined below) but nonnative.

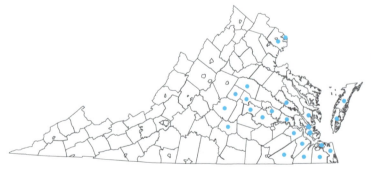

Figure 19-15: Introduced range of southern magnolia, *Magnolia grandiflora* L.

People have planted southern magnolia possibly in every county in Virginia, but in most counties, they have not yet been found to have escaped cultivation. All the dots in the map for the southern magnolia, above, are blue (indicating introduced status). The voucher specimens did not represent a tree clearly in cultivation or a planted landscape tree but one that had naturalized from a seed dispersed from a cultivated tree by a bird or other animal.

Naturalized describes a nonnative plant that can reproduce and persist in nature without human help. The southern magnolia is naturalized in the blue-dotted counties in its range map. About its habitat, the Digital Atlas says, "Much planted, escaped, and naturalized in upland forests and swamps, especially near urban areas and in southeastern Virginia. Infrequent in the Coastal Plain and outer Piedmont; locally common in the Back Bay region."

Native Plants Outside of Academia

Observing and studying nature were nothing new, but outside of academics, appreciation of native plants didn't pick up steam until the 19th century, as new botanical gardens and field guides brought ordinary citizens up close and personal with American native plants. A result was concern, even then, about the damage human activity was doing to the natural world. This led, in part, to the founding of the National Audubon Society in 1905.

Field guides came into their own between the world wars and supplied more information on nomenclature and taxonomy, physical attributes, ecology, and ranges. As the native-plant audience grew, guides became progressively more scientific. Many people can trace their interest in wildflowers and, in particular, native plants, to these guidebooks. They instilled in us the desire to know the plants, to be able to identify them, and to take pride in knowing that natives grow here without anyone's effort. Yet concern about overcollecting and other damage grew.

Natives: Why Now?

In the United States, interest in preserving wildflowers revved up around 1900. That June, William Trelease, director of the Missouri Botanical Garden, spoke in New York to mark his stepping down as vice president of the botany section of the American Association for the Advancement of Science, of which he was past president. He was also the first president of the Botanical Society of America. In closing, he pointedly mentioned the need for "the protection and preservation in every possible way of our native and natural vegetation," calling it "a matter of prime interest to all botanists, since it will probably affect the very prosecution of many of their studies before the next century shall have been closed." He added that this was vital as well to "taxonomists, systematists, physiologists, and those studying plant morphology" (Trelease 1900).

Beginning in the 1950s and gaining momentum in the 1960s and 1970s, the environmental movement resulted in laws and policies designed to rein in and clean up pollution and protect (or in the case of most plants, at least designate) threatened and endangered species. Agencies and organizations were formed or grew to study and better care for the environment. Scientists and agencies whose goal it is to conserve and restore native habitats and the organisms that live in them need easy access to information about those habitats and organisms. As the soil, climate, and other physical features provide the habitats for plant growth, the plants provide the habitats for animals and other plants. Plants are also the basis of food webs, creating the building blocks of nutrients from sunlight, carbon dioxide, other atmospheric gases, and chemical components in the soil. Conservation became more and more allied to ecology, the focus not only on individual species but the variety of habitats, and the range of types of ecological communities that both attract and result from the living things in that area.

The Flora of Virginia

Virginia needed a modern volume describing its plant life and providing a tool for people involved in the conservation of plants and environmental protection. The Virginia Academy of Science was created in 1923 and just three years later formed its Committee on Virginia Flora. It kept alive the idea for a new flora but never managed to produce such a work. The massive amount of effort that would make it possible was finally mustered by the Flora of Virginia Project, formed in 2001 with the considerable logistical and scientific support of the Virginia Department of Conservation and Recreation's Division of Natural Heritage (the Virginia Natural Heritage Program). With funding from the academy, the Virginia Native Plant Society and its chapters and members, many individuals, foundations, and organizations, including many garden clubs, affiliates of both the Garden Club of Virginia and the Virginia Federation of Garden Clubs, the project became reality. Gronovius and Clayton's remarkable book was finally supplanted in 2012, exactly 250 years after the publication of its second edition, by the new and massive Flora of Virginia (Weakley et al. 2012).

The print Flora covers 3,164 species and infraspecific taxa (that is, subspecies and botanical varieties, referred to as "species" here for simplicity's sake) and includes 1,400 illustrations commissioned for the work as aids to identification, as well as keys for identification. Species descriptions include information on habitat, status, phenology (blooming and fruiting times), and botanical and ecological comments to further aid in understanding and identification.

The Flora Project also created an app for smart phones and tablets, making the content of the book accessible to more people, as well as a series of online educational modules (https://floraofvirginia.org/education/flora-educational-modules/).

Be Nice to Natives: Don't Collect Them or Their Parts

Once you identify a plant that has caught your eye and suits your yard or garden, your task becomes to find it for sale at a nursery, since it's better not to collect from the wild; we don't want to love our native plants to death. Sustainability is more than a buzzword; it's the banner under which we expand our appreciation of native plants and their use. Sustainable plants are those capable of continuing to thrive in their native habitat. Many things can undercut sustainability. Apart from the complex threats of human development, the most obvious infractions are collecting native plants or their flowers, seeds, or rootstocks, or, worse, digging the plants out of the wild and transplanting them to your site. This should not be done. Plants are under too many other threats to face affronts from plant lovers. The flowers and seeds are needed in their native habitat, both clearly essential for propagation,

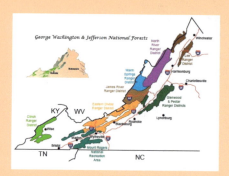

Figure 19-16: National forest areas in Virginia: You cannot remove plant material from protected areas like national forests.

continuation of populations, and the establishment, through seed dispersal, of new populations. All parts of the plants support wildlife, from bees, butterflies, and moths and their larvae to bats, birds, and other vertebrates that depend on plants for food, cover, shelter, nesting materials, and habitat. Plants protect other parts of the environment as well, from slowing or preventing erosion to serving as riparian buffers, filtering and retarding storm runoff from terrestrial habitats into aquatic ones.

"It is never acceptable to dig out wild plant material in nature," says Ashley Moulton, who runs a native-plant operation in Richmond. Moulton formerly coordinated the Chesterfield Extension Master Gardener unit and serves on the boards of the Virginia Native Plant Society and the Flora of Virginia Project. Moulton states "It is illegal to harvest any type of plant material from protected lands, even if they are open to the public." Unfortunately, laws do not prohibit collecting plants on other property. You must remember that if you were to collect on someone else's land without permission, you could be held liable for trespassing. Instead of just following the letter of the law, rely on your own ethics: buy from conscientious sellers who collect and propagate native plants using procedures that encourage sustainability.

Be a squeaky wheel: As you window-shop for natives at any nursery, ask questions. Nurseries are increasingly coming on board with native plants. You want to be sure that they are sourcing their native plants and seed with sustainability in mind. Ask managers where they get their native plants or seeds. In a larger nursery, ask them to show you their natives, and if they don't have any, that's an opening for a conversation.

Learn in the field: Just because you won't be collecting, picking, or digging your own natives doesn't mean you can't enjoy native plants in the wild. It's a good idea to do so because in observing living plants, you get a better idea of their habitats and habits, essential for matching plants to desired sites. Not only do you learn the plants and where they live, you begin to hone your instincts as to which plants like what kinds of places and what plants you'd eventually like to find in a nursery.

You are lucky today in that most people have a virtually weightless, high-quality camera in their pocket: a phone. "Take only pictures, leave only footprints" remains a sensible adage to follow as you explore natives in natural places. Pictures give you a nice permanent record of those beautiful plants. Get close-ups of flowers, leaf edges, seed pods, and fruits. It's also good to back off a bit for a habit shot, illustrating height, posture, and habitat, which you can try to replicate if you buy the plant at a nursery for your garden.

Another popular activity that will take you into the habitats is field trips, including those involving nature journaling. A variety of classes are available, and they usually involve drawing or painting some aspect of a plant or a spot, to which the artist adds notes of observation around the drawing, both narrating the art and complementing it. Some simply sketch or paint, while others only write. The point is to heighten our observational powers about what plants there are, what they look like, how they grow, what animals use them, and where they thrive, all while recalling one's own yard or project.

Choosing Native Plants to Match Your Site

"To a very considerable extent," wrote Robert S. Lemmon in 1940, "success in the growing of native plants in a more or less cultivated state hinges on the application of plain common sense, plus the realization that the great majority of the more desirable species have definite likes and dislikes to which we must defer" (Lemmon 1940). Lemmon was writing in *Wild Flower* on "Plants and Planting Methods for the Native Garden." A naturalist and writer, in 1938 he founded the horticulture magazine *Real Garden* and from 1943 to 1951 was editor-in-chief of *The Home Garden*.

It is common among gardeners to say that "this plant likes partial shade or that one likes wet feet," but what if we considered a semantic shift that better fits an ecological approach? What if we said that a plant's "habitat should provide at least partial shade," or "habitat should not provide soil that is bone dry for extended periods"? The plants are at the mercy of their habitat, and habitat is what you are providing, even if in a "more or less cultivated state." Make sure plants will get what they need before you buy and plant them. This will make them easier to keep.

As with any plants, you may select a native for many reasons: beauty, desired color, appearance, flowering time, leaf shape etc., but first and foremost, it must be chosen to fit a habitat that is conducive to its thriving. Does it need acid soil or alkaline soil; full sun, part sun, or shade? Is it a beach species that you bought and planted in a spot in the mountains?

Siting and Planting Natives

Lemmon gives good advice: "At the very outset you should make a thorough study of the place you propose to work with," he wrote. This is nothing new for gardeners, but it's worth even more serious consideration when you are planting natives. One point is that you want to let the environment and not humans meet the lion's share of their needs.

Once you have explored your site well, you would do well to test the soil from different areas that appear to be distinct from one another. "The physical and the chemical character of the soil may vary sharply in different sections of even a decidedly small area," wrote Lemmon. If they are quite different, there could be different microhabitats that could multiply your prospects for diversity.

A soil test will tell you the pH of the soil of interest, as well as levels of nutrients, including phosphorus, potassium, calcium, magnesium, zinc, manganese, copper, iron, and boron, as well as the soil's ability to retain nutrients. You can change some things by adding chemicals, but if it's natural you're after, honor that and pick a plant that will like your soil as it is.

Soil sample boxes and information forms are available at Virginia Cooperative Extension offices. Analyses are done at the Virginia Tech Soil Testing Laboratory, and results are provided by email.

Resources for Choosing Native Plants

Once you have assessed your site, it's time to decide what natives you want, but it may feel more complicated than with mainstream plants. Because natives are slow getting into the retail stream, the labeling of native plants can be variable or include only the plant name. You should not depend on finding detailed siting and planting instructions on labels like you're used to with big-box-store plants, nor is it always a simple task to find cultivation tips in gardening books. You are fortunate in Virginia that a number of organizations have taken on the task of helping you discover which natives best match your site. Here are some of those sources.

Digital Atlas of the Virginia Flora: Virginia Botanical Associates

The habitat and status information, the county-by-county range maps, and most of the photographs you see in the Flora of Virginia app have been provided by the Virginia Botanical Associates, a consortium of Virginia herbarium curators and botanists who document the occurrence of plants and their habitats around the state. It presents and regularly updates this information in its Digital Atlas of the Virginia Flora (http://vaplantatlas.org/) (Virginia Botanical Associates 2022).

Native Plants for Conservation, Restoration, and Landscaping Project

Figure 19-17: The Native Plants for Conservation, Restoration, and Landscaping Project has produced numerous brochures on Virginia natives.

The Native Plants for Conservation, Restoration, and Landscaping Project (https://www.dcr.virginia.gov/natural-heritage/nativeplants) is a collaboration between the Virginia Natural Heritage program and a number of organizations invested in plant- and nature-related issues. A series of helpful brochures, available as PDFs at that address, was produced listing likely natives for planting in the Coastal Plain, Piedmont, and mountains. You will also find information on planting and restoring grasslands and planting or restoring native vegetation in the riparian zone (riverbanks and stream banks).

Plant Virginia Natives

Aiming to increase awareness, availability, and use of Virginia's native plants, the Plant Virginia Natives Initiative was begun in 2011 by the Virginia Coastal Zone Management Program, part of a federal–state program of the National Oceanic and Atmospheric Administration (NOAA) managed here by the Virginia Department of Environmental Quality. Goals were to make messaging about natives more consistent and to increase the efficiency of using these resources. The Virginia Department of Wildlife Resources became a co-chair of the partnership two years later to help fund and expand the program's reach beyond the coastal zone.

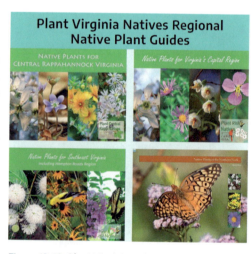

Figure 19-18: Plant Virginia Natives regional native plant guides are a great resource for identifying the native plants of your area.

A key focus of the initiative has been to create regional native-plant marketing campaigns and guides. As of 2022, there are now nine such regional campaigns, with more in the planning stages. Seven have published a guide: Northern Virginia, Upper Piedmont, Richmond and environs, the Central Rappahannock region, the Northern Neck, the Eastern Shore, and Southeast Virginia. Southern Piedmont and Southwest Virginia are developing their guides.

Not only do the guides provide great advice on using natives, but they also beautifully illustrate many natives available for the regions, giving specific information that will be invaluable for matching plants with your site. Habitat needs are part of the species description in the Capital Region guide and are presented in a separate matrix in the Upper Piedmont guide. The guide for the Capital Region gives a photograph and description of a species, with its relationships to pollinators and other insects, and it also gives a list of points that will help you determine whether there's a spot at your site that's like the plant's native habitat. The Upper Piedmont guide offers habitat information in a matrix, directing readers to the descriptions

CHAPTER 19: VIRGINIA NATIVE PLANTS

and images. The other guides provide information in similar formats. For more information on the regional campaigns, or to download PDFs of the guides now available, start at: https://www.plantvirginianatives.org/virginia-regional-native-plant-campaigns-guides.

Virginia Natural Heritage Program Virginia Native Plant Finder

The online plant finder (https://www.dcr.virginia.gov/natural-heritage/native-plants-finder) lets you search by scientific or common name and returns data in a grid. You can also use a more detailed search form and provide information about your site, and it returns a matrix of species that fit. Each species links to its page in the Digital Atlas of the Virginia Flora, which further describes habitat and status, gives a range map, and provides color photographs.

The *Flora of Virginia*: Flora of Virginia Project

What if you like a plant you saw at a native-plant nursery or that you know from a field trip? Before you decide to buy one, you can use the Flora to see how it would fit your site. If you are considering buying a wax myrtle, *Morella cerifera*, you can find it in the Flora and read its description to see if you have the site for it. Both the Flora of Virginia book and mobile app are good resources for identifying and learning more about Virginia's native plants.

Table 19-1: Virginia Native Favorites

Here are some popular Virginia native plants for home gardeners!

Scientific name	Common name	Family, scientific name	Family, common name	Light	Moisture	Native Range	Conditions
Sambucus canadensis var. *canadensis*	Common elderberry	Adoxaceae	Moschatel family	Part shade	Wet	Whole state	Damp to wet soil in fields, clearings, ditches, roadsides, floodplain forests, and swamps;
Rhus glabra	Smooth sumac	Anacardiaceae	Cashew family	Full sun, part shade, shade	Dry	Nearly whole state	Old fields, clearings, fencerows, and roadsides; occasionally in natural woodlands.
Asimina triloba	Pawpaw	Annonaceae	Custard-apple family	Full sun, part shade, shade	Medium	Nearly whole state	Well-drained floodplain forests, mesic to occasionally dry upland forests, wet flatwoods, and swamp hummocks.
Asclepias syriaca	Common milkweed	Apocynaceae	Dogbane family	Full sun	Medium	Whole state	Fields, pastures, roadsides, and other open, disturbed habitats.
Asclepias tuberosa var. *tuberosa*	Butterfly-weed	Apocynaceae	Dogbane family	Full sun	Dry to medium	Whole state	Dry woodlands, clearings, fields, pastures, and roadsides.
Ilex verticillata	Winterberry	Aquifoliaceae	Holly family	Full sun, part shade	Medium to wet	Nearly whole state	Alluvial swamps, seepage swamps, bogs, ponds, and depression swamps; occasionally in well-drained floodplain forests and mesic upland forests.
Arisaema triphyllum ssp. *triphyllum*	Common jack-in-the-pulpit	Araceae	Arum family	Shade	Medium	Whole state	Mesic upland forests, floodplain forests, and swamp hummocks.

Table 19-1: Virginia Native Favorites (continued)

Scientific name	Common name	Family, scientific name	Family, common name	Light	Moisture	Native Range	Conditions
Conoclinium coelestinum	Ageratum	Asteraceae or Compositae	Aster or composite family	Full sun, part shade	Medium	Nearly whole state	Floodplain forests, alluvial swamps, moist to wet meadows, old fields, clearings, and other disturbed, open or shaded sites.
Eurybia divaricata	White wood aster	Asteraceae or Compositae	Aster or composite family	Part shade, shade	Dry to medium	Whole state except eastern counties	Mesic to dry upland forests, woodlands, shaded outcrops, well-drained floodplain forests, seepage swamps, and fens.
Eutrochium purpureum var. *purpureum*	Sweet-scented joe-pye-weed	Asteraceae or Compositae	Aster or composite family	Full sun, part shade	Medium	Nearly whole state	Mesic to dry-mesic upland forests; less frequently in dry forests, woodlands, barrens, well-drained floodplain forests, seepage swamps, and fens.
Helenium autumnale	Common sneezeweed	Asteraceae or Compositae	Aster or composite family	Full sun, part shade	Dry to medium	Nearly whole state	Bogs, fens, seeps, riverbanks and bars, floodplain forests, freshwater and oligohaline tidal marshes, tidal swamps, wet fields and meadows; also in high-elevation grassy balds.
Solidago nemoralis var. *nemoralis*	Gray goldenrod	Asteraceae or Compositae	Aster or composite family	Full sun, part shade, shade	Dry	Nearly whole state	Open forests, woodlands, barrens, clearings, old fields, and road banks; most characteristic of dry soils, but occasionally occurring in seasonally saturated or alternately wet and dry hardpan soils, especially in the Coastal Plain.
Podophyllum peltatum	Mayapple	Berberidaceae	Bayberry family	Part shade, shade	Medium	Whole state	Mesic to dry-mesic upland forests, well-drained floodplain forests, and various moist, disturbed habitats.
Campsis radicans	Trumpet-creeper	Bignoniaceae	Bignonia family	Full sun, part shade	Medium	Nearly whole state	Floodplain forests, swamp forests (alluvial, nonriverine, tidal, and maritime), maritime forests, dune woodlands and scrub, various upland forests, rocky and sandy woodlands, old fields, and fencerows.
Mertensia virginica	Virginia bluebells	Boraginaceae	Borage family	Full sun, part shade	Medium	Central VA and many western counties	Rich soils of well-drained floodplain forests, low-elevation cove forests, and mesic slope forests.
Lobelia cardinalis	Cardinal flower	Campanulaceae	Bellflower family	Full sun, part shade	Medium to wet	Whole state	Floodplain forests, alluvial swamps, seepage swamps, maritime swamps, tidal swamps, tidal freshwater and oligohaline marshes, wet meadows, ditches, and low roadsides.
Stellaria pubera	Star chickweed	Caryophyllaceae	Pink family	Shade	Medium	Whole state except eastern counties	Mesic to dry forests; most abundant on, but not restricted to, base-rich substrates.
Cornus florida	Flowering dogwood	Cornaceae	Dogwood family	Full sun, part shade	Medium	Whole state	Common understory tree in a wide variety of mesic to dry upland forests; also in borders, clearings, old fields, and well-drained floodplains.

Table 19-1: Virginia Native Favorites (continued)

Scientific name	Common name	Family, scientific name	Family, common name	Light	Moisture	Native Range	Conditions
Juniperus virginiana var. *virginiana*	Eastern redcedar	Cupressaceae	Cypress family	Full sun, part shade, shade	Dry	Whole state	Dry upland forests, rocky woodlands, barrens, old fields, fencerows, and sandy soils of the Coastal Plain.
Carex stricta	Tussock sedge	Cyperaceae	Sedge family	Full sun, part shade	Wet	Nearly whole state except southwest mountains and southwest piedmont	In a wide range of wetlands, including bogs, fens, seeps, swamps (all types), wet meadows, beaver ponds, depression ponds, freshwater to oligohaline tidal marshes, and floodplain forests
Scirpus cyperinus	Woolgrass	Cyperaceae	Sedge family	Full sun, part shade	Wet	Nearly whole state	Freshwater and oligohaline tidal marshes, tidal swamps, alluvial swamps (particularly in seasonally flooded sloughs), maritime swamps, interdune swales and ponds, depression swamps and ponds, bogs, fens, seeps, impoundments, beaver wetlands, ditches, wet meadows, and other wet disturbed habitats
Diospyros virginiana	Common persimmon	Ebenaceae	Ebony family	Full sun, part shade	Dry to medium	Nearly whole state	Weedy tree in old fields, fencerows, and roadsides; also scattered in a range of natural habitats, including swamp forests, depression ponds, dune woodlands and scrub, rocky woodlands, and the understory of mesic to dry upland forests.
Kalmia latifolia	Mountain laurel	Ericaceae	Heath family	Part shade	Medium	Whole state	Mesic to dry, acidic forests, woodlands, and shrub balds; often in sandy, rocky, or organic-rich soils; less typically in bogs and seepage wetlands. More or less common throughout, except in the outer and far se.
Rhododendron periclymenoides	Wild azalea	Ericaceae	Heath family	Full sun, part shade	Medium	Nearly whole state	Mesic to dry, acidic forests, seepage swamp hummocks, and stream banks.
Fagus grandifolia	American beech	Fagaceae	Beech family	Full sun, part shade	Medium	Whole state	Mesic to dry-mesic upland forests, very well-drained floodplain terraces, and bluffs; most common on well-drained, acidic, nutrient-poor soils but found in a variety of soils.
Hamamelis virginiana	Witch hazel	Hamamelidaceae	Witch hazel family	Part shade	Medium	Whole state	Mesic to dry upland forests, occurring in a wide range of habitats, elevations, and community types.
Hydrangea arborescens	Wild hydrangia	Hydrangeaceae	Hydrangea family	Part shade	Medium	Nearly whole state	Mesic to dry, usually rocky forests, boulder fields, stream banks, cliffs, and outcrops.
Achillea millefolium	Common yarrow	Asteraceae or Compositae	Aster or composite family	Full sun	Dry to medium	Whole state	Ubiquitous in fields, meadows, roadsides, clearings, mesic to dry upland forests, and other habitats.

Table 19-1: Virginia Native Favorites (continued)

Scientific name	Common name	Family, scientific name	Family, common name	Light	Moisture	Native Range	Conditions
Hypericum prolificum	Shrubby St. John's-wort	Hypericaceae	St. John's-wort family	Full sun, part shade	Medium	Nearly whole state	Dry, open forests, rocky woodlands, barrens, clearings, riverside prairies and outcrops, often on mafic or moderately to strongly calcareous substrates; also in rich floodplain forests, mafic and calcareous fens, and interdune swales.
Sisyrinchium angustifolium	Narrow-leaved blue-eyed-grass	Iridaceae	Iris family	Full sun, part shade	Medium	Whole state	Mesic to dry upland forests, woodlands, fields, meadows, and floodplain forests.
Claytonia virginica	Spring beauty	Montiaceae	Montia family	Part shade	Medium	Nearly whole state	Well-drained floodplain forests, mesic and dry-mesic upland forests, and old fields; most characteristic of, but not restricted to, base-rich soils.
Osmundastrum cinnamomeum var. cinnamomeum	Cinnamon fern	Osmundaceae	Royal fern family	Part shade, shade	Medium to wet	Nearly whole state	Seepage swamps, wet flatwoods, bogs, fens, pocosins, floodplain forests, alluvial and tidal swamps; usually in acidic, often peaty soils but also in base-rich soils of mafic seepage wetlands; occasionally in low-elevation mesic forests and frequently in Northern Red Oak and northern hardwood forests at high elevations.
Sanguinaria canadensis	Bloodroot	Papaveraceae	Poppy family	Part shade, shade	Medium	Nearly whole state	Mesic to dry-mesic upland forests, dry calcareous forests and woodlands, well-drained floodplain forests; most numerous in moderately to strongly base-rich soils.
Chelone glabra	White turtlehead	Plantaginaceae	Plantain family	Part shade	Medium to wet	Nearly whole state	Seeps and seepage swamps, alluvial and tidal swamps, floodplain forests, stream banks, bogs, fens, and wet meadows.
Eragrostis spectabilis	Purple lovegrass	Poaceae or Graminae	Grass family	Full sun	Dry to medium	Nearly whole state	Dune grasslands, scrub, and woodlands; interdune swales, river shores and bars, riverside prairies, dry woodlands and barrens, clearings, fields, roadsides, and other open, disturbed habitats.
Adiantum pedatum	Northern maidenhair fern	Pteridaceae	Maidenhair fern family	Part shade, shade	Medium	Nearly whole state	Base-rich soils of cove forests, mesic and dry-mesic slope forests, well-drained floodplain forests, and calcareous ravines in the Coastal Plain; occasionally on mesic or periodically wet calcareous or mafic boulder fields.
Aquilegia canadensis	Wild columbine	Ranunculaceae	Buttercup family	Full sun, part shade	Medium	Nearly whole state	Dry forests, woodlands, barrens, and rock outcrops throughout; shell-marl slopes, bluffs, and shell middens in the Coastal Plain. Although most numerous on subcalcareous, calcareous, and mafic substrates, in the higher mountains it is more tolerant of acidic soils and varied habitats, including mesic to dry-mesic forests, meadows, and roadsides.

Table 19-1: Virginia Native Favorites (continued)

Scientific name	Common name	Family, scientific name	Family, common name	Light	Moisture	Native Range	Conditions
Thalictrum thalictroides	Rue-anemone	Ranunculaceae	Buttercup family	Part shade	Medium	Nearly whole state	Mesic to dry upland forests and well-drained floodplain forests; grows in a variety of soils, but somewhat restricted to base-rich soils in the Coastal Plain.
Aronia arbutifolia	Red chokeberry	Rosaceae	Rose family	Full sun, part shade	Medium	Nearly whole state	Bogs, fens, seeps, seepage swamps, tidal swamps, acidic alluvial swamps, wet flatwoods, pocosins, and borders of depression ponds; occasionally in mesic or even dry upland forests.
Rosa carolina ssp. *carolina*	Carolina rose	Rosaceae	Rose family	Full sun	Medium to wet	Nearly whole state	Dry-mesic to dry (rarely mesic) upland forests, woodlands, barrens, clearings, old fields, pastures, and roadsides.
Rosa palustris	Swamp rose	Rosaceae	Rose family	Full sun	Wet	Nearly whole state	Swamps (all types), tidal freshwater and oligohaline marshes, interdune swales and ponds, bogs, fens, seeps, and old beaver wetlands.
Mitchella repens	Partridge-berry	Rubiaceae	Madder family	Part shade, full shade	Medium	Whole state	Ubiquitous in dry to mesic forests, woodlands, and on hummocks of bottomland forests and swamps.
Viola pubescens	Yellow violet	Violaceae	Violet family	Part shade	Dry	Nearly whole state	Depends on variety

Figure 19-19: Virginia natives for shade include common jack-in-the-pulpit, star chickweed, white wood aster, mayapple, cinnamon fern, bloodroot, northern maidenhair fern, partridge-berry, and rue-anemone.

Going Native, but to What Degree?

As with any plan for a garden or landscape, it's seldom all-or-nothing, and a range of possibilities awaits each gardener. Starting at the low end of the scale, even a yard that is populated entirely from the garden department of a major building-supply store almost certainly has at least some natives in it. Unless the ground was shaved to the subsoil during development, which does happen, the transition to native gardening has probably already begun: trees that escaped felling during construction, others planted early upon occupation, the obligatory dogwood or two (*Cornus* spp.), or a redbud (*Cercis canadensis*). You may find some phlox a friend passed on, not realizing it was native, or a trumpet creeper (*Campsis radicans*) whose demise you have often pondered but luckily never got around to.

Other than such native accidentals, you may well find that your lot is more typically nonnative: tight foundation plantings of traditional but nonnative standbys like Asian azaleas, Chinese hollies, nandinas, and barberries. You may see hedges of privet or Bradford pears, and walls of nonnative wisterias, Japanese honeysuckle, or English ivy. All of this surrounding a manicured monocultural expanse of a nonnative grass.

Start Slow and Small

As you think about how you can make your yard or community more suited to its natural habitat using native plants, you need to plan. It's generally best to start small. Going a little at a time and being selective is a good rule of thumb. Unless you have a big patch of open field to transform into a native wildflower meadow, you may not want to start by trying for total replacement, at least not at the outset. This will also help you to think now about how your planting will affect conditions once things become established.

Figure 19-20: Azaleas surround the border of this garden.

As you go, consult references to learn which are the more invasive or problematic. What if you have a lot of Chinese privet (*Ligustrum sinense*) and boxwood (*Buxus sempervirens*), both nonnative, and wonder which would be better replaced with natives if you could only replace one? Use the Digital Atlas of the Virginia Flora to help you identify which has been introduced in more counties, therefore likely posing a greater risk of escape. For example, when you search for boxwood on the Digital Atlas range map, you see only six widely spaced counties with dots, all blue, indicating nonnative, though not terribly invasive. Chinese privet is a different story, with a blue dot in nearly every county. With masses of bluish-purple berries attractive to birds, the seeds are often dispersed willy-nilly. Boxwoods pose a lesser risk of escape, and it would therefore be better to remove Chinese privet.

You can also look up nonnative species to see if they appear in DCR's invasive plant list (https://www.dcr.virginia.gov/natural-heritage/invsppdflist). Invasive species identified by DCR are given a rank indicating how much of a threat they pose to the ecosystem. Chinese privet has an invasiveness rank of "high" (yet it is still used in the horticulture industry). The choice is clear: the privet goes.

What if you have azaleas all around your house and are interested in finding native replacements. Removing a few is a more cost-effective option, though some people may choose to uproot them all at once. Even replacing a few can contribute to improving the biodiversity of your landscape.

Figure 19-21: *Rhododendron calendulaceum*, flame azalea is a native alternative to Asiatic azaleas.

Virginia has a lot to offer in the native-azalea department, and azaleas are in a familiar genus: *Rhododendron*. As always, though, check the range map to see whether a species is native to your county. Some species have a restricted range or are mapped only in a few counties.

The following are some native replacements for Asiatic azaleas:

- *Rhododendron arborescens*, smooth azalea, sweet azalea
- *Rhododendron atlanticum*, dwarf azalea
- *Rhododendron calendulaceum*, flame azalea
- *Rhododendron catawbiense*, Catawba rhododendron
- *Rhododendron cumberlandense*, Cumberland azalea
- *Rhododendron maximum*, great rhododendron, great laurel
- *Rhododendron periclymenoides*, pinxterflower
- *Rhododendron prinophyllum*, early azalea
- *Rhododendron viscosum* var. *viscosum*, southeastern swamp azalea

Don't forget the rhododendrons' cousin, the mountain laurel, *Kalmia latifolia*, native to every Virginia county.

Warning Internet Searchers

Always be cautious about where you get information online. Not all websites will have correct information on Virginia native. Look for .edu or .gov sources, or use the resources described above. For example, if you were looking for native plants for hedges, Plant NOVA Natives' page on hedges (https://www.plantnovanatives.org/hedges-and-screens) is a reliable option, suggesting:

- *Carpinus caroliniana*, American hornbeam
- *Cornus amomum*, silky dogwood
- *Itea virginica*, Virginia sweetspire
- *Morella cerifera*, wax myrtle
- *Rhus aromatica*, fragrant sumac
- *Rosa carolina*, Carolina rose
- *Rosa virginiana*, Virginia rose

Why Are Native Plants Important?

As gardeners, we can learn how to transform gardens by using more native plants and, in the process, reconnect natural habitats fragmented by human activity. Planting natives can help invite wild animals to breed, nest, develop, and dine in your native-plant-fortified environments.

With increases in human development and expansion of built areas, native habitats have been fragmented into "islands." These islands can be so small as not to provide enough space for some animals' territory, which ensures a breeding pair plenty of room for raising young and foraging. With these islands, species can be so far apart that mating becomes more difficult, opportunities for mating are more scarce, and genetic diversity of the species in that location diminishes.

Figure 19-22: The Carolina chickadees feed their nestlings nutrient-packed caterpillars.

"The negative impact on habitat connectivity due to anthropogenic activities can cause isolation of populations, with consequences on intercrossing between individuals and effective gene flow," wrote Zubaria Waqar and her colleagues, researchers from the Brazilian state of Bahia (Waqar et al. 2021). "According to genetic variation dynamics, over space and time a few genotypes of a population can become dominant over others due to natural selection, genetic drift, and inbreeding."

"When we design our home landscapes, too many of us choose beautiful plants from all over the world, without considering their ability to support life within our local ecosystems," professor and author Doug Tallamy wrote in "The Chickadee's Guide to Gardening" (Tallamy 2015). He tells how he counted the caterpillars on two trees in his neighbor's yard: a Bradford pear (*Pyrus calleryana* 'Bradford'), from Asia, and a young native white oak (*Quercus alba*) of about the same size. On the native oak, he found 419 caterpillars, representing 19 species. On the Bradford pear, he found one inchworm. The next day he found 233 on the oak, of 15 species, and one caterpillar on the nonnative Bradford pear.

He describes the often toxic, or at least unpalatable, chemical defenses plants have developed over millennia. Some species "have evolved to eat oak trees without dying, while others have specialized in native cherries or ashes and so on," Tallamy writes. "But local insects have only just met Bradford pears, in an evolutionary sense, and have not had the time … required to adapt to [the trees'] chemical defenses. And so, Bradford pears stand virtually untouched in my neighbor's yard."

In Tallamy's example of the chickadee, both parents feed their nestlings caterpillars, bringing one to the nest every three minutes. Tallamy calculates that for 14 hours of feeding time a day, for 16 to 18 days before the nestlings fledge, that's 350 to 570 caterpillars a day, depending on the brood size. "So, an incredible 6,000 to 9,000 caterpillars are required to make one clutch of chickadees." Larger bird species are likely to require even more insects to feed their young.

Some might wonder why the birds can't just feed in wild areas. "That worked in the past, but now there simply is not enough 'nature' left," Tallamy says. "And it shows." You've read about the plight of the monarch butterfly. Birds are hurting too. Rosenberg et al. (2019) reported in *Science* that, since 1970, nearly 3 billion U.S. birds have been lost. That's 29 percent of 1970 levels. "Species extinctions have defined the global biodiversity crisis," they wrote, "but extinction begins with loss in abundance of individuals that can result in compositional and functional changes of ecosystems." The monarch and the birds are proverbial canaries, and they portend worse. "These bird losses are a strong signal that our human-altered landscapes are losing their ability to support bird life," Rosenberg told Gustave Axelson, who heralded the researchers' findings in a blog entry on All About Birds, the site of the Cornell Lab of Ornithology (Axelson 2019). "These results have major implications for ecosystem integrity, the conservation of wildlife more broadly, and policies associated with the protection of birds and native ecosystems on which they depend," Rosenberg and his colleagues wrote (2019).

In recent years, more people are understanding that by planting natives in their landscapes, they can help the environment. They are realizing that their yards present an opportunity for species conservation and are inviting nature in to share their spaces.

Truly Native: Avoid Cultivars and Hybrids

When looking through what's on offer at native nurseries or in native catalogs, you will at some point get down to the nitty-gritty of the *why* of native plants. You may encounter plants marketed as native that have a cultivar name in single quotes on the label or that are hybrids between two plants, one of them possibly a nonnative. Gene combinations resulting from artificial selection or hybridization for certain "more desirable" traits are not considered native.

When looking for plants that have evolved in your county, that are truly native there, you may want to provide native animals the "wild type" of plants, the native genotype with which they have coevolved. A cultivar or a hybrid falls short, as do **nativars**, or cultivars of native species, a term that piques the interest of native-plant people but indicates something otherwise. If you can't find the truly native species at a nursery, wait a while until you do find it.

Here's part of the Virginia Native Plant Society's statement on cultivars:

> "VNPS recognizes that wild-type plants may be difficult to find in the marketplace, and that cultivars and hybrids of native plant species can offer distinctive characteristics which increase their effectiveness in landscape design. However, due to documented cases where the introduction of cultivated plants has negatively impacted natural populations, and because the ecological implications of such plants have not yet been adequately evaluated, we recommend avoiding hybrids and using cultivars only in locations distant from natural areas (e.g., urban gardens) and to exercise caution in the selection of plants that vary significantly from the wild type (e.g., in flower structure, flower color, fruit size and leaf color)."

Case Study: What Native Plants Mean to the Monarch Butterfly

The plight of the monarch butterfly has upped the focus on native plants, the relationship between natives and animals, and the domino effect of environmental crises. It has people planting butterfly weed and other milkweeds (a group of required host plants for monarch larvae and thus for egg-laying by adult females) like never before. In the United States, there are two separate populations of monarch butterflies: the population east of the Rockies (some 99 percent of the North America population), which spends the summer along the eastern U.S. and eastern Canadian border and winters in central Mexico, and the western population, which lives along the Pacific coast and spends the winter in California.

Figure 19-23: The adult monarch butterfly, *Danaus plexippus*, feeds and may lay eggs on this swamp milkweed, *Asclepias incarnata*. Adults feed on plants in addition to milkweeds, but they lay their eggs only on milkweeds, because their larvae cannot mature without eating milkweed tissues.

Figure 19-24: Monarch butterflies spend the winter in Mexico where they roost en masse.

The eastern population faces ecological peril in its summer home in the United States and Canada, in its winter home in Mexico, and in between. As of 2022, the monarch is not listed under the Endangered Species Act, but the U.S. Fish and Wildlife service has determined that listing is warranted (https://www.fws.gov/initiative/pollinators/monarchs), so it may be considered for inclusion soon. Although there is not scientific consensus on the reason for the monarch's population decline, threats include habitat loss and degradation, pesticides, illegal logging, climate change, and the lack of milkweeds.

The eastern monarchs migrate north from Mexico to breed. After three to five short-lived generations have been produced, the season's last generation heads to Mexico to winter, roosting in clusters in the oyamel fir (*Abies religiosa*) forest of the Sierra Madre at 8,000 to 12,000 feet. The monarch differs from other butterflies, which don't migrate such great distances or may overwinter as larvae or pupae. Monarchs could not survive northern winters. (U.S. Department of Agriculture 2022).

Figure 19-25: This monarch larva will metamorphosize through five larval stages, differing in morphology and in banding, before its pupal or chrysalis stage, from which it emerges as a butterfly in about two weeks.

Working for monarchs in the backyard

The U.S. Department of Forestry, U.S. Fish and Wildlife Service, and other federal and state agencies are involved in work to restore monarch habitat. Read more about conservation efforts here (https://www.fws.gov/initiative/pollinators/monarchs). Gardeners can also help make their landscape and their community more favorable for monarchs.

Susan Walton, of the Peninsula Master Naturalist chapter, teamed up with Virginia Department of Transportation Superintendent Kevin Sears to identify and protect patches of milkweed growing on the shoulders of U.S. 17 in Gloucester County. Walton and Sears showed that the answer to this need was as simple as a change in mowing patterns around the milkweed habitat, an action that could be easily replicated in any milkweed-containing shoulder being mowed. Even a milkweed patch that was accidentally cut in early summer would grow again, ready for the last monarch generation of the season.

In 2013, Master Naturalists from the Historic Rivers Chapter, including York and James City counties and Williamsburg, worked to involve students at 10 elementary schools and one high school to build a monarch waystation (https://www.monarchwatch.org/waystations/) (milkweed-containing monarch habitats) at each. Word spread, and outdoor classrooms and pollinator habitats were created at 23 schools. The following year, a total of 650 monarchs were tagged to monitor migration (Virginia Master Naturalist Program 2015).

Virginia Invasives: 8 More Reasons to Plant Native Plants

Nonnative plants can become invasive or harbor pathogens that will affect native species. Here are a few examples of invasive plants that have disrupted our ecosystems.

Kudzu, *Pueraria montana*: Kudzu was once the infamous star of invasive plants in many parts of Virginia. Sadly, it has a lot more company nowadays. A legume native to Asia, kudzu was first brought in as an ornamental and later found use in retarding erosion. It had other ideas and spread rampantly, often engulfing anything in its path. The Nature Conservancy has called it "the invasive vine that ate the South."

Figure 19-26: Dense kudzu vines can cover structures and other plants.

Japanese honeysuckle, *Lonicera japonica*: Nearly everyone in Virginia knows this plant. It's beautiful and sweet smelling, and its nectar is delicious, but don't be fooled. This nonnative has found its way into every county in the state. If you have it in your yard or garden, you have a problem, and it doesn't respect boundaries. The Digital Atlas of the Virginia Flora says, "Nearly ubiquitous in wet to dry forests, old fields, disturbed floodplains, and various open habitats; shade-tolerant and very invasive in many natural community types." It's a back-breaker to get rid of, but it must be done. Try coral honeysuckle, *Lonicera sempervirens*, a favorite of the Ruby-throated Hummingbird.

Tree-of-heaven, *Ailanthus altissima*: Betty Smith might have put this species front and center in *A Tree Grows in Brooklyn*, but this made-to-invade plant is now ubiquitous and destructive in Virginia and beyond. Arriving in the United States via its strawlike seeds, which were used as packing materials to protect fragile porcelain, ailanthus creates those seeds in huge numbers. Making matters worse, the tree sprouts strongly from the roots when is cut down. In addition, it's a preferred host plant for the equally invasive spotted lanternfly. A new threat to Virginia, the planthopper first appeared in the northwestern part of the state in 2018 and has since spread.

Figure 19-27: Tree of Heaven is a host plant for the highly invasive spotted lanternfly.

Chinese wisteria, *Wisteria sinensis*: It is such a shame that many invasives would be beautiful if they weren't so dastardly. Planted for its beauty and fragrance, it broke free to become established in woods, borders, and fencerows, says the Digital Atlas. It's common locally in the eastern half of Virginia. Bite the bullet and pull it out. The similar *Wisteria frutescens* var. *frutescens*, Atlantic wisteria, is native to parts of the Coastal Plain, though it's rare.

Japanese stiltgrass, *Microstegium vimineum*: Another example of something that could be loved it if weren't so damaging, this aggressive destroyer creates a carpet that chokes out everything in its path. Another plant that stowed away as packing material in shipments of porcelain, it is also now common in nearly every Virginia county. Control requires early and close mowing before flowering and seed formation. It's an annual, and its seeds survive in the soil for years, unaffected by herbicides applied directly to the blades of grass.

Hydrilla, *Hydrilla verticillata*: You may be familiar with many of these invasive nonnatives, but hydrilla's an aquatic and possibly not so well known. The Flora of Virginia calls it "[o]ne of our most invasive aquatic weeds, often clogging waterways and boat motors and outcompeting native aquatics." From Africa, it first got a foothold in Florida, probably via the aquarium trade (Virginia Department of Conservation and Recreation and Virginia Native Plant Society 1997).

Autumn olive, *Elaeagnus umbellata*: Another plant that's visually pleasing but on the most-wanted list of nonnative invaders. From Asia, this shrub was imported for wildlife, with whom the fruits are indeed popular, which explains its invasiveness in waste ground and in natural habitats.

Stowaway diseases and pests: Nonnatives can carry diseases or pests for which native plants have not evolved coping mechanisms. Some are well known: Dutch elm disease, the emerald ash borer, the hemlock woolly adelgid, and the infamous chestnut blight. Hitting Virginia's state tree, the flowering dogwood (*Cornus florida*), is the fungal disease dogwood anthracnose. Since the 1970s, native dogwoods have been plagued by anthracnose, caused by the fungus *Discula destructiva* (Miller et al. 2016). The disease was first noticed on native dogwoods near U.S. ports, where it is believed to have entered on dogwood plants from Asia. There, the fungus doesn't cause severe disease in native dogwoods (Miller et al. 2016). By the early 1990s, it had caused major losses and damage in the flowering dogwood, especially in the South (Anderson et al.).

Additional Resources

Online resources

- Virginia Master Naturalist Program: Extension Master Gardeners are already collaborating with Master Naturalists, and there is much more to collaborate on, including native plant–pollinator demonstration gardens, Plant Virginia Natives campaigns, habitat restoration projects involving native plant communities, and educational programs about native plants.
- Virginia Native Plant Society: https://vnps.org/
- Virginia Department of Conservation and Recreation Natural Heritage Program: Information on native plants, invasive species, and Virginia conservation and ecology. https://www.dcr.virginia.gov/natural-heritage/
- Blandy Experimental Farm at the State Arboretum of Virginia: https://blandy.virginia.edu/
- Digital Atlas of the Virginia Flora: http://www.vaplantatlas.org/
- Flora of Virginia Project.: https://floraofvirginia.org/
- Plant Virginia Natives Initiative.: https://www.plantvirginianatives.org/
- USDA's PLANTS Database: https://plants.usda.gov/home
- Virginia Extension Master Gardener Tree Steward Manual: https://vtechworks.lib.vt.edu/handle/10919/103953
- "Wildflower ethics and native plants" Article from the USDA Forest Service https://www.fs.usda.gov/wildflowers/ethics/index.shtml
- North Carolina State University Extension Plant Toolbox: https://plants.ces.ncsu.edu
- Missouri Botanical Garden Plant Finder: https://www.missouribotanicalgarden.org/plantfinder/plantfindersearch.aspx
- Heffernan, K., E. Engle, and C. Richardson. 2014. *Virginia Invasive Plant Species List*. Natural Heritage Technical Document 14-11. Virginia Department of Conservation and Recreation, Division of Natural Heritage, Richmond. https://www.dcr.virginia.gov/natural-heritage/document/nh-invasive-plant-list-2014.pdf. Available March 2022.
- Virginia Department of Wildlife Resources. 2020. *Habitat at Home*, 2020 revision. Text and photography by Carol A. Heiser. https://dwr.virginia.gov/wp-content/uploads/media/Habitat-at-Home.pdf. Available April 2022.
- "Biodiversity for the Birds: Non-native plants in homeowners' yards endanger wildlife, UD researchers report," LaPenta, Dante.

2022.

Books

- Botanical Artists for Education & the Environment. 2014. *American Botanical Paintings: Native Plants of the Mid Atlantic, a Book for Artists and Gardeners.* B.S. Driggers, editor. Lydia Inglett Ltd. Publishing, Hilton Head, South Carolina.
- Capon, B. 2010. *Botany for Gardeners.* Timber Press Inc., Portland, Oregon.
- Darke, R., and D. Tallamy. 2014. *The Living Landscape: Designing for Beauty and Biodiversity in the Home Garden.* Timber Press Inc., Portland, Oregon.
- Finch, B., B.M. Young, R. Johnson, and J.C. Hall. 2012. *Longleaf, Far as the Eye Can See: A New Vision of North America's Richest Forest.* The University of North Carolina Press, Chapel Hill.
- Hamilton, H., and G. Hall. 2013. *Wildflowers & Grasses of Virginia's Coastal Plain.* Sponsored by the John Clayton Chapter of the Virginia Native Plant Society. BRIT [Botanical Research Institute of Texas] Press, Fort Worth.
- Harris, J.G., and M.W. Harris. 2001. *Plant Identification Terminology: An Illustrated Glossary, 2nd ed.* Spring Lake Publishing, Spring Lake, Utah.
- Holm, Heather. *Pollinators of Native Plants: Attract, Observe and Identify Pollinators and Beneficial Insects with Native Plants.* Minnetonka, MN: Pollination Press LLC, 2014.
- Norris, Kelly. *New Naturalism: Designing and Planting a Resilient, Ecologically Vibrant Home Garden.* Beverly, MA: Cool Springs Press, 2021.
- Rainer, T., and C. West. 2015. *Planting in a Post-Wild World: Designing Plant Communities for Resilient Landscapes.* Timber Press Inc., Portland, Oregon.
- Slattery, B.E., K. Reshetiloff, and S.M. Zwicker. 2003, 2005. *Native Plants for Wildlife Habitat and Conservation Landscaping: Chesapeake Bay Watershed.* U.S. Fish and Wildlife Service, Chesapeake Bay Field Office, Annapolis, Maryland. https://dnr.maryland.gov/criticalarea/Documents/chesapeakenatives.pdf. Available April 2022.
- Tallamy, D.W. 2007. *Bringing Nature Home: How You Can Sustain Wildlife with Native Plants.* Timber Press Inc., Portland, Oregon.
- Tallamy, D.W. 2020. *Nature's Best Hope: A New Approach to Conservation that Starts in Your Yard.* Timber Press Inc., Portland, Oregon.
- Tallamy, D.W. 2021. *The Nature of Oaks: The Rich Ecology of Our Most Essential Native Trees.* Timber Press Inc., Portland, Oregon.
- Virginia Department of Forestry. n.d. *Rain Gardens Technical Guide: A Landscape Tool to Improve Water Quality.* Virginia Department of Forestry, Charlottesville. https://dof.virginia.gov/wp-content/uploads/Rain-Gardens-Technical-Guide_pub.pdf. Available April 2022.
- Weakley, A.S., J.C. Ludwig, and J.F. Townsend. 2012. *Flora of Virginia.* Bland Crowder, ed. Foundation of the Flora of Virginia Project Inc., Richmond. BRIT [Botanical Research Institute of Texas] Press, Fort Worth.
- Weakley, A.S., J.C. Ludwig, J.F. Townsend, and G.P. Fleming. 2020. *Flora of Virginia* [mobile app]. Bland Crowder, ed. Foundation of the Flora of Virginia Project Inc., Richmond, and High Country Apps, Bozeman, Montana.

References

- Anderson, R.L., J.L. Knighten, M. Windham, K. Langdon, F. Hedrix, and R. Roncadori. [1994.] Dogwood anthracnose and its spread in the South. USDA Forest Service, Atlanta. https://www.fs.usda.gov/Internet/FSE_DOCUMENTS/stelprdb5447373.pdf. Available March 2022.
- Axelson, G. 2019. Vanishing: more than 1 in 4 birds has disappeared in the last 50 years. All About Birds. Cornell University, Cornell Lab of Ornithology, Ithaca, New York. https://www.birds.cornell.edu/home/bring-birds-back/. Available March 2022.
- Beverley, R. 1705. *History and present state of Virginia.* R. Parker, London.
- Canadian Food Inspection Agency. 2021. Adelges tsugae (hemlock woolly adelgid) – fact sheet. https://inspection.canada.ca/plant-health/invasive-species/insects/hemlock-woolly-adelgid/fact-sheet/eng/

- 1325616708296/1325618964954. Available March 2022.
- Center for Biological Diversity. 2022. Monarch butterfly. Center for Biological Diversity, Tucson, Arizona. https://www.biologicaldiversity.org/species/invertebrates/monarch_butterfly/
- D'Arcy, C.J. 2000. Dutch elm disease, revised 2005. Plant Disease Lessons, American Phytopathological Society, St. Paul, Minnesota. https://www.apsnet.org/edcenter/disandpath/fungalasco/pdlessons/Pages/DutchElm.aspx. Available March 2022.
- Darke, R., and D. Tallamy. 2014. The living landscape: designing for beauty and biodiversity in the home garden. Timber Press Inc., Portland, Oregon.
- Goatley, M., Jr. 2008. What grass should I grow for my lawn? Virginia Cooperative Extension, Virginia Tech, Blacksburg, Virginia, and Virginia State University, Petersburg. Crop and Soil Environmental News, March 2008. https://www.sites.ext.vt.edu/newsletter-archive/cses/2008-03/WhatGrass.html (available 3 March 2022). Available March 2022.
- Frost, C.C. 1993. Four centuries of changing landscape patterns in the longleaf pine ecosystem. Pp. 17–43 in S.M. Hermann (ed.), The longleaf pine ecosystem: ecology, restoration and management. Proceedings of the Tall Timbers Fire Ecology Conference, No. 18. Tall Timbers Research Station, Tallahassee, Florida.
- Hance, J. 2020. Brazil's Atlantic Forest (Mata Atlântica). Mongabay [blog]. https://rainforests.mongabay.com/mata-atlantica/. Available March 2022.
- Hartke, B.B. 2017. Finding fulfillment as a Wildlife Way Station volunteer. Blog. Virginia Native Plant Society, Boyce, Va. https://vnps.org/finding-fulfillment-as-a-wildlife-way-station-volunteer/. Available March 2022.
- Heffernan, K., E. Engle, and C. Richardson. 2014. Virginia invasive plant species list. Natural Heritage Technical Document 14-11. Virginia Department of Conservation and Recreation, Division of Natural Heritage, Richmond. https://www.dcr.virginia.gov/natural-heritage/document/nh-invasive-plant-list-2014.pdf. Available March 2022.
- Hill, E.C. 1943. Conserving the native beauty of Virginia. Wild Flower 20(1): 1–3.
- Lady Bird Johnson Wildflower Center. 2009. Ask Mr. Smarty Plants. [Mr. Smarty Plants replies to a reader's question about replacing azaleas with native plants.] https://www.wildflower.org/expert/show.php?id=3435&frontpage=true. Available 7 March 2022.
- Lemmon, R.S. 1940. Plants and planting methods for the native garden. Wild Flower 14(1):89–94.
- Michaux, F.A. 1810. The North American sylva, or a description of the forest trees of the United States, Canada and Nova Scotia. F.A. Michaux, 1810. Real-time PCR detection of dogwood anthracnose fungus in historical herbarium specimens from Asia. Plos One 11(4): e0154030. https://doi.org/10.1371/journal.pone.0154030. Available March 2022.
- Miller, S., H. Masuya, J. Zhang, E. Walsh, and N. Zhang. 2016. Real-time PCR detection of dogwood anthracnose fungus in historical herbarium specimens from Asia. PloS ONE 11(4): e0154030. https://doi.org/10.1371/journal.pone.0154030.
- National Audubon Society. 2022. History of Audubon and science-based bird conservation. https://www.audubon.org/about/history-audubon-and-waterbird-conservation. Available March 2022.
- Newcomb, L. 1989. *Newcomb's wildflower guide.* Reprint edition. Little, Brown and Company, Boston.
- Palmer, M.J. 2018. Defenders of Mexico's environment chronicle their battles: poet Homero Aridjis and Betty Ferber have spent a lifetime fighting to save endangered species and ecosystems in Latin America. Earth Island Journal, August 8, 2018. Earth Island Institute, Berkeley, California. https://www.earthisland.org/journal/index.php/articles/entry/defenders-of-mexicos-environment-chronicle-their-battles/. Available March 2022.
- Ray, J. 1999. Ecology of a cracker childhood. Milkweed Editions, Minneapolis.
- Ricker, P.L. 1937. A history of the wild flower preservation movement. Wild Flower 14(2): 28–30 and 14(2): 49–53.
- Rosenberg, K.V., A.M. Dokter, P.J. Blancher, J.R. Sauer, A.C. Smith, P.A. Smith, J.C. Stanton A. Panjabi, L. Helft, M. Parr, P.P. Marra. 2019. Decline of the North American avifauna. Science 366(6461): 120–124.
- Rothenberg, J. 2014. In defense of the monarch butterfly: a letter to three nations from poets, writers, scientists, & artists. Poems and poetics [blog]. Jacket 2, Philadelphia. https://jacket2.org/commentary/defense-monarch-butterfly-letter-three-nations-poets-writers-scientists-artists. Available March 2022.
- Solyst, J. 2020. The greatest wildlife comeback you've never seen: saved from near extinction, wild turkeys are now guarded by vigilant wildlife managers. Chesapeake Bay Program, Recent News. https://www.chesapeakebay.net/news/blog/the_greatest_wildlife_comeback_youve_never_seen. Available March 2022.
- Tallamy, D. 2011. A call for backyard biodiversity. Originally published in American Forests magazine, autumn 2009. https://www.americanforests.org/magazine/article/a-call-for-backyard-biodiversity/. Available March 2022.
- Tallamy, D.W. 2007. Bringing nature home: how you can sustain wildlife with native plants. Timber Press Inc., Portland,

- Oregon.
- Tallamy, D.W. 2015. The chickadee's guide to gardening. New York Times, March 11, 2015. https://www.nytimes.com/2015/03/11/opinion/in-your-garden-choose-plants-that-help-the-environment.html. Available March 2022.
- Tallamy, D.W. 2020. *Nature's best hope: a new approach to conservation that starts in your yard.* Timber Press Inc., Portland, Oregon.
- Tallamy, D.W. 2021. *The nature of oaks: the rich ecology of our most essential native trees.* Timber Press Inc., Portland, Oregon.
- Trelease, W. 1900. Some twentieth century problems. Science (New Series) 12(289): 48–62.
- UNESCO. 2008. Twenty-seven new sites inscribed. World Heritage Convention, News, July 8, 2008. UNESCO, Paris. https://whc.unesco.org/en/news/453/, available March 2022.
- U.S. Department of Agriculture. 2022. Monarch butterfly frequently asked questions (FAQs). U.S. Forest Service, Washington. https://www.fs.fed.us/wildflowers/pollinators/Monarch_Butterfly/faqs.shtml. Available March 2022.
- Virginia Botanical Associates. 2022. Digital atlas of the Virginia flora [website]. Virginia Botanical Associates, Blacksburg. http://www.vaplantatlas.org/. Available March 2022.
- Virginia Department of Conservation and Recreation and Virginia Native Plant Society. 1997. Hydrilla. Invasive alien plant species in Virginia [factsheet series]. Virginia Department of Conservation and Recreation and Virginia Native Plant Society. https://www.dcr.virginia.gov/natural-heritage/document/fshyve.pdf.
- Virginia Department of Conservation and Recreation. 2022. Eastern hemlock–hardwood forests. Virginia Department of Conservation and Recreation, Division of Natural Heritage, Richmond. https://www.dcr.virginia.gov/natural-heritage/natural-communities/nctb5. Available March 2022.
- Virginia Department of Conservation and Recreation. 2022. What are native plants? In Native plants for conservation, restoration, and landscaping. Virginia Department of Conservation and Recreation, Division of Natural Heritage, Richmond. https://www.dcr.virginia.gov/natural-heritage/nativeplants. Available March 2022.
- Virginia Department of Forestry. 2022. Emerald ash borer. Virginia Department of Forestry, Forest Health Program. Charlottesville. https://dof.virginia.gov/forest-management-health/forest-health/insects-and-diseases/emerald-ash-borer/. Available March 2022.
- Virginia Department of Forestry. 2022. Emerald ash borer in Virginia: an introduction. Story map. Virginia Department of Forestry, Forest Health Program. Charlottesville. https://vdof.maps.arcgis.com/apps/MapSeries/index.html?appid=e2660c30d9cd46cc988cc72415101590. Available March 2022.
- Virginia Master Naturalist Program. 2015. Giving monarchs a boost in Virginia. Virginia Master Naturalist Program, Charlottesville. http://www.virginiamasternaturalist.org/home/giving-monarchs-a-boost-in-virginia. Available March 2022.
- Virginia Tech. 2022. Virginia Tech Soil Testing Lab. Virginia Tech, Blacksburg. https://www.soiltest.vt.edu. Available March 2022.
- Waqar, Z., R.C.S. Moraes, M. Benchimol, J.C. Morante-Filho, E. Mariano-Neto, and F.A. Amato. 2021. Gene flow and genetic structure reveal reduced diversity between generations of a tropical tree, Manilkara multifida Penn., in Atlantic Forest fragments. Genes 2021, 12, 2025. https://doi.org/10.3390/genes12122025.
- Weakley, A.S., J.C. Ludwig, and J.F. Townsend. 2012. Flora of Virginia. Bland Crowder, editor. Foundation of the Flora of Virginia Project Inc., Richmond. BRIT [Botanical Research Institute of Texas] Press, Fort Worth.
- Weakley, A.S., J.C. Ludwig, J.F. Townsend, and G.P. Fleming. 2020. Hydrilla verticillata [species treatment]. Bland Crowder, editor. Flora of Virginia [mobile app]. Foundation of the Flora of Virginia Project Inc., Richmond, and High Country Apps, Bozeman, Montana.
- Worrall, J.J. 2022. Chestnut blight. In Forest pathology: diseases of forest and shade trees. [website.] https://forestpathology.org/canker/chestnut-blight/. Available March 2022.

Attributions

Written by Bland Crowder, Executive Director Flora of Virginia Project

- Marion Lobstein, Associate Professor of Biology, NVCC-Manassas, Adjunct Professor, Blandy Experimental Farm (2022 peer reviewer)
- Patricia Lust, Professor Emerita, Longwood University and Extension Master Gardener Volunteer (2022 reviser)
- Stacey Morgan Smith, Extension Master Gardener (2022 reviser and editor)

Table 19-1: Virginia Native Favorites: Range information and conditions adapted from the Digital Atlas of the Flora of Virginia (2022).

Image Attributions

- Figure 19-1: "Rhododendron periclymenoides, Pinxter Azalea" Gary P. Fleming. CC BY-NC-SA 4.0.
- Figure 19-2: "Eastern prickly pear cactus." 2021. Assateague Island National Seashore National Park Service. Public Domain.
- Figure 19-3: Oak tree hopper "5576790" Jennifer Carr, University of Florida, Bugwood.org CC BY-NC 3.0 US
- Figure 19-4: "Wild Turkeys" 2018. NPS / Jane Gamble. Public Domain
- Figure 19-5: "White Oak Tree, West Hartford, CT – June 17, 2013" 2013. Msact , Wikimedia. CC BY-SA 3.0
- Figure 19-6: "20140918-NRCS-LSC-0350" USDA. 2014. Flickr. Public Domain.
- Figure 19-7: "Like minded people" 2016. Virginia Cooperative Extension Master Gardener Program. CC BY-NC-SA 4.0.
- Figure 19-8: Eurybia divaricate, DCR-DNH, Gary P. Fleming. CC BY-NC-SA 4.0.
- Figure 19-9: Chimaphila maculata. "Chimaphila maculata1010" by Wasp32. 2016. Wikimedia. CC BY 4.0
- Figure 19-10: "Beautiful, but not a Virginia native: Magnolia grandiflora." Bland Crowder. CC BY-NC-SA 4.0
- Figure 19-11: Cucumber-tree, *Magnolia acuminata* range covers western half of Virginia. Johnson, Devon. 2022. CC BY-NC-SA 4.0. Includes "Map of Virginia Counties and Independent Cities.svg" by Dbenbenn. 2009. Wikimedia. CC BY-SA 3.0. and "*Magnolia acuminata* flower" by John Seiler. Virginia Tech Dendrology. Used with permission. Data from Digital Atlas of the Virginia Flora.
- Figure 19-12: Fraser magnolia, *M. fraseri* range covers western panhandle of Virginia and Highland county. Johnson, Devon. 2022. CC BY-NC-SA 4.0. Johnson, Devon. 2022. CC BY-NC-SA 4.0. Includes "Map of Virginia Counties and Independent Cities.svg" by Dbenbenn. 2009. Wikimedia. CC BY-SA 3.0. and "*Magnolia fraseri* flower" by John Seiler. Virginia Tech Dendrology. Used with permission. Data from Digital Atlas of the Virginia Flora.
- Figure 19-13: Umbrella magnolia, *M. tripetala* range covers western panhandle, west-central Virginia, and eastern-most counties. Johnson, Devon. 2022. CC BY-NC-SA 4.0. Johnson, Devon. 2022. CC BY-NC-SA 4.0. Includes "Map of Virginia Counties and Independent Cities.svg" by Dbenbenn. 2009. Wikimedia. CC BY-SA 3.0. and "*Magnolia tripetala* flower" by John Seiler. Virginia Tech Dendrology. Used with permission. Data from Digital Atlas of the Virginia Flora.
- Figure 19-14: Sweetbay, M. virginiana range covers eastern half of Virginia. Johnson, Devon. 2022. CC BY-NC-SA 4.0. Includes "Map of Virginia Counties and Independent Cities.svg" by Dbenbenn. 2009. Wikimedia. CC BY-SA 3.0. and "*Magnolia virginiana* flower" by John Seiler. Virginia Tech Dendrology. Used with permission. Data from Digital Atlas of the Virginia Flora.
- Figure 19-15: Johnson, Devon. 2022. CC BY-NC-SA 4.0. Includes ""Map of Virginia Counties and Independent Cities.svg" by Dbenbenn. 2009. Wikimedia. CC BY-SA 3.0. and "Southern magnolia — Magnolia grandiflora" by Jim Evans via Wikimedia. 2002. CC BY-SA 4.0. Data from Digital Atlas of the Virginia Flora.
- Figure 19-15: National Forests in Virginia. "George Washington and Jefferson National Forests." USDA Forest Service. Retrieved 2022. Public domain.
- Figure 19-16: The Native Plants for Conservation, Restoration, and Landscaping Project. Johnson, Devon. 2022. CC BY-NC-SA 4.0. Brochure from Native Plants for Conservation, Restoration, and Landscaping Project.
- Figure 19-17: Plant Virginia Natives regional native plant guides. Johnson, Devon. 2022. CC BY-NC-SA 4.0. Thumbnails used under fair use; includes cover thumbnails of Native Plants for Central Rappahannock, Plant Hampton Roads Natives, Native Plants for Virginia's Capital Region, and Native Plants of the Northern Neck
- Figure 19-18: Azaleas surround the border of this garden. "Azalea's at Houston's River Oaks Garden Club" by i_am_jim. 2013. Wikimedia. CC BY-SA 3.0
- Figure 19-19: Virginia Natives for shade. Johnson, Devon. 2022. CC BY-NC-SA 4.0. Includes: "Jack-in-the-pulpit (41416531534).jpg." Will Brown. 2018. Wikimedia. CC BY 2.0; "Star Chickweed – Stellaria pubera im.JPG" Ivy Main. 2011. Wikimedia. CC BY-SA 3.0; "Eurybia divaricata in CT.jpg" Mets501. 2017. Wikimedia. CC BY-SA 4.0; "Mayapple flower 1.jpg" **Wasrts**. 2019. Wikimedia. CC BY-SA 4.0; "Cinnamon Fern Long Valley Farm Carver Creek NC SP 2995 (5682748445).jpg" bobistraveling 2011. Wikimedia. CC BY 2.0; "Bloodroot (Sanguinaria canadensis) – Guelph, Ontario 02.jpg" Ryan Hodnett. 2016. Wikimedia. CC BY-SA 4.0; "Northern Maidenhair Fern.jpg" Schnobby. 2011. Wikimedia. CC BY-SA 3.0; "Mitchella repens Partridge berry Norfolk Connecticut 05112019.jpg" Sesamehoneytart. 2019. Wikimedia. CC BY-SA 4.0; "Thalictrum thalictroides rue anemone.jpg" Dcrjsr. 2012. Wikimedia. CC BY 3.0

CHAPTER 19: VIRGINIA NATIVE PLANTS

- Figure 19-20: *Rhododendron calendulaceum*, flame azalea is a native alternative to azaleas. DCR-DNH, Gary P. Fleming. CC BY-NC-SA 4.0.
- Figure 19-21: The Carolina chickadee eats. "Carolina Chickadee." 2006. Barnes, Dr. Thomas G., USFWS. Public Domain.
- Figure 19-22: The adult monarch butterfly, *Danaus plexippus*. "Danaus plexippus on Asclepias incarnata" by R. A. Nonenmacher. Wikimedia. 2015. CC BY-SA 4.0
- Figure 19-23: Monarch butterflies spend the winter in Mexico where roost en masse. "Monarch butterflies in Santa Cruz." by Brocken Inaglory. 2007. Wikimedia. CC BY-SA 3.0
- Figure 19-24: This monarch larva will metamorphosize through five larval stages. Monarch caterpillar 27 August 2019" by Maria L. Evans. 2019. Wikimedia. CC BY-SA 4.0
- Figure 19-25: Dense kudzu vines can cover structures and other plants. "5471097" Daren Mueller, Iowa State University, Bugwood.org. CC BY 3.0 US
- Figure 19-26: Tree of Heaven is a host plant for the highly invasive spotted lanternfly. "1150026." Chuck Bargeron, University of Georgia, Bugwood.org. CC BY 3.0 US

GLOSSARY

Abiotic factors
> Nonliving factors such as nutrient deficiencies and water or temperature stress

Absorption
> Process by which substances, particularly water and minerals, are moved into the plant. This occurs mainly through the roots in the tip region where root hairs are present, but it may also occur through leaf surfaces.

Accent
> Focal point, something that deliberately stands out from the overall landscape

Adsorption
> Attachment of dissolved or gaseous pollutants to the surface of solids. For example, odors from freezers and refrigerators are adsorbed to baking soda.

Adventitious buds
> Buds arising at sites other than in the terminal or axillary position

Aggregate fruits
> Fruits that come from a single flower with many ovaries

Alternate
> Leaf arrangement where leaves are arranged in alternate steps along the stem with only one leaf at each node.

Ametabolous
> An insect that undergoes slight or no metamorphosis

Angiosperms
> Flowering plants that produce seeds enclosed in a fruit

Annuals
> Plants that pass through their entire life cycle from seed germination to seed production in one growing season, then die

Anvil style shears
> Pruning shears with a sharpened blade that cuts against a broad, flat plate

Aquifers
> Geologic formation that holds and yields usable amounts of water. The water in an aquifer is called groundwater. Aquifers may be categorized into confined aquifers and unconfined aquifers.

Atmospheric humidity
> Amount of water vapor in the air, expressed as a percentage of the moisture saturation of air

Autotrophy

    Ability of plants to manufacture their own food

Axillary buds

    Buds arising in the leaf axils

Balance

    Design principle that refers to an aesthetically pleasing integration of elements; a sense of one part being of equal visual weight or mass to another

Bare root plants

    Perennials that are dug up during their dormant season and sold without soil around the roots

Bark

    A nontechnical term that refers to all the tissues outside the vascular cambium, including the periderm

bedding plants

    Encompass a wide variety of non-hardy, seasonal things like annuals, tropicals, herbs, vegetable transplants, etc.

Bermudagrass

    A fine-bladed, warm-season grass with exceptional drought tolerance that aggressively creeps by both rhizomes and stolons.

Biennials

    Plants that start from seeds and produce vegetative structures and food storage organs the first season and flowers, fruit, and seeds the second season

Binomial nomenclature

    System of naming organisms in which the name is composed of two terms

Biodiversity

    The variety of genes, species and ecosystems in the aggregate, across the larger landscape.

Biological control

    Using living organisms (i.e., natural enemies) to reduce pest populations (typically insects and weeds)

Biotic

    Living agents such as fungi, nematodes, bacteria, and viruses

Blade

    Expanded, thin structure on either side of the midrib of a leaf. The blade is usually the largest and most conspicuous part of a leaf.

Bolt

    flower prematurely

Bracts

    Modified leaf or scale with a flower or flower cluster in its axil. Often brightly colored, as in poinsettias.

Branch

    A stem that is more than one year old and typically has lateral stems

Branch bark ridge

    Prominent ridge of raised bark that forms within the branch crotch

Branch collar

    The swollen area that forms around the base of a branch, often appearing a bit swollen

Broadleaf evergreens

    Angiosperms trees that retain foliage throughout the year

Bud

    Small package of partially preformed tissue which becomes leaves/stems or flowers

Budding

    The union of one bud and a small piece of bark from the scion with a rootstock

Bulbs

    Shortened, compressed, underground stems surrounded by fleshy scales (leaves) that envelop a central bud located at the tip of the stem

Bypass pruners

    Pruning shears with two blades that cut like scissors

C3 plants

    Found in temperate to cold climates with high moisture environments and represent the majority of plant species. They typically are slower-growing plants than C4 plants and use CO_2 less efficiently as a result of an energy-wasting process called photorespiration.

C4 plants

    Found in hot, dry, subtropical to tropical environments. They are fast growers and have higher rates of photosynthesis than C3 plants. Because C4 plants do not photorespire, they are more efficient in fixing CO_2 than C3 plants.

Calyx

    The sepals of a flower

CAM plants

    Found in very hot dry desert areas. Like C4 plants, CAM plants are not susceptible to photorespiration because, unlike C3 and C4 plants, they open their stomata at night, thus conserving water and fixing CO_2 and storing it for use during the day to make sugar.

Cambium

    In woody plants, the layer of cells located between the wood and bark of a stem from which new tissues originate

Cane

A stem that has a relatively large pith (the central, strength-giving tissue of stem) and usually lives only one or two years

Cane habit

Shrub growth habit in which plants spread by sending up erect new branches, called canes, from their base

Caneberries

Fruits that grow on woody stems called canes, for example, raspberries, blackberries, and their hybrids

Cataphylls

The small, leathery, protective leaves that enclose and protect buds, found on rhizomes and are

Cation exchange capacity

A measure of the total negative charges within the soil that adsorb plant nutrient cations

Cell wall

A rigid, structural layer outside the cell membrane in cells of plants, fungi, and some other organisms

Centipedegrass

A coarse-textured stoloniferous warm-season grass that is adapted in southern Virginia from Martinsville to the coast. It is the lowest maintenance, highest density warm-season grass available.

Cerci

Typically paired appendages on the abdomen of many species of insect, typically with sensory function

Chelates

Chemical claws that help hold metal ions, such as iron, in solution, so that the plant can absorb them

Chemical control

Use of pesticides to reduce pest populations. A pesticide is any substance that is used to prevent, destroy, repel, or mitigate any pest

Chilling stress

Stress that occurs in plants sensitive to temperatures in the range of 68-32° F

Chitin

The primary component of the exoskeletons of arthropods such as crustaceans and insects

Chloroplasts

Sites of photosynthesis within cells that contain chlorophylls and carotenoid pigments

Chlorosis

Yellowing of normally green tissue

Clays

The finest soil particles

Climbing roses

> Rose bushes that have flowers more than 2 inches across, borne on wood that is 2 or more years old. Canes are larger and sturdier than those of ramblers

Clones

> Groups of plants that are identical to their one parent and that can only be propagated asexually

coconut coir

> A pH-neutral, non-hydrophobic soil amendment that aerates and improves water retention of soil. Readily renewable and more environmentally friendly than peat moss

Cold stratification

> Process where seeds are exposed to a period of cold temperatures to break their dormancy cycle

Columnar

> Column-like tree form

Complete flower

> A flower with a stamen, pistils, petals, and sepals

Compound leaf

> Leaf composed of several separate leaflets arising from the same petiole

Conifers

> Gymnosperms, mostly evergreen but there are notable deciduous species, that have needle, scale-like, or awl-like foliage

Conservation landscaping

> Landscape principles that apply best practices for conserving water, soil, and existing native plant communities.

Contaminants

> Undesirable substance not normally present, or an usually high concentration of a naturally-occurring substance, in water, soil, or other environmental medium. In more restricted usage, a substance in water that may be harmful to human health.

Cork cambium

> Falls outside the vascular cambium and is responsible for growth that replaces the epidermis in stems and roots.

Cork spot

> Small dimples on the surface of apples, likely caused by lack of calcium availability in the developing fruit

Corms

> A solid, swollen stem whose scales have been reduced to a dry, leaf-like covering. They have shapes similar to bulbs, but do not contain fleshy scales.

Corolla

> The petals of a flower

Cotyledons

    Modified leaves that are found on the embryonic plant and commonly serve as storage organs

Crown

    A region of compressed stem tissue from which new shoots are produced

Crowns

    Region of compressed stem tissue from which new shoots are produced, generally found near the surface of the soil

Cultivar

    Variety bred by people to have desired traits that are reproduced in each new generation (usually through asexual propagation)

Cultural Control

    Modifying or disrupting the pest environment to make it less habitable for a pest

Cuticle

    Protective film covering the outermost layer of epidermis in leaves, some shoots and some other plant organs.

Cuticle (insects)

    The outer covering of the insect, includes most of the material of the exoskeleton

Cutting

    A vegetative plant part which is severed from the parent plant in order to regenerate itself, thereby forming a whole new plant

Day-length

    Duration of light received. For example, Poinsettia, kalanchoe, and Christmas cactus bud and flower only when day-length is short (11 hours of daylight or less).

Day-neutral

    Plants that form flowers regardless of day length

Deciduous trees

    Angiosperm trees that lose their leaves in the fall

Dicots

    Flowering plants with seeds that contain a pair of embryonic leaves (cotyledons). Most of the broadleaf herbs, shrubs, and trees are dicots.

Digger

    Hand tool with a narrow curved or straight blade on the end of a long stick, also called an asparagus knife

Dioecious

    Plants with male and female reproductive organs on separate individuals

Disease triangle

    Represents three factors that interact to produce turfgrass disease: the disease causer, the susceptible grass, and a favorable environment

Drainage

    (1) the natural movement of surface water over a land area to a river, lake or ocean (surface drainage), (2) removal of water from a soil using buried pipelines that are spaced regularly and perforated (subsurface drainage).

Ecosystem

    Biologically diverse communities, combined together with the other non-living (abiotic) elements of the surrounding environment, such as soil, water and sunlight that form a functional system of continuous energy exchange.

Edge

    Places where two habitat types come together.

Endosperm

    Built-in food storage supply in a seed

Enlarged hypocotyl

    Storage organ, the swollen portion of the stem below the cotyledon and above the roots

Erosion

    Detachment and transport of soil particles by water and wind. Sediment resulting from soil erosion represents the single largest source of nonpoint source pollution in the United States.

Evapo-transpiration

    Water lost through stomata when they are open during the day

Evaporation

    Process by which a liquid is transformed to the gaseous state

Extensive rejuvenation

    Pruning technique that involves complete removal of the entire plant 6-10 inches above the ground

Fastigiate

    Tree form that looks like a narrow oval

Ferns

    Class of herbaceous vascular plants that reproduce via spores

Fertility

    The ability of soil to sustain plant growth

Fertilization

    When materials for plant nutrition are supplied to the environment around the plant

Fibrous root system

> Root system in which the primary root ceases to elongate, leading to the development of numerous lateral roots which branch repeatedly and form the feeding root system of the plant

Fine-leaf fescues

> Includes creeping red, hard, and chewing fescues. Exhibits the best tolerance of shade, drought, low-nitrogen, and acid soil

Flooding

> Temporary condition of partial or complete inundation of normally dry land areas from the overflow of inland or tidal waters or from the unusual and rapid accumulation of runoff.

Floricane

> Raspberry and blackberry plants that bear fruits on the second year cane

Flower bud

> A but that contains partially preformed flower tissue

Flower primordia

> The small buds at the end of stems from which flowers develop

Freezing stress

> Stress that occurs in plants sensitive to temperatures below the freezing point of water or 32°F

Galls

> Growth on the external tissues of a plant

Genus

> A group of somewhat closely related individuals (a group name) comprising one or more species

Geophytes

> Herbaceous plants with underground storage organs, rather than fibrous root systems

Gradual rejuvenation

> Pruning technique that removes growth gradually

Groundwater

> Water that fills voids, cracks, or other spaces between particles of clay, silt, sand, gravel or rock within a saturated zone or formation (aquifer) below the soil surface.

Guard cells

> Epidermal cells located around a stoma that help regulate gas exchange by opening and closing

Gymnosperms

> Seed-bearing vascular plants that produce exposed seeds, or ovules, which are usually borne in cones

Habitat

The area within an ecosystem where an animal is able to secure the food, water, cover and space it needs to survive and reproduce.

Hand cultivators

Digging hand tool with tines

Hardening

The process of altering the quality of plant growth to withstand the change in environmental conditions which occurs when plants are transferred from a greenhouse or home to the garden

Hardiness

A plant's ability to withstand low winter temperatures and remain aesthetically pleasing

Heading cuts

Pruning cuts that reduce the height or width of a plant by cutting back lateral branches and removing terminal buds; made at nodal areas either above side branches or buds

Hedge shears

Shears with long, flat blades and relatively short handles, one for each hand

Herbarium

An organized and cataloged collection of such specimens, usually at a university or a museum.

Hoe

Tool with a blade at a right angle to the handle. Examples may be pointed with a heart-shaped blade or have a narrow blade to slice through soil.

Holometabolous

An insect that undergoes complete metamorphosis with four distinct stages of development

Host

A plant that another organism (such as an insect or virus) lives on

Humus

The portion of organic matter that remains after most decomposition has taken place

Hybrid

A genetic cross of two different plants, usually from two different varieties of the same species

Hypocotyl

The portion of a seedling between the radicle and the first leaf-like structure

Infection

To become established on/in the plant and initiate disease development

Infiltration

    Process by which water (surface water, rainfall, or runoff) enters the soil.

Infiltration rate

    Quantity of water that enters the soil surface in a specified time interval. Often expressed as a volume per unit of soil surface per unit of time (in3 per in2 per hour). Soil surface wetness, soil texture, residue cover, precipitation rate, irrigation application, topography, and other factors control the infiltration rate.

Inoculum

    Part of a pathogen that can cause infection

Integrated pest management

    An ecosystem-based strategy that focuses on long-term prevention of pests or their damage through a combination of appropriate control tactics. These tactics can be preventative, curative, or both and are often combined to provide the best possible results.

Intergeneric hybrid

    Cross between two genera (a very rare occurrence)

Internode

    Section of the stem between two successive nodes

Interspecific hybrid

    A cross between different species of the same genus

Intra-specific variation

    Variation within a species

Irrigation

    Controlled application of water to land to supply plant water requirements not satisfied by rainfall

Kentucky bluegrass

    Turfgrass that provides lush, blue-green, fine-bladed lawns. Best suited to areas in and west of the Blue Ridge Mountains and north of Richmond.

Landscape design

    The process of planning and organizing the natural and man-made parts of the landscape into an aesthetic, functional, and environmentally sustainable space

Lateral buds

    Buds borne on the sides of a stem

Lateral root

    Side or branch root that arises from another root. Also called a secondary root.

Leaching

    Removal of dissolved chemicals from soil caused by the movement of a liquid (like water) through the soil

Leaf bud

    Bud composed of a short stem with embryonic leaves

Lesion

    A well defined area of diseased or injured tissue, often dead spots or areas. Lesions are often a primary symptom.

Light intensity

    Influences the manufacture of plant food, stem length, leaf color, and flowering

Light quality

    The spectral distribution of light, or the number of different colored photons emitted by the light source (for example, blues, reds, greens)

Loam

    A textural class of soil that has moderate amounts of sand, silt, and clay

Long-day

    Plants form flowers only when day lengths exceed 12 hours (short nights).

Lopping shears

    Long handled shears that are operated with both hands

Macronutrients

    Chemical elements required in large amounts for plant growth and development. These are: Carbon (C), Hydrogen (H), Oxygen (O), Nitrogen (N), Phosphorus (P), and Potassium (K), Calcium (Ca), Magnesium (Mg), and Sulfur (S).

Mechanical/physical control

    Using hands-on techniques or simple equipment/devices to reduce or prevent the spread of pest populations

Meristem

    An area of cell division and growth Cells in the meristem can develop into all other tissues and organs found in plants.

Microclimates

    Zones of atypical high or low temperatures

Micronutrients

    Chemical elements required in small amounts for plant growth and development. These are: Iron (Fe), Zinc (Zn), Manganese (Mn), Boron (B), Copper (Cu), Molybdenum (Mo), Chlorine (Cl)

Micropyle

    A small pore located in a seed's seedcoat that allows water absorption and gas exchange

Miniature roses

    Rose bush 6 to 12 inches high with tiny blooms and foliage

Monocots

    Grass and grass-like flowering plants with seeds that typically contain only one embryonic leaf

Monoecious

Plants with male and female reproductive organs on the same plant

Mounding habit

Shrub growth habit in which plants often have soft, flexible stems, small leaves, and are often used in mass plantings

Multiple fruits

Fruits derived from a tight cluster of separate, independent flowers borne on a single structure

Nativars

Cultivars of native species

Native plants

Plants that occur in the region in which they evolved.

Net-veined

Leaf venation pattern in which veins branch from the main rib(s), then subdivide into finer veinlets which then unite in a complicated network

Node

The part of the stem where one or more leaves are attached

Nonpoint source pollution

Pollution originating from diffuse sources on the landscape. Examples include runoff from fields receiving manure applications, runoff from urban landscapes, or roadbed erosion in forestry. It has been estimated that NPS pollution accounts for more than one-half of the water pollution in the United States today.

Nucleus

Organelle that contains the genetic information for the organism and controls the activities of the cell

Open pollinated

Seed that is self or cross-pollinated by wind or insects and is produced by isolating plants from other plants of different varieties to produce seed that is "true to type"

Opposite

Leaf arrangement where leaves are positioned across the stem from each other, two leaves at each node.

Organic

Methods that involve growing and maintaining healthy plants without using synthetic (manmade) fertilizers, pesticides, hormones, and other materials

Organic matter

Plant and animal material in varying stages of decomposition present in soil.

Overhead watering

Watering system in which water is sprayed down on crops, directly wetting the crop surface

Palmate

    Leaf shape in which leaflets form and radiate from a single point of attachment

Parallel-veined

    Leaf venation pattern in which numerous veins that run essentially parallel to each other and are connected laterally by minute, straight veinlets

Parent material

    Bottom soil horizon, decomposed rock that has acquired some characteristics of the subsoil and retained some characteristics of the rock from which it weathered.

Peat moss

    Decomposed mosses and other living material found in peat bogs

Peds

    Peds are made up of mineral particles (clay, silt, sand) and organic matter; held together by the electrical charges on the surfaces of the minerals and organic matter

Pendulous

    Tree form in which branches hang down, also called weeping

Perennial

    Plants that live for many years. May be herbaceous or, if significant xylem develops in the stem and the top persists, may be classified as woody.

Perennial ryegrass

    A fine-medium textured grass that mixes well with Kentucky bluegrass

Perfect flower

    A flower with functional stamens and pistils

Perlite

    A sterile, porous soil amendment material produced by heating volcanic rock to approximately 1800°F

Pesticide

    Any substance that is used to prevent, destroy, repel, or mitigate any pest. Can be synthetic (man-made), or natural products derived from plants, microorganisms, or inorganic elements

Petals

    Modified leaves, typically brightly colored, segments of a flower's corolla

Petiole

    Stalk that supports the leaf blade

Phenotypic

    Visual appearance as a result of DNA expression

Phloem

Transport tissue in vascular plants, transports the soluble organic compounds made during photosynthesis to the rest of the plant in a process called translocation

Photosynthesis

Process by which green plants and some other organisms use sunlight to synthesize foods from carbon dioxide and water. Generally involves the green pigment chlorophyll (in green plants) and generates oxygen as a byproduct.

Pinnate

Leaf shape in which leaflets are attached along an extension of the petiole

Pistil

The female part of the plant that consists of the stigma, style, and ovary

Pistillate flowers

Flowers are those that possess a functional pistil(s), but lack stamens

Plant community

The collection of plant populations found in that area

Plant nutrition

The needs and uses of the basic chemical elements in the plant

Plugs

Small squares/circles of sod grown in a tray

Plumule

Embryonic shoot

Point source pollution

Pollutant loads discharged at a specific location from pipes, outfalls, and conveyance channels. Point source discharges are generally regulated through the National Pollution Discharge Elimination System (NPDES) permitting procedures established by the EPA. Point sources can also include pollutant loads contributed by tributaries to the main receiving stream or river.

Pole pruners

Shears with a hooked blade above and a cutting blade beneath. The cutter is on a pole and is operated by a cord or chain pulled downward

Pollutant

Any substance of such character and in such quantities that when it reaches a body of water the effect is to degrade the receiving water perhaps to a point rendering it unfit for some specified designated use

Pollution

Alteration of the physical, biological, chemical, and radiological integrity of water due to human activities , any unwanted contaminating property that renders a water supply unfit for its designated use.

Precipitation

    Rain, sleet, snow, or hail that falls to the earth as the result of water vapor condensing in the atmosphere.

Precocity

    In grafting, the ability of rootstocks to induce fruitfulness. Precocity is measured in apple rootstocks by observing the length of time from planting to when the cultivar produces flowers.

Pregermination

    Sprouting the seeds before they are planted in pots (or in the garden)

Primocane

    Raspberry and blackberry plants that bear fruits on the first year cane (shoot) which are ready for harvest in late summer

Provenance

    Source of plant material

Radicle

    Primary root, first organ to appear when a seed germinates

Rain garden

    A shallow landscaped depression that filters polluted stormwater before it evaporates, evapo-transpires through the plants, or percolates through the soil into the groundwater.

Rake

    Tool with a long handle and crossbar with a toothed comb, helpful in spreading mulches and smoothing seedbeds

Rambler roses

    Rose bushes that have clusters of flowers, each usually less than 2 inches across

Relative humidity

    The ratio of water vapor in the air to the amount of water the air could hold at a given temperature and pressure, expressed as a percent

Respiration

    Process by which plants use the sugars produced during photosynthesis (plus oxygen) to produce energy

Rhizomes

    Specialized stem that grows underground and sends out roots and shoots from nodes

Rhythm

    Design principle of even repetition, and it directs the eye in the landscape through continuity and flow

Riparian

    Pertaining to the banks of a river, stream, or other typically, flowing body of water as well as to plant and animal communities along such bodies of water. This term is also commonly used for other bodies of water, e.g., ponds, lakes.

Root cap
: Outermost tip of the root, consists of cells that are sloughed off as the root grows through the soil

Root hairs
: Projects of root epidermal cells, important in absorption of nutrients, plant anchorage, and more

Rootstock
: In grafting, the piece of shoot that provides the new plant's root system and sometimes the lower part of the stem, the lower portion of the graft

Rose standard
: Tree rose, a Hybrid Tea, Grandiflora, or Floribunda budded at the top of a tall trunk

Rosulate
: A circular arrangement of leaves, usually near the soil (for example, dandelion)

Rotary tiller
: Power toll with a series of rotating tines used for working soil several inches deep

Runner
: A specialized stem that grows on the soil surface and forms a new plant at one or more of its nodes. A type of stolon.

Runoff
: Part of rainfall or snowmelt that does not infiltrate the soil but flows over the land surface toward a surface drain, eventually making its way to a stream, river, lake or an ocean. It can carry pollutants into receiving waters. Also known as stormwater.

Rushes
: Members of the Juncaceae family of flowering plants; distinguishable from grasses and sedges by their round (and frequently unbranched) stems filled with pith (not hollow)

Sand
: Coarser mineral particles of the soil

Scale
: Design principle that refers to the size relationship or proportion between different parts of a landscape. This could be between buildings and plants, plants and plants, or plants and people

Scarification
: Breaking, scratching, or softening the seed coat so that water can enter and begin the germination process

Scion
: In grafting, the piece of shoot with dormant buds that will produce the stem and branches on the upper portion of the graft

Sclerites
: Hardened plates joined together forming the hard surface of insects

Secondary growth

    Growth in lateral meristems that causes increase in girth

Sedges

    Members of the Cyperaceae family of grass-like monocotyledonous flowering plants; distinguishable from rushes and grasses by their triangular stems

Sediment

    In the context of water quality, soil particles, sand, and minerals dislodged from the land and deposited into aquatic systems as a result of erosion.

Sepals

    Small, green, leaf-like structures on the base of the flower that protect the flower bud

Sexual propagation

    Involves the union of the sperm (male) with the egg (female) to produce a seed

Shoot

    A young stem with leaves present

Short-day

    Plants that form their flowers only when the day length is less than about 12 hours in duration.

Shovel

    Tool used for digging and lifting loose soil or other materials

Shrubs

    Perennial woody plants that have one or several main stems, and usually are less than 12 feet tall at maturity.

Signs

    Structures or products of the pathogen itself on a host plant, for example, mold, fungal fruiting bodies, or bacterial slime/ooze

Silt

    Relatively fine soil particles that feel smooth and floury. When wet, silt feels smooth but is not slick or sticky.

Simple fruits

    Fruits that develop from a single ovary

Simple leaves

    Leaves with a leaf blade that is a single continuous unit

Sod

    Upper layer of soil with grass growing, often harvested and rolled

Soluble salts

    Minerals dissolved in water that can accumulate in potted plants

Spading fork

> Digging tool with strong, flat tines that is ideal for breaking and turning heavy soils and for loosening subsoil layers when double digging a bed

Species

> A group of individuals that can be characterized by a set of identifiable characteristics that distinguishes them from other types

Species diversity

> The use of many varied taxa (family, genus, species) within an "area", where an area may range from a residential site to municipal or larger sites

Specific epithet

> The second word of the Latin binomial that usually functions as an adjective (or sometimes named after an individual) and indicates or describes the member of the genus

Spines

> Specialized modified leaves that protect the plant

Sprigs

> The stems from shredded sod. Sprigs should include leaves, a stolon, and roots

St. Augustinegrass

> A coarse-textured stoloniferous warm-season grass that has the best shade tolerance of warm-season grasses.

Stamen

> The male reproductive organ. It consists of a pollen sac (anther) and a long, supporting filament

Staminate flowers

> Flowers that contain stamens, but no pistils

Stolon

> Horizontal stem that is fleshy or semi-woody and lies along the top of the ground

Stomata

> Openings in leaves that allow passage of water and gasses into and out of the leaf. Singular: stoma

Storage leaves

> Serve as food storage organs, found on bulbous plants and succulents

Stress

> Any change in environmental conditions that adversely affects survival, growth, development and yield in plants

Stubble mulch

> A stubble of crop residue left in place for winter

Subsoil

    Usually finer and firmer than the surface soil. Organic matter content of the subsoil is usually much lower than that of the surface layer.

Subspecies

    A grouping within a species used to describe geographically isolated variants

Suckers

    Vigorous shoots growing from the trunk or roots

Surface horizon

    Contains more organic matter than the other soil layers. Organic matter gives a gray, dark-brown, or black color to the surface horizon

Symptoms

    Physical expressions of disease in the host tissue, e.g., changes in color, appearance, integrity, etc.

Tall fescue

    A fine to moderate coarse-textured turfgrass which is tolerant of a wide range of soil types and climatic conditions

Taproot

    Formed when the primary root continues to elongate downward into the soil and becomes the central and most important feature of the root system, with a somewhat limited amount of secondary branching.

Taxon

    Any taxonomic group/category

Temperate

    Perennials native to moderate temperature regions without extreme cold or a tropical climate

Terminal bud

    Buds located at the apex of a stem

Terminal buds

    Buds located at the apex of a stem

Thatch

    An organic mat of stems that forms between the mineral soil and the turfgrass canopy

Thermoperiod

    The daily range of temperatures a plant is exposed to

Thinning cuts

    Also called reduction cuts, pruning cuts that remove branches at their points of origin or attachment

Topping cuts

    Height-reducing pruning cuts made indiscriminately in internode areas

Transpiration

> Process by which a plant loses water, primarily from leaf stomata.

Tree-like shrubs

> Shrubs that have woodier, finely divided branches and can be pruned as a single-trunk or multi-stemmed trees

Trees

> Perennial woody plants, usually with one main trunk and usually more than 12 feet tall at maturity

Trowel

> A small hand-tool for digging

Trunk

> A main stem of a woody plant

Tuber

> Enlarged portion of an underground stem. The tuber, like other stems, has nodes that produce buds.

Tuberous root

> Modified lateral roots that are enlarged to function as an underground storage organ. Found in dahlia and sweet potato.

Tuberous roots

> Underground storage organ

Tuberous stem

> Shortened, flattened, enlarged, and underground stem. Examples are tuberous begonia and cyclamen.

Turbidity

> Measure of the cloudiness or opaqueness of the water expressed in nephelometric turbidity units (ntu). The turbidity is influenced by the amount and nature of suspended organic and inorganic material in water. Typically, higher concentrations of the suspended material equal greater turbidity. The source of turbidity could be sediment (fine sand, silt, and clay), organic material, particles of iron and manganese or other metal oxides, rust from corroding piping, algae, carbonate precipitates, etc.

Turgor

> Turgidity (swelling) and resulting rigidity of plant cells or tissues, typically from the absorption of fluid

Twig

> A stem that is less than one year old and has no leaves since it is still in the winter-dormant stage

Unity

> Design principle created by repetition of shapes, lines or colors, the grouping or arranging different parts of the design to appear as a single unit

Vacuole

> A large liquid-filled cavity within a cell

Variety

A subpopulation of a species that has a distinctive trait that distinguishes it from the rest of the species and occurs in nature

Vascular bundle

Part of the transport system in vascular plants that includes the xylem, phloem, and other tissues

Vascular cambium

The main growing tissue of stems and roots in most plants. It produces the secondary xylem and secondary phloem.

Vegetative bud

A bud that contains partially preformed leaf and stem tissue

Vermicompost

Compost made by worms as they digest plant material

Vermiculite

A sterile, lightweight, mica product used as a soil amendment

Vernalize

Cool the plant in order to encourage flowering

Verticutting

Vertical mowing to remove thatch buildup

Vine

A plant that develops long, trailing stems that grow along the ground unless they are supported by another plant or structure

Voucher specimen

A specimen of a species that depicts clearly its most important physical characteristics and structures.

Water table

The depth at which soils are fully saturated with water, the upper surface of an unconfined aquifer.

Water-holding capacity

The amount of water that a soil can hold for crop use

Watershed

Area that drains or contributes water to a particular point, stream, river, lake or ocean. Watersheds are also referred to as basins. Watersheds range in size from a few acres for a small stream basin, to large areas of the country like the Chesapeake Bay Basin that includes parts of six states.

Watersprouts

Vigorous, usually-upright shoots that grow from the trunk or branches

Well

Deep hole or shaft sunk into the earth to obtain water groundwater.

Wetland

Transitional lands between terrestrial and aquatic systems where the water table is usually at or near the surface, or the land is covered by shallow water. Wetlands are those areas where water saturation is the dominant factor determining the nature of soil development and the types of plant and animal communities living in the surrounding environment.

Whorled

Leaf arrangement where leaves are arranged in circles along the stem.

Wide row planting

Planting in such closely-spaced bands rather than in rows of individual plants

Windbreaks

Plantings of trees and shrubs placed strategically to slow winds

Witch's broom

deformity in a woody plant where a mass of shoots grows from a single point

Woody plants

Perennials (life span ranges from decades to centuries, or in some cases millennia) in which the shoot (above ground portion of the plant) persists during plant dormancy (usually late-autumn to early-spring)

Xylem

Transport tissue in vascular plants, transports water from roots to stems and leaves (also transports nutrients)

Zoysiagrass

A warm-season grass of fine to medium texture that turns brown with the first hard frost in the fall and greens up about mid-May.

VERSION NOTES

This book replaces the 2015 version of the Virginia Master Gardener Handbook. It includes significant changes to organization, factual corrections, content additions, and deletions.

Overall or Major Changes

- Drawings replaced with photos: Drawings have been selectively replaced with real photos. All drawings related to specific insects and plant damage have been replaced.
- Changes to wording and sentence structure throughout as recommended by the 2022 Handbook Review Team in order to improve comprehensibility.
- Corrections to errors and typos throughout.
- Addition of "call out sections" which highlight EMG projects or special horticultural topics.

Chapter Numbering

- Previous Chapter 1 "Introduction to Extension Master Gardenering" has been removed and will be replaced with separate manual
- Combination of previous Chapter 2 "Soils" and Chapter 3 "Nutrient Management" into new Chapter 2 "Soils and Nutrient Management"
- Previous Chapter 9 "Pesticide Use & Safety" replaced by new Chapter 7 "Integrated Pest Management and Pesticide Safety"
- New chapter order
- Addition of Chapter 19 "Virginia Native Plants"

New Chapter Order

- Chapter 1: Botany (Original CH 2)
- Chapter 2: Soils and Nutrient Management (Original CH 3 and CH 4)
- Chapter 3: Entomology (Original CH 5)
- Chapter 4: Plant Pathology (Original CH 6)
- Chapter 5: Abiotic Stress (Original CH 7)
- Chapter 6: Diagnosing Plant Damage (Original CH 8)
- Chapter 7: Integrated Pest Management (Original CH 9)
- Chapter 8: Plant Propagation (Original CH 10)
- Chapter 9: The Vegetable Garden (Original CH 13)
- Chapter 10: Fruits in the Home Garden (Original CH 14)
- Chapter 11: Lawns (Original CH 15)
- Chapter 12: Indoor Plants (Original CH 12)
- Chapter 13: Woody Landscape Plants (Original CH 16)
- Chapter 14: Pruning (Original CH 11)
- Chapter 15: Herbaceous Landscape Plants (Original CH 17)
- Chapter 16: Landscape Design (Original CH 18)
- Chapter 17: Water Quality and Conservation (Original CH 19)
- Chapter 18: Wildlife habitats (Original CH 20)
- Chapter 19: Native Plants (New)

"Call out Box" Topics and Authors:

- Ch 1: Green Spring Gardens "Planting Seeds of Hope" A Master Gardener approach to Therapeutic Gardening Kathleen Wellington, Extension Master Gardener, Green Spring Gardens
- Ch 2: Northern Neck Shoreline Evaluation Program By Ian Cheyne, Extension Master Gardener, Northern Neck
- Ch 3: Tick populations densest in suburban forests By David Gaines, State Public Health Entomologist Virginia Dept. of Health, Office of Epidemiology
- Ch 4: Importance of disinfecting tools to prevent spread of plant disease By Mary Ann Hansen, Extension Plant Pathologist, Virginia Tech
- Ch 9: Lost Crops of Africa for Virginia Farmers By Harbans Bhardwaj, Professor, Virginia State University
- Ch 11: Healthy Virginia Lawns: Grassroots in Chesterfield By Seth Guy, Environmental Educator, Virginia Cooperative Extension, Chesterfield
- Ch 12: Indoor Plants and Toxicity for Pets By Marion Ehrich and Dennis Blodgett, Virginia Maryland College of Veterinary Medicine, Virginia Tech
- Ch 14: Norfolk Master Gardener Crepe Myrtle Pruning By Paulette Crawford, Extension Master Gardener, Norfolk
- Ch 15: Adapting the Garden for Therapeutic Benefits By Phyllis Turner, Extension Master Gardener, Bedford
- Ch 16: More Than Just a Pretty Space By Scott Douglas, Director Hahn Horticulture Garden, Virginia Tech
- Ch 17: From the Rooftops to the Roots – An Integrated Approach to Harvesting Rain Water By Shawn Jadrnicek, Extension Agent, Virginia Cooperative Extension, Roanoke
- Ch 18: Goochland-Powhatan Extension Master Gardener Habitat Demonstration Garden By Linda Toler, Extension Master Gardener, Goochland-Powhatan

Specific Chapter-Level Changes

Chapter 1: Botany

- Moved discussion of taxonomy to end
- Added section on plant cells to beginning
- Replaced many figures with more clear/demonstrative images
- Moved discussion of cultivar, taxon, etc. from "Woody Plants" to "Botany"

Chapter 2: Soils and Nutrient Management

- Combined duplicate discussions of pH
- Addition of images, including Virginia soils map
- Added paragraph on urban soils
- Added paragraph on soil food web
- Added paragraph on Cation Exchange Capacity (CEC)

Chapter 3: Entomology

- Replaced drawings with photos, insect ID lab has reviewed diagrams adapted from the original handbook

Chapter 4: Plant Pathology

- Replaced drawings with photos

Chapter 5: Abiotic Stress

- Addition of discussion of CO_2 and atmospheric CO_2 charts
- Additional diagrams in salinity section

Chapter 6: Diagnosing Plant Damage

- Diagnostic key reviewed and updated

Chapter 7: Integrated Pest Management (New, replaces previous "Pesticide Use and Safety" chapter)

- Chapter rewritten
- Beginning focuses on IPM and second half deals with pesticide safety

Chapter 8: Plant Propagation

- Replaced all diagrams of propagation techniques
- Added coconut coir as an option everywhere sphagnum moss is mentioned

Chapter 9: Vegetables

- Reworded weed section
- Removed pest management in the garden and organic pest control (see new Chapter 7 "Integrated Pest Management and Pesticide Safety" instead)
- Deleted pesticide recommendations and instead refer people to VCE "Pest Management Guide"
- Rewrite of "Plant Health Management" section
- Added paragraph on no-till gardening

Chapter 10: Fruits

- Moved pruning images to pruning chapter

Chapter 11: Turf

- Removed duplicate discussion of turf varieties
- Moved "Grass choices for Virginia beach" from end to the recommended varieties section

Chapter 12: Indoor Plants

- Removal of all plant species care sections; replaced with more general descriptions of types of indoor plants
- Corrections to scientific names

Chapter 13: Woody

- Moved discussion of cultivars, variety etc. to Chapter 1 "Botany"
- Moved discussion of buds to botany
- Addition of woody plant botany section

Chapter 14: Pruning

- Rearranged chapter
- Shortened discussion of pruning tools
- Added pruning fruits images from fruits chapter

Chapter 15: Herbaceous Landscape Plants

- Corrections to scientific names

Chapter 17: Water Quality and Conservation

- Moved and updated section on regulatory agencies
- Corrected statements on cost of irrigation systems/updated irrigation section

Chapter 18: Wildlife Habitats

- Update name change from Virginia Department of Game and Inland Fisheries to Virginia Department of Wildlife Resources
- Updated statements regarding regulatory information

Chapter 19: Native Plants (New)

- New chapter

Made in the USA
Columbia, SC
16 January 2024